Testing Young Children

Contributors

Russell A. Barkley, Ph.D.
Carol A. Boliek, Ph.D.
Robert H. Bradley, Ph.D.
Judith A. Brisby, Ph.D.
Jan L. Culbertson, Ph.D.
Philip W. Davidson, Ph.D.
Merelyn Dolins, Ph.D., R.P.T.
Janna Dresden, M.A.
Betty N. Gordon, Ph.D.
George W. Hynd, Ed.D.
Randy W. Kamphaus, Ph.D.
Alan S. Kaufman, Ph.D.
Morgan P. Kelly, J.D., M.A.
Thomas J. Kenny, Ph.D.
Patricia A. Kleine, Ed.D.
Margaret Lansing, M.Ed.
Lee M. Marcus, Ph.D.
Gary B. Melton, Ph.D.
John E. Obrzut, Ph.D.
Mary L. Peery, Ph.D.
Melissa Ramirez-Johnson, Ph.D.
Cecil R. Reynolds, Ph.D.
Eric Schopler, Ph.D.
Carolyn S. Schroeder, Ph.D.
Margaret Semrud-Clikeman, Ph.D.
Terri L. Shelton, Ph.D.
James T. Webb, Ph.D.
J. Kenneth Whitt, Ph.D.
Diane J. Willis, Ph.D.
Barbara C. Wilson, Ph.D.

Testing Young Children

A REFERENCE GUIDE FOR
DEVELOPMENTAL, PSYCHOEDUCATIONAL, AND
PSYCHOSOCIAL ASSESSMENTS

Jan L. Culbertson, Ph.D.
Diane J. Willis, Ph.D.
General Editors

pro·ed

8700 Shoal Creek Boulevard
Austin, Texas 78758
(512) 451-3246

© 1993 by PRO-ED, Inc.

All rights reserved. No part of this book may be
reproduced in any form or by any means without
the prior written permission of the publisher.

Printed in the United States of America

LIBRARY OF CONGRESS CATALOGING-IN-PUBLICATION DATA

Testing young children : a reference guide for developmental, psychoeducational, and
   psychosocial assessments / Jan L. Culbertson, Diane J. Willis, general editors.
      p.   cm.
   Includes bibliographical references and indexes.
   ISBN 0-89079-550-9
   1. Infants—Psychological testing. 2. Psychological tests for children. 3. Behavioral
assessments of infants. 4. Behavioral assessment of children. I. Culbertson, Janet L.
II. Willis, Diane J.
BF719.6.T47 1992   92-11515
155.42′2393—dc20   CIP

pro·ed

8700 Shoal Creek Boulevard
Austin, Texas 78758

10 9 8 7 6 5 4 3 2 1   92 93 94 95 96

To my parents, Jean and R.L. Culbertson, for their love, support, and guidance.
—*J.L.C.*

In memory of my grandmother, Orpha Bynum, for her support and love all these many years, and to my parents, W.P. "Bill" and Zelma Bynum Willis, for their support, wisdom, and love.
—*D.J.W.*

Contents

Preface	ix
I. NORMAL DEVELOPMENT	
1. Introduction to Testing Young Children *Jan L. Culbertson, Ph.D. and Diane J. Willis, Ph.D.*	1
2. Developmental Considerations in Cognitive Assessment of Young Children *George W. Hynd, Ed.D. and Margaret Semrud-Clikeman, Ph.D.*	11
3. Developmental Theory and Concerns in Personality and Social Assessment of Young Children *Mary L. Peery, Ph.D. and Cecil R. Reynolds, Ph.D.*	29
II. MODELS AND METHODS FOR TESTING YOUNG CHILDREN	
4. Clinical and Psychometric Considerations in the Cognitive Assessment of Preschool Children *Randy W. Kamphaus, Ph.D., Janna Dresden, M.A., and Alan S. Kaufman, Ph.D.*	55
5. Developmental Screening for Preschoolers *Thomas J. Kenny, Ph.D. and Jan L. Culbertson, Ph.D.*	73
6. Assessment of Behavior Problems in Young Children *Carolyn S. Schroeder, Ph.D. and Betty N. Gordon, Ph.D.*	101
7. Assessment of the Home Environment *Robert H. Bradley, Ph.D. and Judith A. Brisby, Ph.D.*	128
III. ASSESSMENT FOR SPECIFIC DISORDERS IN PRESCHOOL CHILDREN	
8. Assessment of Learning and Cognitive Dysfunction in Young Children *Margaret Semrud-Clikeman, Ph.D. and George W. Hynd, Ed.D.*	167
9. Assessment of Young Children with Communication Disorders *Barbara C. Wilson, Ph.D.*	192

10. Assessment of the Young Child with Visual Impairment and Multiple Disabilities
Philip W. Davidson, Ph.D. and Merelyn Dolins, Ph.D., R.P.T.   237

11. Psychological Evaluation of Infants and Young Children with Chronic Physical Illness
J. Kenneth Whitt, Ph.D. and Melissa Ramirez Johnson, Ph.D.   262

12. Assessment of Attention-Deficit Hyperactivity Disorder in Young Children
Terri L. Shelton, Ph.D. and Russell A. Barkley, Ph.D.   290

13. Assessment of Children with Autism and Pervasive Developmental Disorder
Lee M. Marcus, Ph.D., Margaret Lansing, M.Ed., and Eric Schopler, Ph.D.   319

14. Assessment of the Child with Social and Emotional Disorders
John E. Obrzut, Ph.D. and Carol A. Boliek, Ph.D.   345

15. Assessing Gifted and Talented Children
James T. Webb, Ph.D. and Patricia A. Kleine, Ed.D.   383

IV. LEGAL AND ETHICAL ISSUES

16. Ethical and Legal Issues
Morgan P. Kelly, J.D., M.A. and Gary B. Melton, Ph.D.   408

Appendix: Test Directory and Index   427

Test Publisher/Distributor Directory   459

Names Index   461

General Index   473

About the Contributors   482

Preface

Testing Young Children is a natural outgrowth of its preceding companion volumes—*Testing Children, Testing Adolescents, Testing Adults,* and *Testing Older Adults*—in a series that began in 1984. It also is a critically needed book, given the passage of PL 99-457 and the mandate to provide early intervention to infants and young children who are developmentally disabled or at risk for disabilities. Many psychologists traditionally have not been trained to assess children under 3 years of age, yet early intervention units have been or are being formed across the nation to provide early assessment and intervention for high-risk populations.

Testing Young Children was compiled to provide a timely, comprehensive text on assessing young children and their families, especially the child with developmental disorders. An understanding of normal cognitive and emotional development is essential for professionals who evaluate children at risk for developmental disorders. Part I of this text covers normal developmental considerations in the cognitive assessment and personality/social assessment of young children. Throughout these chapters, the reader is provided theoretical information that will assist in the interpretation of assessment data. Hynd and Semrud-Clikeman discuss the continuities and discontinuities in development, the appropriate use of the concept "intelligence" with young children, and the problems with predictive validity of test instruments for preschool children. The chapter by Perry and Reynolds on developmental theory as it relates to personality and social assessment includes information on methods of evaluation, as well as the influence of parental and other environmental factors on the child's functioning.

Part II provides an overview of general models and methods for testing young children. Kamphaus et al. discuss clinical and psychometric considerations in the cognitive assessment of preschool children, including a comparative analysis of the major cognitive instruments for young children. Because most school systems will develop a program of screening for the "Child Find" portion of PL 99-457, the chapter by Kenny and Culbertson will provide a discussion of the strengths and weaknesses of screening tests, an overview of common screening tests that may be used, and a model for a developmental screening program. In their chapter on assessment of behavior problems, Schroeder and Gordon review the classification of behavior disorders in young children and common assessment approaches that can be used in a school or clinic setting. Finally, Bradley and Brisby address the important topic of assessment of the family and home environment. They provide a critical analysis of the assessment approaches available for use and a compelling rationale for the importance of understanding the home environment when working with young children who have developmental disorders.

Part III includes eight chapters covering the assessment of specific disorders in young children. A thorough coverage is given to assessment of the child with cognitive and learning disorders, communication disorders, visual and motor impairment, chronic physical illness, Attention-Deficit Hyperactivity Disorder, autism and pervasive developmental disorder, social and emotional disorders, and gifted and talented abilities. The authors of each of these chapters are leading experts in their field who contribute practical information for the psychologist interested in assessing the young child.

Finally, Part IV deals with legal and ethical issues in assessing young children. Kelly and Melton provide a comprehensive review of pertinent legislation and litigation, special ethical considerations in assessment, guidelines for expert testimony by psychologists, and a special focus on the implications of PL 99-457 for service providers.

Testing Young Children is meant to provide the general methodology and specific approaches for psychological assessment of developmental and behavioral disorders in young children. It also provides a foundation for understanding the influence of the child's family and basic approaches to evaluating the home environment. The focus on early diagnosis and treatment of young children is an important first step in preventing more serious developmental and psychosocial problems.

Jan L. Culbertson
Diane J. Willis
Oklahoma City, Oklahoma

1

Introduction to Testing Young Children

JAN L. CULBERTSON, PH.D. & DIANE J. WILLIS, PH.D.

Never in the history of American education has there been such a focus on the young child. There is a growing national impetus to recognize the developmental needs of the infant and preschool-aged child, to improve our capability for making early diagnosis of disabilities, and to provide early intervention when those disabilities are diagnosed. Not only the needs of the child with disabilities, but also the needs and the importance of the child's family are being considered. The passage of Public Law 99-457 is largely responsible for this new movement. Its provisions call upon psychologists, educators, speech/language pathologists, occupational and physical therapists, social workers, nutritionists, and physicians to provide earlier evaluation and ongoing assessment of the infant and young child. The specialized chapters that follow in this book address the general methodology and specific approaches for the psychological assessment of developmental and behavioral disorders in young children. The purpose of this format is to provide state-of-the-art information for psychologists on assessment of young children, but the discussion also may be useful to professionals of other disciplines who are involved in identification of disabilities.

PUBLIC LAW 99-457

On October 8, 1986, President Ronald Reagan signed into law Public Law 99-457, which brought amendments to the 1975 Education for All Handicapped Children Act (EHA; PL 94-142). These amendments reauthorized the EHA and included a rigorous national agenda relating to more and better services for both young children with special needs and their families (Trohanis, 1989). The law was based on the documented benefits of early intervention and preschool services (Shonkoff & Hauser-Cram, 1987) and recognition of the unique role of families in the development of their children with disabilities (Trohanis, 1989). In order to achieve the goals set forth by the new law, a 5-year phase-in period was included. The final rules and regulations were published in June 1989, and states now should have in place a plan consistent with federal regulations for providing early intervention services. By the time this book is published, all states receiving federal funds through PL 99-457 should be serving all eligible children and their families.

The national agenda set forth by this legislation contains numerous initiatives, such as research, training, educational technology, demonstration and outreach, and technical assistance. However, two major portions of the law, as described in the following sections, are of particular importance for improving and expanding services to infants, toddlers, and preschoolers.

Infants and Toddlers with Disabilities

Title I (Part H of the Act) is an entirely new part of the EHA, which allocated funds to encourage states to establish comprehensive, coordinated, multidisciplinary, interagency programs of early intervention services for infants and toddlers with disabilities. Part H also was developed to facilitate the coordination of payment for early intervention services from federal, state, local, and private sources (including public and private insurance coverage), and to enhance states' capacity to provide quality early intervention services and expand and improve existing early intervention services for infants and toddlers with handicaps and their families. Part H was enacted in recognition of four urgent and substantial needs: (a) to enhance the development of infants and toddlers with handicaps and minimize their potential for developmental delay; (b) to reduce the need for special education and related services after these infants and toddlers reach school age; (c) to maximize the likelihood that individuals with handicaps ultimately will lead productive lives in the community; and, (d) to enhance the capacity of families to meet the needs of infants and toddlers who have handicaps.

States must develop and implement a statewide system of services that consists of 14 minimum components. Included among these components are the following:

1. The state's definition of developmental delay, and its position regarding provision of services to children who are at risk.
2. A central directory of information about intervention services, resources, and experts available in the state.
3. Timetables for serving all eligible children before the beginning of the fifth year of a state's participation under Part H of PL 99-457.
4. A comprehensive Child Find system, including a system for making referrals to service providers and for participation by primary referral sources.
5. A timely, comprehensive, multidisciplinary evaluation of each infant and toddler in the state, ongoing assessment, and use of nondiscriminatory procedures.
6. An evaluation of the needs of the families to assist appropriately in the development of infants and toddlers with handicaps.
7. Individualized family service plans, which include case management services.
8. Interagency agreements that identify and coordinate all available resources within the state, define the financial responsibility of each agency for paying for early intervention services, and procedures for resolving disputes.

Participating states are required to serve children from birth through 2 years of age who are experiencing developmental delays, as measured by appropriate diagnostic instruments and procedures, in one or more of the following areas: cognitive development, physical development (including vision and hearing), language and speech development, psychosocial development, or self-help skills. Early intervention services, as defined in the law, may include family training, counseling, and home visits; special instruction; speech pathology and audiology services; occupational therapy; physical therapy; psychological services; case management services; medical services (only for diagnostic or evaluation purposes); early identification, screening, and assessment services; and health services necessary to enable the infant or toddler to benefit from the other early intervention services. Early intervention services must be provided by qualified personnel, including special educators, speech/language pathologists, occupational therapists, physical therapists, psychologists, social workers, nurses, and nutritionists. Each state must establish a definition of the term *developmentally delayed* that it will use in carrying out its statewide early intervention program. The system is flexible to fit the needs of each state while meeting the 14 criteria designated in the law. An Interagency Coordinating Council, appointed in each state by the governor, advises and assists the state's lead agency in planning and carrying out the comprehensive system of services mandated by Part H of PL 99-457.

Participating states also are required to serve children from birth through 2 years of age who have a diagnosed physical or mental condition that carries a high probability of resulting in developmental problems. This may include chromosomal disorders, neurological abnormalities, inborn errors of metabolism, genetic disorders, congenital malformation of the brain, congenital infections, and sensory abnormalities and impairments or identified syndromes. States also have the option to extend services to infants who are "at risk" for developmental problems. If states have the financial and programmatic resources to extend services to at-risk infants, there are few criteria as to who should be served. Although federal regulations provide guidelines for medical at-risk conditions, such as low birth weight, no guidelines exist regarding social or environmental risk factors such as abusive or neglectful families (Black, 1991). Thus, the law provides the *opportunity* for prevention services to infants and toddlers who do not yet have developmental delay, but these services are not required and it is unclear to what extent they will be included in individual state plans.

Part H of the EHA breaks new ground in federal policy by moving toward a family-centered approach that incorporates both services for the child and services that enable parents to enhance their child's development. These services must include a multidisciplinary assessment of unique needs and the identification of services appropriate to meet such needs, plus a written Individualized Family Service Plan (IFSP), which will determine what services are appropriate for the particular child and his or her family and which is developed by a multidisciplinary team, including the parent or guardian. All eligible children and their families are entitled to ongoing assessment and case management and to the development, implementation, review, and evaluation of the IFSP, and all are covered by a system of procedural standards. The IFSP is based on the rationale that all children are embedded within a family unit, and that both the family's and child's needs must be met for their collective development to be enhanced (Hauser-Cram, Upshur, Krauss, & Shonkoff, 1988).

Numerous studies suggest an important reciprocal relationship between the child's development and the caregiving environment in which he or she is raised (Campos, Barrett, Lamb, Goldsmith, & Stenberg, 1985; Cramer, 1987; Meisels,

1989; Sameroff & Chandler, 1975). These studies are based on the view that influences on a child's development extend beyond genetic capacities to include environmental effects as well (Meisels, 1989). Because development is viewed as a transactional process between the child's genetic endowment and the environment, dysfunctions resulting in disabilities may be precipitated by either the child or the environment. Thus, interventions must take into account contributions from both members of the dyad (Meisels, 1989). The inclusion of family intervention in PL 99-457 addresses this need.

Preschoolers with Disabilities

The part of PL 99-457 that concerns preschoolers with disabilities, referred to as Section 619, amends a previous portion of the EHA. According to Trohanis (1989), it creates enhanced incentives so that all states will provide a free and appropriate public education to eligible 3- to 5-year-olds with disabilities by school year 1991–92. Section 619 includes all requirements of the state's Part B Plan for special education and related services based on PL 94-142, including the definition of *handicapped*, the right to nondiscriminatory testing and confidentiality of records, an Individualized Educational Plan determined by a multidisciplinary team (which includes the parents), and the right to due process. In addition, family services and variations in child programming are encouraged (Trohanis, 1989).

Early childhood education, as mandated by PL 99-457, represents an extremely progressive approach to public policy for young children and their families (Meisels, 1989). The new law includes within the purview of early intervention such elements as prevention, family focus, interdisciplinary cooperation, case management, and use of multiple sources of funding. Thus, PL 99-457 offers expanded access to public programs of treatment, remediation, and prevention for young children (Meisels, 1989). The new initiatives represented by this law require personnel within the educational system to expand and develop their services as well. Therein lies the focus of this book. Psychologists are an important part of the educational system for young children with disabilities and their families. The traditional psychometric and psychological methods for older children must be examined and modified in many ways for application to young children, as there are many special considerations in their assessment.

TESTING YOUNG CHILDREN

Young children present many challenges to the psychologist who is charged with evaluating their intellectual, language, motor, and adaptive functioning. Normal developmental transitions of infancy and early childhood influence childrens' motivation, interest, and cooperation with the testing process. The psychologist experienced in testing school-aged children may expect a young child to exhibit appropriate "testing behavior"—sitting quietly at a desk, attending to the task at hand, and being motivated to complete the tasks presented. Such characteristic testing behavior often is not present in this age group or, if present, is limited to a few brief moments. The psychologist examining young children must be aware of the developmental influences affecting the young child and must be flexible enough to adapt the testing procedures to the special characteristics of the young child.

Developmental Influences

The developmental influences on testing young children may include physiological factors, normal periods of fear or oppositionality, and changing interests related to emerging developmental skills. Physiological factors in infants include colic during the first 2 to 3 months of life, teething (with associated increased irritability), more frequent hunger and need for sleep, and more frequent state changes (i.e., variability between alertness, irritability, drowsiness, and sleep). The practical implications of these physiological factors on the testing situation relate to the brief amount of time in which the infant and young child may be alert and attentive to the testing process. During this brief "window" of time, the examiner must move quickly through a variety of test stimuli while observing the child's behavior to ascertain developmental progress. This requires that the examiner have a thorough familiarity with the test content and procedures, to maximize on the child's brief period of alertness and cooperation. The examiner also must be flexible, with a good sense of timing, to recognize state changes in infants and young children and make appropriate adjustments in the test procedures (Culbertson & Gyurke, 1990). Some physiological factors (e.g., colic, teething) may require postponing the evaluation until the difficult physiologic period has passed.

The developmental process of separation-individuation in young children may involve normal periods during which fears or oppositional behavior are present. The period of 8–12 months in infants is a time when attachment to a primary caregiver is strongest, and the infant may exhibit stranger anxiety. Imagine trying to administer the Bayley Scales of Infant Development (Bayley, 1969) to a 9-month-old who screams and clings to his mother every the time the examiner approaches! During this developmental period, it often is wise to enlist the aid of the caregiver in administering test items, while the examiner coaches the caregiver and maintains a safe distance from the anxious infant. During even later stages of development, the young child may be appropriately anxious when separated from the parents, and it may be helpful to have the parents sit quietly in the examining room during the testing, after they have been coached not to provide help to their child on the test items. The developmental transitions during the toddler years involve a movement from dependence to greater self-reliance and the beginning of compliance to social rules and values (Culbertson & Schellenbach, 1991). It is normal during this developmental period for the toddler to be more negative and to assert his or her will with persistence. The toddler may resist changing activities or may insist on playing with test materials in an idiosyncratic way rather than following the examiner's instructions. Rather than engage in a battle of wills, the examiner must use a flexible approach to testing that encourages the child to play with the test materials in a manner consistent with the test procedures. Because toddlers like to declare toys "mine," and rarely like to give them up willingly, the examiner may modify test instructions from "Give me the doll" to "Put the doll on the table." A toddler who resists changing from one activity to another may be more willing to cooperate if the examiner presents the new activity and test materials before trying to remove the previous materials. Simple modifications of test procedures can result in greater cooperation while maintaining standardized test administration procedures.

Another developmental influence involves the changing interests of the young child as new developmental skills emerge. For instance, when a toddler masters the skill of walking independently, an interest in exploring the environment motorically may supersede his or her interest in language. Language development temporarily may slow while new motor skills and exploration of the environment are mastered. During this period, the toddler may be less interested in fine motor or language test activities than those involving gross motor activity. At a different period of development, language skills may emerge as dominant, and development may progress rapidly. Testing the infant just before or just after this spurt of language development can result in vastly different test performance. The point to be made is that infant and toddler development occurs rapidly, and often in spurts. These normal transitions in development make it difficult to test a young child at one point in time and have a valid predictor of later developmental functioning. It is far safer to conduct serial evaluations of young children at different times during their early years, so that some estimate of the rate of development may be determined. Tracking the rate of development will result in much more accurate developmental data than any single evaluation conducted during the early years.

Environmental and cultural influences on the young child also must be considered when testing young children. Psychologists can expect much more variability in test performance due to environmental influences on infants and preschool children than on older, school-aged children. As Bradley and colleagues point out in chapter 7 of this text, measures of the home environment can be very helpful in understanding a child's developmental functioning. Such factors as the quality of the mother's or father's verbalization, the toys or variety of activities available in the home environment, the restrictiveness of discipline, and the freedom from danger can influence the child's early developmental course. It is very appropriate that PL 99-457 includes a focus on the family of the child with disabilities, and that a family evaluation can be included as part of the Individualized Family Service Plan. Cultural influences also must be considered, as they may affect parenting style and the child's responsivity to the examiner and the testing process. For instance, a young Native American child may make less eye contact, act more shy, and be less verbal with the examiner than Caucasian children, but these differences may represent cultural influences rather than developmental delay. Reviewing the cross-cultural literature regarding the developmental performance of infants who are African-American, Asian-American, Hispanic, and from other cultural groups would be helpful to the prospective examiner.

Because of the many physiological, developmental, cultural, and environmental influences on test performance of infants and young children, there is a need for a high level of examiner proficiency in order to obtain the most reliable and valid test results. This involves an understanding of what each test measures, knowledge of normal developmental transitions in infants and young children, and an understanding of individual differences (Culbertson & Gyurke, 1990). Beyond these issues, there are several basic assumptions about the testing process to be made. These assumptions place psychological testing within the context of the broader evaluation that will be provided for young children under PL 99-457.

The Evaluation Process

It is assumed that psychological testing of infants and young children will be part of a broader evaluation process that involves professionals of other disciplines (e.g., speech/language pathology, occupational and physical therapy, education, medicine), evaluations conducted in different settings (e.g., home, school), and those conducted with different components of the family system (e.g., the parents and the child). However, the psychologist also must obtain information from many sources in order to interpret the child's performance on psychological testing competently. A helpful mnemonic for remembering these various areas of assessment—PIEES—was presented by Weaver (1984) in an earlier volume of this series:

P = Physical functioning
I = Intellectual functioning
E = Emotional functioning
E = Educational functioning
S = Social functioning

Weaver suggested that each psychological evaluation should include attention to these five areas. Although the psychologist does not conduct a physical evaluation of the child, much important information can be obtained from history. A review of medical records or interview with the child's parents can reveal whether the child had birth injuries, illnesses that could have an effect on development, vision or hearing acuity deficits, or a genetic disorder. Intellectual and educational functioning often will be included as part of the formal testing process, but social and emotional functioning may be obtained from parental interview, observations of parent-child interaction, a home visit, or play interview with the child.

The process of conducting a comprehensive evaluation with young children has several steps. The first step involves using an hypothesis-testing approach—that is, ascertaining the presenting symptoms or concerns about the child and then forming hypotheses about what might be causing the symptoms (Culbertson, 1981). For example, a 26-month-old girl presents with a significant delay in speech and language skills. Might she have a generalized delay in all areas of development consistent with mental retardation, a specific language disorder, an emotional problem that has interfered with her expressive communication, or cultural influences that make it difficult for her to express herself verbally with persons other than her family?

Once the hypotheses are formed, the psychologist sets out to test them through data gathering. This process might include interviewing caregivers, observing the child in structured and unstructured situations, observing parent-child interaction, and formal testing. The interview with caregivers should provide a history of the child's medical, family, developmental, educational, behavioral, and past screening or testing background. Prior to beginning formal testing, the psychologist must obtain medical information about the child's visual and auditory acuity and ascertain whether his or her motor functioning will be adequate for the demands of the testing procedures.

Once the hypotheses are determined and a comprehensive history is obtained, the psychologist is ready to decide which tests and procedures should be included in the evaluation. It is important to match the demands of the particular test to the specific characteristics of the child. For instance, if the referral question relates to the intellectual functioning of a language-disordered child, the psychologist will need to include a nonverbal cognitive measure in the test battery. A child with motor incoordination will need to be tested with a measure that does not require timed performance on motor tasks. A task analysis of each test, with regard to the performance demands upon the child as well as the skills measured, will be helpful to the psychologist (Culbertson, 1981).

If any detected sensory or motor deficits might interfere with the child's ability to perform on psychological tests, the testing procedures must be modified to take these into account, and the test results must be interpreted carefully in light of the physical disabilities noted. A child with severe motor dysfunction, such as cerebral palsy, may need special adaptations to stabilize their posture and aid their movements (Willis, Culbertson, & Mertens, 1984; Davidson & Dolins, chapter 10 of this text).

After the child is tested, the family interviewed, and all data are scored, a preliminary report may be prepared to share information with other members of the multidisciplinary team of professionals working with the child and his or her family. Often this multidisciplinary staffing conference can be helpful in interpreting and integrating the psychological data in the context of the broader evaluation of the child. Following this staffing conference, basic impressions of the child's strengths and weaknesses as well as recommendations for intervention or prevention are determined. The final step is a feedback conference with the parents to interpret the results of the evaluation.

Accardo and Caputo (1979) suggested that the communication of diagnostic information to parents should occur at three levels. All are important and may affect the parents' willingness to follow through on the recommendations of the evaluation team. Information first must be communicated at the *cognitive* level. This involves communicating clearly and concisely, in language appropriate for the level of understanding of the parent or other professional. It is wise to avoid psychological jargon when communicating results to laypersons. Next, information must be communicated at an *operative* level. This involves suggesting a plan of treatment, educational or developmental programming, and any needed rehabilitation or supportive services based on the evaluation data. The psychologist at this level attempts to engage the parents' participation in a treatment program. Finally, information must be communicated at an *affective* level. This involves attending to the parents' underlying concerns and emotional reactions to the diagnostic information and the suggestions for treatment. These affective issues must not be overlooked if successful follow through is to occur. Accardo and Caputo (1979) suggest the following guidelines for the feedback conference with parents:

1. Attempt to have both parents present, if available, to relieve the burden on one parent of communicating information to the absent parent.
2. Give the impression of unlimited time, so that parents do not feel rushed and pressured to get through the session quickly.
3. Encourage and expect questions. If parents are silent or nonreactive, pause and ask if they have questions about the feedback.

4. Open the session by restating the parents' questions and concerns, or by asking them to review their perception of their child's development.
5. Rather than beginning the feedback with a diagnostic label or psychometric score, describe the child's behavior, referring to the parents' descriptions whenever possible.
6. Describe the child's performance initially using mental age scores before using an IQ range.
7. Discuss etiology, using extreme caution about any statements that might engender feelings of guilt or responsibility on the part of the parents. If etiology is not known, it is helpful to say so, or to refer the parents to other professionals who may be able to answer parents' questions about etiology.
8. Offer the parents the opportunity for another opinion regarding the child's diagnosis. It is helpful to give parents a list of other competent professionals who can give an independent consultation; to do so may diffuse potential denial of the child's diagnosis and discourage "doctor shopping."
9. At the conclusion of the session, focus on the present situation—the child's current functioning—and avoid trying to predict the child's developmental course across the life span. However, it is also important to avoid giving the parents the impression that certain developmental problems (such as mental retardation) are temporary or can be "cured." It is a challenge to achieve a balance between giving an honest appraisal of the child's functioning and still providing "hope" for the parents.
10. Leave parents with an "open-door policy" so they know the professionals involved are available to answer future questions, review their child's status, and assess the appropriateness of major changes in placement or programming.

This chapter has provided a description of the provisions of PL 99-457, discussion of the special considerations for testing young children, and a model for the evaluation process using the PIEES mnemonic. Attention to the five areas of functioning—physical, intellectual, emotional, educational, and social—is necessary for conducting a comprehensive evaluation of young children. An hypothesis-testing approach to assessment is useful in formulating the plan for the assessment and integrating the data for interpretation following the assessment. Finally, effective communication of the evaluation results to the parents and family of the young child is essential for follow through on appropriate intervention.

REFERENCES

Accardo, P.J., & Capute, A.J. (1979). Parent counseling. In P.J. Accardo & A.J. Capute, *The pediatrician and the developmentally delayed child* (pp. 167–177). Baltimore: University Park Press.

Bayley, N. (1969). *Bayley Scales of Infant Development.* San Antonio, TX: Psychological Corporation.

Black, M.M. (1991). Early intervention services for infants and toddlers: A focus on families. *Journal of Clinical Child Psychology, 20,* 51–57.

Campos, J.J., Barrett, K.C., Lamb, M.E., Goldsmith, H.H., & Stenberg, C. (1985). Socioemotional development. In M.M. Haith & J.J. Campos (Eds.), *Handbook of child psychology: Infancy and developmental psychology* (pp. 783–916). New York: Wiley.

Cramer, B.B. (1987). Objective and subjective aspects of parent-infant relations: An attempt at correlation between infant studies and clinical work. In J.D. Osofsky (Ed.), *Handbook of infant development* (2nd ed., pp. 1037–1058). New York: Wiley.

Culbertson, J.L. (1981). Psychological evaluation and educational planning for children with central auditory dysfunction. In R.W. Keith (Ed.), *Central auditory and language disorders in children* (pp. 13–29). Austin, TX: PRO-ED.

Culbertson, J.L., & Gyurke, J. (1990). Assessment of cognitive and motor development in infancy and childhood. In J.H. Johnson & J. Goldman (Eds.), *Developmental assessment in clinical child psychology: A handbook* (pp. 100–131). New York: Pergamon.

Culbertson, J.L., & Schellenbach, C.J. (1991). Prevention of maltreatment in infants and young children. In D.J. Willis, E.W. Holden, & M. Rosenberg (Eds.), *Prevention of child maltreatment: Developmental and ecological perspectives* (pp. 47–77). New York: Wiley.

Hauser-Cram, P., Upshur, C.C., Krauss, M.W., & Shonkoff, J.P. (1988). Implications of Public Law 99-457 for early intervention services for infants and toddlers with disabilities. *Social Policy Report, 3*(3).

Meisels, S.J. (1989). Meeting the mandate of Public Law 99-457: Early childhood intervention in the nineties. *American Journal of Orthopsychiatry, 59*, 451–460.

Sameroff, A.J., & Chandler, M.J. (1975). Perinatal risk and the continuum of caretaking casualty. In F. Horowitz, M. Hetherington, S. Scarr-Salapatek, & G. Siegel (Eds.), *Review of child development research* (Vol. 4, pp. 187–244). Chicago: University of Chicago Press.

Shonkoff, J., & Hauser-Cram, P. (1987). Early intervention for disabled children and their families: A quantitative analysis. *Pediatrics, 80*, 650–658.

Trohanis, P. (1989, January/February). An overview to P.L. 99-457. *Exceptional Parent*, p. 46.

Weaver, S.J. (Ed.). (1984). *Testing children: A reference guide for effective clinical and psychoeducational assessments*. Austin, TX: PRO-ED.

Willis, D.J., Culbertson, J.L., & Mertens, R.A. (1984). Considerations in physical and health-related disorders. In S.J. Weaver (Ed.), *Testing children: A reference guide for effective clinical and psychoeducational assessments* (pp. 185–196). Austin, TX: PRO-ED.

2

Developmental Considerations in Cognitive Assessment of Young Children

GEORGE W. HYND, ED.D. &
MARGARET SEMRUD-CLIKEMAN, PH.D.

Imagine for a moment that you live in a food-gathering, prehistoric society, where the overriding value is survival of the clan. Everyone, to the fullest extent of their physical abilities, contributes in some meaningful fashion to hunting or gathering food, preparing food, making or mending clothing, or protecting the clan from danger. In such a simple society, most tasks associated with contributing to the daily survival of the clan were relatively easy to learn and, other than those requiring unusual physical skill or perhaps strength, could be mastered by most members of the clan. Those few positions that required unusual skill, such as healing or toolmaking, required considerable training and, because they contributed significantly to the survival of the clan, were positions of high social status.

Contrast this less complex society with that represented by a large industrial nation such as ours. In our pluralistic society physical strength and contributing to the survival of a small isolated clan are not realities that many face. In a democratic society, where one of the goals of public education is to assist everyone to develop to the fullest extent of their abilities, the individual's contribution often is judged by whether or not the person is working to the fullest extent of his or her abilities. Because in a pluralistic society most positions are highly specialized, many individuals are required to master highly skilled tasks. Further, many positions require more than mastery of complex physical skills; they demand considerable mental ability as a prerequisite to mastery.

In the prehistoric society there would be little value in predicting someone's mental ability. On the other hand, an observation of an infant's physical development and perceptual-motor skills may have been helpful in selecting which children would be the best hunters, toolmakers, and so on. As most individuals likely would have had the minimal mental ability to master these physical skills, the assessment of an infant or child's mental ability was not necessary.

However, in our society, where there is a presumption that education assists all children to develop to the fullest extent of their abilities, assessing mental ability has assumed a great deal of importance. It is deemed important because we as a society value the early identification of developmental deviations so that early intervention may be attempted. Moreover, we believe that there is a need to predict the level and rate of learning in both preschool and school-aged children.

Recognizing that our society places great value on the individual and his or her potential to achieve in a rapidly expanding socioeconomic environment, it should be relatively easy to identify those variables that assist us in evaluating developmental maturation and in predicting future performance. If we were still a food-gathering society, a good predictor of hunting ability might have been early physical achievements. We might suppose that the child who runs the fastest, can throw the spear the longest distance, and is physically the strongest would have the greatest potential as a hunter. Performance on these tasks is readily observable and early achievements in this domain are probably good predictors of eventual hunting success as an adult.

However, if we wish to predict how rapidly an infant will develop cognitive skills or how well a preschool child will eventually do in school, which predictor variables does one select? A vast number of other questions also might be asked. For example, are early motor or physical achievements of any predictive value in identifying infants who will mature early or late? How do we identify infants who are exceptionally gifted or early developers? Which variables do we select to identify those children who appear normal during the preschool years but will eventually require extra academic assistance in school? If we can identify those variables that offer good prediction of later performance, does that mean we can potentially accelerate physical or cognitive development by teaching children these tasks and thus accentuate the potential for achievement?

Clearly, the answers to these and related questions are not easy. We live in a vastly more complex world than our distant food-gathering relatives and, consistent with our present values, we need to address more complex issues with regard to assessment and prediction. As will be seen, there are significant theoretical as well as practical issues when one considers what cognitive domains we wish to assess, how these abilities develop over time, and what practical use is served by the assessment results.

To gain an appreciation of these issues and to better understand what is and is not reasonable to expect with regard to the assessment of cognitive development in young children, the following chapter will provide a brief history of the interest in the assessment of individual differences, what is conceptualized as normal development, how we go about developmental and cognitive assessment, and what theoretical models should drive our assessment practices today.

MEASURING COGNITIVE ABILITIES: A BRIEF HISTORY

Early Influences

As Hynd and Obrzut (1986) have pointed out, it was the influence of Franz Joseph Gall, better known as the founder of phrenology, that established the conceptual foundation for the study of cognitive abilities. Gall, writing in the 18th century, proposed that various places in the brain had various functions. He disavowed any connection between metaphysics and cognitive function in man and drew parallels between observed behavior in man and animals. Of great importance was Gall's notion that the convolutions of the brain were specialized, such that our feelings, thoughts, abilities, and traits originated in them.

Unfortunately, Gall is also known for his speculations about the relationship between the shape of the skull and underlying brain processes. He believed that he had localized many human behaviors on the convolutions and, by feeling the bumps and asymmetries of the skull, could tell what parts of the brain (and correlated behavior) were normally or abnormally developed.

Gall made two important contributions. First, he believed that the brain was the seat of our cognitive processes. Second, he thought that our cognitive processes could be categorized by faculties. Thus, scientists could study individual differences in independent faculties or abilities.

Preceding Gall and the publication of his ideas regarding what had been termed *phrenology* by one of his colleagues, was a developing interest in measuring the global ability known as intelligence. The Spanish philosophers were the first to actually devise a working definition and propose ways in which to measure intelligence. Juan Haurte in the 16th century set forth his ideas on intelligence. He believed that intelligence was reflected by docility in learning from a master, inspiration in the absence of extravagance, and understanding and independence of judgment. Primarily because he suggested that accurate measurement of intelligence could be achieved, the writings of Huarte had a great impact on those who followed.

While the Spanish and later the English and French investigators were primarily interested in intelligence, the Germans contributed through their interest in perception. Friedrich Wilhelm Bessel, an astronomer at Königsberg, observed that two scholars obtained slightly different measurements of the passage of a star. Ernst Heinrich Weber followed up on Bessel's observation that small but significant differences could exist in precise measurement in science and concluded from his studies that there existed what he termed "just noticeable differences" in perceptions. In other words, even if the perceptual stimuli were exactly the same, as they were for Bessel's colleagues, individual differences existed such that no two persons would record the same phenomena in exactly the same fashion. This difference was not due to error in judgment but reflected basic, fundamental human individual differences.

Wilhelm Wundt, a German scientist who established the first psychology course at the University of Heidelberg, studied not individual differences but similarities in human perception. The objectivity in measurement Wundt and others brought to the assessment of faculties of human perception and cognition greatly affected those who followed, particularly Charles Darwin and other Englishmen interested in genetics and heredity. Francis Galton best represents the achievements of this period.

Sir Francis Galton: Impact of a Metric Approach

Working in the mid- to late 1800s, Sir Francis Galton was vitally important in further establishing a metric approach in understanding normal and deviant human variability. Galton was Darwin's first cousin, and as a scientist he was interested in how evolution affected the development of genius. Often referred to as the founder of individual psychology, he established the first anthropometric laboratory at London's South Kensington Museum in 1884.

In his use of statistical methods, Galton used the median (most frequent score) and developed percentiles to assess central tendency. He was also the first to discuss the concepts of correlation and regression. Behavioral measures collected in his laboratory included performance on a dynamometer, reaction time tasks, auditory perception tasks, and performance on the Snellen eye chart still used today. Physical measures included, among others, weight, arm span, height, head circumference, head length, and sitting height. Test-retest correlations on these measures were, as one might suspect, quite good, but their predictive validity regarding genius was disappointing to say the least.

The psychological tradition of measurement as developed by Galton had an impact on American scholars. James M. Cattell, who received his doctorate under the direction of Wundt (somewhat in opposition to Wundt's wishes, Cattell did his dissertation on individual differences as opposed to similarities in human reaction time), became familiar with Galton's work while lecturing at Cambridge in England. Cattell returned to the United States, eventually receiving the first appointment as a professor of psychology while at the University of Pennsylvania. In an article written in 1890, Cattell first used the term *mental tests*.

Cattell later moved to Columbia University and continued to develop his investigations into individual differences. Concurrent with these efforts to delineate the scope of human variability on a variety of dimensions was the realization that mental illness and mental retardation were two distinct ailments. With the recognition that the intellectually retarded comprised a distinct subpopulation came the need for a reliable and valid indicator of cognitive ability. Frenchman Alfred Binet met this need.

Alfred Binet: Assessing Cognitive Development

Alfred Binet was born in 1857 in Nice, France, and graduated from the Lycée Saint-Louis with a degree in law in 1878. So impressed with the exciting advances being made at that time in medicine, he decided to pursue a career in medical science, eventually completing his doctoral dissertation on the insect nervous system.

While Galton's work impressed Binet, the latter was convinced that Galton's measures were too basic and narrow to assess higher cognitive abilities. In 1904 Binet was invited by the Minister of Public Instruction to recommend a means of assessing intelligence in children. Working with a colleague, Théodore Simon, the two developed the Measuring Scale of Intelligence, which included 30 items organized in their order of difficulty. The test was revised in 1908 to include 59 items so that children between the ages of 3 to 13 could be assessed. The purpose of this test was to differentiate retarded children from their normal counterparts in the belief that the retarded children could not profit from the existing school curriculum.

Although Binet's scale has been revised numerous times, it still has a profound impact on the construction of tests for preschool and school-aged children even today. Many items appearing on contemporary tests of cognitive ability (e.g., Minnesota Preschool Scale, McCarthy Scales of Children's Abilities) are nearly identical to some of the items appearing on these early Binet scales (Kaufman, 1983).

Controversy over the Measurement of Intelligence

Binet's work and that of his colleagues generated considerable controversy and raised issues that still draw heated debate today. Charles Spearman, for example, suggested that intellectual ability could not be changed through instruction or training. Binet was very disturbed by these views and eloquently responded:

> Some recent philosophers appear to have given their moral support to the deplorable verdict that the intelligence of the individual is a fixed quantity, a quantity which cannot be augmented. We must protest and act against this brutal pessimism. . . . a child's mind is like a field for which an expert farmer has advised a change in the method of cultivating, with the result that in place of desert land we now have a harvest. It is in this particular sense, the only one that is significant, that we say that the intelligence of children may be increased . . . namely the capacity to learn, to improve with instruction. (Skeels & Dye, 1939, p. 116)

Binet also was confronted with the issue of cultural bias when an investigator in Belgium found that children tested there performed substantially better than children tested by Binet in France. When he examined the test results, Binet found that the children in Belgium who took the test "belonged to a social class in easy circumstance." He recognized that normal children from an enriched environment could perform significantly better than children of similar ability who experienced an impoverished or poorly enriched period of cognitive development.

Thus, by the early part of this century it was recognized that developmental and cognitive tasks could be used to rank young children according to a population norm by chronological age. The metric procedures were available to validate these measures, and there were some significant issues that needed to be addressed. Important issues focused on how to assess early abilities, how these early abilities related to those important in learning in an academic setting, whether intelligence was an innate and fixed ability, and how these measures should best be used.

Prior to addressing these historically important and contemporary controversial issues, an understanding of what constitutes normal development is in order. While other chapters in this volume may highlight relevant developmental milestones, the intent here is to demonstrate how multifactored early development is and how difficult it is to devise accurate predictive measures.

Normal Development in Infants and Young Children

Normal neurobehavioral development has been well documented only recently through the careful observation of clinicians and researchers alike. It is critical to understand that behavioral development does not begin at birth; considerable sensory and motor development occurs prenatally.

Prenatal Development

Hooker (1952) examined neurobehavioral development in 131 fetuses, ranging in age from 5 weeks postconception to approximately 45 weeks of gestation. This study found that at or around 10 weeks postconception, most fetuses will respond to oral stimulation, and at about 24 weeks, the sucking reflex is established. At 25 weeks deep tendon reflexes, including both knee and ankle reflexes, are established.

Sensory development also occurs prenatally. At about 8 weeks of gestation, a fetus will respond to tactile stimulation. Hearing structures are formed by approximately 6 months of gestational age. However, reports that prenatal infants can hear apparently are seriously flawed. First, the ear canal of the fetus is filled with a waxy gel that would seriously attenuate hearing. Further, as intrauterine noise level (mother's heart beat, bowel sounds, etc.) is quite high (50-70 dB), it is impossible to know if the infants are responding to sounds perceived or to vibrations felt through the uterine wall during these experiments. More sophisticated experiments in which the fetal heart rate is monitored for stimuli-specific changes suggest that the fetus does respond to auditory stimuli by about the 25th week of gestation. Hynd and Willis (1988) provide a more detailed discussion of these issues.

Consequently, we should conceive of development as ongoing, with considerable sensory and motor development occurring prenatally. Because of the success of neonatal intensive care units, it has been necessary in the past several decades to develop scales to evaluate developmental maturity in premature infants. Knowledge about early neurobehavioral development led to the publication of a number of scales that take between 10-45 minutes to administer. These scales include the Neonatal Behavioral Assessment Scale (Brazelton, 1973), Early Neonatal Neurobehavioral Scale (Scanlon, Brown, Weiss, & Alper, 1974), and the Neurological Assessment of the Preterm and Full-Term Newborn Infant (Dubowitz & Dubowitz, 1981). Basically these scales formalize and standardize as much as possible the neonatal neurological examination and provide a good indicator of developmental fetal maturity (Hynd & Willis, 1988).

Normal Postnatal Neurobehavioral Development

We cannot assess cognitive ability in neonates as presumably their neurological system is not sufficiently developed to integrate sensory stimuli. Consequently, in early development the rapidly developing motor system becomes the focus of assessment procedures. Muscle strength and muscle control develop rapidly, such that by approximately 10 weeks of age many normal infants can hold their head horizontal when held face down. At birth infants typically lie down with their knees drawn up under the abdomen, but by 12 weeks or so they may lie on their abdomens with the head held vertical (looking up) and their weight distributed on their forearms. Strength develops sufficiently rapidly that by 28 weeks they may be able to lean on one arm while lying down.

Postural muscles develop quickly, such that by 10 months most infants can sit unaided and twist their bodies around to pick up things in their environment. Muscles in the limbs develop quickly as well. By 36 weeks many infants can pull themselves into a standing position but do not have enough muscle strength to lower themselves down again. Most 1-year-olds show an active interest in walking and do so on the average by 14 months. By 2 years of age most children can go up and down stairs by themselves, one step at a time. By age 3 they can climb using one foot per stair, yet still need to come down using two feet per stair. By 4 years of age most children can readily go up and down stairs as adults do, one foot per step at a time.

Motor development continues dramatically, and this development is most likely highly correlated with the degree of neurological maturation of those regions of the brain that contribute to these abilities (Hynd & Willis, 1985). By age 2, for example, most children can run but cannot skip. Skipping is a very difficult motor task, and many children do not master it until kindergarten age.

More refined motor development also occurs during this early period. By 6 months most children will be able to transfer an object from one hand to another, and by 10 months the palm grip favored by infants gives way to the more refined pincer grasp in which objects are held between the thumb and forefinger. By 15 months most children can drink from a cup, and by 18 months or so a child may be able to turn the pages in a book. By 3 years of age many children can dress themselves but still cannot tie their shoes, an ability many still fail to master by age 5 or later—perhaps because of the widespread use of Velcro. Toilet training should be completed by 2½ years, and by age 5 about 90% of children can remain dry all night long, although boys may still experience bouts of bed wetting after this age.

Concurrent to these rapidly developing skills, children begin to engage in behaviors with clear relevance to the perceptual-motor tasks required in the early school years. For example, by approximately 2½ years a child should be able to copy a vertical line. By age 3 most children should have mastered copying a circle, and by age 4½ most can draw a square. A triangle is more difficult to draw than a square, and most children can draw one by age 5. Copying a diamond should be mastered by age 6.

Language begins rather inelegantly at about 5–7 weeks, when infants begin producing vowel sounds. By 28–30 weeks many infants can produce consonant-vowel (CV) syllables such as "ba" or "da." By approximately 32 weeks two-syllable words may emerge (e.g., "dada"). At about 14 months of age most children are capable of saying their first meaningful word, and by age 2, several simple-word sentences are reasonable to expect of a normal child. Pronouns also begin to be used in speech at about this time.

The documentation of the emergence of these behaviors in normal infants by Arnold Gesell at Yale University and others helped form the foundation for the development of a number of scales for the assessment of infants and young children. From the brief overview provided so far, one can well imagine how difficult it was to develop reliable measures because, as we have seen, developmentally prominent behaviors range from those related to postural control to the emergence of complex language by age 5 years. In other words, the scales that were to be developed had to focus initially on behaviors more related to overt neurological integrity and then, at the older ages, on more linguistically oriented behaviors, which in turn reflect the ontogeny of the rapidly evolving cognitive-linguistic systems.

Development of Tests for the Infant and Young Child

Because the development of the infant and young child followed a fairly predictable course, it seemed a reasonable task for researchers in the early 1920s and '30s to devise schedules that would allow for an accurate estimation of developmental status. Brooks and Weintraub (1976) correctly noted that early interest in infant testing was spurred on by two forces. The first related to the fact that many well-respected scholars, particularly Darwin, stressed in their writings the importance of studying infants. It was believed that by doing so we could obtain better insights as to those behaviors that separated man from the other primates. Considering the widespread interest in anthropology at this time, it is no wonder that researchers eagerly took up the challenge to study, in an empirical fashion, the developing infant and young child.

A second factor that influenced scholars arose from the social welfare movement. The emergence of social agencies early in this century resulted in widespread programs of adoption. The fact that the medical and biological parental history was poorly known in many of these children prompted a significant need for an assessment device that could distinguish the normal child from one with significant developmental delay. Although few adoptive parents were willing to accept developmentally delayed children, many would take "normal" infants and children. Thus, if a valid and reliable assessment instrument could be developed, the social agency could provide objective evidence of normality to the prospective parents. Also, to a lesser extent, the medical community desired an instrument that could be used for research purposes. With these forces at work, a number of scholars responded to meet the need. The work of Gesell and Bayley are particularly important and deserve mention.

Gesell's and Bayley's Early Contributions

Arnold Gesell, a pediatrician at the Yale Clinic of Child Development, invested approximately 40 years in refining methods to chart behavioral development in infants and young children. Gesell argued that his work was not to develop an intelligence test as Binet had done, but rather to develop scales of mental growth. As mental growth, similar to physical growth, followed an orderly sequence, it should be possible to chart its course over years.

The development of an initial schedule involving 50 children at 10 age levels (0, 4, 6, 9, 12, 18 months; 2, 3, 4, 5 years) resulted in scores in the areas of motor development, language development, adaptive behavior, and personal-social behavior. Important in Gesell's early efforts was the fact that he attempted to use the child's natural responses in a normal environment.

Following this initial effort, Gesell began a much more ambitious longitudinal project in 1927. A very carefully selected sample of normal, white, middle-class children were followed during their first year, at a year and a half, and at each birthday through 5 years of age. An enormous body of data grew, including a detailed medical history, family record, daily records, physical measurements, and so on. All this work resulted in the Gesell Developmental Schedule, appropriate for evaluating a child from 1 month through 6 years of age. Consistent with Gesell's earlier schedule, the developmental items were organized such that four domains of physical and cognitive development were assessed. From this assessment, age scores could be derived within each domain.

Although Gesell's work was very sound in that he reported on the reliability and validity of his scales, its real value lay perhaps in that his careful documentation of development provided a rich source of data for developing other assessment procedures. Within this additional research, the work of Nancy Bayley emerges as important in extending our ability to assess infants and young children.

Gesell was interested primarily in charting the course of development. Bayley's objectives stand in some contrast, addressing instead some very important theoretical and clinical questions highlighted in the works of previous scholars. She was interested in knowing, for example, whether mental development was invariant over age, whether good predictor variables of later cognitive and academic achievement existed, and what the relationship was between early attainments in development and later ones.

To answer these questions she participated in the Berkeley Growth Study and collected longitudinal data on infants and children through 3 years of age. Bayley developed her own test items, but like many other researchers, she also borrowed items from the work of Gesell. The data provided through Bayley's studies suggested that it was possible to develop a reliable test of developmental and mental maturity, but that performance on the items at an early age did not have good predictive value at later ages. In fact, performance on some items during early development correlated negatively with later cognitive achievements.

From her studies, Bayley (1933) concluded that "behavior growth of the early months of infant development has little predictive relation to the later development of intelligence" (p. 74). In fact, only after age 2 did Bayley find much of a relationship to later performance on items that tapped more complex cognitive processes.

The work of these investigators highlights the psychometric procedures and difficulties encountered in developing reliable and valid measures of development and cognitive maturation in young children. Though the need for more refined measures by mid-century was even greater than at the beginning of the century, a realization existed that very important theoretical and practical issues were yet to be resolved.

Issues in Assessing Infants and Young Children

Even though a number of assessment schedules and tests have been developed for use with infants and young children, many problems remain. Some of these pertain to how one conducts the evaluation, while others relate to important psychometric issues.

Clinical Assessment

Consider for a moment how practically difficult it is to obtain a good assessment result with a severely retarded young child. As was noted earlier, children's drawing abilities may be a good indicator of developmental level. For example, in assessing a severely retarded preschooler of 2½ years, one cannot simply ask the child to draw a vertical line as one would a normal 2½-year-old. Rather, the examiner may need to assist the child in grasping the pencil or crayon and model the behavior required. In other words, in trying to obtain the best possible indication of a child's developmental maturity, the examiner must be proactive in attempts to elicit the performance. The more intrusive or assertive the examiner is, however, the more the assessment process itself changes, and the child's resulting performance may be a less valid indicator of his or her actual developmental attainment.

Dealing with children who are developmentally delayed often poses other problems (Strichart & Lazarus, 1986). For example, children of severely delayed ability not infrequently have concurrent behavior problems ranging from extreme difficulty in maintaining attention to self-abusive behavior. To help the child focus his or her limited attentional resources, the examiner may need to divide the assessment into several very short sessions in order to obtain the best estimate of developmental potential. However, as the test may have been normed on children at one sitting, one could question whether it is valid to allow one examinee multiple sessions to maximize the probability of obtaining his or her best performance while requiring a presumably normal child to sit through one long, perhaps tiring assessment session.

The answer to the above question naturally depends on the purpose of the assessment. If one wishes to obtain the most positive estimate of developmental maturity independent of the negative effects of some condition (e.g., severe attentional problems, cerebral palsy), then modifications of the testing session are justified. On the other hand, if one wishes to obtain a sample of whether or not a child can sit still for an hour-long examination and do reasonably well, then breaking up the testing session is not justified.

In clinical practice, of course, the most optimal performance is usually elicited, but it should be clear that by modifying the standardized testing procedures, the clinician runs the risk of obtaining less valid results; consequently, predictions about future performance may be compromised somewhat.

Psychometric Issues

Several important psychometric considerations also deserve consideration. In a clinic setting it is not unusual to be asked to provide an assessment of a child who has had a prior evaluation. Suppose for the sake of discussion that the prior evaluation, conducted at age 5, revealed a developmental age of approximately 4 years and documented severe attentional problems. A year has passed since the evaluation and the child has responded very favorably to stimulant medication prescribed for the attentional problems. The current assessment reveals above-average mental ability, and you are asked to explain why the results of the present assessment are so significantly different from the one provided a year previously.

Many questions can and should be asked. For example, is the difference due to the effects of the stimulant medication? Was the prior test result obtained incorrectly? Were different tests used at the two testing periods? Did the child not feel good the day of the first evaluation and thus do poorly? Or, did the child simply "catch up" developmentally? Although it is unlikely that a truly definitive answer to these questions can be provided, important psychometric issues deserve to be considered in thinking about the possible answers.

If tests are to have any value in charting development or in making predictions, the scores obtained must be reasonably stable, both in terms of performance on intrascale items and over time. The first issue is referred to as *internal consistency,* the second as *test-retest reliability.*

Generally infant scales and tests are reasonably internally consistent. For example, Werner and Bayley (1966) found that correlation coefficients between items on the Bayley Scales of Infant Development (Bayley, 1969) ranged from .51 to .95 for the items through the 1½-year level. Tests given during the first year produced coefficients in the .80 range, which is traditionally judged to be satisfactory.

The test-retest reliability of infant and preschool measures is a major concern.

One of the very significant problems with these instruments is that at different ages, different constructs of development may be measured. In infancy, motor development is assessed primarily, while at the later ages (e.g., 4 to 5 years), the scales assess perceptual-motor and linguistically based cognitive development. Consequently, test-retest reliability over long time intervals (e.g., a year or more) often is not very good.

Further, because these scales and tests must be administered to young children with limited attentional capabilities, they often are composed of relatively few items. The effect of the small number of items is compounded when one considers the many other influences (e.g., chance variation, motivation, or attentional factors) on a child's test performance. These factors likely have a significant effect on the resulting test score, thus lowering the correlation over different testing sessions.

Also, there may be an increasing impact of the environment on a child's cognitive growth over time. As will be discussed in the next section, different effects on cognitive development may be apparent in children depending on whether or not they have been raised in a stimulating environment. Such variability in environmental stimulation can affect test-retest correlations.

Finally, test-retest correlations may be affected by the developmental process itself. Because by adulthood not a great deal of intellectual development takes place during a year's time, we would not expect a great deal of test-retest variation to occur. Infants and young children, however, develop very rapidly, and the evidence suggests that this development may be uneven over time. In other words, an individual child may experience very rapid cognitive development over a 6-month period and then little over the next 3 months.

Generally test-retest correlations with infants are poor, particularly in the very young; it is not unusual to find correlations ranging from -.24 to .44 for 1- to 2-month-old infants. For older infants and young children, test-retest correlations generally increase over development, ranging in the .60 to .85 or higher range (Brooks & Weintraub, 1976). A historically conservative position says that the test-retest reliabilities of these measures is not acceptable until 18 to 24 months of age, and that only after a child is 2 years old should one expect an acceptable correlation across testing sessions (Thorndike, 1940). Considering these psychometric issues, can or should these tests be used to make predictions about later performance?

Early reports on the predictive validity of infant and preschool measures of mental development were very discouraging. Some researchers reported correlations in the .50 range for certain tests to predict scores a year later. Bayley (1933), in her seminal studies, found that scores obtained in the mid-portion of an infant's first year correlated only .22 with his or her score at 2 years.

However, the results obtained from infants and children with either developmental delays or some other serious difficulties (usually of neurological origin) were much more promising. In one of the most methodologically sound studies, Knobloch, Pasamanick, and Sherard (1966) found that scores obtained in infancy on the Gesell Developmental Schedule correlated well with Stanford-Binet scores obtained at later ages. Performance on these measures by neurologically impaired children at 8–10 years produced correlations in the .70 range. The correlations were considerably higher for those children with neurological-developmental problems than for their unimpaired counterparts.

More recent attempts to assess neurodevelopmental status in infants and very young children have led to the use of the Denver Developmental Screening Test (Frankenburg, Dodds, Fandal, Kazuk, & Cohrs, 1975) and the Neonatal Behavioral Assessment Scale (Brazelton, 1973), among other measures. Also, researchers are beginning to more objectively assess other variables that impact significantly on later cognitive attainments, such as socioeconomic status, achievement motivation, social development, and language abilities. However, Honzik's (1976) conclusions are still relevant. With regard to the predictive validity of early measures of infant development, she asserts the following:

1. Scores obtained on early scales of infant development generally are not predictive of later intellectual growth.
2. Adequate prediction of later intellectual levels is only possible after approximately age 2.
3. Regardless of the medical condition, the prediction of later intellectual development is significantly greater among young children with serious delay.
4. A constant, stimulating environment produces the most stable predictive relationships. Infants and young children who live in disruptive and disorganized environments show the least consistency across assessment intervals.

Theoretical Models of Intelligence

To this point the discussion has considered why and how cognitive maturation is assessed in infants and young children, recognizing that the measures used assess components of cognitive ability that are correlated with or reflected in intelligence. The next step then is considering how intelligence is viewed theoretically.

What is it that we believe we are measuring on our tests and scales? Does general ability have an innate component? Is it a fixed quantity? Can it be altered through environmental influences? What are we trying to predict when we administer developmental scales to infants? The simple answer is what Boring (1923) proposed some 60 years ago: "Intelligence is what the tests of intelligence test." Unfortunately, not all test authors have conceived of intelligence in the same fashion.

Binet, for example, believed that intelligence was a collection of faculties that included judgment, common sense, initiative, and adaptability. Wechsler viewed intelligence as comprised of two factors, one verbal and one performance based. Others, such as Guilford, have believed that intelligence derives from numerous multidimensional factors. Vernon proposed a hierarchical theory, comprised of g or innate native intelligence at the highest level, followed by two second-order factors, a verbal-educational one and a practical-mechanical one (Wolman, 1985).

Wechsler's definition is probably the most widely accepted today, even by those who may advance other theories of cognitive processing. He proposed that intelligence

> deals not with mental representations but with relations that may exist between them, and . . . as a cognitive process, intelligence involves primarily the perceptions of relations. . . . this process is independent of the specific modality in which the terms are perceived. For effective functioning intelligence may de-

pend more upon the intactness of some rather than other portions of the brain, but in no sense can it be said to be mediated by any single part of it. (Wechsler, 1958, p. 20)

Though great disagreement may exist among the details of the various models of intelligence, there are basically three perspectives: those who have argued that intelligence is the result of polygenetic endowment, those who suggest a main effects environmental model, and finally those who argue in favor of an interactive or transactional model (Haywood & Switzky, 1986).

Those supporting the notion that genetic endowment contributes most significantly to intellectual capacity cite research that suggests (a) there exist higher correlations between adopted children's IQ and that of their biological parents than with that of adoptive parents (Scarr & Weinberg, 1977); (b) the often striking similarity in intellectual characteristics between identical twins over that of fraternal twins (McAskie, 1978); and (c) the well-documented depression of intelligence in the children of consanguineous relationships. Recent behavioral studies continue to support a substantial genetic stability in cognitive development from 2 years through adulthood (DeFries, Plomin, & LaBuda, 1987).

The position that most human endowment is the product of environmental influences stems from research showing that (a) children's mental development is correlated with the direction of change in their environment (e.g., development is enhanced in an enriched environment and declines in an impoverished one; Switzky & Haywood, 1984); (b) mild and moderate mental retardation unrelated to organic pathology seem to appear almost always in lower socioeconomic levels (Robinson & Robinson, 1976); and (c) IQ scores are highly correlated with educational attainment, and the relationship between IQ and achievement increases with age (Stanovitch, Cunningham, & Freeman, 1984).

A number of scholars argue against these narrow perspectives, however. At a more emotional level, the genetic perspective has been viewed as pessimistic, and, as opponents argue, it offers little incentive for the development of social programs aimed at addressing social impoverishment. Others suggest that such a perspective represents the worst of a racially oriented perspective.

The truth of the matter is that most today would agree that the genetic effects model and the main effects environmental model are too simplistic to explain the range of human variability (Scarr-Salapatek, 1975; Zigler, 1970). As Switzky and Haywood (1984) suggest,

> main effects models may be tenable only for very extreme cases, including those in which the children are profoundly brain damaged and unable to respond to environmental variations, or in which the environment is so disorganized and pathological that all children no matter what their genetic endowments, will have depressed development. (p. 860)

Transactional Perspectives

The transactional model of intelligence recognizes that there must be significant interactions between the genetic phenotype and the environment (Haywood & Switzky,

1986). Evidence in support of this position is gleaned from studies that suggest (a) there exist differential developmental effects on children with birth defects, depending on the rearing environment; (b) the suppressing effects of severe malnutrition on IQ occur in children under 2 years of age, primarily among children from impoverished backgrounds who also experience poor physical growth (Richardson, 1977); and (c) the fact that fetally malnourished infants develop normally only if their rearing environment is supportive (Zeskind & Ramey, 1978).

Basically, the transactional model supposes that an active genetic program asserts itself in one's developmental attainments. At the same time that the genetic endowment provides a path for the course of development, strong environmental influences can facilitate or attenuate this genetically directed program. In fact, the genetic program most likely variably affects not only intelligence but temperament, learning behaviors, the regulation of attention, and other facilitatory or inhibitory behaviors related to successful maturation.

After birth there are significant interactions between the existing genetic program and the infant's environment. The work of Plomin, DeFries, and Loehlin (1977) and Scarr and McCartney (1983) suggests three kinds of genotype-environment interactions. First, a passive kind may exist where the biological parents provide an environment that is correlated to the genotype of the child either in a positive or negative sense. Second, an evocative relationship may exist where the child acquires behavioral responses from others that are more directly influenced by his or her genotype. Finally, a more active effect may occur that represents the child's selective learning from environmental components that may be influenced by his or her genotype yet indirectly related to his or her biological predispositions.

Consequently, one may view the environment as not only a medium for the expression of genetically driven behaviors but as a medium that synergistically and selectively impacts on the maturing organism over the course of development. Conceptually, as a child matures, an evolution may take place in which a passive effect between genotype and environment during infancy gradually yields to a more active genotype-environment interaction by adolescence. Thus, as one matures, biological-genotypical factors increasingly may be selectively reinforced by an active pursuit of experiences consistent with genetic predispositions.

This conceptualization may become clearer if we consider an example of a child who may have a genetic predisposition for learning disabilities specific to reading (see Figure 2.1). If this child lived in our earlier food-gathering society, this predisposition would never become evident. However, because he lives in our demanding pluralistic society where reading is a requisite skill, there is a good chance his genetic predisposition for a learning disability will become evident through his early school years.

In our conceptual model we see that learning behaviors and achievement motivation, as an example, may be affected not only by a predisposition for learning disabilities but by potentiator variables that may impact positively or negatively on genotypic behavior. Risk factors such as poor home environment or poor school environment may impact more negatively on a passive genotype-environment effect early in development but not have such a profound effect later in development when a more active interaction occurs.

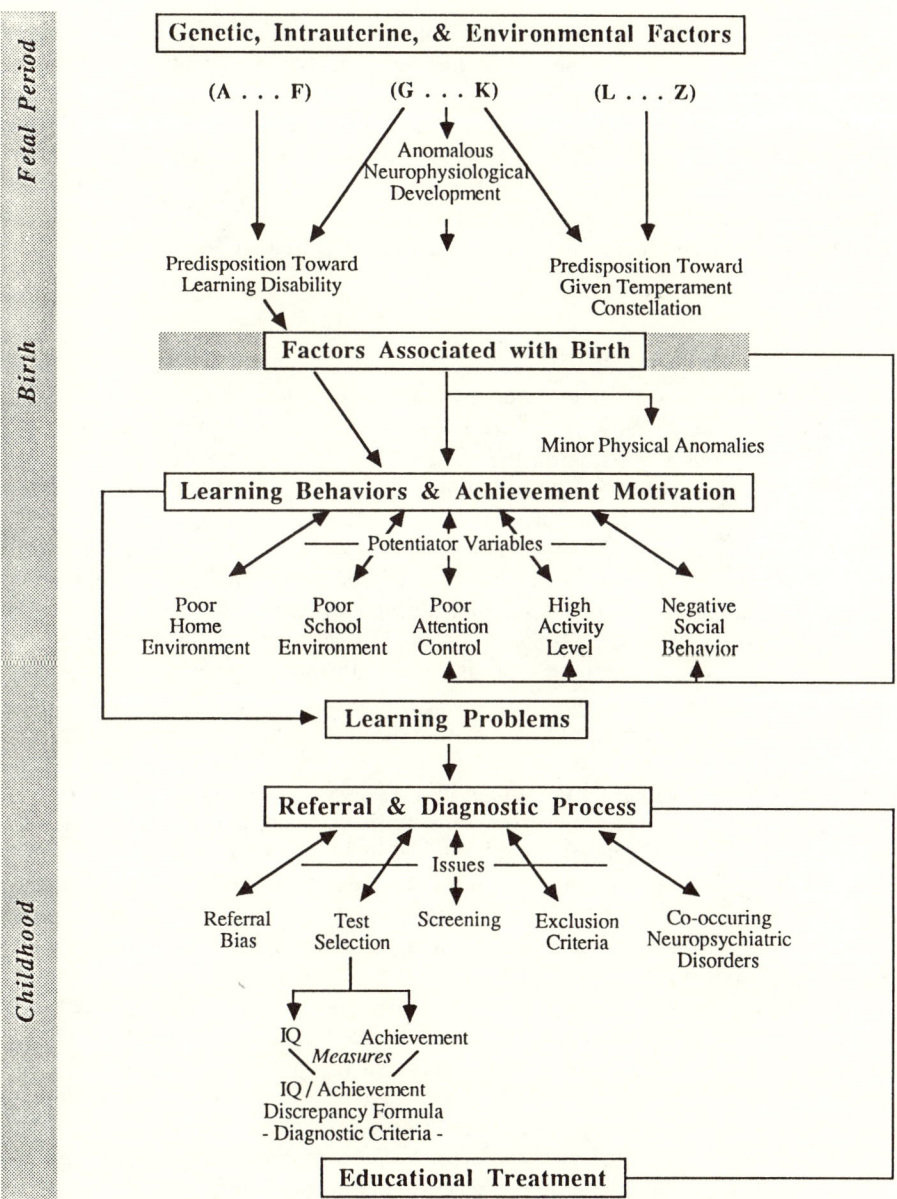

FIGURE 2.1. Neurobiological-sociobehavioral model of learning disabilities, reflecting a transactional conceptualization of development. (Modified from R. Martin, Department of Educational Psychology, University of Georgia, Athens, Georgia, with permission.)

Depending on the cumulative effects of the existing genetic program, potential deviations in neurological organization, and the effects of the potentiator variables, a learning or behavioral problem may well result. Basically this modified transactional model presumes that neurobiological factors, including the existing genetic program, impact most significantly in early development, while sociobehavioral variables modify, attenuate, or accelerate the trajectory of development. Once learning or behavioral problems are identified, then other conceptual and theoretical issues emerge, such as those related to referral bias, test selection problems, screening, and so on.

Implications for Assessing the Infant and Young Child

The implications of such a model for assessment should be evident. Conceptually it makes sense that if we wish to predict future learning or behavioral problems, we must initially focus on the more biologically driven behaviors, such as neonatal reflexes, developmental behavioral attainments, and other early reflections of the genetic trajectory. However, as the child matures and develops cognitive skills, it makes sense to assess not only intelligence as reflected in test scores, but also the valence of other potentiator variables such as socioeconomic status, motivation, attention, social reinforcers, and the impact of the social environment.

Haywood and Switzky (1986) would most likely agree with this position, as they also view the assessment process as requiring a more dynamic and comprehensive process than is most typical in today's schools or clinics. The assessment of the infant may be achieved best through existing developmental schedules. However, as the young child matures, the assessment process should become a multifaceted-multimodal one, in which far more than IQ is assessed. As suggested in our conceptual model, the procedures of assessment may likely result in higher coefficients of predictability if the effects of potentiator variables are evaluated in some formal fashion. In the final analysis, assessment should be not only conceived of as addressing the level of cognitive development attained, but also as requiring an empirical appraisal of environmental and biological potentiator variables that impact on the genetic predispositions.

If the goals of assessment remain unchanged and we continue to provide assessment as we have in the past, it seems that our knowledge regarding the interactions between genotypic behavior and the environment will not have been put to the most productive use. If, however, we modify our practices of assessing young children to better reflect our evolving understanding of human development, we will be able to enhance our potential significantly to predict which children are delayed in development, what synergistic interactions are occurring between their ongoing mental development and their environment, and, perhaps more importantly, what variables have the greatest potential to enhance the trajectory of ontogeny.

References

Bayley, N. (1933). Mental growth during the first three years. *Genetic Psychology Monographs, 14*, 1.
Bayley, N. (1969). *Manual for the Bayley Scales of Infant Development*. San Antonio, TX: Psychological Corporation.
Boring, E.G. (1923, June 6). Intelligence as the tests test it. *The New Republic*, pp. 35-37.
Brazelton, T.B. (1973). *Neonatal Behavioral Assessment Scale*. Philadelphia: Lippincott.
Brooks, J., & Weintraub, M. (1976). A history of infant intelligence testing. In M. Lewis (Ed.), *Origins of intelligence* (pp. 19-58). London: Wiley.
DeFries, J.C., Plomin, R., & LaBuda, M.C. (1987). Genetic stability of cognitive development from childhood to adulthood. *Developmental Psychology, 23*, 4-12.
Dubowitz, L., & Dubowitz, V. (1981). *The neurological assessment of the preterm and full-term newborn infant* (Clinics in Developmental Medicine No. 79). Philadelphia: Lippincott.
Frankenburg, W.K., Dodds, J.B., Fandal, A.W., Kazuk, E., & Cohrs, M. (1975). *Denver Developmental Screening Test* (rev. ed.). Denver, CO: Ladoca Project and Publishing Foundation.
Haywood, H.C., & Switzky, H.N. (1986). The malleability of intelligence: Cognitive processes as a function of polygenic-experiential interaction. *School Psychology Review, 15*, 245-255.
Honzik, M.P. (1976). Value and limitations of infant tests: An overview. In M. Lewis (Ed.), *Origins of intelligence* (pp. 59-95). London: Wiley.
Hooker, D. (1952). *The prenatal origin of behavior.* Lawrence, KS: University of Kansas Press.
Hynd, G.W., & Obrzut, J.E. (1986). Childhood exceptionality: Historical antecedents and present positions in psychology and education. In R.T. Brown & C.R. Reynolds (Eds.), *Psychological perspectives on childhood exceptionality* (pp. 3-27). New York: Wiley.
Hynd, G.W., & Willis, W.G. (1985). Neurological foundations of intelligence. In B.B. Wolman (Ed.), *Handbook of intelligence: Theories, measurements and applications* (pp. 119-157). New York: Wiley.
Hynd, G.W., & Willis, W.G. (1988). *Pediatric neuropsychology*. Orlando, FL: Grune & Stratton.
Kaufman, A.S. (1983). Intelligence: Old concepts—new perspectives. In G.W. Hynd (Ed.), *School psychology: An introduction* (pp. 95-117). Syracuse, NY: Syracuse University Press.
Knobloch, H., Pasamanick, B., & Sherard, E.S., Jr. (1966). A developmental screening inventory for infants. *Pediatrics, 38*(2), 1095-1104.
McAskie, M. (1978). Carelessness or fraud in Sir Cyril Burt's kinship data? A critique of Jensen's factor analysis. *American Psychologist, 33*, 496-498.
Plomin, R., DeFries, J.C., & Loehlin, J.C. (1977). Genotype-environment interaction and correlation in the analysis of human behavior. *Psychological Bulletin, 84*, 309-322.
Richardson, S.A. (1977). Mental retardation in the community: The transition from childhood to adulthood. In P. Mittler (Ed.), *Research to practice in mental retardation. Vol. 1: Care and intervention*. Baltimore: University Park Press.
Robinson, N.M., & Robinson, H.B. (1976). *The mentally retarded child* (2nd ed.). New York: McGraw-Hill.
Scanlon, J.W., Brown, W.U., Weiss, J.B., & Alper, M.H. (1974). Neurobehavioral responses of newborn infants after maternal epidural anesthesia. *Anesthesiology, 40*, 121-123.
Scarr-Salapatek, S. (1975). Genetics and the development of intelligence. In F.D. Horowitz (Ed.), *Review of child development research* (Vol. 4, pp. 34-72). Chicago: University of Chicago Press.

Scarr, S., & McCartney, K. (1983). How people make their own environments: A theory of genotype-environment effects. *Child Development, 54,* 424–435.

Scarr, S., & Weinberg, R.A. (1977). Intellectual similarities within families of both adopted and biological children. *Intelligence, 1,* 170–191.

Skeels, H.M., & Dye, H.B. (1939). A study of the effects of differential stimulation on mentally retarded children. *Proceedings of the American Association of Mental Deficiency, 44,* 114–136.

Stanovich, K.E., Cunningham, A.E., & Freeman, D.J. (1984). Intelligence, cognitive skills, and early reading processes. *Reading Research Quarterly, 19,* 278–303.

Strichart, S.S., & Lazarus, P.J. (1986). Low-incidence assessment: Influences and issues. In P.J. Lazarus & S.S. Strichart (Eds.), *Psychoeducational evaluation of children and adolescents with low-incidence handicaps* (pp. 1–15). Orlando, FL: Grune & Stratton.

Switzky, H.N., & Haywood, H.C. (1984). A biosocial ecological perspective on mental retardation. In N.S. Endler & J. McV. Hunt (Eds.), *Personality and the behavioral disorders* (Vol. 2, pp. 121–147). New York: Wiley.

Thorndike, R.L. (1940). Constancy of the IQ. *Psychological Bulletin, 37,* 167.

Wechsler, D. (1958). *The measurement and appraisal of adult intelligence.* Baltimore, MD: Williams & Wilkins.

Werner, E., & Bayley, N. (1966). The reliability of Bayley's revised scale of mental and motor development during the first year of life. *Child Development, 37,* 39.

Wolman, B.B. (Ed.). (1985). *Handbook of intelligence: Theories, measurements and applications.* New York: Wiley.

Zeskind, P.S., & Ramey, C.T. (1978). Fetal malnutrition: An experimental study of its consequences on infant development in two caregiving environments. *Child Development, 49,* 1115–1162.

Zigler, E. (1970). The nature-nurture issue reconsidered. In H.C. Haywood (Ed.), *Socialcultural aspects of mental retardation* (pp. 230–259). New York: Appleton-Century-Crofts.

3

Developmental Theory and Concerns in Personality and Social Assessment of Young Children

MARY L. PEERY, PH.D. & CECIL R. REYNOLDS, PH.D.

Children's social and emotional growth and development has been approached via a number of different theories and models. Socialization has been represented as discontinuous (occurring in stages) (e.g., Piaget, Freud, and Erikson) as well as in more continuous, ever-evolving terms (e.g., social learning theory, life-span perspective, and an interactional/systems approach). Those who assess young children should be familiar with the major models of cognitive and social development, both their key features and implications as well as the related perspectives for personality assessment. The need to view assessment of personality and affective characteristics from a development perspective is neither new nor widespread. Some authors emphasize developmental theory in assessment of children (e.g., Palmer, 1983), while others simply ignore developmental differences in the meaning of children's responses altogether (e.g., Anderson, 1981).

Factors associated with deviant social development also are important to consider, in particular the impact of stressful life events (such as divorce). Once a framework for normal and pathological socialization is developed, it is possible to elaborate the relationship between cognitive variables and personality assessment, with particular emphasis on a developmental psychopathology perspective to clinical practice and application. Within this perspective, one can see how cognitive, social, and familial factors exert their influence on the choice of a therapeutic approach.

Developmental Models

Psychologists have long been interested in the age-linked changes that children undergo. Through observation and experimentation, theorists have constructed models aimed at representing child growth, maturation, and acquisition of skill. These models vary in theoretical perspective as well as in mechanism. A primary distinction involves whether the developmental model is continuous or discontinuous in nature. Early developmental models were typically discontinuous in that they viewed the child progressing through distinct, step-like changes; each step is defined as a stage, and growth is successive albeit in unit fashion. Later, or more recent, theorists focus on the important role of the environment as an interactive force and see the child's growth as part of a system. These models are classified as continuous because they envision the child's maturation as continuously evolving in a gradual, fluid progression rather than in distinctly marked stages.

The Role of Theory in Assessment

Theory is crucial to assessment because assessment is a science, not an art as many would claim. Theory also is important to personality because the latter is a scientific construct. The assessment process offers an appraisal of the presence, level, and magnitude of some latent trait or attribute. Here we are concerned with the appraisal of personality attributes that can in fact be shown to behave lawfully and that clearly fall within the realm of scientific investigation (e.g., see Eysenck & Eysenck, 1985). Again, assessment is not an art—it is directed by the internalized nomothetic guide of theory and informed by an empirical knowledge base developed over nearly a century of research.

Many may argue, as did Allport (1937) so eloquently, that all human beings are unique, to the point that they cannot be placed properly on a continuum of any trait or ability nor can their behavior be so predicted. Human beings behave in ways determined by how an ability or trait manifests itself and in opposition to other traits, making impossible meaningful predictions from isolated measures of traits or abilities. The present authors have no quarrel with the view that each human being is, in fact, "uniquely unique," but we find ourselves in accord with Eysenck (1952, p. 18) when he argues that, to the scientist investigating personality, "the unique individual is simply the point of intersection of a number of quantitative variables." Because as Eysenck and Eysenck (1985) demonstrate, if human beings are distinguishable on 10 personality dimensions, each with but 10 levels, and assuming independence of these 10 constructs, some 10,000,000,000 different human beings result, each unique. The only way to sort, organize, and understand such an immense problem is through the parsimony of theory.

Once data are gathered about an individual, meaning is assigned to them through theory, bound as it is by error. Some theories are more powerful than others, and all are ultimately wrong to some degree. However, even a theory that makes many inaccurate predictions will be retained until a more powerful one is determined. Weak, even poorly organized theories provide predictions and enhance understanding at levels beyond chance—the level at which we tend to operate when we practice art divined solely from personal experience and anecdotal data.

Theory must be put into practice, and it allows a clinician to select more quickly and accurately the most viable of a myriad assessment interpretations. The primary function of theory in practice is to guide our actions in a systematic fashion. Without a viable set of theories to ground our own behaviors, we become not professionals, not artists, but technicians who are stimulus bound, relying upon trial and error, illusioning relationships, anecdotal data, and ineffective treatment plans when confronting patients with problems not encountered previously (Reynolds, Gutkin, Elliott, & Witt, 1984).

These authors agree, too, with Tomkins (1967), who has argued so well that personality is carefully and lawfully organized and that language serves a useful analogy. Personality is organized as is language with elements of simplicity and many higher degrees of complexity—from letters, words, and phrases to sentences and varying styles, but with a set of rules of combinations that allow the generation of endless novelty (as the Eysencks argue) and a simultaneous redundancy called *styles*. These rules of combinations in personality are our theories.

Theories of personality, of which there are many, are crucial to the process of assessment, particularly clinical assessment, which must fulfill both descriptive and classificatory purposes. Whenever children are considered, however, another layer of complexity must be integrated into the process. Theories of development must be considered in conjunction with personality theory, and here we will review major developmental theories that have clear implications for how we interpret tests, the tools of assessment, as we carry forward the assessment of children's personality and behavior.

The importance of these developmental theories lies not only in the inherent knowledge and organizational base they provide as we seek to understand normal as well as pathological development in children, but also in the implications these models hold for the assessment, diagnosis, and treatment of young children. In understanding and applying the tenets of these theories, we gain a developmental perspective useful in clinical application—an essential component to an effective, individually tailored method for treating children, and a method inherent to "intelligent testing" (e.g., see Reynolds, 1987).

Cognitive Development and Piaget

Jean Piaget, a highly influential writer and theorist of child development, was interested in how intellectual processes develop in young children. Coming from a biological perspective, Piaget sought to understand how children grow and adapt to their environment while gaining knowledge and skill. To Piaget, the child is a microcosm of evolution, possessing an internal drive to seek input actively from the environment. The mechanism by which this drive is propelled consists of adaptation. The child formulates and organizes patterns of behavior or thought, termed *schemas*, by interacting with the environment (i.e., family, peers, situations, etc.). When the child encounters new experiences and information, a process of evaluation and adaptation begins whereby the new experience is either assimilated into an already-existing, compatible schema, or the existing schema is made to adapt to (or accommodate) the new information. With this process, the child continuously seeks to establish and reestablish a state of equilibrium of intellectual processes, maintaining coherence and stability in his or her knowledge of the world (Baldwin, 1968).

To Piaget, this cycle of adaptation moved the child through a series of cognitive stages, each characterized by a type of cognitive process or structure. The progression in cognitive processing was definite, invariant, and true of all children, although they could progress through these stages at different paces. Once a child incorporated knowledge and experience to meet a new stage, the old stage was discarded.

Piaget's model of cognitive development consists of four major stages: sensorimotor (birth to 2 years), preoperational (2 to 7 years), concrete operations (7 to 11 years), and formal operations (11 to 15+ years). Each period entails a characteristic mental process that must be achieved in order for the child to continue to develop and mature (Piaget, 1963).

The sensorimotor period is characterized predominantly by sensory/perceptual and motor activity as the infant searches its environment for input. The infant's basic schemas revolve around survival (e.g., eating, drinking, and sleeping). Through repeated encounters with the environment, he or she grows to physically manipulate and interact with materials, objects, and people. At its peak, this interaction with individuals and objects leads to the infant's attaining the concept of object permanence. The infant learns that objects and people exist though they are not in direct view, and that his or her actions on an object or person are separate from that object or person (Flavell, 1963; Rappoport, 1972).

Preoperational thought is propelled by the child's ever-growing ability to communicate with the world—the acquisition of language. Language not only enhances their ability to gather information, but it also teaches children about representational thought: Thoughts can be expressed by using symbols such as words and actions. The preoperational child, however, remains egocentric in that he or she is able to look at the world solely from his or her own perspective. Other views and roles of an object or person are foreign and inconceivable. Related to this egocentricity is their inability to decenter or simultaneously consider more than a single aspect or feature of a problem. For example, the preoperational child fails to understand how something can be both good and bad; things must be either good *or* bad. Finally, preoperational thought is also irreversible. The question "Why did you hide the toy?" can be very confusing to the preschool child, who cannot reverse the series of steps needed to reason what thought led to hiding the toy (Flavell, 1963).

The concrete operations child is somewhat logical and is able to categorize; however, his or her conceptual understanding is restricted to tangible objects and events. Unlike the preoperational child, the concrete operations child can think back to an earlier event, gain knowledge, and return with insight to the task at hand. Through their newly acquired abilities to reverse operations and take another's perspective, the concrete operations child can generate strategies, organize a sequence of events, and determine alternate ways to meet the same goal. In addition, the concrete thinker understands that while objects may change in shape or form depending on what contains them (e.g., water and sand), their quantitative amount remains the same—the principal of conservation (Rappoport, 1972).

As the child grows, mental processing abilities multiply and develop in leaps and bounds. The child that once incorporated data only through touch and manipulation now performs and reverses operations to generate hypotheses. The child at formal operations thinks abstractly, aesthetically, and flexibly. This child is now an adolescent who can self-evaluate not only his or her own actions, but also those of others. As these upper level cognitive processes continue to develop through adulthood, the formal operations individual becomes in tune with the gray features inherent to most decisions and ideals rather than just their limited black and white components (Baldwin, 1968).

Overall, cognitive development is an encompassing, multifaceted process. Although Piaget's conception of this development has strengths and weaknesses, our purpose is not to critique its merits or deficits but to use the model as a structural base from which to determine (a) how a child's abilities and limitations affect how he or she perceives and interacts with the world at different points in time and (b) how we as therapists can assess, diagnose, and treat the child using a developmentally appropriate method.

Implications for assessment. One can see that assessment of the child will vary in approach depending on his or her capabilities. For example, the preoperational child has developed language, but expression of thoughts and feelings is limited by the extent of language development and by the child's egocentrism. Questions led by the probe "why" will usually receive a response of "I don't know" or an illogical (to the adult mind) answer that appears merely confused because the child cannot reverse mental processes to derive an answer. The concrete operations child is somewhat logical and will be able to respond to questioning so long as the events and experiences are real or (better) are visually represented. The concrete operations child can differentiate self-perspective from other perspective (e.g., mother's perspective) and can think about thinking (i.e., metacognition). Finally, the formal operations child can engage in reflection and evaluation of self and others. The development of abstract thinking helps the child to consider many aspects and perspectives of complex problems and the analysis of these components to make decisions.

In the context of assessment with projective techniques and with unstructured interviews, the child's Piagetian stage should not only become apparent but should influence how the responses are to be interpreted. The failure to use color in formulation of Rorschach responses may be interpreted very differently, irrespective of chronological age, depending upon the "stage" of development present. Preoperational and formal operational children fail to use color for very different reasons, and different interpretations may be called for due to qualitative distinctions in the child's mental processing of the stimuli that are related to intellect and not affect.

Freud's Psychosexual Development

Although Sigmund Freud's psychoanalytic model has been reproached for its lack of scientific integrity, it is worthy to recognize its theoretical value, its contributions to our knowledge of socioemotional maturation, and its impact on personality assessment. According to Freud, behavior is determined by unconscious forces and biological drives. From the time of infancy, the child experiences pleasures and conflicts arising from physical maturation that will influence and form his or her personality. In fact, one of Freud's most important contributions entails the importance of childhood experiences in determining adult psychological adjustment.

Freud stipulated that personality is composed of three components: the id, the ego, and the superego. The id is present from birth and is instilled with the basic instinctual drives. It is intent on immediate gratification and is hedonistic in its desires. Much like an infant or very young child, the id is self-serving and highly immature (Freud, 1960; Rappoport, 1972).

Mechanisms that help to keep the id in check involve the rationalizing and reasoning of the ego. Often prompted into action by feelings of anxiety, the ego seeks to control the id by using effective coping strategies that mediate the stressful situation and relieve anxiety. Currently the concept of the ego is often termed *ego strength*. This concept is included in the interpretation of personality measures such as the Minnesota Multiphasic Personality Inventory (MMPI; Hathaway & McKinley, 1967) and in systems of the Rorschach (Exner, 1974). On the whole, ego strength serves as that volume of internal, usable coping skills, adaptations, and resources available to the individual (Exner, 1974).

Freud termed the human conscience the *superego*. Between the ages of 3 to 5½ years, the superego incorporates and stores moral values learned from the child's environment (primarily from his or her parents). The superego mediates both id and ego, either rewarding via feelings of pleasure and contentment or punishing via guilt. These three components of personality oversee the conflicts and rewards associated with maturation through the five major life stages.

Similar to Piaget's biological perspective of development, Freud's views are based on a medical model. According to Freudian theory, stage-to-stage movement is biologically determined, regardless of the completion of a previous stage. Movement through the stages is invariant and comes to all children due to physical maturation (Baldwin, 1968).

From birth to approximately 1½ years of age, the child's primary focus is eating and/or the exploration of objects with the hands and mouth. Freud called this period in the child's development the oral stage. During this stage, the child derives much pleasure from and can be comforted by oral gratification. In addition to warmth and affection, food is a major reinforcer.

The anal stage was named to denote the conflict experienced by the child as he or she becomes a more independent being. In an effort to socialize the child and teach self-control, the 1- to 3-year-old toddler is introduced to toilet training. Similar to Piaget's preoperational child, the Freudian toddler is rigid in the fight for independence and in wanting to do things by his or her plan.

As children grow and mature, they begin to explore themselves and the world around them. What makes boys different from girls and moms different from dads? During the phallic stage (3 to 5 years of age), Freud proposed that children will engage in masturbatory activity in an attempt to understand and differentiate themselves from others. In particular, Freud felt that the child suffers dissonance from (a) feelings of attachment for the opposite-sex parent and (b) resentment that attention from the favored parent is shared with the other parent. Freud (1960) called this the Oedipus complex for boys and the Electra complex for girls. As the child resolves the need for a total, all-encompassing relationship with the opposite-sex parent, he or she gains attachment with the same-sex parent through a process of identification.

According to Freud, the phallic stage is a crucial period for two other reasons. First, it is during this period that the superego or true conscience develops, as the child is now able to differentiate right from wrong in many situations. Second, the phallic stage is pivotal because the basic personality structure becomes set. Although the child's personality may evolve with time and experience, its basic groundwork has been laid.

During the next six years (ages 6 to 12; latency stage), the child's personality matures as he or she concentrates on acquiring societal values, skills, and roles. Relationships, at this point, are primarily with same-sex peers. As the body develops physically in puberty, endocrinological changes cause a reevaluation of values and relationships (the genital stage). Most children undergo the path to opposite-sex relations and progressively gain in maturity and altruism, becoming less egocentric (Rappoport, 1972).

Within this theory, Freud not only accounted for normal personality development, he also proposed means by which a child developed pathological personality traits. To Freud, pathology was merely an excess or deficit in features of normal development, that is, he placed normality and pathology on a single continuum. As the child grows, interacts with, and experiences life, he or she encounters events that can be traumatic and stressful. As a result of such experiences, the child's unconscious wrestles with reality. When reality is too overwhelming, he or she may feel the need to escape psychologically. If, on the other hand, the situation is perceived as only moderately stressful, the child's coping skills may be sufficient to wade through the conflict and maintain the course of normal development. Such conflicts are felt to result from an *aggregate* of situations, traumas, and unconscious deliberations.

When the unconscious finds reality excessively painful, the ego develops a series of defenses in order to cope with the painful stimuli. These defenses mold or alter consciousness into a form that is less threatening. When painful stimuli elicit the ego's defense mechanisms, one can (a) *repress* or refuse to allow the painful stimuli to reach conscious level (this defense underlies all other defense mechanisms to some extent); (b) perform a *reaction formation* in which the ego substitutes a negative or undesirable emotion with its positive counterpart in an effort to deny anxiety-producing negative feelings toward an object or person; (c) *project* or attribute one's feelings or characteristics to others in an effort to dissipate self-guilt and anxiety; (d) *regress* to a point in time where the self felt more stable and secure; (e) *fixate* one's development (i.e., attempt to halt one's emotional growth) so as to either maintain oneself at a secure point in time or avoid progressing into a foreseeably more demanding, less stable point in development; (f) *sublimate* one's negative or anxiety-ridden feelings into positive, socially acceptable behavior; or (g) *rationalize/intellectualize* the negative experience in an effort to regain emotional equilibrium (Freud, 1960; Jensen, 1985; Rappoport, 1972).

Examples of each of these defenses are found in everyday clinical practice. The child refusing to acknowledge a traumatic event (such as sexual molestation or desertion by a parent) chooses to eliminate or repress these memories from conscious awareness. The child who resents continually being ignored by a parent chooses to acknowledge only love for that parent (reaction formation) and claims that Billy from down the street dislikes his mean parents because they never pay attention to him (projection). The once toilet-trained preschooler experiences parental divorce and finds he or she can no longer stay dry and refrain from "accidents" (regression). A latency-aged child approaching adolescence, junior high school, and relationships with the opposite sex chooses to continue to act his or her present age in an effort to avoid "growing up" and having to deal with frightening new surroundings and experiences (fixation). A child who is socially unsuccessful chooses to concentrate on academics in order to avoid anxiety-producing social situations (sublimation). Finally, a learning disabled youngster who finds it difficult to read relates to his counselor that it does not matter that he cannot read because Johnny, Mary, and Susie cannot do math problems (rationalization/intellectualization).

The extent to which the ego develops defenses rather than age-appropriate, adaptive coping mechanisms determines the extent of pathology. According to Freud, these are the mechanisms that underlie neuroses and psychoses.

Implications for assessment. Freud's psychoanalytic theory has greatly impacted personality assessment and research. First and foremost, he emphasizes the importance of early experiences. From this premise arises the importance of obtaining a thorough developmental history and clinical interview as part of an assessment. The clinician who gathers data pertaining to birth, developmental milestones, temperament, relationships, and social/familial changes gains a wealth of diagnostic and prognostic information.

Second, Freud outlined the importance of identifying and evaluating how an individual chooses to handle stress, anxiety, and trauma. Through personality assessment, we can identify the type and amount of stress and anxiety the child is experiencing, the types of defenses the child uses to help him- or herself cope, the depth of ego development (or to what extent mature coping skills have developed), and the conditions under which the child functions both poorly and successfully. For example, one can address the following questions: Are the child's coping skills so immature that he or she has extremely low stress tolerance? Is he or she easily overwhelmed? Does he or she succeed only when situations are highly structured and predictable?

Third, Freud outlined a stage format of development. Although some may feel that the stage concept of development is stilted, identifying the stage in which the child is functioning can help to determine the child's developmental focus (e.g., What is the predominant "task" at this point in development?), how he or she perceives others, and what is reinforcing or rewarding. For example, is the child self-absorbed and self-satisfying (egocentric), or does he or she relate well to others and appreciate their needs? With whom does the child identify? What things provide the child with pleasure? What conflict(s) is the child experiencing specific to his or her developmental level? How do these developmental factors affect how the child handles changes in his or her environment (e.g., in the family)?

Interpretation of specific responses to test protocols is affected by the child's psychosexual stage. During the phallic and early genital stages, sexually laden protocols are regarded as less pathognomic generally than are similar protocols during the latency period. Of course the form of the expression of sexual preoccupation must be considered as well, and greater specificity of form may be more pathological during the genital than the phallic stage, although a demonstration of great knowledge coupled with aggressive responses during the phallic stage may lead to suspicions of abuse. This is but one example of the consideration of Freudian stage as it impacts test interpretations. The egocentricity of the responses and the use of defenses and their sophistication in projective responses also will be crucial, especially in content approaches to interpretations; purely normative-based interpretations are less but still significantly affected.

Ego Development: Erikson's Psychosocial Stages

As a student of Freud, Erik Erikson founded his theory of personality development on psychoanalysis; however, whereas Freud discussed the id, ego, and superego, Erikson's developmental model centers exclusively on the ego and the forces affecting its growth and maturation. Like Freud, Erikson's model is designed in stage fashion, with each stage characterized by a conflict. The child faces positive and negative alternatives to a conflict at each developmental level as arising from social and cultural interactive forces. Although none of the conflicts is ever resolved completely, positive adjustments at the time the conflict is experienced as well as in later life serve to guide the child on a path to a healthy ego (Erikson, 1963).

Erikson outlined eight stages in personality development. The first, trust versus mistrust (birth to 1 year), emphasizes that the infant must form a secure, stable, and nurturant attachment to the parent in order to view the world as trustworthy. Young children who experience unpredictable, arbitrary, punitive, or unstable parenting develop a sense of mistrust of the environment.

The second stage, autonomy versus shame and doubt (approximately 2 to 3 years of age), delineates the child's growing sense of independence. If the child's environment responds to this growth in autonomy by fostering positive growth, self-respect, and self-confidence, the child will gain a sense of control and mastery over the environment. A child governed by shame-induced guilt will foster feelings of self-doubt.

As the child reaches 4 to 5 years of age, he or she enters the phase of initiative versus guilt. The child develops the initiative to plan, organize, and implement goals, and he or she also grows to recognize the dividing line between fulfilling desires and abiding by rules and restrictions. The environment that dampens a child's spirit, creativity, and innovation through excessive criticism and/or punishment fosters lowered self-esteem and feelings of guilt from failing to perform to a desired level of expectation; the child builds a growing sense of often being or doing wrong. On the other hand, the environment that promotes initiative through responsibility and maturity demands fosters a healthy self-concept.

When the child encounters the early school years (6 to 11 years of age), the family is no longer the only setter of expectations, values, and rules. At this point, two potent environments impact the child's socialization simultaneously; in particular, these socializing forces mold whether the child internalizes a sense of industry or a sense of inferiority.

With adolescence comes the conflict of identity versus role confusion (12 to 18 years of age). Building on the experiences and resolutions gained from past stages, the child now asks, "Who am I?" As the varying roles differentiate and become less clouded, the adolescent's identity integrates into a unified and more productive whole; pieces and roles of an individual—student, son or daughter, and aspiring professional—grow to form one's sense of self. When crises surround the adolescent's identity formation, roles become confused, conflicts arise as to what part of the self will remain and what will be discarded or outgrown, and the future seems more raveled.

As one's identity becomes more stable, it becomes possible to engage in intimate relationships and friendships (early adulthood). With these experiences comes introspection and further self-growth and identity development. Conflicts within oneself that have been poorly resolved will limit the ability to attain intimacy with others and sustain productive relationships. In this case, one may find isolation and emptiness rather than intimacy.

Middle adulthood brings the need to contribute and/or bestow one's knowledge and expertise on society in hopes of guiding the coming generation. Erikson's term *generativity* means to propagate faith and caring in the future. Those who lose sight of their need to give back to society the benefit of one's experiences grow to be self-absorbed and stifled psychologically.

Finally, as the life cycle turns to late adulthood, Erikson finds the conflict of integrity versus despair. Do I feel satisfied with my life experiences or do I resent having so little time left? A sense of integrity is felt by those who see life as fulfilling and purposeful, while those with regrets and resentments feel despair (Erikson, 1963; Rappoport, 1972).

Implications for assessment. Like Freud, Erikson stresses the need to examine ego strength and the maturation of coping skills. Clinicians may wish to investigate psychosocial themes specific to the child's level of development and how these themes color the child's perceptions and relationships. Furthermore, one can evaluate how the social environment surrounding the child influences him or her (e.g., parenting style).

To Erikson a healthy ego meant positive self-concept and self-esteem. The need to analyze and evaluate such areas is evident. Finally, assessment of the child should lead to identifying the presence of identity crises and/or poor resolution of conflicts he or she has had to face. Such themes usually become evident in projective testing.

Even more so than in strictly Freudian approaches, ego strength may need to be assessed in adolescence under an Eriksonian model. However, such constructs as self-reliance and self-esteem become more important at earlier ages and are less independent as constructs. Thus, the emphasis of assessment for the Eriksonian and the choice of technique would be different.

Social Learning Theory

The advent of social learning theory saw an intertwining of psychoanalytic concepts with the mechanics of stimulus-response learning theory (Baldwin, 1968; Maccoby, 1980). Social learning theory is not a translation of Freudian theory into behavioral terms, but rather a means of accounting for mechanisms involved in children's socioemotional development; that is, operationally defining terms such as power and love and the processes that they affect, namely internalization and identification (Sears, Rau, & Alpert, 1965). During the 1960s and 1970s, a band of theorists undertook to examine the role of imitation in young children's learning and development. Although imitation had been studied prior to this point, Bandura and his colleagues sought to define the concept of identification via the mechanisms of imitational learning.

Bandura believed that observational learning was one of the most potent mechanisms of socialization. As the child observes another person, modeling teaches him or her new behaviors. Bandura's (1969, 1971) findings indicate that (a) adults who are previously unknown to the child are more likely to be imitated by the child if the adult is nurturant, and (b) the likelihood of imitation is increased if the model is perceived as powerful by the child (i.e., if the model controls things the child needs or wants, such as food, love, and toys). In addition, Bandura's findings weakened then current S-R conditioning theories by demonstrating that reinforcement was more instrumental in determining whether children *chose* to perform the behavior(s) in the future as opposed to their initial acquisition of the behavior(s). Imitation occurs regardless of whether (a) the model's actions are or are not copied at the time that they were modeled (learning without performance) or (b) the model or the observer receives a reward (learning without reinforcement) (Bandura & Walters, 1963). As a result, parents are no longer merely reinforcers and punishers of behaviors, they are also powerful models. Identification is a process of modeling, and imitation and the rate and path of development results from children spontaneously learning how they are supposed to behave; reinforcement and punishment merely support the performance of learned behaviors (Maccoby, 1980).

Implications for assessment. In applying social learning theory to the assessment of young children, we come to understand not only the content of what the child tells us but also the *process* involved. Process is defined as the underlying psychological mechanisms and dynamics of a response and/or interaction. For example, as the child relates what happens when he or she shares the day's experiences with a parent, the examiner obtains not only the content of the exchange but an appreciation for (a) how the child approached the parent and initiated the conversation, (b) the way the parent responded to the child, and (c) how the child reacted to the parent's response—a sense of the process underlying their interaction. As a result, we also come to understand and appreciate the reciprocal nature of the parent-child interaction.

A social learning perspective also allows us to analyze the child's and the parent's behavior to understand how the dynamics of imitation and observational learning affect their interaction. We observe and evaluate what is reinforcing the behavior of the child and the parent, respectively. Analysis of parent-child dynamics in this manner resembles the approach used by Bandura and his associates in examining the functional processes of aggression and aggressive behaviors. Research in this area finds that parents of aggressive children issue more commands and punish deviant behavior more often (Hetherington & Martin, 1979). It is interesting to note that the proportion of deviant behaviors punished is not significantly different between clinic-referred and nonclinic families; instead, the children of clinic families show higher incidences of deviant behavior. The identified pattern further reveals that parents of aggressive children are more likely to respond positively to deviant behavior (Herbert & Baer, 1972) and react negatively to nondeviant child behavior (Lobitz & Johnson, 1975), establishing no contingency for appropriate behavior. As in this example, social learning theory provides the mechanisms necessary to understanding contingencies in normal and pathological development.

Life-Span Perspective

The life-span theory of development is a continuous model, proposing that one's personality evolves over time through interactions and experiences with the environment. Several factors affect how one adapts and integrates changes in personality, namely temperament, talents, motivation, roles, and coping skills. In addition, no one phase of life is more influential than any other in shaping and/or producing a marked impact on personality development (as opposed to Freud's emphasis on childhood as the most formative period of development relating to later adjustment). Life-span theorists define personality as "that relatively consistent set of thoughts, feelings, and behavior patterns that guide the organization of experience and the direction of new growth" (Newman & Newman, 1980, p. 2).

The life-span perspective takes into account predispositional factors such as temperament (Block, 1971) and motivation (e.g., Maslow's motive hierarchy; Maslow, 1954, 1977) as well as their impact on how the child views the world and interacts with it. For example, with regard to the child's temperament, was he or she (as an infant) easy to care for, slow to warm up, or difficult to comfort (Chess & Thomas, 1973)? Is the child described best as extroverted or as introverted? Regarding motivation, Maslow would stipulate that humans have a needs hierarchy consisting of (a) physiological needs, (b) safety needs, (c) belongingness and love needs, (d) self-esteem needs, and (e) self-actualization needs. Earlier needs are physical and survival oriented, while later ones *(metaneeds)* are more aesthetic. A child who worries about meeting physical and love needs probably will not move past lower levels to meet more aesthetic, self-growth needs, arriving at self-actualization (Maslow, 1977).

The life-span perspective is an encompassing model in that it incorporates many individual theories and perspectives into one framework. It is hoped that the reader will investigate each of these theories more fully, as a true overview of each of these areas is beyond the scope of this chapter.

Implications for assessment. As stated earlier, the life-span perspective borrows from many individual research advances and assimilates them into a working model. It highlights the importance of examining social roles, motivational factors, dispositional factors (such as temperament), and the development of coping skills. In addition, life-span theorists emphasize the equal impact of every phase in development, not just childhood.

Interactional/Systems Approach

The preceding sections have discussed person-oriented models (such as Freudian psychoanalytic development) and recognized environmental theories (such as S-R conditioning theory). The interactional/systems approach to development combines these personological and environmental perspectives, viewing maturation as a "continuously ongoing, bidirectional, person-situation interaction in which the person is the intentional active agent" (Magnusson & Allen, 1983, p. 4). The interaction of person and environment is dynamic, in that one acts on the environment and is also acted upon—a system of reciprocity much like that proposed by social learning theory. Moreover, the environment consists of systems (e.g., a dyad, a family, or a work situation), and person and system(s) are indispensably linked to each other (Magnusson & Allen, 1983). Learning and development result from our interactions with these systems.

With the family as an example of a system, we can assume that (a) each family member has and brings into interactions with the family system his or her own plans, goals, motives, and so forth; (b) within the family system there exist structures of hierarchy and power as well as feedback mechanisms, and these system characteristics shape and reshape individual members of the family; and (c) each family member undergoes developmental changes and exerts behavior(s) that, in turn, continuously influence and change the family as a system. To further the example of the family as a system, we can discuss the parent-child relationship, one level of the family system. The child not only exerts influence on his or her parents through temperament and other inborn characteristics, but parents also impact on the child through love, basic satisfaction of needs, and so forth. The basis of early attachment has been demonstrated to be such a dynamic process (Ainsworth, Blehar, Waters, & Wall, 1978). Furthermore, as the child grows and matures physically, cognitively, and emotionally, these changes are met with reciprocal and dynamic changes in parental attitudes, practices, and expectations that complement changes in the child (Baumrind, 1971; Maccoby, 1980).

The interactional/systems approach has become one of, if not the most, prominent models used to understand emotional development in children and parents, particularly in attempting to understand the mechanisms of the parent-child relationship. In her 1980 American Psychological Association address, Maccoby stressed the need for bidirectional models and interactive/system studies. Developmental studies should no longer seek the mother-child dyad but, instead, should research the father, mother, child, and family as a hierarchical system (Maccoby, 1980).

Implications for assessment. Similar to social learning theory, an interactional/systems approach stresses the reciprocal nature of interaction and the individual inherent to any system. The child is part of a system; he or she is what impacts the parental system and vice versa. Pathology in particular must be understood as part of such a system. An example of the development of behavioral pathology within a system is obtained via Patterson's coercion model. Patterson (1976) proposed that the inappropriate use of rewards and punishments by parents may be responsible for the difficulties encountered in using these behavior modifiers when treating aggressive children (i.e., the children become less responsive to them). Furthermore, Patterson (1977) suggested that the poor parenting skills of these parents creates a family environment that accelerates coercive behaviors. These parents are more likely to be the target of their children's deviant behavior and less likely to be effective in terminating the deviant behavior. Patterson's coercion theory states that a desirable outcome is gained through the use of aversive manipulation by an individual. For example, a mother asks her child to pick up a toy. The child ignores the mother's directive. The mother proceeds to restate her directive more emphatically, raising her voice and becoming more aversive. The child, reacting to his mother's aversive behavior, throws a tantrum. The mother, perceiving herself in an aversive situation, fails to carry through her directive by becoming frustrated and relinquishing her position. Patterson proposes that the mother has been negatively reinforced not to carry through with directives by removing herself from the unpleasant situation. The child has been negatively reinforced to maintain his oppositional behavior by using aversive behavior successfully to undermine parental demands. The child is "the victim and architect of his environment," and the family system becomes a "reinforcement trap" (Patterson, 1976, 1979). Thus, in assessing the referred child, one must evaluate the system as opposed to assessing and treating the child in a vacuum.

PSYCHOMETRIC COGNITIVE DEVELOPMENT AND ASSESSMENT OF CHILDREN'S PERSONALITY

Particularly with regard to children, but true to a lesser extent with adults, intellectual level as determined psychometrically should be considered when interpreting responses to personality assessment techniques. Psychometric models of intelligence are nearly all continuous models of development, finding only quantitative changes in intellect across the age range. The Wechsler scales, the most successful series of individually administered intelligence tests to date, offer an excellent example of the psychometric model of intellectual development. The Wechsler Preschool and Primary Scales of Intelligence–Revised (WPPSI-R; 1989) for ages 3 years to 7 years, 3 months, the Wechsler Intelligence Scale for Children–Third Edition (WISC-III; 1991) for ages 6 years to 16 years, 11 months, and the Wechsler Adult Intelligence Scale–Revised (WAIS-R; 1981) for ages 16 years to 74 years are all formatted according to a dichotomous content-approach to intelligence (yielding a Verbal IQ and a Performance IQ) and measuring it in highly similar ways across the age span of 4 years to 74 years. Only the difficulty level, not the nature of the tasks, changes.

As children move up the intellectual continuum, their level of ability to respond to personality assessment devices increases. Language-based measures become more applicable, and a broader picture of the complex personality structure is possible. A more refined interpretation is possible if data on intellectual ability are available as well.

Responses to many personality assessment techniques are interpreted with reference to age. Projective drawings are clearly age related in quality, complexity, and meaning. Transparencies are considered a bizarre response and are keyed toward indicating potentially psychotic disturbances, but only after about the age of 5 to 6 years. Yet the same drawing, complete with transparencies, would be given very different personality-related interpretation coming from an intellectually normal 4-year-old, an intellectually normal 8-year-old, and a mentally retarded 8-year-old. As the technique becomes more complex, as with the various sentence completion methods and projective story-telling techniques, the influence of the child's level of intellectual skill on the interpretation of his or her responses becomes ever more important. For very young children, many projective tests (especially the Rorschach) are little more than assessments of general mental ability (e.g., see Koppitz, 1982).

Patterns of intellectual ability also should be considered and the law of parsimony applied liberally to test score interpretations. As an example of the latter, these authors recently encountered a psychological case report wherein a lengthy discussion and psychoanalytically based interpretation was offered of a 13-year-old girl's inability to define the word *cave* even after extensive probing by the examiner. What was not discussed, and what explained the incident in a far more terse fashion, was that despite an average nonverbal IQ, the young girl fell near the mentally retarded range in verbal IQ. Neither had the examining psychologist considered the girl's very low verbal IQ in interpreting her rather meager TAT responses, preferring to resort to explorations of her defensiveness, internalization, and inability to recognize her emotions.

Very little has been written about the moderating effects of IQ and specific patterns of intellectual ability on personality test responses. A number of authors want to give personality-based interpretations to patterns on IQ tests (a practice we neither endorse nor encourage but would condemn in most cases we have seen), but few integrate IQ into personality test responses. There is even less research than speculation on these relationships, but it is clear that IQ as determined through traditional psychometric approaches must be considered when interpreting responses to personality traits.

FACTORS ASSOCIATED WITH DEVIATIONS FROM NORMAL DEVELOPMENT

Research has identified a host of factors that play an essential role in deviating normal child development, at times to the point of emotional and behavioral disturbance. A strong association has been found between family variables and childhood psychiatric diagnosis, including such variables as broken homes, single-parent families, parental maladjustment, and marital discord (Offord, 1983). An important etiological factor associated with children developing behavioral disorders is the absence of consistent and mature parent nurturance and involvement (Shaw & Lucas, 1970). Children who experience early parental rejection often do not become adequately socialized. Their moral development is usually impaired, causing them to have an inadequate sense of "right" versus "wrong." Other parent variables related to the development of behavior disturbance include uncontrolled and punitive aggressive acts on the child (Shaw & Lucas, 1970). Severe behavior disorders (such as juvenile delinquency) have been related to parents who were hostile, neglectful, and cruel in punishing their children (Robins, West, & Herjaniz, 1975).

Overall, childrearing practices, consistency, and predictability appear to be highly influential in children's social and emotional adjustment. Via modeling and reinforcement, parents affect the child's growth and level of competence (Sabatino, 1987). Aggressive acts modeled by the parent can increase the chances of the child's developing aggressive tendencies. Furthermore, learning or reinforcing maladaptive communication patterns within a family can cause children to learn coercive, negative communication styles, depicting poor conflict resolution and reactive as opposed to contemplative responses to situations (Minuchin, Montalvo, Guerney, Rosman, & Schumer, 1967). Parental psychopathology also can lead to modeling of poor adjustment and/or inconsistent parenting, particularly if the parent's mental illness is chronic (Willis & Holden, 1987). Finally, feelings of ambivalence toward a child (i.e., a parent who feels uncomfortable with the parental role or is unsatisfied with the child) can lead to maladaptive parental style that creates dysfunction for the child and the family.

Examining this extensive array of research is far too large in scope for the present work; however, an analysis of some key findings is warranted, particularly those findings instrumental to understanding the parent-child relationship.

Negative Life Events

Researchers have found that negative life events (e.g., death in the family, divorce, and financial concerns) and chronic stress and strain (e.g., due to parental employment, unemployment, or marital conflict) can adversely affect children's adjustment and development (Moos & Billings, 1982; Sandler & Block, 1979). Furey and Forehand (1984) found that working mothers report significantly more displeasing child behaviors. This finding becomes more salient if the working mother heads a single-parent household. Hetherington, Cox, and Cox (1977) described the overburdening number of tasks facing the unintact family. Routines and roles fail to be assigned systematically and performed, resulting in a high level of family disorganization. A single-parent family (usually mother-headed) faces many stresses that make the mother susceptible to social and psychological maladjustment. As a single parent, the mother assumes the salient and pivotal family role in dealing with stress, and her adjustment to these stresses plays a determining factor in shaping her children. Also, many broken homes experience financial duress. Preschoolers whose mothers begin work outside the home following a divorce tend to become conduct disordered. The child seemingly undergoes a sense of double desertion, with paternal absence and the mother working. No relationship was found between maternal employment and child behavioral problems if the mother was employed prior to the divorce (Hetherington et al., 1977).

Parental Psychopathology

In exploring the dynamics of child psychopathology, researchers have examined the relationship between child deviance and parental mental illness. It has been established that parents of referred children generally score higher on personality scales such as the MMPI. For example, two scales are consistently found to be elevated across studies: Psychopathic Deviate (Pd) and Hysteria (Hy) (Johnson & Lobitz, 1974). Hetherington and Martin (1979) also found that children who were anxious and withdrawn tended to come from families in which at least one parent (although often both) displayed neurotic behavior. Other investigators consistently have found the presence of personality disorders in parents of maltreated children. Pathological histories had been presented for two, three, or more generations in these families (Oliver, 1985).

The University of Rochester Child and Family Study (URCAFS; Harder, Kokes, Fisher, Cole, & Perkins, 1982) examined the effects of acute versus chronic parent mental illness on child functioning. Children rated less competent came from parents who were chronically impaired and failed to respond to their children. These children tended to have parents evidencing psychotic disturbances as opposed to affective symptomatology. It is likely that the socioemotional and cognitive development also would be less than optimal, given the deprivation of interaction and responsiveness to the child's environment. A single life event such as an acute episode of parent psychopathology was less traumatic to the child than an environment clouded with ongoing and continued strain. Further analyses suggest that the effects of a chronically emotionally unstable parent may be buffered by a balanced emotional relationship with the other parent.

One disorder that has attracted a good deal of attention in regard to child adjustment is parental depression. Researchers have demonstrated a relationship between maternal depressive moods and poor parenting (Orvaschel, Weissman, & Kidd, 1980). First, depression may create in the parent a sense of intolerance for child behaviors. For example, depression may be accompanied by such symptoms as psychomotor agitation, difficulty sleeping and eating, and a disturbed ability to concentrate. In other words, a depressed individual is subject to a deficit in organized cognitive and emotional resources that can (a) serve to lower their tolerance level; (b) lead to correcting behavior that would otherwise be unnecessary; and (c) possibly lead to an increased use of punishment rather than more positive approaches to discipline (Christensen, Phillips, Glasgow, & Johnson, 1983).

Marital Satisfaction

Parental dissatisfaction with the marital relationship has been seen not only to precipitate behavior and emotional problems in children, but also to maintain them (Rogers, Forehand, & Griest, 1981; Satir, 1964).

Family systems analysts have proposed that marital discord is a seed from which child disturbance grows (Christensen et al., 1983). Children with conduct disorders have been found to have parents with unhappy marital relationships and to witness interparental conflict (Johnson & Lobitz, 1974; McCord & McCord, 1959; Rutter, 1974). These parents are characterized as isolated and indifferent to each other, as actively quarreling, or as aggressing against one another. Studies of family interaction in the homes of delinquent children indicate a high degree of marital strife, with husbands frequently verbally abusing their wives. Little conflict or disagreement was noted in the homes of normal parents (Hetherington, Stouwie, & Ridberg, 1971). In their early study on delinquents, the McCords (1959) found that quarrelsome, broken, and neglecting homes ranked highest in rates of delinquency (70%). Thus, not only broken homes but also nuclear homes are seen to relate to an increase in children's antisocial behavior as the quality of the marriage deteriorates (Rutter, 1971).

One of the single largest and most profoundly researched areas of child development involves the effects of marital conflict and divorce on children. Studies involving both referred and nonreferred children have revealed that children having undergone parental divorce show a greater likelihood of manifesting emotional turmoil as conduct disordered behavior (Hetherington et al., 1977). How can this behavioral response tendency be explained? One possibility is

> that children adopt the predominant behavior exhibited by their parents during a crisis and that this becomes a guiding framework for later behavior coping. In the case of divorce—particularly . . . one . . . preceded by considerable acrimony and conflict—anger, aggression and hostility are the behaviors displayed by the parents and adopted by the child. (Hetherington & Martin, 1979, p. 273)

Parental modeling appears to be the key. In comparison, the death of a parent is usually related to depression and anxiety in children (Hetherington, 1972). The parent likewise models withdrawal, depression, and mourning (Felner, Stolberg, & Cowen, 1975).

Several researchers have proposed that it is the conflict projected from marital discord rather than the actual divorce that is essential to the development of conduct-disordered child behaviors (Emery, 1982; Rutter, 1971, 1974). Rutter (1975) reported that boys evidencing delinquent behaviors were more likely to live in intact, unhappy families than in broken harmonious homes. Oltmanns, Broderick, and O'Leary (1977) examined the relationship of marital adjustment and conflict with child deviance and reported significant correlations between discord and conduct disorders, feelings of inadequacy and immaturity, and personality problems. Porter and O'Leary (1980) also reported significant correlations between marital hostility and these same child deviance variables in addition to an association with socialized delinquency. These correlations were significant for boys but not for girls. Whitehead (1979), in a sample of 2,775 seven-year-old English children, found that marital discord was related to negative behavior in girls and boys, although a stronger relationship did exist for boys.

One of the few dynamics investigated in the marital adjustment–child deviance literature involves the perceptions of these parents as related to actual child behavior. O'Leary and Emery (1985) conducted an extensive review of the literature and found that parental perceptions of marital conflict and child behavioral dysfunction were not significantly correlated in the general population yet strongly correlated within treatment-referred populations. Similar findings have been reported suggesting that parents who were experiencing dissatisfaction with their marital relations perceived child behaviors more negatively (Christensen et al., 1983; Ferguson & Allen, 1978; Forehand, Brody, & Smith, 1986; Furey & Forehand, 1984; Griest, Forehand, Wells, & McMahon, 1980) and demonstrated greater difficulty in using positive approaches. These parents equated implementing contingencies with the use of punishment. As an aside, fathers' discomfort (arising from poor personal and marital adjustment) was also related to intolerance of child deviance and to a negative attitude toward positive discipline approaches (Christensen et al., 1983). The interaction of marital adjustment and child behavior has been shown to affect parent perceptions to a greater degree than either of the respective variables in and of themselves (Forehand et al., 1986; Griest et al., 1980).

In summary, a child who is deviant, noncompliant, or disruptive, and concurrently has a mother who is dissatisfied with her marital relationship, is perceived to be more maladjusted; the presence of these two factors is more predictive than the child's behavior problems or the unhappy marriage, respectively. These results are particularly reliable, given that they were replicated across different child behaviors with a young clinic-referred sample and subsequently on a nonreferred sample of adolescents employing different instrumentation (Forehand et al., 1986). Increased parent perceptions of child maladjustment also have been related to poor behavioral treatment outcome and poor treatment generalization (Forehand & Brody, 1985). To further underscore this relationship, it has been found that relieving marital conflict alleviates, if not prevents, child deviance (Oltmanns et al., 1977; Kent & O'Leary, 1976). An additional finding by Kelso and Stewart (1986) suggests that mothers' remarriage may be related to a decrease or resolution of aggressive behavior disorders in children. Boys who no longer evidenced aggressive behaviors had mothers who had been married a greater number of times than mothers of boys with persistent conduct disorder behavior (2:1). Given the poor history of conduct-disordered children (usually marked by antisocial models and conflict-ridden life-styles), these authors suggest that those boys who showed improvement had mothers who had divorced and removed themselves and the children from a disruptive home situation and remarried. These stepfathers tended to be more stable.

Parental Resources

The parental support network involves several elements: the marital relationship, work satisfaction and support, friendships and extended family relations, and extracurricular activities. These areas are conceived as external resources available to the parent, and their importance for psychological and physical well-being has been well documented (Mitchell & Trickett, 1980). Further evidence has been gathered outlining the effects on parental functioning. Social support is felt to enhance parental functioning by (a) delivering emotional support, (b) providing assistance (such as information, advice, or help), and (c) establishing models of social expectations (Belsky, 1984). These elements of support can have a direct impact on child development (e.g., praise from a relative regarding some child-rearing technique) or an indirect effect (e.g., mother's self-esteem is heightened from positive remarks from her husband and co-workers).

The marital relationship has been seen to play a large role in child development. The interactional facet of marriage serves as a social model for the child, and marital conflict affects the parent-child relationship through negative attitudes, increased stress, and dysfunctional interaction patterns. The marital relationship also can exert other influences. Sears, Maccoby, and Levin (1957) observed that mothers' feelings of esteem for their spouses were related to the encouragement and reinforcement they directed at their children. In both sets of research (marital conflict and resource/support literature), the amount of warmth and/or support involved in the marital relationship held some direct or indirect effect on child adjustment. Whether the marital relationship is the most important source of support (as Belsky, 1984, would propose) remains to be determined.

Relatives, friends, and neighbors comprise an important social network from which to obtain support. Access to and support received from these significant others has been shown to have positive effects on parent-child interaction (Hetherington et al., 1977; McLanahan, Wedemeyer, & Adelberg, 1981; Reis, Barbera-Stein, & Bennett, 1986). The presence of such a social network has been associated with mother's greater sense of competence in that she is better able to appreciate the individual differences in her children and appreciate her need to adjust to their developmental capabilities (Abernethy, 1973). An extended social network also has been associated with a decrease in the use of punishment and restrictive attitudes in mothers (Pascoe, Loda, Jeffries, & Easp, 1981). It is hypothesized that the availability and use of a social network helps to enhance self-esteem, which in turn enhances the parents' sensitivity to their child (Belsky, 1984).

It should be noted that the presence of a social network need not always be perceived as positive. Contact with friends and relatives may prove to be stressful if the advice and support received is considered interfering. French, Rodgers, and Cobb (1974) feel that it is the "goodness-of-fit" between the desire for support and support received that explains the interaction best.

The absence of a social network also has been found to impact parent-child relations. Research has shown that problem families tend to be socially isolated (Furey & Forehand, 1984; Gabarino, 1977; Tonge, James, & Hillam, 1975). The occurrence of child abuse tends to run concurrent with social isolation (Gabarino, 1977). Similarly, families producing conduct-disordered children are also withdrawn from community influences (Moore, 1982). Tonge et al. (1975) studied 33 problem families and their social systems. These families displayed marital conflict, sociopathic or psychological illness in the parents, and delinquent children. Moreover, a marked lack of contact with neighbors and relatives was also characteristic of these families. In comparison to control families, problem families also participated in fewer social activities.

The most extensive work in this area was conducted by Wahler and his associates. They pursued lower and middle income families and monitored the number and types of contacts with their community (Wahler, 1980). Middle income mothers had outside daily contacts that outnumbered low income mothers by a margin of 4:1. The majority of these contacts were found to be positive interactions with friends. Outside contacts of low income mothers were predominantly with relatives or agencies offering assistance. The community networks of these mothers were punitive in nature rather than supportive. Wahler came to term these mothers "insular" due to their relative social isolation. An inverse relationship was found between the mothers' daily contacts with friends and the rate of aversive parent-child interactions. Days characterized by high friendship contacts were related to low rates of aversive parent-child behaviors and vice versa. Insular mothers also were more likely to engage in and sustain longer coercive interactions with their children; the coercive interactions were usually more than twice as long as similar interactions of noninsular mothers (Wahler, Hughey, & Gordon, 1981). It was concluded that many families who did not demonstrate and maintain treatment gains failed to do so because of their insular characteristics; that is, because of their limited positive support with the community (Dumas & Wahler, 1983; Wahler, 1980; Wahler & Afton, 1980). Webster-Stratton (1985) also found lack of social support to be a consistent predictor of treatment success or failure. Overall, parents with better psychological resources seem to have more competent children.

A Developmental Approach to Psychopathology

For decades, children were assessed, diagnosed, and treated using adult clinical practices, perspectives, and instruments (Garber, 1984; Sroufe & Rutter, 1984). The developmental models discussed indicate that children are vastly different from adults, and their level of cognitive and socioemotional development determines how they perceive, react to, and adjust to stress, anxiety, and changes in their environment. For example, a 3-year-old and a 10-year-old react quite differently to parental divorce, given their differing cognitive understanding, perspective-taking skills, and expressive and receptive language abilities (terms such as *divorce* and *visitation rights* will be quite difficult for the 3-year-old to understand). The 3-year-old under stress and anxiety due to divorce may regress and become enuretic. This is seen as a more "normal" or less pathological symptom for the 3-year-old than the development of this same behavior for the 10-year-old child. In other words, differing degrees of pathology are inferred due to the different developmental levels of children displaying the same behavior. Developmental psychopathology involves the unification of developmental and clinical perspectives in an effort to assess and elucidate the developmental processes pertaining to the disordered behavior, how the behaviors developed, and how they change and adapt (Masters, 1981).

Incorporating the Developmental Psychopathology Approach into Clinical Application

A child's developmental change poses prescriptions and proscriptions regarding the type of interventions that can be used to enhance functioning, in that developing physical, cognitive, behavioral, and emotional features determine what interventions are efficient, ineffective, and/or contraindicated. The clinician must understand the child and the child's interaction with his or her environment under three capacities: (a) the child as stimulus, (b) the child as processor, and (c) the child as shaper and selector (Kendall, Lerner, & Craighead, 1984).

As discussed previously in examining social learning theory and the interactional/systems perspective, child-environment relationships are reciprocal or bidirectional. The child exerts influence on his or her environment that as a consequence causes a reciprocal effect on the child. As a result, the clinician must assess the child's behavioral and physical stimulus characteristics, how caregivers react to the child, what feedback is returned to the child (i.e., the consequence of the child's behavior), and how the child is affected by this interaction. Intervention strategies that focus on or eliminate any given factor will be ineffective because they fail to capture the essence of the dysfunction inherent to the system, concentrating only on the child or the environment—single units within the system. As the therapist initiates work with the child, it is also wise to recognize that a new system has been formed—a therapist-child system—and to assess the dynamics of this system in a similar fashion.

In defining developmental psychopathology, the child's varying ability to process information was discussed. One can see that the same stressors and/or the same interventions will be processed differently by a child at different points in development. This, in turn, results in differing effects. As such, "not all interventions are equally useful across the life span, and intervention decisions need to coordinate the features of one's chosen strategy with what is known about the [child's] individual developmental trajectory" (Kendall et al., 1984, p. 74). As noted, age is an important but insufficient consideration in this process, and intellectual level also must be addressed as a key developmental index. Kendall et al. (1984) further discuss instances where children's developmental characteristics are crucial to the appropriateness and effectiveness of an intervention. For example, the use of systematic desensitization requires an evaluation of how the child manifests anxiety. Research has shown that young children exhibit crying, screaming, and (at times) a need to be held, while older children exhibit the rigidity and tenseness of muscles characteristic of (or more specific to) adult expressions of anxiety and are far more responsive to treatment using systematic desensitization.

Another example involves teaching verbal and nonverbal self-control strategies in an effort to slow down the thinking of impulsive young children. This intervention requires children to evaluate their plans, strategies, goals, and behaviors; that is, to use their metacognitive awareness. Young children do not begin to develop and/or use such abilities until approximately 7 years of age. The use of such an intervention with a much younger child, chronologically or intellectually, probably would not prove fruitful.

The clinician evaluating the child's roles as shaper and selecter recognizes that a child brings to a given situation competencies, deficits, and perceptions that determine how he or she will react to that situation, and, in return, how factors in the situation will react to and affect the child. Therefore, one would want to assess how the child evaluates (a) the situation's cues and demands (i.e., its rules, structure, etc.); (b) the situation's personal and behavioral characteristics (i.e., the features associated with the people and relationships involved in it); and (c) the extent to which the child recognizes how the environment and human or personal factors match. In turn, one assesses whether the child's ineffectiveness is due to a deficit in knowledge, understanding, or processing of the situation, or if a deficit in the skills needed to successfully mediate, adapt to, and perform in this situation exists. Intervention strategies then would be applied that assisted the child in building skills for self-change, situation change, or both (Kendall et al., 1984).

When a child is referred, the clinician should examine the system in which the child lives, for the child and the problem do not develop in a vacuum. The professional should actively seek to obtain developmental histories, assess personality variables (defined in the broader, European tradition) and system interactions, and assess what the child and the system, respectively, contribute to the referral problem. Such an approach ensures the recognition of children's individual needs and the tailoring of our tools and expertise to meet them.

REFERENCES

Abernathy, V. (1973). Social network and response to the maternal role. *Interactional Journal of Sociology and the Family, 3,* 86–92.

Ainsworth, M.D.S., Blehar, M.C., Waters, E., & Wall, S. (1978). *Patterns of attachment.* Hillsdale, NJ: Erlbaum.

Allport, G. (1937). *Personality.* London: Constable.

Anderson, L.W. (1981). *Assessing affective characteristics in the schools.* Boston: Allyn & Bacon.

Baldwin, A.L. (1968). *Theories of child development.* New York: Wiley.

Bandura, A. (1969). Social-learning theory of identificatory processes. In D. Goslin (Ed.), *Handbook of socialization theory and research* (pp. 10–20). Chicago: Rand McNally.

Bandura, A. (Ed.). (1971). *Psychological modeling: Conflicting theories.* New York: Aldine-Atherton.

Bandura, A., & Walters, R.H. (1963). *Social learning and personality development.* New York: Holt, Rinehart & Winston.

Baumrind, D. (1971). Harmonious parents and their preschool children. *Developmental Psychology, 4,* 99–102.

Belsky, J. (1984). The determinants of parenting: A process model. *Child Development, 55,* 83–96.

Block, J.H. (1971). *Lives through time.* Berkeley, CA: Bancroft.

Chess, S., & Thomas, A. (1973). Temperament in the normal infant. In J.C. Westman (Ed.), *Individual differences in children* (pp. 149–155). New York: Wiley-Interscience.

Christensen, A., Phillips, S., Glasgow, R.E., & Johnson, S.M. (1983). Parental characteristics and interactional dysfunction in families with child behavior problems: A preliminary investigation. *Journal of Abnormal Child Psychology, 11,* 153–166.

Dumas, J.E., & Wahler, R.G. (1983). Predictors of treatment outcome in parent training: Mother insularity and socioeconomic disadvantage. *Behavioral Assessment, 5,* 301–313.

Emery, R.E. (1982). Interparental conflict and the children of discord and divorce. *Psychological Bulletin, 92,* 310–330.

Erikson, E.H. (1963). *Childhood and society* (2nd ed.). New York: Norton.

Exner, J.E. (1974). *The Rorschach: A comprehensive system (Vol. 1).* New York: Wiley.

Eysenck, H.J. (1952). *The scientific study of personality.* London: Routledge & Kegan Paul.
Eysenck, H.J., & Eysenck, M.W. (1985). *Personality and individual differences: A natural science approach.* New York: Plenum.
Felner, R.D., Stolberg, A., & Cowen, E.L. (1975). Crisis events and school mental health referral patterns of young children. *Journal of Consulting and Clinical Psychology, 43,* 305–310.
Ferguson, L.R., & Allen, D.R. (1978). Congruence of parental perception, marital satisfaction, and child adjustment. *Journal of Consulting and Clinical Psychology, 46,* 345–346.
Flavell, J.H. (1963). *The developmental psychology of Jean Piaget.* New York: Van Nostrand.
Forehand, R., & Brody, G. (1985). The association between parental/marital adjustment and parent-child interactions in a clinic sample. *Behavior Research and Therapy, 23,* 211–212.
Forehand, R., Brody, G., & Smith, K. (1986). Contributions of child behavior and marital dissatisfaction to maternal perceptions of child maladjustment. *Behavior Research and Therapy, 24,* 43–48.
French, J., Rodgers, W., & Cobb, S. (1974). Adjustment as person-environment fit. In G. Cochlo, D. Hamberg, & J. Adams (Eds.), *Coping and adaptation* (pp. 243–245). New York: Basic.
Freud, S. (1960). *A general introduction to psychoanalysis.* New York: Washington Square Press.
Furey, W.M., & Forehand, R. (1984). An examination of predictors of mothers' perceptions of satisfaction with their children. *Journal of Social and Clinical Psychology, 2,* 230–243.
Gabarino, J. (1977). The human ecology of child maltreatment: A conceptual model for research. *Journal of Marriage and the Family, 39,* 721–735.
Garber, J. (1984). Classification of childhood psychopathology: A developmental perspective. *Child Development, 55,* 30–48.
Griest, D.L., Forehand, R., Wells, K.C., & McMahon, R.J. (1980). An examination of differences between nonclinic and behavior-problem clinic-referred children and their mothers. *Journal of Abnormal Psychology, 89,* 497–500.
Harder, D.W., Kokes, R.F., Fisher, L., Cole, R.E., & Perkins, P. (1982). Parent psychopathology and child functioning among sons at risk for psychological disorder. In A.L. Baldwin, R.E. Cole, & C.P. Baldwin (Eds.), *Parental pathology, family interaction, and the competence of the child in school* (Monographs of the Society for Research in Child Development, 47[5, Serial No. 197]).
Hathaway, S.R., & McKinley, J.C. (1967). *The Minnesota Multiphasic Personality Inventory manual.* Minneapolis, MN: National Computer Systems/PAS Division.
Herbert, E.W., & Baer, D.M. (1972). Training parents as behavior modifiers: Self-recording of contingent attention. *Journal of Applied Behavioral Analysis, 5,* 139–149.
Hetherington, E.M. (1972). Effects of paternal absence on personality development in adolescent daughters. *Developmental Psychology, 7,* 313–326.
Hetherington, E.M., Cox, M., & Cox, R. (1977). The aftermath of divorce. In J.H. Stevens, Jr., & M. Matthews (Eds.), *Mother-child, father-child relations* (pp. 108–125). Washington, DC: N.A.E.Y.C.
Hetherington, E.M., & Martin, B. (1979). Family-interaction. In H.C. Quay & J.S. Werry (Eds.), *Psychopathological disorders in childhood* (2nd ed., pp. 50–83). New York: Wiley.
Hetherington, E.M., Stouwie, R., & Ridberg, E.H. (1971). Patterns of family interaction and child rearing attitudes related to three dimensions of juvenile delinquency. *Journal of Abnormal Psychology, 77,* 160–176.
Jensen, L.C. (1985). *Adolescence: Theories, research, applications.* New York: West.
Johnson, S.M., & Lobitz, G.R. (1974). The personal and marital status of parents as related to

observed child deviance and parenting behaviors. *Journal of Abnormal Child Psychology, 3,* 193-208.
Kelso, J., & Stewart, M.A. (1986). Factors which predict the persistance of aggressive conduct disorder. *Journal of Child Psychology and Psychiatry, 27,* 77-86.
Kendall, P.C., Lerner, R.M., & Craighead, W.E. (1984). Human development and intervention in childhood psychopathology. *Child Development, 55,* 71-82.
Kent, R.N., & O'Leary, K.D. (1976). A controlled evaluation of behavior modification with conduct problem children. *Journal of Consulting and Clinical Psychology, 44,* 386-396.
Koppitz, E.M. (1982). Personality assessment in the schools. In C.R. Reynolds & T.B. Gutkin (Eds.), *The handbook of school psychology* (pp. 273-295). New York: Wiley.
Lobitz, C.W., & Johnson, S.M. (1975). Parental manipulation of the behavior of normal and deviant children. *Child Development, 46,* 719-726.
Maccoby, E.E. (1980). *Social development: Psychological growth and the parent-child relationship.* New York: Harcourt Brace Jovanovich.
Magnusson, D., & Allen, V.L. (Eds.). (1983). *Human development: An interactional perspective.* New York: Academic Press.
Maslow, A.H. (1954). *Motivational personality.* New York: Harper.
Maslow, A.H. (1977). A theory of metamotivation: The biological rooting of the value-life. In H.M. Chiang & A.H. Maslow (Eds.), *The healthy personality* (pp. 18-37). New York: Van Nostrand.
Masters, J.C. (1981). Developmental psychology. *Annual Review of Psychology, 32,* 117-151.
McCord, W., & McCord, J. (1959). *Origins of crime.* New York: Columbia University Press.
McLanahan, S., Wedemeyer, N., & Adelberg, T. (1981). Network structure, social support, and psychological well-being in the single-parent family. *Journal of Marriage and the Family, 43,* 601-612.
Minuchin, S., Montalvo, B., Guerney, B.G., Rosman, B.L., & Schumer, F. (1967). *Families of the slums: An exploration of their structure and treatment.* New York: Basic.
Mitchell, R., & Trickett, E. (1980). Task force report: Social networks as mediators of social support. *Community Mental Health Journal, 16,* 27-44.
Moore, D.R. (1982). Childhood behavior problems: A social learning perspective. In J.R. Lachenmeyer & M.S. Gibbs (Eds.), *Psychopathology in childhood* (pp. 48-65). New York: Gardner Press.
Moos, R.H., & Billings, A.G. (1982). Conceptualizing and measuring coping resources and processes. In L. Goldberg & S. Breznitz (Eds.), *Handbook of stress: Theoretical and clinical aspects* (pp. 10-13). New York: Macmillan.
Newman, B.M., & Newman, P.R. (1980). *Personality development through the life span.* Monterey, CA: Brooks/Cole.
Offord, D.R. (1983). Classification and epidemiology in child psychiatry: States and unresolved problems. In P.D. Steinhauer & Q. Rae-Grant (Eds.), *Psychological problems of the child in the family* (2nd ed., pp. 89-94). New York: Basic.
O'Leary, K.D., & Emery, R.E. (1985). Marital discord and child behavior problems. In M.D. Levin & P. Satz (Eds.), *Developmental variation and dysfunction* (pp. 113-121). New York: Academic Press.
Oliver, J.E. (1985). Successive generations of child maltreatment: Social and medical disorders in the parents. *British Journal of Psychiatry, 147,* 484-490.
Oltmanns, T.F., Broderick, J.E., & O'Leary, K.D. (1977). Marital adjustment and the efficacy of behavior therapy with children. *Journal of Consulting and Clinical Psychology, 45,* 724-729.
Orvaschel, H., Weissman, M., & Kidd, K.K. (1980). Children and depression: The children of depressed parents, the childhood of depressed patients, depression in children. *Journal of Affective Disorders, 2,* 1-16.

Palmer, J.O. (1983). *The psychological assessment of children* (2nd ed.). New York: Wiley-Interscience.
Pascoe, J.M., Loda, F.A., Jeffries, V., & Easp, J.A. (1981). The association between mother's social support and provision of stimulation to their children. *Developmental and Behavioral Pediatrics, 2,* 15-19.
Patterson, G.R. (1976). The aggressive child: Victim and architect of a coercive system. In L.A. Hamerlynck, L.C. Handy, & E.J. Mash (Eds.), *Behavior modification and families: Vol. 1. Theory and research* (pp. 36-50). New York: Brunner/Mazel.
Patterson, G.R. (1977). Mothers, the unacknowledged victims. In J.H. Steven, Jr., & M. Matthews (Eds.), *Mother-child, father-child relations* (pp. 12-30). Washington, DC: N.A.E.Y.C.
Patterson, G.R. (1979). A performance theory for coercive family interaction. In L.G. Cairns (Ed.), *Social interaction: Methods, analysis, and illustration* (pp. 40-47). Chicago: University of Chicago Press.
Piaget, J. (1963). *The psychology of intelligence.* New Jersey: Littlefield, Adams.
Porter, B.P., & O'Leary, K.D. (1980). Marital discord and childhood behavior problems. *Journal of Abnormal Child Psychology, 98,* 287-295.
Rappoport, L. (1972). *Personality development: The chronology of experience.* Glenview, IL: Scott, Foresman.
Reis, J., Barbera-Stein, L., & Bennett, S. (1986). Ecological determinants of parenting. *Family Relations, 35,* 547-554.
Reynolds, C.R. (1987). Intelligent testing. In C.R. Reynolds & L. Mann (Eds.), *Encyclopedia of special education* (Vol. 2, pp. 855-857). New York: Wiley-Interscience.
Reynolds, C.R., Gutkin, T.B., Elliott, S.W., & Witt, J.C. (1984). *School psychology: Essentials of theory and practice.* New York: Wiley.
Robins, L.N., West, P., & Herjaniz, B. (1975). Arrests and delinquency in two generations: A study of urban families and their children. *Journal of Child Psychology and Psychiatry, 16,* 125-140.
Rogers, T.R., Forehand, R., & Griest, D.L. (1981). The conduct disordered child: An analysis of family problems. *Clinical Psychology Review, 1,* 139-147.
Rutter, M. (1971). Parent-child separation: Psychological effects on the children. *Journal of Child Psychology and Psychiatry, 12,* 233-260.
Rutter, M. (1974). Epidemiological and conceptual considerations in risk research. In E.J. Anthony & C. Koupernik (Eds.), *The child in his family: Children at psychiatric risk* (pp. 61-63). New York: Wiley.
Rutter, M. (1975). *Helping troubled children.* New York: Plenum.
Sabatino, D.A. (1987). Behavior disorders. In C.R. Reynolds & L. Mann (Eds.), *Encyclopedia of special education* (Vol. 1, pp. 193-196). New York: Wiley.
Sandler, I.N., & Block, M. (1979). Life stress and maladaptation of children. *American Journal of Community Psychology, 7,* 425-440.
Satir, V. (1964). *Conjoint family therapy.* Palo Alto, CA: Science and Behavior Books.
Sears, R.R., Maccoby, E.E., & Levin, H. (1957). *Patterns of child rearing.* Evanston, IL: Row Peterson.
Sears, R.R., Rau, L., & Alpert, R. (1965). *Identification and child rearing.* Stanford, CA: Stanford University Press.
Shaw, C.R., & Lucas, A.R. (1970). *The psychiatric disorders of childhood* (2nd ed.). New York: Appleton-Century-Crofts.
Sroufe, L.A., & Rutter, M. (1984). The domain of developmental psychopathology. *Child Development, 55,* 17-29.
Tomkins, S.S. (1967). The ideology of research strategies. In D. Jackson & S. Messick (Eds.), *Problems in human assessment* (pp. 633-641). New York: McGraw-Hill.

Tonge, W.L., James, D.S., & Hillam, S.M. (1975). *Families without hope: A controlled study of 33 problem families.* Ashford, Kent: Headly Brothers.

Wahler, R.G. (1980). The insular mother: Her problems in parent-child treatment. *Journal of Applied Behavior Analysis, 13,* 207–220.

Wahler, R.G., & Afton, A.D. (1980). Attentional processes in insular and noninsular mothers: Some differences in their summary report about child behavior problems. *Child Behavior Therapy, 2,* 25–41.

Wahler, R.G., Hughey, J.B., & Gordon, J.S. (1981). Chronic patterns of mother-child coercion: Some differences between insular and noninsular families. *Analysis and Intervention in Developmental Disorders, 1,* 145–156.

Webster-Stratton, C. (1985). Predictors of treatment outcome in parent training of conduct disordered children. *Behavior Therapy, 16,* 223–243.

Wechsler, D. (1981). *Wechsler Adult Intelligence Scale–Revised.* San Antonio, TX: Psychological Corporation.

Wechsler, D. (1989). *Wechsler Preschool and Primary Scales of Intelligence–Revised.* San Antonio, TX: Psychological Corporation.

Wechsler, D. (1991). *Wechsler Intelligence Scale for Children–Third Edition.* San Antonio, TX: Psychological Corporation.

Whitehead, L. (1979). Sex differences in children's responses to family stress: A re-evaluation. *Journal of Child Psychology and Psychiatry, 20,* 247–254.

Willis, D.J., & Holden, E.W. (1987). Emotional disorders. In C.R. Reynolds & L. Mann (Eds.), *Encyclopedia of special education* (Vol. 1, pp. 603–607). New York: Wiley.

4

Clinical and Psychometric Considerations in the Cognitive Assessment of Preschool Children

RANDY W. KAMPHAUS, PH.D., JANNA DRESDEN, M.A., &
ALAN S. KAUFMAN, PH.D.

This chapter is presented as a primer for the beginning assessment clinician. In this context assessment clinicians may encompass a range of professional groups working with children, including speech/language pathologists, psychologists, educational evaluators, nurses, and others. More specifically, the discussion that follows is designed for the clinician involved in cognitive assessment.

Although factors such as test selection and interpretive skill are crucial for the accurate assessment of young children, an equally critical variable is the examiner's ability to develop a working relationship with the child. This skill at establishing rapport is essential for testing all clients, especially young children. Once clinical skills are mastered, then knowledge of psychometrics becomes preeminent. Some psychometric pitfalls are common to the clinical assessment of children of all ages, but certain phenomena are more relevant to the assessment of preschoolers. Examiner difficulties with the "basics" or essential aspects of psychometric knowledge constitute some of the most common problems.

The overview that follows first addresses the skills necessary for developing a working relationship with young children and their parents that is conducive to testing. Next, measurement "basics" such as derived scores will be considered, along with other psychometric concepts that seem to cause problems for the users of cognitive tests. Rather than focusing on numbers and formulae, however, the emphasis here is on understanding the psychometric issues, as a lack of such knowledge becomes the precursor of misinterpreted assessment results.

CLINICAL CONSIDERATIONS

All assessment situations involve an interaction between the characteristics of the examiner, the characteristics of the examinee, and the location (in time and space) of the assessment. These variables are extremely important and are essentially independent of the psychometric instrument being used (Sarason, 1954). The examiner must consider the nature of these variables and their possible impact on his or her performance when planning and evaluating an assessment of a young child.

Characteristics of Examinees

Although all children are different, there are specific ways in which most young children are similar to each other and different from older children and adults. These traits, known as developmental characteristics, necessitate that examiners possess special skills and sensitivity in order to conduct an assessment of a young child. Although their characteristic spontaneity and lack of pretense make young children a delight to encounter socially, these aspects present very real challenges to those who deal with them in more structured settings.

Young children view the world differently from adults and older children and so have a different view of the assessment process. More specifically, children under the age of 5 or 6 tend to be egocentric and unable to take the perspective of another person. Because young children can understand only their own feelings and needs, they are less likely to be motivated by extrinsic rewards and often are less compliant than older children (Lidz, 1983). Even though young children typically want to please adults, it is nearly impossible for them to put the needs of others ahead of their own. Clearly, motivating a young child to participate in an assessment can be quite challenging, an issue to which we shall return.

Several other developmental characteristics also relate to the behavior of young children in assessment situations. The physical development of these young subjects requires a high level of activity, and they may have trouble sitting still for long periods of time (Lidz, 1983). Dealing with this straightforward problem may require considerable ingenuity on the part of the examiner. Also, many children of this age require naps (Paget, 1983) and/or frequent snacks, so testing sessions must be scheduled to accommodate these needs.

One of the major developmental tasks of the preschool years is the ability to separate successfully from significant adults. As many children continue to struggle with this issue, the assessment process will be complicated by the difficulties involved in being away from a parent or trusted teacher (Lidz, 1983).

The cognitive capabilities of young children also differ from those of older children and create challenges for the examiner. Preschoolers can perceive or focus on only one dimension of an object at a time (e.g., height *or* width). They can remember only a few pieces of information at a time, and do not know how to use mnemonic strategies to increase their memory capacity. They do not understand the principle of transitivity; that is, knowing that $A > B$ and $B > C$ does not imply to them that $A > C$. Preschoolers do not understand concepts of time, or even such relational terms as *alike* or *different,* and often do not have well-developed expressive verbal skills (Kaufman & Kaufman, 1983; Lidz, 1983).

Finally, the behavior of young children simply is more variable than that of older children (Lidz, 1983) and, in addition, they are much more susceptible to the influence of extraneous variables. The characteristics of the examiner and of the environment exert more control over the performance of children, especially young ones, than they do on the performance of adults (Anastasi, 1988).

Examiner Characteristics

Examiner characteristics, a significant variable in the effective assessment of young children, can be described in three dimensions or types: demographic characteristics, personality and appearance, and examiner expectations.

Individuals who assess young children may vary by age, race, ethnicity, native language, gender, and social class. These demographic differences tend to elicit different responses from young children. For example, children may perform better for younger examiners than for older ones. However, the process by which examiner characteristics (demographic as well as others) influence children's behavior is not well understood. Clearly, however the process is complex and interactive; for example, age of examiner may be relevant only for certain types of children and under certain testing conditions (Barber, 1973; Anastasi, 1988; Epps, 1974; Sarason, 1954). Thus we have a warning about the importance of the demographic characteristics of an examiner, but few clear guidelines about how to minimize their impact. The two specific recommendations one can glean from the literature relate to the negative consequences that occur when young black children are tested by white examiners (Epps, 1974) or when children from linguistic minorities are tested by individuals unfamiliar with the child's language and culture (Figueroa, 1990). These results seem to indicate that children are likely to perform better when examined by adults who share their background on as many dimensions as possible. In addition, examiners who are familiar to the children seem to elicit better performances (Anastasi, 1988; Epps, 1974).

Research on the effect of examiner personality on young children's performance also has yielded results that emphasize the interactive nature of the process. The personality of the examiner interacts with the personality of the examinee as well as with the type of test and the purpose of the assessment (Anastasi, 1988).

However, a fairly clear view emerges of what might be called an "optimizing style" or set of personality characteristics that most likely will elicit optimum performance from young children (Epps, 1974). These characteristics include being friendly, cheerful, relaxed, warm, and natural (Anastasi, 1988); reassuring and encouraging (Anastasi, 1988; Epps, 1974); and patient (Paget, 1983). Note that these attributes describe a style or approach more than a personality. It is unreasonable to expect that all examiners will have identical or even similar personalities, nor are children so brittle as to be able to deal effectively with only one type of person. Most children can work effectively with any adult who is sincerely interested in them, who genuinely enjoys their company, and who makes every effort to be responsive to their needs and temperament.

An examiner's appearance also may play a significant role in the assessment of a young child. Examiners must present a professional image to parents and teachers while being ready to conduct an assessment on the floor. Simple clothing allows for a variety of activities while preventing the possibility that bright colors or elaborate jewelry will distract examinees from the assessment tasks.

Examiner expectations about how well a child will perform on a test may be communicated unintentionally to the child and thus have an impact on his or her actual performance (Anastasi, 1988). However, this phenomenon probably is not as pervasive as was once believed (Barber, 1973), nor is it unavoidable. Research suggests that the *halo effect,* as these expectations are called, can be minimized, not by denying that we form these opinions, but by being expressly aware of them and making every attempt to avoid their impact by closely following standardized procedures (Sattler, 1988).

In conclusion, it appears that a variety of examiner characteristics can influence the results of an assessment. These variables have more impact with difficult tests, novel tasks, tasks utilizing ambiguous stimuli (Anastasi, 1988), and in situations where the child is experiencing a high level of anxiety (Epps, 1974). Obviously a great many variables interact in complex ways to determine the outcome of an assessment.

Characteristics of the Environment

The importance of environmental variables was pointed out by Sarason (1954), who stated that there exists an

> unstated but oft made assumption that a test measures something independent of the conditions or time of measurement. In these terms a test presumably is like an x-ray: regardless of the conditions external to the patient (the immediate environment) the "thing" being studied (e.g., a bone, intelligence, fantasy) can be observed in splendid isolation—a statement which is true neither for a test nor for an x-ray. (p. 59)

As with examiner variables, young children have been found particularly susceptible to variations in the environment, which necessitates that professionals pay close attention to aspects of the environment and their potential influence on young examinees. In contrast to the literature on examiner characteristics, the discussion in the area of environmental variables has focused almost exclusively on a description of the optimal testing environment (Anastasi, 1988; Paget, 1983; Sattler, 1988). To provide an optimal testing environment,

1. The testing room should be
   a. free from interruptions;
   b. pleasantly, but minimally, decorated so as not to distract the child;
   c. well lit (but without being too bright, and there must be no glare);
   d. adequately ventilated;
   e. quiet, with no noise from adjoining rooms;
   f. a few degrees cooler than a room meant for adults, as children have higher body temperature than adults; and
   g. sparsely furnished, to minimize possible distractions.
2. The furniture should be
   a. comfortable, and
   b. child sized (a table 36 inches long and 20–24 inches wide with adjustable height is best). Elbows should rest on the table and feet on the floor (if the child's feet do not touch the floor, put a box under them to avoid a restless feeling).

3. The materials should be
   a. child sized (i.e., large crayons);
   b. well organized and accessible to the examiner;
   c. placed directly in front of the child and set up so that he or she can reach only the materials needed for the current task;
   d. set up so that the examiner can use the manual effectively without its becoming a barrier between him- or herself and the child; and
   e. set up so that the examiner can use the scoring sheet efficiently, but the child cannot see it.

Another environmental variable involves the timing of the assessment. As was mentioned earlier, sleeping and eating routines must be considered when scheduling an evaluation of a young child. In addition, examiners need to consider the possible impact of activities that precede the assessment (Anastasi, 1988). Children are likely to behave differently in an assessment situation if the preceding activity has been a boisterous outdoor time or a quiet story time.

Finally, no other persons should be present in the testing room. The presence of others, especially parents, is likely to distract young examinees and make it difficult for them to concentrate on the test (Paget, 1983).

Planning an Assessment

The planning stage is absolutely essential to a successful assessment and has both conceptual and practical aspects. The necessary conceptual planning involves learning about the background and presenting problem of the child and thus placing the testing session in context. Each assessment must be viewed as an "individualized investigation" (Lidz, 1983), and the examiner must carefully consider the purpose of the assessment, who has requested it, and the stresses and supports the child experiences on a daily basis. Only by considering all of these factors can the examiner truly understand the total situation and be prepared to conduct an assessment.

Advance preparation also is crucial from a practical perspective. The examiner must be totally comfortable with the instructions for all of the tests to be used and must have the materials organized so that smooth and swift (and sometimes unanticipated) transitions can be made between tasks (Paget, 1983). These skills are necessary so that the examiner can concentrate fully on the child's needs and responses rather than on the presentation of materials or instructions. Because the behavior of young children can be variable, examiners must be prepared to be flexible; the ability to be so while adhering to standardized procedure requires a high level of expertise. The development of this expertise comes from a great deal of supervised practice (Anastasi, 1988).

Conducting an Assessment

The complex process of conducting an assessment involves a number of different aspects. The first step occurs when the examiner meets the child; these few moments constitute a critical period for establishing rapport with the child. The examiner's second task is to introduce the tests in such a way that the child is interested in them and motivated to perform well. Perhaps the most difficult aspect of conducting an assessment is keeping the child on task throughout the session. Finally, dealing with specific problems and "debriefing" the child at the close of the session also represent important assessment components.

Establishing Initial Rapport

Because all children are different, the style or approach that best facilitates establishing initial rapport will vary from child to child (Kaufman & Kaufman, 1983). Some children may feel most comfortable with a quiet and gentle approach, while others may enjoy a lively and outgoing examiner. However, a sincere and thoughtful examiner who treats children with respect and pays close attention to a few simple, but important, guidelines will be successful with most children:

1. Place yourself at the child's eye level before you begin talking (Sattler, 1988); squatting is preferable to bending over.
2. Introduce yourself to the child and ask what you should call him or her (Sattler, 1988).
3. Do not be overly demonstrative or intrusive; allow the child to make the first move (Anastasi, 1988).
4. Be honest and direct, explaining to the child exactly what will happen during the session.
5. Speak clearly, avoiding both a "cutesy," high-pitched voice and an overly technical, adult style of conversation (Paget, 1983; Sattler, 1988).

If the examiner must go to the child's classroom or day-care room to collect him or her, it is important not to ask the child to leave in the middle of an activity or as a preferred activity is about to begin (Sattler, 1988). To the extent possible, the examiner should spend some time in the classroom just watching the child. This will facilitate the familiarization process *and* likely will add a great deal to the examiner's understanding of the assessment results. When it is time to begin the session, the examiner should not ask the child if he or she is ready to go—this violates the old adage of never giving children a choice unless they do, in fact, have one. Instead, one should approach the child with positive, confident anticipation and simply state that now it is time to go (Paget, 1983). The examiner may wish to tell the child that they will be playing some games together or that his or her help is needed to gather some information. The specific words are not particularly important, but rather the approach that will make a difference.

If the child is brought to the examiner, it is helpful to begin the conversation with a neutral or "easy" topic such as the weather. Especially useful for starting conversations in these situations are concrete objects such as fish tanks or appealing toys.

Creating Interest and Motivation

Motivating young examinees requires that the examiner have an understanding of how the child perceives the assessment from a cognitive perspective and how he or she feels about being assessed. This knowledge will enable the examiner to present the various tasks in an interesting, nonthreatening manner. The plan for the entire session and the requirements of each task as it is presented should be thoroughly explained to the child. Testing should begin as soon as the child seems ready in order to maximize the time before he or she gets tired (Sattler, 1988). Tasks should be presented as games, *not* as tests, and it is generally useful to begin with subtests that are appealing and relatively easy (Anastasi, 1988; Sattler, 1988).

Keeping the Child on Task

The primary tool for keeping children on task is simply the reinforcement of on-task behavior. The examiner should use approval liberally, taking care to praise the process, *not* the product (Anastasi, 1988). Children should be rewarded for their effort, not for correct responses. Such comments as "I see you're really thinking hard" or "I can tell you're really trying" can be valuable reinforcers. It is important, however, that praise of this type be spontaneous and genuine, not redundant or perfunctory. Physical contact, used appropriately, also can be reinforcing and motivating to a child. A pat on the arm or even a hug can show children that you like them and want them to try to do their best.

Examiners find it easier to keep children on task by keeping the testing sessions brief (Anastasi, 1988) and by making allowances for different needs whenever possible. Some subtests can be done on the floor in a different part of the room, and the order of the tasks can be varied to suit the individual child. For example, shy or anxious children are likely to perform best when the initial tasks are unstructured, play-type procedures without obvious right and wrong answers, while highly active children benefit from beginning with structured activities that help them to focus their attention. It does make sense in most cases, however, to alternate tasks demanding close attention with those that are more play-like and/or emphasize motor skills (Paget, 1983).

Another area where testing sessions can be modified to suit individual needs lies in the pacing or tempo of the assessment. Some children do best with a slow and relaxed pace, while others need to move very swiftly from one subtest to the next in order to keep their attention on the tasks. Examiners should be attentive to signs of boredom, fatigue, or overstimulation and adjust the tempo or length of the testing session accordingly.

Children also should be allowed to respond in their own way and at their own pace. Knowing how to handle very slow examinees or those who frequently say they don't know the answer requires a great deal of sensitivity (Paget, 1983). On the one hand, children should not be urged to respond before they are ready, but on the other, those who reply that they don't know generally should be encouraged to try again (Sattler, 1988). It is sometimes difficult to know what to do, but when a child hesitates or says "I don't know," the examiner first should make sure that the directions have been understood and then urge the child to try again.

A final technique for keeping children on task comes with the judicious use of breaks. Some children will be refreshed by a chance to get up and stretch for a moment, others will lose their concentration and have difficulty getting back to work. The examiner should use breaks in such a way that they maximize the child's ability to perform well on the tests. Although one should let children work steadily if they seem to be doing well, it is the examiner's responsibility to watch for any signs of discomfort and offer the shy child an opportunity to use the bathroom or get a drink of water. Active or restless children frequently will request breaks or the opportunity to play again with some favorite materials. These requests can be granted upon completion of other tests, thus serving as rewards for appropriate behavior (e.g., "You may have another drink of water as soon as we finish this game"). In this way the examiner maintains control while being responsive to the needs of the child.

Problems in the Assessment Process

Most problems in the assessment process can be avoided by following the guidelines outlined thus far, by providing clear limits, and by redirecting any inappropriate behavior. When a child becomes uncooperative and is clearly not doing his or her best, the examiner should confront the child directly, but not angrily, and verbally acknowledge the situation (Paget, 1983; Sattler, 1988). The examiner should attempt to discuss the situation with the child but should not try to change the behavior through negative comments or comparisons with other children (Sattler, 1988).

If an assessment is proving totally unproductive, the examiner may want to terminate the session before the child is completely miserable or before the examiner has lost control. However, the offer to terminate a session and reschedule may have a variety of results: The child may begin to cooperate more fully, he or she may accept the offer and a subsequent session may prove more productive, or the termination may simply reinforce the child's uncooperative behavior and produce even more difficult future testing sessions (Paget, 1983). Thus one should evaluate the situation very carefully before offering to terminate a session.

TESTING INFANTS

The assessment of children under 24 months of age typically involves different psychometric instruments and some further modifications in the standard assessment procedure. The most notable difference in the assessment of infants is that their mothers typically are present during the testing session and are an integral part of the process. This requires that the examiner develop a good rapport with the mother as well as with the baby. In fact, rapport with the mother is probably more important. The latter will be facilitated by making eye contact, smiling, and approaching her in a direct and friendly manner. The reason for the assessment and/or more neutral topics such as the weather and parking difficulties may provide good material for an opening conversation. It is also important to explain the testing procedures thoroughly at the outset and to continue to do so at each step.

As was discussed previously, the examiner should be aware of the context surrounding the individual testing session. This is particularly important when testing infants because the examiner has the opportunity during the session to provide the parent with some information about his or her child. For example, the examiner may use the session to model appropriate interaction with an infant for a parent whose parenting skills need strengthening, or he or she may highlight the child's capabilities in order to reassure an overly anxious parent.

Scheduling, a significant consideration with preschoolers, is crucial with infants. Young infants may have only an hour or two of alert time each day, and it is imperative that examiners attempt to schedule testing for this time. Unfortunately, predicting these alert times often is very difficult and thus makes the testing of infants very tricky indeed. In any case, a testing session should not be scheduled during regular nap or feeding times.

Essentially the same recommendations regarding the environment hold for infants as for preschoolers, with the addition of several suggestions. The floor should be carpeted, and the setting should have comfortable places for a young infant—a quilt on the floor and an infant seat, for example. If the clinic or facility does not make infant seats available, the examiner can ask the mother to bring the infant to the testing session in his or her own car seat and use that one instead.

Because infants have such brief periods when they are happy and alert, the examiner must pace the session carefully and be extremely flexible. The pace of the session must be very rapid in order to catch as much optimal behavior as possible *and* very calm and gentle in order not to overstimulate the baby. Too many repetitions of an item or too many items in too little time can overwhelm babies and cause them to fall apart. Flexibility can take many forms—the examiner may have to follow a toddler around the room, administering whatever item seems most likely to attract his or her attention. The key to flexible, swift, yet relaxed test administration is a very thorough knowledge of the instrument and total familiarity with the materials. This enables the examiner to move rapidly from one item to another while focusing on the child, thus maximizing the likelihood that he or she will perform up to the level of true capability.

PSYCHOMETRIC ISSUES

Types of Scores

Today the types of scores produced by cognitive tests expand continuously. In the early days of Binet and others, the mental age score stood as the only one of relevance. Not until the time of World War I did the IQ score become a part of the intellectual assessment enterprise (Kamphaus, in press). Since these early days the psychometric properties of cognitive tests have become more sophisticated and complex. A reflection of this complexity is the ever-increasing number of scoring options.

Raw scores. The first score a clinician usually computes is the raw score. On most cognitive tests these are simply comprised of the number of items correct or the total number of points earned on individual items. The term *raw* is probably apropos for these scores, in that they give little information as to how the examinee's performance compares to that of his or her peers. As such, raw scores are not helpful for the most desired type of interpretation—norm-referenced interpretation. Just knowing that a child solved four items correctly on a test offers no insight because of the lack of a standard or norm. The information that consumers and professionals need most is how this raw score compares to the "average" or some other normative standard. Hence, psychometricians have invented numerous other scores to give this desired norm-referenced comparison.

Standard scores. The most popular type of score for cognitive tests is the standard score, which converts raw scores to a distribution with a set mean and standard deviation, and equal units along the scale. The typical standard score scale used for cognitive tests has a mean set at 100 and the standard deviation at 15. By having equal units along the scale, standard scores are very powerful for statistical analyses and useful for making comparisons across tests. The equal units (or intervals) characteristic of standard scores are clear when inspecting the norm tables of various tests. For Kaufman Assessment Battery for Children (K-ABC; Kaufman & Kaufman, 1983) composite scores or Wechsler (e.g., 1991) IQs, the distance between 55 and 70 is the same as that between 70 and 85, which is the same as between 85 and 100, and so forth. (See the sample K-ABC protocol depicted in Figure 4.1.)

Standard scores also are particularly useful for cognitive test interpretation because they allow comparisons among various subtests or composites yielded by the same cognitive test. In other words, they facilitate profile analysis and interpretation of a young children's intraindividual strengths and weaknesses (see Figure 4.1). Most modern cognitive tests use standard scores for their composites that have a mean of 100 and a standard deviation of 15. The notable exceptions to this are the McCarthy Scales of Children's Abilities (McCarthy, 1972) and the Stanford-Binet Intelligence Scale, Fourth Edition (Stanford-Binet; Thorndike, Hagen, & Sattler, 1986), the standard scores of which have a mean of 100 and standard deviation of 16.

Other popular standard score scales include Wechsler's *scaled score* metric for subtest scores. Scaled scores have a mean of 10 and a standard deviation of 3 (see Figure 4.1, where the K-ABC uses the same scaled score metric for its subtests). Again, the Stanford-Binet is an outlier in that its subtest scores have a mean of 50 and standard deviation of 8. *T-scores* and *NCEs* (normal curve equivalents) are not commonly used in cognitive assessment. The important similarity to remember about the various standard scores is that they simply represent different ways of doing the same thing: expressing young children's scores in terms of their distance from the mean or average along an equal interval scale.

Percentile ranks. A particularly useful score for cognitive test interpretation is the percentile rank, which gives an individual's relative position within the norm group (Lyman, 1963). Percentile ranks are very useful for communicating with parents, administrators, educators, and others who do not have an extensive background in scaling methods (Lyman, 1963). It is very easy for parents to understand that if their child received a percentile rank of 50, he or she scored better than approximately 50% of the norm group and worse than approximately 50% of the norm group. This type of interpretation works well so long as the parent understands the difference between percentile rank and percent of items passed.

Percentile ranks have one major disadvantage in comparison to standard scores: They have unequal units along their scale. For example, the difference between the first and fifth percentile rank (see the percentile rank scale depicted just below the Achievement scale bar graph at the bottom of Figure 4.1) is *larger* than the difference between the 40th and 50th percentile ranks. In other words, percentile ranks in the middle of the distribution tend to *overemphasize* differences between standard scores, whereas percentile ranks at the tails of the distribution tend to *underemphasize* differences in performance. An example follows to show how confusing this property of having unequal units can be.

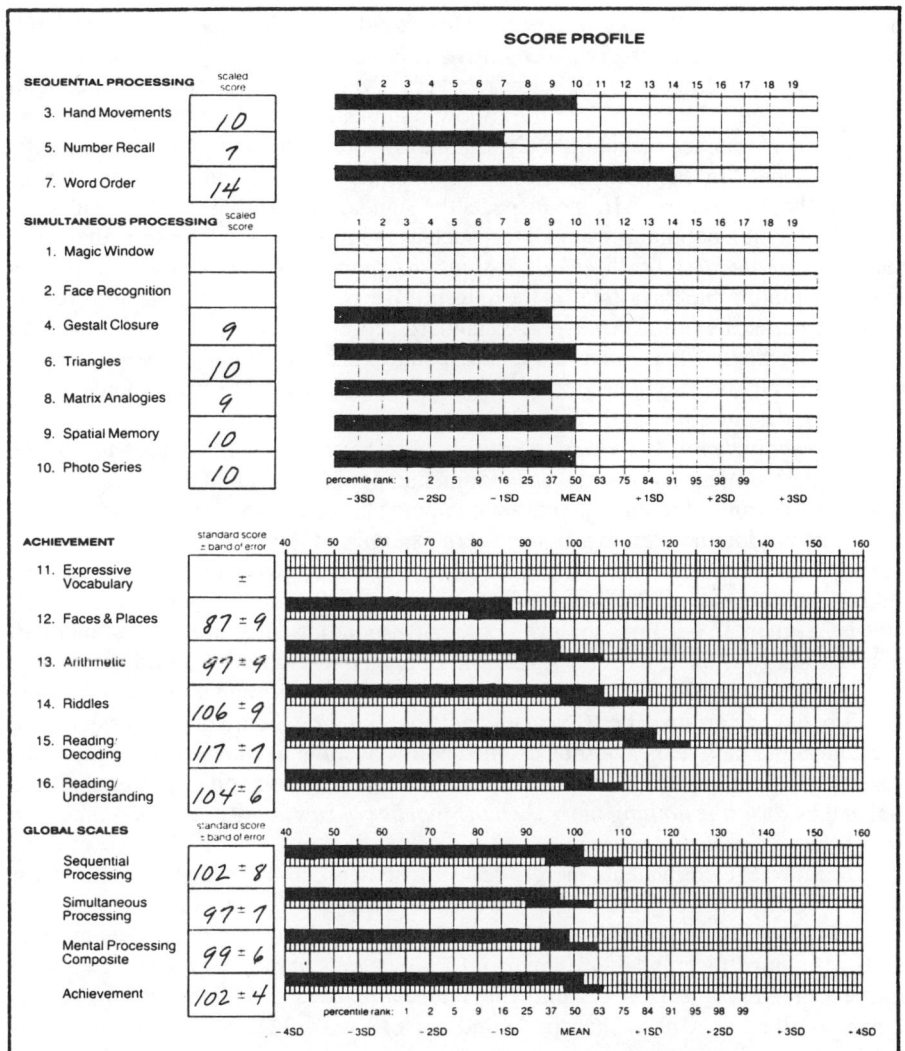

FIGURE 4.1. Completed K-ABC record form. (From Figure 4.11 in *K-ABC Administration and Scoring Manual* by A.S. Kaufman and N.L. Kaufman, 1983, Circle Pines, MN: American Guidance Service. Copyright 1983 by A.S. Kaufman and N.L. Kaufman. Adapted by permission.)

Consider the following question: 'How would you describe a child who obtained a percentile rank of 25 on a cognitive test: well above average, above average, average, below average, or well below average?" Most often clinicians respond with "below average." Then consider the follow-up question: "How would you rate the cognitive performance of a child with a standard score of 90, using the same classification system?" In this latter case most clinician describe the child as being "average" or "below average." If one inspects the standard score to percentile rank conversion table of a popular preschool test such as the K-ABC, however, one discovers that a *percentile rank of 25 equals a standard score of 90* (see Figure 4.1)! This graphic example portrays one of the interpretive problems with percentile ranks, their unequal scale units. An average standard score, for example, can be made to sound much worse when converted to a percentile rank. As a result, when percentile ranks could be misleading used to describe a child's performance, they should not be employed, despite some of their obvious advantages.

Age equivalents. Individual cognitive tests have a long history of using age equivalents (AE), developmental ages, or mental ages (MA), all of which refer to the same type of score. Age equivalents are computed based on the performance of every age group used in the norming of a test. For example, if the average raw score for 7-year-olds on a cognitive test is 24, then 24 becomes the raw score that yields an age equivalent of 7 years. If the average raw score on the same cognitive test for 10-year-olds is 32, then 32 becomes the raw score corresponding to an age equivalent of 10 years. It follows, then, that if a 7-year-old obtains a raw score of 32 on a cognitive test, his or her age equivalent on this cognitive test is 10 years and thus above average for his or her age group. The 10-year-old who obtains a raw score of 24 is assigned an age equivalent of 7 years and thus deemed below average in comparison to other 10-year-olds. The important thing to remember about the derivation of age equivalents is that they *describe nothing more than the number of raw score points obtained by a particular age group.*

Because age equivalents merely reflect whether a child obtained a high or low raw score, they typically are prone to overinterpretation (Lyman, 1963). A common scenario would be to consider the 7-year-old who obtained an age equivalent of 10 years as having "the mind of a 10-year-old," which may or may not be the case. What is true is that this 7-year-old certainly obtained *more items correct* than the average 7-year-old. Whether he or she has the "mind" of a 10-year-old is open to debate, and is not measured directly by the mental age score.

Age equivalents also are problematic on a technical level because they have different standard deviations at each age level, with a trend for larger standard deviations with increasing age (Anastasi, 1988). As such, age equivalents have unequal units along their scale and, just as with percentile ranks, powerful statistical methods cannot be used with them.

Grade equivalents. Grade equivalents (GE) present another type of developmental norm, these derived specifically for plotting growth through the academic curriculum. Unfortunately grade equivalents may not be the best score for this purpose as they share all of the interpretive and technical weaknesses of age equivalents. Computed identically to age equivalents, they also do not indicate a particular level of curricular knowledge. Instead they simply indicate whether a child has obtained a higher or lower raw score than his or her particular grade-reference group. The following examples of students Tonya and Tracy illustrate the problem with grade equivalents:

Tonya, a very intelligent first-grader, obtained a grade equivalent of 3.4 (third grade, fourth month) on the mathematics portion of an academic achievement test on which each item measured a progressively higher level of mathematics knowledge. Her performance (where 1 = correct and 0 = incorrect) on every item is shown below:

Item	Score
1.	1
2.	1
3.	1
4.	1
5.	1
6.	0
7.	0
8.	0

Raw score = 5

Tracy, a third-grader of about average cognitive ability, also obtained a grade equivalent of 3.4 (third grade, fourth month) on the same mathematics test. Her performance is shown below:

Item	Score
1.	1
2.	0
3.	0
4.	1
5.	0
6.	1
7.	1
8.	1

Raw score = 5

Note that Tonya and Tracy obtained the same raw scores on the achievement test and, consequently, the same grade equivalents. Tonya's parents, however, may easily misinterpret her grade equivalent, thinking that if she has a third-grade equivalent, then perhaps she should be advanced to that grade level in mathematics. This, however, does not appear to be warranted, because although the two children received the same raw score and grade equivalents, they achieved them in very different ways, with Tracy showing considerably more mathematical knowledge (albeit with a tendency to make some "silly" errors) than Tonya. It is also clear that Tonya has not mastered the higher level skills. As was demonstrated at the outset, *grade equivalents do not necessarily indicate the level of curricular knowledge or expertise that an individual child possesses.* They simply indicate a level of performance. In addition, as was the case with age equivalents, grade equivalents do not have equal units along their scale.

Latent trait scores. A proposed solution to the problems of age equivalents and grade equivalents is *latent trait methodology,* also referred to as *item response theory* (Anastasi, 1988). Latent trait scores are developmental norms like GEs and AEs, with one exception: They have equal units along their scale. These scores, frequently referred to as "scaled scores" on academic achievement tests, are designed for the same purposes as GEs—tracking growth through curriculum. Now, however, they are beginning to be used more in clinical assessment of cognitive and other skills. At this point in their development they do not solve the interpretive problems of grade equivalents or age equivalents as far as providing an estimate of curricular knowledge or mental development, but they do offer one interpretive "plus": Obtaining the same difference between scaled scores from year to year indicates a similar level of growth in curricular knowledge.

Again an example is in order. Lionel obtained the following grade equivalents and scaled scores:

	Grade 1	Grade 2	Grade 3	Grade 4
Grade equivalent	1.7	2.6	3.8	4.5
Scaled score	240	260	280	300

One can say, based on the scaled score information, that this child seems to be progressing at about the same rate from year to year, because scaled scores have equal units along the scale. A teacher, however, cannot say that Lionel is making the same gains every year based on his GEs because GEs have unequal units along their scale.

Another notable characteristic of scaled scores is that they are not useful for making comparisons across subtests or composites. If a child, for example, obtains a scaled score of 392 in mathematics and 377 in reading, it does not necessarily follow that he or she is better in mathematics than in reading. Each score scale applies only to a particular "latent trait."

Many more scores could be described here, but this may not be necessary. The basics already covered—standard scores, percentile ranks, and developmental norms—appear in most cognitive tests for preschoolers. Sometimes, however, the score is unrecognizable. At such times clinicians should be prepared to read the fine print of manuals, determine the basic characteristics of a score scale, and then see how the score scale fits with those described here. Unfortunately, many test manuals do not provide enough information on scaling. In these cases independent reviews of the test (such as those found in Buros and in Keyser and Sweetland's *Test Critique* series) may help.

Reliability

The reliability of a test refers to the degree to which its scores are free from errors of measurement (American Educational Research Association, American Psychological Association, & National Council on Measurement in Education, 1985). Of particular interest to cognitive test users is the issue of stability, or the degree to which a preschooler's cognitive test scores are likely to be similar from one measurement to the next. Various theories of intelligence (Kamphaus, in press) all suggest that cognitive ability is a fairly stable trait over the course of development. If an individual shows an extremely high level of intelligence, it is likely to remain this way barring any unusual circumstances.

The reliability of a cognitive test is expressed by the computation of a reliability coefficient, which is a special type of correlation coefficient (Anastasi, 1988). One essential difference between reliability coefficients and correlation coefficients is that the former typically are not negative, while it is eminently possible to have a negative correlation coefficient. Reliability coefficients range, then, from 0 to +1. Reliability coefficients represent the amount of reliable variance associated with a test. In other words, a reliability coefficient is not squared, as is the case with correlation coefficients, to calculate the amount of reliable variance (Anastasi, 1988). For example, the reliable variance of a test with a reliability coefficient of .90 is 90%.

The error variance associated with a test also is easy to calculate; one simply subtracts the reliability coefficient from 1 (perfect reliability). Taking the previous example, the error variance for a test with a reliability coefficient of .90 is 10% (1 − .90).

The most popular method for computing the stability of cognitive test scores is the *test-retest method*. Here the same test, for example the Stanford-Binet, is administered to the same group of individuals under the same or similar conditions over a brief period of time (typically 2 to 4 weeks). The correlation between the first and second administrations of the test is then computed, yielding a test-retest reliability coefficient that ideally is very close to 1.0, usually somewhere between .90 and .98.

Another type of reliability coefficient often reported in cognitive test manuals is an *internal consistency* coefficient. This is very different from test-retest or stability coefficients in that it does not assess directly the stability of the measure over time. Internal consistency coefficients assess what the name implies—the average correlation among the items in a cognitive test (in other words, the homogeneity of the test item pool). Internal consistency coefficients are valuable primarily because they are inexpensively produced (they require only one administration of the test) and serve as *good estimates* of test-retest or stability coefficients. Typical formulae used for the computation of internal consistency coefficients include split-half coefficients, Kuder-Richardson Formula 20, and coefficient alpha (Anastasi, 1988).

On occasion there are differences between internal consistency and test-retest coefficients that can affect cognitive test interpretation. It is possible, for example, for a test to have both a relatively poor internal consistency coefficient and a strong test-retest coefficient. One sees an example of this in the Gestalt Closure subtest of the K-ABC, which has a very heterogeneous item pool. Its internal consistency coefficients fall in the .60 to .70 range, but its test-retest coefficient is in the .80s. Because internal consistency coefficients are imperfect estimates of stability coefficients, both should be recorded in the manual for a cognitive test (see also AERA, APA, & NCME, 1985).

Clinicians who use cognitive tests should be especially cognizant of factors that can affect reliability. Foremost among these is test length (Nitko, 1983). The longer the test, the more likely the clinician will obtain an accurate assessment of a preschooler's cognitive skill. This is why short forms of cognitive tests are generally frowned upon. Other factors that the clinician should keep in mind when estimating the reliability of a test for a particular child include the following:

1. Reliability is affected by homogeneous ability levels. Differentiating among the very gifted and severely impaired may be difficult, as these individuals represent a very small range of scores (Nitko, 1983).
2. Reliability can change for different ability levels. A test that is very reliable for gifted students should not be considered as reliable for mentally retarded students in lieu of research evidence for samples of children diagnosed as mentally retarded (Nitko, 1983).
3. Reliability can suffer when there is a long interval between assessments (Nitko, 1983).
4. Characteristics of the child can affect reliability, including his or her age, fatigue, and other factors. As is discussed in other chapters, the reliability of cognitive measurement drops precipitously at preschool age levels.

Why Test Scores Differ

A frequently perplexing problem for clinicians is having to explain why two or more sets of cognitive test scores for the same child differ, sometimes substantially. This becomes a frequent question in preschool assessment at the time when a child is reevaluated. A number of psychometric reasons account for changes in scores, including the age of the norms, floor and ceiling effects, age at which the child was first tested, item content differences, and reliability of gain/difference scores.

Age of norms. One of the most important characteristics of norm tables is that they must be recent. A comprehensive analysis of changes in Stanford-Binet and Wechsler norms from the years 1932 to 1978 (Flynn, 1984) highlights the problem of using antiquated norms. Flynn (1984) concluded that the American population became about 1 standard deviation (15 standard score points) "smarter" over an approximately 50-year period. In other words, the norm tables became "tougher" with each succeeding decade, in the sense that a child had to obtain a higher raw score every time a test was renormed to obtain the same standard score that he or she had obtained previously. If a child, for example, took an intelligence test normed in the 1940s in 1956 and correctly answered 13 vocabulary items, he or she may have obtained a scaled score of 10. A child taking the vocabulary subtest on the revised edition of that same intelligence test (this one normed in the early 1970s) and answering 13 items correctly may obtain a scaled score of only 8 or 9. This occurs because the trend is for new norm samples to yield a higher standard. One of the first things to look for when selecting a cognitive test for use is the date of the data collection for the sample. If the standardization sample is 10 years old or more, then the clinician should be wary of the accuracy of the norms for current use.

Floor and ceiling effects. Floor effects occur when the test being administered to a child lacks enough easy items to allow him or her to obtain a raw score (i.e., the child gets all of the items wrong). Conversely, ceiling effects occur when a test lacks difficult items, resulting in the child obtaining a perfect score. The problem of no adequate range of difficulty frequently is encountered in clinical assessment. Floor and ceiling effects become problematic in that if a child obtains either a perfect score or a zero raw score, his or her cognitive ability has not been measured adequately. The examiner then does not know how far the child's ability lies below the lowest item or how far it supersedes the highest item. Clinicians most likely will encounter problems with insufficient floor and ceiling near the extremes of a test's age range (e.g., for 2½- and 8-year-olds on the McCarthy Scales).

Correlations between tests. Certainly one of the most straightforward reasons for test score differences is the possibility that the two tests are not highly correlated. As was mentioned earlier, cognitive test composite scores typically have reliability coefficients in the .90s. As a result, when a child is administered the same test twice, his or her scores are likely to be similar. If, on the other hand, the child takes two different cognitive tests, his or her scores likely will differ more, simply because a cognitive test typically correlates more with itself than it does with other cognitive tests.

Item content differences. Cognitive tests can be based on a variety of theories that dictate item and subtest selection. Some tests may place a premium on verbal skills, others on motor skills. The child with cerebral palsy, for example, may perform very differently on two cognitive measures, depending on the content of the items—verbal versus nonverbal.

Reliability of gain/difference scores. Gain scores are computed by subtracting a preschooler's first score on a cognitive test from his or her second score. These figures commonly are referred to as *gain scores* because the outcome tends to be slightly higher on the second testing (a gain) in test-retest reliability studies. Difference scores subsume gain scores. The term *difference score,* however, is usually used in conjunction with comparing composite scores within a test or across tests. An example of a difference score would be the difference between verbal and performance scores on the Wechsler Intelligence Scale for Children–Third Edition (Wechsler, 1991).

When interpreting score differences one should keep in mind that difference scores and gain scores are inherently less reliable than composite or subtest scores (Anastasi, 1988). Specifically, a gain or loss from one test administration to another is a difference score. *Difference scores possess the error variance of both tests used* in producing the difference. Being aware of the increased error associated with difference scores, clinicians frequently attribute small differences between composite scores to chance variation.

Practice effects. Practice effects, which may explain small differences in scores between cognitive tests, are observed when scores improve (a gain score) due to familiarity with the test items. The size of practice effects is usually less than 10 standard score points. They are considerably larger for less verbal (i.e., performance) tests and smaller for verbal tests.

Based on the preceding discussion, the examiner thus has several psychometric hypotheses to consider when differences between cognitive tests occur.

The clinical and psychometric concepts discussed in this chapter are "basic" ones that should be familiar to all professionals engaged in diagnostic practice with preschoolers. These essential concepts provide a foundation that can be built upon with strong academic training and supervised experience. The preschool assessment enterprise requires the highest levels of clinical acumen and psychometric expertise.

REFERENCES

American Educational Research Association, American Psychological Association, & National Council on Measurement in Education. (1985). *Standards for educational and psychological testing*. Washington, DC: American Psychological Association.
Anastasi, A. (1988). *Psychological testing* (6th ed.). New York: Macmillan.
Barber, T.E. (1973). Pitfalls in research: Nine investigator and experimenter effects. In R.M.W. Travers (Ed.), *Second handbook of research on teaching* (pp. 382–404). Chicago: Rand McNally.
Epps, E.G. (1974). Situational effects in testing. In L.P. Miller (Ed.), *The testing of black students: A symposium* (pp. 17–29). Orlando, FL: Harcourt Brace Jovanovich.
Figueroa, R.A. (1990). Assessment of linguistic minority group children. In C.R. Reynolds & R.W. Kamphaus (Eds.), *Handbook of psychological and educational assessment of children: Vol. 1. Intelligence and achievement* (pp. 671–696). New York: Guilford.
Flynn, J.R. (1984). The mean IQ of Americans: Massive gains 1932 to 1978. *Psychological Bulletin, 95*, 29–51.
Kamphaus, R.W. (in press). *Clinical assessment of children's intelligence*. Newton, MA: Allyn & Bacon.
Kaufman, A.S., & Kaufman, N.L. (1983). *K-ABC administration and scoring manual*. Circle Pines, MN: American Guidance Service.
Keyser, D.J., & Sweetland, R.C. (Eds.). (1984–92). *Test critiques* (Vols. I–IX). Austin, TX: PRO-ED.
Lidz, C.S. (1983). Situational effects in testing. In L.P. Miller (Ed.), *The testing of black students: A symposium* (pp. 41–51). Englewood Cliffs, NJ: Prentice-Hall.
Lyman, H. (1963). *Test scores and what they mean*. Englewood Cliffs, NJ: Prentice-Hall.
McCarthy, D. (1972). *McCarthy Scales of Children's Abilities*. San Antonio, TX: Psychological Corporation.
Nitko, A. (1983). *Educational tests and measurement: An introduction*. New York: Harcourt Brace Jovanovich.
Paget, K.D. (1983). The individual examining situation: Basic considerations for preschool children. In K.D. Paget & B.A. Bracken (Eds.), *The psychoeducational assessment of preschool children* (pp. 51–62). Orlando, FL: Harcourt Brace Jovanovich.
Sarason, S. (1954). *The clinical interaction, with special reference to the Rorschach*. New York: Harper.
Sattler, J.M. (1988). *Assessment of children* (3rd ed.). San Diego, CA: Author.
Thorndike, R.L., Hagen, E.P., & Sattler, J.M. (1986). *Guide for administering and scoring the Stanford-Binet Intelligence Scale: Fourth Edition*. Chicago: Riverside.
Wechsler, D. (1991). *Wechsler Intelligence Scale for Children–Third Edition*. San Antonio, TX: Psychological Corporation.

5

Developmental Screening for Preschoolers

THOMAS J. KENNY, PH.D. & JAN L. CULBERTSON, PH.D.

Screening is an important first step in the process of identifying potential developmental and behavioral problems. The process is defined as sorting out from among a presumably normal population those individuals at risk for a certain disorder. The purpose of screening is not to diagnose a disorder or to plan a treatment approach, but rather to suggest to the professional *when* and *whom* to refer for further diagnostic evaluation. The importance of screening is not diminished by its nondiagnostic function; this critical process aids early detection and facilitates early referral for evaluation and subsequent intervention.

Medical professionals commonly use screening in the course of primary care. For example, the physician who conducts a well-child examination on an infant will screen for hydrocephalus by measuring the infant's head circumference. The screening approach is simple, quick, and highly reliable in determining which infants are at risk for the disorder of interest. Infants whose head circumference exceeds a certain dimension will be considered at risk for hydrocephalus and most likely will be referred for a more detailed diagnostic evaluation. Likewise developmental screening (i.e., assessing language, motor, cognitive, adaptive, and personal-social skills) can, and should, be done commonly in the course of caring for the preschool-aged child. However, because developmental disorders are extremely complex, such screening may not be as simple and quick as for some medical disorders. It is important to understand the nature of the developmental disorders being screened for, the sensitivity and specificity of the many screening tools available for use, and the special considerations regarding the screening process.

Four primary issues arise in considering developmental screening of young children:

1. Why should developmental screening be done?
2. Who should do the screening?
3. How should the screening be done?
4. What tools are available for the screening?

A careful examination of these factors should lead to more effective screening, which in turn could be a major step in facilitating optimal developmental outcome in young children.

DEVELOPMENTAL SCREENING—WHY?

The case for early detection and early intervention with developmentally delayed children has been justified and detailed in many publications. Although early educational intervention may not help a youngster with severe mental retardation become normal, there is ample evidence to support the positive effects of early intervention in supporting the families of the handicapped, providing environmental stimulation that is appropriate for the child's level of functioning, preventing worsening of the disabilities, and enhancing the ability of the child to develop to the fullest extent of his or her potential. Screening is the first, and therefore the most important, step in the process of early identification of developmental disorders. Screening provides the key to the door of a wide range of professional services available to handicapped children and their families, a door that will remain closed unless the child's problems are detected. A well-developed screening program for preschool children can work to benefit their long-term development. In addition to this compelling reason for screening, other events and issues also converge to give additional impetus.

There is a need for determining more accurate estimates of the incidence and prevalence of all types of developmental disorders. Professionals estimate that at least 10% of all children may have a handicapping condition that will affect their optimal development. Mental retardation occurs in 2.5% of the population. The incidence of speech/language disorders is estimated to range from 0.5% to 2.5%. Some reports suggest that 10% of school-aged children may have some form of learning disability. Physical, sensory, and emotional problems add untold numbers of children to the group at risk for developmental problems. Yet, the figures cited are just estimates. There is no systematic, reliable body of data that indicates the actual number of children with developmental problems. Obtaining these data is a critical first step in effectively planning the services required to meet the needs of children with handicaps. Of equal importance is the fact that the individual child in need of services usually is not identified early in the course of the handicap. A program of comprehensive, systematic developmental screening would ameliorate these problems.

Another factor that underlies the need for a comprehensive system of screening is the passage of two federal laws mandating educational and related services for the handicapped—PL 94-142 and the more recent PL 99-457. Implicit in these two laws is the mandate for early identification of children with developmental delays and handicaps. The earlier legislation, PL 94-142, has been called "an educational Bill of Rights" because it requires the provision of a free and appropriate education for handicapped children. The law lists specific handicaps, including mental retardation, physical and sensory handicaps, learning disabilities, language disorders, and emotional problems.

The more recent legislation, PL 99-457, requires providing educational and related services from birth through the preschool years to children who have, or are at risk for, handicapping conditions. This downward extension of the earlier Education for All Handicapped Children Act (PL 94-142) makes clear the import of early intervention and therefore early screening and evaluation. The significant provision of PL 99-457 regarding serving children "at risk" for a developmental disorder (even if they do not yet show signs of the disorder) suggests that more children than ever before may receive early intervention services. Examples of "at-risk" children include those born with an obvious genetic disorder (e.g., Down's syndrome) that is associated with cognitive delay, or those whose birth history places them at risk (e.g., extreme prematurity). The full impact of this recent legislation is yet to be determined, as school systems only now are developing plans for implementing the law. However, it is clear that in order to serve preschool children who are handicapped and at risk, schools must have a plan for identifying the children who need to be served.

The answers to the question, "Why should developmental screening be done?" are clear. Developmental screening can

1. benefit the long-term development of children;
2. help in developing a reliable database for the incidence of developmental disorders in children, and therefore facilitate program planning to meet the service needs of these children;
3. assist in implementing recent federal legislation that mandates services for preschool children who are handicapped and at risk; and
4. provide the first step in early intervention for young children who are handicapped and at risk.

DEVELOPMENTAL SCREENING—WHO?

At least three professional disciplines—medicine, education, and psychology—play a significant role in developmental screening. Each has a mix of advantages and disadvantages that impact developmental screening.

Medicine

In the medical discipline, physicians have experience as primary care providers as well as a history of continuity of care with their patients. Both of these factors are essential components of a comprehensive screening system. A primary care provider typically is the first person contacted by the consumer, in this case the patient. In the medical model, the primary care provider is the gateway into the system. People are accustomed to "going to the doctor," and parents usually take their children to the pediatrician for a series of well-child visits. As a result, primary care physicians, usually pediatricians, are in an optimal position to do systematic developmental screening because they have access to the population of young children for whom such screening is needed. The American Academy of Pediatrics recommended in 1951 that developmental screening be a regular part of routine well-child visits. These visits occur at regularly scheduled intervals, give the pediatrician repeated access to the child, and enable repeat screening in the event of a questionable result.

The advantages inherent in the medical system unfortunately have not been used successfully. In a survey of a large group of pediatricians, Smith (1978) found that 97% of those responding to the survey felt that developmental screening was important, but only 15% to 20% of the respondents screened more than 10% of their patients. In another study, Carr and Stephens (1964) found that 91% of the pediatricians using developmental screening tests were administering them to children previously identified as having developmental problems. Fischler and Tancer (1984), in their survey of pediatricians, found that 90% believed they should include developmental screening in well-child care, but nearly half of those responding felt they did not have the time to do the testing. Smith (1978) also reported that the time required to administer a developmental test, estimated at 20 minutes, was a major deterrent to the pediatrician. Although the pediatrician is well situated to do developmental screening, the studies cited indicate that only a small percent of them regularly screen their patients and that most of the tests are administered to children already known to have problems. Therefore, those children with subtle developmental disabilities or those at risk are the least likely to be tested.

Another obstacle to developmental screening relates to the training of medical professionals. Although physicians (particularly pediatricians) receive some training in developmental screening during medical school and/or residency, the training often is rather cursory and may result in improper administration and interpretation of screening tests. Physicians may have a tendency to use screening tests to "diagnose" rather than to detect those children who need to be referred for further testing. Also, a preponderance of medical literature supports the use of nonstandardized screening tests that either lack or have poor reliability/validity studies (e.g., see Kenny et al., 1990; Levine et al., 1980). These obstacles in physician training may result in mislabeling or failing to detect developmental disorders in young children.

Education

The discipline of education, especially special education, also has a major role in early screening. PL 94-142, referred to as the "education for all handicapped" law, mandates not only identifying children who are handicapped, but also providing them with special educational services. From the standpoint of efficiency, education is the discipline with the most to gain from the development of an effective screening system. In an effort to meet the requirements of the federal laws, many school systems have developed "Child Find" programs, which represent an attempt to extend preschool services to children with handicapping conditions. Children referred to Child Find are evaluated, and if the assessment determines they have a handicapping condition, an Individualized Educational Plan (IEP) is developed for them. The strength of education is in the provision of intervention/remedial services. In almost all handicapping conditions, the educational system has a role in the provision of services. Some children may need medical care, others physical therapy, speech therapy, and so forth, but all of them will require educational services. One can question the effectiveness of remedial education programs or early intervention programs, but the fact remains that they are a required part of the services provided to children.

The discipline of special education has several advantages related to developmental screening: expertise with intervention programs, a mandated role as a service provider to handicapped children, an understanding of developmental issues, and longitudinal contact with children. A basic problem that education must overcome lies in the passive nature of its evaluation procedures. Traditionally children present themselves to the school for entry and only then are referred for evaluation. In many circumstances this evaluation does not take place unless a preexisting problem is documented or the child has difficulty in school. Such a system is not optimal for the identification of preschoolers or other children at risk for handicapping conditions. Child Find attempts to remedy this shortcoming, but as presently operated the process still requires an external trigger—a person to identify and report the suspect child. Mass screening of preschool children is not at this time typical, so that the educational system still remains largely a passive participant in the screening process.

The consequence of an effective screening program may represent a potential conflict-of-interest situation for education. Both PL 94-142 and PL 99-457 mandate services to children with handicapping conditions, but the provision of these services results in increased educational expense and the need for specially trained teachers, support staff, and more space. Failure to provide these services places an educational system in a position to lose federal monies. If the school system does not have adequate resources in personnel or funds, one way of staying in compliance with the federal laws would be to limit the number of children identified as needing services. This situation is a potential "catch-22" for school officials. Finally, the field of education places more emphasis on teaching than on identifying or diagnosing, so that school systems have not developed the cadre of personnel needed to carry out a comprehensive screening program.

Psychology

As a discipline, psychology has much to contribute to a program of developmental screening: It offers the greatest expertise in psychometric assessment and the most experience in administering and interpreting tests. Psychologists' research training and knowledge of research methodology can be useful in devising a comprehensive system to identify the target population. A knowledge of child development and familiarity with the issues of parenting and the effects of the environment on child functioning are other valuable assets of psychologists' training.

The main obstacle psychology must face in the area of developmental screening is the lack of a primary care orientation. In practice, psychologists usually function as specialists receiving referrals from other sources. Like educators, psychologists are passive or reactive participants in this identification/referral process.

Multidisciplinary Coordination

Combining the strengths of each of the three disciplines into a coordinated effort for developmental screening makes sense. The medical discipline provides the primary care orientation and early access to young children, while psychology provides knowledge of psychometric evaluation and research expertise. Psychologists are in a position to train physicians on proper screening procedures and help them improve their knowledge of when and whom to refer. Educators may rely on both physicians and psychologists to help handicapped children enter the educational system for services, but educators are the experts in devising appropriate special education programs to meet the needs of these children. Other disciplines, such as speech/language pathology, physical medicine, nursing, and social work also may contribute to the developmental screening process.

Obstacles to this multidisciplinary coordination include the different terminology used by specific disciplines, differences in theoretical orientation toward developmental disorders and their etiology, and different goals/interests related to working with the handicapped. At times professionals from different disciplines may engage in turf battles over who "owns" the handicapped child and his or her family, and whose information is more important in helping the child. These obstacles to multidisciplinary cooperation typically result from lack of familiarity with the role and contributions of the other disciplines, plus ineffective communication. Fortunately, since PL 94-142 was passed in 1975, provisions for multidisciplinary coordination have been inherent in the care of handicapped children who enter the public school system. Likewise, PL 99-457 now provides for multidisciplinary coordination in serving younger children at risk for handicapping conditions, and this paves the way for developing a coordinated screening effort. Cross-disciplinary exchange of information, discussions as to which discipline can offer what services, and the organization of effective collaboration among disciplines can occur. These discussions must address such issues as how to access the target population, how to organize the screening program, what abilities to evaluate, and which screening tools to use. The remainder of this chapter addresses these issues and concludes with a proposal for an optimal screening system.

Developmental Screening—How?

Problems Involved in Screening

In order to determine how to do developmental screening, it is necessary to consider the problems involved in the process. The first problem relates to our ability to predict developmental handicaps, from what age and over what length of time. The literature on developmental follow-up indicates significant problems with the process of prediction (Aylward & Kenny, 1979). Factors affecting prediction/identification include the variability of functions that can be tested at various ages. For example, motor functions can be tested at an earlier age than language skills. The variability of developmental rates between individuals is another complication, as is the possibility of compensation or recovery of function affecting the outcome. Sameroff (1975) highlighted the interactive effects of the environment on development, which presents another possible complication to long-term prediction. For example, a child with a mild handicap might have different manifestations depending on the strength of the environment. In a disorganized home the problem would be exaggerated, while in a stable environment, it might not be expressed.

Another complication relates to the tests available at each age and what they measure. When attempting to test a very young child, the process could be limited by the developmental skills operational at that time and the need for an adequate sample of those skills to be tested. One result of this situation is the emphasis on motor development in most tests developed for infants and young children. The early acquisition of motor functions provides a broad enough range of skills to measure at a very young age. The situation with language is almost the reverse. At an early age there is little language to measure, and such measurement is difficult. In effect, motor development virtually peaks out before language development is effectively measured. This problem was apparent in the use of the Denver Developmental Screening Test

(DDST; Frankenburg & Dodds, 1967), where language items are sparse in the early months. Although the Denver II (Frankenburg et al., 1990) improves on this situation by increasing the number of language items in the early months, the problem is not eliminated.

To put this in practical terms, consider the following example. A 3-year-old child with a language delay is administered the Denver II. This child performs relatively well on the test because up to the 3½-year level, many of the items require limited language use and are mostly motor or imitative in nature. In the first 3½ years of the test range, only five items involve expressive language. In the next year, there are five more items in this short age span. Giving the test at 3½ years would not fully identify the child's language problems, and the results would be negative (or normal). Testing the child at 4½ years would produce very different results, as the number of language items increases markedly. Thus, the child's performance would be lowered significantly because of the increased emphasis on a single skill—language. Comparing the test results at the two ages would produce weakened reliability and lower predictive validity. To take this example further, consider the possibility that the child's language problem is transient or that the child learns to compensate for the problem, and the predictive validity is further reduced. Add to these problems the impact of the environment on a child's development and it is easy to understand the limited predictive capacity of early developmental screening.

Most of the noted complications to prediction are associated with the use of one-time or episodic developmental assessment. One way to minimize these problems is to use multiple screens on a systematic basis, which would impact on the issues of developmental variability, the sample of skills operational at any age, and the possibility of compensation or recovery. However, to make multiple screenings of large numbers of children practical, one must consider the training required to do the screening, the time needed to accomplish the screening, and the cost involved in the process.

Cost-Effectiveness

As discussed previously, the members of many professional disciplines could be trained to do screening, but using professionals in such a large-scale process is not cost-effective unless each screening involves very little time. When providing training for screening, one must consider not only the time to learn the process but also that required to administer and score the tests. As most screening measures do not demand advanced degree training, given adequate instruction in the specific procedures, these measures may be used by nonprofessionals or paraprofessionals such as office receptionists, nursing assistants, teacher's aides, students, and parents. The best screening approach would stratify the expertise required for the program, beginning with the least professional and ending with the professional in the role of interpreter/decision maker.

As an example, a clerk at the health clinic administers the screening test or supervises the child's parent in completing the protocol, then collects and scores the test information. The results are given to the physician/educator/psychologist, who reviews the results and makes the appropriate decision about further evaluation. Such a plan requires that the screening instrument be simple enough that minimal training would result in uniform and valid administration and screening. In addition, the results must be such that decision making is simple. This would involve a cutoff score or a classification system that identifies children in need of further evaluation. A good screening test should take no more than an hour or two to learn to administer, and should require little or no professional training to administer and score accurately.

Studies examining the use of the Denver Developmental Screening Test consistently reported objections to the length of time required to administer and score it (Smith, 1978; Fischler & Tancer, 1984), estimated to be about 20 minutes. These findings suggest that the professional time required for screening should be less than 20 minutes and/or one should use a stratified approach as described earlier for the screening process.

Cost effectiveness might also be increased by using different levels of screening, with "prescreening" techniques used initially and "formal screening" techniques reserved for those children who appear to be at risk on the prescreening measures. The prescreening process should take very little professional time—reviewing questionnaires filled out by parents, inquiring about the child's developmental milestones, or considering the risk factors that might impact the child's developmental outcome (e.g., premature gestation, birth complications, illnesses associated with developmental sequelae, poor nutrition, low socioeconomic status). Information obtained from the prescreening should indicate to the professional when to engage in formal screening procedures.

Formal screening involves an investment of time in direct interaction with the child and/or parents, and use of a formal screening instrument, such as the Denver II. Formal screening tests may be further subdivided into "primary," "secondary," and so on. Primary formal screening tests have wide utility for a broad population of children in terms of the range of developmental skills measured, the age range covered, and the level of accuracy in classifying children as normal or at risk. The Denver II also would be a good example of a primary screening test. Secondary formal screening tests have a more narrow focus, such as language functioning. They would be used after the primary screening test has indicated a concern in a specific area, such as language, and when further information regarding the delayed area is required.

Use of the different levels of screening assures cost-effectiveness in that the prescreening, which is done routinely on all preschool children, requires little professional time. Formal screening, which is more time-consuming, is reserved for those children already deemed to be at risk on the basis of some prescreening process. Regardless of the approach used, cost-effectiveness will depend on such factors as the time and training required for developmental screening, whether professionals or paraprofessionals do the direct screening, and the effectiveness of the screening instruments in detecting those children actually at risk for developmental disorders.

Goals of Screening

Before undertaking development of a screening system, one must understand the differences between the goals of screening and the goals of a full evaluation. Specifically, a screening test is expected to classify rather than diagnose, and to do so involves test characteristics that are not as well measured by the standard concepts of correlation that produce validity and reliability estimates.

Most psychometric studies stress the need to determine strong correlational relationships between a test and another standard, either an outcome criterion or an already accepted test. In evaluating an intelligence test, this is a necessary procedure because the test must demonstrate stability over the entire range of items measured and, usually, the factor to be measured is assumed to have a normal distribution. A screening test reduces the focus to classification rather than comparison; that is, it is more important that a subject is in a particular class than that the distribution of scores is similar. Two tests can have a good correlation even if the scores on one are 10 or 15 points higher than the other, as long as the distribution of these scores is similar—usually a normal or bell-shaped curve. Similarly, the tests can correlate if the same number of subjects fall at certain points on the distribution.

In screening tests both of these correlational measures could be very misleading. The screening test is not useful if it does not classify the subject correctly. The proportion of subjects at a given level is not as important as the fact that the test puts a subject in the same category consistently. For example, to classify a child as retarded using a screening measure compared to the Wechsler Intelligence Scale for Children–Third Edition (WISC-III; Wechsler, 1991) would require not that 2.5% of the subjects on the screening test score in the retarded range, but that those children identified as retarded by the screening test be the *same* children who produce IQs below 70 on the WISC-III. This concept, referred to as *test sensitivity and specificity*, is the standard by which to judge screening tests as opposed to correlational measures of validity and reliability.

Sensitivity is defined as the ability of a test to classify abnormal results as abnormal and is illustrated by Figure 5.1. A test with high sensitivity would be the most accurate in detecting those children who actually have a developmental disability, so that appropriate referral can be made for diagnostic evaluation. Specificity refers to a test's ability to identify normal performance as being normal, also illustrated in Figure 5.1. A good screening test optimally should have high specificity as well as sensitivity, to avoid referring normal children for unnecessary diagnostic evaluations.

Figure 5.1 illustrates a hypothetical screening of 100 children, in which a subsequent diagnostic test reveals that 90 children are normal and 10 are abnormal. The screening test has relatively good sensitivity in that it correctly categorized 9 of the 10 children as abnormal. The screening test's specificity is slightly lower; of the 90 children who were normal, the screening test correctly identified 80 of them. This means that 10 children were erroneously referred because they were labeled "abnormal" on the screening. However, the screening measure missed only one child who subsequently was found to be abnormal.

Sensitivity and specificity essentially reflect a test's ability to place children in the correct group, which then determines the next appropriate action (i.e., referral or nonreferral). This process also can be demonstrated by what is called a *hit rate* (the percent of children correctly identified as handicapped as opposed to those who are incorrectly identified). There are four hit rate classifications: correct referral, overreferral, correct nonreferral, and underreferral.

Diagnostic Test Results

	NORMAL	ABNORMAL	
Screening Test Results NORMAL	A ($n = 80$)	B ($n = 1$)	81
ABNORMAL	C ($n = 10$)	D ($n = 9$)	19
	90	10	

$$\text{SENSITIVITY} = \frac{D}{B + D} \times 100 = .90$$

$$\text{SPECIFICITY} = \frac{A}{A + C} \times 100 = .89$$

FIGURE 5.1. Illustration of test sensitivity and specificity in a hypothetical screening of 100 subjects.

In screening situations, the largest number of children should fall into the correct nonreferral category, which is the "normal" group. The correct referrals reflect the power of the test to predict accurately children who are abnormal. The other two classifications represent the test error rate, overreferral being a result that is abnormal on screening but normal on a complete evaluation, and underreferral being a normal screening result on a child who actually is determined to be abnormal. Both of these factors are important in effective screening, but underreferral is the more critical in that it represents children who should be receiving special help but are not identified by the screening process. Overreferral is a lesser problem in that the outcome is not harmful; a child simply is referred for an evaluation that he or she does not need, the cost of which is measured in professional time and expense as well as in anxiety caused to parents and children. Overreferral is inefficient but better than failing to identify a child who is abnormal. As a result, a good screening test can tolerate some degree of overreferral if this lowers the rate of underreferral.

SCREENING TESTS

Among the numerous screening tests available, the choice depends on the population to be screened, the types of disorders being screened for, and the resources available for intervention in the child's community. The discussion that follows will incorporate a representative sample of the most researched and most commonly used instruments in the following categories: developmental tests, language tests, school readiness tests, visual-motor tests, and tests of adjustment or behavior (see Table 5.1). All of these measures have the potential to identify handicapping conditions, but they approach the task in slightly different ways.

TABLE 5.1

Commonly Used Screening Tests

Test	Age Range	Administration	Description
DEVELOPMENTAL			
Battelle Developmental Inventory	Birth to 8 years	Individually administered; 10–30 minutes (screening test)	Five areas: personal-social, adaptive, motor, communication, and cognitive. The whole battery can be used, but there is a screening version.
Denver II	Birth to 6 years	Individually administered; 20 minutes	Four areas: language, fine motor, personal-social, and gross motor.
Developmental Profile II (DPII)	Birth to 9 years	Parent report; 20–40 minutes	Five areas: physical, self-help, social, academic, and communication.
Early Child Development Inventory	1 to 3 years	Parent report; 10 minutes	Seven development scales: self-help, fine motor, expressive language, comprehension, memory, and letters; also includes adjustment and symptom scales.
Minnesota Child Development Inventory (MCDI)	Birth to 6 years	Parent report; 20 minutes	Eight areas: general development, gross motor, fine motor, expressive language, comprehension-conceptual, situation comprehension, self-help, and personal-social.
Minnesota Infant Development Inventory	Birth to 15 months	Parent report; 10 minutes	Five areas: gross motor, fine motor, language, comprehension, and social.
Minnesota Preschool Inventory	3 to 6 years	Parent report; 10 minutes	Same developmental scales as above. Determines child's readiness to enter school.
Minnesota Pre-Kindergarten Inventory	4½ to 5½ years	Parent report; 20 minutes	Same developmental scales as above. Determines child's educational development and school readiness.
Pediatric Evaluation of Educational Readiness (PEER)	4 to 6 years	Individually administered; 45 minutes	27 rating scales; must be done with a physical exam. Physician administered.
Revised Denver Preschool Developmental Questionnaire (R-PDQ)	Birth to 6 years	Parent report; 20 minutes	Developed from the DDST. Four areas: fine motor, language, personal-social, and gross motor.

Continued

TABLE 5.1 *(continued)*

COMMONLY USED SCREENING TESTS

Test	Age Range	Administration	Description
LANGUAGE			
Bankson Language Screening Test	4 to 8 years	Individually administered; 25 minutes	17 subtests; questionable validity and reliability.
Early Language Milestone Scale (ELM)	Birth to 3 years	Individually administered; 15–20 minutes	Three areas: auditory expressive, auditory receptive, and visual skills.
Reynell Developmental Language Scales (2nd rev.)	1 to 6 years	Individually administered; 15–25 minutes	Three scales: verbal comprehension A, verbal comprehension B, and expressive language. No formal validity, limited information on reliability.
Test of Early Language Development (TELD)	3 to 8 years	Individually administered; 15–20 minutes	Yields a total score with individual scores in receptive language, expressive language, semantics, and syntactic forms.
SCHOOL READINESS			
Kerby Learning Modality Test, Revised	5 to 11 years	Individually administered; 15 minutes	Three areas: visual, auditory, and motor. Requires special training to score, used for educational planning.
Riley Preschool Developmental Screening Inventory	3 to 5 years	Individually administered; 10 minutes	Measures school readiness. No reliability or validity data. Not well designed, not comprehensive.
VISUAL-MOTOR			
Developmental Test of Visual-Motor Integration (3rd rev.)	2 to 18 years	Individually administered; 15–20 minutes	24 geometric forms; yields developmental age, standard score, and percentile.
Motor-Free Visual Perception Test	5 to 9 years	Individually administered; 10 minutes	Five categories: spatial relations, visual discrimination, figure ground, closure, and memory.
Slosson Drawing Coordination Test	1 year to adult	Individually administered; 10–15 minutes	12 figures; no evidence of validity.

Continued

TABLE 5.1 (*continued*)

COMMONLY USED SCREENING TESTS

Test	Age Range	Administration	Description
BEHAVIOR, ADJUSTMENT			
Child Behavior Checklist	2 to 16 years	Individually administered or parent report; 10–30 minutes	Two forms: one for 2- to 3-year-olds, one for 4- to 16-year-olds.
Conners Parent Rating Scale–Revised	3 to 17 years	Parent report or checklist; 20 minutes	Five areas: conduct, learning, psychosomatic, impulsivity/hyperactivity, and anxiety.
Conners Teacher Rating Scale–Revised	3 to 17 years	Teacher report or checklist; 10–15 minutes	Three areas: conduct, hyperactivity, and inattention-passivity.
Eyberg Child Behavior Inventory	3 to 17 years	Parent report or checklist; 10–15 minutes	36 behaviors rated on a 7-point scale, denoting frequency of occurrence and whether each behavior is a problem.
Parenting Stress Index	Infant to 10 years	Parent report; 20–30 minutes	Comprehensive coverage; yields 7 child domain and 8 parent domain scores plus total score.
Sutter-Eyberg Student Behavior Inventory	3 to 5 years	Teacher report or checklist; 10–15 minutes	36 behaviors rated on a 7-point scale, denoting frequency of occurrence and whether each behavior is a problem

Tests of Development

To screen effectively for developmental disorders, the tests, by definition, must be broad in scope. They may be either "prescreening" measures or formal screening measures, so long as they cover a broad range of developmental skills and a broad age range in children. These tests typically assess such skills as gross and fine motor functioning, language and communication, personal/social development, memory, and adaptive behavior. The categories vary among tests but generally include those mentioned.

The Denver II (Frankenburg et al., 1990), as mentioned previously the revised version of the Denver Developmental Screening Test (DDST), probably is the best known and most widely used example of a primary screening test. The original DDST was developed in 1967 and widely disseminated to pediatric centers. The revised version retains the original format but is improved in several ways: increased number of language items, updated norms, modifications in interpretation to increase test sensitivity, and improved training procedures.

The Denver II is designed to be used with children from birth to 6 years of age. It consists of 125 tasks arranged into four areas of development: personal-social, fine motor–adaptive, language, and gross motor. The Denver II manual clearly and simply explains the test procedures, including administration and scoring. It is designed to be used by a variety of professionals and paraprofessionals. To improve accuracy in administration and interpretation of the Denver II, the authors suggest that persons who administer the test be thoroughly familiar with the testing materials and procedures, undergo a formal training program, and pass a proficiency test. However, professionals experienced in screening with the DDST most likely will find strong generalization from the original to the revised edition, as long as they become thoroughly familiar with the new administration and interpretation guidelines in the manual.

The Denver II items can be scored by direct observation, administration of item, or parent report. Each item is scored on a bar that indicates the ages at which 25%, 50%, 75%, and 90% of the normative group passed a specific test item. Test items are grouped by age in each category so that the examiner can start the administration at a level near the child's age. The child's performance on the Denver II can be interpreted as advanced, normal, caution (i.e., when a child fails or refuses an item on which the age line falls on or between the 75th or 90th percentile), delayed (i.e., when a child fails or refuses an item that falls completely to the left of the age line), or no opportunity (i.e., when the parent says the child has not had an opportunity to try a particular task). A "Normal" outcome for the Denver II occurs when the child has no delays and a maximum of one caution score. An "Abnormal" outcome occurs when the child has two or more delays. A "Questionable" outcome occurs when there is one delay and/or two or more cautions. The authors recommend referral of the child for diagnostic evaluation if screening yields an Abnormal result, although this decision must be made with consideration of the child's clinical history.

The Denver II has a number of advantages as a screening instrument. It is easy to administer and score, and the items are well selected to interest the child. The instrument covers an appropriate age range for screening and can be administered serially to a child to monitor development over time. As noted, the revision has brought a number of improvements. One of the major concerns of the DDST was its limited sample of language items. Borowitz and Glascoe (1986) evaluated the DDST as a speech and language screening test and found that in a group of 18- to 66-month-old children, the test failed to identify more than half of those with language problems. Therefore, professionals who used the DDST as a primary screening test for preschool children also needed a "secondary," or more narrowly focused, language screening test in order to avoid the problem of underreferral. This problem has been addressed on the Denver II, as the language items now outnumber each of the other types of items.

Another improvement relates to the changes in interpretation of the Denver II, which are likely to increase the test's sensitivity. In a review of the research on the DDST, Bauchner and Greer (1987) pooled the results of several studies to evaluate the test's predictive validity. They determined that the DDST had an overall sensitivity of 20% and specificity of 93%. The most serious concern was their finding that the DDST failed to identify approximately 15% of the children who later had a poor outcome. Research must now demonstrate if the Denver II is better than the DDST in this regard, but the changes in interpretation appear to be a step in the right direction for addressing this problem.

The updated normative sample, which was diversified according to age, race, place of residence (urban, semirural, rural), and mother's educational level, also presents an improvement over the now-dated 1967 version. The increased attention given in the Denver II manual to examiner training and standardized administration should improve the accuracy of the test as well. A training tape is available, as are training workshops and a proficiency test for examiners.

One final problem remains with the Denver II—the length of administration and its impact on physicians. Smith (1978) concluded that a major obstacle to the regular use of the DDST was the physician's perception that it takes too long to administer (about 20 minutes). This is a factor to consider in recommending the revised version as well, as it is approximately the same length. However, few if any screening tests are briefer and still retain the positive qualities of the Denver II for detecting those children who are developmentally at risk. The Denver II is one of the best tools available, if one is cautious about obtaining appropriate training in its administration and interpretation.

Another test developed for use by physicians is the Pediatric Examination of Educational Readiness (PEER; Levine & Schneider, 1982). This test is part of a series developed by Melvin Levine to encourage pediatricians to become involved in developmental evaluation. The PEER is designed for children from 4 to 6 years of age and produces 27 rating scores, covering such areas as gross and fine motor ability, orientation, processing efficiency, attention, sequential learning, and linguistics. In his work on these tests, Levine maintains that they are not screening tests and that they should be used in conjunction with other evaluations. However, aspects of the test design and application are similar to those of screening measures.

The PEER has the problem of being costly in terms of time and training. The test takes nearly an hour to administer, not including the physical examination that should be part of the evaluation. In addition, the complexity of the administration and scoring are such that interrater reliability is acceptable only after extensive training and practice. The determination of a cutoff is somewhat arbitrary in that Levine suggests that local norms be developed. An evaluation of a companion test for school-aged children, the Pediatric Early Elementary Examination, revealed poor sensitivity and specificity (Kenny et al., 1990), and other investigators have questioned the utility of the PEER as a screening measure (Palmer, Garner, Lifschitz, Wilson, & Williamson, 1990). However, the extensive time and training required are probably the most significant impediment to using the PEER as a screening test.

The Battelle Developmental Inventory (Newborg, Stock, Wnek, Guidubaldi, & Svinicki, 1984) is a relatively new test designed to be used with children from birth to 8 years of age. It measures five main areas—personal-social, adaptive, motor, communication, and cognition—and yields a variety of scores, including both age equivalents and standard scores. Using the full battery (all items in each area) can take over an hour to complete, but a screening test also is included that requires only 10 to 20 minutes to administer. One purpose of the Battelle is to identify children with handicapping conditions, but the test actually is focused more on educational issues such as school readiness and the planning of educational programs.

Another approach to developmental screening that is gaining attention and acceptance is the use of parental reports to measure development. With these instruments parents answer a series of questions covering a variety of developmental tasks, and their responses produce a developmental profile of the child. The parent report approach has the major advantage of reducing professional administration time to near zero. Concerns about the use of these instruments center on questions related to the parents' accuracy of reporting, parental bias, the reading level required for the test, and the related concept of the parents' understanding of the questions. Recent research on a variety of tests generally has negated these concerns (Burgess, Asher, Doucet, Reardon, & Daste, 1984; Dean & Steffan, 1984; Eisert, Spector, & Shankaran, 1980; Gottfried, Guerin, Spencer, & Meyer, 1984; Kenny, Hebel, Sexton, & Fox, 1987; Knobloch, Stevens, Malone, Ellison, & Risenberg, 1979).

In response to concerns about the time requirements of the standard Denver screening test, Frankenburg and associates modified the DDST to utilize parent report. This new test, a shortened version, was named the Revised Prescreening Developmental Questionnaire (R-PDQ; Frankenburg, 1986), modified so that test items can be answered by parent response rather than requiring actual administration of the item. In reporting the development of the original PDQ, Frankenburg, Van Doornick, and Liddell (1976) found that the parent's response to the test questions achieved a high level of agreement when measured against actual item administration. They concluded that the PDQ was an effective prescreening tool that significantly reduces the professional time required to screen young children.

The same study also reported reasonable agreement between the PDQ and the DDST in classifying children's performance. The PDQ was found to be well received by parents, and parental education and socioeconomic status were not thought to significantly affect reliability in responding to the questions (though Frankenburg later acknowledged that parent reliability in responding is questionable when educational level falls below 12th grade). A problem with the Frankenburg approach to the PDQ is that, as it was developed from the original DDST, in the validating studies PDQ performance was compared to performance on the DDST. As a result, the PDQ is a "shortcut" to the DDST but retains the problems associated with the original. The study does not deal with the PDQ's sensitivity or specificity, an acknowledged problem in the DDST, but does suggest a loss of efficiency associated with the reduction of the item sample.

Burgess et al. (1984) compared the PDQ, a modification of the PDQ, and the Alpern-Boll Developmental Profile II (Alpern, Boll, & Shearer, 1980), finding that the PDQ predicted performance on the DDST. However, the PDQ had only a 50% sensitivity level and a 62% specificity level. The PDQ also showed an overreferral rate of 30% while still having a problem with underreferral. Of the three measures, the Alpern-Boll had better sensitivity and specificity with a higher hit rate.

The Minnesota Child Development Inventory (MCDI), developed by Ireton and Thwing (1974b), is a parent-report measure that has gained increased recognition. The MCDI was developed to be used from birth to 6 years and contains 320 questions divided into eight areas: general development, gross motor, fine motor, expressive language, comprehensive-conceptual, situation comprehension, self-help, and personal-social. The MCDI has been used with high-risk infants (Eisert et al., 1980;

Saylor & Brandt, 1986), developmental screening (Byrne, 1987; Colligan, 1980; Ireton, Thwing, & Currier, 1977), and preschool screening (Colligan, 1981; Sturner, Funk, Thomas, & Green, 1982). Kenny et al. (1987) found the MCDI correlated well with the McCarthy Scales of Children's Abilities (McCarthy, 1972). In a study in volving 369 three-year-olds, the MCDI achieved a sensitivity of 70% and a specificity of 79% when compared to the McCarthy, using a General Cognitive Index of 80 or less and a cutoff score on the MCDI as criteria. With the same criteria the MCDI had a 79.1% hit rate for correct classification, with a false positive rate of 17.3% and a false negative rate of 3.6%. These data suggest that the MCDI is more efficient than the DDST or the PDQ.

New versions of the MCDI have been developed that are briefer and targeted to a more restricted age range. The Minnesota Infant Development Inventory (MIDI; Ireton & Thwing, 1974c) can be used from birth to 15 months and contains 75 items divided into five test areas: gross motor, fine motor, language, comprehension, and personal-social. The Early Child Development Inventory (ECDI; Ireton & Thwing, 1974a), for children from 1 to 3 years of age, contains 60 items in the developmental scale plus a 24-item symptom and behavior problem list. The Minnesota Preschool Inventory–Form 34 (Ireton & Thwing, 1974d) can be used with 3- to 6-year-olds to determine children's readiness to enter school. Parents use this multiple-item, paper-and-pencil inventory to review their child's development, adjustment, and symptoms.

The Minnesota Pre-Kindergarten Inventory (Ireton & Thwing, 1974d) is suitable for children ages 4½ to 5½ years, screening for educational development and school readiness. This 150-item, paper-and-pencil inventory is completed by the parent to assess seven areas of development: self-help, fine motor, expressive language, comprehension, memory, letter recognition, and number comprehension. There are also four adjustment scales (Immaturity, Hyperactivity, Behavioral Problems, and Emotional Problems) as well as four symptom scales (Motor, Language, Somatic, and Sensory). The adjustment and symptom scales are a potentially useful feature that have yet to be evaluated. Freeland (1988) compared parent reports of problems on the adjustment scales with psychologists' ratings and found significant correlations. There also was agreement on problem patterns and a significant relationship to the child's score on the McCarthy Scales.

The previously mentioned Developmental Profile II (DPII; Alpern et al., 1980), also referred to as the Alpern-Boll Scale, is a 1980 revision of the original 1972 test. The DPII is briefer than the original due to eliminating items used for 10- to 12-year-olds. The present version is for children from birth to 9 years of age. The DPII contains 186 test questions, grouped by age level into five test areas: physical, self-help, social, academic, and communication. The test is administered individually by an interviewer and takes 20 to 40 minutes to complete. The administration is simple enough to be done by a nonprofessional, and this reduces the demand for professional time and related cost. Compared to the DDST, the DPII is better at predicting language delay (Harper, 1985) and in reducing the rate of overreferral (Burgess et al., 1984). In a review of the DPII, White (1985) raised questions about the test's standardization sample and the use of the IQ Equivalency Score, but concluded that the test is good at screening young children to determine the need for further evaluation.

Tests of Intelligence-Cognition

The use of intelligence tests as predictors of school achievement has historical precedence going back to the origins of psychometric testing. In developing one of the earliest intelligence tests, Binet and Simon had as a goal the prediction of school performance of children entering the Paris school system. The underlying concept was to produce a measure that would assess the child's developmental status and compare that measure to school performance. What emerged became a test of cognitive functioning that considered intelligence to be composed of a variety of specific abilities, most or all of which would impact on school performance. In its simplest form, the approach postulates cognitive functioning or intelligence as the central factor in learning. In the broadest sense, the construct is still operational. If we could choose only one type of test to predict school performance, the intelligence test would be the most successful instrument.

While we can accept or debate this concept, the utility of intelligence tests for developmental screening raises special issues. First, an IQ score is a composite of a number of different abilities averaged together into a global, rather than specific, index. The IQ is good at indicating problems such as mental retardation, but is less useful for more specific areas such as motor or language functioning. Because both motor and language deficits are listed as handicapping conditions in the special education system, they need to be screened; an intelligence test is less effective in these areas.

In addition, intelligence tests are designed to measure the spectrum of cognitive functioning, including gifted abilities, and to do this requires a continuous distribution of scores. A screening test can be focused on the "problem" end of the continuum and needs only a cutoff score. For example, the Wechsler Preschool and Primary Scales of Intelligence–Revised (Wechsler, 1989) yields an IQ that reflects the subject's position in relation to the total population, but the Denver II produces a cutoff score that indicates problems by specific areas. To achieve comprehensive screening, an intelligence test likely would have to be augmented by other screening techniques that would identify motor or language problems. A child with cerebral palsy could score in the average range on an IQ test but need special education services because of motor problems associated with the cerebral palsy.

Added to the concerns already mentioned about screening for intelligence is not having appropriate tools for such screening. Historically the practice of screening for intelligence was more common, but it would not be recommended practice today. However, some of the tests used historically for screening intelligence should be discussed for the sake of reader information.

A common approach to IQ screening in the past involved using picture vocabulary tests. The best known of these measures is the Peabody Picture Vocabulary Test–Revised (PPVT-R; Dunn & Dunn, 1981). The original was developed in 1959 and enjoyed widespread use (as has the revised edition) as a clinical and research tool. The PPVT-R is easy to learn, simple to administer and score, and yields results in the form of a standard score, percentile, stanine, and age equivalent. The test can be used from 2½ years to adulthood. To administer this test, the examiner says a word while the subject looks at a plate with four pictures on it. One picture is a correct match for the word spoken by the examiner, and the subject completes the task by pointing to the picture matches the stimulus word.

The PPVT-R is a useful test because of its ease of administration and scoring. The test is enjoyable, usually attracts and holds children's interest, and it serves the appropriate age range for screening. In addition, parallel forms allow for repeated evaluations without confounding practice effects. These factors combine to make the PPVT-R a useful test of receptive vocabulary, and a helpful addition to a more complete diagnostic test battery for children. However, the practice of using the PPVT-R as a screening for intelligence is not currently accepted.

A number of other tests, such as Gardner's (1979) Expressive One-Word Picture Vocabulary Test, are similar to the PPVT-R but less well known, designed, or reliable. In general they offer no benefits over the PPVT-R and have some additional problems.

The Slosson Intelligence Test (SIT; Slosson, 1981b) is a screening instrument for children aged 2 weeks to 18 years. It is individually administered and takes 10 to 20 minutes to complete. Designed to parallel the Stanford-Binet Intelligence Scale, Form L-M (Terman & Merrill, 1960), the present form was introduced in 1981 as a revision of the 1963 version, but most of the changes are minor. Little information is provided on validity or reliability, and the SIT is a highly verbal measure. Thus, children with a normal IQ but a specific language deficit may score poorly on this test. Reynolds (1985) reported that the SIT is a psychometrically poor measure of general intelligence; it also would not be recommended for screening of intelligence.

A more detailed coverage of issues relating to cognitive assessment can be found in chapter 8 of this volume. The reader who is interested in screening those children at risk for cognitive deficits is directed to the general developmental tests discussed in the previous section.

Language Tests

Language and communication skills long have been considered key predictors of success in our society. The role of language in educational achievement, business, and interpersonal relations is well accepted. Realizing the importance of language to successful achievement makes screening for communication problems a high priority, but effective screening of these skills is one of the most difficult assessments.

As noted earlier in this chapter, the first obstacle to assessing language is the relatively late onset of the skill. A comparatively wide range of motor skills is operational by 1 year of age, but at that same age only precursors of language and communication are measurable. A surge in language development occurs between 3 and 5 years, which makes it more reasonable to assess language skills, but problems with accurate assessment still linger at these ages. All developmental functions have some variability in onset, which makes it difficult to discriminate a developmental delay from a deficit. For example, walking may occur as early as 9 months or as late as 15 months, both within the range of normal variability. Speech and language, even with its late onset, shows an equally large span of acceptable variability, so that preschool prediction of problems is further compromised. Another age-related variable to consider is that certain speech or language problems are transient, occurring frequently at a particular age but often outgrown. Stuttering and articulation difficulties exemplify these problems.

The strong interrelationship between communication disorders and cognitive deficits further complicates the use of language tests. The majority of mentally retarded children likely will have problems in speech or language, making it necessary to glean reliable information about a child's cognitive level before determining if he or she has a specific language problem or a more global delay. The interactive effect of language and intelligence on IQ test scores is most difficult to separate in the 3- to 5-year age range. The reader is referred to chapter 9 in this volume for a more thorough discussion of evaluating the communication-disordered preschool child.

As a consequence of the complexity of assessing language problems, the tests available usually require a greater degree of expertise than most screening tests. Many of these tests are best used by speech/language pathologists, and even with that level of training tend to take longer than other screening tests. Language screening tests generally would be viewed as "secondary" or more narrowly focused screening instruments, applied after the "primary" tests or when only a focal problem in speech/language skills is suspected.

The Bankson Language Screening Test (Bankson, 1977) for children ages 4 to 8 requires minimal training to use and can be completed in 20 to 30 minutes. Basically designed to measure expressive language, the test also covers other areas such as auditory and visual-perceptual skills. Picture stimuli present test items based on a model that includes the morphological, syntactic, and semantic aspects of language necessary for linguistic performance. The results determine appropriate areas for follow-up diagnostic assessment and identify initial language areas in need of remediation. The test authors provide evidence of reasonable concurrent validity, but predictive validity has not been demonstrated. As a result, the Bankson test must be used with caution.

The Test of Early Language Development (TELD; Hresko, Reid, & Hammill, 1982), designed for use with children from 3 to 8 years of age, measures receptive and expressive language, semantics, and syntactic forms. This test is easy to learn and administer and takes about 20 minutes to complete. As with the Bankson, the TELD provides limited data on validity and reliability, and the test authors caution users on the appropriate use of the test.

The Reynell Developmental Language Scales–Second Revision (Reynell, 1979) provide another means of screening language skills, this in children ages 1 to 6 years. This test assesses expressive language and verbal comprehension, and is used for evaluation of early development. In addition, it is suitable for use with hearing impaired children. Again, there are no reliability or validity data available for this test, and the user is thereby cautioned.

Finally, the Early Language Milestone Scale (ELM; Coplan, 1983) is a more recently designed measure, patterned after the Denver Developmental Screening Test and developed by a physician for use by physicians and other professionals concerned with the language development of young children. The scale covers the age range from birth to 3 years, presuming that this is the period when most language delays are missed by medical professionals. Indeed, this is the age range in which language items on the DDST are most sparse, and the ELM provided a much more detailed range of items to measure before the Denver II was available to use. The ELM is a 41-item, paper-and-pencil screening instrument divided into three subscales: auditory expressive, auditory receptive, and visual skills. Like the Denver II, the items are grouped by age range, graphically displayed so that one can determine at what ages 25%, 50%, 75%, and 90% of the normative population passed that item. If the child fails to pass items that 90% of the peer group can achieve, then those items are considered failed.

There are some scoring and interpretation differences between the ELM and the Denver II, but generally it is an easily administered and scored test. The ELM is gaining popularity with physicians as a supplemental measure to the Denver II, particularly to cover the language areas in younger children. The scale is norm referenced, and percentile values for the expected age of emergence of each item are provided. Reliability and validity data currently are lacking for this test, as for the other language measures discussed, so again the examiner is advised to interpret results with caution.

Screening for Academic Readiness

Tests of academic readiness have long appeared in preschool screening. These tests have reasonable ability to determine a child's functioning in areas related to school performance, but there are limitations to their use. In a screening program, such a test would not provide sufficient coverage of the range of handicapping conditions, such as cognitive, language, or motor problems. As a result, academic screening tests must be used in conjunction with other screening instruments. A more central problem lies in the similarity between readiness tests and achievement tests. It has been argued that readiness tests reflect only the child's *opportunity* to have learned the skills tested rather than his or her *ability* to learn the material. This may be conceived of as the difference between disadvantage and disability.

The Riley Preschool Developmental Screening Inventory (Riley, 1975) is used in Grades PreK–1 to measure readiness to attend school and to identify children most likely to need assistance adjusting to normal school situations. This is a multiple-item observational test, providing ratings on the child's developmental age and self-concept and determining serious developmental and maturational problems. Suggested cutoff scores are provided, but the test lacks adequate reliability and validity data. The Riley test has been used widely in Head Start programs for counseling regarding school readiness.

The Kerby Learning Modality Test, Revised (Kerby, 1980) is appropriate for ages 5 to 11 years and addresses strengths and weaknesses in three primary learning modalities: visual, auditory, and motor activity. The test consists of a variety of classroom work samples arranged in eight subtests: visual and auditory discrimination, visual and auditory closure, visual and auditory memory, and visual and auditory coordination. This test purportedly is used to identify children with learning disabilities, but it is not sufficiently broad or validated for that purpose. It may likely be useful in planning teaching strategies for working with children who have learning weaknesses in the areas measured.

Screening for Visual-Motor Skills

Visual-motor coordination comprises an area of functioning that has been long associated with developmental and learning problems. A number of tests are available to assess this area such as the Developmental Test of Visual-Motor Integration (Beery, 1982/1989), the Slosson Drawing Coordination Test (Slosson, 1981a), and the Motor-Free Visual Perception Test (Colarusso & Hammill, 1972). The narrow focus of these measures requires that they be used with other screening instruments; however, they are useful measures of specific deficits in need of treatment.

Screening for Behavioral Problems and Adjustment

Problems with adjustment or behavior are found in a significant number of preschool-aged children. One study reported behavior problems occurring in 7% to 10% of a sample of 3-year-olds (Richmond, Stevenson, & Graham, 1975). Rutter (1975) reported that, over the course of 1 year, 5% to 15% of children have an emotional or behavioral problem severe enough to disrupt their functioning in everyday life. The high prevalence rate of behavioral disorders, and their adverse effect on learning, indicate the need to screen consistently for their presence. The clinician will find a number of excellent instruments for such purposes; several are reviewed briefly here but discussed in greater detail in chapter 6 of this volume.

The Conners Parent Rating Scale–Revised (Goyette, Conners, & Ulrich, 1978) is a parent-report checklist that comes in two versions, one of which has 98 items and the other, 48 items. The briefer version would be appropriate for screening. This test is used appropriately for children 3 to 17 and takes approximately 20 minutes to complete. Although used primarily to screen for hyperactivity, parents' responses are categorized into five behavior problem areas: conduct, learning, psychosomatic, impulsivity/hyperactivity, and anxiety. This scale is helpful in discriminating hyperactivity and conduct problems in young children.

A corollary to the Conners parent scale is the Conners Teacher Rating Scale–Revised (Goyette et al., 1978). The short version of this scale is designed to screen for three areas of problem behavior in the classroom setting: conduct, hyperactivity, and inattention/passivity. This teacher-report checklist also is appropriate for children 3 to 17 years of age, has 28 items, and takes 10–15 minutes to complete. Studies have demonstrated a strong positive correlation between parent and teacher versions of the Conners scale. It is useful to obtain information from both teachers and parents in a screening program because a child's activity and attention levels may vary by setting. Screening programs that obtain information across a variety of settings and from a variety of informants more likely will pick up on developmental or behavioral problems than those using a single setting or source of information.

The Conners scales are the most well known and widely used screening instruments in the area of attention deficit and hyperactivity in children (Edelbrock & Rancurello, 1985). They are frequently cited as the criteria for inclusion in research studies, and there is widespread evidence for their validity in discriminating normal from hyperactive samples of children (Edelbrock & Rancurello, 1985). However, Ullman, Sleator, and Sprague (1985) have criticized the use of the Conners scales due to confusion regarding the cutoff scores for various versions of the scales. However, publication of a technical manual for the current revised versions of the parent and teacher scales has clarified the norms and factor structure (Conners & Blouin, 1980; Goyette et al., 1978; Trites, Blouin, & Laprade, 1982).

The Eyberg Child Behavior Inventory (ECBI; Robinson, Eyberg & Ross, 1980) is a well-researched and useful instrument for determining the number of problem behaviors a child has, their intensity (or frequency of occurrence), and parental perception of difficulty in managing them. Consisting of 36 common behavior problems reported to occur in young children, the ECBI asks parents to rate each of these problems as it pertains to their own child. Cutoff scores determine if the child's problems fall in the clinically significant range (which suggests referral for intervention) or not. The scale is appropriate for children ages 3 to 17, and it takes 10–15 minutes to complete.

The ECBI also has a classroom corollary, the Sutter-Eyberg Student Behavior Inventory (SESBI; Funderburk & Eyberg, 1987). This scale is standardized for use with 3- to 5-year-old children and follows the same format as described for the ECBI. It is especially useful for classroom screening because of its brevity, the careful research underlying it, and the ability to compare its results to those of the ECBI. Both the ECBI and SESBI have proven effective in documenting the progress made in intervention programs for behaviorally disturbed children and their parents.

The Child Behavior Checklist (CBCL; Achenbach & Edelbrock, 1983) is a carefully constructed, empirically derived scale with a great deal of research indicating its validity and reliability. There are two forms of the test, one for 2- to 3-year-old children and the other for 4- to 16-year-olds. The scale is a quite lengthy parent-report measure, taking up to 30 minutes to complete. It yields information about the child's social competence (including number and types of social activities and relationships, and learning ability) and behavior problems. Because of its length, it may not be as useful for screening as either the Conners or the ECBI scales if one suspects a disruptive behavior disorder. However, the Achenbach CBCL is broader than the ECBI and Conners, and taps a number of internalizing emotional or behavioral problems as well as the more externalizing or disruptive problems. Although usually completed by the parents, there is a teacher version of the Child Behavior Checklist as well.

Because child emotional and behavioral problems often reflect problems in the family, it is helpful to conduct screening of the child's environment. The Parenting Stress Index (PSI; Abidin, 1983) is a parent report that provides information regarding the parent's perception of stresses related to child characteristics (e.g., activity level, demandingness, ability to reinforce the parent), parent characteristics (e.g., depression, sense of isolation, relationship to spouse), and life events. PSI information is not usually obtained in other screening tests and therefore can be quite useful in a comprehensive screening program (limited perhaps by its length). The reader also is referred to chapter 7 in this volume for a more detailed discussion of family assessment.

Model for a Comprehensive Screening Program

Given the issues discussed thus far, an ideal screening program must target the preschool population, provide for early and repeated screenings with tests having a high level of sensitivity and specificity, and be cost-effective in terms of the professional time needed to complete the screening process.

In the United States, the health care system provides the earliest and most frequent access to preschool children and their parents. It is logical, therefore, that the initial screening program be based within this system, which includes public health facilities, private pediatric or family medicine practices, and hospital-based clinics. The essential prerequisite to this medical-based screening program is that the persons doing the screening (a) be well trained to appropriately administer, score, and interpret the screening tests utilized, and (b) be knowledgeable about community resources for referral when further diagnostic evaluation is needed. This necessitates a strong multidisciplinary orientation, with the participating health care professionals understanding the expertise of psychologists, speech/language pathologists, and educators in the diagnosis and treatment of developmental and behavioral disorders.

The proposed screening program would be developed through collaboration of the psychologist and physician, along with the health care staff. Together these professionals would discuss the mechanisms of the screening program and devise a schedule and procedures for carrying out the screening. The psychologist would take the lead in familiarizing the health care staff with the screening instruments that are available and appropriate to use. This should be done to secure their cooperation, to equip them to explain the screening program to parents, and to get their input about potential problems. The psychologist also should have a schedule for the screening, a method for triggering the screening, and a data collection and recording system.

Once the screening program is ready to begin, the nurse or receptionist who schedules well-child visits would refer to a schedule in each child's chart indicating the date for the next developmental screening. When the well-child visit is scheduled, copies of the screening or prescreening instruments would be placed in the child's chart. A practical choice would be a parent-report measure, such as the PDQ or one of the Minnesota Child Development Inventory scales, which cover a broad range in terms of age and developmental skill areas. The results of this "prescreening" measure should indicate to the professional whether a formal screening is necessary at that time.

To monitor the possibility of parental or environmental problems affecting the child's development, the Parenting Stress Index might be used as a second part of the screening process. When the parent checks in for the appointment, he or she would be given the parent-report screening measures to complete while waiting for the regular health examination. The receptionist or other health care staff would be available to answer any questions from the parent.

If the clinician determined the child was at risk for developmental problems, based on either the prescreening measure or historical information provided by the parent, a formal developmental screening then would be scheduled. If the prescreening measure was normal, then the child would be scheduled for another prescreening at his or her next well-child visit.

This approach allows for frequent, systematic, and cost-effective screening during the first months and years of life. The use of repeated assessments of development would provide the broadest sample of skills and identify problems as early as possible. For example, repeated screening would be more likely than a single testing to make an early identification of problems in a late-developing skill such as language. Also, professionals would be better able to study the child's developmental pattern over time, which improves the accuracy of predicting developmental problems. Finally, repeated screenings allow the professional to better evaluate the role of the environment in facilitating or inhibiting development. The child's developmental pattern is the equivalent of a growth chart; as with physical growth, findings of excessive variability or significant shift in the rate of development may be important.

The psychologist plays an important role in this hypothetical screening program, not only in the initial planning and training stages but also in the data analysis. The psychologist may devise a comprehensive data collection system for screening information obtained in the health care system. Analysis of these data may provide insight into the incidence of developmental disorders as well as the characteristics associated with the early manifestations of developmental problems. Pairing the physician and psychologist to carry out the screening program requires some changes in the typical practice mode of each. The physician must become a more active part of the screening process, and the psychologist must be willing to move into a more primary care environment.

However, the advantages of working collaboratively outweigh the disadvantages in terms of a more effective program. The multidisciplinary collaboration with educators, speech/language pathologists, and occupational and physical therapists should begin at the point of referral for further diagnostic evaluation and intervention. There are legal, practical, and humanistic reasons for professionals, parents, and systems to join together to carry out an effective developmental screening program. However, the potential benefit to children is the simplest and most compelling reason to do so.

REFERENCES

Abidin, R.R. (1983). *Parenting Stress Index.* Charlottesville, VA: Pediatric Psychology Press.

Achenbach, T.M., & Edelbrock, C. (1983). *Manual for the Child Behavior Checklist and Revised Child Behavior Profile.* Burlington, VT: University of Vermont, Department of Psychiatry.

Alpern, G.D., Boll, T.J., & Shearer, M.S. (1980). *Developmental Profile II.* Aspen, CO: Psychological Development Publications.

Aylward, G.P., & Kenny, T.J. (1979). Developmental follow-up: Inherent problems and a conceptual model. *Journal of Pediatric Psychology, 4,* 331–343.

Bankson, N.W. (1977). *Bankson Language Screening Test.* Baltimore, MD: University Park Press.

Bauchner, H.C., & Greer, S.W. (1987). The Denver Developmental Screening Test: How good is its predictive validity? *American Journal of Diseases of Children, 141,* 368.

Beery, K.E. (1982/1989). *Revised administration, scoring, and teaching manual for the Developmental Test of Visual-Motor Integration.* Cleveland, OH: Modern Curriculum Press.

Borowitz, K.C., & Glascoe, F.P. (1986). Sensitivity of the Denver Developmental Screening Test in speech and language screening. *Pediatrics, 78,* 1075–1078.

Burgess, D.B., Asher, K.N., Doucet, H.J., Reardon, K., & Daste, M.R. (1984). Parent report as a means of administering the Prescreening Developmental Questionnaire: An evaluation study. *Journal of Developmental and Behavioral Pediatrics, 5,* 195–200.

Byrne, J.M. (1987, August). *Clinical validity of the Minnesota Child Development Inventory: A developmental perspective.* Paper presented at the 95th Annual Meeting of the American Psychological Association, Washington, DC.

Carr, J., & Stephens, E. (1964). Pediatricians and developmental tests. *Developmental Medicine and Child Neurology, 6,* 614–620.

Colarusso, R.P., & Hammill, D.D. (1972). *MVPT—Motor-Free Visual Perception Test manual*. Novato, CA: Academic Therapy Publications.

Colligan, R.C. (1980). The Minnesota Child Development Inventory as an aid in the assessment of developmental disability. *Journal of Clinical Psychology, 33,* 162–163.

Colligan, R.C. (1981). Prediction of reading difficulty from parental preschool report. *Learning Disability Quarterly, 4,* 31–37.

Conners, C.K., & Blouin, A.G. (1980, August). *Hyperkinetic syndrome and psychopathology in children*. Paper presented at the 89th Annual Meeting of the American Psychological Association, Montreal, Canada.

Coplan, J. (1983). *Early Language Milestone Scale*. Austin, TX: PRO-ED.

Dean, R.S., & Steffan, J.E. (1984). Direct and indirect pediatric screening measures. *Journal of Pediatric Psychology, 9,* 65–76.

Dunn, L.M., & Dunn, L.M. (1981). *Peabody Picture Vocabulary Test–Revised*. Circle Pines, MN: American Guidance Service.

Edelbrock, C., & Rancurello, M. (1985). Childhood hyperactivity: An overview of rating scales and their applications. *Clinical Psychology Review, 5,* 429–445.

Eisert, D.C., Spector, S., & Shankaran, S. (1980). Mothers' report of their low birth weight infants' subsequent development on the Minnesota Child Development Inventory. *Journal of Pediatric Psychology, 5,* 353–364.

Fischler, R.S., & Tancer, M. (1984). The primary physician's role in care of developmentally handicapped children. *Journal of Family Practice, 18,* 85–88.

Frankenburg, W.K. (1986, May). *Revised Denver Prescreening Developmental Questionnaire*. Paper presented at the Ambulatory Pediatric Association Meeting, Washington, DC.

Frankenburg, W.K., & Dodds, J.B. (1967). The Denver Developmental Screening Test. *Journal of Pediatrics, 71,* 181–191.

Frankenburg, W.K., Dodds, J.B., Archer, P., Bresnick, B., Maschka, P., Edelman, N., & Shapiro, H. (1990). *Denver II Screening manual*. Denver, CO: Denver Developmental Materials.

Frankenburg, W.K., Van Doornick, W.J., & Liddell, T.N. (1976). The Denver Prescreening Developmental Questionnaire (PDQ). *Pediatrics, 57,* 744–753.

Freeland, C.A. (1988). *The utility of the behavior and symptom items on the Minnesota Child Development Inventory*. Unpublished manuscript.

Funderburk, B., & Eyberg, S. (1987). *Standardization of a teacher rating scale of conduct problem behaviors in preschool children*. Unpublished manuscript, University of Florida, Gainesville.

Gardner, M.F. (1979). *Expressive One-Word Picture Vocabulary Test*. Novato, CA: Academic Therapy Publications.

Gottfried, A.W., Guerin, D., Spencer, J.E., & Meyer, C. (1984). Validity of Minnesota Child Development Inventory in screening young children's development status. *Journal of Pediatric Psychology, 9,* 219–230.

Goyette, C.H., Conners, C.K., & Ulrich, R.F. (1978). Normative data on the revised Conners Parent and Teacher Rating Scales. *Journal of Abnormal Child Psychology, 6,* 221–236.

Harper, D.C. (1985). Developmental Profile II. In J.V. Mitchell, Jr. (Ed.), *The ninth mental measurements yearbook* (pp. 466–468). Lincoln, NE: Buros Institute of Mental Measurements.

Hresko, W.P., Reid, D.K., & Hammill, D.D. (1982). *Test of Early Language Development (TELD)*. Austin, TX: PRO-ED.

Ireton, H., & Thwing, E. (1974a). *The Early Child Development Inventory*. Minneapolis, MN: Behavior Science Systems.

Ireton, H., & Thwing, E. (1974b). *Manual for the Minnesota Child Development Inventory*. Minneapolis, MN: Behavior Science Systems.

Ireton, H., & Thwing, E. (1974c). *Minnesota Infant Development Inventory.* Minneapolis, MN: Behavior Science Systems.
Ireton, H., & Thwing, E. (1974d). *Minnesota Pre-Kindergarten Inventory.* Minneapolis, MN: Behavior Science Systems.
Ireton, H., & Thwing, E. (1974e). *Minnesota Preschool Inventory.* Minneapolis, MN: Behavior Science Systems.
Ireton, H., Thwing, E., & Currier, S.K. (1977). Minnesota Child Development Inventory: Identification of children with developmental disorders. *Journal of Pediatric Psychology, 2,* 18-22.
Kenny, T.J., Gaes, G., Saylor, W., Grossman, L., Kappelman, M., Chernoff, R., Toler, S., & Majer, L. (1990). The Pediatric Early Elementary Examination: Sensitivity and specificity. *Journal of Pediatric Psychology, 15*(1), 21-26.
Kenny, T.J., Hebel, J.R., Sexton, M.J., & Fox, N.L. (1987). Developmental screening using parent report. *Journal of Developmental and Behavioral Pediatrics, 8,* 8-11.
Kerby, M.L. (1980). *Kerby Learning Modality Test-Revised.* Los Angeles, CA: Western Psychological Services.
Knobloch, H., Stevens, F., Malone, A., Ellison, P., & Risenberg, H. (1979). The validity of parental reporting of infant development. *Pediatrics, 6,* 872-878.
Levine, M., & Schneider, E.A. (1982). *Pediatric Examination of Educational Readiness.* Cambridge, MA: Educators Publishing Service.
Levine, M. (1985). *Manual for the Pediatric Examination of Educational Readiness.* Cambridge, MA: Educators Publishing Service.
Levine, M., Oberklaid, F., Ferb, T., Hanson, M., Palfrey, J., & Aufseeser, C. (1980). The Pediatric Examination of Educational Readiness: Validation of an extended observation procedure. *Pediatrics, 66,* 341-349.
McCarthy, D. (1972). *Manual for the McCarthy Scales of Children's Abilities.* San Antonio, TX: Psychological Corporation.
Newborg, J., Stock, J.R., Wnek, L., Guidubaldi, J., & Svinicki, J. (1984). *Battelle Developmental Inventory.* Allen, TX: DLM Teaching Resources.
Palmer, D.J., Garner, P.W., Lifschitz, M.H., Wilson, G.S., & Williamson, W.D. (1990). An exploratory study of the structure and validity of Pediatric Examination of Educational Readiness (PEER) factors. *Journal of Developmental and Behavioral Pediatrics, 11,* 317-321.
Reynell, J. (1979). *Reynell Developmental Language Scales-Second Revision.* Berkshire, England: NFER-Nelson.
Reynolds, W.M. (1985). Slosson Intelligence Test. In J.V. Mitchell, Jr. (Ed.), *The ninth mental measurements yearbook* (pp. 1403-1404). Lincoln, NE: Buros Institute of Mental Measurements.
Richmond, N., Stevenson, J., & Graham, P. (1975). Prevalence of behavior problems in 3 year old children: An epidemiological study in a London borough. *Journal of Child Psychology and Psychiatry, 16,* 272-281.
Riley, C.M. (1975). *Riley Preschool Development Screening Inventory.* Los Angeles: Western Psychological Services.
Robinson, E.A., Eyberg, S.M., & Ross, A.W. (1980). The standardization of an inventory of child conduct problem behaviors. *Journal of Clinical Child Psychology, 9,* 22-28.
Rutter, M. (1975). *Helping troubled children.* New York: Plenum.
Sameroff, A.J. (1975). Early influences on development: Fact or fancy? *Merrill-Palmer Quarterly, 21,* 267-294.
Saylor, C.F., & Brandt, B.J. (1986). The Minnesota Child Development Inventory: A valid maternal report form for assessing development in infancy. *Journal of Developmental and Behavioral Pediatrics, 7,* 308-313.

Slosson, R.L. (1981a). *Slosson Drawing Coordination Test*. East Aurora, NY: Slosson Educational Publications.
Slosson, R.L. (1981b). *Slosson Intelligence Test*. East Aurora, NY: Slosson Educational Publications.
Smith, R.D. (1978). The use of developmental screening tests by primary care physicians. *Journal of Pediatrics, 93,* 524–527.
Sturner, R.A., Funk, S.G., Thomas, P.D., & Green, J.A. (1982). An adaptation of the Minnesota Child Development Inventory for preschool developmental screening. *Journal of Pediatric Psychology, 7,* 295–306.
Terman, L.M., & Merrill, M.A. (1960). *Stanford-Binet Intelligence Scale, Form L-M*. Chicago: Riverside.
Trites, R.L., Blouin, A.G., & Laprade, K. (1982). Factor analysis of the Conners Teacher Rating Scale based on a large normative sample. *Journal of Consulting and Clinical Psychology, 50,* 615–623.
Ullman, R.K., Sleator, E.K., & Sprague, R.L. (1985). A change of mind: The Conners Abbreviated Rating Scales reconsidered. *Journal of Abnormal Child Psychology, 13,* 553–565.
Wechsler, D. (1989). *Manual for the Wechsler Preschool and Primary Scales of Intelligence–Revised*. San Antonio, TX: Psychological Corporation.
Wechsler, D. (1991). *Wechsler Intelligence Scale for Children–Third Edition*. San Antonio, TX: Psychological Corporation.
White, S. (1985). Developmental Profile II. In J.V. Mitchell, Jr. (Ed.), *The ninth mental measurements yearbook* (pp. 468–469). Lincoln, NE: Buros Institute of Mental Measurements.

6

Assessment of Behavior Problems in Young Children

CAROLYN S. SCHROEDER, PH.D. & BETTY N. GORDON, PH.D.

Most children in the process of growing up will have emotional and behavioral problems that are transient in nature and due to the stresses of adapting to family and societal expectations. A major parenting task is to help children manage and gain control over normal developmental events, such as toilet training, being told "no," starting school, becoming involved in community activities, and dealing with sibling and peer relationships. Children and parents also must cope with unexpected events, such as hospitalization, divorce, poverty, abuse, and death. For all of this pressure to adapt and cope, it is heartening that epidemiological studies find rather consistently that over the course of any one year, only 5% to 15% of children suffer from an emotional or behavioral problem that is severe enough to interfere with their functioning in everyday life (Rutter, 1975). The clinician's task is to identify and treat those children who suffer from emotional and/or behavioral problems that do interfere with their development.

In dealing with children's behavior problems, the goal of the assessment process should be to "provide a picture of the child that is informative, accurate, and useful in both the understanding and modification of child behavior disorders" (Ollendick & Hersen, 1984, p. 6). To accomplish this goal, one must not only directly observe and record the child's behavior but also take into account those ecological, social, cultural, biological, and developmental factors that influence him or her. The clinician choosing methods to assess for clinically relevant childhood behaviors and the potential influences on these behaviors often feels like a juggler balancing an ever-increasing number of objects of different shapes and sizes! The discussion that follows will present guidelines for the classification and assessment of behavior problems in young children.

Portions of this chapter have appeared in "Developmental Assessment in Clinical Practice: From Assessment to Intervention" by B.N. Gordon and C.S. Schroeder in *Developmental Assessment in Clinical Child Psychology: A Handbook* edited by J.H. Johnson and J. Goldman, 1990, Elmsford, NY: Pergamon; and in *Assessment and Treatment of Childhood Problems: A Clinician's Guide* by C.S. Schroeder and B.N. Gordon, 1991, New York: Guilford.

CLASSIFICATION OF BEHAVIOR PROBLEMS

Diagnosis refers to the different ways of classifying and delineating disorders. Currently there is no one classification system for children's behavioral problems that is accepted and employed by all health care professionals. The choice of a classification system usually is based on (a) the purpose of the classification and (b) the characteristics of the children to be classified (i.e., age, type, and severity of problems; Martin, 1988). A number of behaviorally oriented mental health workers, including the authors of this chapter, use a classification system that provides descriptive categories for behavior problems, such as toileting problems, sleep problems, negative behavior, and so forth (Chamberlin, 1974; Korpela, 1973; Schroeder, Gordon, Kanoy, & Routh, 1983).

Table 6.1 presents an example of the classification system used by Schroeder and her colleagues to describe the common behavior problems referred to psychologists in a primary health care setting (Schroeder, Gordon, Kanoy, & Routh, 1983). This approach does not lead to a determination that a child has a particular disorder but rather describes the degree to which one or many characteristics are evident (Kazdin, 1987). In applying this approach to diagnosis, we use interviews, rating scales, and observations to delineate specific behaviors of the child, the family, and the broader environment in which he or she lives and plays. In this way one gets a picture of an individual child, how his or her behavior compares to other children the same age, and how that behavior is viewed by the family and others in the wider environmental setting. This leads to a judgment about the significance of the behavior problem and, if necessary, the appropriate treatment.

In contrast, psychiatric diagnostic systems usually focus on more severe behavioral problems, often termed *behavioral disorders.* These systems are products of a medical model that views very deviant behavior as a function of biological determinants (Martin, 1988). They rely on clinical observations to identify discrete constellations of behavior or syndromes. The task of diagnosis is to identify which symptoms are present, if any, and then to assign or rule out the presence of discrete disorders (Kazdin, 1987). The most commonly used system in the United States is the revised third edition of the *Diagnostic and Statistical Manual of Mental Disorders,* or DSM-III-R (American Psychiatric Association, 1987). DSM-III-R diagnoses are made according to "diagnostic criteria" which are specific behaviors and symptoms. In addition to diagnostic criteria, the DSM-III-R manual supplies information concerning the prevalence, complications, familial patterns, and predisposing features of many of the diagnostic categories.

DSM-III-R lists nine overall diagnostic categories that may apply to infants, children, or adolescents: Developmental Disorders, Disruptive Behavior Disorders, Anxiety Disorders, Eating Disorders, Gender Identity Disorders, Tic Disorders, Elimination Disorders, Speech Disorders, and Other Disorders. Each of these nine diagnostic categories contain various specific diagnoses. For example, the diagnostic category of "Disruptive Behavior Disorder" contains the specific diagnoses of (a) Attention-Deficit Hyperactivity Disorder, (b) Conduct Disorder, and (c) Oppositional Defiant Disorder.

The DSM-III-R manual also indicates that there are some adult diagnostic cate-

TABLE 6.1

DEFINITIONS OF PROBLEM BEHAVIOR CATEGORIES

Problem Category	Definition
Negative behaviors	Won't listen to parents, doesn't obey, has tantrums, is bossy and demanding, cries, whines.
Toileting problems	Has toilet-training problems—soiling, enuresis, encopresis.
Developmental delays	Shows perceptual-motor problems, slow development, lack of school readiness, speech problems (stuttering), is overly active.
School problems	Hates school, is not doing well in school, has learning problems, shows aggression toward teacher.
Sleep problems	Won't go to bed, won't take naps, wakes during the night, has nightmares, has night terrors.
Personality problems	Lacks self-control, has no motivation, won't assume responsibility, lies, steals, is dependent, has difficult temperament.
Sibling/peer problems	Won't share, has no friends, is aggressive toward peers or siblings, fights a lot, shows sibling rivalry.
Divorce, separation	Involves custody, visitation schedule, adjustment, and how to tell child.
Infant management	Has problems feeding and/or nursing, cries all the time (colic), has difficult temperament.
Family problems	Parents disagree on discipline, mother feels isolated, marital conflict and/or child abuse present.
Sex-related problems	Wears opposite-sex clothes, has no same-sex friends, lacks sex-appropriate interests, has gender identity problems, suffers sexual abuse.
Food/eating problems	Is a picky eater, won't eat certain foods, eats too much.
Specific fears	Fears dogs, the dark, trucks, etc.
Bad habits	Bites nails, has tics, sucks thumb.
Parents' negative feelings	Parents don't like child, get no enjoyment from child.
Physical complaints	Complains of headaches, stomachaches.
Adoption/foster care	Needs advice on possible placements, what to tell child.
Moving	Needs preparation for new home, adjustment to moving.
Death	Has problem understanding the concept, adjusting to death, talking about death.
Giftedness	Needs special programs, appropriate stimulation.

Note. Adapted from Schroeder, Gordon, Kanoy, & Routh, 1983.

TABLE 6.2

AGE OF ONSET AND PREVALENCE OF DSM–III–R CATEGORIES OF DISORDERS RELEVANT FOR CHILDREN 0 TO 7 YEARS

Disorders	Age of Onset	Prevalence
DEVELOPMENTAL DISORDERS		
Mental Retardation	Birth	1%
Pervasive Developmental Disorders	Before 3 years	10 to 15 per 10,000
Autism	Before 3 years	4 to 5 per 10,000
Language and Speech Disorders		
Developmental Articulation Disorder	3 to 6 years	10% below 8 years
Developmental Expressive Language Disorder	Before 3 years for severe forms	No info for 0 to 7 years
Developmental Receptive Language Disorder	Before 4 years	No info for 0 to 7 years
Motor Skills Disorder		
Developmental Coordination Disorder	Preschool	6% of 5- to 11-year-olds
DISRUPTIVE BEHAVIOR DISORDERS		
Attention-Deficit Hyperactivity Disorder	Before 4 years	3%
Oppositional Defiant Disorder	Precursors in preschool years	No info
ANXIETY DISORDERS		
Separation Anxiety Disorder	Preschool years	Common
Avoidant Disorder	As early as 2½	Uncommon
Overanxious Disorder	No info	Common
EATING DISORDERS		
Pica	12 to 24 months	Occasional
Rumination Disorder of Infancy	3 to 12 months	Very rare
GENDER IDENTITY DISORDERS		
Gender Identity Disorder of Childhood	Before 4 years	Uncommon

Continued

TABLE 6.2 (*continued*)

AGE OF ONSET AND PREVALENCE OF DSM–III–R CATEGORIES OF DISORDERS RELEVANT FOR CHILDREN 0 TO 7 YEARS

Disorders	*Age of Onset*	*Prevalence*
TIC DISORDERS		
Tourette's Disorder	As early as 1 year	0.5 per 1,000
Transient Tic Disorder	As early as 2 years	No info
ELIMINATION DISORDERS		
Functional Encopresis	By age 4	1% of 5-year-olds
Functional Enuresis	By age 5	7% males, 3% females at 5 years
SPEECH DISORDERS NOT ELSEWHERE CLASSIFIED		
Stuttering	2 to 7 years	5%
OTHER DISORDERS		
Elective Mutism	Before 5 years	Rare
Reactive Attachment Disorder	Before 5 years	No info

gories that are appropriate for children because the essential features are the same for children as adults (e.g., Schizophrenia, Mood Disorders). Table 6.2 lists the DSM-III-R disorders that usually appear during the first 7 years of life. It is recognized that many children who come to the attention of clinicians have problems that do not warrant a diagnosis of a mental disorder. With the DSM-III-R system these can be categorized as Parent-Child Problems, Childhood or Adolescent Antisocial Behaviors, or Other Specified Family Circumstances.

The DSM-III-R classification system is relatively new and thus has not been thoroughly critiqued for its usefulness. This version as well as earlier versions of the system, however, have been criticized for using behavioral criteria that do not correspond well to empirically derived clusters of behavioral symptoms (Achenbach, 1980; Rutter, 1988). It also could be argued that some of the criteria used for a DSM-III-R diagnosis (e.g., violation of minor rules, often loses temper) are common among many children, and it is questionable whether all of these children truly evidence a psychiatric disorder. Clearly further empirical work is needed to develop a reliable and valid system of classification for childhood disorders. The reader is referred to an edited volume by Rutter, Tuma, and Lann (1988) for a review and critique of classification systems as they relate to childhood disorders.

In spite of the potential problems in using a classification system like DSM-III-R, it is important for the clinician to be aware of the system and the criteria used to diagnose the more extreme disorders of early childhood. It is equally important to remember that as Chess and Thomas (1978) state, "no single aspect of the child or environment—whether it be intellectual level, temperament, parental characteristics, relationships to sibs and peers, etc.—no matter how important in general, is necessarily a significant etiological factor in every instance of problem behavior development" (p. 229). In other words, one must be cautious about giving a child a diagnosis that may imply a prediction about future adjustment, as it is only the rare case in which this can be done. The young child's behavior is constantly evolving and changing through each interaction with the environment, and this dynamic interaction precludes most such predictions.

PREVALENCE OF BEHAVIOR PROBLEMS

Prevalence studies on problems during the early years of childhood are sparse. Chamberlin (1974) surveyed a group of 200 middle class mothers of preschool children. Of these, 60% to 70% reported concerns about one or more behaviors, including stubbornness, toilet training, "getting into things," bedtime and sleep, sibling-peer problems, whining, nagging, temper tantrums, activity level, inhibited behavior, dressing, speech, and annoying habits. Twenty percent of the 4-year-olds were considered to have a significant behavioral or emotional problem. Richmond, Stevenson, and Graham (1975) interviewed mothers of 88 randomly selected 3-year-old children in London and estimated 7% to have moderate to severe problems, and 15% to have mild problems. In this study there were no sex differences, although a similar study found significantly more boys had problems than girls (Behar & Stringfield, 1974). Richmond et al. (1975) found that language delay in 3-year-old children was associated with behavior problems, as did Jenkins, Bax, and Hart (1980). The latter study also indicated that the children with language delays were likely to have difficulty learning to read and write.

Jenkins et al. (1980) studied 412 preschoolers and found that the percentage of parents worried about their children was highest at 3 years of age (23%). The problems these children had included difficulty in management, the child demanding too much attention, and the occurrence of temper tantrums. Although food fads and poor appetite also were more common at age 3, the parents did not view them as significant problems.

In a follow-up of children from the New York Longitudinal Study (NYLS), Thomas and Chess (1977) found that for 34 of 47 children with behavior disorders, onset occurred before the age of 6. Only one new case developed between the ages of 9 and 12 years. In the NYLS the behavior problems in the younger children were sleep disturbances, temper tantrums, and maladaption to the rules of social living. By school age the problems centered on peer relationships and learning.

Another study (Schroeder, Gordon, Kanoy, & Routh, 1983) conducted over a 9-year period looked at the 2,008 behavioral and emotional problems for which parents sought help from psychologists in a pediatric primary care setting. Table 6.3 gives the percentage of concerns by category for those parents who used the psychological services compared with a random sample of 523 parents with children ages 1 month to 10 years of age who did not use the psychological services. From the table it is clear that parents had similar concerns, whether or not they consulted with the psy-

TABLE 6.3

PERCENT OF PARENTAL CONCERNS WITHIN A RANDOM SAMPLE AND USERS OF PSYCHOLOGY SERVICES

Parental Concerns	Random Sample (n = 523)	Service Users (n = 2,008)
Negative behaviors	12%	15%
Toileting	2	10
Personality or emotional problems	6	10
School problems	2	9
Sleep problems	4	8
Developmental delays	4	7
Sibling/peer problems	6	7
Divorce/separation	1	7
Family problems	6	4
Infant management	1	3
Specific bad habits	6	3
Specific fears	7	2
Sex-related issues	3	2
School problems	4	2
Physical complaints	4	2
Parents' negative feelings for child	4	2
Death	6	1
Eating problems	6	1
Moving	3	1
Adoption/foster care	5	1
Guidance of gifted child	8	1
Miscellaneous	3	1

Note. Adapted from Schroeder, Gordon, Kanoy, & Routh, 1983.

chology staff. It could be that while a behavior is bothersome for many parents, it often is not seen as severe enough to talk about with a professional. Negative behaviors were the most troublesome for both groups of parents, supporting what others have found (Chamberlin, 1974). Guidance of a talented child, specific fears, bad habits, sibling/peer problems and family concerns/problems, food/eating problems, and concerns about death all caused considerable concern for the random sample, particularly when one considers that parents' use of the psychological service for these areas is relatively low. Toileting, school problems, and divorce-related problems were less often reported as concerns in the random sample than among the service users. Additionally, different problems seemed to peak at different ages, with developmental problems of eating, sleeping, toileting, and developmental delays reported as concerns more often in the preschool years, and problems around socialization reported in the school years. Negative behavior did not appear to center around the "terrible twos" but rather was a concern of parents of children at all age levels. The greatest number of problems occurred in the 2- to 4-year-old group, with years 5 and 6 being relatively calm, and another peak of problems occurring between the ages of 7 to 10 years.

In summary, it is important to note that estimates of prevalence of children's behavioral and emotional problems depend on the classification system used to define "behavioral and emotional" problems. In general one can conclude from the studies reviewed and others (Cullen & Boundy, 1966; Earls, 1980; Knorring, Andersson, & Magnusson, 1987) that at any point in time up to 50% of children will evidence at least one specific problem behavior such as fears or bedwetting, that 5–15% will evidence a repertoire of specific behavior problems, and that less than 1% will evidence a severe psychological disorder. Rolf and Harig (1975) surveyed risk studies and follow-up studies and concluded that the most vulnerable children at any age are (a) those with deviant parents (e.g., schizophrenics); (b) those with unsocialized, aggressive behavior; (c) those with severe social, cultural, economic, and nutritional deprivation in their environment; and (d) those with physical and intellectual handicaps.

Framework for the Assessment Process

It is commonly accepted that the foundations for many complex behaviors are laid within the first 7 years of life. During this time the emergence of language, peer relationships, gender identity, self-esteem, play skills, motor abilities, and cognitive skills sets the stage for increased and often intense interactions between the child and his or her environment. As the extent of the child's interaction with the environment increases, so do problems and parental concerns. The clinician will come in contact, therefore, with rather minor, transitory, and circumscribed problems as well as emotional and behavioral problems that may handicap the child's developmental progress significantly. A major task in the assessment process is to determine (a) which problems are transient and need no intervention or only minor environmental changes, (b) which are likely to persist and need a more thorough evaluation and careful monitoring, and (c) which problems require referral for further evaluation or treatment.

The challenges in assessing the behavior of young children are numerous because of only a few clearcut disorders of childhood (e.g., autism) that are qualitatively different from normal behavior. For most behaviors, particularly in the young child, one must judge whether the behavior is more or less than one would expect in a particular environment and is, therefore, abnormal or deviant. Graham (1980) cogently states that to make the judgment that a behavior is abnormal, one has to know (a) a great deal about normal child development as well as the social and cultural setting in which the behavior is occurring, and (b) that the behavior negatively impacts on the child, family, or wider society.

The professional also must remember that children are developing constantly and that behavior at one age might be perceived as normal while at another it would seem abnormal. As previously noted, a surprising number of children are reported to have a high rate of what appears on the surface to be behavior problems. Lapouse and Monk's (1959) epidemiological study of 482 children aged 6 to 12 years is a good example of this. Mothers reported that 43% of the children had seven or more fears, 80% lost their tempers at least once a month, and that 28% had nightmares. Are these behaviors normal or abnormal? In order to determine this, it is necessary to determine the frequency and intensity of the behavior and how it affects the child and his or her environment.

Another important issue to consider when assessing young children is that certain behaviors are more predictive of future adjustment or maladjustment than others (Schroeder, Gordon, Kanoy, & Routh, 1983). Also, this prediction changes developmentally. What is predictive at one age is not necessarily so at another. Intelligence in early childhood, for example, is not predictive of intelligence later in childhood, but later childhood intelligence is predictive of adult intelligence. Also, many behaviors such as sleep disturbances, timidity, overdependence, and anxiety are considered significant in the preschool years but not predictive of later emotional disturbance or social adjustment (Kohlberg, LaCrosse, & Ricks, 1972). On the other hand, antisocial behaviors such as lying and the quality of peer relations are important predictors for later social behaviors (Furman, 1980). Temperament, or the behavioral style of a child's interaction with the environment, also is important to consider in the prediction of future problems (Schroeder, Gordon, Kanoy, & Routh, 1983; Thomas & Chess, 1977). As Furman (1980) points out, this does not mean that we should not treat behaviors that are interfering with a child's current adjustment but do not happen to be predictive of future problems. Priority, however, should be given to determining the cause of and effective treatment for behavior known to have predictive validity.

Clearly one must take many factors into account when identifying the emotional and behavioral problems of children. Some method of systematically collecting and organizing information during the assessment process is critical. Schroeder and her colleagues (Gordon & Schroeder, 1990; Schroeder, 1979; Schroeder, Mesibov, Eastman, & Goolsby, 1981) describe a behaviorally oriented system for the assessment of children's behavioral problems that is based on Rutter's (1975) work (see Figure 6.1). This system focuses on the specifics of the behavior of concern, as well as taking into account other aspects of the child, family, and environment that influence the behavior. It provides a framework for planning an assessment, choosing instruments or techniques for gathering information, and summarizing the assessment data. This framework can be used with any person concerned about a child, including parents, teachers, or caregivers. It should be obvious, however, that assessing problems of young children always necessitates the involvement of the parents in the assessment process.

FIGURE 6.1. A framework for assessing child behavioral problems. (*Note.* Adapted from Schroeder, Gordon, Kanoy, & Routh, 1983.)

I. THE INITIAL CONTACT
   Identify the problem. Send out questionnaires or checklists.

II. CLARIFICATION OF THE REFERRAL QUESTION
   After the parent has told you the problem, be certain that you both are thinking about the same problem. Do this by reflecting what the parent said: "It sounds like you are concerned about your child getting up in the night, as well as the different ways you and your husband are handling the situation."

III. THE SOCIAL CONTEXT
   A child is referred because someone is concerned, which doesn't mean the child needs treatment or that his or her behavior is the problem. Ask, "Who is concerned about the child?" "Why is this person concerned?" "Why is this person concerned now versus some other time?" Listen to the parents' affect in describing the problems; are they overwhelmed, depressed, nonchalant?

IV. GENERAL AREAS TO ASSESS
   A. Development
   B. Environment
   C. Consequences of the behavior
   D. Physical status

V. SPECIFIC AREAS TO ASSESS
   A. Persistence of the behavior
   B. Changes in the behavior
   C. Severity of behavior
   D. Frequency of behavior
   E. Situation specificity
   F. Type of problem

VI. HOW BEHAVIOR AFFECTS CHILD AND OTHERS
   A. Who is suffering?
   B. Does it interfere with the developmental process?

VII. INTERVENTION OPTIONS
   A. Development
      1. Teach new responses to the child, parent, or school.
      2. Change the behavior by increasing or decreasing it.
   B. Environment
      1. Change the cues that set off or prevent the behavior from occurring.
      2. Change the emotional atmosphere.
      3. Change parental expectations, attitudes, or beliefs.
   C. Consequences of the behavior
      1. Change the parent's responses to the behavior.
      2. Change others' responses to the behavior.
      3. Change the payoff for the child.
   D. Physical
      1. Intervene in the cause of the problem.
      2. Treat the effect of the problem.

Steps in the Assessment Process

The Initial Contact

The initial contact most often is a telephone conversation during which the behavior(s) of concern are identified. This contact usually is followed by gathering general information about the child and family through questionnaires and rating scales. (Specific instruments will be discussed in the next section.) These instruments provide information that sets the stage for an interview with the family. The clinician then proceeds by developing and testing various hypotheses about the nature of the problem and how he or she might best intervene.

Clarifying the Referral Question

Although clarifying the referral question may seem an obvious step, its importance cannot be overemphasized. The clinician and the referral source, whether a teacher, parent, or someone else, must agree on the issues to be addressed by the assessment before assessment procedures can be selected. It is often the case that parents or teachers have questions that are not well articulated or of which they are not even aware. Once the issues are clarified, the clinician must then decide which questions he or she can adequately or appropriately address, and these must be agreed upon by the parents and/or teacher. The information gathered in the assessment process will be useful only to the extent that there is agreement on what is being asked.

Determining the Social Context of the Problem

As Furman (1980) states, child behaviors must be viewed in the wider context of societal attitudes and values, which vary by culture and with time. Thomas, Chess, Sillen, and Mendez (1974) found, for example, that middle class children were more likely to be referred for problems during the preschool years, while children from working class Puerto Rican families were referred most heavily during the early school years. Cultural values also can determine the focus of intervention. In some cultures, for example, aggression may be sanctioned for survival purposes. The goal for a child from this culture would be to learn to discriminate inappropriate and appropriate settings for aggression rather than to decrease the level of aggression.

On a more narrow scale, the accepted or common behavior in one social setting might be considered deviant or atypical in another. A case example given by Routh and Schroeder (1981) illustrates this point. The mother of a 3-year-old frantically asked for help in stopping her child's occasional masturbation while watching TV in the afternoons. When asked why she was concerned now versus some other time she blurted out, "My mother-in-law is coming to visit next week!" This mother did not view her child's behavior as deviant, but she viewed its occurrence in an upcoming social context (grandmother's visit) as inappropriate.

General Areas to Assess

In assessing children's behavioral problems, it is important to keep in mind the general areas where things can go wrong, which are (a) the child's developmental status, (b) the child's environment, (c) the consequences of the child's behavior, and (d) the child's physical status.

Developmental status. Knowledge of the child's developmental status allows the clinician to evaluate the behavior relative to that of other children of the same age or developmental level. What might be considered a problem at one stage in development might be quite normal at another. The job of the clinician is to judge whether the behavior of concern is more or less than one would expect of any child at that age and in that environment. A 4-year-old who wets the bed, for example, would not be considered to have a problem, but a 10-year-old would. Nightmares and fear of the dark are quite typical at age 4 but not in older children (Ollendick & Hersen, 1984). Also, the frequency of almost all problem behaviors changes developmentally (Hartup, 1970; Mussen & Eisenberg-Berg, 1977). Thus, some behaviors can change in the appropriate or desired direction without any intervention. For example, physical aggression reaches a peak during the preschool years and then declines (Feshbach, 1970). Thus, the time when a behavior occurs in a child's life is as important as the behavior itself.

The preschool years also present a critical time for the identification of children with developmental problems. Children with disorders such as mental retardation, autism, language disorders, and childhood schizophrenia often are referred for assessment because they fail to achieve the parents' expectations for development or they exhibit unusual or problem behaviors. Families of children with identified developmental handicaps often find the preschool years to be a time of great stress (Schroeder, Gordon, & Hawk, 1983). Because the developmentally disabled child typically has a difficult time accomplishing normal developmental tasks such as toileting training, each developmental milestone requires a new adjustment for parents. It is obvious that knowledge of normal development would be critical in the assessment of these children.

Environment. The child's environment provides the setting conditions for the behavior in question and may be the appropriate target for intervention rather than the behavior itself. Events such as parental divorce, a death in the family, or an impending move often can lead to the appearance of behavior problems in young children. Additionally, it is important to remember that children rarely refer themselves for assessment or treatment (Schroeder, Gordon, Kanoy, & Routh, 1983). Rather, they are referred because someone, usually an adult, is concerned about their behavior (Ross, 1981).

The perspective of the referring person must be taken into account. In the Isle of Wight study (Rutter, Tizard, & Whitmore 1980), for example, teachers and parents reported the same frequency of problems, but they reported them for entirely different children! Other work (Hingst, 1981) has demonstrated that parents and children often perceive problems differently. The referring person may lack information about children's development, may have emotional problems, or may be experiencing stress, all of which can distort one's perception of a child's behavior. Forehand, King, Peed, and Yoder (1975), for example, found that low parental tolerance, high expectations for child behavior, marital stress, and family problems influenced parents' perception of their child's behavior. Wahler's (1980) work shows that a mother's perception of her child's behavior is highly correlated with the type of environmental interaction (positive or coercive) she has just experienced.

In assessing this area it is important to gather information about various members of the family and their relationships with the child. Sensitivity to the affect expressed by parents is also important. Two mothers, for example, both described their 3-year-old daughters as anxious and fearful. One parent was calm, in control of herself, and using good judgment in attempting to deal with the problem. The other, however, was extremely upset, tearful, and unable to view the problem objectively. Each parent presented a different focus for the assessment/intervention process.

Consequences. Assessing the consequences of the behavior includes finding out how the parents currently are managing it, the techniques tried previously, and the "payoff" for the child. Lack of careful assessment of the situation usually leads to parents responding to suggestions by saying "Yes, but we've tried that and it didn't work." Assessing consequences of the behavior also can involve looking at its consequences for parents and others in the child's environment. Some behaviors might be totally acceptable to the family but interfere with the child's functioning in the environment. For example, a 5-year-old who is not toilet trained because his parents did not want to "pressure" him would be likely to suffer negative consequences when he started school.

Physical status. The clinician must be aware of the child's current physical status as well as his or her medical history. Assessment of problems in this area also requires that the clinician have some knowledge of the emotional/behavioral effects of physical conditions. An example of this arose with a 6-year-old girl referred by her parents because she was moody, impulsive, and having difficulty in school. In the course of the assessment the examiner found that a member of the mother's family recently had been diagnosed as having Fragile X chromosomal disorder. A review of the literature on this disorder revealed that females are the carriers of the defective gene and that there is a phenotype for these females. The child's behavioral profile showed many of the characteristics of the female Fragile X carrier, and the family was referred for a genetic evaluation (Gordon & Schroeder, 1990).

Specific Areas to Assess

In addition to the general assessment areas just described, specific areas to consider include (a) the persistence of the behavior (how long has it been going on?); (b) changes in the behavior (is it getting worse?); (c) severity (is the behavior very intense or dangerous, or "low level" but annoying?); (d) frequency (has the behavior occurred only once, twice, or many times?); (e) situation specificity (does the behavior occur only at home, or in a variety of settings?); and (f) the type of problem (is the problem a discrete behavior or a set of diffuse symptoms?). Information about these areas can be gathered by direct questioning and by asking questions about daily routines, including bedtime, sleeping, morning behavior, dressing and bathing, mealtime behavior, play behavior, and so forth. The parents' expectations for the child also will become clear in the course of gathering this information.

The above format should not be seen as a rigid system. Rather, it is offered as a logical and systematic way to generate and test hypotheses and plan intervention for children's problems. The information can be gathered from a variety of sources using many different methods. A quick review of the "specific areas to assess" list will alert the clinician to any information missed on a particular problem. Table 6.4 illustrates the use of this framework in assessing the referral of a 6-year-old girl who was disrupting her class in school.

114 BEHAVIOR PROBLEMS

TABLE 6.4

THE ASSESSMENT PROCESS IN A BRIEF CASE EXAMPLE

Areas to Assess	*Assessment*
I. THE INITIAL CONTACT	A first-grade teacher makes a referral for a 6-year-old girl who, once or twice a week, becomes distraught, walks in circles, and cries inconsolably.
II. CLARIFICATION OF THE REFERRAL QUESTION	"It sounds like Jane is disrupting the class and you're not able to give her or the other children the attention they need. You're also wondering why she seems so genuinely distraught one or two times a week."
III. THE SOCIAL CONTEXT	A review of the child's record indicates that her parents are separated and she is living with her father. The father is contacted and told of the teacher's concern.
A. Listen to affect	"I had so hoped this wouldn't happen again in Jane's new school. I don't know what I can do to help her."
B. Who is concerned?	The teacher is concerned for both Jane and the other children. The father says, " I have been worried about Jane for the last 2 years, but generally her teachers and I have been able to calm her down."
C. Why now?	Jane just started in a new school.
IV. GENERAL AREAS TO ASSESS	
A. Development	"Jane is a very bright child, rarely gives any problem at home. She has friends in the neighborhood and generally likes going to school. Recently she started wetting herself during the day and having nightmares at night."
B. Environment	"Her mother and I have been divorced for 3 years and went through a terrible custody battle. Jane visits her mother every Wednesday and every other weekend. She hates to go, reports being left alone, and is afraid of some of her mother's friends."
C. Consequences	"I tell Jane that the court says she has to visit her mother, that she should love her mother and have a good time. I also have told her not to act up in school because it gets me in trouble."
D. Physical	"While Jane is generally healthy, in the last 3 months she has been to the doctor because of her wetting and nightmares. She also has complained of stomachaches. I also should tell you that social services

Continued

TABLE 6.4 *(continued)*

THE ASSESSMENT PROCESS IN A BRIEF CASE EXAMPLE

Areas to Assess	*Assessment*
D. Physical *(cont.)*	investigated my ex-wife's charges against me for sexual abuse, which were not true. Recently Jane's doctor called social services because Jane had a number of bruises when she came home from a visit with her mother."
V. SPECIFIC AREAS TO ASSESS	
A. Persistence	"Jane has been upset since the divorce 3 years ago."
B. Changes in behavior	"She has never liked to visit her mother, but in the last 3 months it has gotten to the point where I have to force her to go."
C. Severity of behavior	"The night before she goes to visit her mother she has become very upset, doesn't listen to me, and has a very hard time getting to sleep. Sometimes she has nightmares."
D. Frequency of behavior	"These problems only seem to occur when she has to visit her mother."
E. Situation specificity	"Jane used to be upset only at home, but now it's happening at school, too. I also think she looks sad a lot of the time."
F. Type of problem	This child's behavior is indicative of significant emotional distress. It is likely to have serious consequences for her functioning and development unless immediate intervention occurs.
VI. EFFECTS OF PROBLEM	
A. Who is suffering?	The child, the teacher, and other children in school.
B. Interference with development	The behavior is already interfering with Jane's adjustment at school. Most important, her emotional needs are not being met. Further, she has few appropriate alternatives available to express her feelings.
VII. WHERE TO INTERVENE?	The severity of this child's behavior and the complexity of the situation warrant an immediate referral for further evaluation and treatment. In the meantime, the father and teacher could work together to provide more emotional support within the school environment on the days Jane visits her mother. The father also could tell her that it's OK to be upset if she's feeling bad on those days. Jane's father and teacher could give her specific ways to express her feelings, such as drawing, working with clay, or simply talking to them.

116 BEHAVIOR PROBLEMS

METHODS FOR GATHERING INFORMATION

One can see clearly from the preceding framework that assessment of behavior problems in the preschool years necessitates a multimethod approach. It also is essential for clinicians to choose methods for assessment that are empirically based and developmentally sensitive (Ollendick & Hersen, 1984). As Eyberg (1985) so aptly points out, "objective measurement of specific behaviors helps us make independent judgments of the child's psychopathology and enhances our communication with other professionals" (p. 135). The choice of methods for gathering information is vast, and this section will cover some of the instruments and techniques most commonly used with preschoolers (summarized in Table 6.5). The reader also is referred to Gabel (1981), Rutter et al. (1988), Weaver (1984), and other chapters in this volume for more comprehensive reviews of available instruments.

Developmental Screening Instruments

Screening for physical and developmental problems is important in order to gain a developmental perspective on behavioral problems. This process also potentially will identify a group of children who are likely to have emotional or behavioral problems, as children with physical and developmental handicaps are at higher risk for these problems (Schroeder, Gordon, & Hawk, 1983). The following are commonly used instruments for measuring developmental status.

The Denver II (Frankenburg & Dodds, 1990) measures the personal, social, fine and gross motor, language, and adaptive abilities of children ages birth to 6 years. It provides a means of identifying potential problem areas for further evaluation. This instrument is individually administered and is most commonly used by pediatricians and pediatric nurses as a routine screening device. The scores yield a profile of the child's development relative to expectations for children the same age.

The Minnesota Child Development Inventory (Ireton & Thwing, 1972) was developed for pediatricians and other health care professionals as a means of evaluating the developmental, self-help, and personal-social status of preschool children. It is completed by the parents of children ages 1 to 6 years and consists of 320 yes/no questions concerning the child's behavior. The scores are plotted on a profile, giving the child's standing in relationship to same-age peers in the areas of general development, gross and fine motor, expressive language, comprehension-conceptual, situation comprehension, self-help, and personal-social.

The Vineland Adaptive Behavior Scales (Sparrow, Balla, & Cicchetti, 1984) measure the personal and social sufficiency of individuals from birth to adulthood. This instrument commonly is used with mentally retarded and handicapped individuals, but it also provides useful information about the development of young children. It is administered through a semistructured interview with parents and covers communication, daily living skills, socialization, and motor skills. Scores yield a profile of development relative to children the same age.

Behavioral Rating Scales and Checklists

Although most of the instruments designed to screen for developmental problems include some measure of personal-social development, they are generally of

TABLE 6.5

Instruments for the Assessment of Child Development and Behavior Problems

Instrument	Ages	Purpose
Child Behavior Checklist	2 to 16 years	To assess behavior competencies and problems. Covers social history, interests, school performance, and behavior problems.
Conners Parent Rating Scale–Revised	3 to 17 years	To assess hyperactivity in children. Includes behaviors reflecting conduct problems, learning problems, psychosomatic problems, impulsivity, and anxiety.
Conners Teacher Rating Scale–Revised	3 to 17 years	To assess hyperactivity in children in classrooms. Includes factors reflecting conduct problems, hyperactivity, and inattention-passivity.
Denver II	Birth to 6 years	To screen for physical and developmental problems. Measures personal, social, fine and gross motor, language, and adaptive abilities.
Eyberg Child Behavior Inventory	2 to 17 years	To screen for conduct problem behaviors. Gives an intensity and problem score.
Minnesota Child Development Inventory	1 to 6 years	To evaluate general development, gross and fine motor, expressive language, comprehension-conceptual, situation comprehension, self-help, and personal-social skills.
Parenting Stress Index	Birth to 10 years	To measure stress in the parent-child relationship. Covers stress due to characteristics of the child and parent, as well as general life stress.
Personality Inventory for Children	3 to 16 years	To assess aspects of personality. Covers adjustment, development, family relations, anxiety, social skills, achievement, somatic concerns, delinquency, psychosis, intellect, depression, withdrawal, and hyperactivity.
Preschool Behavior Questionnaire	3 to 6 years	To measure behavior problems in a preschool setting. Covers hostile-aggressive, anxious-fearful, and hyperactive-distractible behaviors.
Sutter-Eyberg Student Behavior Inventory	3 to 5 years	To measure conduct problem behaviors in the preschool setting. Gives a problem and intensity score.
Vineland Adaptive Behavior Scales	Birth to 18 years	To measure personal and social sufficiency. Covers communication, daily living skills, socialization, and motor skills.

limited value in the assessment of this area. The clinician will want to include some direct measures of the child's behavior and the family's functioning. In order to be most useful in clinical practice, rating scales and checklists must provide adequate normative data and cutoff points so that decisions about individual children can be made (Eyberg, 1985). Although a selection of these measures is described here, the reader is referred to Barkley (1988) for a more thorough review of child behavior rating scales.

The Child Behavior Checklist (CBCL; Achenbach & Edelbrock, 1983) consists of two forms, one for ages 2 to 3 and one for ages 4 to 16. Parents rate a number of child behaviors (both positive and negative) on a 3-point scale as "not true," "somewhat or sometimes true," or "very true or often true" for their child. The scores provide a profile of the child's behavior relative to other children the same age and sex. Additionally, summary scores representing "internalizing" or "externalizing" problems are calculated. The CBCL has been carefully constructed and has generated considerable research indicating its validity for screening for problems in preschoolers and measuring the effects of treatment (Achenbach & Edelbrock, 1983).

The Conners Parent Rating Scale-Revised (Goyette, Conners, & Ulrich, 1978) requires parents of children ages 3 through 17 to rate 48 behaviors on a 4-point scale. Although designed for assessing hyperactivity in children, it provides a profile of child behavior in five categories: conduct problems, learning problems, psychosomatic problems, impulsivity-hyperactivity, and anxiety. There also is a cluster of items that make up a Hyperactivity Index. Scores on this measure have been shown to discriminate hyperactive from normal children (Conners, 1970) and to be sensitive to the effects of drug treatment (Barkley, 1981).

The Conners Teacher Rating Scale-Revised (Goyette et al., 1978), also designed for children ages 3 to 17, consists of 28 items on three scales (conduct problem, hyperactivity, and inattentive-passive) that are rated by teachers. This scale has demonstrated reliability and validity for discriminating conduct problems and hyperactivity, and for monitoring treatment effects, but it is not useful for other types of child problems.

The Eyberg Child Behavior Inventory (ECBI; Robinson, Eyberg, & Ross, 1980) consists of 36 common behaviors that are problematic for parents. Parents rate each behavior on a 7-point frequency scale and also indicate whether each behavior is a problem for them. The ECBI is very simple, quick to complete, and appropriate for use with any parents, including those with poor reading skills. Research has provided considerable evidence of its reliability and validity in screening for behavior problems (e.g., Eyberg & Ross, 1978) and in evaluating the effects of treatment (e.g., Eyberg & Robinson, 1982).

The Parenting Stress Index (PSI; Abidin, 1983) provides a measure of the magnitude of stress in the parent-child interaction. Parents rate 101 items on a 5-point scale, and scores are summed to form 13 subscale scores in two broad domains—stress that results from characteristics of the parent, and stress that results from characteristics of the child. Items cover areas such as the marital relationship, parental depression, parental attachment to the child, various aspects of the child's temperament, and the degree to which the child is reinforcing to the parent. The PSI has generated considerable research, and its validity in discriminating clinic from nonclinic children has been demonstrated (Martin, 1988; Mash, 1983). This measure is particularly helpful in screening for problems in the child's family that may be related to the behavior problems and that can be evaluated further as the assessment progresses.

The Personality Inventory for Children (Wirt, Lachar, Klinedinst, & Seat, 1977) is the childhood equivalent of the Minnesota Multiphasic Personality Inventory (MMPI). It consists of 600 true/false items that are completed by parents. Separate norms and profiles are available for boys and girls ages 3–5 and 6–16 for 14 clinical subscales and 2 validity subscales. Although this is an extremely well-constructed and standardized measure, its length makes it less useful than some other shorter instruments.

The Preschool Behavior Questionnaire (Behar & Stringfield, 1974) is a 30-item checklist designed for use by preschool teachers. Each item is rated on a 3-point scale, and scores are obtained for three subscales: Hostile-Aggressive, Anxious-Fearful, and Hyperactive-Distractible. This questionnaire was standardized on a large population of children ages 3 to 6, and it has been shown to discriminate clinic from nonclinic subjects.

The Sutter-Eyberg Student Behavior Inventory (SESBI; Funderburk & Eyberg, 1987) was designed for use with the school-aged child but recently has been standardized for use with preschoolers (ages 3 to 5). It follows the format of the Eyberg Child Behavior Inventory (ECBI) in requiring teachers to rate 36 child behaviors on two dimensions—frequency of occurrence and identification as a problem. Some items are similar to those on the ECBI, others reflect behaviors typically reported as problems by teachers. The SESBI has been shown to discriminate between normal children and those referred for behavior problems.

In addition to these standardized instruments, parent records can be useful in providing information about the actual day-to-day functioning of the parent and child. The format of a parent daily log can be quite variable, depending on the behaviors of interest. The present authors use a log sheet on which parents record appropriate and inappropriate behavior on a daily basis and give their child a rating from 0 to 10, with 10 being best (see Figure 6.2). On the reverse side, parents record the antecedents and consequences of behaviors identified as specific problems. This record helps both parents and clinician determine what the child is actually doing (in contrast to what the parents *think* he or she is doing). It also helps the parents recognize when progress occurs.

Interviews

Parent interviews set the stage for understanding the parents' perception of the problem and how it has affected both the child and themselves within the family. In this interview the clinician can specify in concrete, objective terms what each of the parents sees as the problem and can glean information about who is concerned and why they are concerned now versus some other time. It also provides an opportunity to follow up on information gathered from the checklists and questionnaires completed before the parents come into the clinic. At this time the clinician begins to generate hypotheses about the nature of the problem behavior, follows up on these hypotheses by getting further information from the parents, and determines what

FIGURE 6.2. Sample parent daily log.

Record a brief summary of both appropriate and inappropriate behavior each day. Give each day's overall behavior a rating from 0 to 10, with 0 being "dreadful" and 10 being "fantastic"!

Date	Appropriate Behavior	Inappropriate Behavior	Rating
9/19/88	Helped feed the dog.	Hit the baby.	
	Played by himself.	Had a tantrum.	
		Threw food at lunch.	5
9/20/88	Cleared the table.	Dropped plates.	
	Went to bed without fussing.		8

Specific Events Causing Concern

Date: 9/19/88   *Time:* 5:30 p.m.

What happened? I was in the kitchen fixing dinner. He wanted something to eat. I said "No." He screamed, and as he ran out of the kitchen, he hit the baby sitting in the high chair.

What did you do? I yelled at him! I ran after him but he hid in his room.

Child's reaction: He cried and said nasty things about me. He also said no one loved him. I felt bad.

other areas need to be assessed as well as what methods to use. The framework presented in the previous section can serve to guide the interview and help the clinician decide what questions need to be asked. A number of structured parent interviews also are available, and the reader is referred to Holland (1970), Jacob and Tennenbaum (1988), and O'Leary and Johnson (1979).

While much has been written recently about interviews with children (Boggs & Eyberg, 1988; Edelbrock & Costello, 1988; Eyberg, 1985; Gross, 1984), the strategies suggested are most useful with older children. Interviewing and actually obtaining useful information from preschool children is challenging, to say the least! As Eyberg (1985) points out, information preschoolers provide verbally often lacks reliability and validity. Observation and assessment of the child at play, however, can be a valuable source of information about how the preschooler perceives his or her world. Play is an extremely important part of development in the preschool years (Schroeder, Gordon, & Hawk, 1983). In summarizing a statement by Susanna Miller, Rutter (1975) noted the many purposes that play can accomplish for the young child:

> [in pretend play] the child may be exploring his feelings, lessening his fears, increasing his excitement, trying to understand a puzzling event by graphic representations, seeking confirmation of a hazy memory or altering an event to make it pleasant to himself in fantasy. (p. 75)

Thus observation of the preschool child's play can give information about his or her intellectual development, language development, feelings, thoughts, social relationships, and current concerns and anxieties (Schroeder, Gordon, & Hawk, 1983). It is useful to provide the child with opportunities to interact with a variety of age-appropriate toys and to vary the degree of structure during the play observation.

Direct Observation of Behavior

Direct observation is the hallmark of a behavioral approach to assessment (Eyberg, 1985) and can be done in a variety of settings, utilizing a variety of methods. Barkley (1981), Barton and Ascione (1984), as well as Reid, Baldwin, Patterson, and Dishion (1988), describe in detail various methods for conducting behavioral observations. In the assessment of child behavior problems, observation of the parent-child interaction is extremely important. Various methods for structuring and recording these observation sessions have been proposed (see for example, Eyberg & Robinson, 1983; Mash, Terdal, & Anderson, 1973; Patterson, Ray, Shaw, & Cobb, 1969), all of which vary in their complexity. There is general agreement, however, that the important dimensions of the interaction are (a) the extent to which the parent gives the child positive versus negative feedback, and whether that feedback is contingent on the child's behavior; (b) the number of demands placed on the child; (c) the number of questions asked; and (d) the child's compliance or noncompliance to parental demands. Most observations typically last 10 to 20 minutes and include both structured and unstructured time.

Observation of the child's behavior at home or in school is also important, as children often exhibit very different behavior in these two environments. Although the same recording methods used in the clinic could be applied in the naturalistic setting, one typically conducts the latter observations for longer periods of time, observing the child engaged in a variety of activities. A good manner in which to begin the observation process is simply to keep a running record of the behavior as it occurs in 1-minute segments of time. In this way the clinician quickly can determine the salient behaviors of the child, his or her peers, or the adults in the situation. This allows one then to record the frequency and duration of those particular behaviors. The reader is referred to chapter 7 in this volume, which describes a structured system for observation in the home, as well as to Jacob and Tennenbaum (1988).

CASE EXAMPLE

(The following case example illustrates the use of the assessment framework and some of the methods of gathering information described in the preceding sections.)

A mother called the psychologist at the suggestion of her friends, saying that her $3\frac{1}{2}$-year-old son was causing a "few" problems and that the problems occurred primarily with her. She asked to come in for an appointment to get some specific suggestions on handling his negative and oppositional behavior.

Prior to the initial interview the parents were asked to complete a questionnaire focusing on demographic information, developmental milestones, caregivers, school and social activities, what the parents saw as the primary problem, what they had previously been told about the behavior, and their perception of the cause of the problem. Each of them also was asked to complete an Eyberg Child Behavior Inventory and a Parenting Stress Index, and the mother additionally was asked to keep a daily log for 1 week prior to the initial interview. She returned the completed forms and checklists before the interview so that they could be scored and reviewed by the clinician. While the father completed the forms and supported the mother in seeking help, he elected not to come to the interview because he saw the situation as primarily the "mother's problem."

The child, Henry, was the older child of an upper middle class family in which the mother was a full-time homemaker. The parents also had a 9-month-old girl. Henry's developmental milestones had occurred within normal limits, with speaking in sentences emerging by 24 months. He was cared for primarily by his mother; babysitters were limited to the occasional evening out and no problems were reported during those times. Likewise, his three mornings a week at a preschool were problem free, although the teachers initially reported that they had to be rather "firm" in their expectations. Henry often was invited to spend time with friends in their homes, and while these went well, difficulties were reported when friends visited him. At these times Henry was described as very active, getting into things that were forbidden and in general creating chaos. Henry's father, who was 15 years older than the mother, thoroughly enjoyed his son, often taking him on full-day outings with only minor problems. He felt that the mother simply was "too nice" and should be firmer with Henry.

The major problems, as described by the mother, were "not listening," "refusing to do as requested," and "talking back." While all of these behaviors occurred primarily with her, they were beginning to occur with others in the family. Henry's mother stated that she viewed much of his behavior as normal for an active, bright boy, but recent comments from her friends and family about his escalating negative behavior pushed her to talk with a professional. She further indicated that she was hoping to get confirmation that everything was really OK with Henry.

On the Eyberg Child Behavior Inventory, the mother gave Henry an Intensity score of 189 and a Frequency score of 5, indicating that she perceived Henry as engaging in a significant amount of inappropriate noncompliant behavior but did not consider the behavior to be significantly problematic for her. The father described Henry within the normal range for both Intensity and Frequency scores. On the Parenting Stress Index, the responses of both mother and father fell within the normal limits, with the exception that the father's score for Child Adaptability and the mother's score for Competence were both above the 90th percentile (high scores on the PSI are problematic). Sample entries on the mother's daily logs read "Henry hit his grandfather on the shin with a baseball bat" and "Henry scraped a knife across the kitchen wall."

Henry appeared in the clinic wearing an Army camouflage outfit, cowboy hat and boots, and two six-shooters, and he was toting a toy machine gun. He greeted the clinician with "I'm going to shoot your eyes out." The clinician responded with a firm, "We don't talk like that in my office," to which Henry quickly responded in a contrite voice, "Oh, I'm sorry." Direct observation of parent-child interaction indicated a mother who gave a high rate of noncontingent positive reinforcement, placed few demands on her child, and tried to get compliance through reasoning. Henry placed many demands on his mother and rarely complied to her requests. There were also many positive interactions between Henry and his mother, and they seemed to enjoy playing together. Henry's play was observed to be age appropriate, his interactions with the clinician after the initial negative statement were positive, and he readily complied with the clinician's requests to clean up the toys and so forth.

In order to determine the extent of the problems and the frequency of their occurrence, the mother was asked to describe a typical day for Henry, from the time he got up in the morning to the time he went to bed. She described Henry as managing many routine events such as eating and bathing with ease, but when any demands were placed on him, he would refuse to comply. The mother spent much of her time rearranging her schedule in order to avoid confronting him. This was becoming increasingly difficult as her 9-month-old baby demanded more attention. Although she was clearly exhausted from the effort of caring for her children, she felt that this was simply part of being a mother.

In determining where things were going wrong for this mother and child, it appeared that physically the child was in good health, that developmentally he was on target, but that his mother's expectations for him and for herself were creating and maintaining much of the inappropriate behavior. Further, her very poor management techniques actually were increasing the problem behavior. The fact that the behavior occurred primarily with the mother and was just beginning to generalize to other adults close to him indicated a rather circumscribed problem. While Henry's mother indicated that she was not suffering from the behavior, it was clear that its continuation could only have a negative effect on their relationship and on the child's ability to function in the wider environment. As the child was beginning to generalize the negative interactions to other adults in his life, this could lead to their avoiding interactions with him and consequently decrease his opportunities to develop appropriate social skills.

The psychologist recommended that the parents attend classes on child development and management and that both of them be involved with Henry in a series of treatment sessions to increase the positive parent-child interactions, to set age-appropriate limits, to increase compliance on Henry's part, and to determine a consistent method of discipline. The father was asked to come in for an interview prior to giving these recommendations so that his view of the problem could be further explored. He agreed to this as well as to the recommendations. He felt that coming to an agreement on management techniques would ultimately decrease the conflict over Henry's behavior.

The framework given for assessing behavior problems in the young child provides clinicians with a hypothesis-testing, multimethod approach for getting "an accurate picture" of the child, his or her family, and the larger societal environment. The dynamic interaction of the child with the environment requires clinicians to have a clear understanding of normal child development, a repertoire of valid and reliable assessment instruments, skills in interviewing parents and children, and the ability to observe the child's behavior objectively in multiple settings. This is a challenging task!

REFERENCES

Abidin, R.R. (1983). *Parenting Stress Index manual.* Charlottesville, VA: Pediatric Psychology Press.
Achenbach, T.M. (1980). DSM-III in light of empirical research on the classification of child psychopathology. *Journal of the American Academy of Child Psychiatry, 19,* 395–412.
Achenbach, T.M., & Edelbrock, C. (1983). *Manual for the Child Behavior Checklist and Revised Child Behavior Profile.* Burlington, VT: University of Vermont, Department of Psychiatry.
American Psychiatric Association. (1987). *Diagnostic and statistical manual of mental disorders* (3rd ed. rev.). Washington, DC: Author.
Barkley, R. (1981). *Hyperactive children: A handbook for diagnosis and treatment.* New York: Guilford.
Barkley, R. (1988). Child behavior rating scales and checklists. In M. Rutter, A.H. Tuma, & I.S. Lann (Eds.), *Assessment and diagnosis in child psychopathology* (pp. 113–155). New York: Guilford.
Barton, E.J., & Ascione, F.R. (1984). Direct observation. In T.H. Ollendick & M. Hersen (Eds.), *Child behavioral assessment: Principles and procedures* (pp. 166–194). New York: Pergamon.
Behar, L., & Stringfield, S. (1974). A behavior rating scale for the preschool child. *Developmental Psychology, 10,* 601–610.
Boggs, S.R., & Eyberg, S.M. (1988). Interviewing techniques and establishing rapport. In A. LaGreca (Ed.), *Childhood assessment: Through the eyes of a child* (pp. 85–108). Newton, MA: Allyn & Bacon.
Chamberlin, R.W. (1974). Management of preschool behavior problems. *Pediatric Clinics of North America, 21,* 33–47.
Chess, S., & Thomas, A. (1978). Temperamental individuality from childhood to adolescence. In S. Chess & A. Thomas (Eds.), *Annual progress in child psychiatry and child development* (pp. 223–232). New York: Brunner/Mazel.
Conners, C.K. (1970). Symptom patterns in hyperactive, neurotic, and normal children. *Child Development, 41,* 667–682.
Cullen, K.J., & Boundy, B.E. (1966). The prevalence of behavior disorders in the children of 1,000 western Australian families. *The Medical Journal of Australia, 2,* 805–808.
Earls, R. (1980). Prevalence of behavior problems in 3-year-old children. *Archives of General Psychiatry, 37,* 1153–1157.
Edelbrock, C., & Costello, A.J. (1988). Structured psychiatric interviews for children. In M. Rutter, A.H. Tuma, & I.S. Lann (Eds.), *Assessment and diagnosis in child psychopathology* (pp. 87–112). New York: Guilford.
Eyberg, S.M. (1985). Behavioral assessment: Advancing methodology in pediatric psychology. *Journal of Pediatric Psychology, 10,* 123–139.
Eyberg, S.M., & Robinson, E.A. (1982). Parent-child interaction training: Effects on family functioning. *Journal of Clinical Child Psychology, 11,* 130–137.
Eyberg, S.M., & Robinson, E.A. (1983). *Dyadic parent-child interaction coding system: A manual.* (Psychological Documents, Vol. 13, #2582)
Eyberg, S.M., & Ross, A.W. (1978). Assessment of child behavior problems: The validation of a new inventory. *Journal of Clinical Child Psychology, 7,* 113–116.
Feshbach, S. (1970). Aggression. In P.H. Mussen (Ed.), *Carmichael's manual of child psychology* (3rd ed., vol. 2, pp. 159–260). New York: Wiley.
Forehand, R., King, H.R., Peed, S., & Yoder, P. (1975). Mother-child interactions: Comparison of a non-compliant clinic group and a non-clinic group. *Behavior Research and Therapy, 13,* 79–84.

Frankenburg, W.K., & Dodds, J.B. (1990). *Denver II*. Denver, CO: Denver Developmental Metrics.
Funderburk, B., & Eyberg, S. (1987). *Standardization of a teacher rating scale of conduct problem behaviors in preschool children*. Unpublished manuscript, University of Florida, Gainesville.
Furman, W. (1980). Promoting social development: Developmental implications for treatment. In B.B. Lahey & A.E. Kazdin (Eds.), *Advances in clinical child psychology* (Vol. 3, pp. 1–40). New York: Plenum.
Gabel, S. (1981). *Behavioral problems in childhood*. New York: Grune & Stratton.
Gordon, B.N., & Schroeder, C.S. (1990). Developmental assessment in clinical practice: From assessment to intervention. In J.H. Johnson & J. Goldman (Eds.), *Developmental assessment in clinical child psychology: A handbook* (pp. 251–267) Elmsford, NY: Pergamon.
Goyette, C.H., Conners, C.K., & Ulrich, R.F. (1978). Normative data on the revised Conners Parent and Teacher Rating Scales. *Journal of Abnormal Child Psychology, 6,* 221–236.
Graham, P. (1980). Epidemiological studies. In H.E. Quay & J.S. Werry (Eds.), *Psychopathological disorders of childhood* (2nd ed., pp. 185–209). New York: Wiley.
Gross, A.M. (1984). Behavioral interviewing. In T.H. Ollendick & M. Hersen (Eds.), *Child behavioral assessment: Principles and procedures* (pp. 61–79). New York: Pergamon.
Hartup, W.W. (1970). Peer interaction and social organization. In P.H. Mussen (Ed.), *Carmichael's manual of child development* (3rd ed., vol. 2, pp. 361–456). New York: Wiley.
Hingst, A.G. (1981). Children and divorce: The child's view. *Journal of Child Psychology and Psychiatry, 10,* 161–164.
Holland, C.J. (1970). An interview guide for behavioral counseling with parents. *Behavior Therapy, 1,* 70–79.
Ireton, H., & Thwing, E. (1972). *Minnesota Child Development Inventory*. Minneapolis, MN: Behavior Science Systems.
Jacob, T., & Tennenbaum, D.L. (1988). Family assessment methods. In M. Rutter, A.H. Tuma, & I.S. Lann (Eds.), *Assessment and diagnosis in child psychopathology* (pp. 196–231). New York: Guilford.
Jenkins, S., Bax, M., & Hart, H. (1980). Behavior problems in preschool children. *Journal of Child Psychology and Psychiatry, 9,* 5–18.
Kazdin, A.E. (1987). *Conduct disorders in childhood and adolescence*. Newbury Park, CA: Sage.
Knorring, A.L., Andersson, O., & Magnusson, D. (1987). Psychiatric care and course of psychiatric disorders from childhood to early adulthood in a representative sample. *Journal of Child Psychology and Psychiatry, 28,* 329–341.
Kohlberg, L., LaCrosse, J., & Ricks, D. (1972). The predictability of adult mental health from childhood behavior. In B.B. Wolman (Ed.), *Manual of child psychopathology* (pp. 1217–1286). New York: McGraw-Hill.
Korpela, J.W. (1973). Social work assistance in private pediatric practice. *Social Casework, 54,* 537–544.
Lapouse, R., & Monk, M.A. (1959). Behavior deviations in a representative sample of children: Variations by sex, age, race, social class, and family size. *American Journal of Orthopsychiatry, 34,* 436–446.
Martin, S.L. (1988). *The effectiveness of a multidisciplinary primary health care model in the prevention of children's mental health problems*. Unpublished doctoral dissertation, University of North Carolina, Chapel Hill.
Mash, E. (1983). Parental perceptions of child behavior problems, parenting self-esteem, and mothers' reported stress in younger and older hyperactive and normal children. *Journal of Consulting and Clinical Psychology, 51,* 88–99.

Mash, E.J., Terdal, L.G., & Anderson, K. (1973). The Response Class Matrix: A procedure for recording parent-child interactions. *Journal of Consulting and Clinical Psychology, 40,* 163–164.

Mussen, P., & Eisenberg-Berg, N. (1977). *Roots of caring, sharing and helping: The development of prosocial behavior in children.* San Francisco: W.H. Freeman.

O'Leary, K.D., & Johnson, S.B. (1979). Psychological assessment. In H.C. Quay & J.S. Werry (Eds.), *Psychopathological disorders of childhood* (2nd ed., pp. 210–246). New York: Wiley.

Ollendick, T.H., & Hersen, M. (1984). An overview of child behavioral assessment. In T.H. Ollendick & M. Hersen (Eds.), *Child behavioral assessment: Principles and procedures* (pp. 3–19). New York: Pergamon.

Patterson, G.R., Ray, R.S., Shaw, D.A., & Cobb, J.A. (1969). *A manual for coding family interactions.* New York: Microfiche Publications.

Reid, J.B., Baldwin, D.V., Patterson, G.R., & Dishion, T.J. (1988). Observation in the assessment of childhood disorders. In M. Rutter, A.H. Tuma, & I.S. Lann (Eds.), *Assessment and diagnosis in child psychopathology* (pp. 156–195). New York: Guilford.

Richmond, N., Stevenson, J.E., & Graham, P.J. (1975). Prevalence of behaviour problems in 3-year-old children: An epidemiological study in a London borough. *Journal of Child Psychology and Psychiatry, 16,* 277–287.

Robinson, E.A., Eyberg, S.M., & Ross, A.W. (1980). The standardization of an inventory of child conduct problem behaviors. *Journal of Clinical Child Psychology, 9,* 22–28.

Rolf, J.E., & Harig, P.T. (1975). Etiological research in schizophrenia and the rationale for primary intervention. In S. Chess & A. Thomas (Eds.), *Annual progress in child psychiatry and child development* (pp. 402–422). New York: Brunner/Mazel.

Ross, A.W. (1981). *Child behavior therapy.* New York: Wiley.

Routh, D.K., & Schroeder, C.S. (1981). Masturbation and other sexual behaviors. In S. Gabel (Ed.), *Behavioral problems in childhood* (pp. 387–392). New York: Grune & Stratton.

Rutter, M. (1975). *Helping troubled children.* New York: Plenum.

Rutter, M. (1988). DSM-III-R: A postscript. In M. Rutter, A.H. Tuma, & I.S. Lann (Eds.), *Assessment and diagnosis in child psychopathology* (pp. 453–464). New York: Guilford.

Rutter, M., Tizard, J., & Whitmore, K. (Eds.). (1980). *Education, health, and behaviour.* New York: Robert Krieger.

Rutter, M., Tuma, A.J., & Lann, I.S. (Eds.). (1988). *Assessment and diagnosis in child psychopathology.* New York: Guilford.

Schroeder, C.S. (1979). Psychologists in a private pediatric practice. *Journal of Pediatric Psychology, 4,* 5–18.

Schroeder, C.S., Gordon, B.N., & Hawk, B. (1983). Clinical problems of the preschool child. In C.E. Walker & M.C. Roberts (Eds.), *Handbook of clinical child psychology* (pp. 296–334). New York: Wiley.

Schroeder, C.S., Gordon, B.N., Kanoy, K., & Routh, D.K. (1983). Managing children's behavior problems in pediatric practice. In M. Wolraich & D.K. Routh (Eds.), *Advances in developmental and behavioral pediatrics* (Vol. 4, pp. 25–86). Greenwich, CT: JAI.

Schroeder, C.S., Mesibov, G., Eastman, J., & Goolsby, E. (1981). Preventive services for children: A model. In A.W. Burgess & B.A. Baldwin (Eds.), *Crisis intervention theory and practice: A clinical handbook* (pp. 128–135). Englewood Cliffs, NJ: Prentice-Hall.

Sparrow, S.S., Balla, D.A., & Cicchetti, D.V. (1984). *Vineland Adaptive Behavior Scales.* Circle Pines, MN: American Guidance Service.

Thomas, A., & Chess, S. (1977). *Temperament and development.* New York: Brunner/Mazel.

Thomas, A., Chess, S., Sillen, J., & Mendez, O. (1974). Cross-cultural study of behavior in children with special vulnerabilities to stress. In D.F. Ricks, A. Thomas, & M. Roff

(Eds.), *Life history research in psychopathology* (Vol. 3, pp. 53–67). Minneapolis: University of Minnesota Press.

Wahler, R.G. (1980). The insular mother: Her problems in parent-child treatment. *Journal of Applied Behavior Analysis, 13,* 207–219.

Weaver, S.J. (Ed.). (1984). *Testing children: A reference guide for effective clinical and psychoeducational assessments.* Austin, TX: PRO-ED.

Wirt, R.D., Lachar, D., Klinedinst, J.E., & Seat, P.D. (1977). *Multidimensional description of child personality: A manual for the Personality Inventory for Children.* Los Angeles: Western Psychological Services.

7

Assessment of the Home Environment

ROBERT H. BRADLEY, PH.D. & JUDITH A. BRISBY, PH.D.

Throughout most of the history of psychology, measurement has focused on the individual. The legacy of the last 20 years, however, has changed this perspective. New theories, new therapies, new interventions have refocused the efforts of measurement in both medicine and the behavioral sciences. We have widened the angle of our lens to include the context of individual actions: the cultural milieu, community settings, interactions among individuals, and so forth. Consequently, those involved in evaluating young children often will desire (or be mandated to perform) an assessment of the home environment.

A RATIONALE AND MODEL FOR ENVIRONMENTAL ASSESSMENT

Research during the middle of the 20th century made clear that children's health and development are closely tied to the environments they encounter. Evidence also was mounting that children's achievement, adjustment, and health status could be improved by being exposed to more nearly "optimal environments" (Bloom, 1964; Bowlby, 1969; Caldwell, 1968; Hunt, 1961). The work of Bloom (1964) and Hunt (1961), in particular, gave rise to the belief that the power of the environment is greatest during the early years of life, when development is most rapid. This body of research propelled changes in theory, measurement, and practice, both clinical and educational, as related to children, including the implementation of programs such as Head Start; Home Start; Women, Infants, & Children (WIC); and Early Periodic Screening, Diagnosis & Treatment (EPSDT).

Research findings on the link between the quality of environment a person encounters and his or her behavior and development continued to accumulate throughout the world during the 1960s and 1970s. Studies indicated that the general relationship between optimal environment, optimal health, and optimal development seems to hold across cultures and across the life span (Bradley & Tedesco, 1982; Cravioto & DeLicardie, 1972; Riccuiti & Dorman, 1981). One of the most significant contributions to the literature during this period was the review published by Clarke and Clarke (1976) that established the importance of the environment beyond the first few years of life.

Drillien's (1964) study of premature infants provides a classic example of findings on the environment/development relationship through the mid-1970s. When children in her study reached the age of 4 years, the developmental quotient (DQ) was found to differ within each birth-weight group for each social class. The greatest difference—33 DQ points—occurred between the smallest infants from the lowest social class and the smallest infants from the highest social class.

In 1971 another classic study appeared, this on the children of Kauai (Werner, Bierman, & French, 1971). In this study a variety of prenatal and perinatal data were collected from a cohort of children born in 1955 on the island of Kauai in Hawaii. The sample consisted of 698 children, diverse by ethnicity and social status. Demographic, family stability and structure, health, and developmental measures also were taken, including measures of the family environment. Results indicated that perinatal complications were *consistently related to later impaired development only when combined with persistently poor environmental circumstances.* Werner and her colleagues also observed that maternal education was one of the most significant factors in determining the course of a child's development.

This constellation of events, capped off by Sameroff and Chandler's (1975) seminal review of factors influencing the development of biologically at-risk children, made clear that future investigations of children's health and development and plans for interventions aimed at improving these areas should include a consideration of their social and physical surroundings. The idea of human development occurring as a result of a dynamic, multileveled set of transactions between individuals and their environments found strong support among researchers in the social and behavioral sciences. Several elaborate ecological/developmental models were proposed in the decade following Sameroff and Chandler's classic article (Bronfenbrenner, 1979; Lerner, 1986; Ramey, MacPhee, & Yeates, 1982). Belsky (1983) presented a smaller ecological model that might serve as a useful guide to both working with parents and children and identifying significant measures to study child health and development.

Belsky's model (shown in Figure 7.1) is very useful for practicing professionals because it depicts child development as dynamically intertwined with the parenting process (i.e., some of those aspects of the environment assumed to be most intimately connected to child behavior and development). It suggests a route, other than direct medical or behavioral interventions, through which one might influence the course of child development; specifically, facilitating good parenting. Further, it identifies a set of factors through which one might facilitate good parenting; namely, the world of work, marital relationships, the family's social network, and individual parent characteristics. Belsky provides evidence that these kinds of factors are, indeed, related to the quality of parenting a child receives, with marital quality given the highest valence in his analysis. This chapter adopts the architecture of Belsky's model, with one modification, in order to structure a discussion about family environment measures.

Figure 7.2 displays this modified model of human development. Added to the Belsky model is one other set of variables, the physical environment. There is substantial evidence that a child's physical environment can influence both behavior and development (Wachs & Gruen, 1982). Furthermore, aspects of the physical environment also can be the subject of counseling and intervention in pediatric and early childhood settings.

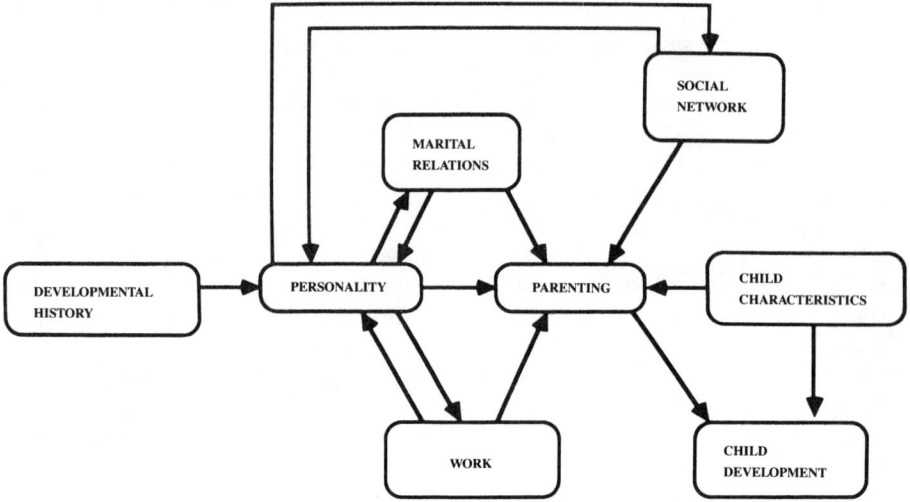

FIGURE 7.1. Belsky's process model of the determinants of parenting. (From "The Determinants of Parenting: A Process Model" by J. Belsky, 1983, *Child Development, 55,* pp. 83–96. Copyright 1983 by The Society for Research in Child Development, Inc. Used by permission.)

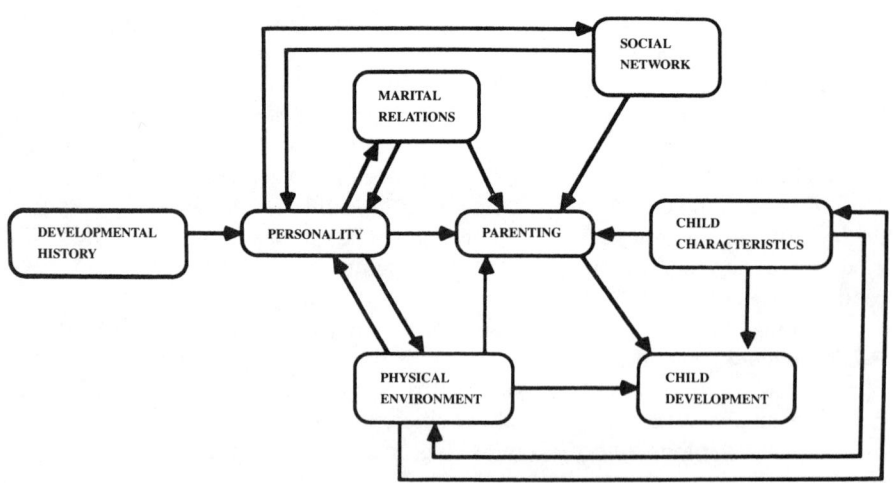

FIGURE 7.2. Modification of Belsky's process model of parenting.

COLLECTING AND USING INFORMATION ABOUT A CHILD'S ENVIRONMENT TO MAKE DECISIONS

While there is near universal agreement on the value of obtaining information about a child's environment as part of an overall assessment, no such universal agreement exists on what factors to consider in choosing such measures or on how to use them. Should they be treated in much the same manner as measures of the characteristics of individuals? Are there fundamental differences? The answer is not entirely clear.

What does seem clear at this time is that researchers and practicing professionals intend to *use* environmental measures in ways similar to how they have used developmental measures. Researchers are using them in an effort to better understand and predict behavior, development, and health status. Practitioners are using them to help establish "risk," prescribe "interventions," and determine the success of treatment programs. *As measurement is essentially an applied enterprise, use more than form determines how a measure should be validated.* Thus, the procedures that have been developed to construct and validate measures of individual development generally would appear appropriate to apply to measures of human environments. In that regard judgments about the utility of environmental instruments are made with reference to the type of decision one must arrive at on the basis of information obtained. Three primary types of decisions derive from information gleaned in environmental measures: screening, diagnosis, and program effectiveness (evaluation). The literature on these types of measurement decisions in medicine, the social sciences, human services, and education is so well established that only a brief review of key features is necessary.

Screening

Screening is basically a dichotomous process that leads to deciding whether some action needs to be taken in behalf of the person screened. Professionals in health, human service, and education agencies have attempted to use environmental measures to make many screening-type decisions—Does a child's home background pose a threat to his later school success? Does the parent's history of violence pose a risk for child maltreatment? Is the level of lead present in the house likely to result in long-term health problems? However, although there are established procedures for conducting validation studies on screening instruments (Stangler, Huber, & Routh, 1980), unfortunately few environmental measures have undergone the necessary psychometric analyses to validate their use for such screening purposes. An exception is the screening study of the HOME Inventory done by Bradley and Caldwell (1977).

Diagnosis

A more complex use of environmental measures is diagnosis. The purpose of screening is to determine *whether* some action (e.g., further testing, referral, effort to find an intervention) should be taken; the purpose of diagnostic testing is to determine *which type* of intervention is needed. It is a classification or placement decision. Should one place the child in an early education program? Should one make home visits to teach the mother better ways of stimulating the child? Should one provide stable employment to parents so that they can afford to give the child more enriching experiences? The decision regarding an appropriate placement or treatment often requires far more detailed information than that available from a brief screening instrument. Not surprisingly, the type of validating procedures needed for a diagnostic instrument are generally quite different from those needed for a screening instrument.

If evidence for the "screening validity" of most environmental measures is limited, evidence for the "diagnostic validity" of such measures is almost unheard of. The dearth of such information is particularly disturbing in light of the requirements under PL 99–457: For each young handicapped child, an Individualized Family Service Plan must be developed for the family, aimed at assisting the ability of the family to provide for the needs of the child.

Evaluation

The third major type of decision that can be made using environmental measures pertains to program or treatment effectiveness, technically called *evaluation*. If the environment is the target of the intervention, then the focus of the evaluation is on changes in the environment. Measures that can reflect changes in the environment resulting from the intervention are needed.

Bloom and his colleagues (1971) have split evaluation decisions into two large categories, formative and summative. Formative evaluation takes place *during* the treatment, attempting to answer the question, "How is the treatment doing in terms of accomplishing its 'in route' objectives?" (i.e., is it proceeding as expected and is it having the kind of effects desired?). The answers to these questions allow interveners to decide whether to continue the intervention as originally planned or to modify it, slow down, go back, speed up, or perhaps stop it altogether. To be useful as a formative evaluation instrument generally requires fairly detailed information, information tagged to specific program goals and anticipated intermediate outcomes. For example, has the mother reduced the rate of negative reinforcement to the point where more positive discipline techniques can be employed? Is the family in at least weekly contact with the Down's syndrome support group? To be valid, environmental measures often must be sensitive to rather small changes in rather narrowly defined environmental conditions. Instruments that might be quite good at identifying general patterns of strengths and weaknesses in the environment (i.e., they are good for diagnostic purposes) may not have items that are sensitive enough to register improvement on program goals (i.e., they are of limited value for formative evaluation purposes).

The other subcategory under evaluation is summative evaluation, done either at the end of the total intervention or at the end of a phase of intervention. It answers the question, was the program successful? Can we terminate the intervention or go on to the next phase? In one important respect the kind of information needed from summative evaluation instruments is like that for formative evaluation instruments; both are tied to program goals. They differ in that the information needed for summative instruments is tied to ultimate or final goals, not intermediate ones. As a rule summative evaluation measures need not be as detailed or sensitive as formative evaluation tools. They may need to reflect only a representative sampling of goals or to reflect that the environment reached a previously established level or point for success (e.g., Dad no longer spanks the kids every time they are disobedient, or the family is now in reasonably regular contact with extended family members and social organizations).

SOCIAL SUPPORT

Vulnerable but Invincible is Werner and Smith's (1982) transcendent follow-up to the classic *Children of Kauai*. In it they describe the children, followed from infancy, as adolescents. Among the things observed about these children was that if the family had a strong social network available, then it more often was able to provide the kind of stimulating, nurturing, and predictable environment needed for good development. The potential of strong social networks to contribute to the well-being and adaptive functioning of adults, and subsequently to the development of children, has received considerable attention in the last decade. Studies of social networks, together with studies of other aspects of the broad domain called social support, have proliferated. The status of the social support construct among professionals working with families and children has been articulated cogently by Dunst and Trivette (1988): "The stress buffering and health promoting influences of social support have been so well documented . . . that it is now almost axiomatic to state that social support promotes well-being as well as lessens the likelihood of emotional and physical distress" (p.1). There remains some uncertainty, though, about the exact relationship between social support, stress, and human adaptive functioning (Barrera, 1986). Does social support help prevent stress? Does it ameliorate the effects of stress? Does stress lead to a deterioration of perceived support or to a reduction of its effectiveness? Nonetheless, there is a general consensus that social support has several positive effects, summarized by Bruhn and Philips (1984) thusly: (a) social support fulfills the human need to belong; (b) social support modifies the effects of negative stress; (c) social support restores hope and morale; and (d) social support enhances one's ability to use skills in new situations.

One of the most significant efforts to bring together the vast literature on social support in such a way that it might be applied with clients is found in the work of Dunst and Trivette (1988). They suggest that the support domain is comprised of five major components: relational support, structural support, constitutional support, functional support, and support satisfaction.

Relational support refers to the existence and quantity of social relationships. One might attempt to assess it by asking questions like, what kind of job do you have? Are you married? How many persons do you see regularly? What organizations do you belong to? These questions get at the simple existence and breadth of social relationships a person has. *Structural support* deals with the "nature" of social relationships between people thought to be important for interactions to be supportive (e.g., density of social network, stability of relationships, reciprocity among network members, etc.). *Functional support* refers to the source, type, quantity, and quality of help or assistance available. It may be in the form of informational, emotional, or instrumental aid. *Constitutional support* concerns the congruence between the type of support available and the type of support needed. One might think of it as resonance. Momma-in-law's offer to prepare dinner every night may not be exactly what the parents wanted in trying to cope with two careers and two teenagers. The final area of support is the most ephemeral of all: *support satisfaction*. How many times have you been in the position that you have found something that by outward appearance seems to fulfill all the necessary criteria, have all the right elements, perform all the right functions, be suited to identified needs, yet you still conclude, "but I just don't like it"? So it is with receiving support. There is a very subjective quality to it. Satisfaction is personal and emotional.

TABLE 7.1. MEASURES OF SOCIAL SUPPORT

Name and Source	Contents and Format	Administration and Scoring	Major Strengths
Arizona Social Support Interview Schedule (Barrera, 1983a, 1983b) A Spanish form is available.	Interview that uses both open-ended responses and rating scales for satisfaction and need. Seven questions with four parts each: A. Available network B. Utilized network size C. Support satisfaction D. Support need	Interview. Scoring somewhat involved. Each area has a separate summed score.	Well-structured interview. Allows some depth of information beyond scores. Taps four different domains.
Family Support Scale (Dunst, Trivette, & Jenkins, 1987)	18 items, 5-point scale used. Assesses helpfulness of six different sources of support: A. Informal kinship B. Social organizations C. Formal kinship D. Immediate family E. Specialized professional F. Generic professional	Paper-and-pencil test. Could be read to a nonreader. Provides total score and six subscale scores.	Simple, clear items. Generally good reliability. Good scale construction procedures followed. Well organized.
Interview Schedule of Social Interaction (Henderson, Byrne, & Duncan-Jones, 1981)	52 items. Multiple-choice responses. Assesses both available support and perceived adequacy of support. Four main areas assessed: A. Availability of attachment B. Perceived adequacy of attachment C. Availability of social integration D. Perceived adequacy of social integration	Interview schedule. Scoring system provided.	Content appears appropriate and directions are clear. Useful for a broad array of respondents. Reasonable reliability.

As appealing as the social support construct is, as compelling as arguments are about its centrality in family functioning, it is not easy to measure with precision. There have been a number of useful critiques of social support measures (Barrera, 1986; Cohen & Wills, 1985; Dean & Linn, 1977; Tardy, 1985; Vaux, Riedel, & Stewart, 1987). Neither the general nor the specific criticisms offered by these researchers will be reiterated here. Table 7.1 lists a number of social support measures that appear to have properties that might make them useful for applied purposes. Brief summary comments are made about each in the table.

Major Weaknesses	Screening Uses	Diagnostic Uses	Evaluation Uses	Research Uses
Lengthy. Requires trained interviewer. Limited information on how to interpret scores.	Limited potential. Too long.	Some potential. The four areas assessed provide a reasonably comprehensive portrait of support. Limited validity data available.	Limited potential. Scores not easily attached to program goals.	Good potential for elaborate studies of social support. However, few validity data are available.
Limited information on how to interpret scores, but suggested for intervention discussions.	Quite promising. Short, quick. Useful validity information available.	Limited but promising. Rather short for detailed diagnosis but items cover a broad range.	Limited potential. Perhaps useful as a pre/post test. Does not provide fine-grained, detailed information on specific goals.	Good validity information. Content validity appears good.
Requires an interviewer. Some items appear stilted and may be difficult for some respondents to comprehend. Scoring procedures difficult to follow.	Too lengthy for this purpose.	Some potential. Assesses four areas and separates availability of support from quality of perceived support. Little validity data available.	Limited potential. Might be used in pre/post type design. Limited data on this use.	Could be useful in research that deals with attachment and social integration themes. Generally good psychometrics.

Continued

TABLE 7.1. MEASURES OF SOCIAL SUPPORT (*continued*)

Name and Source	Contents and Format	Administration and Scoring	Major Strengths
Inventory of Social Support (Trivette & Dunst, 1987a)	18 items using 5-point rating scale for amount of contact with various groups; 12 items indicating who provides support.	Paper-and-pencil test. Scoring directions available from test developers.	Extensive coverage of groups providing assistance. Clear items.
Inventory of Socially Supportive Behavior (Barrera, 1981)	40 items, 5-point rating scale.	Paper-and-pencil test, results in a total score. Score sheet provided.	Good reliability. Moderate length. Clear directions.
Maternal Social Support Index (Pascoe, Loda, Jeffries, & Earp, 1981)	Seven items with pre-established responses. A. Social support B. Task orientation C. Affection D. Community involvement E. Use of helping professions	Brief interview. Respondents answer questions using pre-established categories. Scoring key provided. Results in a total score.	Short. Good organization. Items clear, wording simple.
Norbeck Social Support Questionnaire (Norbeck, Lindsey, & Carrieri, 1982, 1983; Norbeck, 1980/1982)	Respondent must list names of contacts and rate how helpful they are. Three scores derived: A. Total Functional B. Total Network C. Total Loss	Paper-and-pencil test. Could be read to nonreaders.	Well organized. Easy to read and score. Good reliability.
Perceived Social Network Inventory (Oritt & Paul, 1985)	Assesses seven areas: A. Perceived network size B. Initiation of support-seeking behaviors C. Perceived availability of support D. Satisfaction with support E. Perceived multidimensionality F. Perceived support reciprocity G. Perceived network conflict	Paper-and-pencil test. Scoring procedures vary, depending on part of scale being scored.	Reasonable reliability. Could easily be completed by a competent reader.

Major Weaknesses	Screening Uses	Diagnostic Uses	Evaluation Uses	Research Uses
No information on scoring interpretation. May be too difficult for someone with limited reading skills.	Short enough but doesn't appear designed for this purpose.	Limited potential. No subscales. Individual items may help identify strategies for increasing assistance client receives.	Very limited potential.	Designed mostly for clinical purposes, but some useful validity data on uses with families with handicapped.
Language difficult for poor readers.	Moderate potential. Length good. Moderate correlations with outcomes.	Very limited potential. Gives only a single total score.	Very limited potential.	Some potential. Generally good correlations with appropriate measure.
Limited information on scale's psychometric properties. Limited information on how to interpret scores. Some items may be vague due to breadth of focus.	Potentially good due to brevity. Some evidence to support this use.	Very limited potitital. Too few items to help target intervention. No data available for this purpose.	Very limited potential. May be useful in simple pre/post type design. No data available for this purpose.	Could be useful in studies where only a broad measure of social support is required. May be useful in studies where a paper-and-pencil measure is not feasible.
Rather long. Limited information on how to interpret scores. Limited sample used.	Some potential. Validity data available. A bit long.	Limited potential; no subscales and discriminant validity information.	Very limited potential.	Some criterion validity information available but limited cross-validation on more representative samples.
Total score from PSNI probably not interpretable. Too difficult for poor reader. Directions and organization not good. Scoring neither clear nor easy. No time frame given in directions.	Rather lengthy for this purpose.	Somewhat limited potential but assesses seven areas that might help plan targeted interventions.	Somewhat limited potential but is possible to measure increases on a number of dimensions that could be targets of intervention.	Some evidence for construct and discriminant validity. Insufficient evidence for content validity.

Continued

TABLE 7.1. MEASURES OF SOCIAL SUPPORT *(continued)*

Name and Source	Contents and Format	Administration and Scoring	Major Strengths
Perceived Social Support: PSS-Fa for Families and PSS-Fr for Friends (Procidano & Heller, 1983)	Two 20-item scales scored yes/no. Assesses perceived needs for support, information, and feedback.	Paper-and-pencil test. Underlined responses are scored 1 point. A total 20 points possible on each scale. Could be read to a nonreader.	Brief scale. Clear items. Easy to use. Good reliability.
Personal Network Matrix (Trivette & Dunst, 1987b)	Three-part measure. Part I—persons with whom one has contact; Part II—persons who help provide for listed needs; Part III—dependability of network members.	Respondent must list persons contacted, how they fulfill needs, and how dependable they are. Scoring and profiling possible; directions available from test developers.	Provides extensive information about one's social network.
Social Support Appraisals (Vaux, Phillips, Holly, Thomson, Williams, & Stewart, 1986)	23 items using 4-point rating scale. Assesses three areas: A. Social support appraisals B. Social support resources C. Distress and well-being	Paper-and-pencil test. Easy to read. Three scores computed by simply: A. Totaling 23 items B. Totaling the 8 "family" items C. Totaling the 7 friend items D. Totaling the 8 "other" items	Good reliability. Short easy-to-read items. Simple to complete.
Social Support Behaviors Scale (Vaux, Riedel, & Stewart, 1987)	45 items for both family and friends, 5-point rating scale. Assesses five areas: A. Emotional B. Socializing C. Practical D. Financial E. Advice/guidance	Paper-and-pencil test. Could be read to nonreader. Scores derived by summing responses for each of five areas.	Directions clear. Easy to use. Reliability good. Good content validity.
Social Support Questionnaire (Sarason, Levine, Basham, & Sarason, 1983)	27 items, each rated on a 6-point scale. Assesses both amount of perceived support and satisfaction with support. 12-item version also available.	Paper-and-pencil test. Scores derived by summing number of persons listed and dividing by number of items. Same procedure used in deriving a score for perceived satisfaction.	Directions clear. Content appears appropriate. Good psychometric data available. Reasonable evidence for reliability and validity.
Support Functions Scale (Dunst & Trivette, 1987)	Two forms—one 12-item, one 20-item; 5-point rating scale. Assesses types of assistance a person needs.	Paper-and-pencil test. Could be read to a nonreader. Total score. Scoring procedures available from authors.	Simple, clear items. Good reliability. Careful scale construction.

Major Weaknesses	Screening Uses	Diagnostic Uses	Evaluation Uses	Research Uses
No information on how to interpret scores. No time frame given. Used only with college students.	Brevity and simplicity make it potentially useful, but limited validity data available.	Quite limited potential for this purpose due to brevity.	Quite limited potential except perhaps as a simple pre/post test measure.	Some evidence for validity. Has been used with a variety of populations.
Hard for person with limited skills to complete. Some clinical skill needed to make use of information.	Very limited potential. Not the measure's intent. Too long.	Some potential, given extent of information and the fact that client profiles can be developed. Limited validity data.	Limited potential. Not designed to evaluate client progress.	More a clinical than a research instrument.
Instructions not very clear. Some items ambiguous. Limited normative sample. Directions for interpreting scores lacking.	Moderate potential due to brevity and ease of administration but no direct validation.	Somewhat limited potential but does assess three areas that might help identify specific needs of clients.	Very limited potential.	Substantial criterion and construct validity information available.
No procedures given regarding how to interpret scores. No time frame in directions. Limited normative sample.	Moderate potential. Not long, but no direct evidence that it is useful for this purpose.	Somewhat limited potential but does assess five areas that could be used to establish intervention.	Quite limited potential.	Content validity information is available. Some criterion validity data are available.
Some items wordy. Poor readers may have difficulty. Some items confusing. Time-consuming. Short form more concise. Limited information on how to interpret scores.	Long form has limited potential due to cumbersome write-in format. Short form has good potential, but little use to date with clinical populations to determine validity.	Moderate potential for long form. Some suggestive validity information. Scoring procedures not optimal for diagnosis.	Limited potential except as general pre/post measure.	Some useful validity data available. Good psychometric information available.
No scoring procedures.	Promising. Short scale. Good general validity information.	Promising. Items tap different areas of potential need.	Quite limited potential. No data available on this type of application. Targeted to families with handicapped members.	Some evidence for validity.

Life Stress

The purported value of social support lies in its ability to protect an individual from the deleterious consequences of stress (Haggerty, 1980). Figure 7.3, taken from Cohen and Wills (1985), depicts a model of the relationship between stress and illness/maladaptive behavior. According to some theories, experiencing a major change in life or experiencing a traumatic event often creates stress (Holmes & Rahe, 1967). The *accumulation of strains* from such experiences may cause an individual to expend considerable psychological energy to achieve a satisfactory level of adjustment. The general connection between stressful life events and disease seems amply documented (Dean & Linn, 1977). Moreover, there are clues that experiencing stressful life events directly affects the behavior of the stressed person.

Some people have to cope with yet another type of strain, *chronic strain* (Cohen & Wills, 1985). Conditions such as poverty, marital conflict, work overload, chronic illness, and the like may require continual behavioral adjustment. Chronic strain also may interfere with a person's performance at work, as a parent, in the community, and so forth (Pearlin & Lieberman, 1979). (See again the model of development depicted in Figure 7.2.)

The exact relationship between either type of stress and child-rearing practices, as depicted in Figure 7.2, is not well established. Though in general people living in chronic negative conditions like poverty and marital discord score lower on measures of parenting, there are significant numbers of exceptions to any general rule (Bloom, 1964; Bradley & Caldwell, 1978). Similarly, while a study by Justice and Duncan (1976) found that parents who experienced high levels of life stress were more likely to abuse their children, Bradley, Casey, and Wortham (1984) found no relationship between stressful life events in a matched sample of lower income families, half of whom had nonorganic failure-to-thrive children, the other half of whom had children with normal growth rates.

Although the relationship of stress (be it from the accumulation of stressful life events or from conditions that produce chronic strain) to parental behaviors and children's development is not yet fully delineated, the potential value of including measures of stressful life events in pediatric, human service, and educational settings would appear substantial. A number of attempts have been made to measure and quantify the degree of stress an individual or family experiences, most notably stressful life events measures. However, stress has not been easy to quantify. Several issues have been raised concerning the content and scoring of life events measures:

1. whether a single set of items should be used with all categories of respondents, regardless of age, gender, ethnicity, cultural background, etc.;
2. whether the time period during which the event should have taken place is the previous 3 months, 6 months, 12 months, or longer;
3. whether items that could be symptoms of disease, rather than precursors of disease, should be eliminated;
4. whether items should be weighted or not; and
5. whether weights should be determined subjectively or objectively.

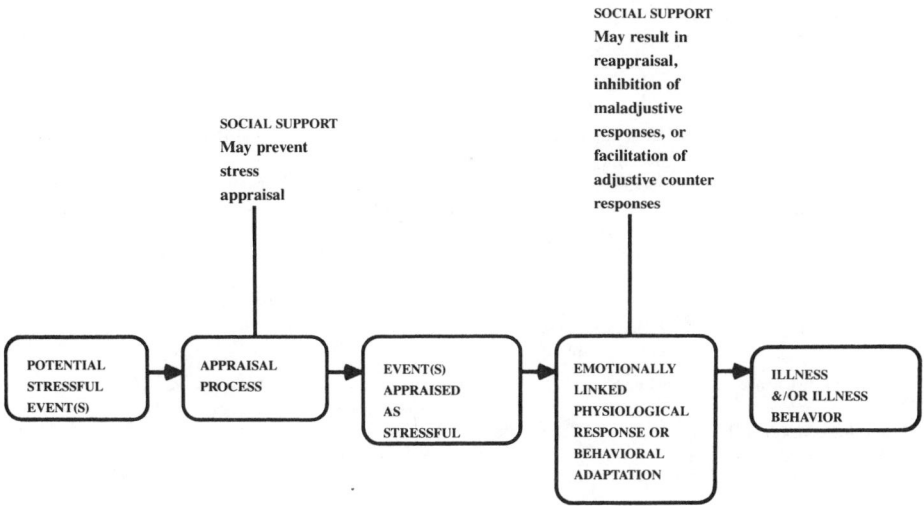

FIGURE 7.3. Two points at which social support may interfere with the hypothesized causal link between stressful events and illness. (From "Stress, Social Support, and the Buffering Hypothesis" by S. Cohen and T. Wills, 1985, *Psychological Bulletin, 98,* 310–357. Copyright 1985 by the American Psychological Association. Used by permission.)

Neither the empirical nor the qualitative evidence to resolve most of these issues has been forthcoming.

Table 7.2 presents brief descriptions of some life events measures. Although some substantive questions remain regarding the best way to measure life events, a number of reasonably reliable instruments exist. Most also show at least moderate correlations with measures of health and development.

Clinicians often have difficulty deciding whether to use a life events scale, which scale to use, or how to use it. Part of the difficulty derives from uncertainty regarding how life events like those included on most measures are related to psychological processes. Dohrenwend and Shrout (1985) present five different models of life stress processes, each of which has different implications with respect to the type of measure that may be most useful in either a research or an applied setting:

1. Victimization—cumulations of stressful life events lead to psychopathology.
2. Vulnerability—preexisting personal dispositions and social conditions mediate the causal link between stressful life events and psychopathology.
3. Additive Burden—personal dispositions and social conditions make independent contributions to psychopathology.
4. Chronic Burden—recent life events have no adverse consequences on personal dispositions and social conditions.
5. Process—the presence of a disorder increases the likelihood of stressful life events, which in turn increases the likelihood of further disorder.

TABLE 7.2 MEASURES OF LIFE EVENTS

Name and Source	Contents and Format	Administration and Scoring	Major Strengths
Adolescent Family Inventory of Life Events and Changes (A-FILE) (McCubbin, Patterson, Bauman, & Harris, 1982)	50-item yes/no format, designed for adolescents. Assesses six areas: A. Transitions B. Sexuality C. Losses D. Responsibilities E. Substance use F. Legal conflict	Paper-and-pencil test. All items deal with past 12 months; 27 deal with time prior to 1 year.	Short, easy to read and respond to. Good definitions of scales. Content appears appropriate for teens. Reliability acceptable.
Adolescent Life Change Events Scale (Yeaworth, York, Hussey, Ingle, & Goodwin, 1980)	31 items	Paper-and-pencil test. Administration and scoring procedures available from test developers.	Easy to score. Appears pertinent to age group. No reliability data available.
Family Inventory of Life Events (McCubbin, Patterson, & Wilson, 1982)	71 yes/no items assess- ing nine types of strains: A. Intrafamily B. Marital C. Pregnancy and childbearing D. Financial E. Work-family transition F. Illness and family care G. Losses H. Family legal violations I. Transitions in and out	Paper-and-pencil test. Total score is obtained by summing the number of "no" responses. Scores obtained for *both* recent and more distant life events. Could be read to nonreaders.	Items clear and appear relevant. Easy to complete. Acceptable reliability. Well organized.
Junior High Life Experiences Survey (Swearingen & Cohen, 1985)	39 items. Report events for last 6 months, then catego- rize as negative, posi- tive, or neutral, then rate on a 7-point scale.	Paper-and-pencil test.	Targeted to early adolescence. Easy to complete. Some reliability data. Provides measure of perceived impact.
Life Event Record (Coddington, 1972)	Scale has four versions: A. Preschool B. Elementary C. Junior High D. High School	Paper-and-pencil test. Must be completed by parent of young child.	Items seem pertinent to targeted age group. Easy to read. Normative data with scoring ranges given for different age, gender, SES, etc., groups. Large normative samples; quite diverse.

Major Weaknesses	*Screening Uses*	*Diagnostic Uses*	*Evaluation Uses*	*Research Uses*
Some items require reading capability at junior high level. Little information on how to interpret scales.	Potential generally good. Length OK. Not much evidence on this specific use.	Some potential. Six areas might allow targeting of intervention. No information validating this use.	Limited potential. Content generally not the focus of intervention.	Some potential. Some reasonable validity data available, albeit most correlations are low.
Only used with Caucasians. Little information provided to aid in interpreting scores.	Potential pretty good. Short scale. However, no direct validity data for this purpose were presented.	Potential limited. No subscales that might help identify strengths and weaknesses.	Potential limited. Items not likely targets of intervention.	Might be useful in a research protocol that required only a general sampling of life events. Validity data limited.
No information on how to interpret scores. No information on how to deal with recent versus more distant events. Some unevenness in quality of subscales based on use of factor analysis.	Potential good. Rather brief and easy to complete. Specific data to support this use not given, but related data suggest usefulness.	Some potential. Several subscales could be used to target intervention. Some useful psychometric data given for subscales.	Potential limited. May be useful for general monitoring of family change more than true evaluation of program effectiveness.	Some useful normative data and psychometric evidence. Care needed if scores reported at subscale level due to brevity and unevenness of subscale quality.
Not used often. Too little information on scoring. Limited sample.	Some potential. Brief scale with some validity data.	Limited potential. No subscores.	Not designed for this purpose.	Useful for junior high schools. A few validity studies available.
Parental judgments about some items may not jibe with child judgments, leading to validity concerns. Wording sometimes is unusual. Limited validity data.	Potential moderate. More validity data for this use needed.	Potential limited. No subscales to detect strengths and weaknesses.	Potential limited. Items not likely targets of intervention.	Items pertinent to age of child so might have place in studies of children. Potential differences between parent and child perceptions of events could limit utility.

Continued

TABLE 7.2. MEASURES OF LIFE EVENTS (*continued*)

Name and Source	Contents and Format	Administration and Scoring	Major Strengths
Life Events: Stressors & Stress (Belle, 1982)	Three parts: Part I—asks respondent to list five significant things that occurred in past 2 years and how stressful; Part II—107 items about stressful events. Assesses 10 areas: A. Environment B. Education C. Work D. Money E. Intimate relationships F. Children G. Health/well-being H. Mental health I. Law J. Personal activities Part III deals with things not covered in I and II.	Detailed interview. Some items open-ended. Each item rated yes/no, then an 8-point rating scale used to indicate degree of perceived stress.	Provides a very detailed portrait of stressful life events. Questions generally are clear.
Life Experiences Survey (Sarason, Johnson, & Siegel, 1978)	57 items—47 for all respondents, 10 for students; 7-point rating scale to indicate type and degree of impact.	Paper-and-pencil test. Scores developed for both number of life events plus impact. Separate scores for positive events and negative events. Sum of the two is total change score.	Clear, easy items. Moderate reliability.
Life Stress Scale (Egeland, Breitenbucker, Dodds, Pastor, & Rosenberg, 1979)	43 items. Designed to assess changing life events for mothers when their infants are 12 to 18 months old. Directions for administering unclear.	Interview schedule. Preestablished response categories.	Questions appear appropriate for lower class groups for which they were designed.

HOME ENVIRONMENT 145

Major Weaknesses	Screening Uses	Diagnostic Uses	Evaluation Uses	Research Uses
Requires a considerable expenditure of time and more expertise to administer than most other measures. May induce fatigue in some respondents. Rating the degree of felt stress for someone else dubious.	Length of scale makes it inappropriate for screening.	Some potential. Does not have true subscales but assesses 10 different areas. There are many items and respondent indicates amount of stress felt. Thus, it may help target an intervention.	Limited value except as a kind of clinical monitoring device.	Greatest potential may be for clinical research. Limited volume of validity data for most uses.
Limited information on interpretation. Use with low SES families not clarified.	Potential good. Short scale but several scores derived. Limited validity for this purpose.	Some potential. Provides two subscores plus assessment of impact. Validity data lacking.	Very limited potential. Not designed for this purpose.	Some validity studies available.
Requires interviewer. Little on how to interpret scales. Reliability unclear. Detailed scoring criteria given.	Limited potential due to length. No data available to support this use.	Limited potential. No separate subscores developed.	Some potential due to length and the fact that each item has multiple score points.	Some potential but validity data largely unknown.

Continued

TABLE 7.2. Measures of Life Events (*continued*)

Name and Source	Contents and Format	Administration and Scoring	Major Strengths
List of Recent Experiences (Henderson, Byrne, & Duncan-Jones, 1981)	71 items across 12 areas: A. Illness, injury, accident B. Bereavement C. Pregnancy or childbirth D. Changes in relationship E. Separation F. Changes in living conditions G. Studying or school H. Work situations I. Financial situation J. Legal difficulties K. Disappointments L. Continuous worry or stress (Each item rated as acute or chronic if experienced.)	Initial response is a closed form. Then interviewer asks respondent to give date, duration, and description of event. Event is then rated on a 10-point scale. A total events score is obtained.	Thorough directions. Clear items. Comprehensive coverage. Strong section on work employment. Reliable.
Multidimensional Assessment of Stressful Life Events Among Adolescents (Newcomb, Huba, & Bentler, 1981)	39 items answered yes/no; seven areas covered: A. Family/parents B. Accident, illness C. Sexuality D. Autonomy E. Deviance F. Relocation G. Distress	Paper-and-pencil test. Scoring done by simply summing the number of "yes" responses.	Short, easy-to-read items. Well organized. Directions for completing test clear. Questions relevant for adolescents. Reliability acceptable given length of subscales.
Psychiatric Epidemiology Research Interview (Dohrenwend, Krasnoff, Askenasy, & Dohrenwend, 1978)	102 items	Paper-and-pencil test. No scoring directions given.	Items clear and easy to read. Substantial validity data.
Revised Life Event Questionnaire (Norbeck, 1984)	79 items assess 10 areas: A. Health B. Work C. School D. Residence E. Love and marriage F. Family and close friends G. Parenting H. Personal and social I. Financial J. Crime and legal matters	Paper-and-pencil test. No scoring procedures given. Could be read to nonreaders. For use with females.	Manageable length. Content appears appropriate. Acceptable reliability. Most items clear. Separate items that focus on parenting.

Major Weaknesses	Screening Uses	Diagnostic Uses	Evaluation Uses	Research Uses
Very lengthy. Could be tiring to complete. Requires an interviewer. Some questionable item placements.	Too lengthy to be used for this purpose.	Some potential. Assesses many areas and provides detailed reactions to each event experienced. Little specific data available for this use, though.	Some potential. The fact that the respondent provides several reactions to each event experienced is significant. Little data dealing with this use, however.	Generally good psychometric properties. Quite comprehensive. Some good validity data. Good normative information.
No items that deal with drugs or their use. No specific scoring directions given.	Potential good. Brief and easy to follow. Evidence for specific screening purposes not given.	Some potential. Several subscales that could be used to target intervention. Evidence not yet developed, though.	Potential limited except as a simple pre/post evaluation.	Psychometrically sound. Some useful validity data available. Appears to have content validity for adolescents.
Limited information on scoring and interpretation.	Limited potential due to length. No specific validity data for this purpose.	Limited potential in that there are no subscores for targeting intervention. May be useful in concert with other measures.	Very limited potential. Not intended for this purpose.	Substantial canon of previous studies using PERI. Theory based.
Two questions for males only. Clustering of some items seems questionable. Little information on how to interpret score. Vocabulary on some items too difficult for broad use.	Moderate potential. A little longer than optimal for screening. Useful validity data to support its use for this purpose.	Some potential. Assesses 10 areas, and each appears to be reliable. Little specific evidence to support this use, however.	Limited potential. Has 10 areas to focus on for evaluation purposes, but does not index perceived stress, a more likely target for intervention.	Some useful validity data available. Generally acceptable psychometrics.

Not all of these models find equal support in the available scientific literature. However, the model of life stress that one espouses, together with the goals one has for measurement, are likely to have as significant an influence on the type of life events measure one chooses as the technical characteristics of the instrument itself.

PARENTING/THE HOME ENVIRONMENT

In the ecological model of early development presented in Figure 7.2, three variables are depicted as directly influencing child development: the child's own characteristics, the parenting, and the physical environment. In this schema parenting is conceived rather broadly to include those objects, events, and transactions that take place in the home. Some are emitted by the parent, others are controlled by the parent, and some are simply permitted by the parent to exist in the general surroundings of the child's home. In all cases, however, these "inputs" represent concrete occurrences in the child's life, and, as such, they are presumed to have "direct" influence (see Figures 7.4 and 7.5). Though sometimes referred to as "environmental processes," they stand in contrast to the processes operationalized in such measures as the Moos Family Environment Scale (FES; Moos, 1974). The FES is not a direct measure of environmental "inputs" to a child so much as it is a measure of attitudes toward or perceptions of the environment. The remainder of this chapter is devoted to a discussion of those "environmental inputs" that appear related to children's development and a description of some home environment instruments used to index them.

Recently we identified five major components of caregiving that appear critical to optimal health and development in children. These five processes (or *inputs* as we term them) consist of both direct actions done to assist the child and indirect, regulatory activities done so that the most appropriate direct action can be taken. Comprehensive assessments of caregiving environments should include attention to each:

1. Sustenance—environmental elements needed to ensure both survival and a level of biological integrity needed for physical and psychological development.
2. Stimulation—sensory data that engage attention and provide information.
3. Support—activities that promote social and emotional well-being, that provide humans motivational preparation for encountering other environments.
4. Structure—the organization of objects, events, policies, and social encounters through time and space.
5. Surveillance—monitoring the whereabouts, activities, and circumstances surrounding a person.

Cognitive Home Environment

Transactions and events within the family environment that facilitate cognitive capability have been called the cognitive home environment (Bradley, 1986a). It includes such factors as the quality and quantity of language used, the emphasis placed on intellectuality in the home, the variety of sensory and social experiences available, and the extent to which parents encourage achievement. There have been

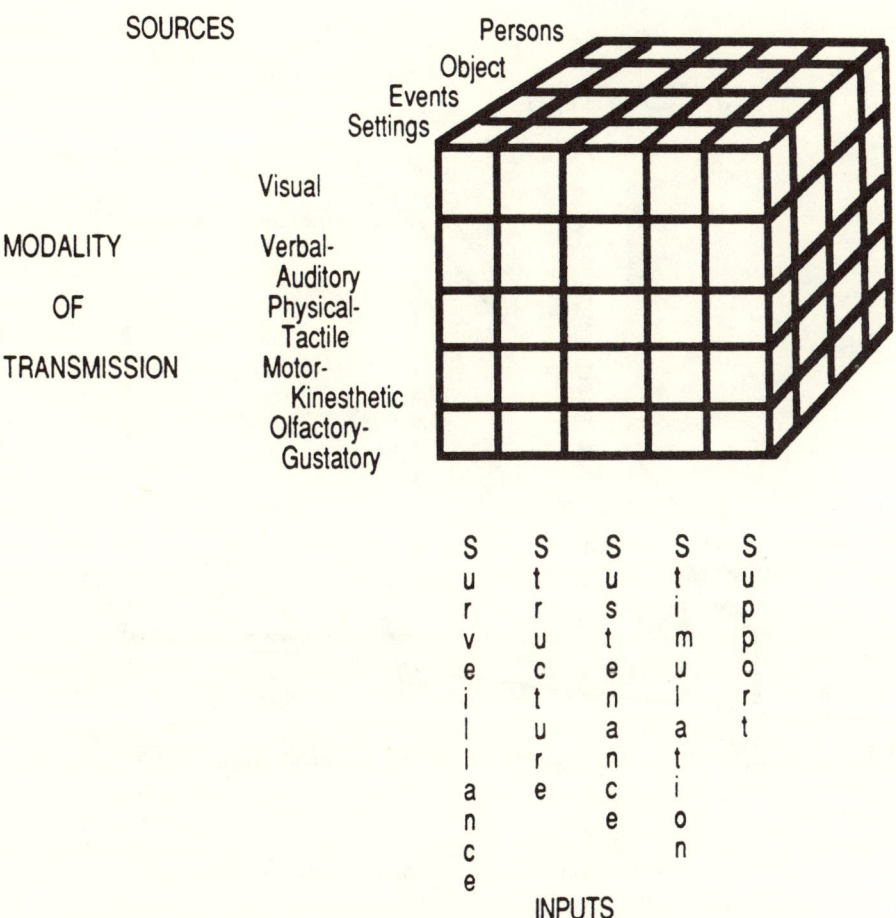

FIGURE 7.4. Taxonomic scheme for structural features of environmental processes.

many studies of these types of factors and their relationship to cognitive and language measures (Bradley & Tedesco, 1982; Kagan, 1984; Wachs & Gruen, 1982). The studies reviewed indicated that the amount and quality of language used by parents is related to children's mental and language competence throughout the preschool and school years (Elardo, Bradley, & Caldwell, 1977; Henderson, Bergan, & Hurt, 1972; Marjoribanks, 1972; Wachs, Uzgiris, & Hunt, 1971; Wulbert, Inglis, Kriegsman, & Mills, 1975). By contrast, the parent's encouragement of intellectual pursuits and intellectuality only appears significant after children enter school (Bloom, 1964; Hanson, 1975; Marjoribanks, 1972).

Evidence supporting the value of variety in sensory stimulation harkens back to the classic studies of Skeels and Dye (1939) and Dennis (1973). In general the findings show that this home environment factor is important from infancy through

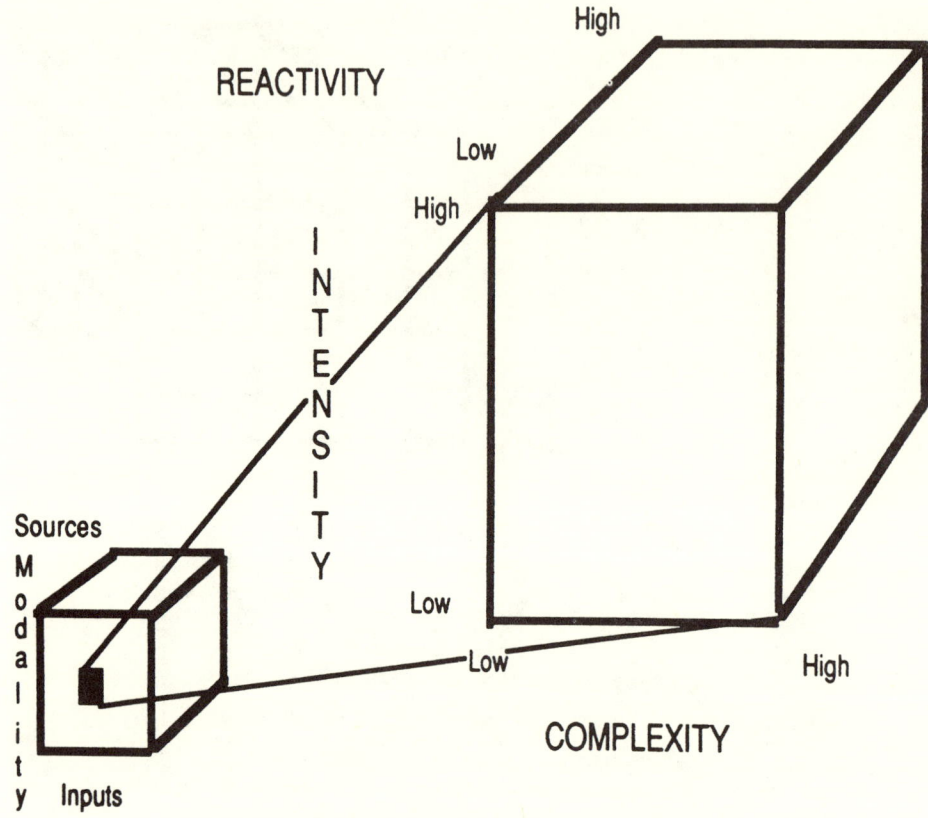

FIGURE 7.5. Taxonomic scheme for dynamic features of environmental processes.

adolescence (Davé, 1963; Elardo, Bradley, & Caldwell, 1975; Henderson et al., 1972; Moore, 1968; Wachs, 1976, 1978; Yarrow, Rubenstein, & Pederson, 1975).

A fourth feature of the child's cognitive home environment is parental encouragement of achievement. Research by White and Watts (1973) makes the importance of parental encouragement during infancy clear. McCall, Appelbaum, and Hogarty (1973) found that parental encouragement of achievement in the first 3 years of life was associated with increases in IQ through age 17. In a study of 11-year-old boys, Marjoribanks (1972) observed a substantial correlation between press for achievement and scores on both number and verbal abilities. Support for the value of parental encouragement of or demands for achievement for their children can also be found in the theory of achievement motivation propounded by McClelland, Atkinson, Clark, and Lowell (1953).

Socioemotional Home Environment

Certain encounters between persons in the home, certain events that occur in the home or that are arranged by family members, and certain efforts made by family members to organize the environment serve to promote or to interfere with the child's social and emotional development. These occurrences, referred to as the socioemotional home environment, have been the subject of inquiry for decades (Wachs & Gruen, 1982). The most commonly examined factors in this domain are parental responsiveness, warmth, and nurturance within the family, restrictiveness, and discipline practices.

Perhaps no other aspect of a child's environment has received as much attention as parental responsiveness (i.e., the extent to which parents both anticipate and appropriately react to a child's needs and interests). Studies of both humans and animals provide substantial support for the centrality of parental responsiveness in promoting long-term social and emotional well-being. The data indicate an especially significant impact in the early years (Bradley, Caldwell, & Rock, 1988; Clarke-Stewart, 1973; Elardo et al., 1977; Henderson et al., 1972; Tulkin & Covitz, 1975; Yarrow et al., 1975). Evidence also indicates the importance of *appropriate responsiveness*. In the case of some medically fragile children, who themselves might be underresponsive or undemonstrative, there is a tendency of parents to "overanticipate" the child's needs (i.e., to act before the child has had the opportunity to express those needs). As a result the children may not learn the connection between their actions and what the environment offers. These conditions do not promote a sense of efficacy and trust, and may lead to a kind of "learned helplessness."

The recent work of Rohner (1986) has given renewed emphasis to the importance of parental warmth and nurturance. His cross-cultural studies demonstrate the value of parental caresses and expressions of positive affect toward children. Such warm behaviors positively impact the child's mood, adjustment, and display of adaptive behavior. In contrast to research findings that show parental warmth having a generally positive impact on children's socioemotional development, research typically shows that restrictiveness has a mildly negative impact (Bradley & Caldwell, 1976; Engel & Keane, 1975; Kagan & Freeman, 1963).

Closely related to the issue of restrictiveness is that of discipline. Results on this subject are mixed, with discipline practices such as punishment, use of fear to control, and strictness all showing modest negative correlations with children's development (Baumrind & Black, 1967; Bayley & Schaefer, 1964; Bradley & Caldwell, 1978; Kagan & Freeman, 1963). In summarizing this research, however, it is important to state that most studies did not include many cases of prolonged or severe physical punishment. Studies of maltreatment provide evidence of much more pronounced and long-term ill effects (Egeland & Sroufe, 1981). Additionally, Baumrind (1978) has described three clusters of parenting behaviors, which she has labeled *authoritative, authoritarian,* and *laissez faire.* These clusters of behavior appear to be more consistently related to child social and emotional outcomes than most individual parent behaviors.

The final component of the social environment that was reviewed was parents' encouragement of independence and responsibility. The studies examined showed little evidence that early encouragement of independence facilitates development (Gordon, 1974; Hanson, 1975; McCall et al., 1973). By contrast, there is some evidence that an emphasis on acting independently in middle class families during the school years may have a modest positive impact on development (Hanson, 1975;

Marjoribanks, 1972). Recent studies of "latch key" children suggest that the amount of misbehavior or difficulty a child gets into is related to the kind of arrangements parents make for keeping in touch with the whereabouts and activities of their children (Steinberg, 1986).

Physical Home Environment

The third major type of environmental inputs consists of objects, pieces of equipment, structures, physical conditions and appearances of the house, and arrangements of physical materials within the home. Collectively these have been referred to as the physical environment (Wachs & Gruen, 1982). The most often-examined aspects of the physical environment include toys, learning materials, level of sensory input, and the extent to which the environment is arranged so as to promote health, well-being, and adaptive functioning.

Over the past two decades there have been a number of studies attesting to the value of a child's access to a variety of toys and materials within the home environment (Bradley et al., 1988; Bradley & Caldwell, 1976; Clarke-Stewart, 1973; Moore, 1968; Wachs, 1976; Wulbert et al., 1975). Important attributes of useful materials appear to be variety and responsiveness to child investigation and manipulation (Yarrow et al., 1975; Wachs, 1978). Effective toys and materials are those that allow the expression of curiosity and mastery motivation (Gottfried, 1986). Renewed attention to the work of Vygotsky (1978) has made clearer how toys can function to promote intellectual development at different points in the early life span, including their use as basic stimuli and as props in imaginative play. Bradley (1986b) provided a model depicting a variety of ways that toys alone, and toys in the context of social encounters, may serve to promote joy and development in children. Almost the entire canon of studies available on the impact of toys, materials, and equipment on children's development has been done on children without handicapping conditions. Nonetheless, clinical reports suggest that the availability of appropriate adapted equipment and toys for children with developmental handicaps is especially important. As Hunt (1961), and more recently Lerner (1986), have argued, it is the "match" or "fit" between child and environment that is important for optimal development.

Distinct from specific objects and events that a child encounters is the envelope of auditory and visual stimulation that constantly surrounds a child in the home. One of the background variables that has been investigated most thoroughly in the past several years is nonspecific background noise. Findings generally show that high noise levels are associated with poorer cognitive scores, poorer school performance, decreased coping ability, and depression (Altman & Wohlwill, 1978; Wachs, 1976, 1978). On the other hand, there is evidence that too little sensory stimulation can also lead to functional difficulties (Dennis, 1973).

Parents provide indirect support for development by organizing the environment so that the child can receive maximum benefit. Parke (1978) has noted that this role may even be more important than that of stimulator, as infants spend far more time interacting with the inanimate environment than they do interacting socially. Unfortunately, the number of studies of specific ways that families organize the objects, events, materials, and so forth in the home is small. The largest volume of studies treats the organization issue rather globally (e.g., households simply are characterized as being more or less organized). The information available suggests that organization of time and space may be especially important in low income homes (Bradley, Caldwell, Rock, Casey, & Nelson, 1987; Bradley & Caldwell, 1987), and that, perhaps, after some threshold is reached, additional levels of organization may not have as great an impact on development (although strong conclusions about the literature are not warranted at present). Appropriate organization of objects, equipment, furniture, and so on to promote access and mobility are likely to be particularly important for children having visual or orthopedic handicaps.

No environmental process measure presently available captures all of the processes or elements of the environment described in the sections immediately preceding. The majority deal with only a few of the factors mentioned, some only one. The more broadly focused instruments derive from a number of different theoretical perspectives and utilize a number of different approaches to data collection. Several of the available measures have undergone useful psychometric studies and a few have been cross-validated on additional samples. But none has been normed on a broadly representative sample—largely due to the great expense incurred in such norming efforts. The remainder of this section is devoted to a discussion of some of the theoretical frameworks used to construct environmental process measures and the various approaches used to collect data for these instruments. In addition, details about specific instruments and their potential usefulness are given.

It has been the better part of 25 years since the seminal works of Hunt (1961) and Bloom (1964) ushered in the current era of measuring children's environments. A number of different broad-scale environmental process measures have been constructed in the intervening years and a number of different conceptualizations of environment/development relations have served as a basis for scale construction. Several instrument developers have utilized the "need-press" theory of Murray (1938) in designing home environment scales, among them Bloom and his students at the University of Chicago (1964), Davé (1963), Henderson et al. (1972), Keeves (1972), Radin (1971), Laing and Sines (1982), Marjoribanks (1972), and Wolf (1965). Most of these scales, save for the HELPS scale constructed by Henderson and his colleagues, are rather lengthy. Data to score items are obtained most often by interviewing the child's caregiver in the home.

A second major influence on the development of environmental process measures is the work of Barker and Wright (1954). Their approach is to quantify human ecologies so that minute details of life events can be reconstructed for purposes of analysis. The Barker-Wright methodology begins with a stream of behavior, a narrative account of objects and actions occurring during a specified time period. The accounts are later coded into an elaborate system of categories to suit the needs of the person who is to interpret the information about the environment. The Human Interaction Scale and the Object Interaction Scale, designed by White and Watts (1973) for the Harvard Preschool Project, leaned heavily on the Barker-Wright approach. These two scales were part of a thorough examination of differences in the homes of successful versus unsuccessful preschoolers. The extensive observations and codings typically required of these types of ecological measures generally makes them inappropriate for screening purposes. It even makes them an expensive approach for diagnosis. By contrast, such techniques might be especially valuable for formative evaluation, as means of monitoring the success of a parent-oriented intervention.

Information theory, operant learning theory, and especially theories of intrinsic motivation were used by Yarrow et al. (1975) at the National Institute of Mental Health to produce their measure of the home environment. Scores on this measure were related both to children's scores on the Bayley Scales of Infant Development and to children's goal-directed behavior. The scale is of moderate length and results in several subscores. Thus, it might prove useful for either screening or diagnostic purposes.

By comparison, Bromwich (1976) drew principally from the research on attachment and reciprocal interactions to design the Parent Behavior Progression. The PBP requires extensive observation of parental behavior and was designed as a means of improving parenting skills. It is atypical in that it is "hierarchical" in structure; specifically, parents generally are categorized as being at one of three levels in terms of the quality of their parenting. The first level, called the "affective" base, is presumed essential for more advanced levels of parenting. The Parent Behavior Progression was designed to be used in a diagnostic fashion and might also be useful for both formative and summative evaluation purposes, depending on the goals of one's parent education program.

Relatively few of the well-known environmental process measures devote significant attention to the physical aspects of the home environment. Perhaps the most notable exception to this rule is the Purdue Home Stimulation Inventory (PHSI; Wachs, 1978). Through a combination of observations and interview questions, the PHSI indexes such things as objects, furnishings, arrangements of physical materials, background noise, and lighting in the home environment. Wohlwill (1983) issued one of the most recent organizing schemes that might be useful for designing measures of the physical environment. It includes ideas about affordances in the environment, complexity, diversity, regularity, and intensity of environmental inputs. Incorporation of all Wohlwill's ideas into a single measure would require rather extensive observations, but those interested in understanding a child's environment might find the scheme useful.

Environmental Process Measures

Because the number of environmental process measures has increased substantially in the past 25 years, it is not easy to generalize about them. The following brief summary is offered as a way of highlighting some key generalizations about environmental process instruments:

1. Most home environment measures were designed initially for use in research studies. Their value for applied uses like screening, diagnosis, and evaluation is largely unknown.
2. The content of environmental process measures varies widely. Thus, it is not appropriate to presume that the measures are equivalent. Selection of measures for applied uses will be determined by the fit between scale content and the specific needs of the user.

3. Nearly every measure reviewed is limited in terms of the age range for which it is appropriate and there is serious question whether the measures are applicable to sociocultural groups other than those for which they were developed.
4. Items on environmental process measures have been developed using a variety of different theories and bodies of empirical and clinical research. At present there appears to be no one theory that is sufficiently encompassing in breadth and detail to serve as the exclusive base for environmental measures.
5. The factor structure of most environmental process measures has not been well established. Moreover, there generally has been naive application of factor analysis in scale construction.
6. Criterion and construct validity studies for most environmental process measures are limited. And, there has been little effort at cross-validation with different groups or in different settings.
7. The relative merits of using total scores or part scores from environmental process measures has not been evaluated. The decision on which to use will depend partly on the specific uses intended.

There are a number of elaborate theoretical models (e.g., Lerner's "goodness of fit" model) that are rich with potentially useful ideas for creating environmental process measures. Their very richness may make designing useful applied measures a formidable task. But components from these models might well serve as a basis for some successful applied scales.

The HOME Inventory

Perhaps the most widely used home environment measure is the Home Observation for Measurement of the Environment (HOME) Inventory (Caldwell & Bradley, 1984). Currently there are three versions of the inventory. The version designed for use with families of infants and toddlers contains 45 items clustered into six subscales: Parental Responsivity, Acceptance of Child, Organization of the Environment, Play Materials, Parental Involvement with Child, and Variety in Stimulation. The version designed for families with children in early childhood contains 55 items clustered into eight subscales: Learning Materials, Language Stimulation, Physical Environment, Parental Responsivity, Encouragement of Social Maturity, Stimulation of Academic Behavior, Variety of Stimulation, and Physical Punishment. The version for families with children in middle childhood contains 59 items clustered into eight subscales: Parental Responsivity, Encouragement of Maturity, Emotional Climate of the Home, Learning Materials, Provision for Active Stimulation, Family Participation in Developmentally Enriching Experiences, Paternal Involvement, and Physical Environment. Scoring of items is based on a combination of observation and semistructured interview questions. The inventory is administered in the home in the presence of the child, the child's primary caregiver, and whomever else is available during the home visit.

Elardo and Bradley (1981), Bradley (1982), and Bradley and Caldwell (1988) have reviewed nearly 100 studies done with the HOME involving a diversity of samples and an array of different health and development outcomes for children. Thus, there is substantial information on the scale's construct and criterion validity, including studies of its screening efficiency and its use as a summative evaluation instrument.

OTHER MEASURES IN THE FAMILY SYSTEMS DOMAIN

The area of family measurement has grown dramatically over the last two decades. In addition to assessments of the conditions directly impacting on family functioning and assessments of family circumstances and behavior that directly impact the child, other areas of family assessment often are useful when either working with or trying to understand family life and its likely relationship to child development. Although it is not the purpose of this chapter to examine these other areas of family assessment in great detail, brief descriptions of some of the better known and potentially more useful measures are offered to illustrate the rich array of instruments available.

Parenting Stress Index

One of the most widely used measures in the family systems domain is the 120-item Parenting Stress Index (PSI; Abidin, 1983). The test materials state that the PSI was designed to identify parent-child systems under stress and at risk for the development of dysfunctional parenting behaviors or behavior problems in the child involved. Items fall into three broad categories. The child domain consists of 47 items, each rated on a 5-point scale, that deal with issues of adaptability, acceptability, demandingness, mood, distractibility/hyperactivity, and the degree to which the child reinforces the parent. High scores on this scale purportedly make it difficult for the parent to engage in good parenting behavior. The parent domain consists of 54 items, also rated on a 5-point scale. These items deal with depression, attachment, restrictions, sense of competence, social isolation, relationship with spouse, and health. The remaining 19 items are life stress events like those found on other life events measures.

The Parenting Stress Index was designed for use in clinical settings. There is a considerable literature using this instrument that supports its construct validity. The PSI manual contains substantial psychometric and normative information. In general the scale appears reliable. There is limited information at present establishing a link between scores on the PSI and actual parenting behaviors independent of global factors like social status or family configuration. The length of items and the vocabulary contained in them makes using this measure questionable with parents of limited reading ability.

Family Adaptability and Cohesion Evaluation Scales

The Family Adaptability and Cohesion Evaluation Scales (FACES), developed by Olson, Portner, and Bell (1982), has become a classic in the family measurement field. FACES II contains 30 items, reduced from a much longer (111-item) original version. Items also were made shorter and easier to read so that children as young as 12 can respond to them. The scale is designed to be given twice, thus allowing family members (preferably all of them) to describe both how they perceive their family and how they ideally would like to see the family. Member satisfaction with the family system can be judged by comparing these two descriptions (perceived versus ideal).

Responses are charted so that families can be typed in terms of their *cohesion* (disengaged to enmeshed) and *adaptability* (chaotic to rigid). Cutting points on these two dimensions have been established for both adults and adolescents. FACES II has been subjected to numerous psychometric analyses and shows generally good test characteristics. Specifically, it has been shown to discriminate among extreme, mid-range, and balanced families in several clinical problem groups. It was normed on a sample of over 2,000 and has been used in many clinical and empirical studies. FACES III (Olson, Portner, & Lavee, 1987) is a shorter (20-item) version of FACES II.

Olson and his colleagues also have produced a number of other measurement devices for describing family conditions. They include the Quality of Life scale (40 items), with both adult and adolescent versions, the Family Satisfaction Scale (14 items), and the Family Strengths Scale (12 items).

Coping Health Inventory for Parents

The same research group that produced the Family Inventory of Life Events and the Family Inventory of Resources for Management also designed a coping measure for parents: the Coping Health Inventory for Parents (CHIP; McCubbin, Patterson, & Wilson, 1982). The CHIP records what parents find helpful or not helpful to them in the management of family life when one or more of its members is ill or has a medical condition requiring continued medical care. Responses to the 45 items result in scores on three coping patterns: (a) maintaining family integration, cooperation, and an optimistic definition of the situation; (b) maintaining social support, self-esteem, and psychological stability; and (c) understanding the medical situation through communication with other parents. Answers are circled on the actual questionnaire form and a coding column is provided with spaces for the total scores on each of the three coping patterns. Three methods for examining and interpreting scores are given in the test manual, plus separate profiles are provided for mothers and fathers. Psychometric characteristics appear reasonably good.

Family Needs Scale

Dunst, Trivette, and their colleagues (1987, 1988) at the Western Carolina Center, developers of the Family Support Scale and Support Functions Scale, have constructed a series of family measures designed to assist those who work with families with handicapped members. These researchers/clinicians often begin the process of enabling and empowering families by assessing their needs using the 41-item Family Needs Scale (Dunst, Cooper, Weeldreyer, Snyder, & Chase, 1987), which indexes the need for six different types of resources. This scale is quickly and easily completed by respondents or can be read to them if necessary. Psychometric analyses show high internal consistency. The scale has undergone several validity studies and appears to have good scale properties, though it is limited in so far as normative information is concerned. Among other scales developed in this series are the Resource Scale for Teenage Mothers (Dunst, Leet, Vance, & Cooper, 1987), a 31-item scale designed for the specific needs of adolescent mothers, and the Family Resource Scale (Leet & Dunst, 1987).

Practical Considerations for Assessment of Families

Within the neighborhood of educational and psychological measurement, family environment measures are very much the "new kid on the block." The theories needed to support approaches to measurement are, as a rule, in early stages of development. The techniques used to appraise aspects of the family environment have been borrowed from other measurement domains and are in a rapid state of evolution. The technical adequacy of many measures has not been established, and the validity of most measures for given applied and research purposes has yet to be determined. Given these conditions, the "context of measurement" must be managed so as to achieve the maximum level of validity from the information obtained.

Establishing the Proper Climate for Data Collection

In all areas of measurement, the test administrator needs to establish a respectful and businesslike climate. Some amount of rapport building is necessary to accomplish even the most menial of measurements tasks. The practical measurement question is, what must the administrator do to establish the level of rapport needed to ensure valid measurement in a given situation? For most of the types of measures discussed in this chapter, the role of the administrator is *not* like that of a census taker or poll taker. The questions one asks are often about rather sensitive matters: attitudes toward friends and family members, relationships, the perceived impact of major life events, and so forth. Moreover, the items may well require the family member to consider some psychological issues previously given very little serious thought. Candid, thoughtful (i.e., valid) responses to such questions require a relaxed atmosphere as well as trust and credibility between administrator and family member. In essence, the administrator must convey a sense of genuine interest in the respondent and an empathy toward the respondent's situation. At the same time the administrator cannot appear presumptuous about the respondent's feelings or concerns, nor should he or she go beyond the bounds required for objective measurement. This means that it may not always be wise to plunge immediately into a long series of questions on a questionnaire, or to press on with question after question even though the respondent indicates an interest in elaborating on a response or changing the course of the conversation somewhat. It may even be useful to engage in true two-way conversation for awhile—outside the rigid confines of items on a questionnaire—so long as the conversation does not interfere with the respondent's objective reporting and the administrator does not imply some service to follow that, in fact, cannot be delivered. It means that one must listen to what the respondent is conveying and not just collect answers to items on a questionnaire.

Length of Test Instruments and Home Visits

There is an acronym often used in planning research studies that appears equally applicable in planning valid measurement protocols: KISS (Keep it simple, stupid!). The point is, don't require anything more from the respondent than is necessary to get the information considered critical from the standpoint of the service or study. It is common, especially in research studies, for persons to include extra measures or more comprehensive measures than are strictly needed for purposes of the study (i.e., there is a concern that one might possibly need the information at a later time). Some of the measures described previously are rich in the breadth and detail of information they provide. But, if one has no predetermined need for such breadth and detail, it may be better to choose a less time-consuming measure. In both clinical settings and research studies, one often is trying to get a variety of different types of measures from a family. The more types of information one needs to get from a respondent, the more problematic become time-consuming individual measures. Fatigue, respondent inattentiveness, and the like pose serious threats to the validity of measurement. In sum, the cost of gathering more information may be less accuracy in the information obtained about critical issues.

Content, Format, and Style of Measurement

It is accepted as axiomatic in the field of measurement that measures are not valid per se but rather only for certain purposes. A corollary to this proposition is that measures are valid only insofar as they are used appropriately in a given instance. For this reason, the content, the format, and the style of measurement may go a long way to determining the validity of the measure when it is used with a particular person at a particular time. To estimate the validity of a specific measure for a given audience, one must first know the audience. Will the items on the measure be clear and comprehensible? Will the directions be clear and easy to follow? The length of items on some of the measures described above, the level of vocabulary contained in the items, the complexity of directions for completing the measure, and so on may well be beyond the capabilities of persons without a 10th-grade or better reading ability. Many of the scales developed by Dunst and his colleagues at the Western Carolina Center and by McCubbin and his colleagues in the Family Social Services center at the University of Minnesota provide excellent illustrations of clear, simple items and easy-to-follow directions.

A related issue is *relevance*. Many of the measures in the family environment domain were designed by middle class professionals with middle class orientations. What they consider important sources of family support may be largely irrelevant to families living in certain economic conditions or from certain cultural backgrounds. Similarly, things considered stressful to many middle class families may not even be an issue for some poor families or single-parent families. Some types of support or stress may be so far removed from a family's everyday experiences that they simply aren't salient aspects of their consciousness. In their excellent approach to enabling and empowering families, Dunst and his colleagues start with the premise that success with the families begins by coming to understand their particular needs and concerns, not by presuming that supports and stresses are universal. From the standpoint of measurement, this may mean that one should field test any instrument being considered for use on the type of families one intends to use it with. The present authors have been embarrassed more than once by a family member snickering at an item. Asked to explain their reaction, they replied in essence that the question was "dumb!" Examples of some scales that have attempted to target a specific audience by addressing relevant questions are the Junior High Life Experiences Survey (Swearingen & Cohen, 1985), the Resource Scale for Teenage Mothers (Dunst, Leet, Vance, & Cooper, 1987), and FACES II.

Another component of items that often helps the respondent to provide a more meaningful response is whether a timeframe for the event or action under question is specified. Although many life events measures do identify a timeframe for the respondent (e.g., the last 6 months, or last year), most social support and coping measures do not. It is often difficult for respondents to reflect back on the salience of an event that happened many years prior. They even may have difficulty either recalling the event accurately or their reaction to it. Finally, it simply may confuse respondents as to whether the item refers to now, the recent past, or to their whole lifetime. Scales developed by McCubbin, by Barerra, by Dunst, and some others specify a timeframe for respondents, thus making it easier to obtain a consistent response.

In scales with closed item formats, the number and types of choices a respondent can make impacts on both their comfort in responding and the validity of the response. The yes/no choices on life events measures seem to present few problems to most respondents; a particular life event either did or did not occur. However, the same yes/no choice often seems inappropriate to respondents on a social support or coping type measure, which more often describe the *frequency* of actions. If a particular action occurred sometimes but not others, how should a person respond? The simple yes/no choice itself becomes ambiguous and thus so does the response (does it mean "Yes, most of the time" or "Yes, always"?). Greater comfort and greater validity are probably obtained with items that allow three or more choices (e.g., Olson's Quality of Life scale). By contrast, if the respondent has limited cognitive capabilities, too many choices make the task of responding too difficult. The result may be to ignore certain options, to respond without giving due consideration to the item, or simply not to respond.

Scoring

A final area of practical concern in the family environments domain relates to scoring. Many of the measures reviewed did not provide clear directions for scoring; and the large majority provided little information on how scores should be used or interpreted. As a rule, the procedures for scoring life events scales were clear. But, even these measures generally lacked information on interpreting the scores. The implication for most measures seemed to be that clinical judgment could be used in interpreting scores, but the guidance needed to execute such judgment was not provided. This lack may be especially critical in the social support domain. Does family member X have enough support? A surplus? Is there a risk due to too little support? Should some action be taken? The decision maker finds little information with which to make such judgments.

The measurement of the family environment is an exciting new arena for both researchers and practitioners in education, health, and human services. Many useful measures already have appeared and some have become part of the fabric of everyday professional practice. They have changed our understanding of human development and have helped shape new kinds of research models and clinical practices. The theories to which these measures are wedded persist in a rapid state of growth.

The arena of family measurement also presents a challenge. Many technical problems in these measures remain to be fully resolved, and the information base needed to make scores interpretable for those working with families is not now sufficient. Nonetheless, family measures are now firmly part of the scene. As theory, research, practice, and measurement in this area continue to grow and enhance one another, family measures will become an ever larger and more important part of the process of assessing young children.

REFERENCES

Abidin, R.R. (1983). *Parenting Stress Index.* Charlottesville, VA: Pediatric Psychology Press.
Altman, I., & Wohlwill, J. (Eds.). (1978). *Children and the environment.* New York: Plenum.
Barker, R., & Wright, H. (1954). *Midwest and its children.* Evanston, IL: Ron Peterson.
Barrera, M. (1981). *Notes on the ISSB.* Unpublished manuscript, Arizona State University, Department of Psychology, Tempe.
Barrera, M. (1983a). *Arizona Social Support Interview Schedule.* Unpublished manuscript, Arizona State University, Department of Psychology, Tempe.
Barrera, M. (1983b). *Notes on deriving network indices from the ASSIS.* Unpublished manuscript, Arizona State University, Department of Psychology, Tempe.
Barrera, M. (1986). Distinctions between social support concepts, measures and models. *American Journal of Community Psychology, 14*(4), 413–445.
Baumrind, D. (1978). Parental disciplinary patterns and social competence in children. *Youth and Society, 9,* 239–276.
Baumrind, D., & Black, A. (1967). Socialization practices associated with dimensions of competence in preschool boys and girls. *Child Development, 38,* 291–327.
Bayley, N., & Schaefer, E. (1964). Correlations of maternal and child behaviors with the development of mental abilities: Data from the Berkeley Growth Study. *Monographs of the Society for Research in Child Development, 29*(Whole No. 6).
Belle, D. (1982). *Life Events Measure: Stressors and Stress.* Cambridge, MA: Deborah Belle Stress and Families Project, Harvard University Graduate School of Education.
Belsky, J. (1983). The determinants of parenting: A process model. *Child Development, 55,* 83–96.
Bloom, B. (1964). *Stability and change in human characteristics.* New York: Wiley.
Bloom, B., Hastings, J., & Maudaus, G. (1971). *Handbook on formative and summative evaluation of student learning.* New York: McGraw-Hill.
Bowlby, J. (1969). *Attachment and loss: Vol. 1. Attachment.* New York: Basic Books.
Bradley, R. (1982). The HOME Inventory: A review of the first 15 years. In W. Frankenburg, N. Anastasiow, & A. Fandal (Eds.), *Identifying the developmentally delayed child.* Baltimore: University Park Press.
Bradley, R. (1986a). Assessing the family environment of young children. In H. Fitzgerald, B. Lester, & M. Yogman (Eds.), *Theory and research in behavioral pediatrics* (Vol. III, pp. 47–105). New York: Plenum.
Bradley, R. (1986b). Play materials and intellectual development. In A. Gottfried & C. Brown (Eds.), *Play interactions* (pp. 227–252). Lexington, MA: Lexington Books.
Bradley, R., & Caldwell, B. (1976). Early home environment and changes in mental test performance in children from six to thirty-six months. *Developmental Psychology, 12,* 93–97.
Bradley, R., & Caldwell, B. (1977). Home Observation for Measurement of the Environment: A validation study of screening efficiency. *American Journal of Mental Deficiency, 81,* 417–420.

Bradley, R., & Caldwell, B. (1978). Screening the environment. *American Journal of Orthopsychiatry, 48*, 114–130.

Bradley, R., & Caldwell, B. (1987). Early environment and cognitive competence: The Little Rock study. *Early Child Development and Care, 27,* 307–341.

Bradley, R., & Caldwell, B. (1988). Using the HOME Inventory to assess the family environment. *Pediatric Nursing, 14*(2), 97–102.

Bradley, R., Caldwell, B., & Rock, S. (1988). Home environment and school performance: A ten-year follow-up and examination of three models of environmental action. *Child Development, 59*, 852–867.

Bradley, R., Caldwell, B., Rock, S., Casey, P., & Nelson, J. (1987). The early development of low-birthweight infants: Relationship to health, family status, family context, family processes, and parenting. *International Journal of Behavioral Development, 10*(3), 301–318.

Bradley, R., Casey, P., & Wortham, B. (1984). Home environments of low SES non-organic failure-to-thrive infants. *Merrill-Palmer Quarterly, 30*(4), 393–402.

Bradley, R., & Tedesco, L. (1982). Environmental correlates of mental retardation. In J. Lachenmeyer & M. Gibbs (Eds.), *The psychology of the abnormal child* (pp. 155–188). New York: Gardner.

Bromwich, R. (1976). Focus on maternal behavior in intervention. *American Journal of Orthopsychiatry, 46,* 439–446.

Bronfenbrenner, U. (1979). *The ecology of human development.* Cambridge: Harvard University Press.

Bruhn, J., & Philips, B. (1984). Measuring social support: A synthesis of current approaches. *Journal of Behavioral Medicine, 7*(2), 151–169.

Caldwell, B. (1968). On designing supplementary environments for early child development. *BAEYC Reports, 10,* 1–11.

Caldwell, B., & Bradley, R. (1984). *Home Observation for Measurement of the Environment.* Little Rock: University of Arkansas at Little Rock.

Clarke-Stewart, A. (1973). Interactions between mothers and their young children: Characteristics and consequences. *Monographs of the Society for Research in Child Development, 38*(Whole Nos. 6–7).

Clarke, A.M., & Clarke, A.D. (1976). *Early experience: Myth and evidence.* New York: Free Press.

Coddington, R.D. (1972). The significance of life events as etiologic factors in the diseases of children–II: A study of a normal population. *Journal of Psychosomatic Research, 16,* 205–213.

Cohen, S., & Wills, T. (1985). Stress, social support, and the buffering hypothesis. *Psychological Bulletin, 98*(2), 310–357.

Cravioto, J., & DeLicardie, E. (1972). Environmental correlates of severe clinical malnutrition and language development in survivors of Kwashiorkor or Marasmus. In *Nutrition: The nervous system and behavior* (Scientific Publication No. 251, pp. 73–94). Washington, DC: Pan-American Health Organization.

Davé, R. (1963). *The identification and measurement of environmental process variables that are related to educational achievement.* Unpublished doctoral dissertation, University of Chicago.

Dean, A., & Linn, N. (1977). The stress-buffering role of social support. *Journal of Nervous and Mental Disease, 165,* 403–417.

Dennis, W. (1973). *Children of the creche.* New York: Appleton-Century-Crofts.

Dohrenwend, B.S., Krasnoff, L., Askenasy, A., & Dohrenwend, B.P. (1978). Exemplification of a method for scaling life events: The PERI Life Events Scale. *Journal of Health and Social Behavior, 19,* 205–229.

Dohrenwend, B., & Shrout, P. (1985). "Hassles" in the conceptualization and measurement of life stress variables. *American Psychologist, 40*(7), 780–785.

Drillien, C. (1964). *The growth and development of the prematurely born infant.* Baltimore, MD: Williams & Wilkins.

Dunst, C., Cooper, C., Weeldreyer, J., Snyder, K., & Chase, J. (1987). Family Needs Scale. In C.J. Dunst, C.M. Trivette, & A.G. Deal, (Eds.), *Enabling and empowering families: Principles and guidelines for practice* (pp. 193–195). Cambridge, MA: Brookline Books.

Dunst, C.J., Leet, H.E., Vance S.D., & Cooper, C.S. (1987). Resource Scale for Teenage Mothers. In C.J. Dunst, C.M. Trivette, & A.G. Deal, *Enabling and empowering families: Principles and guidelines for practice* (pp. 145–146). Cambridge, MA: Brookline Books.

Dunst, C., & Trivette, C. (1987). Support Functions Scale. In C.J. Dunst, C.M. Trivette, & A.G. Deal (Eds.), *Enabling and empowering families: Principles and guidelines for practice* (pp. 152–158). Cambridge, MA: Brookline Books.

Dunst, C., & Trivette, C. (1988). Assessment of family and community support. In S. Meisels & J. Shonkoff (Eds.), *The handbook of early intervention* (pp. 326–349). New York: Cambridge University Press.

Dunst, C.J., Trivette, C.M., & Jenkins, V. (1987). Family Support Scale. In C.J. Dunst, C.M. Trivette, & A.G. Deal, *Enabling and empowering families: Principles and guidelines for practice* (pp. 196–199). Cambridge, MA: Brookline Books.

Egeland, B., Breitenbucker, M., Dodds, M., Pastor, D., & Rosenberg D. (1979). *Life Stress Scale and scoring manual.* Minneapolis, MN: University of Minnesota, Mother-Child Research Project.

Egeland, B., & Sroufe, A. (1981). Developmental sequelae of maltreatment in infancy. In T. Ridly & D. Cicchetti (Eds.), *Developmental perspectives on child maltreatment.* San Francisco: Jossey-Boss.

Elardo, R., & Bradley, R. (1981). The Home Observation for Measurement of the Environment: A review of research. *Developmental Review, 1,* 113–145.

Elardo, R., Bradley, R., & Caldwell, B. (1975). The relation of infants' home environments to mental test performance from six to thirty-six months: A longitudinal analysis. *Child Development, 46,* 71–76.

Elardo, R., Bradley, R., & Caldwell, B. (1977). A longitudinal study of the relation of infants' home environments to their language development at age three. *Child Development, 48,* 595–603.

Engel, M., & Keane, W. (1975, April). *Black mothers and their infant sons: Antecedents, correlates, and predictors of cognitive development in the second and sixth year of life.* Paper presented at the Biennial Meeting of the Society for Research in Child Development, Denver, Colorado.

Gordon, I. (1974). *An investigation into the social roots of competence: Final report to the National Institute of Mental Health.* Unpublished manuscript, University of Florida, Gainsville.

Gottfried, A. (1986). Intrinsic motivational aspects of play experiences and materials. In A. Gottfried & C. Brown (Eds.), *Play interactions* (pp. 81–100). Lexington, MA: D.C. Heath.

Haggerty, R. (1980). Life stress, illness and social supports. *Developmental Medicine and Child Neurology, 22,* 391–400.

Hanson, R. (1975). Consistency and stability of home environmental measures related to IQ. *Child Development, 46,* 470–480.

Henderson, R., Bergan, J., & Hurt, M. (1972). Development and validation of the Henderson Environmental Learning Process Scale. *Journal of Social Psychology, 88,* 185–196.

Henderson, S., Byrne, D., & Duncan-Jones, P. (1981). *Neurosis and the social environment.* Sydney, Australia: Academic Press.

Holmes, T.H., & Rahe, R.H. (1967). The Social Readjustment Rating Scale. *Journal of Psychosomatic Research, 11,* 213–218.

Hunt, J. (1961). *Intelligence and experience.* New York: Ronald.

Justice, B., & Duncan, D. (1976). Life crisis as a precursor to child abuse. *Public Health Reports, 91,* 110–115.

Kagan, J. (1984). *The nature of the child.* New York: Basic Books.

Kagan, J., & Freeman, M. (1963). Relation of childhood intelligence, maternal behaviors, and social class to behavior during adolescence. *Child Development, 34,* 889–911.

Keeves, J. (1972). *Educational environment and student achievement.* Stockholm, Sweden: Wiksell.

Laing, J., & Sines, J. (1982). The Home Environment Questionnaire: An instrument for assessing several behaviorally relevant dimensions of children's environments. *Journal of Pediatric Psychology, 4,* 425–449.

Leet, H.E., & Dunst, C.J. (1987). Family Resource Scale. In C.J. Dunst, C.M. Trivette, & A.G. Deal (Eds.), *Enabling and empowering families: Principles and guidelines for practice* (pp. 139–141). Cambridge, MA: Brookline Books.

Lerner, R. (1986). *On the nature of human plasticity.* New York: Cambridge University Press.

Marjoribanks, K. (1972). Environment, social class, and mental abilities. *Journal of Educational Psychology, 43,* 103–109.

McCall, R., Appelbaum, M., & Hogarty, P. (1973). Developmental changes in mental performance. *Monographs of the Society for Research in Child Development, 38*(Whole No. 3).

McClelland, D., Atkinson, R., Clark, R., & Lowell, E. (1953). *The achievement motive.* New York: Appleton.

McCubbin, H.I., Patterson, J.M., Bauman, E., & Harris, L.H. (1982). Adolescent-Family inventory of Life Events and Changes (A-FILE). In D.H. Olson, H.I. McCubbin, H. Barnes, A. Larsen, M. Muxen, & M. Wilson, *Family inventories: Inventories used in a national survey of families* (pp. 89–98). St. Paul, MN: University of Minnesota, Family Social Science.

McCubbin, H.I., Patterson, J.M., & Wilson, L.R. (1982). FILE: Family Inventory of Life Events and Changes. In D.H. Olson, H.I. McCubbin, H. Barnes, A. Larsen, M. Muxen, & M. Wilson, *Family inventories: Inventories used in a national survey of families* (pp. 80–88). St. Paul, MN: University of Minnesota, Family Social Science.

Moore, T. (1968). Language and intelligence: A longitudinal study of the first eight years. Part II: Environmental correlates of mental growth. *Human Development, 11,* 1–24.

Moos, R. (1974). *Family Environment Scale: Preliminary manual.* Palo Alto: Consulting Psychologists Press.

Murray, H. (1938). *Exploration in personality.* New York: Oxford University Press.

Newcomb, M., Huba, G., & Bentler, P. (1981). A multidimensional assessment of stressful life events among adolescents: Derivation and correlates. *Journal of Health and Social Behavior, 22,* 400–415.

Norbeck, J.S. (1980/1982). *Social Support Questionnaire.* San Francisco: Author.

Norbeck, J.S. (1984). Modification of Life Event Questionnaires for use with female respondents. *Research in Nursing and Health, 7,* 61–71.

Norbeck, J.S., Lindsey, A.M., & Carrieri, V.L. (1982). The development of an instrument to measure social support. *Nursing Research, 30*(5), 264–269.

Norbeck, J.E., Lindsey, A.M., & Carrieri, V.L. (1983). Further development of the Norbeck Social Support Questionnaire: Normative data and validity testing. *Nursing Research, 32*(1), 4–9.

Olson, D.H., Portner, J., & Bell, R. (1982). FACES II: Family Adaptability & Cohesion Evaluation Scales. In D.H. Olson, H.I. McCubbin, H. Barnes, A. Larsen, M. Muxen, & M. Wilson, *Family inventories: Inventories used in a national survey of families* (pp. 5–27). St. Paul, MN: University of Minnesota, Family Social Science.

Olson, D.H., Portner, J., & Lavee, Y. (1987). Family Adaptability and Cohesion Evaluation Scale (FACES-III). In K. Cocoran & J. Fischer (Eds.), *Measures for clinical practice: A source book*. New York: Free Press.

Oritt, E.J., & Paul, S.C. (1985). The Perceived Support Network Inventory. *American Journal of Community Psychology, 13*(5), 565–581.

Parke, R. (1978). Children's home environments: Social and cognitive effects. In I. Altman & J. Wohlwill (Eds.), *Children and the environment*. New York: Plenum.

Pascoe, J.M., Loda, F.A., Jeffries, V., & Earp, J. (1981). The association between mothers' social support and provision of stimulation to their children. *Developmental and Behavioral Pediatrics, 2*(1), 15–19.

Pearlin, L.I., & Lieberman, M.A. (1979). Social sources of emotional distress. In R.G. Simmons (Ed.), *Research in community and mental health* (Vol. 1, pp. 217–243). Greenwich, CT: JAI.

Procidano, M.E., & Heller, K. (1983). Measures of perceived social support from friends and from family: Three validation studies. *American Journal of Community Psychology, 11*(1), 1–24.

Radin, N. (1971). Maternal warmth, achievement motivation, and cognitive functioning in lower class preschool children. *Child Development, 42*, 1560–1565.

Ramey, C., MacPhee, D., & Yeates, K. (1982). Preventing developmental retardation: A general systems model. In L. Bonds & J. Joffe (Eds.), *Facilitating infant and early childhood development*. Hanover, NH: University Press of New England.

Riccuiti, H., & Dorman, R. (1981, October). *Interaction of multiple-risk factors contributing to high-risk parenting*. Paper presented at the Johnson & Johnson Pediatric Roundtable on High-Risk Parenting, Key Biscayne, FL.

Rohner, R. (1986). *The warmth dimension: Foundations of parental acceptance-rejection theory*. Beverly Hills, CA: Sage.

Sameroff, A., & Chandler, M. (1975). Reproductive risk and the continuum of caretaking casualty. In R. Horowitz, M. Hetherington, S. Scarr-Salapatek, & G. Siegel (Eds.), *Review of child development research* (Vol. 4, pp. 187–244). Chicago: University of Chicago Press.

Sarason, I.G., Johnson, J.H., & Siegel, J.M. (1978). Assessing the impact of life changes: Development of the Life Experiences Survey. *Journal of Consulting and Clinical Psychology, 46*(5), 932–946.

Sarason, I.G., Levine, H.M., Basham, R.B., & Sarason, B.R. (1983). Assessing social support: The Social Support Questionnaire. *Journal of Personality and Social Psychology, 44*(1), 127–139.

Skeels, H., & Dye, H. (1939). A study of the effects of differential stimulation on mentally retarded children. *Proceedings of the American Association on Mental Deficiency, 44*, 114–136.

Stangler, S., Huber, C., & Routh, D. (1980). *Screening growth and development of preschool children: A guide for test selection*. New York: McGraw-Hill.

Steinberg, L. (1986). Latchkey children and susceptibility to peer pressure: An ecological analysis. *Developmental Psychology, 22*, 433–439.

Swearingen, E., & Cohen, L. (1985). Measurement of adolescents' life events: The Junior High Life Experiences Survey. *American Journal of Community Psychology, 13*(1), 69–85.

Tardy, C. (1985). Social support measurement. *American Journal of Community Psychology, 13*(2), 187–202.
Trivette, C., & Dunst, C. (1987a). Inventory of Social Support. In C.J. Dunst, C.M. Trivette, & A.G. Deal (Eds.), *Enabling and empowering families: Principles and guidelines for practice.* Cambridge, MA: Brookline Books.
Trivette, C., & Dunst, C. (1987b). Personal Network Matrix. In C.J. Dunst, C.M. Trivette, & A.G. Deal (Eds.), *Enabling and empowering families: Principles and guidelines for practice.* Cambridge, MA: Brookline Books.
Tulkin, S., & Covitz, F. (1975). *Mother-infant interaction and intellectual functioning at age six.* Paper presented at the Biennial Meeting of the Society for Research in Child Development, Denver, CO.
Vaux, A., Phillips, J., Holly, L., Thomson, B., Williams, D., & Stewart, D. (1986). The Social Support Appraisals (SS-A) Scale: Studies of reliability and validity. *American Journal of Community Psychology, 14*(2), 195–219.
Vaux, A., Riedel, S., & Stewart, D. (1987). Modes of social support: The Social Support Behaviors (SS-B) Scale. *American Journal of Community Psychology, 15*(2), 209–237.
Vygotsky, L. (1978). *Mind in society: The development of higher psychological processes* (trans. by M. Cole, V. John-Steiner, S. Scribner, & E. Souberman). Cambridge, MA: Harvard University Press.
Wachs, T. (1976). Utilization of a Piagetian approach in the investigation of early experience effects: A research strategy and some illustrative data. *Merrill-Palmer Quarterly, 22,* 11–29.
Wachs, T. (1978). The relationship of infants' physical environment to their Binet performance at 2½ years. *International Journal of Behavioral Development, 1,* 51–65.
Wachs, T., & Gruen, G. (1982). *Early experience and human development.* New York: Plenum.
Wachs, T., Uzgiris, I., & Hunt, J. (1971). Cognitive development in infants from different age levels and different environmental backgrounds: An explanatory investigation. *Merrill-Palmer Quarterly, 17,* 283–317.
Werner, E., Bierman, J., & French F. (1971). *The children of Kauai.* Honolulu, HI: University of Hawaii Press.
Werner, E., & Smith, R. (1982). *Vulnerable but invincible: A study of resilient children.* New York: McGraw-Hill.
White, B., & Watts, J. (1973). *Experience and environment.* Englewood Cliffs, NJ: Prentice-Hall.
Wohlwill, J. (1983). The concept of nature: A psychologist's view. In I. Altman & J. Wohlwill (Eds.), *Behavior and the natural environment.* New York: Plenum.
Wolf, R. (1965). The measurement of environments. In A. Anastasi (Ed.), *Testing problems in perspective.* Princeton, NJ: Educational Testing Service.
Wulbert, M., Inglis, S., Kriegsman, E., & Mills, B. (1975). Language delay and associated mother-child interactions. *Developmental Psychology, 2,* 61–70.
Yarrow, L., Rubenstein, J., & Pederson, F. (1975). *Infant and environment.* Washington, DC: Hemisphere.
Yeaworth, R., York, J., Hussey, M., Ingle, M., & Goodwin, T. (1980). The development of an adolescent life change event scale. *Adolescence, 15*(57), 91–97.

8

Assessment of Learning and Cognitive Dysfunction in Young Children

MARGARET SEMRUD-CLIKEMAN, PH.D. &
GEORGE W. HYND, ED.D.

The assessment of young children ages 3 to 6 is fraught with potential pitfalls. These difficulties are exacerbated when evaluating children with suspected exceptional educational needs. The assessment of preschool children requires a working knowledge of behaviors and cognitive skills appropriate for certain developmental levels. This knowledge cannot be obtained informally. Rather, it is essential that the examiner have direct experience with children of various ages because some behaviors that would be pathological in older children are normal for younger ones. Development during this period of childhood is often fast and uneven.

Young children progress by means of an internal "biological-developmental clock," whereby developmental tasks are completed within a broad frame of reference, each building on past experience. Piaget's concept of assimilation/accommodation appears to be particularly apt here. The child will absorb and transform environmental information within the framework that is individually appropriate, plus assimilate information that is relevant for his or her current stage of development. Therefore, developmental profiles may be radically different between children and yet be essentially normal. The purpose of psychoeducational assessment of preschool children is to determine how far from the norm the child may be and if this difference is aberrant or within normal limits.

Given the wide variability of normal development, one readily can see the difficulties for accurate assessment that arise when preschool children with possible mental retardation or the precursors to learning disabilities are referred for evaluation to clinical and school specialists. Because it is inadvisable to utilize a preschool IQ measure for diagnostic predictions of future academic performance (Telzrow, 1984), the assessment should be multimodal and include measures of different areas of development. This chapter will seek to (a) identify the many variables that can impinge on assessment of preschool children, (b) delineate differences between developmental delay, mental retardation, and the precursors of learning disability as opposed to normal development, (c) provide an overview of often-used assessment instruments, and (d) provide suggestions of workable assessment guidelines for practitioners.

Definitions

Developmental Delay and Mental Retardation

The terms *developmental delay* and *mental retardation* often are used interchangeably and, as such, frequently are confusing to both parents and teachers. The American Association on Mental Deficiency (AAMD) defines mental retardation as "significantly subaverage general intellectual functioning existing concurrently with deficits in adaptive behavior, and manifested during the developmental period" (Grossman, 1983, p. 11). There are four categories of mental retardation in this classification—mild, moderate, severe, and profound. The majority of cases fall into the mild category, followed by moderate, severe, and profound (Sattler, 1988).

As Sloan and Birch (1955) suggest that the mild level of classification is generally not distinguished before school age, it is reasonable to understand the propensity for using the term *developmental delay* with possibly mentally retarded preschoolers. Fotheringham (1983) suggests that for those preschoolers who perform in the mild mentally retarded range, the diagnosis of developmental delay may be more appropriate for two reasons. First, even though the behaviors are indicative of retardation, the child may be too young for a definitive diagnosis and, consequently, should be followed over time to chart developmental progress. Second, other disorders (e.g., delayed speech and language skills, cerebral palsy, environmental deprivation, seizures) may adversely affect test results.

Given the physical and intellectual growth spurts often seen in very young children, it would be unfortunate to identify them prematurely as mildly mentally handicapped, particularly as such labels can have potentially harmful effects (Lerner, Mardell-Czudnowski, & Goldenberg, 1981). Fotheringham (1983) suggests that developmental delay is a more tentative diagnosis that allows for learning disorders, poor environmental situations, or a host of other conditions. Continued evaluation, including observations and parent-teacher interviews, may allow the practitioner to arrive at an appropriate final diagnosis.

A case example will help illustrate this point. A 3-year-old child brought into a school system for evaluation scored 2 standard deviations below age level on cognitive, speech/language, gross motor, visual-perceptual, and adaptive behavior measures. The multidisciplinary team arrived at a tentative diagnosis of speech/language delay coupled with overall developmental lags. The boy consequently was enrolled in an early childhood–exceptional education program that provided speech/language services and occupational and physical therapy. The school psychologist consulted frequently with the teacher and parents. After 3 months of intensive intervention and observation, it was found that the child not only had frequent occurrences of wax buildup in his ears (thus attenuating hearing and subsequent auditory processing), but he possibly also was experiencing petit mal seizures. Referral to an otolaryngologist confirmed the need for tubes, and a neurologist prescribed seizure medication. Following these medical interventions, the child made good progress and eventually was dismissed from special education services.

Although an extreme case, the preceding is representative of the numerous variables that can impinge significantly on a preschooler's performance. In children with more significant retardation, diagnostic assessment is not as difficult, and more medical complications are typically present. Particularly when confronting children with mild mental handicaps, the evaluator must be cognizant of possible effects of environmental, familial, and/or medical interactions.

Learning Disability

Public Law 94-142 defines *learning disability* as "a disorder in one or more of the basic psychological processes involved in understanding or in using language, spoken or written, which may manifest itself in an imperfect ability to listen, think, speak, read, write, spell, or to do mathematical calculations" (*Federal Register,* 1977, p. 65083). These guidelines also require a significant discrepancy between achievement and ability in one or more skill areas. In considering this definition, one cannot help but notice that the emphasis on academic achievement makes this definition very difficult to apply to preschool children. How does one differentiate achievement at this level with the attainment of cognitive/developmental skills?

Academic underachievement has often been defined as a discrepancy between a child's achievement test results and his or her ability or aptitude. But this is clearly not appropriate for preschool children; they have not been in school and have not been exposed to formal academic tasks. Boehm and Sandberg (1982) suggest that the intent of PL 94-142 is to identify children with potential learning problems as "at risk" and to develop appropriate interventions for them. Significant difficulties with visual-motor tasks, auditory comprehension, and listening skills, as well as inefficient problem-solving and reasoning skills, have been suggested as possible precursors to future reading problems (Torgesen, 1981). The adept clinician will investigate these areas with children referred for possible learning problems.

Preschool children who are referred for learning disability evaluations generally fall into one of two groups—language/auditory delays or visual-spatial-motor delays. Given the fact that preschoolers present at a preacademic stage of development, the referral question often involves either an inability to learn colors, numbers, the letters in their name, and so forth, or, as in the case of motor development problems, difficulty in copying simple shapes or writing their name, motor clumsiness, or any combination thereof.

Assessment Issues

It is important for the practitioner to recognize the assessment issues that may negatively impact a young child's performance. Preschoolers represent a special population, and, as is well documented (Sattler, 1988), both examiner and child variables can affect their performance.

Examiner Characteristics

From the start the examiner must be sensitive to a child's reactions to the testing situation itself. Even the initial approach can affect subsequent performance. Experience in clinical practice suggests it is wise to approach the child slowly and to modulate the distance as he or she shows willingness to establish eye contact. In addition, it is helpful to bend down to the child's eye level rather than literally "talking down" to him or her.

If the child does not have a choice about coming with the examiner, he or she should not be offered one. As statements such as "Do you want to come with me to play a game?" can be thus misleading, it is far better to say something like "We are going now to play some games." If the child resists coming, allow the parent to accompany him or her for the beginning of the assessment. Often children become absorbed in the task and the parent is able to leave. However, examiners should not be averse to allowing the parent to remain if this is necessary to ensure appropriate cooperation. Of course, these behaviors should be noted in the protocol. At times it is helpful to have the father bring the child, particularly if separation from the mother has been an issue in the past.

A related examiner variable is the need to be conversant with expectations for various developmental levels. Children commonly show normal variations in different areas of development. Toward this end it can be very helpful for the beginning practitioner to spend time in a day-care or preschool setting, actively participating with the children, in order to appreciate the wide variations of "normal" behavior at this age. Along the same lines, inexperienced examiners can become so interested in a child's performance that the process he or she has used to attain the outcome is ignored. Yet determining the child's learning and/or information-processing style can be very important, particularly for an assessment to help suggest possible remedial needs.

The examiner must be very familiar with the assessment instruments he or she intends to use, a point that may well seem self-evident. However, if the examiner is searching for materials or busy reviewing the manual, it will become extremely hard to maintain rapport with the preschool child. Moreover, anyone who has ever tested children in this age group knows how flexible and creative one must be in order to elicit responses. For example, a child who is shy often may not answer questions. Sometimes the use of puppets or modeling may help produce answers from otherwise recalcitrant children. Then, too, stickers, Cheerios, or a walk can serve as powerful reinforcers for attempting difficult tasks. When making decisions about critical issues such as possible mental retardation or learning difficulties, it is imperative to elicit the child's best performance on these tasks.

Child Characteristics

When assessing the preschool child, it is important to be an adept observer. General appearance, for example, can provide invaluable information; children who come to the assessment dirty, tired, or complaining of hunger may indicate possible home problems. Separation of the child from his or her parents offers another good opportunity for observation. Overly dependent or clingy behaviors may signify immaturity, lack of confidence, or other potential problems.

Observed attention span presents a significant variable in determining a child's readiness for learning and/or ability to respond. Obviously a child who cannot attend to stimuli for any length of time may well have difficulty integrating environmental information and/or performing on assessment instruments; thus an extremely short attention span that goes unnoticed can seriously affect test results and lead to inappropriate conclusions. Examining such a child is best performed in short periods, with much reinforcement to alleviate the effects of short attention span on test results.

A child that the present authors evaluated provides an example of this approach. This young child was unable to focus on any task for more than 30 seconds. She already was on Ritalin (a stimulant), plus additional medication for seizures. We found that changing tasks quickly, providing frequent breaks, and testing her over several sessions not lasting more than 10 minutes resulted in more accurate results. This child had been tested previously in another clinic, obtaining a General Cognitive Index of 75 on the McCarthy Scales of Children's Abilities (McCarthy, 1972). In the school setting, where the above procedures were followed, she achieved a score of 121 on the same test. Such an improvement offers a provocative illustration of the interaction of child and examiner variables.

A child's speech and language presents another variable that can affect performance dramatically. It is obviously poor practice to test a child with a speech and/or language delay on a heavily verbal measure and believe that this score reflects that child's cognitive development adequately. The assessment instead should include measures from all domains. At times, measures that require little verbalization and/or auditory comprehension (i.e., Columbia Mental Maturity Scale, Burgemeister, Blum, & Lorge, 1972; Leiter International Performance Scale, Leiter, 1948; Pictorial Test of Intelligence, French, 1964) should be considered. Unfortunately, many of these tests must be supplemented, as they are either outdated or poorly normed. However, they can provide observational information and point to other domains that can be assessed independently.

A final variable to consider is the child's affect. Is he or she withdrawn, anxious, or shy? Children who are overly friendly also should be noted. In addition, the parent's affect may be informative. A very talkative, anxious, or withdrawn parent can influence, in turn, the child's approach to the assessment process. Likewise, a parent who accepts the assessment as normal may well have a child who is very cooperative and relaxed. If necessary the clinician should feel free to set another appointment time to discuss the evaluation process with the parent, particularly as to what information the evaluation can or cannot provide. As will be discussed in the next section, a preassessment interview often can partially alleviate the normal anxiety a parent feels.

One can readily see that both examiner and child characteristics interact during any assessment process. It is important to control this interaction so that the information derived from the evaluation reflects the child's ability, not just the situation. Preschool children are rewarding to work with and generally open and friendly once they acclimate themselves to the situation. It is the responsibility of the examiner to make the assessment process as free from anxiety or negative experience as possible.

The Assessment Process

Psychoeducational assessment should be thought of as a process rather than a product. Through this process the clinician tests hypotheses as to the underpinnings of the child's current functioning. The goal of the assessment is not to arrive at a series of numbers, but rather to provide insight into the child's learning processes. Applying a hypothesis-testing approach is most apt for preschoolers, particularly because their development is in a very dynamic state and no one battery can anticipate all developmental variations. Through the judicious use of various assessment and interview techniques, the clinician can arrive at suggestions for appropriate interventions.

As most preschoolers are not in a standardized school setting, parents are most often the referral sources, but referrals also may originate with preschool and/or daycare teachers, observant pediatricians, or close relatives. When initially receiving a referral from a concerned parent, it is critical to obtain an in-depth interview. Information regarding the course of pregnancy and delivery, age of mastery of early developmental milestones, illnesses and/or head injuries, school experiences, and family composition become important areas of investigation. A suggested interview format is provided in the appendix to this chapter.

Parents frequently also need reassurance. They may harbor considerable concern, particularly if the child is the oldest in the family, that something is drastically wrong. Moreover, parents often blame themselves for all the problems the child is experiencing. It has been found helpful to provide information about both normal development and what developmental delays mean for the child and the family. If the parents' cooperation can be enlisted, the evaluation process goes much more smoothly and is likely to produce more accurate results.

The second step in any evaluation should be an observation of the child in some customary setting. Day care or nursery school offer a chance to see the child in a structured work time, play time, and snack, but in the case of a child who does not attend either situation, fruitful observations can be carried out at home, in Sunday school, or on a playground. Obviously this step involves more time than some evaluators may choose or be allowed to spend. However, invaluable information, such as a child's ability to relate in a small group, take turns, interact, react to frustration, and demonstrate independent skills, can be lost if such observations are not part of the evaluation.

By setting the scene with the significant adult, the examiner can observe how the child solves problems and deals with novel situations in a familiar environment. Moreover, as the adult can provide much useful information, in the event that interventions are recommended consultation already has begun. Often, too, the teacher or parent thereby feels more a part of the evaluation, with the result that interventions more likely are arrived at and carried out jointly. As PL 94–142 states, previous interventions must be attempted prior to consideration for special education services. Observations and consultation can document attempts at remediation prior to enrollment in special education programs.

Selecting the Battery

The next step in the evaluation process is to select a battery of tests and begin the formal assessment. Table 8.1 presents many options open to the examiner evaluating young children for learning and cognitive dysfunction. The use of a consistent battery presupposes that each child shows the same difficulties and thus each should be examined in the same fashion. Experience and common sense, though, argue that this is just not the case. For some children one measure of visual-motor skills may be sufficient, while for others it may be important to delineate the particular areas of weakness. Kaufman and Kaufman (1977) suggest that the goal of psychoeducational assessment is to determine the child's strengths as well as weaknesses, so that the strengths can help build a program of intervention most matched to the child's needs. Thus, an examiner may administer only selected subtests of some measures in an attempt to match the child's needs to the test instrument rather than the other way around.

As stated previously, although children can present with a myriad difficulties, these generally manifest as auditory-verbal, visual-perceptual-constructive, or some combination of both. Therefore, each assessment requires clinicians to choose thoughtfully, selecting appropriate instruments that will provide maximum information in the minimum amount of time. It may well be worth the time spent to conduct a screening of the child before continuing with a more formal assessment. Several instruments can offer information about the child's current level of functioning. The Denver II (Frankenburg & Dodds, 1990), the McCarthy Screening Test (Taylor, Slocumb, & O'Neill, 1979), and the Kaufman Short McCarthy Scales of Children's Abilities (Kaufman & Kaufman, 1977) all yield developmental levels and can indicate whether further evaluation is warranted and in what areas specifically.

For preschool children found to be at risk for possible learning disability, it is important to utilize an overall cognitive measure. Those presented in Table 8.1 are well-validated, standardized psychometric instruments. Generally, young children benefit from the use of either the McCarthy Scales of Children's Abilities (McCarthy, 1972) or the Kaufman Assessment Battery for Children (K-ABC; Kaufman & Kaufman, 1983). Both of these measures are engaging and provide verbal as well as performance measures. The McCarthy Scales also yield a measure of perceptual performance and quantitative skills, while the Kaufman battery provides a nonverbal mental composite. For children with language-based learning problems, this nonverbal processing measure may be most useful (Telzrow, 1984).

If the K-ABC is used, the examiner should administer a separate measure of visual-motor integration skills. In addition, as the K-ABC does not require a great deal of language during the assessment (Kaufman & Kaufman, 1983), the examiner should supplement with language measures such as the Vocabulary, Similarities, and Comprehension subtests of the Wechsler Preschool and Primary Scales of Intelligence–Revised (WPPSI-R; Wechsler, 1989), the Vocabulary subtest of the Stanford-Binet Intelligence Scale, Fourth Edition (Thorndike, Hagen, & Sattler, 1986) or the Peabody Picture Vocabulary Test–Revised (PPVT-R; Dunn & Dunn, 1981) as possibilities. If these scores are low, particularly if the K-ABC Mental Processing Composite is average or above, referral to a speech pathologist should be pursued.

Although the McCarthy Scales and the K-ABC may measure similar constructs, some research suggests that these tests may tap areas apart from general cognitive ability that vary substantially. A study of high-risk preschoolers by Lyon and Smith (1986) found that scores between the K-ABC and McCarthy were very similar (Mental Processing Composite = 85.9 vs. General Cognitive Index = 86.3). However, the correlation between the two scales was .59, suggesting that while these two measures assess somewhat similar psychometric constructs, a significant amount of variance is not accounted for. Therefore, it may well be good clinical practice to utilize parts of these two tests to customize the assessment to the particular child.

TABLE 8.1. SELECTED PRESCHOOL ASSESSMENT INSTRUMENTS

	Age	Type	Time (Minutes)	Cognition	Verbal	Quantitative
GENERAL COGNITIVE						
Cognitive Skills Assessment Battery	4–5	Norm	20–25	X		
Differential Ability Scales	2½–5-11	Norm	30–50	X	X	X
Kaufman Assessment Battery for Children	2½–12½	Norm	60–75	X	X	X
McCarthy Scales of Children's Abilities	2½–8½	Norm	60–75	X	X	X
Stanford-Binet Intelligence Scale, Fourth Edition	2–18+	Norm	60–90	X	X	X
Wechsler Preschool and Primary Scales of Intelligence–Revised	3–7¼	Norm	45–60	X	X	X
SCREENING						
Denver II	Birth–6	Screen	15–20	X	X	X
Developmental Activities Screening Inventory	Birth–5	Screen	20–40	X		
Kaufman Short McCarthy Scales of Children's Abilities	2½–8½	Norm	20–30	X	X	X
McCarthy Screening Test	4–6½	Norm	20–30		X	X
LANGUAGE						
Assessment of Children's Language Comprehension	3–8	Norm	10–15		R	
Environmental Language Inventory	1–2	Norm	30–40		E	
Carrow Elicited Language Inventory	3–8	Norm	45		E	
Houston Test for Language Development	0–4½	Norm	30–60		X	
Peabody Picture Vocabulary Test–Revised	2½–18	Norm	20		R	
Preschool Language Scale–Revised	1½–7	Criteria	30		X	
Test for Auditory Comprehension of Language	3–7	Norm	20		R	
Test of Early Language Development	3–8	Norm	25–30		X	
Test of Language Development	4–9	Norm	30–45		X	
Utah Test of Language Development	0–4	Criteria			E	
ADAPTIVE BEHAVIOR						
AAMD Adaptive Behavior Scale–School Edition	3–17		30		X	X
Adaptive Behavior Inventory	5–19		20–25		X	
Scales of Independent Behavior	Birth–Adult	Norm	NR		X	X
Vineland Adaptive Behavior Scales	Birth–18	Norm	60–90		X	X

	Developmental Areas Measured				Scores Provided			
Perception/ Fine Motor	Gross Motor	Readiness	Social- Behavior	Self- Help	Standard Scores	Percentiles	Age Equivalent	Other
						X		
X					X	X	X	Nonverbal scale available
X		X			X	X		
X	X				X	X	X	
X					X			
X					X	X	X	
X	X						Age cutoffs	
X							X	Also used for physically/multiple handicapped, visually impaired
X	X				X	X		
X	X				X	X		
X						X		
					X			
						X		
							X	
					X	X	X	
					X		X	
						X	X	
					X	X	X	
					X	X	X	
							X	
X	X		X	X	X	X		Separate tables for EMR and TMR
		X	X	X	X	X		
X	X		X	X	X	X	X	
X	X		X	X	X	X	X	

Continued

TABLE 8.1. Selected Preschool Assessment Instruments (*continued*)

	Age	Type	Time (Minutes)	Cognition	Verbal	Quantitative
PREACADEMIC						
Battelle Developmental Inventory	Birth–8	Norm	60	X	X	X
Bracken Basic Concept Scale	2½–7½	Norm	25–30		X	X
Brigance Diagnostic Inventory of Early Development	Birth–7	Criteria		X	X	X
Developmental Profile II	Birth–8	Criteria	25–30	X	X	X
Early Intervention Developmental Profile	1–5	Criteria	60	X	X	X
Gesell Developmental Schedule	Birth–7	Adaptive	30		X	
Learning Accomplishment Profile (Diagnostic)	Birth–6	Norm	60–90	X	X	X
Minnesota Child Development Inventory	1½–6	Norm	30	X	X	X
Portage Guide to Early Education	Birth–6	Criteria	30–45	X	X	X
Preschool Attainment Record	Birth–7	Norm	20–30	X	X	X
FINE MOTOR						
Bender Visual Motor Gestalt Test	3–11-11	Norm	10–15			
Developmental Test of Visual-Motor Integration	3–18	Norm	10–15			
Motor-Free Visual Perception Test	4–8	Norm	10			
Purdue Perceptual-Motor Survey	PreK–Gr. 8		60–75			
Southern California Sensory Integration Tests	4–8	Norm	75–90			
GROSS MOTOR						
Bruininks-Oseretsky Test of Motor Proficiency	4½–14½	Norm	20–30			
Gross Motor Assessment for Children	2–6½	Norm	20			
Motor Control Process Checklist	4,6,8	Criteria	20–30			
Williams Preschool Motor Development Checklist	3–6	Screen	15–20			

LEARNING & COGNITIVE DYSFUNCTION

Developmental Areas Measured					Scores Provided			
Perception/ Fine Motor	Gross Motor	Readi- ness	Social- Behavior	Self- Help	Standard Scores	Percentiles	Age Equivalent	Other
X	X	X	X	X	X	X		
	X				X	X	X	
X	X	X		X			X	
X	X			X				
X	X	X		X			X	Also appropriate for retarded, physically handicapped, hear/visual impaired
X	X						X	
X	X			X			X	
X					X	X		
X	X	X	X	X				
X	X		X		X			
X					X	X	X	
X					X	X	X	Also appropriate for hearing impaired questionable reliability
X							X	
X	X							
X					X			
X	X				X	X	X	
X	X						Age cutoffs	
X	X					X		Performs task 4 times to 75% proficiency
	X					X		Checklist

Again, examiners should think of the assessment as hypothesis-testing detective work and adapt the instruments to the child rather than the child to the instruments.

The possibility of markers for a learning disability profile on the K-ABC currently is being researched. Lyon and Smith (1986) found the Sequential Processing mean was lower than the Simultaneous Processing mean (86.6 vs. 88.0). Similarly, Kamphaus and Reynolds (1987) found that learning disabled children generally produce their lowest scores on the Sequential Processing and Achievement scales. Telzrow's (1984) research indicates the possibility of a profile suggestive of learning disability in preschoolers similar to the one found by Lyon and Smith (1986) and Kaufman and Kaufman (1983). Unfortunately no current published research substantiates this pattern of strengths and weaknesses in preschool children.

Two other cognitive measures often are utilized for preschool assessment. The recent WPPSI-R's floor is adequate after age $3^{1}/_{4}$ and its ceiling is appropriate before $6^{1}/_{2}$ (Gyurke, 1991). In this revision, standardization and stratified sampling from minority groups was obtained, and items found to be biased were eliminated. Therefore, due to extensive administration time, the WPPSI may be most helpful when the examiner uses selected subtests to further investigate areas of weakness (or strength) rather than just routinely applying the whole scale in the individual appraisal of preschool children. The Stanford-Binet, Fourth Edition is relatively new, and research is just now addressing its utility for special populations. Sattler (1988) found that there is a limited floor to this edition for children ages 2 and 3. Moreover, the test has a long administration time, which may tax even the most cooperative preschooler, with fewer manipulative tests in the younger ages than the McCarthy Scales or the K-ABC; again, selected subtests may be utilized rather than the full battery. With the new Stanford-Binet, technical limitations have been found, with a limited floor present for preschoolers, and the administrative directions can be difficult to utilize (McCallum, 1991).

In summary, any of these measures may be appropriate depending on the needs of the child. The McCarthy Scales and the K-ABC were developed especially for younger children and may appeal more to a child with learning delays. The McCarthy's inclusion of gross and fine/perceptual motor scales provides a more inclusive measure of all domains. Examiners can select only these scales from the total battery and use them in combination with the K-ABC or the Stanford-Binet. One should be cautious in interpreting the Stanford-Binet, Fourth Edition, especially with very young children. Both the latter and the WPPSI-R present difficulty in length of test and tasks. Both may contribute subtests that one can use separately from the entire battery.

A related and important area of battery selection concerns the level of developmental skill attainment, and various appropriate instruments appear in Table 8.1. These tests and profiles differ in the areas assessed, type of information provided, amount of training needed by the examiner, and administration time required. If the purpose of the assessment is to determine an overall level of current functioning, examiners may find it most time efficient to utilize a measure such as the Developmental Profile II (Alpern, Boll, & Shearer, 1980) and the Portage Guide to Early Education (Bluma, Shearer, & Frohman, 1976). All of these measures assess verbal, quantitative, and fine and gross motor skills, but among them only the Portage Guide provides information as to preacademic skill attainment.

If the latter is of interest, the Bracken Basic Concept Scale (Bracken, 1984) and the Brigance Diagnostic Inventory of Early Development (Brigance, 1978) provide such a measure. For a quick assessment of preacademic skills, the Bracken scale and/or the Portage Guide may be most appropriate. Further, the Bracken also provides standard scores that are directly comparable to measures of general cognitive ability. Another option here is using the K-ABC Achievement subtests. Factor analysis has shown that these subtests relate to general knowledge rather than factual knowledge (Kamphaus & Reynolds, 1987). Perhaps the strongest argument for using the K-ABC Achievement test is the availability of a ready comparison between the Mental Processing Composite, Sequential Processing, and Simultaneous Processing, with tables provided regarding the significance of any differences.

For an actual description of which developmental areas are delayed, other profiles provided in Table 8.1 may be more appropriate. Often these are administered by special education teachers and thus may be unnecessary for the clinician to use. However, the other professionals outside of education should become familiar with these various measures, particularly for the developmental information they can yield.

Assessment of Receptive and Expressive Language

Verbal skills present another important area when assessing preschool children with possible learning delays. Prior to assessment the child's hearing should be screened. Moreover, a child who has frequent ear infections may stand at particular risk for deficits in auditory comprehension, auditory discrimination, or verbal delays. The developmental history obtained prior to the examination should inquire about the child's history with ear infections, tubes, and so on. If weaknesses emerge in the verbal area, the adept examiner can apply various other instruments to further delineate possible areas of difficulty.

Children with expressive delays may understand more than they are able to say. The PPVT-R offers an efficient way to determine if receptive language skills are intact. Tallal and Curtis (1988) found that children with receptive language delays in preschool were at higher risk for later learning disabilities than were children with expressive delays. This finding makes intuitive sense, as much learning is accomplished through listening and doing; the child with difficulty understanding language therefore may experience severe delays in development, with the possibility of high frustration. A brief description of a case involving receptive language delays may help to illustrate this point.

Jason was referred initially at 3 years of age for temper tantrums and noncompliance to his parents' commands. His speech was understandable, although often not relevant to the topic at hand. An evaluation showed average visual-spatial ability with severe receptive language delays, as well as a failure to comply with adult direction. His hearing was normal. Jason was referred for language therapy as well as participation in a half-day preschool program for exceptional educational need. He made good progress once behavioral management techniques were in place and became more successful in communicating both with his peers and adults. Three years later he was placed in a learning disabilities classroom, with part-time enrollment in a regular kindergarten program. Jason continued to experience difficulty with understanding language and with reading readiness skills. His math readiness skills were at grade and age expectations.

Further evaluation of children with significant language and/or speech delays should be conducted by a speech pathologist. Not only can this professional provide a comprehensive evaluation and appropriate intervention, but he or she also can provide parent training in facilitation of speech/language skills. Some of the more common instruments used for such an assessment appear in Table 8.1.

Motor Assessment

Fine and gross motor skills often can be assessed quickly prior to a formal evaluation. As stated previously, the McCarthy Scales provide measures of both these areas. If another instrument is used, the examiner should include a separate assessment of motor skills. Moreover, if a child (particularly a preschooler) shows delays in these areas, it is important to delineate his or her strengths and weaknesses, as much of early learning and socialization takes place via these motor skills. For fine/perceptual motor skills, the Developmental Test of Visual-Motor Integration (Beery, 1982) offers a relatively quick and accurate measure. For children with motor difficulties, and even those with normal motor skills but deficient visual-perceptual skills, the Motor-Free Visual Perception Test (Colarusso & Hammill, 1972) can yield very helpful information for future programming. On the other hand, the Southern California Sensory Integration Tests (Ayres, 1980) and the Purdue Perceptual-Motor Survey (Roach & Kephart, 1966) require a high level of training, are time-consuming, and may be more appropriate for an occupational therapy assessment.

Gross motor assessment also can be accomplished fairly quickly. The Gross Motor Assessment for Children in Early Childhood (Early Childhood Motor Development Committee, 1986) or the Motor Control Process Checklist (McClenaghan & Gallahue, 1978) are both readily available and require little training. For children with suspected gross motor delays, these two tests may be sufficient. Moreover, observation of the child on the playground may yield as much information as a formal assessment. If severe motor problems are present, though, it may be more appropriate to refer the child for a physical therapy evaluation.

Assessment of Mentally Retarded Children

Generally the assessment of mildly mentally handicapped children progresses similarly to that of those with average potential but suspected learning delays. Assessment of overall cognitive ability, preacademic skills, and fine and gross motor skills is appropriate. Given the earlier caution of diagnosing children with mild mental retardation as retarded at a young age, often these children are diagnosed as developmentally delayed. Kamphaus and Reynolds (1987) suggest that the rationale for administering an ability measure to a low ability child is first to determine that he or she is at risk for academic failure and then to produce a learning environment that will reverse this risk. In order to accomplish this goal, a complete assessment of the child's current functioning is necessary, including parent interviews, observations, tests of different developmental areas, and measures of adaptive behavior.

Interviewing the parents is very important when assessing for possible developmental delay. Age of attainment of early developmental milestones, environmental experiences, illnesses (especially high fevers and/or seizure activity), and the occurrence of head injuries (such as concussion, fracture, etc.) are significant areas to investigate. Although Reschly (1982) suggests that children with mild mental retardation do not often present with definite cause, the interview can help to delineate areas of parental concern, particularly in the area of parenting skills and knowledge of the developmental process.

It is imperative here to evaluate adaptive behavior. Not only does this make for good clinical practice, but most states require it. *Adaptive behavior* has been defined by the American Association on Mental Deficiency (Grossman, 1983) as behavior that is appropriate to meet the demands of the child's environmental and social situation. For preschoolers this behavior translates into maturational attainment. Adaptive behavior encompasses a wide range, including expressive and receptive language, socialization, self-help skills, fine and gross motor abilities, and preacademic attainment. For preschool children it is particularly important to interview the parent(s) using one of the adaptive behavior scales listed in Table 8.1. The clinician also may want to interview the day-care and/or preschool teacher, if available. If not, it may be helpful to administer the adaptive behavior scale with the child to ascertain what skills he or she does have. Of course, some areas may be impossible to assess directly, such as "sleeping behavior," but most components of adaptive behavior are amenable to direct observation by a skilled examiner. This latter course is especially important when the assessment involves parents who are neither able nor willing to accurately describe their child's behavior.

The Vineland Adaptive Behavior Scales (Sparrow, Balla, & Cicchetti, 1984) is the most commonly used such measure. Age norms begin at birth, and standard scores are provided so that direct comparison with ability measures is possible. The Scales of Independent Behavior (Bruininks, Woodcock, Weatherman, & Hill, 1984) also assess adaptive behavior from birth. Although less research is available on this instrument, it does assess skills in domains similar to those of the Vineland. Therefore, both of these instruments are appropriate for use with preschoolers.

Sattler (1988) cautions against the idea that adaptive behavior scales are as psychometrically precise as cognitive ability measures, due to difficulties with norming and standardization practices. He suggests that these scales should be used as guides rather than for determining the presence of retardation. Moreover, clinical judgment and multidisciplinary input are vital in arriving at a diagnosis.

A related issue arises with the possible existence of concurrent behavioral problems. It is not unusual for mentally retarded children to present with disruptive behavior. Philips (1967) found that mentally retarded individuals are at higher risk for maladaptive behavior in all periods of their lives. Therefore, the clinician should be cognizant of these behavioral deviations as well as prepared to assist parents with them. A case illustration may help to underscore this point.

Danny was referred for evaluation at 4 years of age due to parental and pediatrician concerns. His possible learning problems were coupled with severe behavior problems of temper tantrums, noncompliance, and poor social skills. Language skills appeared normal. Assessment showed a WPPSI Full Scale IQ of 60 (Verbal IQ=65, Performance IQ=58). Receptive language (as measured by the PPVT) produced an age level of 3-0, with expressive language slightly higher at 3-6. Danny's expressive language, however, was characterized by tangential speech, difficulty with abstract language concepts, and poor expressive vocabulary. His preacademic skills were delayed by approximately 1 year, although Danny possessed some factual knowledge above this level. These skills often emerged in an automatic fashion, as though by rote memory. This knowledge also did not generalize to related topics. Behaviors were difficult to manage as Danny would not remain seated, often refusing to complete tasks, repeatedly challenging the examiners, and acting physically aggressive toward the examiners.

Evaluation produced a tentative diagnosis of developmental delay with co-occurring behavioral disturbance and speech and language delay. Danny was enrolled in a generic program for children with early childhood exceptional educational needs. When reevaluated prior to first grade, Danny's Full Scale IQ was 62 (Verbal IQ=65, Performance IQ=51) on the Wechsler Intelligence Scale for Children, with adaptive behavior scores commensurate with these abilities. At that time, he was placed in a mildly mentally handicapped program that offered behavioral and speech/language support. Danny's behavior continued to be difficult to manage both at home and school. These patterns continued throughout his school career and most likely followed him into adulthood.

Although, as with the normal population, a wide variation in behavior occurs with retarded individuals, examiners need to be aware of the frequent co-occurrence of problematic behaviors with mental retardation. Simner (1983) reviewed the literature on early signs of later school failure and found that behaviors such as short attention span and high distractibility were the best predictors of learning difficulties. Although a comprehensive examination of social and behavioral measures is beyond this chapter, the Child Behavior Checklist (Achenbach & Edelbrock, 1983) and Burks' Preschool Behavior Rating Scales (Burks, 1983) have been found helpful as screening devices.

When assessing severe and profoundly retarded preschoolers, the examiner often must be inventive and flexible. Most cognitive tests do not provide enough floor to their subtests for the assessment of these children, especially at the preschool age. Therefore, the use of infant measures of development is often indicated. The Bayley Scales of Infant Development (Bayley, 1969) is a measure for the age period of 2 months to 2½ years that provides a mental development index and a psychomotor development index. Both of these indices are reported in mental age scores, and the manual cautions against the use of the ratio IQ for the Bayley. The materials are bright, colorful, and manipulative. In addition, this test provides a systematic way of recording observations of the child's behavior and social skills.

Matheny, Dolan, and Wilson (1974) found that the behaviors of goal directedness, attention span, object orientation, and objectivity were related to mental scores on the Bayley Scales. These particular behaviors are important for the assessment of this special population. Although an IQ is not derived, an estimate of the child's developmental attainment is provided. Again, the astute clinician's observations of the child is helpful for diagnosis. Often it is helpful to enlist the assistance of another professional, such as a speech pathologist or occupational therapist, in the administration of the Bayley Scales, due to the very short attention span of the very young severely retarded child.

Recently one of the present authors evaluated a 5-year-old suspected of severe mental retardation. No previous evaluation had been conducted due to the child's extremely short attention span and physically aggressive behavior. The examiner enlisted the assistance of a teacher of severe and profoundly retarded children and administered the Bayley Scales. It was necessary to restrain the child by a seat belt in a chair. All testing materials had to be kept out of his reach, as did the examiner's hair and glasses, which were inviting stimuli. The examiner placed herself in front of the child, at eye level. The teacher sat to one side and contained the child as best she could.

The child's score on the mental developmental index was 18 months (a delay of 51 months), and his psychomotor index was 21 months (a delay of 48 months). Adaptive behaviors, as measured by the Vineland Adaptive Behavior Scales, also fell in this range, with the exception of social skills, which were slightly higher. Language assessment, conducted by a speech pathologist, documented skill attainment at approximately the 12-month level. Subsequent recommendations for this child included full-day attendance in a program for severe and profound mental retardation, with daily speech and language therapy and occupational and physical therapy support. Children with severe and profound retardation are particularly challenging to evaluate, and the clinician should be prepared to conduct the evaluation in short segments and in a familiar environment for the child.

Other measures that can be considered for use with the severely or profoundly retarded preschooler are the Merrill-Palmer Scale (Stutsman, 1931), the Columbia Mental Maturity Scale (Burgemeister, Blum, & Lorge, 1972), and the Cattell Infant Intelligence Scale (Cattell, 1940). However, these tests have inherent difficulties. The Cattell test has outdated norms, while the Columbia Mental Maturity Scale scores are not comparable to those produced on the WPPSI, WISC, or Stanford-Binet (Sattler, 1988). However, each of these instruments can be utilized for the information they provide rather than for the score. At times the clinician needs to be less interested in a resulting score and more so in what the child actually can do.

From the overview provided in this chapter, one can readily see that the evaluation of exceptional preschoolers is often difficult. However, the intelligent examiner will be cognizant of the many potential difficulties and act to prevent their occurrence rather than simply reacting after the fact. Children with developmental lags/possible mild mental retardation and children with possible learning disabilities present similar educational problems and assessment goals; that is, to provide interventions that may prevent the future development of even more severe psychoeducational difficulties. Assessment of these children must be conducted sensitively and flexibly in order to ensure an accurate and educationally useful diagnosis.

Analysis of strengths as well as weaknesses is imperative. In addition, one should ascertain the child's method of problem solving. Once the evaluation has been completed, it may be instructive to go back to some items that posed problems and attempt to determine the child's method of approaching a problem. In this context, diagnostic teaching can be fruitful. By developing tasks similar to ones failed in the assessment and then seeking to teach the task, one can learn how the child approaches the task, if verbal rehearsal is utilized, if the child is able to shift cognitive set, and how he or she reacts to frustration. All of these behaviors are important for the implementation of an effective intervention program.

The clinician who seeks to evaluate preschool children also needs a thorough grounding in developmental theory and practice. Preschools and day-care centers often are open to offers for volunteer help. The beginning student, or the clinician of limited experience with this age group, will find such time well spent when called upon to determine the needs of a young child with suspected exceptional educational needs. Practice and experience will help determine which of the preceding suggestions may be relevant to individual settings. The adept practitioner always remains open to new methods and measures and enjoys utilizing those that best fit his or her needs. Moreover, he or she will adapt them to fit the individual needs of a child.

References

Achenbach, T.M., & Edelbrock, C. (1983). *Manual for the Child Behavior Checklist.* Burlington, VT: University of Vermont, Dept. of Psychiatry.

Alpern, G.D., Boll, T.J., & Shearer, M.S. (1980). *Developmental Profile II.* Aspen, CO: Psychological Development Publications.

Ayres, A.J. (1980). *Southern California Sensory Integration Tests.* Los Angeles, CA: Western Psychological Services.

Bayley, N. (1969). *Manual for the Bayley Scales of Infant Development.* San Antonio, TX: Psychological Corporation.

Beery, K.E. (1982). *Revised administration, scoring, and teaching manual for the Developmental Test of Visual-Motor Integration.* Cleveland, OH: Modern Curriculum Press.

Bender, L. (1938). A visual motor gestalt test and its clinical use. *American Orthopsychiatric Association Research Monograph,* No. 3.

Bluma, S., Shearer, M., & Frohman, A. (1976). *Portage Guide to Early Education* (rev. ed.). Portage, WI: Portage Project.

Boehm, A.E., & Sandberg, B.R. (1982). Assessment of the preschool child. In C.R. Reynolds & T.B. Gutkin (Eds.), *The handbook of school psychology* (pp. 294-333). New York: Wiley.

Boehm, A.E., & Slater, B.R. (1981). *The Cognitive Skills Assessment Battery* (2nd ed.). New York: Teachers College, Columbia University.

Bracken, B.A. (1984). *Bracken Basic Concept Scale.* San Antonio, TX: Psychological Corporation.

Brigance, A.H. (1978). *Brigance Diagnostic Inventory of Early Development.* North Billerica, MA: Curriculum Associates.

Bruininks, R.H. (1978). *Bruininks-Oseretsky Test of Motor Proficiency.* Circle Pines, MN: American Guidance Service.

Bruininks, R.H., Woodcock, R.W., Weatherman, R.F., & Hill, B.K. (1984). *Scales of Independent Behavior.* Allen, TX: DLM Teaching Resources.

Burgemeister, B.B., Blum, L.H., & Lorge, I. (1972). *Columbia Mental Maturity Scale* (3rd ed.). San Antonio, TX: Psychological Corporation.

Burks, H.F. (1983). *Burks' Preschool and Kindergarten Behavior Rating Scales.* Los Angeles: Western Psychological Services.

Carrow, E. (1973). *Test for Auditory Comprehension of Language.* Austin, TX: Urban Research Group.

Carrow, E. (1974). *Carrow Elicited Language Inventory.* Austin, TX: Author.

Cattell, P. (1940). *Cattell Infant Intelligence Scale.* San Antonio, TX: Psychological Corporation.
Colarusso, R.P., & Hammill, D.D. (1972). *Motor-Free Visual Perceptual Test.* Novato, CA: Academic Therapy Publications.
Crabtree, M. (1969). *Houston Test for Language Development.* Houston, TX: Houston Test Co.
Doll, E. (1966). *Preschool Attainment Record.* Circle Pines, MN: American Guidance Service.
Dunn, L.M., & Dunn, L.M. (1981). *Peabody Picture Vocabulary Test–Revised.* Circle Pines, MN: American Guidance Service.
Early Childhood Motor Development Committee. (1986). *Gross Motor Assessment for Children in Early Childhood.* Madison, WI: Wisconsin Department of Public Instruction.
Elliott, C.D., Murray, D.J., & Pearson, L.S. (1990). *The Differential Ability Scales.* San Antonio, TX: Psychological Corporation.
Federal Register. (1977). *Regulations implementing Education for All Handicapped Children Act of 1975.* Washington, DC: U.S. Government Printing Office.
Fewell, R.R., & Langley, M.B. (1984). *Developmental Activities Screening Inventory (DASI-II).* Austin, TX: PRO-ED.
Foster, R., Giddan, J., & Stark, J. (1969). *Assessment of Children's Language Comprehension.* Palo Alto, CA: Consulting Psychologists Press.
Fotheringham, J.B. (1983). Mental retardation and developmental delay. In K.D. Paget & B.A. Bracken (Eds.), *The psychoeducational assessment of preschool children* (pp. 176–204). New York: Grune & Stratton.
Frankenburg, W.K., & Dodds, J.B. (1990). *Denver II.* Denver, CO: Denver Developmental Materials.
French, J.L. (1964). *Manual: Pictorial Test of Intelligence.* Boston: Houghton Mifflin.
Grossman, H.J. (1983). *Manual on terminology and classification in mental retardation* (American Association on Mental Deficiency). Baltimore: Garamond/Pridemark Press.
Gyurke, J.S. (1991). The assessment of preschool children with the Wechsler Preschool and Primary Scales of Intelligence–Revised. In B. Bracken (Ed.), *The psychoeducational assessment of preschool children* (pp. 86–106). Boston: Allyn & Bacon.
Hresko, W.P., Reid, D.K., & Hammill, D.D. (1982). *Test of Early Language Development.* Austin, TX: PRO-ED.
Ireton, H., & Thwing, E. (1974) *Minnesota Child Development Inventory.* Minneapolis, MN: Behavior Science Systems.
Kamphaus, R.W., & Reynolds, C.R. (1987). *Clinical and research applications of the K-ABC.* Circle Pines, MN: American Guidance Service.
Kaufman, A.S., & Kaufman, N.L. (1977). *Clinical evaluation of young children with the McCarthy Scales.* New York: Grune & Stratton.
Kaufman, A.S., & Kaufman, N.L. (1983). *Kaufman Assessment Battery for Children: Interpretive manual.* Circle Pines, MN: American Guidance Service.
Knobloch, H. (1980). *Manual of developmental diagnosis.* New York: Harper & Row.
Lambert, N.M., Windmiller, M., Tharinger, D., & Cole, L.J. (1981). *AAMD Adaptive Behavior Scale—School Edition.* Monterey, CA: CTB/McGraw-Hill.
Leiter, R.G. (1948). *Leiter International Performance Scale.* Chicago: Stoelting.
Lerner, J., Mardell-Czudnowski, C., & Goldenberg, D. (1981). *Special education for the early childhood years.* Englewood Cliffs, NJ: Prentice-Hall.
Lyon, M.A., & Smith, D.K. (1986). A comparison of at-risk preschool children's performance on the K-ABC, McCarthy Scales, and Stanford-Binet. *Journal of Psychoeducational Assessment, 4,* 35–43.

MacDonald, J.D. (1978). *Environmental Language Inventory.* Columbus, OH: Charles E. Merrill.
Matheny, A.P., Jr., Dolan, A.B., & Wilson, R.S. (1974). Bayley's Infant Behavior Record: Relations between behaviors and mental test scores. *Developmental Psychology, 10,* 696-702.
McCallum, R.S. (1991). The assessment of preschool children with the Stanford-Binet Intelligence Scale: Fourth Edition. In B. Bracken (Ed.), *The psychoeducational assessment of preschool children* (pp. 107-132). Boston: Allyn & Bacon.
McCarthy, D. (1972). *McCarthy Scales of Children's Abilities.* San Antonio, TX: Psychological Corporation.
McClenaghan, B., & Gallahue, D. (1978). *Fundamental movement: A developmental and remedial approach.* Philadelphia: Saunders.
Mecham, M.J., & Jones, J.D. (1978). *Utah Test of Language Development* (rev. ed.). Salt Lake City, UT: Communication Research Associates.
Mercer, J.R., & Lewis, J.F. (1978). *Adaptive Behavior Inventory for Children: System of Multicultural Pluralistic Assessment.* San Antonio, TX: Psychological Corporation.
Newborg, J., Stock, J.R., & Wnek, L. (1984). *Battelle Developmental Inventory.* Allen, TX: DLM Teaching Resources.
Newcomer, P.L., & Hammill, D.D. (1977). *Test of Language Development.* Austin, TX: PRO-ED.
Philips, I. (1967). Psychopathology and mental retardation. *American Journal of Psychiatry, 124,* 29-35.
Reschly, D.J. (1982). Assessing mild mental retardation: The influence of adaptive behavior, sociocultural status, and prospects for nonbiased assessment. In C.R. Reynolds & T.B. Gutkin (Eds.), *The handbook of school psychology* (pp. 346-372). New York: Wiley.
Roach, E.G., & Kephart, N.C. (1966). *The Purdue Perceptual-Motor Survey.* San Antonio, TX: Psychological Corporation.
Sanford, A.R., & Zelman, J.G. (1981). *Learning Accomplishment Profile.* Winston-Salem, NC: Kaplan Press.
Sattler, J.M. (1988). *Assessment of children's intelligence and special abilities* (3rd ed.). San Diego, CA: Author.
Simner, M.L. (1983). The warning signs of school failure: An updated profile of the at-risk kindergarten child. *Topics in Early Childhood Special Education, 3,* 17-27.
Sloan, W., & Birch, J.W. (1955). A rationale for degrees of retardation. *American Journal of Mental Deficiency, 60,* 258-264.
Sparrow, S.S., Balla, D.A., & Cicchetti, D.V. (1984). *Vineland Adaptive Behavior Scales.* Circle Pines, MN: American Guidance Service.
Stutsman, R. (1931). *Mental measurement of preschool children.* Yonkers-on-Hudson, NY: World Book.
Tallal, P., & Curtis, S. (1988). From developmental dysphasia to dyslexia: A neurodevelopmental continuum. *Journal of Clinical and Experimental Neuropsychology, 10,* 19.
Taylor, R.L., Slocumb, P.R., & O'Neill, J. (1979). A short form of the McCarthy Scales of Children's Abilities: Methodological and clinical applications. *Psychology in the Schools, 16,* 347-350.
Telzrow, C.F. (1984). Practical applications of the K-ABC in the identification of handicapped preschoolers. *The Journal of Special Education, 18,* 311-324.
Thorndike, R.L., Hagen, E.P., & Sattler, J.M. (1986). *Guide for administering and scoring the Stanford-Binet Intelligence Scale: Fourth Edition.* Chicago: Riverside.
Torgesen, J.K. (1981). The relationship between memory and attention in learning disabilities. *Exceptional Education Quarterly, 2,* 51-59.

Wechsler, D. (1989). *Manual for the Wechsler Preschool and Primary Scales of Intelligence–Revised.* San Antonio, TX: Psychological Corporation.
Williams, H. (1974). *Williams' Preschool Motor Development Checklist.* Unpublished manuscript, University of Toledo.
Zimmerman, I.L., Steiner, V.G., & Pond, R.E. *Preschool Language Scale.* San Antonio, TX: Psychological Corporation.

Appendix. Outline of Interview for Preschool Children[1]

Interviewer: _____ Date: _____

Examiner: _____ Respondent: _____

Child's name: _____ (mother/father/other) _____

A. REFERRAL

    1. Clarification:

    2. What does referral agent want from assessment?

	Name	Age	Age at birth of Client
B. IDENTIFICATION DATA			
1. Client	_____	___	N/A
2. Father	_____	___	_____
3. Mother	_____	___	_____
4. Siblings	_____	___	_____
	_____	___	_____
	_____	___	_____
5. Others in home	_____	___	_____
	_____	___	_____

C. RESIDENCE

    Street address _____

    City _____ State _____ ZIP _____

    Type of dwelling: (circle) apartment / single home / farm / other _____

---

[1] Developed by Roy P. Martin, Department of Educational Psychology, University of Georgia. Reproduced by permission.

D. EDUCATIONAL AND WORK HISTORY

	Years Education	Work Type	Dates
1. Father	_____	_____	_____
	_____	_____	_____
2. Mother	_____	_____	_____
	_____	_____	_____

E. DEVELOPMENTAL MILESTONES (*=important)

Behavior	Normal Range	Age Attained
1. Head control while vertical	2.5 months (1 to 5)	_____
2. Rolls from front to back	4.5 months (2 to 6)	_____
3. Rolls from back to front	6.4 months (4 to 10)	_____
4. Sits alone steadily	6.6 months (5 to 9)	_____
*5. Crawls or scoots	8.0 months (6 to 12)	_____
6. Pulls to standing position	8.1 months (5 to 12)	_____
*7. Walks alone	11.7 months (9 to 17)	_____
8. Walks up stairs	16.1 months (12 to 23)	_____
9. Walks down stairs (both feet on each tread)	25.8 months (19 to 30)	_____

Language Development	Normal Range	Age Attained
1. Startles to sharp noises	0 to 3 months	_____
2. Interest in sounds	3 to 7 months	_____
3. Understands first words	7.5 months (6.5 to 9)	_____
*4. Says "dada" or equivalent	7.9 months (6.5 to 9)	_____ (Word: __)
*5. Speaks first word	14 months (12 to 24)	_____ (Word: __)
*6. Names one object	17.8 months (13 to 27)	_____ (Word: __)
*7. Speaks first sentence	24 months (16 to 30)	_____ (Sentence: _____)

Other

*1. Weaned	4 to 5 months	_____(bottle/breast)
*2. Toilet trained	24 to 30 months	_____
*3. Dresses self (except tying shoes)	4 to 5 years	_____

F. HEALTH HISTORY

1. Pregnancy: Length _____ Problems _____

2. Delivery: Labor length _____ Problems _____

3. Child's first 2 weeks: Problems _____

4. Health since first 2 weeks: Problems _____

5. Other health-related problems (e.g., sight, teeth, orthopedic): _____

G. SOCIAL RELATIONSHIPS (circle description; make comments)

   1. With sibs: good / average / poor _____

   2. With peers: good / average / poor _____

   3. With mother: good / average / poor _____

   4. With father: good / average / poor _____

H. CHILD MANAGEMENT TECHNIQUES

   1. Type: _____

   2. Agreement between parents: agree / some disagreement / considerable disagreement
      Comments: _____

I. EMOTIONAL DEVELOPMENT

   1. Fears: (list) _____

   2. Activity level: high / average / low _____

   3. Emotional intensity: high / average / low _____

   4. Other areas of concern: _____

J. EDUCATIONAL HISTORY

	Amount of Time per Day	*Dates*	*Adjustment*
1. Day care	_____	_____	_____
	_____	_____	_____
2. Preschool	_____	_____	_____
	_____	_____	_____

K. FAMILY DYNAMICS

   1. Quality of marriage: good / average / poor _____

	Type	*Dates*
2. Stress on family since birth of client:	_____	_____
	_____	_____

L. Other (not previously mentioned):

_____

_____

9

Assessment of Young Children with Communication Disorders

BARBARA C. WILSON, PH.D.

For those professionals involved in the early identification of developmental disabilities, the federal legislation that mandates the availability of public education for handicapped preschool children (PL 99–457) is a further validation of the position we have taken over the years: that cognitive as well as physical deficits may be identified early in a child's life, and that appropriate intervention should be made available in order to enhance development in all areas. The presence of any disability can have an effect on many levels of development within the child and his or her family. The effect of a communication disorder may have major ramifications in terms of cognitive development, psychosocial adjustment, and in emotional growth and development. The diminished ability of a family member, and particularly a young child, to express or to comprehend spoken language must place great stress on the family system, creating yet further distress for the child and those who must care for and live with him or her.

The numbers of children so affected, specifically those with primary developmental language disorders as opposed to those with language disorders embedded in the autistic and mental retardation syndromes, is not insignificant, with estimates ranging from 3% (Allen & Bliss, 1978) to 8.5% (Wolpaw, Nation, & Aram, 1977), the latter translating into approximately 1 out of 12 otherwise normally developing children. The careful identification of sometimes subtle deficits in these children can make a difference in providing timely intervention or in avoiding inappropriate identification of such a child as retarded, autistic, or emotionally disturbed. Sometimes the distinctions are not always clear. Thoughtful interpretation of the data, historical, observational, and psychometric, is critical but not always enough. There are real diagnostic dilemmas, which will be taken up later in this chapter.

BACKGROUND, ETIOLOGY, AND SYMPTOMATOLOGY

Communication disorders encompass a range of developmental disabilities, including developmental language disorders or developmental dysphasia, autism, mental retardation, and pervasive developmental disorder (PDD). For our purposes, the discussion here will address primarily the assessment and early detection of developmental language disorders (DLD), with consideration of some of the issues surrounding autism, PDD, and mental retardation in terms of differential diagnosis. Within this context DLD is defined as resulting from "deficits at the level of receiving, processing, and/or expressing language, and our basic assumption . . . is that failure to develop language is always, except in rare instances of extreme environmental deprivation, the consequence of neurological dysfunction" (Rapin & Wilson, 1978, p. 13). Exclusionary criteria include a hearing loss sufficient to limit acquisition of speech and language and primary emotional disorders. Most definitions also exclude from the diagnosis of DLD those children with mental retardation or those presenting clear evidence of neurological deficits beyond what might be considered developmental in origin (e.g., cerebral palsy), although there are arguments to be made that children with one disability may have a second co-occur independently (i.e., children may have measles *and* a broken leg).

Background

Formal recognition of developmental aphasia or DLD as a clinical entity did not occur until the mid-19th century, although there are much earlier references to the acquired aphasias. The earliest treatise providing a description of the aphasias was included in a discussion of localization of brain function and is found in the Edwin Smith Surgical Papyrus, written circa 2500–3000 B.C. (Breasted, 1930). The Hippocratic writings of the fourth and fifth centuries B.C. provided more elaborate descriptions of these acquired language deficits (Gibson, 1962; McHenry, 1969). However, it was not until 1853 that William Wilde, an otologist, made the first documented reference to children he had seen in his practice who were "dumb but not deaf" (Wilde, 1853), and only as recently as 1937 did Samuel Orton, well known for his pioneering work in dyslexia, lay the groundwork for an appreciation of the neurological basis of developmental disorders, in which he included child language disorders (Orton, 1937). A good deal of work followed in the '50s and '60s that provided clinical descriptions of various aspects of DLD and theories as to the pathogenesis and etiology of the disorders (e.g., Benton, 1959, 1964; Hardy, 1965; Ingram & Reid, 1956; McGinnis, 1963; Myklebust, 1954; Morley, 1957; Strauss, 1954), and the study of developmental language disorders took on a life of its own.

Where Do These Disorders Come From?

The field has gone well beyond the descriptive stage in a relatively short span of time, considering how fairly recent was the appreciation of the disorder as a clinical entity. A great deal of research is being directed to issues of the origins of DLD. At this point, contrary to some of the prevailing winds of the 1930s, there is general consensus that DLD represents atypical central nervous system function. Early notions regarding the neurological basis for DLD were reflected in Vaisse's position that "congenital aphasia" was due to the same kinds of focal lesions that accounted for the acquired aphasias in adults (Benton, 1959). Since then, the major theories regarding the neurological basis for the disorder include developmentally determined abnormal hemispheric dominance and interhemispheric interaction (LeBrun & Zangwill, 1981; Zaidel, 1979), abnormal structure of the brain (Dalby, 1975; Hauser, Delong, & Rosman, 1975), and genetic contributions (Decker & DeFries, 1980; Decker, 1982; Garvey & Mutton, 1973). At this point, however, the etiology and pathogenesis of DLD are still unclear. Some evidence exists that aspects of the disorder may be genetic, and there is still some question as to the possible contribution of early compromise of the developing brain.

What Do These Disorders Look Like?

At the behavioral level, disorders in receptive, expressive, and receptive/expressive language have been well described, with research focusing on the characteristics of the disorders as manifested by deficits in specific aspects of cognitive and linguistic functions (see especially Aram & Nation, 1982; Berry, 1969; Morley, 1957, 1965, 1967; and Wyke, 1978, for in-depth discussions and overviews of the disorders, and Culbertson, 1981; Frumkin & Rapin, 1980; Kamhi, 1981; Morehead & Ingram, 1973; Nation & Aram, 1982; Tallal & Piercy, 1978; Tallal, Stark, & Mellits, 1985; and Wilson, 1986, for discussions of specific aspects of the disorders). The literature is voluminous; the few references just noted address but some of the major areas of concern, ranging from auditory processing to patterns of neuropsychological function.

A detailed description of the characteristics of DLD is beyond the scope or intent of this chapter. However, in general terms developmental language disorders manifest themselves as (a) receptive disorders, characterized by the apparent inability or deficient ability to comprehend vocal language and, in some instances, accompanied by a limited ability to comprehend linguistically meaningful visual stimuli; (b) expressive disorders, characterized by the inability or deficient ability to express thoughts in vocal language and, in some instances, accompanied by a limited ability to use gestures or to sign for communicative purposes; (c) some combination of receptive and expressive disorders; or (d) a deficiency in the pragmatics of language (i.e., in communicative intent and communicative competence), which frequently are seen as a component of expressive language but that may co-occur with receptive disorders as well. Each of these types of disorders may have diverse presentations and diverse etiologies. For example, some children cannot produce adequate sentences because of disorders of semantic, syntactic, or phonologic output (Leonard, 1979), while others cannot produce sentences because of a severe developmental verbal apraxia, a disorder of *voluntary movement* of the articulators for speech that is resistant to remediation (Darby, 1985, pp. 113–132). At the receptive level, some children have difficulty because of deficits in syntactic comprehension (Aram & Nation, 1975, p. 112), while others experience increased difficulty as a function of sentence length (Tallal, 1975).

CLASSIFICATION OF DLD

At present the profession generally acknowledges that DLD is not a unitary syndrome. As clinicians and researchers have increased their understanding of these disorders, it has become apparent that clinically recognizable patterns of cognitive and linguistic function and dysfunction exist that may be systematic enough to differentiate DLD children into clinically meaningful subgroups. Although there is a history of attempts at classifying the acquired aphasias going back to the last century (Kertesz, 1979), none has yet gained general acceptance and the search goes on.

Given the rather recent emergence of DLD as a recognized clinical entity, approaches to classification of the disorders have only recently begun to be developed. The potential ramifications of a typology of DLD in terms of remedial paradigms, prediction, evaluation of efficacy of intervention, and brain-behavior research cannot be underestimated. In her review of research in child language disorders, Ludlow (1980) has suggested that research in the area of child language disorders will continue to be limited in its replicability and in its usefulness until a generally accepted classification develops.

Typology 1: Aram and Nation, 1975

Until the seminal study by Aram and Nation (1975), attempts at developing a typology of DLD had been limited to clinical descriptions (de Ajuriaguerra et al., 1976; McGinnis, 1963; Myklebust, 1954). In 1975 Aram and Nation published the first data-based, quantitative classification study that explored comprehension, production, and repetition with reference to phonologic, semantic, and syntactic characteristics in a DLD sample. Their study involved 47 preschool children whose comprehension, formulation, repetition, semantics, syntax, and phonology were examined using a set of 14 standardized language measures. Six statistically coherent patterns were isolated through factor analysis and described as Nonspecific Formulation-Repetition Deficit, Generalized Low Performance, Repetition Strength, Specific Formulation-Repetition Deficit, Comprehension Deficit, and Phonologic Deficit. The relatively small number of subjects and the absence of clinical and empirical validation studies, although limiting the applicability of their results, in no way minimizes the importance of this initial classification study; it was ground breaking in its recognition of recurrent patterns of language performance and processing deficits in a heterogeneous group of children with disordered language.

More recently, Wolfus, Moscovitch, and Kinsbourne (1980) used linguistic and neuropsychological measures to identify two subgroups of DLD, Expressive and Expressive-Receptive, but their study was based on only 19 children who were not well defined.

Typology 2: Rapin and Allen, 1983

Eight years after Aram and Nation's (1975) study, Rapin and Allen (1983) presented still another DLD typology; their model identifies six subtypes based on patterns of psycholinguistic variables. This model is clinically derived, based on observations of interactions between child and parent or child and other adult. Briefly described, their clinically identified subtypes include a Disorder of Phonologic Decoding, namely Verbal Auditory Agnosia, in which all aspects of expressive and receptive vocal language are impaired; Disorders of Phonologic Encoding including Verbal Dyspraxia, in which all aspects of expressive vocal language are impaired, and a Phonologic Programming Deficit Disorder; a Disorder of Morpho-Syntactic Encoding and Decoding, namely a Phonologic-Syntactic Deficit Disorder; Disorders of Higher Level Processing, including a Semantic-Pragmatic Deficit Disorder and a Lexical Syntactic Deficit Disorder. This model provides rich clinical descriptions of linguistic subtypes of DLD that appear to be clinically coherent in that the descriptions "match" children that we see clinically, but it awaits the kind of quantification that will permit validation and reliable clinical diagnosis from one clinician to the next. The subtypes are defined and described in detail in the 1983 Rapin and Allen paper.

Typology 3: Wilson and Risucci, 1986

The most recent attempt at a DLD typology stems from a neuropsychological approach that aspires to both clinical and statistical coherence (Risucci, 1984; Wilson & Risucci, 1986), relying at this point on results of standardized neuropsychological and language measures. One of the aims in developing this classification is to provide a method that will be useful in the early identification of DLD subtypes. The developers plan to do this by delineating neurocognitive patterns that they believe are related to psycholinguistic subtypes within some as yet unspecified set of brain-behavior relationships. The model as presented provides a heuristic framework for the generation of hypotheses in neurocognitive and brain-behavior domains, offering a step in the direction of data-driven approaches to remedial paradigms. It is a clinically derived and empirically validated "first generation" typology, still in the development stage, but already it has demonstrated the ability to predict subtype-related acquisition of reading skills in the early grades (Wilson & Risucci, 1986).

In more recent external validation studies, affect sensitivity (Black-Van Santen, 1989) and pragmatic abilities and aspects of social play (Webb, 1988) have been shown to be systematically related to subtype membership. Currently the model is based on quantitative data only, which limits its usefulness in clearly defining some aspects of the subtypes. Systematic observational data are required in order to make sense of some of the quantitative data, and the Speech-Language Inventory Questionnaire (SLIQ; Tortolani, Murray, Risucci, & Wilson, 1986) is an observational scale being developed for this purpose. The latter provides data on the characteristics of expressive language, including phonology, formulation, grammar, and pragmatics. Reliability studies are nearing completion, and once concluded, information derived from the SLIQ will become an additional source of data used in the definition of the DLD subtypes and in the validation studies to follow. The most recent experimental version of the SLIQ appears in Appendix A.

Ten subtypes were identified by initial clinical sorts of neurocognitive profiles. There were insufficient numbers available at the time of the initial study to validate each of the subtypes, although such a validation study is planned as numbers permit. Several subsets of receptive disorders and, similarly, expressive disorders were combined for purposes of validation. Only those subtypes that were included in the validation study are presented. In each instance it is doubtless the case that the subtypes as presented in this chapter can be further defined in terms of possible deficits in processing, motor planning, semantic and/or syntactic comprehension, temporal sequencing, and so on, particularly because subsets were combined that do, indeed, appear to have defining characteristics. This typology is presented in more detail here because it is the one referred to in the case studies to follow:

1. *Receptive Disorders,* which may or may not include a mild expressive component:
    a. *Auditory Comprehension Disorder*—relatively diminished abilities in the

decoding of verbally presented material in contrast to visually presented material of equivalent cognitive-linguistic complexity.
  b. *Auditory and Visual Comprehension Disorder*—relatively diminished abilities in the decoding of verbal material and of visually presented material with linguistic loading, in contrast to well-preserved abilities in visual-spatial and memory functions.
  c. *Verbal Auditory Agnosia (VAA)*—a special case of auditory comprehension disorders, which represents a profound vocal language decoding disorder presumed to be limited to an inability to decode phonology and accompanied by a resultant severe expressive disorder. Children with VAA acquire language through sign and through reading. Expressive skills are, of course, poor, but may improve somewhat with appropriate and intensive intervention (see Darby, 1985, pp. 70–72; Rapin, Mattis, Rowan, & Golden, 1977). (This group is not specifically identified by the profiles used in classification; it is here that observational and historical data are necessary in making the finer cut.)
2. *Expressive Disorders,* which may or may not include a mild receptive component:
  a. *Formulation Disorder*—characterized by auditory memory and retrieval deficits and difficulties in formulating sentences (i.e., in the precise verbal production of the thoughts to be expressed). Comprehension typically is spared, as are visually mediated functions. (Frequently deficits are observed in morphosyntactic usage and, in a small subset, disordered pragmatics.)
  b. *Organization Disorder*—neuropsychological profile shows no pattern of deficits. This subgroup is characterized by generally average to well above average abilities in all areas, but difficulties appear in organizing the content and sometimes the order within sentences. The deficit is usually rather subtle. (There are more likely to be mild to moderate deficits in pragmatics in this group, and although there may be deficits in grammar, it is not as prevalent as in the Formulation Disorders, of which this may be a subset.)
  c. *Developmental Verbal Dyspraxia*—a special case of expressive disorders, characterized by an inability to produce intelligible running speech due to deficits in speech programming. (As with Verbal Auditory Agnosia, this group cannot be identified at present by the profiles used in the classification. Addition of the results of a neuro-oromotor examination and/or Blakeley's [1980] Screening Test for Developmental Apraxia of Speech, as well as observational data, are required to delineate this group from other significant expressive disorders.)
3. *Mixed Disorders,* which may or may not include expressive components:
  a. *Auditory Comprehension and Auditory Short-Term Memory Disorder*—auditory comprehension and auditory short-term sequential memory are impaired relative to visually mediated functions.
  b. *Auditory Comprehension and Auditory and Visual Short-Term Memory Disorder*—auditory comprehension and short-term sequential memory in

both modalities are deficient relative to visual cognitive and spatial abilities.

c. *Global Auditory and Visual Comprehension and Memory Disorder*—comprehension and short-term sequential memory in both auditory and visual modalities are deficient. The Global group usually manifests expressive deficits. Visual-spatial functions are intact and auditory perceptual abilities vary independently.

Each of these three classification systems shares commonalities that cut across the instruments and methods of clinical appraisal used in each of the studies and reinforces the position that there are, indeed, systematic patterns that can be differentiated and used in the identification of subtypes of DLD. Table 9.1 presents the subtypes identified by the three studies and indicates those that appear to be similar in major characteristics across the three.

Although the development of a DLD typology that meets appropriate clinical and statistical criteria is of great interest and will be very useful when available, the clinical identification of children with DLD is, of course, a separate issue. Such

TABLE 9.1

COMMONALITIES AMONG THREE DLD TYPOLOGIES

Wilson & Risucci, 1986	Rapin & Allen, 1983	Aram & Nation, 1975
Auditory Comprehension Disorder	Semantic-Pragmatic Disorder	Repetition Strength Pattern
Auditory and Visual Comprehension Disorder	Semantic-Pragmatic Disorder	Repetition Strength Pattern
Auditory Comprehension and Auditory Short-Term Memory Disorder	Phonologic-Syntactic Disorder	Nonspecific Formulation-Repetition Disorder
Auditory Comprehension and Auditory and Visual Short-Term Memory Disorder	Phonologic-Syntactic Disorder	Nonspecific Formulation-Repetition Disorder
Global Auditory and Visual Comprehension and Memory Disorder	—	Generalized Low Pattern
(Auditory Verbal Agnosia)	Auditory Verbal Agnosia	Generalized Low Pattern
Formulation Disorder	Lexical-Syntactic Disorder	—
Organization Disorder	Lexical-Syntactic Disorder	—
Auditory Memory and Retrieval Disorder	Phonologic Production and Speech Planning Disorder	Syntactic and Speech Programming Disorder
(Developmental Verbal Dyspraxia)	—	—

identification may be made by a language pathologist, a psychologist with a developmental background, or a physician with an understanding of normal language development and its deviations. Although a language pathologist is certainly required for a recise definition of the specifics of the language disorder in a given child, with an eye to remedial planning, an evaluation by a neuropsychologist or developmental psychologist can provide useful and sometimes sufficient information to identify the presence of the disorder.

AN APPROACH TO THE NEUROPSYCHOLOGICAL ASSESSMENT OF DLD

The model to which this author subscribes begins with an appreciation of the *referral issues* for the information they may contain relative to the development of hypotheses to be addressed during the formal evaluation. Similarly, a review of the *history* may provide relevant diagnostic information or provide the basis for hypotheses that will help to guide the assessment. The *selection of methods and procedures of clinical appraisal,* modified as the evaluation proceeds, is to some extent informed initially by the information gained in the first interview in which the referral issues and history are reviewed. Both *formal test scores* and *clinical observations* are taken into consideration as the assessment progresses, because how a child arrives at a given score is usually as significant as the score itself.

This approach to assessment does not rely on a standard battery, although the initial set of measures may be the same for a given age group. Rather, it is shaped by the data as they emerge and is based on a branching, "if-then" hypothesis-testing approach in which, as a deficit or relative inefficiency in function is detected, the examiner asks "why?" This generates hypotheses to address the question, and measures or clinical methods are selected to test these hypotheses. If, for example, a child does poorly on most aspects of auditory comprehension tasks, questions that should arise include those regarding memory (did the child remember the question long enough to process it?), retrieval (can the child rapidly retrieve verbal information in order to produce a response?), auditory perception of language (can the child discriminate one speech sound from another, for example?), hearing acuity (does the child have a hearing loss, perhaps transient, due to serous otitis media?), and expressive language skills (does the child have trouble formulating or organizing language?). If these functions are examined in a systematic fashion and appear to be intact, then perhaps the problem *is* at the level of comprehension. (For a more complete discussion of this process-oriented approach to assessment, see Wilson, 1986.)

Referral Issues and Review of History

The preschool child with developmental problems that do not involve frank physical findings or clear indications of significant disability typically is brought to clinical attention (a) by parents who think "something is wrong" and are frightened and anxious lest you agree with them, (b) by preschools in which the teacher has noted something of concern and has alerted the parents, (c) by language pathologists and audiologists to whom the child was referred to rule out speech or hearing problems and who are asking for a differential diagnosis in the less clear instances of DLD, or (d) sometimes by physicians who are alert to the issues of language development. The questions posed and the descriptions provided of the behaviors of concern can be the beginning point of a mystery story that you may have to solve.

Frequently parental descriptions of the yet-to-be diagnosed DLD child include statements such as "He doesn't listen," "He doesn't like TV," or "He doesn't like me to read to him." (Does he understand what he hears? Has he a hearing problem?) "He seems to understand everything, but he doesn't do the things I tell him to do." (Does he *really* understand everything? Does he *remember* things he is told to do?) "There are days he seems to understand everything and other days he acts like he doesn't." (Does he *really* understand on Day 1, or does he have a conductive hearing loss on Day 2?) "I know he understands what we say to him, but he has such trouble answering questions or telling us things." (Formulation or organizational deficits? Problems with retrieval?) "He tries to talk to us, but we can't understand what he is saying." (Hearing loss? Phonological disorder? Verbal dyspraxia?) "He doesn't play with other children and sometimes he acts as though we were not here." (Hearing loss? Autism?)

The referrals from professional sources generally are requesting (a) some indication of cognitive level in order to rule out mental retardation in instances of significant DLD, or (b) a differential diagnosis when DLD, retardation, autism, or PDD are under consideration. Instances will arise in which parental concerns and those of the referring source differ. Both are informative, and both should be addressed. Regardless of the source of the referral, it is most useful to try to get as precise a statement of the referral issues as possible. It saves time and provides focus.

A careful review of the history collected from parents or other informed caregivers, supplemented by birth records, other hospital and medical records, and results of other evaluations (speech, hearing, psychological, psychiatric, etc.), may provide important diagnostic information and certainly provides material for questions. When the child has attended a preschool program, one also should request information from the teacher. (The questionnaire used by this author and her colleagues for this purpose is reproduced in Appendix B.) However, although most clinicians take extensive histories, much of the information we collect, as it turns out, may be of interest but perhaps not very helpful.

In the assessment of preschool children for DLD, one can ask focused questions related to history that may provide both information suggesting risk for some *unspecified* developmental problems as well as information *specific* to the disorder in question. General such "red flags" include prematurity, which places a child at risk for unspecified developmental problems, or a history of prolonged febrile seizures beginning in the first year of life, which would indicate a higher risk for mental retardation (Nelson & Ellenberg, 1978). The presence of delayed language milestones (e.g., first words were not uttered until 23 months of age) should raise questions about hearing loss, a communication disorder of one kind or another, or retardation, perhaps prompting a multidisciplinary evaluation. Similarly, a history of neonatal meningitis, typically treated with ototoxic drugs, should make one suspect a hearing loss and request appropriate audiological assessment prior to any further evaluations.

More specific to the identification of DLD, a history of frequent occurrences of serous otitis media is notable because of the growing literature that suggests a strong relationship between such a history, concomitant conductive hearing loss, and the presence of DLD (Kavanagh, 1986; Needleman, 1977; News Note, 1985). The presence of learning disabilities in the family history must raise the possibility of DLD (Owen, 1978). A history of significant feeding problems during infancy and drooling past the age of teething in a child with expressive language deficits should alert the clinician to a possible oral motor dysfunction contributing to or defining the disorder (Abbs, Hunker, & Barlow, 1983; Morris, 1982; Sheppard, 1987). The reader is referred to Berenberg (1977), Shaffer and Dunn (1979), and Thompson and O'Quinn (1979) for additional information regarding relationships between early historical data and developmental problems.

In sum, the collection and review of referral information and historical data, other pertinent evaluations, observations, and reports, and the additional information obtained in a preliminary parent interview constitute the initial steps in the evaluation. These data are as important as those derived from formal clinical assessment measures, as they place the child in a medical, developmental, and psychosocial context and provide for the next steps in the assessment.

Behavioral Observations

Information about the child's behavior and adjustment comprises a critical part of any evaluation. In addition to observations that the clinician would make during the assessment sessions, he or she should create an opportunity for observing the parent and child together and, if possible, the child interacting with other children, perhaps in a playroom at the clinic or perhaps in a visit to the child's preschool. Such luxuries of time and space are not always available, but when they are, the kind of information they yield is immeasurably important. When a parent says that the child "doesn't behave like that at home (or at school)," typically he or she is right. The artificiality of a one-to-one testing situation opens only a very small window into a child's behavioral style. Examinees described as "hyperactive" in group situations may be very manageable in the testing milieu, when stimulation is reasonably well controlled and the examiner can help him or her focus, and focus again. Children with receptive disorders may do better in a one-to-one format because the examiner, sensitive to the child's distress, may slow down the rate of speech, shorten sentences, and in other ways create a situation that facilitates language processing. Place these same children in a group situation, or even at home with ambient noises and a "normal" language environment, and they might become lost and unable to deal with the language demands.

If such observations are not possible, it is important to obtain a careful and detailed description of the child's functioning abilities in a variety of situations. In addition, administration of the Child Behavior Checklist (CBCL; Achenbach & Edelbrock, 1983), the Personality Inventory for Children (Wirt, Lachar, Klinedinst, Seat, & Broen, 1985), or the Behavioral section of the revised Vineland Adaptive Behavior Scales (Sparrow, Balla, & Cicchetti, 1984) will provide information as to the *informant's perception* of the child's behavior and possible indications of significant or emerging problems. This information is important in any diagnostic endeavor. A preschooler is as prone as anyone else to adjustment problems in response to, for example, environmental situations or an awareness of the disability.

Formal Assessment

Tests and Constructs

Psychological assessment should be guided by a conceptual framework that helps both in the selection of measures and in the interpretation of data. The framework discussed here is process oriented, emphasizing the neuropsychological functions or processes of interest and not the tests to be given. "What do you want to look at?" is our standard response to "What test should I give?" If one thinks about cognitive functions and selects or devises constructs that describe them (e.g., short-term auditory memory, visual-spatial abilities, word retrieval), it becomes possible then to select specific subtests that tap those functions, such as the Sentence Repetition task of the Stanford-Binet Intelligence Scale (Thorndike, Hagen, & Sattler, 1986), Block Designs on the Wechsler Preschool and Primary Scales of Intelligence-Revised (WPPSI-R; Wechsler, 1989), or Verbal Fluency on the McCarthy Scales of Children's Abilities (1972). This works reasonably well if the tests selected are carefully task analyzed to ensure that most of what a test does is what your construct demands. As there probably are no unidimensional tests, the clinician usually has to settle for as close to a "pure" measure as he or she can find. Tests do not always measure only what the manuals say they do, or at least not at first.

Significant constructs to consider in the assessment of young children referred for possible communication disorders include the following:

1. Auditory discrimination (for like-sounding words)
2. Auditory perception (relates to phonological awareness, including, for example, the ability to blend speech sounds and accurately repeat nonwords)
3. Auditory sequential memory (relates to the ability to repeat both linguistically organized and nonmeaningful verbal strings; that is, sentences in contrast to a series of nonsense words or digits)
4. Word retrieval (relates to the ability to rapidly access one's lexicon in response to semantic or [later] phonemic cues)
5. Auditory cognition (relates to the ability to decode vocal language and make an appropriate vocal or nonvocal response. One can conceptualize increasing levels of auditory cognitive abilities as the linguistic demands increase. Apparent deficits in this domain may be related to one or more of the auditory-based constructs noted above.)
6. Visual discrimination (relates to the ability to perceive differences of increasing complexity in visual stimuli)
7. Visual-spatial function (relates to the ability to analyze and synthesize visually presented stimuli. Tasks may or may not require constructional abilities and may involve meaningful [puzzles depicting real things] or nonmeaningful [block patterns] stimuli.)
8. Visual confrontation naming (word retrieval to a pictorial stimulus)
9. Visual cognition (relates to the ability to decode visually presented material in which the task makes cognitive/linguistic as well as other visually based demands. Increasing conceptual demands call for higher levels of visual-cognitive abilities. Deficits in this domain may be related to deficits or

relative inefficiencies in linguistic [verbal mediation] as well as visual discrimination and visual-spatial abilities.)
10. Visual sequential memory (relates to the ability to reconstitute a sequence of briefly exposed visual stimuli)
11. Fine motor skills (relates to eye-hand coordination and motor dexterity)
12. Graphomotor skills (relates to the ability to produce paper-and-pencil representations spontaneously and from copy)
13. Praxis (relates to the ability to mimic a series of movements or to produce a series of voluntary movements on command in response to verbal or visual stimuli)

To assess each of these constructs, with the exception of fine motor function, stimuli may be representational or nonrepresentational. It is useful to present both classes when possible, as the efficiency of a child's verbal mediation skills can make a systematic difference in performance across modalities.

Table 9.2 presents the preceding constructs along with a selection of subtests that one might use to assess them. Using this particular approach, that is, relying on constructs to drive the evaluation rather than tests, one can substitute measures one for another to tap any given function, so long as the subtests have been carefully analyzed in terms of task demands. It is also helpful when time permits to administer more than one measure of a given construct; because of the sometimes uneven reliability of instruments, examiners, and average preschool children, clinicians may be more confident of a result if it can be seen more than once. In the event of significant discrepancies, one might repeat the statistically more reliable measure at another time or at the end of a session.

A Common Metric

At the conclusion of such an assessment, one is left with a number of scores from different tests, each of which has its own metric. For example, the WPPSI has a mean scaled score of 10 and a standard deviation of 3; the Illinois Test of Psycholinguistic Abilities (ITPA; Kirk, McCarthy, & Kirk, 1968) has a mean scaled score of 36 with a standard deviation of 6; the McCarthy Scales have no standard or scaled mean subtest scores, but provide means and standard deviations for each of the subtests as a function of age. It is difficult to conceptualize a pattern of neuropsychological functions with such an array of unrelated scores, and even more difficult to communicate such information to those not conversant with the tests. Because all the tests this author and her colleagues use in the formal assessment phase of the evaluation are standardized, and the means and standard deviations are provided in the test manuals, we have adopted the course of converting all subtest scores into a common metric, the percentile. We do so by going from the test score to a z score and then to a percentile, using the following formula:

$$Z = \frac{X - M}{\sigma}$$

where X is the child's score, M is the mean score of the standardization sample given in the manual, and σ is the standard deviation associated with that mean. The conver-

TABLE 9.2

EXAMPLES OF ALTERNATIVE SUBTEST COMPOSITION
OF NEUROPSYCHOLOGICAL CONSTRUCTS AND CLINICALLY DEFINED FACTORS
AND MODALITIES INVOLVED IN STIMULUS AND RESPONSE MODES

Constructs	Clinical Factor	Subtest	S-R Modes
Auditory perception (AP) (phonologic awareness)	AP1	ITPA[1] Auditory Closure	Auditory-vocal
	AP2	GFW[2] Sound Blending	Auditory-vocal
		GFW Sound Mimicry	Auditory-vocal
Auditory discrimination	AD-Q	GFW[3] Quiet	Auditory/visual-motor
	AD-N	GFW Noise	Auditory/visual-motor
Auditory cognition	AC1	WPPSI-R[4] Similarities	Auditory-vocal
		ITPA Auditory Association	Auditory-vocal
		McCarthy[5] Opposite Analogies	Auditory-vocal
	AC2	K-ABC[6] Riddles	Auditory-vocal
	AC3 (greater formulation demands)	S-B[7] Vocabulary	First seven items; auditory/visual-vocal then auditory-vocal
		S-B Comprehension	First six items; auditory/visual-vocal then auditory-vocal
		WPPSI-R Vocabulary	Auditory-vocal
		WPPSI-R Comprehension	Auditory-vocal
	AC4	Token Test[8] 1,2,3	Auditory/visual-motor
	AC5 (heavy memory load)	Token Test 4	Auditory/visual-motor
	AC6 (increased syntactic comprehension)	DTLA-P[9] Oral Directions	Auditory/visual-motor
		Token Test 5	Auditory/visual-motor
Auditory semantic retrieval (ASR)	ASR	McCarthy Verbal Fluency	Auditory-vocal
		CELF-R[10] Word Association	Auditory-vocal
Auditory memory (AM)	AM1 (representational, linguistic)	S-B Memory for Sentences	Auditory-vocal
		WPPSI-R Sentences	Auditory-vocal
	AM2 (nonrepresentational)	ITPA Auditory Sequential Memory	Auditory-vocal
		S-B Digits	Auditory-vocal
		McCarthy Digits (F)	Auditory-vocal
		DTLA-P Digit Sequence	Auditory-vocal

Continued

TABLE 9.2 *(continued)*

EXAMPLES OF ALTERNATIVE SUBTEST COMPOSITION
OF NEUROPSYCHOLOGICAL CONSTRUCTS AND CLINICALLY DEFINED FACTORS
AND MODALITIES INVOLVED IN STIMULUS AND RESPONSE MODES

Constructs	Clinical Factor	Subtest	S-R Modes
	AM3 (formulation demands often exceed memory demands)	McCarthy Verbal Memory 2 (use with probe questions)	Auditory-vocal
		CELF-R Listening to Paragraphs	Auditory-vocal
Visual discrimination	VD	H-N[11] Picture Identification	Visual-motor
		PTI[12] Form Discrimination	Visual-motor
		DTLA-P Letter Sequence–Type I	Visual-motor
Visual-spatial ability	VSP1 (nonrepresentational)	WPPSI-R Block Designs	Visual-motor
		McCarthy Blocks	Visual-motor
	VSP2 (representational)	McCarthy Puzzles	Visual-motor
	VSP3 (representational)	K-ABC Gestalt Closure	Visual-vocal
Visual cognition	VC1	WPPSI-R Picture Completion	Visual-vocal
	VC2	ITPA Visual Reception	Visual-motor
		H-N Picture Identification	Visual-motor
	VC3	ITPA Visual Association	Visual-motor
		H-N Picture Association	Visual-motor
		PTI Similarities	Visual-motor
		DTLA-P Conceptual Matching	Visual-motor
	VC4	K-ABC Photo Series	Visual-motor
	VC5 (significant formulation demands)	S-B Absurdities	Visual-vocal
	VC6	ITPA Manual Expression	Visual-motor
Visual semantic retrieval	VSR (interpret judiciously re actual vocabulary demands)	Boston Naming Test[13] (age 5+)	Visual-vocal
		PPVT-R[14]	Visual-vocal
Visual memory	VM1 (representational, sequential)	H-N Visual Attention Span	Visual-motor
		S-B Memory for Objects (from 4–10)	Visual-motor
		DTLA-P Object Sequences	Visual-motor

Continued

TABLE 9.2 *(continued)*

EXAMPLES OF ALTERNATIVE SUBTEST COMPOSITION
OF NEUROPSYCHOLOGICAL CONSTRUCTS AND CLINICALLY DEFINED FACTORS
AND MODALITIES INVOLVED IN STIMULUS AND RESPONSE MODES

Constructs	*Clinical Factor*	*Subtest*	*S-R Modes*
Visual memory *(continued)*	VM2 (nonrepresentational, sequential)	ITPA Visual Sequential Memory	Visual-motor
		H-N Bead Memory	Visual-motor
		S-B Beads	Visual-motor
		H-N Memory for Color	Visual-motor
	VM3 (nonsequential)	PTI Immediate Recall	Visual-motor
Fine motor ability	FM	Purdue Pegboard[15]	Visual-motor
		H-N Bead Stringing	Visual-motor
Graphomotor function	GrM1 (nonrepresentational)	McCarthy Draw-A-Person	Visual-motor
		WPPSI-R Geometric Designs	Visual-motor
		DTLA-P Draw-A-Person	Visual-motor
	GrM2 (representational)	McCarthy Draw-A-Person	Visual-motor
		DTLA-P Draw-A-Person	Visual-motor
Praxis	Pr1	K-ABC Hand Movements	Visual-motor
		ITPA Manual Expression (if poor score on VC5, consider dyspraxia)	Visual-motor
	Pr2	DTLA-P Motor Directions	Auditory-motor

[1] Illinois Test of Psycholinguistic Abilities (Kirk, McCarthy, & Kirk, 1968)
[2] Goldman-Fristoe-Woodcock Auditory Skills Battery (Goldman, Fristoe, & Woodcock, 1986)
[3] Goldman-Fristoe-Woodcock Test of Auditory Discrimination (Goldman, Fristoe, & Woodcock, 1970)
[4] Wechsler Preschool and Primary Scales of Intelligence–Revised (Wechsler, 1989)
[5] McCarthy Scales of Children's Abilities (McCarthy, 1972)
[6] Kaufman Assessment Battery for Children (Kaufman & Kaufman, 1983)
[7] Stanford-Binet Intelligence Scale: Fourth Edition (Thorndike, Hagen, & Sattler, 1986)
[8] Token Test for Children (DiSimoni, 1978)
[9] Detroit Test of Learning Abilities–Primary (Hammill, 1985)
[10] Clinical Evaluation of Language Fundamentals–Revised (Semel, Wiig, & Secord, 1987)
[11] Hiskey-Nebraska Test of Learning Aptitude (deaf and hearing norms) (Hiskey, 1966)
[12] Pictorial Test of Intelligence (French, 1964)
[13] Boston Naming Test (Kaplan, Goodglass, & Weintraub, 1978)
[14] Peabody Picture Vocabulary Test–Revised (Dunn & Dunn, 1981)
[15] Purdue Pegboard (Wilson et al., 1982, preschool norms)

sion table is entered with the calculated z score, and the percentile is read out. Such a z-to-percentile table appears in Appendix C.

Profile Development

If more than one score is available to represent a given construct, we take the median or midpoint of the scores and plot that percentile as the score representing the construct. When the scores are clearly discrepant, the score from the test with the better reliability statistics is the one used. The profile is plotted in terms of constructs plotted as a function of percentile score.

Assessment of Infants and Toddlers

Although one cannot assess infants and toddlers for the presence of a developmental language disorder as speech and language are not at the disposal of most of the age range under consideration, it is possible to detect potential precursors and to alert families and physicians to the possibilities. In that way, regular follow-up evaluations may be provided either to confirm or disconfirm these possibilities as the child grows into preschool age and the developmental requirements in the language domain become more demanding.

What are the high risk indicators? What should one expect in terms of normal language milestones? First, if the infant shows abnormal feeding patterns that seem to involve inadequate or inappropriate oromotor function, a careful examination should be conducted by one who understands infant oral reflexology and developmental patterns. Such deficits, if discovered, may herald nothing, a more generalized pattern of motor abnormalities, or the early signs of apraxia. They are not diagnostic signs at this stage of development but rather signals that prespeech development should be monitored. If the infant displays a questionable response to speech or environmental sounds and a less than average amount of vocalization, or has a history of ototoxic drugs, hearing should be tested until the possibility of a hearing loss is ruled out. If hearing is demonstrated to be normal, based on crib or behavioral audiometry and evoked potential studies, the child's speech development should be monitored. VAA has an early onset.

A few standardized instruments are available for the evaluation of speech and language in children under 2 years of age. Those used most often are the Sequenced Inventory of Communication Development (SICD; Hedrick, Prather, & Tobin, 1984), the Bzoch-League Receptive-Expressive Language Scale (REEL Scale; Bzoch & League, 1971), and the Communication scale of the revised Vineland. All of these measures are based on parent or caregiver report. Information obtained on the basis of such reports may be very useful or very unreliable, and thus should be supplemented with one's own observations. Additionally, there are many checklists and observational scales available to help screen and monitor speech and language development (see particularly Miller, 1983, and Darby, 1985). What follows is a very short list of the major speech and language behaviors that should emerge between 6 months and 2 years of age (a version of the developmental scale proposed by Miller, 1983). This does not replace a more detailed inventory if problems are noted or suspected, but it does provide a schedule of major milestones as a first step in the identification of possible problem areas:

1. At 6 months, an infant should be able to
   a. orient to sounds in the environment;
   b. repeat syllables beginning with bilabial sounds (e.g., "ma ma ma," "ba ba ba");
   c. maintain vocalizations such as cooing and babbling for a minute and a half or better;
   d. vary the intonation of vocal production; and
   e. make discrete tongue movements, allowing for the production of d and n sounds.
2. At 12 months, an infant should be able to
   a. understand his or her own name and the name of a family member who is present;
   b. call "mama" and "papa" referentially, not often and with limited, but generally recognizable, intelligibility;
   c. imitate speech sounds; and
   d. take turns in vocal play and in peek-a-boo games.
3. At 18 months, a toddler should be able to
   a. understand single words and names of things he or she can see;
   b. produce several intelligible words;
   c. demonstrate an increase in vocalization with communicative intent;
   d. make requests and signify rejection with motor or vocal behavior; and
   e. comment on events in the here and now.
4. At 24 months, a toddler should be able to
   a. understand at least a two-word utterance, such as "Get bottle";
   b. demonstrate understanding of action-object relation;
   c. produce words, including action verbs and refer to objects not present;
   d. demonstrate a vocabulary of at least 20 words;
   e. regularly produce two-word phrases; and
   f. ask for names of things and places.

These chronological guidelines are considered outside limits of the normal range of acquisition. If a child is not demonstrating these behaviors at the given time intervals, careful evaluation is clearly indicated. Although the absence or delay in the acquisition of language milestones is not sufficient evidence of a present or incipient developmental language disorder, it is certainly an indication that something may be amiss and should be taken seriously at any age level at which such delays are noted. They may indicate just delays, particularly the earlier milestones, that will clear up as development progresses, but others may relate to environmental issues or may reflect static or progressive neurological disorders. Language delays can indicate delayed or deficient development of a more global nature. When the problem is of sufficient concern following a careful evaluation, most states provide intervention programs that can address a range of developmental issues, and parents should be helped to access such programs.

What is true for diagnostic statements when we talk about preschool children is even more true when discussing infants and toddlers. We don't know very much about the outcomes of developmental vagaries noted in the first 2 years of life. Predictions are less reliable, particularly concerning cognitive issues, and standardized assessment instruments are all but nonexistent. We need to be prudent in what we tell parents and others. It is certainly fair and indeed more than appropriate to state that one is watching thus-and-so because there are concerns about aspects of development, but that there is no firm statement of diagnosis or prognosis to be made. The issue usually relates to rate of development, something that clinician and parents can watch together.

CASE STUDIES

Beth W.

Beth was referred for evaluation at 3 years, 10 months of age by a pediatric neurologist because of reported delays in acquisition of language in the presence of otherwise normal development. The referral question had to do with her current level of cognitive development, really a differential diagnosis between mental retardation and DLD. Prenatal history was noncontributory; birth history was benign. There was no family history of delayed language, learning disabilities, retardation, or neurological diseases. The W.'s have two older children and an 18-month-old, all developing normally. The results of the neurological examination and thorough medical examinations at regular intervals were entirely negative except for a history of severe and frequent episodes of serous otitis media, which have persisted until the present time. According to Mrs. W., the pediatrician "did not believe in myringotomies," a procedure that places evacuation tubes in the ear(s) to provide for drainage, and the condition had been treated with decongestants over the years.

The developmental information of note is a history of "very late" talking, first words not appearing until 20 months of age and two- and three-word phrases at about 23 months. All other milestones were attained at age-appropriate intervals. Mrs. W. described Beth as a quiet but delightful child, full of curiosity and feeling more and more the impact of her limited communication skills. She had been attending a regular nursery school several mornings a week, but Mrs. W. felt that it had become too much of a strain because of her language problems; Beth was returning home tired and irritable. The preschool teacher had commented on Beth's initial friendliness, willingness to try new things, and apparently good cognitive skills in nonverbal areas, but she agreed that things became progressively more difficult for her as time went on. Frustration and anger had been increasingly evident in the 3 months prior to the evaluation. At home, the family members had worked out ways of dealing with Beth's difficulties, including the development of an informal "sign" language.

The history strongly suggests a developmental language disorder, defined or contributed to by an ongoing history of serous otitis media. The nursery school teacher and Mrs. W. had the impression that Beth had otherwise good intelligence, although a more generalized developmental disorder still would need to be ruled out. The initial evaluation sessions, then, would best deal with an assessment of cognitive abilities in both verbal and performance areas, with particular attention paid to speech and language skills, both expressive and receptive, and other parameters of communication (e.g., pragmatics). As there were some concerns about increasing frustration and anger, careful attention would need to be given to matters of behavior and adjustment, particularly because children with language disorders are at high risk for psychiatric disorders (Beichtman, 1985; Cantwell & Baker, 1977; Cantwell, Baker, & Mattison, 1980); a referral for psychiatric evaluation might be appropriate.

Given the history, a complete audiological evaluation was necessary in order to rule out the presence of a hearing loss prior to the initiation of any other evaluation. As such an evaluation had never been done, there had been no monitoring of Beth's hearing acuity before, during, or after bouts of the otitis. The report from the audiologist indicated that the audiological evaluation found normal hearing at the time of the examination, but given the history and current status of Beth's ears, hearing might fluctuate in response to accumulation of fluid. Referral was made to a pediatric ENT (ear, nose, and throat) specialist, who recommended that myringotomies be performed as soon as possible.

The neuropsychological evaluation was then undertaken, prior to the surgical procedure, with follow-up testing planned for some months following surgery. Beth was initially somewhat anxious and shrank into her chair, but by the end of the first session she appeared to feel less threatened, and although she continued to be somewhat shy, she related in a friendly manner despite the demands made on her limited linguistic skills. Things became difficult for her during the administration of the auditory-verbal items, at which times she became visibly anxious, twirled a lock of her hair between her fingers, and gave minimal eye contact. She knew when she was in trouble. In spite of the obvious stress she was experiencing, Beth's behavior throughout the assessment was characterized by good attention and cooperation. She produced limited spontaneous speech and brief and grammatically immature verbal responses. It was clear that Beth did not always understand what was being said to her, so that her responses were frequently tangential or perseverative, often disorganized and unintelligible. When presented with nonverbal tasks or those that required a minimum of verbal comprehension or expression, her demeanor changed and she became more spontaneous in her movements, facial expression, and vocalization. She paid a good deal of attention to the examiner's face, both for assistance in understanding what was being said (lip reading?) and for some reading of how she was doing.

Subtests of the McCarthy Scales, the ITPA, and the Pictorial Test of Intelligence (PTI; French, 1964) were chosen for the initial phase of the assessment in order to make some determination about her level of abilities in verbally and visually mediated areas. Initial results indicated deficiencies in both auditory cognitive abilities and auditory memory, except for repetition of digits. This task requires repetition but neither comprehension, as for the story repetition task, nor good grammar, as a facilitator for sentence repetition. Visually mediated skills were within the average range except for some aspects of visual cognitive abilities and a heavily language-loaded visual memory task, which is facilitated by rapid retrieval of labels and other aspects of verbal mediation. Based on these findings, it was necessary to determine whether the retrieval skills useful in some of the visual and verbal tasks (memory,

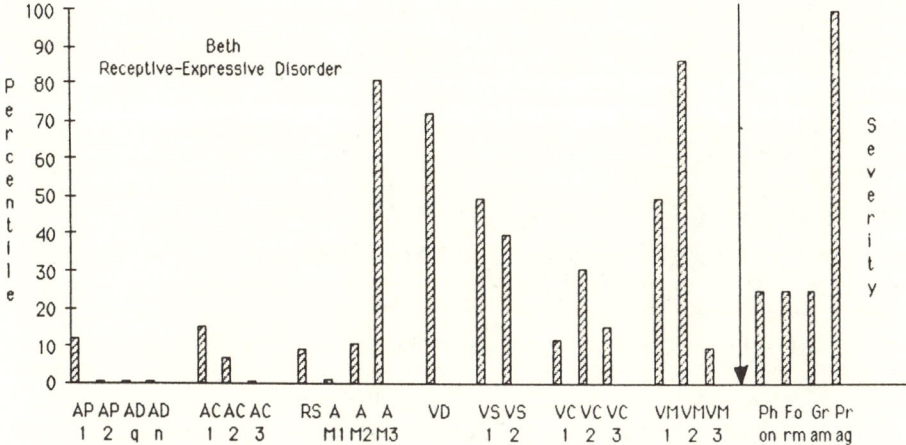

FIGURE 9.1. Neuropsychological profile of Beth, aged 3 years, 10 months. Significant receptive disorders were evident, and expressive language was compromised by organizational deficits and associated retrieval problems and by significantly compromised phonology and grammar. Pragmatic abilities were excellent. Beth's language disorder was characterized as a receptive-expressive disorder.

naming, grouping and categorization skills) were deficient, and what auditory discrimination and aspects of auditory perception looked like, as these are prerequisite skills for any more cognitively demanding auditorily presented material.

The retrieval measure, in this instance the Verbal Fluency subtest of the McCarthy Scales, yielded a score in the deficient range. Measures of auditory discrimination under both quiet and noisy background situations and measures of sound blending, auditory closure, and sound mimicry yielded scores ranging from the eighth percentile to scores below the first percentile (indicated by the asterisk on the profile). Clearly the more complex verbally presented material was not being adequately processed, and verbal responses were compromised further by inadequate retrieval strategies from an inadequate lexicon. In addition to the psychometric measures, the SLIQ was completed at the conclusion of the evaluation. Beth's SLIQ data indicate severe deficiencies in *observed* language abilities in interactive situations in the areas of phonology, formulation/organization, and grammar, with essentially normal pragmatics. These data, psychometric and observational, are presented in profile form in Figure 9.1. (Table 9.3 provides a key to the factors and constructs illustrated in Figures 9.1, 9.2, and 9.3.)

Results of fine motor and graphomotor assessment, not included in the profile, were within age expected ranges. Oromotor screening did not reveal deficits in Beth's voluntary control of her articulators, so that her limited intelligibility seemed not to be a function of motor deficiencies. One might hypothesize that some of the less adequate visual-cognitive and visual memory tasks were negatively influenced by Beth's inadequate acquisition of linguistic concepts and verbal mediation strategies, and that she had been functioning as an intermittently hearing impaired child, which

TABLE 9.3

KEYS TO FIGURES 9.1, 9.2 AND 9.3

Constructs	Factors	Subtests
Auditory perception (AP)	AP1	ITPA Auditory Closure
	AP2	ITPA Sound Blending
Auditory discrimination (AD)	AD-Q	GFW Quiet
	AD-N	GFW Noise
Auditory cognitive (AC)	AC1	WPPSI-R Similarities ITPA Auditory Association
	AC2	WPPSI-R Information ITPA Auditory Reception
	AC3	WPPSI-R Vocabulary WPPSI-R Comprehension
Auditory memory (AM)	AM1	WPPSI-R Sentences McCarthy Verbal Memory
	AM2	McCarthy Verbal Memory
	AM3	ITPA Auditory Sequential Memory
Retrieval (RET)	RS	McCarthy Verbal Fluency
Visual discrimination (VD)	VD1	H-N Picture Identification PTI Form Discrimination
Visual spatial (VSp)	VSp1	WPPSI-R Block Design H-N Block Patterns
	VSp2	McCarthy Puzzle Solving
Visual cognitive (VC)	VC1	WPPSI-R Picture Completion ITPA Visual Reception
	VC2	ITPA Visual Association H-N Picture Association PTI Similarities
	VC3	ITPA Manual Expression
Visual memory (VM)	VM1	H-N Visual Attention Span
	VM2	H-N Memory for Color ITPA Visual Sequential Memory
	VM3	PTI Immediate Recall

contributed to her poor phonology and generally inadequate language skills. Final results indicated that Beth's nonverbal cognitive abilities were solidly within the average range in spite of her less adequate visually mediated cognitive-linguistic skills. Her auditory-verbal cognitive abilities were within the borderline range, easy to understand in the face of severely deficient auditory perceptual skills. Based on history, observation, and formal assessment, Beth was identified as having a primary developmental language disorder characterized by deficits in both receptive and expressive areas, a member of the Wilson-Risucci Auditory and Visual Semantic Comprehension Disorder subtype. Overall cognitive abilities were considered to have been compromised by the language disability and probable fluctuating hearing loss. There was the potential for increased abilities in the auditory-verbal and linguistically loaded visually mediated areas as hearing improved and as appropriate speech-language and educational services were provided.

In the parent-informing conference, the results were reviewed and implications for daily function in school and at home were discussed. The recommendations included (a) a follow-up on the recommendation for myringotomies, which was done within 2 weeks of the conference; (b) a referral to a speech/language therapist for further evaluation of speech/language functions and for the initiation of speech therapy while a referral to a preschool program for children with language disorders was set in motion; (c) a Total Communication program, including Signing Exact English to assist Beth in the acquisition of concepts and grammatical structure of the language, with sign cuing as an assist in acquiring a visual representation of phonologic aspects of language (participation recommended for therapist, school, and family); (d) referral for evaluation of Beth's emotional status, given the response to stress that she had already demonstrated; and (e) a reevaluation in 1 year to monitor her progress.

By way of follow-up on the immediate postevaluation events, speech therapy was initiated following the surgical procedure. The report from the therapist indicated inadequate speech discrimination, limited lexicon, and significant phonological deficits, sometimes rendering speech unintelligible unless the contexts were shared. There were deficits in every aspect of language other than pragmatics. The therapist implemented the recommended Total Communication program, to which Beth responded enthusiastically and which was continued in the preschool program. The therapist reported slow but steady progress over a 5-month period, at which time Beth was placed in a full-day preschool program for language disordered children.

Beth was followed from age 3 years, 10 months through her 15th birthday at annual then biennial intervals. Her verbal skills did increase over the years, but the discrepancy between auditory-verbal and visually mediated functions continued to be present. At 15 years of age, Beth's VIQ of 90 reflected an increase from the borderline to average level; her PIQ had increased from low average to within the solidly average range, 112. The discrepancy between the two scores is significant and reflects the discrepancies in her day-to-day functional abilities. Her speech was generally intelligible but had a muffled quality. Phonology was still deficient, and when Beth attempted to communicate a lengthy, complicated message, she sometimes became borderline intelligible, and her sentence and grammatical structure deteriorated. Receptive abilities, although greatly improved, still left her vulnerable to misunderstanding what was being said or asked. She was a very pretty youngster, friendly and popular, but her social group of choice was, in general, lower functioning than she. She did not understand humor or nuances. Academic skills were hard won and never attained the levels commensurate with her cognitive abilities. Her continuing deficiencies in all aspects of reading (i.e., phonics, decoding, and comprehension) reflect the well-documented relationship between language and reading; Beth's "label" was changed from Speech/Language Impaired to Learning Disabled at the end of third grade. Expressive writing in ninth grade indicated creative ideas, but inadequate language skills constrained her ability to develop them adequately. Beth had been involved in play therapy from ages 5 to 6, then in group counseling at 11, and finally in individual psychotherapy from age 13 on, for all of the reasons that deficient receptive and expressive language abilities would suggest. Although progress had been made in all areas over the years, Beth and her family continue to live with the ramifications of DLD.

Mark H.

Mark was referred at 4 years, 1 month of age for evaluation by his Pre-K teacher because of his "inability to play with other children" and unwillingness to participate in some of the classroom activities, notably such things as "show and tell." He would try to hide under his table in the classroom during some activities, and although he played alongside other children, he rarely initiated discussion and in general talked very little. He did not demonstrate classically autistic behaviors, although there was said to be a slight remoteness about him. There seemed to be little doubt that he understood what was being said, and he was thought to have above average conceptual abilities as demonstrated by his creative play and constructional abilities. The question was whether Mark was demonstrating an emotional or behavioral disorder, or whether he had some kind of language problem that the school had not been able to identify.

Mrs. H. reported an uneventful pregnancy and delivery, confirmed by review of the medical records. Neonatal history was noncontributory. All developmental motor milestones were normally acquired; first words and short phrases reportedly occurred on target as well. Mrs. H. commented that Mark has "plenty of language" but doesn't talk very much, even at home, and when he does, he seems to have difficulty "getting things straight." Family history revealed that Mrs. H. had an M.A. in education and her husband, Dr. H., an advanced degree in engineering. He was described as "not very talkative" and, according to his recollections, he, too, had been considered a "slow talker" and something of a "loner" during much of his school career. In fact, Dr. H. seemed to have a residual expressive problem of his own; his sentences were halting, and verbal tics such as "umm" and "you know" were distributed throughout his conversation, not uncommon fillers for those who have some trouble putting language together. He may have had word-finding problems as well, but there did seem evidence of a mild expressive problem.

The history suggests the possibility of (a) an autistic spectrum disorder or (b) an organization or formulation deficit in expressive language with compromised pragmatics, perhaps familial. Given the real absence of standardized measures of expressive language beyond the one-word level, the evaluation would need to focus on the elicitation of as much language as possible, with verbatim responses recorded for review. Although there seemed little question about Mark's receptive skills, these, too, would need to be carefully assessed for the presence of subtle deficits. The possibility of discrepancies between processing modalities would need to be determined, as would the possibility of a referral to child psychiatry in the event that "poor pragmatics" turned out to be something more clearly on the autistic spectrum. As with all suspected communication disorders, an audiological examination was requested; results confirmed the presence of normal bilateral hearing.

Mark entered the testing situation with some reserve but a good deal of curiosity. He gave good eye contact, was attentive to what was being said, but offered no spontaneous language until the last of four testing sessions. He was clumsy at "conversing" in terms of topic maintenance or conversational turn taking and kept his responses as brief as possible. What became clear as we moved along was that Mark had considerable difficulty in organizing responses to *wh-* questions or to open-ended questions in general. He found it a real problem to put new thoughts or complex thoughts into acceptable form and frequently gave up in the middle with a wave of his hand and mounting frustration. Practiced verbal material was easier for him, and he could do reasonably well in conventional language-demand situations, talking about the here and now in simple, declarative sentences. Although he did demonstrate inadequate pragmatic skills, there seemed no reason to suspect an autistic spectrum disorder, and he was far too competent to be considered for a diagnosis of PDD. He was well related and had clearly demonstrated communicative intent. Further demonstration of this subtle language problem in conjunction with overall good cognitive skills would suggest that Mark might be one of the children who would fit into the Organization Deficit subtype as described in the Wilson-Risucci classification, the rule stating that there may be no more than one score below the average range for inclusion in this group.

Figure 9.2 presents the results of Mark's formal assessment. Scores range from superior to average in both the verbal and nonverbal domains. The single score falling below the average range was obtained on auditory discrimination in the noisy condition. This was administered twice to corroborate the results. The score appears reliable and may reflect either an incipient attentional deficit or a rapid "stimulus overload" in the auditory modality, something to monitor in classroom situations.

Beyond the formal test instruments, tasks were devised to encourage Mark to produce spoken language and to try to converse. He did not seem able to do very well with the latter except in rather concrete terms, although in certain situations he was clearly interested in providing information for comment. Asking him about his favorite TV program, his little brother, or his classroom, providing him with things to play with, and encouraging a running description of what he was doing elicited a good number of responses. A classroom visit seemed potentially helpful, as his language behavior with his peers was of more relevance perhaps than his one-on-one interaction with an adult who was manipulating the situation. A careful review of Mark's elicited and spontaneous utterances in both situations indicated the presence of poorly constructed sentences, with errors both of syllable sequence within words (metathetic errors) and in order of words, and general difficulty in organizing the content of what he wanted to say.

In response to the Verbal Memory 2 subtest of the McCarthy Scales, in which

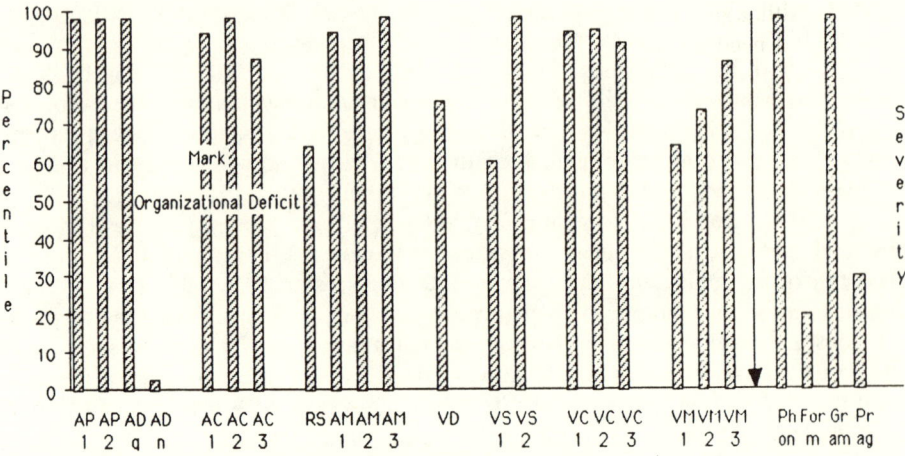

FIGURE 9.2. Neuropsychological profile of Mark, aged 4 years, 1 month. Formal assessment results indicated high average to superior skills in all areas except auditory discrimination in a noisy surround. Scaled observational data indicated excellent formulation and grammar, poor formulation, and mild to moderate deficits in pragmatic abilities. Mark's subtle but real language disorder was identified as an expressive organizational deficit.

the child is to tell back a brief story just heard, Mark's response was "the boy . . . the letters he got . . . the lady . . . the letters, she dropped and the wind . . . she was glad of the boy"—this from a child who clearly understood the content and had superior cognitive abilities. Again, in response to a request to talk about his trip to the zoo, "You go on a train and you . . . there are . . . you could see ephalunts and you could . . . there are things to feed them . . . zebras and bears could be and . . . ." When talking about what he was doing, Mark's sentences were short but generally more precise. He was doing some excellent block construction in his classroom, combining the blocks with other toys. "This will be a bridge. And this is the train that goes over it. It goes to the station. There is this guy in the caboose and here is the train driver. If I could make a mountain, the train could go on it." The presence of "things" to talk about seemed to help him get organized. His vocabulary and sentence content were not up to expectations, but the accompanying pretend play suggested that much more was going on in his head then he could comfortably talk about.

In sum, the results of the evaluation indicated the presence of a subtle expressive language disorder, perhaps familial, characterized by organizational problems and accompanied by compromised pragmatic abilities. Results of the SLIQ indicated intact phonology and grammar, with moderate deficiencies in formulation/organization and in pragmatics.

In the parent conference, with his teacher present, the results of the evaluation were reviewed. Everyone's feelings about Mark's excellent cognitive skills were confirmed. The presence of an organizational language disorder was discussed and a speech/language evaluation was recommended for a more detailed assessment of the disorder. Although the recommendation for placement in a special preschool program for DLD children was discussed, the parents chose to have Mark remain in his current placement, a private school that went through high school and was aimed at high functioning children, with language therapy provided privately, to be coordinated with his teacher. They accepted a referral to child psychiatry for evaluation because, at a behavioral level, Mark had begun to demonstrate his frustration in maladaptive ways in the classroom. His pulling away from his group was in part dictated by his inability to communicate easily, but his parallel rather than cooperative play was becoming more and more the norm. How much of his behavior was based in biological temperament, perhaps with a familial contribution, remained an open question. A behavioral rather than traditional psychotherapeutic approach was ultimately recommended and proved effective. Speech/language therapy was provided twice a week, with monthly conferences with the school built into the treatment plan. This course was continued until the end of first grade, at which time the therapist "dismissed" Mark.

There are several important points to be made about a child such as this, with an expressive disorder and no apparent receptive component; the problem is too often minimized or ignored. Although not as frequently as with receptive disorders, expressive problems can lead to behavioral or emotional problems and need to be recognized on those grounds alone. In addition, data resulting from a longitudinal study of DLD children (Wilson, Wilson, Risucci, & Wheeler, 1989) suggest that children with profiles such as Mark's move along academically in the early grades, typically experiencing little or no difficulty in the acquisition of reading. However, they appear to encounter a good deal of difficulty when they are expected to produce original written material. Here, as with the receptive problems, the organization problems do not really go away; they surface in another, related domain.

This was the case with Mark. At 14 years of age, he had improved his expressive vocal language to the point where he could carry on a conversation with little difficulty. Vocabulary usage was not as good as his lexicon would suggest, his sentences tended to be adequate but short, and although the pragmatic aspects of his language has improved greatly and he was no longer self-isolating, neither was he a very social young man. It is not possible to know how much of this was related to his earlier language difficulty, how much to biological temperament, or how much to environmental factors. Each likely made a contribution. He excelled in math and read 1 year above grade level with good comprehension. It was in expressive writing that his earlier problem resurfaced. He was unable to produce anything like grade-level written work. Spelling, usually good, became variable, handwriting was less adequate, and vocabulary usage deteriorated. There were too many things to put into place at the same time. He wound up producing "baby" sentences, not very well put together. Private tutoring centered around Mark's devising an outlining format that would work for him and permit him to address his attention to content rather than what should come next.

Georgia R.

Georgia was referred at 3 years of age by the pediatrics in-patient service to which she had been admitted because of a reported seizure disorder. The referral issue had to do with a request for an estimate of cognitive level and a differential diagnosis. The child psychiatry department had raised questions about autism, PDD, and retardation. The child's history was taken from the mother, who had brought her to the emergency room several days earlier, stating that Georgia had experienced an epileptic seizure. At that time Mrs. R. also described "peculiar behavior" that may have been descriptions of absence seizures, which according to Mrs. R. happened frequently, and the child was admitted for a workup.

The neurological examination yielded negative results except for noting that Georgia seemed developmentally delayed in language and in poor contact. Her EEG was normal. The history obtained from her mother indicated an essentially normal pregnancy and delivery. No difficulties occurred during the neonatal period. Motor milestones were acquired at the outside limit of normal; Georgia did not walk independently until 17 months. Speech had never developed; although cooing and some babbling were noted at age-appropriate levels, vocalizations tapered off by 24 months of age. Standard audiological examinations had been attempted in the past without success. Although the family believed that she could hear, Mrs. R. had questioned the level of Georgia's comprehension from early on. They never had questions about her communicative intent within the family, nor of her awareness of what was going on around her. Mr. and Mrs. R. described Georgia's behavior at home in terms of what she could not do in the language area, and how she was able to manage in others. They described her ability to "read" faces for clues as to what was wanted and to respond to and to use gestures with her family, but they noted her unwillingness to use gestures outside of her home. They described a child who related appropriately to her family and some frequent visitors, but who became a different child when strangers appeared. This had developed over time, Georgia becoming less able or less motivated to attempt interactions with those outside of her home.

The parents had taken Georgia for rounds of evaluations from the time she was 18 months old and were given a range of diagnoses, from childhood schizophrenia to mental retardation and disorders in between. Still in search of a diagnosis, and with a range of conflicting recommendations, no intervention had been provided up to the point of hospital admission. Some time after Georgia was discharged from the hospital, Mrs. R. admitted that there had been no seizures. At the conclusion of her last visit with the pediatrician, the mother had been advised to institutionalize Georgia, who would get worse, not better, and who had no real potential for development. Before they would consider the option of a residential placement, the R.'s decided to obtain one final but comprehensive evaluation. Their request for hospital admission was denied because the child was not ill, and an in-patient admission was not deemed necessary. They, particularly Mr. R., were frightened and angry, and did not understand what was wrong with their child. It was then that Mrs. R. concocted the story about a seizure disorder and obtained the comprehensive evaluation she sought, with all consultant services in the same place and able to confer conveniently about this diagnostic dilemma.

Prior to the neuropsychological evaluation, brain stem and cortical auditory-evoked responses were assessed and appeared normal, so that hearing could be presumed intact. Georgia was observed in the playroom on the pediatrics floor on several occasions before the neuropsychological evaluation was undertaken. Although she did not interact with the other children in the playroom, she always migrated to the area in which someone or some group of children were playing. She ignored any invitation on the part of the others to join them but stayed close by and watched. Eye contact was fleeting and her facial expression was generally "flat" when she was approached by strangers, but she became somewhat more spontaneous and expressive when she was with people that she knew. Several nurses on the floor developed relationships with Georgia, and although she never initiated an interaction, she did attempt gestural communication in response to communicative attempts on their parts. They described the interactions as variable, in that she would be "with them" at one point and inaccessible at others.

In the playroom and by herself, Georgia indulged in rather high-level symbolic play. With the help of a set of small toy figures, she created little worlds in which people did real things. For example, she played with the house, furnished a kitchen, and had a "mommy" doll at the stove, who brought pretend food to the table at which sat a "daddy" doll and a baby in a little chair. There was a scenario in which "Daddy" took dishes to the sink and then left the house, and "Mommy" put the baby to bed. Although some autistic children demonstrate high-level play, it is usually those who demonstrate reasonable use of language, which Georgia had not done at that point. Her block constructions were elegant but she moved off from any activity when another child attempted to join her.

Georgia appeared to be very fearful initially, and only over time was she able to cooperate in the assessment. The formal evaluation extended over many brief sessions, sometimes several a day, and yielded no score on any auditory-verbal measure. Georgia appeared to understand no vocally presented language. She responded reasonably well to gestures, and produced a few meaningful ones herself, including facial expressions for "More," "I don't like it," "Something to drink," and "Go away." She began to indicate "I don't understand" by opening her eyes very wide and looking very hard, almost staring, at the examiner.

With regard to the formal assessment, Georgia produced performances within the average range for her age on those subtests for which she understood the directions. Results of her evaluation appear in Figure 9.3. Graphomotor ability, which is solidly within the average range, was included because we were interested in presenting as broad a picture as possible of what her abilities were. Georgia was unable to comply with any of the auditory-verbal tasks, apparently because she did not understand the questions and/or could not produce language. She could be led into imitation of some sounds and word approximations. Her phonology was poor on imitation and she volunteered no vocal production other than humming when she was engaged in manipulative tasks. Simple within-semantic-category match (e.g., ITPA Visual Reception, ball-to-ball paradigm) was accomplished within the average range, but the associative and higher level conceptual tasks were beyond her abilities, either in comprehending the task and/or in having the concepts available to her. She was able to manage the non-representational visual-spatial tasks (e.g., Hiskey-Nebraska Block Patterns), but, for whatever the reason, she could not do so on representational items such as Puzzles from the McCarthy Scales. She was unable to perform either the representational or non-representational visual sequential memory tasks, but scored within the average range memory load of one item. Oromotor function was examined and found to be entirely normal.

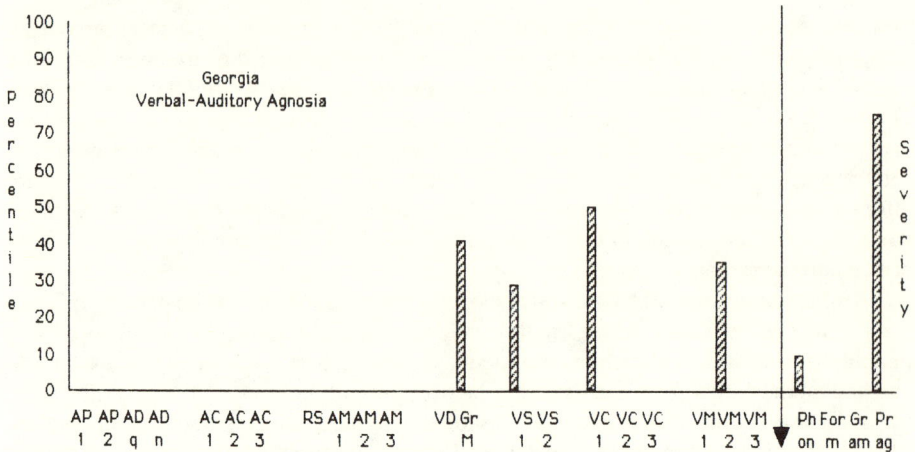

FIGURE 9.3. Neuropsychological profile of Georgia, aged 3 years. Georgia was unable to comprehend spoken language, to respond to standardized test items, and to produce intelligible speech. She performed within the average range on some visually mediated subtests and demonstrated adequate pragmatics but severely deficient phonology. Her inability to produce running speech precluded evaluation of formulation and grammar. Georgia's language disorder was identified as verbal-auditory agnosia.

The diagnoses that could be considered at this point included mental retardation, a global language disorder, a place on the autistic spectrum, PDD, or auditory verbal agnosia (VAA). A review of the data suggested that mental retardation could be ruled out because all of the cognitive functions that could be assessed were found to be within the normal range of abilities. Most children with the global disorder do use vocal language, however inadequate, and do have some receptive abilities, however limited. Further, their pragmatic abilities are typically not as deficient as other aspects of language. None of these characterizations were true of Georgia. Although there were those clinicians who continued to opt for a diagnosis of autism at the conclusion of the comprehensive evaluation, it was our position that Georgia demonstrated the VAA syndrome with less adequate pragmatics in terms of communicative intent than often the case, although even this had to be modified in light of her interactions with a chosen few. The hallmarks of VAA include severe receptive deficits, with late onset of speech that is typically sparse or sometimes absent. Children with this deficit may develop a gesture language and acquire language through sign and by reading. It occurs in "epileptic aphasia" and may be associated with frank EEG abnormalities. (For a review and discussion of the VAA literature, see Rapin et al., 1977).

If one checks off the cardinal features of autism instead of taking a gestalt-like impressionistic view, one finds the diagnosis of autism less and less compelling (see DSM-III-R, pp. 38–39). Eight of a list of 16 items must be presented to meet the DSM-III-R criteria, and even if one agrees with the DSM-III-R definition, which many do not, Georgia did not qualify. She did meet criteria A-4 (no or abnormal social play), A-5 (gross impairment in ability to make peer friendships), B-1 (no mode of communication), although this seemed to be true only for people she did not know because she used gestures sometimes, and D (onset during infancy). Alternatively, a diagnosis of PDD could have been considered. However, as defined in DSM-III-R, such a diagnosis also would not work because Georgia was too competent in other areas to qualify. In addition, although she showed an impairment in reciprocal social interaction and verbal communication skills, it was more a quantitative than a qualitative issue as specified in the DSM-III-R description. Further, although she surely had a major deficit in verbal communication skills, she had rudimentary gestures available that she used for communicative purposes.

The diagnosis of VAA was appealing for a variety of reasons. It best fit the data and, although leading to a prediction of significant difficulties in a hearing-speaking world, it offered a less dire prognosis than usually conferred by autism. This had meaning not only for the parents but also for those clinicians who would be working with Georgia; like it or not, self-fulfilling prophesies have a way of coming true. Many of us unwittingly are affected by the hopefulness of an outcome; the more positive, the greater one's motivation seems to be. As the recommendations would be the same regardless of the diagnosis, nothing would be lost.

With the consensually arrived at diagnosis of VAA and a frank discussion of the meaning of this diagnosis with Georgia's parents, a series of recommendations were made that included (a) speech therapy to commence immediately, with an emphasis on sign language (it would be necessary for the family to learn sign as well, for this likely would be Georgia's main mode of communication); (b) enrollment in a preschool program that would provide a Total Communication program, with individual therapy to be provided until that time; and (c) a targeted behavior modification program with the parents instructed in its delivery, to be initiated within the Department of Child Psychiatry and to become part of the preschool program on admission. The first goals were to increase eye contact, to foster initiation of social play, and to attempt vocalizations in conjunction with signs. The latter was abandoned in a short time because it seemed to interfere with acquisition of signs (whether this occurred on an emotional basis or had to do with intermodal processing could not be determined). The decision was made to go with reinforcement of spontaneous vocalizations and to concentrate on Georgia's development in other areas. An assessment of the probability of vocal language could be addressed down the road.

Georgia learned to sign very quickly and was highly motivated to communicate with the adults in her environment. Expression of affect and communicative intent were deemed to be within the normal range after approximately 4 months in the preschool program. It took the better part of a year for her to become involved in anything resembling social play and to demonstrate prosocial behavior with her peers. She accomplished this slowly and warily, and one wonders what experiences, real or imagined, she must have had with peers to have created such a negative impact. Georgia was seen annually until she was 12 years old. She was maintained in a special education setting but because of state regulations was not permitted assignment to a "deaf education" sign class (as she was not actually deaf, although functionally so). She was identified as speech/language impaired, sat in a classroom of speaking children, and was assigned a full-time aide who signed and acted as a translator for her. In spite of this less than optimal arrangement, Georgia acquired academic skills and at 12 was functioning at a third- to fourth-grade level in all academic areas.

Georgia made slow but steady progress in all areas. Although she remained rather shy with peers, she did have some school friends. They managed to communicate in spite of all of the obstacles. Her real social life was centered around an after-school group sponsored by a local private school for the deaf. They encouraged participation from all quarters. Most of the children in the group ranged from 7 to 15 and most of them signed. The activities were nonacademic and involved a variety of activities that reinforced social skills and "team" efforts. Although Georgia was able to produce some vocal language, mostly single words that were reasonably intelligible, she chose not to use them and relied on being a member of a sign-language community. From a vocational point of view, she will probably find herself in a work situation in which hearing impaired and deaf people would find employment.

At 10 years of age, she had been referred for psychotherapy because of the beginnings of social withdrawal and depression. The family located a therapist who was fluent in sign, and he reassured them that Georgia's distress was reality based, as her realization of the extent of her disability found its way home. He believed that she would come to terms with it and continue to go forward. She was still in therapy at the time of the most recent reevaluation, now done in tandem with a signing language therapist. Georgia indicated that she was doing better and was once again becoming involved with a circle of friends and enjoying it.

In every instance, clinical observation and historical information must be involved in the final decisions about "what a child is." To make diagnostic statements is to take on a great deal of responsibility for what happens next to a child and to that child's family. It is very important therefore to include all information in any diagnostic deliberation and, where possible, to make regular follow-up a part of the treatment plan. This allows for modification of recommendations and sometimes of diagnosis, and it certainly provides an important source of learning for the evaluator; nothing is more educational than longitudinal evaluations. It is also important to be able to say out loud that one cannot make a definitive diagnosis at a given point in time and to review the alternatives, recommending an intervention program and regular and frequent visits until the interactive effects of maturation, environment, and intervention help to clarify the picture. Professional responsibility mandates providing the most reliable information possible at the conclusion of an evaluation, although sometimes that is "I don't know. Let's keep on trying to find out."

Parents of young children with developmental disabilities need an advocate who understands child development and who, in this particular instance, understands the diagnostic and prognostic ramifications of developmental language disorders, including their impact on the family. Parents who learn that their young child has a disability of some kind typically will respond with anger, fear, guilt. If they perceive the problem to be significant, regardless of the reality of the situation, they will mourn for the child that they did not have, and they need time and support during that period. The more ambiguous the situation, the more anxiety producing, and it is often the parents' anxiety in such instances that pressure an evaluator to produce a diagnosis when there is none, or to be more reassuring than they should be, or to be brusque and try to help the parents "snap out of it." Empathy is what is needed, not sympathy; this is a fine distinction, but a meaningful one. Until a child with an identified disability is in an appropriate treatment program and other support systems are available to the family, it may be you, the evaluator and perhaps identifier of the disorder, who should take up the advocacy role and be there to help the child and family obtain the intervention services and support that is needed. Responsibility need not and probably should not end with the signed report and parent conference. If more needs to be done to help obtain what is needed, then be there to help get it done.

REFERENCES

Abbs, J., Hunker, C., & Barlow, S. (1983). Differential speech motor subsystem impairments with suprabulbar lesions: Neurophysiological framework and supporting data. In W.R. Berry (Ed.), *Clinical dysarthria* (pp. 21–56). San Diego: College-Hill Press.

Achenbach, T.M., & Edelbrock, C. (1983). *Child Behavior Checklist and Revised Child Behavior Profile.* Burlington, VT: University of Vermont, Department of Psychiatry.

Allen, D.V., & Bliss, L.S. (1978). *Evaluation of procedures for screening preschool children for signs of impaired language development* (Report No. 1-NS-2355). Bethesda, MD: National Institutes of Health.

American Psychiatric Association. (1987). *Diagnostic and statistical manual of mental disorders* (rev. 3rd ed.). Washington, DC: Author.

Aram, D.M., & Nation, J.E. (1975). Patterns of language behavior in children with developmental language disorders. *Journal of Speech and Hearing Research, 18,* 229–241.

Aram, D.M., & Nation, J.E. (1982). *Child language disorders.* St. Louis, MO: Mosby.

Beitchman, J.H. (1985). Speech and language impairment and psychiatric risk. *Psychiatric Clinics of North America, 8,* 721–735.

Benton, A.L. (1959). Aphasia in children. *Education, 79,* 408–412.

Benton, A.L. (1964). Developmental aphasia and brain damage. *Cortex, 1,* 40–52.

Berenberg, S.R. (Ed.). (1977). *Brain: Fetal and infant.* The Hague, The Netherlands: Martinus Nijhoff.

Berry, M.F. (1969). *Language disorders of children.* New York: Meredith Corp.

Black-Van Santen, L. (1989). Relationship between language disorder subtype and social-emotional functioning in children 3 to 5. *Dissertation Abstracts International, 50,* 8910782.

Blakeley, R.W. (1980). *Screening Test for Developmental Apraxia of Speech.* Tigard, OR: C.C. Publications.

Breasted, J.H. (1930). *The Edwin Smith surgical papers.* Chicago: University of Chicago Press.

Bzoch, K., & League, R. (1971). *Bzoch-League Receptive-Expressive Emergent Language Scale.* Austin, TX: PRO-ED.

Cantwell, D.P., & Baker, L. (1977). Psychiatric disorders in children with speech and language retardation. *Archives of General Psychiatry, 34,* 583–591.

Cantwell, D.P., Baker, L., & Mattison, R.E. (1980). Factors associated with the development of psychiatric disorders in children with speech and language retardation. *Archives of General Psychiatry, 37,* 423–426.

Culbertson, J. (1981). Psychological evaluation and educational planning for children with central auditory dysfunction. In R.W. Keith (Ed.), *Central auditory and language disorders in children* (pp. 13–29). Houston: College-Hill Press.

Dalby, M.A. (1975). *Air studies in language-retarded children: Evidence of early lateralization of language function.* Paper presented at the First International Congress of Child Neurology, Toronto.

Darby, J.K. (Ed.). (1985). *Speech and language in neurology: Childhood disorders.* Orlando, FL: Grune & Stratton.

de Ajuriaguerra, J., Jaeggi, A., Guignard, F., Kocher, F., Maquard, M., Roth, S., & Schmid, E. (1976). The development and prognosis of dysphasia in children. In E.M. Morehead & A. Morehead (Eds.), *Normal and deficient child language* (pp. 345–385). Baltimore, MD: University Park Press.

Decker, S.N. (1982). Reading disability: Is there a heredity pattern? In R.N. Malateska & L.C. Hartlage (Eds.), *Neuropsychology and cognition* (Vol. 2, pp. 420–430). The Hague, The Netherlands: Martinus Nijhoff.

Decker, S.N., & DeFries, J.C. (1980). Cognitive abilities in families with reading disabled children. *Journal of Learning Disabilities, 13,* 9.

DiSimoni, F.G. (1978). *Token Test for Children.* Allen, TX: DLM Teaching Resources.

Dunn, L.M., & Dunn, L.M. (1981). *Peabody Picture Vocabulary Test–Revised.* Circle Pines, MN: American Guidance Service.

French, J.L. (1964). *The Pictorial Test of Intelligence.* Boston: Houghton Mifflin.

Frumkin, B., & Rapin, I. (1980). Perception of vowels and consonant-vowels of varying duration in language impaired children. *Neuropsychologia, 18,* 443–454.

Garvey, M., & Mutton, D.E. (1973). Sex chromosome aberrations and speech development. *Archives of Disease in Childhood, 48,* 937.

Gibson, W.C. (1962). Pioneers of localization of function in the brain. *Journal of the American Medical Association, 80,* 944–951.

Goldman, R., Fristoe, M., & Woodcock, R.W. (1970). *Goldman-Fristoe-Woodcock Test of Auditory Discrimination.* Circle Pines, MN: American Guidance Service.

Goldman, R., Fristoe, M., & Woodcock, R.W. (1986). *Goldman-Fristoe-Woodcock Auditory Skills Battery.* Circle Pines, MN: American Guidance Service.

Hammill, D.D. (1985). *Detroit Tests of Learning Aptitude–Primary.* Austin, TX: PRO-ED.

Hardy, W.G. (1965). On language disorders in young children: A reorganization of thinking. *Journal of Speech and Hearing Disorders, 30,* 3–16.

Hauser, S.L., DeLong, R., & Rosman, P. (1975). Pneumographic findings in the infantile autism syndrome: A correlate with temporal lobe disease. *Brain, 98,* 677.

Hedrick, D.L., Prather, E.M., & Tobin, A.R. (1984). *Sequenced Inventory of Communication Development* (rev.) Seattle: University of Washington Press.

Hiskey, M.S. (1966). *The Hiskey-Nebraska Test of Learning Aptitude.* Lincoln, NE: Union College Press.

Ingram, T.T.S., & Reid, J.F. (1956). Developmental aphasia observed in a department of child psychiatry. *Archives of Disease in Childhood, 31,* 161–172.

Kamhi, A. (1981). Nonlinguistic symbolic and conceptual abilities of language impaired and normally developing children. *Journal of Speech and Hearing Research, 24,* 446–453.

Kaplan, E., Goodglass, H., & Weintraub, S. (1978). *The Boston Naming Test.* Philadelphia, PA: Lea & Febiger.

Kaufman, A.S., & Kaufman, N.L. (1983). *K-ABC: Kaufman Assessment Battery for Children.* Circle Pines, MN: American Guidance Service.

Kavanagh, J.F. (Ed.). (1986). *Otitis media and child development.* Parkton, MD: York.

Kertesz, A. (1979). *Aphasia and associated disorders: Taxonomy, localization, and recovery.* New York: Grune & Stratton.

Kirk, S.A., McCarthy, J.J., & Kirk, W.D. (1968). *Illinois Test of Psycholinguistic Abilities.* Urbana: University of Illinois Press.

LeBrun, Y., & Zangwell, C. (1981). *Lateralization of language in the child.* Lisse, The Netherlands: Swets & Zeitlinger.

Leonard, L.B. (1979). Language impairment in children. *Merrill-Palmer Quarterly, 25,* 205–232.

Ludlow, C. (1980). Children's language disorders: Recent research advances. *Annals of Neurology, 7,* 497-507.
McCarthy, D. (1972). *McCarthy Scales of Children's Abilities.* San Antonio, TX: Psychological Corporation.
McGinnis, M.A. (1963). *Aphasic children: Identification and education by the association method.* Washington, DC: Alexander Graham Bell Assn.
McHenry, L.C. (1969). *Garrison's history of neurology.* Springfield, IL: CC Thomas.
Miller, J.F. (1983). Identifying children with language disorders and describing their language performance. *ASHA Reports, 12,* 61-74.
Morehead, D.M., & Ingram, D. (1973). The development of base syntax in normal and linguistically deviant children. *Journal of Speech and Hearing Research, 16,* 330-352.
Morley, M.E. (1957). *The development and disorders of speech in childhood.* Edinburgh, Scotland: Livingstone.
Morley, M.E. (1965). *The development and disorders of speech in childhood* (2nd ed.). Baltimore, MD: Williams & Wilkins.
Morley, M.E. (1967). *The development and disorders of speech in childhood* (3rd ed.). Baltimore, MD: Williams & Wilkins.
Morris, S. (1982). *The normal acquisition of oral feeding skills: Implications for assessment and treatment.* Central Islip, NY: Therapeutic Media.
Myklebust, H.R. (1954). *Auditory disorders in children: A manual for differential diagnosis.* New York: Grune & Stratton.
Nation, J.E., & Aram, D.M. (1982). The diagnostic process. In N.J. Lass, J.L. Northern, D.E. Yoder, & L.V. McReynolds (Eds.), *Speech, language, and hearing* (Vol. 2, pp. 443-460). Philadelphia, PA: Saunders.
Needleman, J. (1977). Effects of hearing loss from early recurrent otitis media on speech and language development. In B.F. Jaffee (Ed.), *Hearing loss in children: A comprehensive test* (pp. 640-649). Baltimore, MD: University Park Press.
Nelson, K.B., & Ellenberg, J.H. (1978). Prognosis in children with febrile seizures. *Pediatrics, 61,* 720-727.
News Note. (1985). Pediatrics Academy address on language-otitis media link. *American Speech and Hearing Association, 27,* 12.
Orton, S.T. (1937). *Reading, writing, and speech problems in children: A presentation of certain types of disorders in the development of the language faculty.* New York: Norton.
Owen, F.W. (1978). Dyslexia: Genetic aspects. In A.L. Benton & D. Pearl (Eds.), *Dyslexia: An appraisal of current knowledge* (pp. 265-284). New York: Oxford University Press.
Rapin, I., & Allen, D.A. (1983). Developmental language disorders: Nosologic considerations. In U. Kirk (Ed.), *Neuropsychology of language, reading, and spelling* (pp. 155-184). New York: Academic Press.
Rapin, I., Mattis, S., Rowan, A.J., & Golden, G.G. (1977). Verbal auditory agnosia in children. *Developmental Medicine and Child Neurology, 19,* 192-200.
Rapin, I., & Wilson, B.C. (1978). Children with developmental language disability: Neurological aspects and assessment. In M.A. Wyke (Ed.), *Developmental dysphasia* (pp. 13-41). New York: Academic Press.
Risucci, D.A. (1984). *Empirical validation of a typology of language impaired preschool children.* Unpublished doctoral dissertation, Hofstra University, Hempstead, NY.
Roach, E.G., & Kephart, N.C. (1966). *The Purdue Perceptual-Motor Survey.* San Antonio, TX: Psychological Corporation.
Semel, E.M., Wiig, E.H., & Secord, W. (1987). *Clinical Evaluation of Language Fundamentals-Revised.* San Antonio, TX: Psychological Corporation.

Shaffer, D., & Dunn, J. (Eds.). (1979). *The first year of life: Psychological and medical implications of early experience.* New York: Wiley.

Sheppard, J.J. (1987). Assessment of oral motor behaviors in cerebral palsy. *Seminars in Speech and Language, 8,* 57–70.

Sparrow, S.S., Balla, D.A., & Cicchetti, D.V. (1984). *Vineland Adaptive Behavior Scales.* Circle Pines, MN: American Guidance Service.

Strauss, A.A. (1954). Aphasia in children. *American Journal of Physical Medicine, 33,* 93–99.

Tallal, P. (1975). Perceptual and linguistic factors in the language impairment of developmental dysphasia: An experimental investigation with the Token Test. *Cortex, 9,* 196–205.

Tallal, P., & Piercy, M. (1978). Defects of auditory perception in children with developmental dysphasia. In M.A. Wyke (Ed.), *Developmental dysphasia* (pp. 63–84). New York: Academic Press.

Tallal, P., Stark, R., & Mellits, D. (1985). The relationship between auditory temporal analyses and receptive language development: Evidence from studies of developmental language disorder. *Neuropsychologia, 23,* 314–322.

Thompson, R.J., Jr., & O'Quinn, A.N. (1979). *Development disabilities.* New York: Oxford University Press.

Thorndike, R.L., Hagen, E.P., & Sattler, J.M. (1986). *Stanford-Binet Intelligence Scale: Fourth Edition.* Chicago: Riverside.

Tortolani, B.C., Murray, S., Risucci, D.A., & Wilson, B.C. (1986). *Scales for the Assessment of Language Sample Questionnaire (SLIQ): Experimental Version.* Manhasset, NY: Northshore University Hospital–Cornell University Medical Center.

Webb, K. (1988). *Social and communicative competence in language disordered preschool children.* Unpublished doctoral dissertation, New York University, New York.

Wechsler, D. (1989). *Wechsler Preschool and Primary Scales of Intelligence–Revised.* San Antonio, TX: Psychological Corporation.

Wilde, W. (1853). *Practical observations on aural surgery.* London, England: Churchill.

Wilson, B.C. (1986). An approach to the neuropsychological assessment of the preschool child with developmental deficits. In S.B. Filskov & T.J. Boll (Eds.), *Handbook of clinical neuropsychology* (Vol. 2, pp. 121–171). New York: Wiley.

Wilson, B.C., Iacoviello, J.M., Wilson, J.J., & Risucci, D. (1982). Purdue Pegboard performance in normal preschool children. *Journal of Clinical Neuropsychology, 4,* 19–26.

Wilson, B.C., & Risucci, D.A. (1986). A model for clinical-quantitative classification: Generation 1. Application to language-disordered preschool children. *Brain and Language, 27,* 281–309.

Wilson, B.C., Wilson, J.J., Risucci, D.A., & Wheeler, F. (1989). *Academic performance of children with developmental language disorders: Expressive writing and spelling abilities.* Manuscript in preparation.

Wirt, R.D., Lachar, D., Klinedinst, J.E., Seat, P.D., & Broen, W.E., Jr. (1985). *Personality Inventory for Children–Revised.* Los Angeles: Western Psychological Services.

Wolfus, B., Moscovitch, M., & Kinsbourne, M. (1980). Subgroups of developmental language impairment. *Brain and Language, 10,* 152–171.

Wolpaw, T., Nation, J.E., & Aram, D.M. (1977). Developmental language disorders: A follow-up study. In M.S. Burns & J.R. Anderson (Eds.), *Selected papers in language and phonology: Vol. I. Identification and diagnosis of language disorders.* Evanston, IL: Institute for Continuing Professional Education.

Wyke, M.A. (Ed.). (1978). *Developmental dysphasia.* New York: Academic Press.

Zaidel, E. (1979). The split and half brains as models of congenital language disability. In C.I. Ludlow & M.E. Doran-Quine (Eds.), *The neurological bases of language disorders in children: Methods and directions for research* (National Institutes of Health Pub. No. 79-440, pp. 55–89). Bethesda, MD: National Institutes of Health.

Appendix A.
Speech-Language Identification Questionnaire (SLIQ)

Copyright © 1985, 1987 by B.C. Tortolani, S.S. Murray, D.A. Risucci, and B.C. Wilson.

Child's Name _____ I.D.# _____

Date of Administration _____ Birth Date _____ C.A. _____

Site _____

Rater's Name _____ Occupation _____

Rating based on: (Please indicate one) _____ Direct Observation

_____ Parent Report

_____ Teacher Report

_____ Other (Specify)

_____

INTRODUCTION

The Speech-Language Identification Questionnaire, or SLIQ (sounds like "slick"), has been designed as a screening instrument for the early identification of children at risk for language disorders.

The items identify potential problems in the areas of speech production, auditory comprehension, grammar and morphology, pragmatics, formulation and expressive content. Where it was felt to be helpful, explanatory comments and examples have been provided for individual items. Careful listening to what the child actually says is essential; the natural behavior of most people is to provide closure when listening to others speak; that is, to think that they have heard a plural "s" because they expect it to be there. Training exercises are recommended in order to develop the necessary listening skills when the SLIQ is administered by direct observation. Such things as listening to taped recordings of the child with the availability of printed translations to check against later is one method of sharpening up one's listening skills.

For purposes of determining interrater reliability, we are interested in having the SLIQ completed by as many people as possible on any given child, including parents and teachers; we ask that the project examiner (e.g., speech/language pathologist, neurologist, psychologist) complete the SLIQ on the basis of parent or teacher report only when absolutely necessary. Either "Yes," "No" or "DK" (DK=Don't Know) should be circled for each item.

Finally, after administering the SLIQ, please take the time to complete the final portion which asks for a judgment to be made as to what the examiner feels are the primary and secondary most contributory causes of the child's problems, if any.

Thanks.

SPEECH-LANGUAGE IDENTIFICATION QUESTIONNAIRE

1. Does the child attempt to engage others in play activities verbally or nonverbally?   Yes   No   DK

2. Does the child greet others verbally or gesturally? (Ex.: "Hi!" or wave.)   Yes   No   DK

3. Does the child respond when spoken to? (Verbal or nonverbal responses are accepted.)   Yes   No   DK

4. Does the child attempt spontaneously to share information or discoveries with parents, siblings, peers, or others? (Nonverbal sharing is accepted. Ex.: Pointing excitedly to objects.)   Yes   No   DK

5. Does the child spontaneously ask for what s/he needs or wants? (Nonverbal requests, such as pointing or taking someone to the desired object are acceptable.)   Yes   No   DK

6. Is the child's attention better when playing with blocks, puzzles, or sand than during story telling?   Yes   No   DK

7. Does the child follow 2-part directions without gestural cues? (Ex.: Get your lunchbox and come to the circle. Turn off the T.V. and come to the table.)   Yes   No   DK

8. Are the child's responses (nonverbal or verbal) relevant to the situation?   Yes   No   DK

9. Does the child use gesture, sign language, or facial expression to communicate?   Yes   No   DK

10. Is most of what the child says intelligible to strangers? (Occasional unintelligible words or phrases are acceptable, but most sentences should be intelligible.)   Yes   No   DK

11. Is the child reticent about talking? (The concern is not about general shyness but self-consciousness attributable to an awareness of difficulty making him/herself understood verbally.)   Yes   No   DK

12. Does the child become angry or frustrated as a result of difficulty communicating? Yes No DK

13. Is the child able to imitate simple words said to him? (Can the child say, "car," "dog" or "cookie" when asked?) Yes No DK

14. Is the child verbal? (That is, does the child use words to express him/herself?) Yes No DK

    Note: If the answer to #14 is *No,* stop here

15. Does the child spontaneously name objects or actions during play or outings? Yes No DK

16. Are the child's comments responsive to the specific question or situation? (The issue is whether the child FULLY understands language. Comments slightly off target are indicators.) Yes No DK

17. Does the child speak like a telegram omitting words? (Ex: "Ball street" to mean "The ball went into the street.") Yes No DK

18. Does the child use verb forms correctly? (Omission of the "-ing," "is," "are," or "ed" or misuse of irregular forms; such as, "comed" or "camed" for came. Any verb errors require a NO answer to this question.) Yes No DK

19. Are plural forms used accurately? (Examples of plural errors: mans, mens, mouses, mices, two doggie.) Yes No DK

20. Does the child use the negatives "not," "can't," and "don't"? (All 3 are required.) Yes No DK

21. Are pronouns used correctly? (Ex.: 'His' rather than 'Hims,' 'her' and 'she' for girls and 'him' and 'he' for boys, etc.) Yes No DK

22. Does the child use nonspecific labels repeatedly? (The issue here is difficulty recalling noun labels. Examples of nonspecific labels: it, this, thing, etc.) Yes No DK

23. Does the child use nonspecific verbs repeatedly? (Difficulty recalling specific verb labels can result in repeated use of "do" or other general verbs for tie, open, fix, etc. Ex.: "Do my shoe." "Do my thermos." "Do my toy.") Yes No DK

24. Does the child substitute descriptive phrases or gestures for nouns or adjectives? (Ex.: "Santa Claus tree" for Christmas tree.) Yes No DK

25. Does the child sometimes use words that don't exactly fit the sentence? Yes No DK

26. Is the order of words within the child's sentences appropriate? ("Why *is it* raining?" rather than "Why *it is* raining?) Yes No DK

27. Does the child use incomplete sentences? Yes No DK

28. Does the child stop in the middle of a sentence, unable to finish? Yes No DK

29. Does the child speak haltingly? (That is, does the child stop or rephrase as if groping for the right words?) Yes No DK

30. Are words spoken fluently? (Whole word repetitions, sound repetitions, prolongations of sounds, numerous ums, or other verbal fillers are considered dysfluencies. A word may be repeated no more than once and only an occasional "um" is acceptable.) Yes No DK

31. Does the child seem to have difficulty putting his ideas into words? Yes No DK

32. Is the child able to recount two or three elements of a prior experience? (The event must be a new one, in contrast to a recurrent one. A trip to the planetarium is a new event; taking a bath is a recurrent one.) Yes No DK

ESTIMATION OF PROBLEM AREA/S

If you feel able to do so, please indicate which aspects of language from those listed below best characterize the child's major problem area(s).

The following is a brief description of the categories being addressed.

Auditory Comprehension—The child does not seem to understand spoken language at an age appropriate level.

Grammar and Morphology—The child appears to have difficulty using appropriate grammatical forms, such as plurals, -ing, and other modifications of word forms which alter their meaning.

Pragmatics—The child shows little interest in communicating, has difficulty following conversational rules, or has difficulty in using vocal or gesture language for basic communicative functions such as requesting, rejecting, modifying the behavior of others, sharing or gaining information, or expressing feelings.

Phonology—The child has difficulty in producing intelligible sequences of sounds. This is to be differentiated from normal developmental errors of articulation.

Oromotor Function—The child appears to have difficulty controlling the oral musculature, or cannot imitate movements of the articulators, resulting in imperfect speech production.

Retrieval—The child appears to have difficulty in finding the precise words that are needed, often resulting in less than adequate expressive language.

Formulation—The child appears to have difficulty in stringing words together, or in putting ideas into fluent phrases.

If you think that more than one area is significantly involved, please rate them as to the extent of their contribution to the problem. The number *1* would indicate the *major* contributor, *2*, the next most important. Please do not rate more than two items. If there is no evident problem, please check the line after "No Problem."

Auditory Comprehension _____ Formulation _____

Grammar and Morphology _____ Word Retrieval _____

Oromotor Function _____ Pragmatics _____

Phonology _____ No Problem _____

Appendix B. Preschool Performance Questionnaire

Child's name _____ Date of birth _____

School _____ Age group or class _____

Address _____

_____

_____

Phone _____

1. Describe any difficulties the child has. What makes this child "different" from others in the class?

_____

_____

_____

_____

2. How long has the problem been noted? Was it identified by previous school personnel?

_____

_____

_____

3. Describe any techniques or methods that have been used to handle problems; length of time alternative methods have been used; success or failure of such methods:

_____

_____

_____

4. Describe this child's assets and positive qualities:

_____
_____
_____
_____
_____
_____

5. Describe the classroom environment:

Structured _____ Unstructured _____

Group instruction _____ Individualized instruction _____

Number of children _____

6. School Readiness:

	Level of Performance	Comments
Number skills	_____	_____
Writing	_____	_____
Reading readiness	_____	_____

7. *Please rate the child in the following areas:*

	Problem	No Problem
Behavioral maturity	_____	_____
Teacher dependency	_____	_____
Compliance to rules and routines	_____	_____
Aggressiveness	_____	_____
Peer relationships	_____	_____
Attention span	_____	_____
Activity level		
Hyperactive	_____	_____
Hypoactive	_____	_____
Following verbal directions	_____	_____

Speech production _____ _____

Expressive language development _____ _____

Fine muscle control (writing, dressing, cutting) _____ _____

Large muscle control (walking, running, climbing) _____ _____

8. Does the child currently receive (or has child received in the past) any special services (such as speech)? Please describe (dates, amounts of time per week, focus):

_____
_____
_____
_____
_____
_____
_____

9. Has the child had any evaluations (speech, psychology, hearing, etc.)? If so, state which (if reports are available, please attach):

_____
_____
_____
_____
_____

10. Proposed school placement for next semester or year. Indicate grade or age group and type of class:

_____
_____

11. What questions would you like answered as a result of this evaluation?

_____
_____
_____
_____

12. Please provide any additional information or comments that might help our understanding of this child:

_____
_____
_____
_____
_____
_____
_____
_____

Completed by _____

Title _____

Date _____

Thank you for your cooperation.

Appendix C. Z Scores to Percentiles

%	Z Score	%	Z Score	%	Z Score
1	−2.326	39	−.279	77	.739
2	−2.054	40	−.253	78	.772
3	−1.881	41	−.227	79	.807
4	−1.751	42	−.202	80	.842
5	−1.645	43	−.176	81	.878
6	−1.555	44	−.151	82	.915
7	−1.476	45	−.125	83	.954
8	−1.405	46	−.100	84	.994
9	−1.341	47	−.075	85	1.037
10	−1.282	48	−.050	86	1.080
11	−1.228	49	−.025	87	1.127
12	−1.175	50	.000	88	1.175
13	−1.127	51	.025	89	1.228
14	−1.080	52	.050	90	1.282
15	−1.037	53	.075	91	1.341
16	−.994	54	.100	92	1.405
17	−.954	55	.125	93	1.476
18	−.915	56	.151	94	1.555
19	−.878	57	.176	95	1.645
20	−.842	58	.202	96	1.751
21	−.807	59	.227	97	1.881
22	−.772	60	.253	98	2.054
23	−.739	61	.279	99	2.326
24	−.706	62	.305		
25	−.6745	63	.331		
26	−.643	64	.358		
27	−.613	65	.385		
28	−.583	66	.412		
29	−.553	67	.440		
30	−.524	68	.468		
31	−.496	69	.496		
32	−.468	70	.524		
33	−.440	71	.553		
34	−.412	72	.583		
35	−.385	73	.613		
36	−.358	74	.643		
37	−.331	75	.6745		
38	−.305	76	.706		

10

Assessment of the Young Child with Visual Impairment and Multiple Disabilities

PHILIP W. DAVIDSON, PH.D. & MERELYN DOLINS, PH.D., R.P.T.

Young children with visual impairment, blindness, multisensory impairment, motor impairment, or motor and sensory impairments are among the most complex and difficult to evaluate because their disabilities involve limitations on input and output systems, complicating the psychologist's goal of determining potential abilities. Their disabilities often preclude the use of standard measurement instruments, necessitating instead modification and nonstandard usage coupled with clinical observations. Few psychologists have had extensive experience in the evaluation or treatment of such children, further limiting their capacity to gather clinical data. And the child may have associated secondary disabling conditions, such as behavior problems, which may confound results.

Davidson and Legouri (1986) have examined some of these issues, recommending the interdisciplinary team approach as the best practice for evaluating sensorily impaired children. Such a team can include specialists in motor dysfunction, speech and language pathology, and medicine, as well as other disciplines, and can facilitate a better understanding of the child and more effective program planning and follow-up treatment.

Such teams may not always be accessible and the psychologist may be asked to evaluate such a child alone; therefore, the practices recommended in this chapter are applicable to either solo or interdisciplinary practice. However, professionals in such a circumstance must recognize the situation as an unfortunate compromise, undoubtedly insufficient to answer all the questions being raised about the child's developmental or social and adaptive functioning.

PREVALENCE OF VISUAL AND MOTOR DISABILITIES

Goldstein (1980) estimated the incidence of blindness in persons of all ages in the United States as 21.6 per 100,000 population. About 10% of these cases are under age 20. An estimated 50,000 children under 20 are blind or visually impaired (Gold-

---

Preparation of this chapter was supported in part by Grant 13156 from the Administration on Developmental Disabilities, Office of Human Development Services, USDHHS, to the first author.

stein, 1980), and of this number, only one out of four cases is reported during the child's first 5 years of life (Kahn & Moorhead, 1973).

Congenital infections, and most particularly congenital rubella, can cause damage to the central nervous system that result in visual, auditory, and motor impairments (Willis & Holden, 1990). The rubella epidemic of 1963–64 caused about 20,000 cases of infected newborns, a small number of whom were both deaf and blind. Since 1964 only sporadic occurrences of congenital rubella have been reported, and the number of children under 5 years who are both deaf and blind is very small (Ziring, 1983).

There are four major categories of disorders in which motor impairment is the primary presenting disability: nonprogressive brain abnormalities, such as cerebral palsy; neural tube defects, such as myelomeningocele (also called spina bifida cystica); muscle tissue disease, such as muscular dystrophy; and connective tissue disease, such as juvenile rheumatoid arthritis.

About .002% of the general population is estimated to have some form of cerebral palsy. This group of dysfunctions is highly correlated with a history of prenatal or perinatal insult. The resultant clinical expression of the brain insult and its severity will depend upon the etiology and timing of the lesion. For example, a much greater percentage of premature babies will present with specific types of cerebral palsy.

Spina bifida cystica occurs in approximately 1 to 2 per 1,000 live births; there are about 11,000 young children in the United States with this congenital anomaly. And about 1 per 1,000 children will get juvenile rheumatoid arthritis (Wilhelm, Johnson, & Eisert, 1986).

Duchenne's muscular dystrophy, the most common form of the dystrophies to affect young children, has a prevalence of 1 per 25,000 live births (Menkes, 1985). It is congenital and sex linked (almost invariably affecting males), as well as progressive and terminal.

Diseases that affect the motor system also may be accompanied by disabilities in sensory functioning. For example, about 12% of children with juvenile rheumatoid arthritis have chronic nongranulomatous uveitis (inflammation of the uveal tract) that may lead to blindness (Cassidy, 1985).

Recent data have indicated increased rates of survival among certain categories of children at high risk for motor or sensory handicaps. These trends are indicative of improved prenatal and perinatal care, advances in medical technology to treat very low birth weight infants born with complications that threaten their health and development, and improved postnatal, long-term medical and developmental services to such children and their families.

These trends also have influenced the awareness of the health and education communities of the diverse, complex, and often overwhelming management needs of multiply handicapped infants and young children. As a result, the psychologist is more likely than ever before to be asked to evaluate such children and assist in case planning, follow-up, and management for them and their families.

There is an increased expectation of significant and persistent developmental disabilities in such children compared to nonaffected peers. There may or may not be concomitant emotional or behavioral disorders. Estimating the frequency of such associated problems is complicated by (a) the recent shift from institutional to community-based services, and (b) complexities in separating true effects on development and behavior from spurious testing resulting from the use of evaluation techniques not suited to children with motor or sensory deficits. For additional information on physical and health-related disorders, see Willis, Culbertson, and Mertens (1984).

The Young Child with Visual Impairment

Case Study

TC is the 4-year-old first and only child of upper middle class parents, reported to be a happy and well-adjusted youngster. Referred for a psychological evaluation to determine his cognitive, perceptual, and language functioning, he is suspected of developmental disability by his parents, who note delays in the appearance of developmental milestones.

TC is the product of a 28-week-gestation pregnancy. His Apgar scores were 3 at 1 minute, 5 at 5 minutes, and 6 at 10 minutes. He was intubated and transferred to the hospital's neonatal intensive care unit, where he spent the next 4 months. During the hospital course, TC developed severe respiratory distress syndrome (RDS) and required a high O_2 environment in an oxyhood for 8 weeks. His lung disease finally resolved, and he was discharged to his parents' care at age 5 months.

Prior to discharge, TC was examined by an ophthalmologist and reported to have a Grade III Retinopathy of Prematurity (ROP). He also had an abnormal brain stem visual evoked potential test. Cryotherapy to reattach his retinae, detached as a consequence of ROP, was performed but not successful. The parents were warned that TC might later develop visual impairment or blindness.

Ages of onset of TC's developmental milestones were properly corrected to reflect his 12-week premature delivery. He sat up at 3 months (corrected gestational age), rolled from back to front at 5 months and from front to back at 6 months. He began babbling at 7 months. He did not reach for objects until 10 months and stood alone at 15 months. He took his first steps at 26 months. By age 24 months, TC's expressive vocabulary had reached about 50 words. He now talks in three- to six-word sentences. He has a mild articulation disorder.

TC's ophthalmologist has determined that his vision is impaired secondary to ROP, and that he is not totally blind. However, this physician cannot tell how much TC can see or what his visual functioning will be like as he grows older.

TC's pediatrician, noting his delayed milestones, encouraged the parents to seek this evaluation and to consider enrolling TC in a preschool program for children with visual impairments. He has suggested that TC may also have cognitive impairments related to his prematurity, but the parents are convinced that TC is intellectually normal.

TC presents a not uncommon history. About 7% of live births are premature. Of that number, between 10% and 15% are very low birth weight and the products of gestational periods of 28 to 32 weeks. About 80% of such youngsters will present with ROP. The number of this group that may eventually present with associated developmental delays secondary to visual impairment is thought to be small, but definitive data are not yet available.

Complicating TC's presentation is the history of severe and protracted RDS. His delivery is also suggestive of some degree of hypoxia, known to be associated sometimes with generalized developmental delays. No doubt this history, coupled with his observed motor milestone delays and articulation disorder, worried TC's pediatrician. Few pediatricians or family practitioners have seen more than a few blind children and would probably not have the experience to distinguish delays in development due to hypoxia from those related to visual impairment.

TC's developmental milestones reflecting functions relating to vision are delayed, but those not involving visual guidance appeared within normal expectation. Fraiberg (1977) has reported that blind infants frequently show such a pattern, distinct from those youngsters with generalized developmental disability who often show delays in all milestones.

Gathering History Data

Gathering the history prior to evaluating a blind youngster must include components that would occur for any child, such as early developmental course, medical factors that might influence development, social and emotional history including incidence of behavioral problems, and any educational history that might be available from a preschool, nursery, or day-care program. In addition, some special considerations are important:

Visual functioning. Data should be gathered concerning the child's visual status, including visual acuity, visual field defects, eye movement disorders (strabismus, esotropia, or exotropia), evidence of brain stem function, and cortical processing of visual information. It is common that visually impaired children may have both impaired acuity and eye movement deficits, complicating both evaluation and performance in educational or social settings. Also, blindness is not a unitary condition: children with acuity between 20/200 and 20/600 Snellen are considered partially sighted and have substantial usable vision. For instance, magnification, special devices, and enlarged visual stimuli may be employed to normalize such children's visual capability. However, children with Snellen acuity less than 20/600 are considered virtually blind. Some may have some light perception that permits discrimination of edges, such as corners of a room or objects from backgrounds, while others may be totally blind. In either case, such children will function in large part without vision and must rely upon haptic perception and on audition for the perception of form and space.

The point during development in which the visual impairment occurred should be noted. There is an important distinction made between children who are born blind and those who lose sight later in early childhood. Those children with congenital loss must rely upon nonvisual modalities during sensorimotor development. Such youngsters may show deficits in concept formation that depends upon vision (Witkin, Birnbaum, Lomonaco, Lehr, & Herman, 1968), whereas they may simultaneously display more accurate haptic and auditory discrimination than youngsters blinded later in life, who have relied upon vision to develop spatial and form concepts Davidson & Legouri, 1986; Hatwell, 1978).

Hatwell (1966) has argued that the point in age demarcating congenital blindness is about 18 to 24 months, generally coinciding with Piaget's sensorimotor intelligence period. Age at loss of vision, as a variable, interacts with the degree of the loss. The more vision lost, the greater the importance of the distinction.

Causes of blindness. There are many causes of childhood blindness (Davidson & Legouri, 1986), some correlated with important behavioral and emotional characteristics that may influence the child's performance in a testing setting as well as at school and home. For instance, a high positive correlation has been reported between superior intelligence and retinoblastoma—cancer of the eye (Levitt, Rosenbaum, Willerman, & Levitt, 1972; Witkin, Oltman, Chase, & Friedman, 1971). Also, Chase (1972) and Scharf and Adams (1984) have related blindness caused by retrolental fibroplasia (now called retinopathy of prematurity) to a higher incidence of autistic behavior compared to children blinded from other causes. The correlation may be misleading, however, because it is quite likely that both the blindness and the autistic behavior may be related to an unknown third cause. Blindness caused by congenital rubella is almost always accompanied by sensorineural deafness (Ziring, 1983), and many children with cerebral palsy and other neuromotor deficits may have a variety of eye movement disorders.

Adaptive behavior, orientation, and mobility. Children with visual impairments may demonstrate delays in the emergence of self-help and adaptive skills, in part due to the role played by vision in such tasks and in part due to secondary dependency on others (Davidson & Legouri, 1986). Orientation in space, obstacle avoidance, and mobility in both confined environments (such as indoors) and in open space may all be limited.

Adjustment and behavior. Children with severe visual impairments frequently develop stereotyped, ritualistic body and limb movements, sometimes referred to as *blindisms.* Although the origin of such behaviors is not known, they are thought to represent a compensatory response to reduced sensory stimulation (Eichel, 1978). Other maladaptive behaviors seen frequently in young, visually impaired children may include adjustment reactions and increased anxiety level.

Establishing Rapport

Beyond typical procedures that the examiner would adopt to establish rapport with any young child, special considerations will apply to the visually impaired youngster:

1. Children with severe visual impairment may demonstrate difficulty separating from caregivers, in part due to introduction of a new environment that cannot be assimilated as rapidly as would occur with a seeing child. To reduce this probability, we recommend allowing the caregiver to enter the testing room with the child and remain as long as necessary.
2. Unfamiliarity with the new environment sometimes increases blind children's social verbal responses. Initiating structured testing may be delayed by such behavior, but the examiner may wish to allow some time for the child to talk freely before beginning.

3. Auditory, vibrotactual, and haptic stimuli will distract the child who is blind. Testing should take place in an unusually quiet environment. The room should have few obstacles, and furniture should have few or no moving parts.
4. When interacting with the child, the examiner should minimize gestures and other nonverbal cues, employing either verbal directions or verbal directions coupled with tactual cues.
5. In conversation, children who are visually impaired and blind often use verb phrases associated with visual experience. For instance, the child may say, "Let me *look at* that ball." There is no need for the examiner to avoid such references out of a concern that they may offend the child.

Designing the Test Battery

Davidson and Legouri (1986) and Collins-Moore & Osborn (1984) have provided a comprehensive review of tests appropriate for use with children who are visually impaired and blind. They also have discussed strategies for designing a battery. In addition, Bullard and Barraga (1971) have catalogued components of evaluation instruments that may be applied to visually impaired preschool children. Our purpose here will be to highlight those issues that relate to the young child.

The typical comprehensive examination of a child such as TC should include an evaluation of cognitive and perceptual ability, adaptive behavior, personal-social development, adjustment, visual and auditory functioning, and caregiver-child interactions. Very few standardized instruments are available to evaluate the young blind or visually impaired child in any of these areas. The examiner may be forced to modify or truncate standardized instruments, or combine standardized procedures with criterion-referenced scales and structured clinical observation. We shall illustrate this approach with specific reference to TC's case.

Cognitive, language, and perceptual ability. TC's age of 4 years permits the examiner to consider using the Perkins-Binet Tests of Intelligence for the Blind (Davis, 1980). This descendent of the Hayes-Binet Intelligence Test developed in the early part of the 20th century is standardized on both partially sighted and blind populations and is appropriate for children 3 through 18 years old. It has separate forms for partially sighted and blind children, requiring the examiner to be familiar with two different sets of administration procedures, tasks, and record forms. Its standardization samples are adequate, it is well understood by educators of children who are blind and visually impaired, and it yields a mental age and IQ distributed similarly to the Stanford-Binet Intelligence Scale, Form L-M (Terman & Merrill, 1973).

If TC had more adequate usable vision, the examiner might consider the McCarthy Scales of Children's Abilities (McCarthy, 1972). This well-standardized test is in wide use for assessing cognitive functioning in sighted children. It has very few subtests that demand fine visual discriminations. For children functioning at a lower cognitive level than TC, one would consider first trying the Perkins-Binet. If a floor effect is observed during administration of the first few items, the Reynell-Zinkin Developmental Scales for Young Visually Handicapped Children (Reynell & Zinkin, 1979) may serve as an alternative. For blind infants with usable vision, any of the tests of infant intelligence may be tried, such as the Bayley Scales of Infant Development (Bayley, 1969), the Griffiths Mental Development Scales (Griffiths, 1978), or the Cattell Infant Intelligence Scale (Cattell, 1960). The Denver II (Frankenburg & Dodds, 1990) may also serve as a clinical examination protocol. Some infants who are blind may be unable to complete tasks on these tests that demand vision. Hence caution must be exercised in drawing conclusions about level of functioning for such children.

Adaptive behavior. TC's skills of daily living and adaptive functioning can be assessed with the Maxfield-Bucholtz Social Maturity Scale for Blind Preschool Children (Maxfield & Bucholtz, 1958). The examiner may wish to supplement administration of this scale with a review of the child's orientation and mobility skills. The child may be asked to move about the testing room while the examiner notes his or her abilities to avoid obstacles and explore the room. The typical preschool child who is blind should be able to explore independently without numerous collisions, and to discriminate and verbally identify features of the environment. Also, the examiner can give spatial directions to the child, such as locating a particular landmark or following a three-stage command requiring mobility. The child who refuses these requests should not be forced to comply.

Personal and social development. TC has no history of adjustment reactions or other maladaptive behavior. If he had, one might consider administering Part II of the AAMD Adaptive Behavior Scale (Nihira, Foster, Shellhaas, & Leland, 1974) as a means to identify maladaptive behaviors of highest concern. The history did not note stereotyped behaviors, but TC should be observed to verify that such behaviors are in fact not present. TC may be interviewed in a play setting and his parents interviewed to determine if he has any other unusual behaviors that might be expected as a function of his cause of blindness. In addition, the examiner may consider administering the Child Behavior Checklist (Achenbach & Edelbrock, 1981) and the Parenting Stress Index (Abidin, 1990) to identify maladaptive family functioning.

Functional vision. The ophthalmological data for TC give few clues to his functional vision. Barraga and Collins (1979) define functional vision as including optical and optical/perceptual discrimination; recognition and identification; visual memory, spatial perception; and visual-motor coordination. Davidson and Legouri (1986) review a variety of techniques to assess such functions, including a test of color vision and a test of near vision. In addition, we recommend assessing two domains: visual tracking and visual target location.

Both functions can be observed while rolling a ball toward the subject from different quadrants of the visual field (periphery and midline). The observer should note (a) the point at which the ball is fixated by watching the child's eye movements and (b) whether or not the child reaches and prehends the approaching target. One also may use balls of varying sizes to establish approximate functional acuity thresholds. The procedure should be repeated with the ball placed at stationary distances from the subject to control for the possible influences of movement. The examiner also may note the degree of haptic exploration the child undertakes once the ball is prehended. If there is evidence of differentiated haptic exploration, then the examiner may wish to present a variety of small objects for identification, discrimination, or memory functioning, employing a two-choice or three-choice discrimination paradigm. Eye movement disorders may cause the child to reorient a target to place it in foveal vision of one eye or the other, and such behavior should be noted. Finally, in very young children, or in children with severe visual impairments, tracking may be elicited by a pinpoint light source.

Auditory acuity. The child's audition should be evaluated in a formal audiological screening. Functional audition can be assessed informally by noting the child's responsiveness to verbal cues. In very young blind children, auditory functioning may be established by observing an orienting response and subsequent habituation to an auditory stimulus.

Interpreting and Reporting Results

The examiner should be sensitive to interpreting evaluation data in light of the differential diagnosis in cases such as TC's, whose referral stemmed in part from confusion over the magnitude and scope of his noted developmental delays. Underlying this question, of course, is the inevitable and comprehensible wish of parents to predict the future. TC's medical history suggested possible global developmental disability, including mental retardation and perhaps neuromotor deficits.

Sufficient data should have resulted from the psychological assessment to be uniquely useful in resolving the differential diagnosis and in helping parents and other professionals caring for TC to place his current developmental status in proper context to plan for the future. Measures of both global intellectual functioning and visual and visual-perceptual functions should help to distinguish between global and specific deficits.

The evaluation data should be interpreted also to assist parents and other professionals associated with the child in planning for needed intervention services. The psychological evaluation may not be sufficient to draw all conclusions. Motor deficits, delayed or abnormal speech or language functioning, or achievement weaknesses may suggest the need for further assessments by a physical therapist or an occupational therapist, speech/language pathologist, or a special educator. Mobility and orientation deficits may suggest referral to an orientation and mobility specialist (usually available through not-for-profit local agencies serving persons with blindness and visual impairment).

If TC's data suggested significant deficits, the examiner might consider preschool special education programming for him. Fraiberg (1977) reported positive effects of early intervention on ameliorating developmental delays secondary to visual loss. Recent increases in the incidence of children with ROP-related vision loss have prompted increases in preschool programs specialized for children with visual impairments. In addition, agencies usually maintain itinerant educational services in local educational programs. Such agencies also may provide specialized counseling for parents.

Communication of results to TC's pediatrician should include a timely and understandable written report. Also, the examiner should establish a rapport and seek the pediatrician's collaboration in gaining referrals for additional services and in monitoring follow-up for TC.

Finally, the communication of findings to TC's parents should include both the youngster's current status and the need for current intervention. A plan should be made for case management that includes parents, physician, and examiner to assure that needed services are obtained and effective. Continued developmental assessments during his early school years should also be anticipated as a means for monitoring his progress.

The Child with Multisensory Impairments

Case Study

AB is a 2½-year-old product of a full-term pregnancy that was marked by maternal exposure to a friend who was ill with rubella (German measles) during the first trimester. Delivery was normal and the immediate postpartum course was unremarkable. AB was discharged after 1 week. However, a blood test for prenatal infections revealed a positive titer for rubella. At AB's first well-child check at 1 month, the family pediatrician explained to his parents that visual and auditory deficits, coupled with developmental disability, could result from this infection, and admonished them to monitor the baby's progress carefully. Since then, the parents have been very concerned, to the point where they report overindulgence of AB. They do not allow their son to want for any need and frequently perform things for him rather than listen to his temper tantrums.

AB's developmental milestones all occurred within normal limits, except for his speech and language. He seems to show little interest in sound production, has never used expressive language, and seems not to respond consistently to others' voice responses. The parents report that AB "hears," citing as evidence his head turns to loud noises. He seems to stare into others' faces. He does not yet use single words but does babble. He gestures to make his wants known and appears to have spontaneously adopted a small number of symbolic manual signs (such as pointing to his mouth to indicate hunger). Occasionally he strings signs together to form two-word or three-word manual sentences.

AB's hearing was recently screened, showing a bilateral loss. A subsequent complete audiological evaluation revealed a moderate to severe bilateral sensorineural hearing loss. There is no history of middle ear disease, ruling out an additional conductive hearing loss. Therefore, hearing aids were recommended, but the parents were reluctant to fit them until his behavior concerning eyeglasses has been resolved.

Visual tracking, fixation, response to light, and form perception are all functional according to AB's parents. He is followed by an ophthalmologist, who reported acuity deficits bilaterally and has prescribed glasses. AB resists wearing his glasses and has broken several pairs since receiving the prescription when he was 14 months old. His parents have sought assistance from the pediatrician in managing this behavior, but nothing seems to have reduced it. The ophthalmologist also diagnosed nystagmus in both eyes, a gaze disorder causing disconjugate eye movements. Behaviorally, AB appears to have difficulty retaining objects at near distances in the foveal visual fields of both eyes simultaneously. Thus, when he fixates, he may appear to be looking away from the object. His parents report that when AB gets older, the ophthalmologist plans eye muscle surgery to correct this problem.

Aside from his tantrums, AB is reported to be an affectionate youngster who is responsive to physical contact and social interaction. Nevertheless, his parents are concerned about the possibility of autism, having read about associations between rubella and pervasive developmental disorders. They are convinced that his vision and hearing contribute less to his developmental status than the presumed autism.

Rubella is one of a number of infectious diseases that can be transplacentally transmitted from a pregnant woman to her fetus. Other common infections in this category include toxoplasmosis, cytomegalovirus, herpes simplex B virus, and Epstein-Barr virus (mononucleosis). The acronym TORCH is often used to refer to this group of diseases, although grouping them obscures their different pathogenesis and sequelae. (For a review of the developmental impact of childhood infections, see Peloquin & Davidson, 1988; for etiological factors contributing to abnormal development, see Willis & Holden, 1990.)

Developmental and physical anomalies are most likely to occur as a result of prenatal infections if the illness was transmitted to the fetus during the first 12 to 14 weeks of gestation. Auditory impairments are the most common sequelae of prenatal rubella infections, but a substantial number of such children also sustain visual deficits or blindness (Ziring, 1983). Hearing losses are almost always sensorineural. Visual deficits including eye movement and gaze disorders are common. When blindness occurs, it is usually centrally mediated rather than a result of end organ dysfunction.

In the most severe cases of hearing loss, substantial delays in language and speech development may occur. In fact, AB's behavior is suggestive of deafness. He has developed no verbal communication, signs some of his needs, and appears more attentive to visual rather than auditory stimulation during social interaction.

Youngsters with rubella-related sensory deficits frequently exhibit behavioral disorders, including tantruming. A small number of the most affected children (the so-called deaf-blind child) also may display associated autistic-like features (Chess & Fernandez, 1976). But AB's lack of expressive language and behavioral problems do not fit the pattern seen in the classical presentation of autism. He is socially interactive, attempts to communicate through manual signing, has few stereotyped behaviors, and does not have the typical pattern of late-onset loss of already developed expressive speech found in autism. On the other hand, the history of overindulgence may suggest a behavioral exacerbation of temper tantruming.

Gathering History Data

In a severely affected deaf-blind youngster, mental retardation and other developmental disabilities may occur. In very young children, it is quite difficult for the examiner to distinguish between global delays due to the multiple sensory impairments and those due to more global central nervous system deficits. The examiner should seek historical data to help clarify these two alternatives prior to planning the evaluation.

The most important information to gather relates to the child's hearing. Psychological testing should not be undertaken for a child like AB until a complete audiological evaluation has taken place. Screening data are insufficient to pinpoint the child's hearing status. Treating a child with a severe bilateral sensorineural hearing loss as a hearing child during a psychological examination will inevitably lead the examiner to reach an incorrect diagnosis.

Also, ophthalmological data are extremely relevant to test development. Specifically, information on both acuity and eye movement disorders will be important. In AB's case, it appears that the gaze disorder, and not acuity, is an issue for his performance.

A behavioral history should be taken from the parents, designed to identify behavior disorders, as should the child's reinforcement history. Also, pediatrician's records should be requested to determine the primary health care provider's perception of the child's development and behavior, as well as any interventions being monitored.

The parents should be queried about how they communicate with their child. Parents are often the only ones who can accurately identify modes of communication not ordinarily obvious to the casual observer. They also may be able to characterize the child's temperament and suggest best practices for interaction.

Establishing Rapport

Many of the issues and techniques discussed for the visually impaired or blind child will apply to establishing rapport with the young child with multiple sensory impairments. There are several additional considerations in cases such as AB:

1. AB's young age, coupled with his sensory deficits and poor communication, suggest the need to have at least one caregiver with whom he is familiar accompany him to the examination room and remain with him throughout the assessment. This practice is doubly important in cases of behavioral difficulties, when the mere act of requesting separation from a caregiver could cause a tantrum that might interfere substantially with accomplishment of the assessment.
2. The excessive concern expressed by AB's parents suggests arranging for both of them to observe the evaluation, even if both are not in the testing room. Testing in a room equipped with one-way observation is helpful in later interpretation of data to the parents.
3. Attention should be paid to the child's hearing loss. The examiner should remain directly in front of the child as much as possible, using gestures as well as vocal instructions.
4. The examiner should establish limits at the outset of the examination for both parents and child, in light of AB's behavior problem.

Designing the Test Battery

AB presents as a deaf child and must be treated that way in designing a psychological evaluation. At the outset, the psychologist should recognize the need for a speech and language evaluation, conducted by a qualified speech/language pathologist. The psychologist's data on general cognitive functioning, functional vision, adaptive behavior, and adjustment should be gathered as closely in time to the speech and language assessment as practicable to facilitate comparison of findings.

Functional vision. Visual functions should be evaluated as described for the child with only visual impairment. With AB, we are more concerned with understanding his gaze disorder. Techniques should be adopted to determine where to place objects in his visual fields to facilitate both near and distant visual prehension and visually guided behaviors. Reaching for objects in various quadrants, at varying distances, will help identify positions in space at which AB has difficulty identifying targets. Identity may be established nonverbally by requesting that he look at, or prehend, a specific target on command.

Cognitive ability. AB's age and sensory impairments limit the selection of standardized tests to measure his cognitive potential. In AB's case, sufficient visual acuity exists to enable selecting instruments with visual stimuli. Hence, visual items from the Bayley Scales might be employed, and a composite age equivalent score calculated based on the age levels of the tasks. Developmental checklists such as the Learning Accomplishment Profile (Sanford, 1974) have developmentally sequenced items that can be used selectively. In either case, one can report no standardized measure.

The psychologist's options are reduced to a limited number of behavioral checklists and functional analyses of behavior in cases where both vision and hearing are severely impaired. The best checklist option for deaf-blind children is the Callier-Azusa Scale (Stillman, 1975). Davidson and Legouri (1986) recommend serial observations of such children to establish a rate of developmental progress.

Adjustment and behavior problems. AB's behavior problems should be observed if possible. Often a playroom affords an environment more likely to elicit a broad range of the child's behavior. Structured and unstructured play interviews are possible in this setting. Also, the psychologist may wish to ask parents to record data at home and return for successive visits until enough information has been collected to characterize the child's problem.

Adaptive behavior. The AAMD Adaptive Behavior Scale (Nihira et al., 1974) or the Vineland Adaptive Behavior Scales (Sparrow, Balla, & Cicchetti, 1984) may be used for children with AB's visual functioning. Other information about adaptive behavior may result from the child's developmental history and from other checklists such as the Callier-Azusa Scale.

Interpreting and Reporting Results

Ideally the estimation of AB's cognitive ability will involve simultaneous interpretation of psychological and speech and language data. Information from both domains is necessary to distinguish between global developmental disability and deficits due to hearing loss.

As is true for many multiply handicapped children, evaluation and treatment of behavioral problems may be an important role for the psychologist. In AB's case, data from the evaluation should bear upon both his temper tantruming and his unwillingness to wear glasses (and potentially, hearing aids). The psychologist should examine the data to distinguish between attention seeking, frustration, maladaptive communication, or more complex psychiatric disorders as explanations for the behavioral disorders. In addition, planning for follow-up should stem from the evaluation. Of critical importance for AB is the development of a behavior treatment plan to facilitate tolerance of sensory aids.

Communicating findings to parents must assure a better understanding of the nature of the child's multiple disability and empower them to continue to act as the child's advocate. In AB's case, that will require distinguishing between physical, behavioral, and psychological causes for his delays. Complex discussions such as this may require multiple visits and should also be coordinated with the family physician (Rockowitz, Davidson, & Hoekelman, 1987). These sessions should serve to assist parents in accepting their child's disabilities and finding resources in the community to address his or her many needs.

The Child with Physical Disabilities

Children with physical disabilities may or may not have significant motor deficits that interfere with performance of psychological functions. Moreover, some physically disabled children have primary motor impairments together with associated sensory deficits. This section is divided into three parts: the first discusses cerebral palsy, the most complex of multiple handicapping conditions; the second presents a child with spina bifida, involving motor and sensory deficits; and the third part describes assessment approaches for children with primary motor disabilities.

Case Study: Cerebral Palsy

RA is a 5-year-old boy with a diagnosis of severe spastic quadriplegic cerebral palsy. He is nonambulatory, with gross and fine motor functioning below the 3-month age level, and requires total care of personal daily needs such as feeding, bathing, and dressing. His voluntary movements are dominated by reflex patterns, so that he is unable to coordinate his head and eyes or use visual regard in reaching for or toward an object. His legs, trunk, and head push into extension, and his arms are either stiffly extended or assume a "fencing" position in conjunction with head and lower limb posturing, when he attempts to make isolated movements. Sudden loud sounds or changes in light, as well as heightened emotionalism, produce an increase in massive movement patterns. There is frequent need for adjusting and repairing his wheelchair due to the pressure and strength of these movements. He has been fitted with long leg braces that lock at the knees.

RA has no functional expressive language, and he is unable to produce speech sounds consistently due to dyscoordination of oral-motor and facial musculature. If relaxed and properly positioned, and in familiar surroundings, he will nod by dropping his head to his chest, or smile. However, RA's mother and her family speak to him in Spanish and English, and consider him to understand both. She speaks to him in an age-appropriate manner, using statements and questions related to ongoing or shared experiences to which he needs only provide a yes (or no) response. Therapists and teachers consider him "smart" and report that he seems to understand and laugh at subtle adult interchanges. He has been in a class for severely disabled, low functioning preschool children.

Previous psychological testing has been inconclusive. The psychologist noted that despite the severity of his handicap, RA is accepted by his mother and her family and included in the large extended family functions.

At his preschool program, the speech/language pathologist and the occupational therapist have developed an augmentative communication system requiring him to activate a buzzer with his knee or visually scan a series of choice boxes to produce consistent yes/no responses to communicate his needs. These methods have been unsuccessful, and the therapists raise questions as to RA's intellectual ability, visual memory, and discrimination.

RA is the firstborn child of the first pregnancy of a 16-year-old Puerto Rican woman. She enrolled in a metropolitan hospital clinic only after the first trimester. She was diagnosed then with anemia and complied with subsequent prenatal care instructions. The term pregnancy was uneventful. RA's birth weight was normal, but his delivery was difficult. There was evidence of meconium staining, and he required immediate but minimal respiratory assistance. His 1- and 5-minute Apgar scores were 3 and 6. This traumatic event resolved rapidly, and he was placed on room air within 24 hours. He was discharged to his mother's care at 7 days of age.

When RA was 8 months old, his mother reported difficulty in feeding him due to poor sucking and swallowing. His pediatrician also noted delay in early motor milestones, poor head and trunk control, hyperreflexive responses, and abnormal muscle tone. He required assistance to roll from back to stomach and was unable to maintain sitting posture. He was then referred to a neurologist, who confirmed the probable diagnosis of cerebral palsy. However, the extent of his disabilities were not made explicit until he reached 18 months of age.

RA is in good health, and his hearing is normal. A recent ophthalmological examination found that he needs corrective glasses. He requires orthopedic surgery to repair a painful dysplastic (dislocated) left hip.

In addition to his wheelchair and braces, RA requires specially adapted feeding equipment and techniques to avoid aspiration of food and drink. The occupational therapist has arranged for a toilet seat and bathing equipment. Until the diagnosis of hip dysplasia, he was placed in a tilt-table, which provided needed restraints and compensated for his lack of postural or muscular control. He then was able to be placed in a semierect position, but could tolerate standing for only 20-minute periods. It required two staff members an equal 20 minutes of time to position him appropriately. However, he was most able to respond consistently with smile or nod of his head when standing in this position.

Cerebral palsy is not a disease entity but a descriptive term that refers to nonprogressive disorders of the sensorimotor system due to prenatal, perinatal, or postnatal brain damage. Risk factors in RA's case include poor prenatal care early in the pregnancy, chronic maternal anemia, and perinatal respiratory distress, all likely contributing to a deprivation of O_2. Diagnostic classifications within cerebral palsy are usually based on (a) distribution of the area of the body in which there is motor involvement, (b) a descriptive term of the form of the motor dysfunction, and (c) the degree or severity of the disordered movement. The diagnostic categories, although somewhat variable in criteria, generally are based on neurological findings or the known course of the effects of brain pathology or lesions.

As noted, distribution indicates the areas of the body showing evidence of sensorimotor impairment. Quadriplegia, as in RA's case, refers to involvement of the entire body, which includes facial, oral-motor, visual, and sphincter musculature. Diplegia indicates that the major disability is present in the trunk and lower limbs, with some dysfunction in the rest of the body, while paraplegia specifies that only the lower extremities are affected. Hemiplegia, the most common form of distribution of cerebral palsy, indicates one entire side of the body, including face and trunk, is involved, although usually the upper extremity (hand and arm) is most affected. Monoplegia, referring to disordered movement in one limb, is a rare finding.

Although diagnosis is based primarily on motor dysfunction, disruption or loss of sensory information may complicate or accompany the motor effects. For example, with deficits in the proprioceptive and kinesthetic sense, the child has difficulty knowing where a limb is in space or how the limb's movement is coordinated with the rest of the body. This may be particularly evident in the way the hemiplegic child maintains the affected arm flexed at elbow and wrist and held close to the trunk. In addition, the child may experience interference with cutaneous messages, leading to an inability to differentiate light or deep touch or an unwillingness to explore and manipulate objects with the affected hand.

The description of the movement disorder (i.e., the symptomatology due to location and effect of the brain lesion) is based on the form of the abnormal movements, posture, or tone. Spasticity, the most common form of cerebral palsy, is characterized by heightened or hyperreflexive responses and an imbalance in control of the relaxation/excitation of affected muscle groups. Thus, there is dyscoordination in the timing and patterns of muscle actions, which are needed for the child to produce smooth, flexible movement. The child may be unable to initiate actions or move out of certain positions. Unequal muscle pull about certain joints (knees and ankles, particularly) or imbalance of postural musculature or bony structures of the spine can produce contractures, deformities, dislocation of limbs (as in RA's case), or scoliosis. Limitations of movement may be increased due to obligatory reflex patterns when the child attempts voluntary actions or in response to sudden shifts in environmental stimuli, such as a loud noise. Postural or balance responses of the trunk may be delayed or impaired, providing for a poorly stabilized base from which to move the limbs. Muscular dysfunction can affect visual, oral-motor, and facial systems, and complicate the respiratory system as well.

Athetosis (or dyskinesia) is the second most prevalent diagnosed type of cerebral palsy. The athetoid child has disorganized, jerky, uncontrollable movements of his or her head and limbs. The tone or muscular tension fluctuates throughout the limbs, producing large circular or writhing movements. The arms are generally more severely involved than the legs, so that although the child may be ambulatory, there is danger of frequent falls and a helmet may be needed for protection. The child may have better control of those voluntary movements either close to or most distal from the body, and most difficulty in controlling actions that require combinations of flexion and extension. Desktop activities, then, may be very difficult for the athetoid child. The child may have difficulty jointly coordinating vision and head position, and so will have visual tracking difficulties. Support of the head and trunk in a sitting position may be needed in order to give the child greater head and shoulder control.

There is a high probability that hearing loss will be associated with athetosis. Because oral-motor musculature also may be affected, speech can be unintelligible or delayed due to the combination of dysarthria and hearing deficit. Athetosis is not consistently associated with mental retardation.

Flaccid or hypotonic cerebral palsy is most often an early diagnosis of an infant with central nervous system dysfunction that will later develop into spasticity or athetoid movement. Persistence of hypotonia in preschool children is usually bilateral and associated with severe mental retardation, seizure disorders, and cortical sensory deficits. One also sees depressed responsiveness to environmental stimuli in these children, particularly evident in their lack of orienting or anticipatory behaviors to common or repetitively experienced daily events such as when dressed or lifted up. The child may be totally reliant on adults for care, although ability for movement and muscle control is present.

Ataxia is probably the most difficult type of cerebral palsy to diagnose. Primarily a disorder of balance and postural coordination (equilibrium) rather than of muscular control, ataxia is due to damage within the cerebellum. The child evidences difficulty in the direction, speed, and placement of a limb, or in the ability to regain postural stability when weight is shifted, as when taking a step. The difficulty is usually greater in the legs and trunk than in the upper extremities.

The classic sign of the ataxic preschooler is that of a wide-based or toe clawing stance or side-to-side shift during gait. The ataxic child will continue to be clumsy and unable to readily shift postural position in sitting, standing, or on all fours. One may see tremoring when he or she produces voluntary or intentional movement. Ataxia may also present with nystagmus, hearing deficits, or speech delay.

Recently there has been greater use of the diagnostic category of mixed type cerebral palsy, combining features of spasticity and athetosis. This may reflect greater sensitivity to subtle changes in variability of the movement disorder as the child develops through preschool years.

The diagnostic characterization of cerebral palsy is completed with a clinical description and determination of the severity of the disorder—mild, moderate, or severe.

Design of the Evaluation in Cerebral Palsy

One important goal of the evaluation of a child with multiple disabilities is always to estimate his or her cognitive, language, and perceptual abilities, independent of limitations that the neurological disorder places on processing or integrating information, or of limitations on performance imposed by neuromuscular dysfunction. In practice, as this goal is often difficult to achieve, there is a high probability of diagnostic error.

An accurate and valid estimation of cognitive functioning will depend on the psychologist's knowledge of or access to data concerning the child's sensorimotor, perceptual, and speech/language abilities. Testimony from family, teachers, and therapists who know the child well should be gathered carefully. Methods developed by other disciplines to enhance the child's sensory-perceptual processing and muscular control should be considered to maximize his or her performance. For example, Velcro or adhesive material may be used to secure objects to the test table to minimize interference with task performance by motor overflow. Also, test materials may be adapted (e.g., choice boxes) via lighted switches or a joystick to enable the child to respond to a task or indicate consistent yes/no responses. Use of such equipment might require a period of training or teaching prior to an actual assessment session (Davidson, Adams, Schroeder, & Tyler, 1978). Consideration should also be given to the time of day, effect of medication, if any, and the need for alternating the child's position to reduce fatigue. Repeated observations in situations familiar to the child (e.g., classroom) and scheduling of multiple short test sessions may be particularly important to assess a multiply disabled youngster. Also, the evaluation should include all adaptive equipment prescribed for the child's use. RA's motor control and ability to produce yes/no responses in a supportive standing position is indicative of the importance for a valid assessment of achieving proper positioning in the client's own adaptive equipment.

Personal and social development. The child with multiple disabilities may be at risk for abnormal adjustment, temperament, behavior, or social interaction. These abnormalities may result from (a) difficulty in establishing bonding with the caregiver; (b) emotional lability, hyperactivity or heightened anxiety, excitability, or arousal secondary to disorganization of movement; (c) inconsistent responsiveness to social cues due to motor deficits; or (d) effects on behavior of persistent and early seizures.

Caregiver-child interactions may reveal some of these deficits. The parents' attempts to assist the neurologically impaired infant to calm or organize his behavior may meet with failure. Often these children do not "cuddle" or respond to parental soothing techniques. The multiply handicapped youngster usually has difficulty feeding and drinking, requiring food to be of a particular consistency to avoid aspiration. Thus, he or she may be difficult for parents to feed, placing stress on interactions during this time. The examiner, therefore, might wish to include a feeding session in the observation. Attempts by caregivers to communicate with the child should be noted.

Adaptive behavior. Adaptive behavior may be assessed by means of parent questionnaire. The AAMD Adaptive Behavior Scale has been designed to accommodate the presence of some physical disabilities and may be preferable to other standardized questionnaires. The Parenting Stress Index and the Callier-Azusa Scale (discussed earlier for use with deaf-blind children) may also prove useful.

Cognitive and perceptual skills. Very few standardized tests of intelligence will be useful with young children who are multiply disabled. Most such tests demand either a verbal or a consistent motoric response to a sufficient portion of test items to prevent administration of such items to these children.

The Pictorial Test of Intelligence (French, 1964), the Leiter International Performance Scale (Leiter, 1948), and the Peabody Picture Vocabulary Test–Revised (Dunn & Dunn, 1981) all can be administered to children with minimal motor functioning and no verbal expressive language. These tests also have few timed items. The examiner can adapt any of them to substitute a gaze for a pointing response, facilitating administration to children with poor upper extremity control or coordination.

In some cases, administration of these tests may require major modification that will depart from testing parameters and preclude the use of test norms. For example, inconsistent responding from a child like RA forced by motor deficits may necessitate extending floor and ceiling requirements for subtests. Drawing a sample of responses below a floor or above a ceiling may also reveal important trends in error patterns related to a specific task component or requirement (e.g., errors may occur more often when the stimulus is in a particular orientation or order). The examiner also may wish to use test items as a means for studying problem-solving strategies. For instance, a failed task may be used to teach the child the desired response while the examiner notes errors and interprets the child's learning style.

Recent advances in adapting the measurement of infant visual recognition memory to clinical settings have been reported by Fagan and his associates (Fagan & Singer, 1983). The Fagan Test, involving preferential looking responses, has been shown to correlate with more traditional measures of intelligence and may prove useful as a screening tool for some children with physical disabilities.

In children whose disabilities are so severe that they prevent the use of standardized instruments, the examiner may wish to employ behavioral checklists (Wilson, 1984) or design a functional analysis of behavior such as described by Davidson et al. (1978). Specifically, one-choice or multichoice discrimination of objects, pictures, or abstract representations can provide a measure of receptive vocabulary that indirectly estimates cognitive level. Also, such tasks can be modified to include a memory component by delaying the presentation of the matching stimuli in a traditional match-to-sample paradigm. Finally, these tasks may provide suggestions for educational intervention.

Case Study: Spina Bifida

CF is a 4-year-old boy, born with a myelomeningocele between the fifth lumbar and sacral vertebrae that was closed surgically on the first day of life. At that time, magnetic resonance imaging (MRI) revealed hydrocephalus, which was treated by placement of a ventricular-peritoneal shunt. The shunt required revision several times as CF developed lethargy and seizures. It now functions effectively. CF's head circumference is within normal limits.

CF has hearing within normal limits. An ophthalmological examination showed amblyopia (unequal visual acuity) for which he now wears an eye patch. CF has been fitted with long leg braces and is now ambulatory with the assistance of a walker. He is incontinent of both bowel and bladder. Early developmental milestones were delayed, whether or not they were related to motor functions. Since enrollment in a infant stimulation program at age 14 months, he has made steady progress in both verbal and nonverbal functions and in self-care skills. However, a recent speech and language evaluation indicated a 6-month delay in receptive language and a 1-year delay in expressive speech. CF's oral facial musculature is weak and he has oral cavity malformations, including a high-arched palate, which produce feeding difficulties. He also shows perceptual deficits in tasks involving form identification and matching, sorting by shape or color, and difficulty in drawing and copying. His teachers report that CF has a short attention span. His intelligence has never been evaluated.

Congenital malformation and extrusion of spinal neural tissue from the bony arch support (myelomeningocele) results in loss of motor and sensory functioning. The areas affected depend on the level of the spinal lesion and specific nerve roots that have been preserved. As in CF's case, lack of motor innervation results in loss or reduction of muscle tissue (atrophy) and reduced bone growth, impaired circulation, and deformities due to imbalance of muscle strength about the joints. Skeletal deformities may be present due to absence or malformation of bone structure or depletion of muscular mass. Because of loss of sensation, the child can be easily injured (e.g., burned) without knowing it, resulting in skin breakdown and ulceration, accompanied by a danger of serious infection.

Although not well understood, intrauterine growth of neural tissue is related to development of other bone or organ systems. For example, cleft palate, congenital cardiac (particularly of heart ventricles), and upper gastrointestinal tract abnormalities are associated with myelomeningocele. The child may also have physical anomolies or deformities, including scoliosis and "club feet." CF displays hydrocephalus (enlargement of the ventricular spaces due to inadequate drainage of cerebrospinal fluid), the most common abnormality associated with spina bifida. Surgical implantation of a drainage shunt from the affected ventricular area to the peritoneal cavity is the treatment of choice. As the child matures, there may be evidence of further malformation of lower brain structures and tethering of the spinal cord at its terminus. These complications can produce seizures and interfere with swallowing and breathing mechanisms. They may also cause abnormal cranial nerve responses, leading to deficits in visual or facial sensorimotor functioning.

Bladder and bowel incontinence are serious problems for all children with myelomeningocele because, for the most part, the nerves that control these functions reside at the sacral spinal level. Bowel training and timing plus a special diet, although only somewhat effective, presents the only currently available noninvasive treatment for fecal incontinence. Chronic urinary incontinence is usually associated with urinary tract infections and can lead to renal failure. Thus, young children with myelomeningocele generally require catheterization four times per day; older ones may be taught to self-catheterize.

Most children with spina bifida have normal intelligence. However, there is increasing evidence of the frequent occurrence in this population of specific learning disabilities (Horn, Lorch, Lorch, & Cullata, 1985; Liptak et al., 1988). Upper body motor coordination, eye-hand functions, and perceptual performance seem to be affected in children with spina bifida, especially if it is associated with hydrocephalus (Anderson & Plewis, 1977; Turner, 1986).

As in CF's case, malformation of oral structures and malfunction of oral-facial musculature may be associated with impairments of speech and language. Feeding disorders may result from the same etiology.

Caregivers of the child with myelomeningocele face continual stresses from coping with the child's numerous multisystem medical and rehabilitative needs. These stresses may become overwhelming and lead to serious family dysfunction.

Design of the Evaluation in Spina Bifida

In general, the psychological evaluation of the young child with spina bifida will approximate procedures used for young children without disabilities. In addition to estimating overall cognitive ability, objectives of the evaluation should include (a) identification of an occult or manifest learning disability; (b) measurement of adaptive and self-care skills, with special reference to those functions most likely to be at deficit (in turn dependent upon level of lesion) in such children; and (c) personal-social adjustment skills, with special reference to the functioning of the family.

In most geographic locations, the young child with spina bifida will be followed by a specialized, multidisciplinary clinic. Information on the child's medical, psychosocial, educational, perceptual-motor, mobility, and communication status will almost always be available through this resource and should be gathered to assist in planning the evaluation and in interpreting the resulting data.

If the child has been enrolled in a preschool or elementary school program, the examiner should obtain any available performance data, with special reference to evidence that might suggest a learning disability. The examiner should also include a social history, gathered from the caregivers, as a means to identify special management problems that may result in family stress.

There are no special problems associated with this disorder in establishing rapport between examiner and child. The only special problem that may impact on rapport involves the child's mobility and seating requirements. The examiner should anticipate any special needs and arrange beforehand for necessary equipment or access to appropriate testing space. Some children with spina bifida have been described as verbose or having "cocktail party" language usage, while others may appear nonresponsive or sullen (Liptak et al., 1988). The examiner may wish to accommodate this possibility by beginning evaluation sessions with a period of open-ended conversation or with free play in a playroom setting.

Cognitive and perceptual abilities. The assessment battery should reflect the psychologist's objective of identifying a possible learning disability. Thus, the McCarthy Scales of Children's Abilities may be considered for the youngest preschoolers, while the Stanford-Binet Intelligence Test, Fourth Edition, (Thorndike, Hagen, & Sattler, 1986), the Wechsler Preschool and Primary Scales of Intelligence–Revised (WPPSI-R; Wechsler, 1989), or the Kaufman Assessment Battery for Children (K-ABC; Kaufman & Kaufman, 1983) provide options for the older preschooler or young school-aged child. Because of the potential for ceiling effects, these tests are preferable to the Wechsler Intelligence Scale for Children–Third Edition (Wechsler, 1991; Vance, Paparella, & Prazza, 1983). Comparison of verbal and performance sections or subscales of these tests will assist in defining specific deficits in language or in perceptual functions.

Perceptual deficits associated with visual-motor integration may be revealed through isolating cognitive factors from motor functions. Two approaches may apply. First, the examiner may adopt tests that require only visual responses, such as the Pictorial Test of Intelligence or Raven's Coloured Progressive Matrices (Raven, Court, & Raven, 1985). Results then can be compared to conventional tests discussed above. Or the examiner may employ neuropsychological tests, such as the Halstead-Reitan Neuropsychological Test Battery for Children (Reitan Neuropsychology Laboratory, 1979).

Adaptive behavior. The child's adaptive abilities may be evaluated by means of either the Vineland Adaptive Behavior Scales or the AAMD Adaptive Behavior Scale–School Edition (Lambert, Windmiller, Cole, & Tharinger, 1981). The examiner may also wish to combine these quantitative data with information from a history and clinical observations drawn from testing or playroom sessions.

Personal and social development. Personal-social and behavioral data also can result from playroom observations and from historical information. The examiner may wish to employ a limited battery of projective tests, including puppet play, a kinetic family drawing (Burns & Kaufman, 1972), the House-Tree-Person test (Buck, 1966), a series of figure drawings, or more formal instruments such as the Children's Apperception Test (CAT; Bellak & Bellak, 1976). The Parenting Stress Index will assist in determining family functioning.

Assessing Children with Other Physical Disabilities

Infants and young children with muscular or joint and bone disorders that do not involve primary central nervous system dysfunction typically manifest motor disabilities. Such disorders include muscular dystrophy and juvenile rheumatoid arthritis.

Some forms of muscular dystrophy have a congenital origin and early onset, followed by slow progression or by short bursts of deterioration of ability. In some forms, the child may never develop certain fine and gross motor skills. As noted previously, the more commonly seen form is Duchenne's muscular dystrophy, an inherited disease usually affecting males. Initial symptoms usually appear between ages 2 to 5 years, manifested by increasing weakness of pelvic and lower limb muscle groups, with deterioration of gross motor skills. Difficulty may be experienced in getting up from the floor or from a chair, walking up stairs, or running. Generally the increasing muscular weakness, especially under exertion, affects the respiratory and cardiac systems, and the child is increasingly subject to infections. Changes in strength and imbalance of muscle pull on the joints (especially evident in knees and ankles, at first) produce contractures and deformities. There is wasting of some muscle groups and hypertrophy (enlargement) of others, which differ depending on type of muscular dystrophy. Involvement of hands and elbows may interfere with self-care and school-related activities. Effects on the upper extremities usually do not occur until later in childhood or adolescence.

Because Duchenne's muscular dystrophy is a terminal, sex-linked, recessive characteristic, affected children may have witnessed other family members decline and die. This pattern can have devastating effects on the child's adjustment and the family's coping abilities. Many children with Duchenne's muscular dystrophy have normal intelligence. However, some develop mental retardation secondary to central nervous system deterioration (Menkes, 1985).

Other, rarer diseases of the young child that affect movement include connective tissue disorders, such as juvenile rheumatoid arthritis, and congenital disorders of growth or malformation of bone and joints, such as arthrogryposis or osteogenesis imperfecta. These diseases may be accompanied by limitation of movement, reduction of strength, and pain or danger of fracture. Surgery, splinting, frequent hospitalizations, and painful therapeutic and diagnostic procedures, although problems faced by many motorically handicapped children, are especially difficult in these diseases. They may fear movement of any kind. Children with these disorders often appear depressed and listless, evidencing flat affect, withdrawal, and poor motivation.

Awareness and sensitivity to the medical and emotional concerns of the family and child will prepare the psychologist in planning for the family interview and will contribute to helping establish rapport with the child. Choice of assessment instrument and the degree of standardization in presenting the test will depend on the physical demands of the testing items or situation. For example, a child who has limited motion of shoulder, elbow, and hands might require objects to be placed in a particular position for optimal accessibility. The child should be observed for signs of weakness, fatigue, and difficulty in closing his or her hand for grasp and release. Choice of verbal assessment might be considered if there is marked inability to manipulate objects. Social responsiveness and informal visual and auditory attention might provide a less formal area of assessment of an infant for whom movement is impeded or painful. Current "screening tests" using recognition and visual attention (e.g., Fagan Test) might be utilized for more informal observations. The examiner should consult with physical and occupational therapists for equipment that positions or provides support to enable the child to use his or her muscles/joints to optimal advantage. Periodic alterations of position might reduce the effects of fatigue, as might scheduling testing in shorter time periods or in the morning or after naps.

Interpretation and Reporting of Assessment Data

Our approach to the assessment of cognitive, perceptual, social-adaptive, and behavioral-adjustment functioning in the young multiply handicapped child is based on ascertaining potential rather than only comparing performance to standardized scores or age equivalent norms. Judgment of the child's potential can be derived from (a) observations made across situations, (b) assessments made following instructional sessions, and (c) the child's responses to a sampling of modified test items, when feasible.

Beyond computing standardized scores, the examiner should note the form of responses exhibited by the child in a variety of situations, with special attention to alternate methods of communication the child adopts. Different tasks, stimulus situations, or social settings may evoke consistent changes in a nonverbal child's excitation level, activity level, degree of alertness, or facial expression—including smiling, grimacing, or eye widening or narrowing. Such consistent changes may indicate understanding of, or attention to, ongoing events, as well as serve as methods to communicate with the examiner. Use of such methods may differ depending on the sensory modality involved in task performance, and such differences should be noted.

Open-ended tasks with few limits or demands on the child may evoke different responses than demanding or highly structured situations. The child's ability to cope with frustration also can be measured by noting the effects of such different settings on excitation, compliance, and attention. In addition, the examiner should attempt to assess the child's intentionality to complete tasks or comply with their demands for those that require motoric responses. Qualitative observations may help the examiner to distinguish between cognitive deficiency and motor inability. For certain tasks, reports of results from one session will not suffice. The examiner should regard data from multiple sessions that reveal rate and quality of learning as appropriate indicators of functional levels and potential.

Most parents believe they know their children better than any professional. In the case of the child with a physical disability, parents are frequently the only ones who "understand" the child's attempts to communicate, and thus they may be particularly sensitive to information about his or her abilities communicated during an interpretive conference (Rockowitz et al., 1987). The examiner should use parental history in designing the evaluation, should consider having parents observe the evaluation, and enlist parents' help in interpreting the data. If these actions are taken, the interpretive conference may serve as a summing up, rather than a presentation of new information that may surprise parents or not fit their perceptions of the child, and thus be unacceptable.

REFERENCES

Abidin, R.R. (1990). *Parenting Stress Index* (3rd ed.). Charlottesville, VA: Pediatric Psychology Press.
Achenbach, T., & Edelbrock, C. (1981). Behavioral problems and competencies reported by parents of normal and disturbed children aged 4 through 16. *Monographs of the Society for Research in Child Development, 46* (Series No. 1).
Anderson, E., & Plewis, I. (1977). Impairment of motor skills in children with spina bifida cistica and hydrocephalus: An exploratory study. *British Journal of Psychology, 68,* 61-70.
Barraga, N., & Collins, M. (1979). Development of efficiency in visual functioning: Rationale for a comprehensive program. *Journal of Visual Impairment and Blindness, 73,* 212-216.
Bayley, N. (1969). *Bayley Scales of Infant Development: Birth to three years.* San Antonio, TX: Psychological Corporation.
Bellak, L., & Bellak, S.S. (1976). *Children's Apperception Test.* Larchmont, NY: C.P.S.
Buck, J.N. (1966). *House-Tree-Person (H-T-P Technique) revised manual.* Los Angeles: Western Psychological Services.
Bullard, B., & Barraga, N. (1971). Subtests of evaluation instruments applicable for use with preschool visually handicapped children. *Education of the Visually Handicapped, 3,* 118-122.
Burns, R.C., & Kaufman, S.H. (1972). *The Kinetic Family Drawing (KFD).* New York: Brunner/Mazel.
Cassidy, J. (1985). Juvenile rheumatoid arthritis. In W. Kelley, E. Harris, S. Ruddy, & C. Sledge (Eds.), *Textbook of rheumatology* (Vol. 2, 2nd ed., pp. 1247-1271). Philadelphia, PA: Saunders.
Cattell, P. (1960). *Cattell Infant Intelligence Scale.* San Antonio, TX: Psychological Corporation.
Chase, J. (1972). *Retrolental fibroplasia and autistic symptomatology.* New York: American Foundation for the Blind.
Chess, S., & Fernandez, P. (1976). Temperament and the rubella child. In Z.S. Jastrzembska (Ed.), *The effects of blindness and other impairments on early development.* New York: American Foundation for the Blind.
Collins-Moore, M.S., & Osborn, K.N. (1984). Assessing the visually handicapped child. In S.J. Weaver (Ed.), *Testing children: A reference guide for effective clinical and psychoeducational assessments* (pp. 137-160). Austin, TX: PRO-ED.
Davidson, P., Adams, W., Schroeder, C., & Tyler, D. (1978). A case study: Educational assessment and planning for a severely involved, non-verbal quadriplegic client. *Journal of Pediatric Psychology, 3*(2), 67-71.

Davidson, P., & Legouri, S. (1986). Assessment of visually impaired children. In R.J. Simeonsson (Ed.), *Psychological and developmental assessment of special children* (pp. 217-240). Boston, MA: Allyn & Bacon.

Davis, C. (1980). *Perkins-Binet Test of Intelligence for the Blind.* Watertown, MA: Perkins School for the Blind.

Dunn, L.M., & Dunn, L.M. (1981). *Peabody Picture Vocabulary Test-Revised.* Circle Pines, MN: American Guidance Service.

Eichel, V. (1978, April). Mannerisms of the blind: A review of the literature. *Journal of Visual Impairment and Blindness,* pp. 125-130.

Fagan, J., & Singer, L. (1983). Infant recognition memory as a measure of intelligence. *Advances in Infant Intelligence, 2,* 31-78.

Fraiberg, S. (1977). *Insights from the blind: Studies of blind and sighted infants.* New York: Basic Books.

Frankenburg, W.K., & Dodds, J.B. (1990). *Denver II.* Denver, CO: Ladoca Project and Publishing Foundation.

French, J.L. (1964). *Pictorial Test of Intelligence.* Chicago: Riverside.

Goldstein, H. (1980). The reported demography and causes of blindness throughout the world. *Advances in Ophthalmology, 40,* 1-99.

Griffiths, R. (1978). *Griffiths Mental Development Scales.* High Wycombe, England: Test Agency.

Hatwell, Y. (1966). *Privation sensorielle et intelligence.* Paris, France: Universitaires de France.

Hatwell, Y. (1978). Form perception and related issues in blind humans. In R. Held, H. Leibowitz, & H.-L. Teuber (Eds.), *Handbook of sensory physiology* (Vol. 8, pp. 489-519). New York: Springer-Verlag.

Horn, D., Lorch, E., Lorch, R., Jr., & Culatta, B. (1985). Distractibility and vocabulary deficits in children with spina bifida and hydrocephalus. *Developmental Medicine and Child Neurology, 27,* 713-720.

Kahn, H., & Moorhead, W. (1973). *Statistics on blindness in the model reporting area* (DHEW Publication (NIH) 73-427). Washington, DC: National Eye Institute.

Kaufman, A.S., & Kaufman, N.L. (1983). *Kaufman Assessment Battery for Children (K-ABC).* Circle Pines, MN: American Guidance Service.

Lambert, N.M., Windmiller, M., Cole, L., & Tharinger, D. (1981). *AAMD Adaptive Behavior Scale-School Edition.* Austin, TX: PRO-ED.

Leiter, R.G. (1948). *Leiter International Performance Scale.* Chicago: Stoelting.

Levitt, E., Rosenbaum, A., Willerman, L., & Levitt, M. (1972). Intelligence of retinoblastoma patients and their siblings. *Child Development, 43,* 939-948.

Liptak, G., Bloss, J., Briskin, H., Campbell, J., Hebert, E., & Revell, G. (1988). The management of children with spinal dysraphism. *Journal of Child Neurology, 3,* 3-20.

Maxfield, K., & Bucholtz, S. (1958). *A social maturity scale for blind preschool children: A guide to its use.* New York: American Foundation for the Blind.

McCarthy, D. (1972). *McCarthy Scales of Children's Abilities.* San Antonio, TX: Psychological Corporation.

Menkes, J. (1985). *Textbook of child neurology* (3rd ed.). Philadelphia, PA: Lea & Febiger.

Nihira, K., Foster, R., Shellhaas, M., & Leland, H. (1974). *AAMD Adaptive Behavior Scale* (rev. ed.). Austin, TX: PRO-ED.

Peloquin, L.J., & Davidson, P. (1988). Psychological sequelae of infectious diseases in children. In D. Routh (Ed.), *Handbook of pediatric psychology* (pp. 222-257). Philadelphia, PA: Guilford.

Raven, J.C., Court, J.H., & Raven, J. (1985). *Coloured Progressive Matrices.* London, England: H.K. Lewis.

Reitan Neuropsychology Laboratory. (1979). *Halstead-Reitan Neuropsychological Test Battery for Children*. Tucson, AZ: Author.

Reynell, J., & Zinkin, P. (1979). *Reynell-Zinkin Developmental Scales for Young Visually Handicapped Children*. Windsor, England: NFER-Nelson.

Rockowitz, R., Davidson, P., & Hoekelman, R. (1987). Communications with parents and patients. In R. Hoekelman, S. Blatman, S. Friedman, N. Nelson, & H. Siedel (Eds.), *Primary pediatric care* (pp. 48-51). St. Louis, MO: Mosby.

Sanford, A. (1974). *Learning Accomplishment Profile*. Winston-Salem, NC: Kaplan Press.

Scharf, L., & Adams, K. (1984). Long-term neuropsychological impact of retrolental fibroplasia: A review and implications. *Journal of Pediatric Psychology, 9*(3), 303-316.

Sparrow, S.S., Balla, D.A., & Cicchetti, D.V. (1985). *Vineland Adaptive Behavior Scales (VABS)*. Circle Pines, MN: American Guidance Service.

Stillman, R. (1975). *Assessment of deaf-blind children: The Callier-Azusa Scale*. Dallas, TX: Callier Center for Communication Disorders.

Terman, L.M., & Merrill, M.A. (1973). *Stanford-Binet Intelligence Scale, Form L-M*. Chicago: Riverside.

Thorndike, R.L., Hagen, E.P., & Sattler, J.M. (1986). *Stanford-Binet Intelligence Test, Fourth Edition*. Chicago: Riverside.

Turner, A. (1986). Upper limb functioning of children with myelomeningocele. *Developmental Medicine and Child Neurology, 28*, 790-798.

Vance, B., Paparella, C., & Piazza, C. (1983). *Wechsler Intelligence Scale for Children-Revised (WISC-R)*. Novato, CA: Academic Therapy Publications.

Wechsler, D. (1989). *Wechsler Preschool and Primary Scales of Intelligence-Revised*. San Antonio, TX: Psychological Corporation.

Wechsler, D. (1991). *Wechsler Intelligence Scale for Children-Third Edition*. San Antonio, TX: Psychological Corporation.

Wilhelm, C., Johnson, M., & Eisert, D. (1986). Assessment of motor-impaired children. In R.J. Simeonsson (Ed.), *Psychological and developmental assessment of special children* (pp. 241-278). Boston: Allyn & Bacon.

Willis, D.J., Culbertson, J.L., & Mertens, R. (1984). Considerations in physical and health-related disorders. In S.J. Weaver (Ed.), *Testing children: A reference guide for effective clinical and psychoeducational assessments* (pp. 185-196). Austin, TX: PRO-ED.

Willis, D.J., & Holden, E.W. (1990). Etiological factors contributing to deviant development. In J.H. Johnson & J. Goldman (Eds.), *Developmental assessment in clinical child psychology* (pp. 38-57). New York: Pergamon.

Wilson, J. (1984). Cerebral palsy. In S. Campbell (Ed.), *Pediatric neurological physical therapy* (pp. 353-413). New York: Churchill Livingston.

Witkin, H., Birnbaum, J., Lomonaco, S., Lehr, S., & Herman, J.L. (1968). Cognitive patterning in congenitally totally blind children. *Child Development, 39*, 767-786.

Witkin, H., Oltman, P., Chase, J., & Friedman, F. (1971). Cognitive patterning in the blind. In J. Hellmuth (Ed.), *Cognitive studies* (Vol. 2, pp. 16-46). New York: Brunner/Mazel.

Ziring, P. (1983). The child with hearing impairment. In M. Levine, W.B. Carey, A.C. Crocker, & R.T. Gross (Eds.), *Developmental and behavioral pediatrics* (pp. 770-777). Philadelphia, PA: Saunders.

11

Psychological Evaluation of Infants and Young Children with Chronic Physical Illness

J. KENNETH WHITT, PH.D. & MELISSA RAMIREZ JOHNSON, PH.D.

Advances in pediatric treatment regimens and aggressive life support procedures continue to reduce the mortality of chronically ill infants and young children. While many children live reasonably unrestricted lives and achieve satisfactory social adaptation, problems incurred from having a chronic physical disorder (e.g., asthma, diabetes, cancer, renal disease, epilepsy, muscular dystrophy, cystic fibrosis, hemophilia, sickle cell disease, cardiac problems, bronchopulmonary dysplasia, juvenile rheumatoid arthritis) may seriously affect a young child's developmental competence.

In general, psychological assessment in pediatric health care settings serves to define the young child's adaptive capacities—as well as deviations in motor, perceptual, cognitive, language, behavioral, social, and/or emotional functioning—for use in case management and intervention planning (Magrab & Lehr, 1982). To these ends, pediatric psychologists utilize observations of child behavior and interaction, child and family interviewing, and standardized psychological instruments, including tests of developmental and intellectual functioning, neuropsychological procedures, social/emotional and personality assessment methods, behavior rating scales, and measures of family system functioning.

Chronic illness impacts the child's adaptive functioning through the direct effects of the disease process, developmental deviations due to treatment interference, disruptions of normal patterns of family system functioning, and/or via the emotional stresses of illness adaptation. Psychologists seeking to evaluate young children with chronic illness must become familiar with the natural history of each disease, as well as the specific challenges that medical treatment and the health care system pose to child and family coping. Potent illness factors, including disease severity and course, effects of hospitalization, illness comprehension, pain intrinsic to disease and treatment procedures, side effects of medication, and medical regimen interferences with normal child and family routines, each may undermine a family's capacity to maintain the child's developmental trajectory (Whitt, 1984).

Specific questions face the psychologist assessing young chronically ill children and their families, and three key purposes, or assessment goals, arise: (a) evaluating child and family adjustment to chronic illness and treatment; (b) defining the primary impact of the illness, as well as secondary effects of treatment and iatrogenic developmental interferences associated with medical interventions; and (c) monitoring, or longitudinal tracking, of the developmental competence of high-risk infants and young children. For more exhaustive surveys of individual test instruments and assessment procedures than are possible or appropriate here, the reader is referred to companion chapters in this volume as well as works by Bettenburg (1985), Sattler (1988), Simeonsson (1986), Tramontana and Hooper (1988), Tuma (1982), and Weaver (1984).

CHILD AND FAMILY ADJUSTMENT TO CHRONIC ILLNESS

The pediatric psychologist is frequently asked to evaluate the child and family adjustment to chronic illness. Coping with painful procedures, anxious reactions to treatment demands, comprehension of illness, prolonged uncertainty regarding the child's future, illness-related disruptions of the family system routines, and the shift of a family's social support relationships in the home and community to include the pediatric health care team are but a few of the challenges that face the child with chronic illness and his or her family. (For discussions of illness adaptation variables, see also Brantley, Stabler, & Whitt, 1981; Cohen & Lazarus, 1979; Drotar, 1981; Johnson, 1979; Patterson & McCubbin, 1983; Pless & Roghmann, 1971; Pless & Pinkerton, 1975; Routh, 1988; Vernon, Foley, Sipowicz, & Schulman, 1965; Varni & Wallander, 1988; Whitt, 1984; Willis, Elliott, & Jay, 1982.)

Reactions to Stressful Procedures and Illness Pain

One goal of evaluation is to distinguish stress responses that are a natural part of adaptation to illness from the signs of more serious developmental psychopathology. For many young children, the illness experience includes the necessity for invasive and painful medical procedures, in addition to repeated "minor" stresses such as rectal temperatures or finger sticks for blood drawing. Both major and "routine" procedures have significant psychological meaning to young children (Mattsson, 1972). Consideration of the situation specificity of the distress behaviors that prompt psychological evaluation often enables the psychologist to determine whether the "problem behaviors" represent an adjustment reaction to exceptional stressors or a deviation from age-appropriate coping. The results often clarify the need for psychotherapeutic intervention to facilitate child and family adjustment, as opposed to a more circumscribed focus on coping with specific medical procedures.

Jane is a 3-year-old girl hospitalized for treatment of a stubborn infection, which required daily injections of antibiotic directly into the shunt draining her hydrocephalus. Her persistent, somewhat anguished, crying during this procedure was disturbing to the medical staff. A consulting psychologist noted Jane's otherwise appropriate emotional and developmental functioning; aside from the procedures, she seemed well adjusted to the hospital, had playful relationships with both staff and other children, cuddled warmly with her mother during visits, and verbalized clearly both her dislike of needles and her enjoyment of playroom activities.

This child's protests—which quickly ended once each procedure was complete—seemed maladaptive, mostly as a stressor for the staff who had to listen. Crying, even screaming, may be an age-appropriate channel for active, even vigorous expression of distress over events that a young child cannot fully understand, avoid, control, or otherwise master. The staff was encouraged to accept the realistic basis for her distress, while maintaining matter-of-fact communication and supportive relationships during procedures. Efforts to suppress her crying were not recommended. Rather, "doctor play" was initiated to provide opportunities for Jane to clarify her perceptions of, and actively master, these events. Although she fussed during injections, Jane remained cheerfully engaged with the staff outside the treatment room and did well upon discharge.

Pain resulting from the disease process itself, as from sickle cell crises, bleeding into joints with hemophilia, or malignant tumor growth, is a particularly difficult problem for assessment. Family and physician apprehensions about potential addiction may lead to underprescribing pain medications, necessitating increased, but adaptive, pain behavior to obtain "relief." On the other hand, secondary gains from interactions around pain communication may also increase the frequency of these complaints. Behavioral observations and diary records of pain behaviors often help define psychological management options, which may link effective doses of medication with behavioral strategies such as distraction, relaxation, hypnosis, or guided imagery (Gardner & Olness, 1981; Hilgard & LeBaron, 1984; Ross & Ross, 1988).

Comprehension of Illness

Child and family coping requires sufficient understanding of the illness to justify undergoing the required treatment procedures. A child's misconceptions of the medical condition (e.g., growing up with "sick as hell anemia," "a demon in my belly," or "die-of-beetes") cannot help but adversely affect child adjustment. Fortunately, children's misconceptions, fears, and/or fantasies regarding the illness, treatment, and potential outcome can be elicited by direct inquiry and, once known, alleviated by careful, age-appropriate communication (for cognitive and social determinants of children's comprehension of illness, see, e.g., Bibace & Walsh, 1980, 1981; Perrin & Gerrity, 1981; Simeonsson, Buckley, & Monson, 1979; Whitt, Dykstra, & Taylor, 1979; and Whitt, 1982).

A child's perception of illness begins to take shape even before the diagnosis (e.g., the word "cancer") has been introduced. Preliminary "meaning" is drawn from the child's experiences of the hospitalization; diagnostic or treatment procedures (such as painful bone marrow aspiration or lumbar punctures, blood drawing, surgery, or radiation treatments, which require lying alone in a room filled with noisy equipment); and the initial patterns of medical team communication and responses to the child's behavior. Social cues obtained from disruptions of family system functioning and "readings" of parental distress also "clarify" the significance of illness. Children often say "I know that I'm very sick (or dying) because people treat me differently. I can even get away with hitting my little sister. My parents would have never let me get away with that if I was well!"

Child Emotional Adjustment

The issues central to the young child's emotional adjustment are complex and varied, but may be understood in the context of the attachment, bodily mastery, environmental exploration, emotional separation and individuation, and peer play tasks that characterize the development of infants and young children.

For example, behaviors ranging from anger and whining to passivity and withdrawal in the infant, toddler, and preschooler may be related to separations that disrupt the important attachment interactions between the infant and caregivers. Or, illness and treatment events, such as orthopedic casting and traction, dependence upon life-support or dialysis technology, and other restrictions of mobility may limit opportunities for normal exploration, development of a sense of autonomous mastery and independence, and tension release through playful motor activity. Some children (e.g., with spina bifida, significant cerebral palsy, or tethered to an oxygen hose) cope with continuous restrictions. Others face intermittent restrictions, such as the bleed for a child with hemophilia, the painful crises of sickle cell disease, or periodic dialysis for the child with renal insufficiency or failure. Creative development of alternative channels for stimulation and modes of exploration (e.g., physical contact, rocking, changes of scenery, music, puppet and fantasy play) may lessen the distress of these restrictions and resultant distress (Bergmann & Freud, 1965; Johnson, 1979; Johnson, Whitt, & Martin, 1987).

Children whose temperament or preillness adaptational style requires more structured family system routines and anticipation of changes may be especially vulnerable if hospital routines and treatment demands do not allow time for preparation strategies. Also at risk are very malleable children who acquiesce to demands so quietly that they do not signal, through outward apprehension or behavior, their distress. They may, therefore, elicit neither supportive adult intervention nor interactions that might enhance their comprehension of illness and repertoire for coping with treatment procedures.

As noted in the case above, a young child may evidence disquieting distress behavior (tears, anxiety, vomiting, withdrawal, avoidance, aggression) even to anticipation of arrival at the pediatric clinic; yet, his or her adaptive functioning at home, interactions within the family system, and age-appropriate mastery of social developmental challenges in the community may be entirely within normal limits. Or, the reverse may be observed.

Often adjustment is thwarted by uncertainty regarding the child's ultimate outcome. Even for chronic, potentially life-threatening illness, group survival statistics do not predict the prognosis for an individual child. The realistic challenge is often coping with uncertainty of outcome rather than accepting and planning for death. For example, even younger children with cancer usually realize the potential threat to life inherent in their diagnosis. However, having grappled with the information necessary to justify and explain the treatment regimen, they often choose not to focus on the illness, treatment, or even threat of death. This "adaptive denial" is not psychopathologic; it serves to refute neither the illness nor need for treatment (Lazarus, 1981). Rather, this common adaptation serves to maintain hope, a focus on the future, and a satisfactory quality of life in spite of illness and treatment interferences.

Parent Coping and Family System Functioning

The parents' feelings and coping strategies also affect the child's adaptation. Attempts to determine a child's adaptation to illness require an understanding of family system functioning as well the roles and feelings of "surrogate family" figures, including physicians, nurses, and other staff members who may mitigate the impact of illness on a young child.

The child's survival is the paramount consideration for most parents, especially those with children in pediatric intensive care (PICU) settings (Johnson & Helm, 1988). However, even if, objectively, the child's prognosis is good, parents may not be comforted by statements that "90% of babies with this condition survive"; even a 10% chance that their baby may die can seem intolerable.

A related worry concerns the child's future functioning and potential ability to live an independent life, even when the child is still an infant. Many parents, especially those whose child is at risk for significant developmental or physical handicap, are acutely aware of the difference between looking after a young child, for whom some dependency is appropriate and natural, and providing support for an impaired adult, for whom adequate resources may be far more scarce.

The parent's provision of supportive buffering between the child and the medical care system during hospitalization is thought to maximize adaptation of the child from 0 to 3 years of age. As a result, parental rooming-in has evolved at progressive pediatric medical centers throughout the world. However, situations occur when attachment fails so completely that child neglect, abuse, or abandonment may ensue. Failure to visit a child in the intensive care nursery even when practical assistance is offered, not working to prepare for the baby's homecoming even when specific homecoming dates are set, and noncompliance with medical instructions may be warning signs of this problem. Distinguishing attachment disorders from environmental limitations, especially lack of transportation and the need to maintain employment in low income families, can be difficult, but collaboration between the psychologist and social work professionals within the hospital and in the community is often helpful.

Feelings of guilt and self-blame are common and, at times, debilitating. While determining causality may be a helpful way for parents to regain a sense of control and perspective of the situation, excessive guilt can paralyze them, leaving a legacy of helplessness and depression more devastating than the realities of the child's illness. Many parents also experience a loss of pleasure in and enjoyment of daily family and married life. Parents may not realize the degree to which the family's adaptation to their child's illness may have altered time for recreation or to be alone. Yet, these changes can have consequences for the well-being of all members of the family system, including siblings. Balancing the demands of medical care regimens against the maintenance of the family's normal routines and obligations requires flexible coping strategies (Johnson, Gershowitz, & Stabler, 1981). Daily chest physical therapy for the child with cystic fibrosis, or the constant attention to oxygen and monitoring equipment for the child with bronchopulmonary dysplasia, exemplify the often overwhelming health care tasks that many families face. The temptation to focus only on the illness and its treatment is often extremely compelling.

Michael is a 5-year-old whose registration for school was marked by an increasing frequency of temper tantrums at home and somatic complaints whenever away from his parents. He has nearly completed treatments for acute lymphocytic leukemia, which was diagnosed when he was 3 years of age. Although Michael's illness course had been relatively smooth and he has remained in a continuous remission following induction over 2 years ago, his parents limit most activities outside the home. Shopping trips, church attendance, and most other outings were avoided for fear of his vulnerability to infection if he came into contact with other people—especially other children—outside the immediate household. As a result, Michael has become accustomed to being attended to by an adult family member at all times. He rarely has had the opportunity to play with other children his age.

Potential problems can arise whenever families begin to lower their expectations for child functioning below that which is realistic, or if they persist in expecting higher performance from a child than he or she can possibly maintain. Young children with growth delay secondary to endocrine, renal, or cardiac problems often seem younger than their chronological age, tempting parents to omit the behavioral limits, language expectations, and social input they normally would provide. In other cases, a family's sense of the vulnerability and fragility of their child contributes to an implicit decision to set aside expectations for developmental and social progress until the child is "completely well." Discussion of functioning based on cognitive or developmental testing may help realign parental expectations.

A lack of normal limits and structure is one of the more serious psychosocial effects experienced by the chronically ill child. For a number of psychological and practical reasons, it may be very difficult for parents to discipline such a child, but the lack of firm limits and consistent environmental structure can be confusing and anxiety-provoking for him or her. However well intended, alterations of normal limits and guidelines for behavior, as well as the implied failure to address preparation for the future, only increase a chronically ill child's sense of isolation and vulnerability.

The issues of "reentry," which are salient in the school-aged child's adaptation to chronic illness, translate to "entry" into peer play for young preschool children. These social activities may raise parental apprehensions as they confront events they cannot personally monitor. However, children require not only physical health but also skills in peer interaction, competence, industry, and emotional well-being, which cannot be developed in social isolation.

Normal peer contacts, so important to the development of interpersonal skills and emotional maturity, may be denied the young chronically ill child. In some cases, for example, such as a child with chronic lung disease or on immunosuppressive therapy, isolation may be a medical necessity. The child's perceptions of social competence, an aspect of self-esteem based on mastery of age-appropriate physical tasks and social relationships outside the boundaries of the family system, may underlie adjustment problems in chronically ill children as they reach preschool age. The self-esteem reflected in the normal bouncy, irrepressible 4-year-old may be lacking in a chronically ill child who has not had opportunities to integrate play interactions with peers.

Techniques for Assessing Emotional Adjustment to Illness

Clearly, the preceding discussion implies that child and family system competence and current developmental challenges be considered in the assessment of illness adaptation. These questions extend assessment beyond "testing" the child to include evaluation of the context of stressors and the quality of available emotional support.

In many situations in which the psychologist is asked to assess child adjustment to chronic illness, the timeframe is compressed compared to traditional evaluations. The psychologist must gather background data, often from the medical chart and informal discussions with medical personnel, formulate hypotheses, decide on an assessment strategy, and carry out the initial assessment, sometimes in the hour allotted to a clinic appointment. If initial rapport is good and practical considerations allow it, subsequent, more leisurely follow-up visits can be scheduled and a longer term relationship established. However, a flexible array of (quick and easy) approaches is needed.

Some "emergent" situations require very brief coping style and personality assessment based on interview techniques alone. Rather than being intimidated by the intensity of the crisis situation, or prompted to relinquish one's diagnostic role because traditional testing is inappropriate, the psychologist can make use of the tendency of relationships to develop quickly in times of crisis to formulate, at the very least, working hypotheses that may guide case management and intervention; a few sensitively asked questions may elicit much of the necessary information.

Behavioral observations are often the foundation of an initial assessment. A grasp of normal infant-toddler behavior and emotional expression is essential to compare observed behaviors with those expected from the child's chronological age and developmental level. Vital behavioral cues are found in ease of separation; positive or negative affect as expressed through crying, whining, or laughter; initiations of social interactions; level of motor activity and attention span; play behaviors; self-stimulatory behaviors; and poor frustration tolerance expressed through tantrums or withdrawal. Equally important are the parents' interactions with the child, with each other, and with the school or medical staff.

Play interviews, both unstructured and structured, extend the process of behavioral observation. A playroom, or the clinician's office, should be furnished with sufficient age-appropriate play and fantasy materials so that the child's solitary and peer play (S. Greenspan, 1981; Lansky, List, Lansky, Cohen, & Sinks, 1985) can be evaluated. Structured observational scales, such as the ratings of play and feeding situations (e.g., Ainsworth, Bell, & Stayton, 1971; Barnard, 1978) also may be useful.

Interviews with parents are fundamental throughout all stages of data gathering. Parents often are excellent observers of their children's preillness coping behavior and can provide crucial information about the child's adaptation outside the hospital or clinic. Their reports of the child's normal daily routine (including what goes smoothly, as well as points of difficulty), changes in social interactions, eating, and sleep behaviors, and the child's spontaneous comments about the illness are important. The clinician will need to judge when parents may be projecting their personal reactions onto the child, denying signs of distress because of their own pain, or adjusting expectations to inappropriately low or high levels. However, even contradictions between observed behavior and parent report will provide valuable information and should not be allowed to justify neglecting the parents' perspective. Questionnaires such as the Parenting Stress Index (Abidin, 1983), FACES III (Olson, 1986), Impact of Illness Scale (Stein & Reissman, 1980), Family Routines Inventory (Jensen, James, Boyce, & Hartnett, 1982), HOME (Caldwell & Bradley, 1979), Family Environment Scale (Moos, 1974), and child health locus of control measures (cf. Parcel & Meyer, 1978) help structure the focus of these information-gathering sessions.

The standardized developmental testing situation, especially with the parent present and reacting to the child's successes or failures, often provides important information on how a child relates to adults, responds to a more structured situation, tolerates challenge and frustration, and asserts autonomy and organizes behavior, as well as pinpointing developmental level. These variables not only suggest how the child is adjusting to life with chronic illness but also may identify strengths to be built on or weaknesses to be dealt with to improve coping.

Behavior checklists move assessment beyond the interview and observation stage. A number of excellent instruments are available, and though norms for chronically ill children are rarely published, one can determine how much and in what way a child's profile differs from his peers. The Child Behavior Checklist (Achenbach & Edelbrock, 1981, 1983), the Parenting Stress Index, and the Eyberg Child Behavior Inventory (Eyberg & Ross, 1978) represent a few of the useful instruments for the chronically ill young child.

Social maturity scales such as the Vineland Adaptive Behavior Scales (Sparrow, Balla, & Cicchetti, 1984) and measures of self-perceptions of social competence (e.g., Harter, 1983) also help evaluate the degree to which a chronic illness may impact a child's ability to carry out age-appropriate social behaviors. Interpreted in combination with an understanding of a child's level of cognitive and motor development, they can help assess whether the illness, and the child and family's understanding of it, is affecting the child's ability to reach his potential for independent functioning.

DEVELOPMENTAL SEQUELAE OF ILLNESS AND MEDICAL INTERVENTIONS

As noted previously, pediatric psychological evaluations are often prompted by "problem" behaviors (e.g., disorders of conduct, mood, feeding, sleep) that may signal a young child's difficulty coping. However, direct cognitive effects of the disease process and/or indirect developmental interferences due to treatment also may threaten normal growth and development. These sequelae are a frequent focus of pediatric psychology assessment and research.

Direct Effects of the Disease Process

Developmental delay, learning disability, and mental retardation are associated with many physical disorders of, or syndromes that affect, the central nervous system (CNS). The clinical symptomatology of epilepsy, lupus cerebritis, pediatric AIDS, and Reye's syndrome, to name but a few disorders, may include deficits that are defined and monitored utilizing neuropsychological assessment procedures.

The potential neurodevelopmental effects of many other chronic conditions are undetermined but are the subject of research at many medical centers. For example, recent reports suggest children with sickle cell disease may develop perceptual-motor deficits, perhaps due to the cumulative impact of microvascular events (small strokes) within the brain (Fowler et al., 1988; Chapar, 1988).

The natural (untreated) course of chronic renal insufficiency in infants includes progressive impairment of physical growth (height, weight, and head circumference), slowed neurodevelopmental progress, serious CNS symptomatology, and death (Kleinknecht, Broyer, Huot, Marti-Henneberg, & Dartosis, 1983; Rotundo et al., 1982). Early identification of developmental deviations that herald apparently irreversible CNS impairments may influence pediatric management, exerting a potential impact on infant mortality and morbidity. Changes in a developmental "growth curve" may identify (in concert with physical growth parameters, clinical signs, and laboratory results) infants and young children at risk for slowing development who may benefit from earlier institution of kidney dialysis and/or new transplantation technology, which grafts adult kidneys into infants weighing as little as 10 kilograms.

Children with hemophilia who have been infected by the human immunodeficiency virus (HIV) during treatment due to contaminated (prior to April 1985) blood products also illustrate the need for psychological assessment to define direct illness effects. Some of these children exhibit neurodevelopmental problems in spite of being asymptomatic for other symptoms of AIDS (Ultmann et al., 1987; Pizzo et al., 1988; Epstein et al., 1986). Neuropsychological results that confirm the presence of silent, subtle CNS impairments may suggest the need for future treatments that cross the blood-brain barrier, in order to reach the CNS and provide effective intervention against "smoldering" HIV infections of brain tissue.

Medical Complications Associated with Premature Birth

Many infants born prematurely are at high risk for illness effects on development. A brief introduction to the ongoing medical issues and potential developmental outcomes of these children, along with references to be pursued by the examiner who finds these children in his or her practice, may be useful. Because of rapid advances in neonatal intensive care, the population of survivors of birth as early as 24 to 26 weeks' gestation is increasing. A premature baby's developmental outlook depends heavily both on how early in gestation the birth occurred and on the complications suffered. The literature on predicting outcome for these children is complex and confusing (Page, 1986; Holmes, Reich, & Pasternak, 1984). The general consensus is that severe developmental disabilities occur in relatively small proportions of prematures, except for the very lowest birth weight categories, where the risk is much higher. More subtle dysfunctions, such as language delays, learning disabilities, and attention deficit disorders, are more common (Allen & Jones, 1986).

Developmental disabilities in preterm babies may be related to several factors, including medical complications secondary to the intensive care environment. Chief among medical complications of prematurity are intracranial hemorrhage and bronchopulmonary dysplasia (BPD). A third complication, a condition known as retinopathy of prematurity or ROP, will not be discussed in this chapter because its major sequelae, visual impairment, is discussed in chapter 10 of this volume. However, the assessor should be alert to the potential for visual difficulties in infants who have had oxygen therapy in the nursery.

Intracranial hemorrhage, or bleeding within the brain, occurs in premature babies when tiny, fragile capillaries, present in the immature brain, rupture, perhaps due to factors related to the stress of early delivery. If the bleeding is limited in quantity, the child generally has a normal prognosis. Bleeding that results in persistent enlargement of the ventricles in the brain is associated with a higher level of disability, particularly motor disability (Bozynski et al., 1984). Some children with this condition develop hydrocephalus, which requires shunting, a procedure that diverts cerebrospinal fluid through a tube to other body cavities in order to relieve pressure in the brain. This procedure has its own complications and requires close medical follow-up. Extension of the bleeding into the brain itself may lead to periventricular leucomalacia (PVL), a condition with a very high incidence of motor and mental disabilities (Stewart et al., 1987; Guzzetta, Shackelford, Volpe, Perlman, & Volpe, 1986).

It is important for the psychologist assessing these children in NICU follow-up clinics or in the school community to be familiar with these conditions and aware of the child's diagnosis and its potential implications. Infants also should be followed by a pediatric physical therapist, who can monitor subtle motor abnormalities that can herald the presence of cerebral palsy. Conversely, transient motor abnormalities and neurological immaturity noted in premature babies often resolve during the first few months of life; thus, overly aggressive diagnosis also should be avoided.

The second major medical threat to prematures, BPD, results from the need to use mechanical respirators to sustain life when the lungs are very immature. An unfortunate side effect of this therapy is, in some instances, chronic lung damage that requires supplemental oxygen therapy for months or longer. These children are also at higher risk for developmental disabilities, feeding disorders, and growth delay (Yu, Orgill, Lim, Bajuk, & Astbury, 1983). As younger and younger infants are kept alive through improved medical technologies, BPD may affect increasing numbers of them. While some children with this problem need continued hospital care, others are discharged from the hospital on short- to long-term oxygen therapy. Constant adult vigilance is needed to prevent life-threatening interruptions to the oxygen supply, while concurrently working to extend environmental boundaries beyond the limits of oxygen tubing. Development of ordinary speech may be difficult and feeding is especially problematic, especially for children who require tracheostomies.

Side Effects of Medical Treatment

Because many medical regimens have the potential for disrupting cognitive processes and/or behavior, psychological assessment offers benchmarks for physical responses to, and side effects of, medical care treatment. Pediatric or school psychologists are often challenged to distinguish behavioral and emotional reactions from the disease process or side effects of treatment. For example, consider the following dilemma: The family of a child with hemophilia has recently learned of his seropositive HIV status; should anxiety or depression in this child be treated as an emotional disorder, accepted as a temporary but expected emotional reaction to family system or individual stress, or pursued as a manifestation of HIV-related activity in the brain?

Phenobarbital, a commonly used drug for treating infants and young children with seizures, has been reported to contribute to increased distractibility, labile emotional status, and poor behavioral self-control. Are behavior problems in these children due to static encephalopathy associated with epilepsy, medication effects, or ineffective discipline within the family system? Similarly, high doses of steroid drugs used in some treatment regimens may have side effects that resemble organic brain syndrome, with behavioral and affective disorganization, as well as changes in physical appearance due to increase in appetite. In each case, psychological assessment strategies may shed light on the etiology of these problem behaviors.

Subtle learning disabilities have been identified as potential late effects in children with leukemia, suggesting the cumulative effects of neurotoxic chemotherapy and/or radiation (Moss, Nannis, & Poplack, 1981; Whitt et al., 1984). Yet, it was these same treatment procedures that, through the prevention of cancer growth in the "safe harbor" of the central nervous system, dramatically increased survival statistics. Prospective psychological monitoring—which is an integral part of treatment protocols designed by the two major children's cancer study groups in the United States—promotes the early identification of these sequelae and provides valuable criteria for selection among new therapeutic regimens that are otherwise equal in long-term efficacy. Likewise, initial AIDS research findings suggest that neuropsychological measures of CNS functioning may be among the sensitive indicators of response to experimental drugs (e.g., AZT) by persons who are HIV seropositive but asymptomatic for AIDS (Grant et al., 1987; Pizzo et al., 1988).

Other factors may confound the identification of illness impact on children's intellectual performance. For example, cognitive deficits might antedate the onset of chronic illnesses rather than being caused by the disease process or treatment. Clearly, the complexity of the phenomena requires multimodal assessment and a comprehensive history that discriminates between past and current developmental issues. A combination of behavioral observations within the context of both the family and health care systems and baseline testing using neuropsychological measures (carefully selected to identify subtle but pathognomic signs of CNS pathology) are also valuable aspects of these assessments.

In addition to direct effects of the illness process and medication side effects, treatment regimens may interfere with opportunities for cognitive, social, emotional, or family system development. These effects may begin with the very youngest patients, those in the neonatal intensive care unit (NICU).

There is increasing evidence that the NICU experience itself may have implications for developmental outcome. For example, infants whose nervous systems are designed for the dark, quiet, gently oscillating and snugly enclosed environment of the uterus are suddenly thrust into a brightly lit, often noisy setting where they may be restrained in a spread-eagled, supine position on a flat bed and subjected to frequent, painful interventions. Much research and clinical effort is currently being devoted to alterations in nursery care that may combat these problems. Efforts to protect babies from noise and light, position them in developmentally appropriate ways, and use infant behavioral cues to guide care and handling are showing potential for improving outcome (Als et al., 1986). However, environmental effects on development continue to be an important issue for those assessing infants. Higher levels of irritability, decreased attention span, delays in motor milestones, and other issues may continue to be problems for intensive care nursery graduates and may foreshadow later difficulties in behavioral organization and learning (Als, 1985; Aylward, 1982; Telzrow, Kang, Mitchell, Ashworth, & Barnard, 1982).

The opportunities for developmental interferences continue as the infant gets older. Consider the iatrogenic interference with mastery of normal tasks of infant development illustrated by the following case example:

Jennifer is an 11-month-old baby referred for evaluation of withdrawn, "autistic-like" behavior following her transfer from a neonatal intensive care unit to an infant-toddler pediatric ward. Her pediatric resident also raised concerns about her level of development, as well as a pattern of regurgitating and rechewing food observed by the ward nursing staff over the previous week.

The pediatric resident and chart review revealed that Jennifer was the Twin A survivor of a pair born 9 weeks premature. A previous child had died of sudden infant death syndrome (SIDS). Not surprisingly, Jennifer's mother had expressed anxiety about "getting too close" to another child whose life was threatened.

Shortly after delivery Jennifer developed respiratory distress that precipitated transfer to a medical center, where she required up to 100% oxygen using prolonged mechanical ventilation. She had a stormy course, which included development of congestive heart failure and systemic infections. She had fed poorly, required nasogastric feedings to gain weight, and had a feeding gastrostomy surgically placed. At 11 months of age, Jennifer continued to require continuous supplemental oxygen for her chronic lung disease.

The evaluation and intervention process included psychological testing of developmental status; behavioral observations by the psychological consultant and nursing staff; clarification of parental attachment; initiation of planning for stimulation and feeding activities by physical therapy, recreation therapy, and psychology; and consideration of primary care nursing and referral for a surrogate "lap parent" to create a greater consistency of caregiver for Jennifer.

Initial observations revealed several important features. First, Jennifer's significant oxygen requirement due to her bronchopulmonary dysplasia necessitated her receiving supplemental oxygen through a plastic hood that entirely covered her head except for a small opening for her neck. The hood presented a major impediment to normal visual-motor exploration. For example, Jennifer could insert her hand up into the hood neck opening only far enough to suck on her fingers. She was observed to reach to scratch her blanket, and she attempted to pull a soft stuffed animal into the hood neck opening. However, Jennifer's hood blocked her successful mastery of the next developmentally appropriate challenge (cf. Piaget); that is, combining these two maneuvers by first reaching to manipulate an object and then putting that object into her mouth. Jennifer's efforts to place any object into her mouth were prevented by the smallness of the opening at the neck, or, more poignantly, blocked as her hand collided against the plastic, halting its trajectory toward her mouth—thus effectively interfering with the normal mechanism of object exploration for a child of her adjusted age. The results of a modified Bayley Scales of Infant Development demonstrated significant delays in fine and gross motor function, but also identified strengths in visual alertness and imitation.

Illness symptomatology and the oxygen hood also limited Jennifer's repertoire for successful state regulation and self-comforting responses. Her ability to communicate distress and to signal caregiving through crying was limited; opportunities to use oral-motor activity (e.g., sucking her fingers or chewing on toys) for self-comforting were blocked by her hood. Not surprisingly, the temporal patterns of her rumination suggested that this substitute oral-motor event served as a specific, adaptive effort at tension discharge rather than indicating developmental psychopathology.

As her developmental interferences were recognized, Jennifer's "problem" behaviors seemed more an effect of procedures that thwarted her attempts to master normal developmental challenges and less a result of poor emotional adjustment, although limitations in parental visitation and the lack of a primary care nurse were noted. A primary intervention was to provide for Jennifer's oxygen requirements while also broadening her "world," allowing more consistent interpersonal contacts and helping her utilize mechanisms already existent in her repertoire for self-comfort and exploration. Collaborative efforts were undertaken to "wean" her oxygen requirements sufficiently to use a tent over her body, rather than the hood, for supplemental oxygen delivery. Once allowed the freedom of the tent within which to explore, Jennifer quickly displayed age appropriate oral-motor exploration of objects and her rumination ceased.

As Jennifer's condition improved, the psychologist encouraged the use of a stroller-based oxygen unit that utilized nasal prongs. She began to spend time out of her crib, opening up opportunities for interpersonal interactions and exploration of novel stimuli. Strategies for self-comforting through play developed, and an increasingly sensitive communication system emerged between Jennifer, her identified primary nursing caregivers, and her family. Observations of her reactions to these interventions were also important aspects of the evaluation process.

Iatrogenic interferences occur whenever the process of medical treatment limits the capacity of a child and/or family system to successfully master the challenges and tasks that characterize normal infant and child development. Potential for iatrogenic developmental interferences, as well as vulnerabilities and resilience of infants and young children, can be explored by defining age-specific developmental tasks that children must master at each stage of development.

S.I. Greenspan (1981) described infant developmental stages of homeostasis (age 0 to 3 months); attachment (2 to 7 months); somatic-psychological differentiation (3 to 10 months); and behavioral organization, initiative, and internalization (9 to 24 months). Although it is beyond the scope of this chapter to describe these stages in depth, each involves discrete tasks that must be mastered, based on the maturation of new competencies of the parent-child dyad, and that may be thwarted by specific interferences of illness, treatment, and/or involvement with the health care system. Within the homeostasis stage, the competent infant accepts caregiving via adequate suck, cuddling, state control and modulation of arousal, attainment of regular sleep-wake cycles, and signaling (e.g., loud crying when hungry) to bring the caregiver into proximity. The attachment stage is characterized by sensitive, contingent, and reciprocal communication between the infant and caregiver. Within the behavioral organization stage, motoric competence enables physical exploration that separates the child from the caregiver, requiring self-regulation of affect, arousal, and behavior as well as fueling a sense of mastery, competence, and confidence, often expressed as an insistent, "I do it myself!" Medical limitations on motoric exploration, such as orthopedic casting, have obvious implications for this process.

As previously noted, interaction between an infant and caregiver is particularly susceptible to interference by early childhood illness. The dyadic nature of the infant developmental tasks increases the infant's vulnerability to poor "coping" whenever the caregiver is unavailable to provide the normal supportive care and act as a buffer between the infant and the environment. Physical separation of a child from his or her caregiver due to having been airlifted to a distant tertiary care medical center, admitted to a PICU where visitation policies may not promote unlimited parent contact, or monitored by an array of intimidating life-support equipment poses inherent risk to the development of emotional attachment between infant and caregiver.

Serious feeding disorders are a frequent consequence of disease, particularly for children requiring treatment in the first 2 years of life. Although a "battle of the spoon" is often evident, it may be premature to conclude that behavioral, rather than direct illness effects or developmental interference, is the cause. For example, the effects of infant renal disease include impairment in appetite, changes in taste, and alterations in gastrointestinal hunger sensations that normally cue learning to eat (as a result of dialysis procedures, which utilize the peritoneal cavity for fluid exchange). Large daily doses of poor-tasting oral medications also may establish the stimulus conditions for learning to resist, rather than seek, oral intake. Early life experiences for children with other illnesses may include nasogastric or gastrostomy tubes for feeding. These procedures, which are often mandated due to CNS immaturity or serious breathing difficulties, may alter the opportunity to learn about feeding during the developmentally appropriate period. Decisions to introduce feeding tube procedures when the infant or young child is just beginning to recognize hunger sensations, link satiation of these cues with "successful" oral feedings, and begin to help by "good swallowing" and rudimentary mastery of finger foods require careful consideration. Helping the infant acquire these skills while attaining adequate nutrition is a continuing challenge at most pediatric settings. Psychological assessment serves to define the developmentally appropriate behaviors and effective context in which to facilitate more competent feeding.

Longitudinal Monitoring (Tracking) of Developmental Competence

Adjustment to illness involves a network of medical, family, and community sociocultural systems that change over time. Thus, a program of longitudinal monitoring of developmental competence (including direct illness and/or treatment effects, iatrogenic developmental interferences, child and family adaptation to illness, and mastery of normal developmental challenges) is an integral part of the interdisciplinary team management approach at many pediatric medical centers (cf. Brantley et al., 1981).

The goals of these programs include (a) definition of the interrelationships between the illness and psychological development; (b) identification of children and families who are at risk for developmental or adjustment problems; (c) clinical differentiation of the characteristics that affect coping; (d) recommendations for intervention to enhance child emotional and social development; and (e) referral for special treatment of children who also evidence developmental delay or psychopathology (Magrab & Lehr, 1982).

Although the prospective tracking approach may be applied to many disorders, it is especially crucial in the follow-up of infants and young children who have suffered serious illness at birth. The following case example illustrates some of the clinical aspects of this assessment strategy:

Sally is a 3-year-old girl who was born at 32 weeks gestation with Rh disease, which left her with severe lung damage. After 5 months in the neonatal intensive care unit (NICU) and a month on the pediatric floor, she was discharged home with a tracheostomy, continuous oxygen therapy, heart and respiratory monitors, a gastrostomy tube, and round-the-clock nursing care. After multiple rehospitalizations for respiratory infections, Sally improved enough to warrant closing her tracheostomy just 3 months ago.

Sally continues to receive oxygen via nasal cannula. Her pediatrician voices concern to the psychologist about Sally's reliance on the gastrostomy tube for feeding, also wondering if her delayed language development indicates mental retardation. Sally's parents, on the other hand, describe her 20-word vocabulary with great pride. They see new progress since the tracheostomy closure and are very happy with Sally's newfound ability to walk with support. They worry mostly about her nutrition: "If only she could feed herself, she would be on her way to being normal." A call to Sally's community-based early intervention program reveals slow but steady progress in motor and verbal skills, but continued resistance to oral eating.

The psychologist begins by administration of the McCarthy Scales; however, Sally's skills are not sufficient to complete most of the initial items. Her fine motor skills appear to be compromised by a mild athetoid pattern, and her language appears only to be at an 18-month level. The Bayley Scales of Infant Development provide indications of general competence, with the exception of fine motor dexterity, at the 18-month level. These results do not explain for the psychologist the origin of Sally's eating problems, which could be related to oral-motor dysfunction from cerebral palsy, from interferences with normal oral-motor development due to her lengthy oral intubation and subsequent tracheostomy, or from behavioral factors related to unfamiliarity with oral eating.

After explaining to the parents that Sally is still quite a few months behind her age level and still requires developmental intervention, the psychologist refers her for speech/language, occupational, and physical therapy evaluations. These assessments conclude that Sally has the physical capacity for oral feeding but has an aversion to oral stimulation. A therapy plan is designed and instituted to decrease Sally's oral tactile sensitivity and to teach her feeding skills. After several weeks the psychologist discovers that little progress has been made; Sally is resistant to the activities suggested and gets upset when demands are made upon her. Moreover, when she becomes agitated, her oxygen requirements increase and she develops breathing problems.

In an interdisciplinary team conference, it becomes clear that no reinforcement contingencies have been discovered that effectively reward the desired feeding behaviors. Sally often seems out of control. The team decides to back off from feeding to address behavioral compliance, including sitting in a seat and completing tasks, at a developmental level expected of an 18-month-old child who also has Sally's emotional needs and respiratory limitations. Sally begins to make progress in therapy.

Importance of Continued Longitudinal Follow-up

Despite several previous evaluations and regular developmental intervention, Sally's parents had a poor understanding of her capabilities and developmental needs.

In part this was due to their use of denial and other coping strategies; in addition, Sally's isolation from other children, necessitated by infection-control needs, limited their opportunities for developmental comparisons.

It is important to recognize the possibility of change over time when following a high-risk infant. Studies of preterm babies offer conflicting evidence about whether it is more likely that these children will show decreases (Hunt, 1979) or increases (Kitchen, Ford, Rickards, Lissenden, & Ryan, 1987) in their developmental scores over time—making it even more critical to follow individual children closely on a continuing basis.

Effects of Ongoing Medical Problems on Developmental Status

The severity of Sally's medical problems made it difficult to assess her intellectual and motoric potential. Because of her inability to tolerate frustration or even mild discipline without behavioral reactions that led quickly to serious respiratory problems, her capacity for behavioral organization necessary to master new developmental tasks was severely compromised. As in many such children, long-term mechanical ventilation and tracheostomy directly interfered with oral-motor functioning, leading to feeding and language delays that were beyond those due to the anoxic brain damage she suffered in the neonatal period. Although these developmental interferences were not as dramatic as those experienced by Jennifer, they were nonetheless crucial to development and required ongoing assessment.

Adaptation of Psychological Measures to Developmental Needs

Although Sally was 3 years old, instruments designed for her age level were inappropriate for her assessment needs. The goal of assessment was to understand her developmental needs rather than to obtain a standardized IQ score. Thus, shifting to a measure that provided tasks on which she could succeed, as well as items that were too difficult, proved useful. Certain aspects of development, such as fine motor skills, needed to be considered separately from cognitive development in order to avoid bias due to physical handicap. (See Wilhelm, Johnson, & Eisert, 1986, for issues that may affect testing of children with motor handicaps, including techniques of handling and positioning, fatigue, and the appropriateness of timed items.)

"Vulnerable Child" Issues in Developmental Assessment

Because Sally's parents had real and appropriate concerns about her survival, they had introduced constraints that limited her past experience. She had never played with other children, had to share or take turns, had to wait while hungry for a meal, been able to "make messes" outside, or even had the opportunity to run freely across an open space, due to her ever-present oxygen hose. Developmental preschool had not been an option because of the danger of respiratory infections. Thus, any prognostic statements about her future potential needed to be undertaken cautiously due to differences in her experiences from those of a healthy child.

Although the classic "vulnerable child syndrome" (Green, 1986) does not apply here in the strictest sense because Sally's parents' fears about her death had a realistic basis, conceptual adjustments for these dynamics, difficulties with limit setting, and options for autonomy needed to be made when evaluating her development.

Need for Interdisciplinary Team Cooperation

Sally's functioning could not be evaluated comprehensively without communication with and input from the pediatrician, physical and occupational therapists, speech pathologist, home care nurse, home developmental specialist, and her parents. Assessment of her underlying physical ability to perform test items, the impact of motor deficits, appropriate positioning, behavioral compliance, and environmental demands and opportunities needed to be addressed on an interdisciplinary basis.

Practical Considerations in Assessing the High-Risk Infant

Several guiding principles may be useful to the psychologist planning to longitudinally track children within this population. A high-risk infant follow-up clinic should be interdisciplinary in nature, with access provided to the infant's complete medical history. The physician is an important collaborator for the pediatric psychologist or applied developmentalist because accurate understanding of past and current medical problems is necessary for both the selection of appropriate assessment instruments and interpretation of results. A physical therapist's skills help monitor the effects of prematurity on motor development, assess the impact of motor skills on the results of cognitive testing, and assist in appropriate positioning that allows each child to perform optimally. Occupational therapists contribute a view of the child's fine motor function and may assist in sorting out fine motor from cognitive delays. Speech/language pathologists should be available, as language delay is a common finding and often heralds later, more global developmental problems. In addition, speech/language pathologists are able to assess emerging speech-language skills in infancy (Bzoch & League, 1970). Because hearing loss may be a complication both of prematurity and of disorders in the full-term newborn (Hendricks-Munoz & Walton, 1988), infant audiological evaluation should be available, and the team's index of suspicion for hearing problems must be high.

An awareness of the child's family situation is crucial for an adequate assessment; it appears for many groups of high-risk and chronically ill infants that socioeconomic and caretaking influences may better predict developmental outcome than medical factors (Holmes et al., 1984; Sigman, Cohen, Beckwith, & Parmelee, 1981). Consideration of the home environment is also important before interpreting cognitive test results. For example, a Mental Development Index of 80 on the Bayley Scales in an infant from a college-educated, well-functioning family may imply more biological risk than a similar score in an infant from a less advantaged family. Formal tools such as the HOME or Parenting Stress Index may be very useful in determining how parents are coping with the stresses of both ordinary life and caring for a chronically ill infant. Clinical interviews by the psychologist or a clinical social worker focus on the parents' economic resources, their social supports, their capacity to manage stress, their ability to interact with their child, and their own parenting histories.

The psychologist should, if possible, have input into the schedule for tracking chronically ill and high-risk infants. It is difficult to suggest an optimal system for tracking all such children. Taken together, the literature in this area (Holmes et al., 1984; Klein, Hack, Gallagher, & Fanaroff, 1985; Vohr & Garcia Coll, 1985; Kitchen et al., 1987) suggests that the psychologist might best avoid implementation of rigid protocols, while striving for regular follow-up that takes into account medical and psychosocial risk, intensity of intervention, test results, and family resources. Follow-up should begin at least midway into the first year for infants with chronic medical complications and continue until school entry; individual clinical needs will guide decisions about interim frequency and intensity of these assessments.

When assessing the preterm infant, careful consideration must be given to the chronological age used in calculating test results. Biologically the premature child is indeed younger than the full-term baby with the same birthday. If a child is born at, for example, 30 weeks gestation, should 10 weeks be subtracted from his or her chronological age when computing a Mental Development Index on the Bayley Scales? If so, how long should such correction be carried out? Arguments have been advanced for differing procedures (L. Siegel, 1983; Forslund & Bjerre, 1985; Rossetti, 1986; Wilson, 1987), and competent practitioners correct for varying lengths of time. The twin errors of overdiagnosis and missing real problems are both important to avoid, as unnecessary parental anxiety or omitting potentially helpful interventions are both undesirable outcomes. The evidence suggests that correcting for prematurity, especially during the first year, is an appropriate strategy as long as the total picture of the child's physical and social environment is considered in making referral decisions. A reasonable compromise is to compute and record both corrected and uncorrected scores. The corrected score will be the most accurate assessment of the child's potential for the first year. During the second year, clinical judgment will indicate the appropriateness of intervention if the uncorrected score is far below average. As the child approaches 2 years of age, the two scores become so similar that the difference is no longer statistically or clinically significant—at this point, the uncorrected score may become more appropriate.

A final caveat in the evaluation of high-risk infants involves the special challenge of remaining objective when a single evaluator, especially one who has known the child and family since the child's birth or soon thereafter, is conducting the follow-up. Despite the advantages for clinician and family of such a system, one must be especially careful to avoid the "halo effect." There may be an emotional investment in finding normal development in a beloved "miracle baby" whom one has watched grow following life-threatening complications. Conversely, an examiner who is well aware of a child's risk factors and history of problems may expect less of the child and actually deflate, rather than inflate, their scores (Field, 1981). Rigorous adherence to the correct examination procedure, working with colleagues from the same and other developmental disciplines, careful calculation of both corrected and uncorrected scores, and frequent opportunities to test normal children can each help ameliorate these problems.

Measures for Longitudinal Monitoring

Selection of the appropriate assessment instruments is important with the populations of high-risk infants and chronically ill children, and will vary depending on the age, developmental status of the child, and clinical question being posed for tracking. Although questions are often raised about the predictive value of psychological assessment in infancy, several investigators have found encouraging continuities between early and later evaluations (Maisto & German, 1986; L.S. Siegel, 1983).

A variety of instruments assessing cognitive, behavioral, language, motor, and social/adaptive functions are available for the infant-through-preschool population. Reviews of these options (Aylward, 1988; Francis, Self, & Horowitz, 1987; Minde & Minde, 1986; Rossetti, 1986; Simeonsson, 1986) reveal that measures vary in their range of applicable ages, psychometric characteristics, and theoretical underpinnings. The psychologist in a medical setting might develop a core battery that is practical for administration within the limited time and space available, allows continuity of follow-up over as long a period as possible, and provides an adequate base of normative, predictive psychometric data. The pediatric psychologist often does not have the luxury of either "one at a time" scheduling or the opportunity to plan ahead for a particular child. Rather, a number of children are likely to be scheduled for a day's clinic; staffing for each child may consist of a review of the chart and a brief discussion with the physician before entering the room. The appropriate instruments for each of the children to be assessed must be quickly available, often having been transported from the psychologist's "home base." Some of the most frequently used and practical instruments in the experience of the authors will be outlined here, with the understanding that alternative approaches may be equally valid.

To begin with the very youngest group, an ideal situation is for the psychologist to be a member of the NICU clinical care team, evaluating infants while they are still hospitalized. Certification on the Brazelton Neonatal Behavioral Assessment Scale (Brazelton, 1984) will allow the assessor to describe the individual neurodevelopmental characteristics of the high-risk infants. Ideally, knowledge of specialized instruments such as the Assessment of Preterm Infant Behavior (Als, Lester, Tronick, & Brazelton, 1982) will permit a sophisticated understanding of the behavioral organization of the more fragile, premature infants. Data from such assessments are useful not only for helping caregivers and parents understand the environmental needs of these infants, but also may guide decisions about referral to early intervention and community support programs as well as influence the frequency and intensity of developmental follow-up.

As infants return for follow-up clinic visits, the psychologist assesses the adequacy of the child's developmental progress in the context of existing medical and environmental challenges. The most frequently used instrument in the United States appears to be the Bayley Scales of Infant Development (Bayley, 1969). This tool, which provides both a Mental and Motor Developmental Quotient, possesses a large literature, samples a variety of behaviors, and is useful for children at developmental levels ranging from a month of age to 30 months. The recent manual supplement (Rhodes & Bayley, 1984) is useful for improving the accuracy and consistency of administration technique. Especially when the examiner is faced with a squirming toddler or soon-to-be-hungry infant, smooth and confident administration is a must.

Other nations may use different instruments, such as the Griffiths Mental Development Scales (Griffiths, 1978) used in Great Britain. Other tools, such as the Hawaii Early Learning Profile, the Carolina Curriculum for Handicapped Infants, the Virginia EMI, the Learning Accomplishment Profile, and the Brigance Diagnostic Inventory of Early Development (Brigance, 1978), may be useful in developing programming ideas, although they were not designed primarily for psychometric assessment purposes. The Ordinal Scales of Psychological Development (Uzgiris & Hunt, 1975) and the Cattell Infant Intelligence Scale (Cattell, 1960) have utility for clinical and research purposes, but they are not likely to be as practical for general use in high-risk infant follow-up clinics as the Bayley Scales, due to their more limited psychometric properties. Instruments with a strong neurological component, such as the Infant Neurological International Battery (Ellison, Horn, & Browning, 1985), or pediatric focus, such as the Gesell Developmental Screening Inventory (Knobloch, Stevens, & Malone, 1980), may be useful in particular settings.

A relatively new pair of instruments, the Mullen Scales of Early Learning (MSEL) for birth to age 3 and the companion Scales of Early Learning for ages 3 to 7, has been designed to allow more systematic evaluation of gross motor competencies and their impact on other areas of functioning (Mullen, 1984). These instruments allow separate assessment of skills within the receptive and expressive organization of visual and language domains. The MSEL may be of particular value with preterm or otherwise handicapped infants for whom it is often critical to clarify the relative contribution of motor, cognitive, and language factors to functioning.

Another innovative approach, the Fagan Test of Infant Intelligence (Fagan, 1986), utilizes visual recognition memory techniques to evaluate infants up to 1 year of age. It shows promise in predicting intellectual outcome in high-risk infants, although it is not designed to provide the range of intervention programming information offered by measures such as the MSEL.

As infants and toddlers reach preschool age, new instruments are necessary. The 30–60 month age group, especially with mild handicaps, presents particular challenges in test selection. Many of these children are not old enough or advanced enough for the Wechsler scales, with their useful organization into subscales and separate verbal and performance scores. Although no single measure will be ideal for all children, the McCarthy Scales of Children's Abilities (McCarthy, 1972) are often a good choice for this age group. Although the younger, mildly impaired child may have difficulty succeeding on a sufficient range of items, a broad range of skills is sampled, and a profile discriminating among verbal, perceptual-performance, memory, and motor areas may be derived. In addition, programming suggestions useful for preschools or parents can be based on the information provided by this test.

The Stanford-Binet Intelligence Scale, Form L-M (Terman & Merrill, 1973) has utility for obtaining scores for entry into special programs and for tracking progress in the young chronically ill child. However, it is outdated and presents problems both for the child with fine motor delays and the nonverbal child. The recently revised fourth edition (Thorndike, Hagen, & Sattler, 1986) warrants consideration but is still new enough that its practical utility remains to be determined.

The Kaufman Assessment Battery for Children (K-ABC; Kaufman & Kaufman, 1983) may be an appropriate tool for the young chronically ill and high-risk populations, due to its emphasis on the information processing style of the child. As more data are collected on the use of the K-ABC with this population, it may become even more useful.

By the age of 5, information should be available on each child that will direct his or her assessment needs, creating a more specific task than that presented by the busy high-risk infant follow-up clinic. Hooper (1988) discusses other procedures, such as the Reitan-Indiana Neuropsychological Test Battery for Children (Reitan, 1969), which may be useful in evaluating the neuropsychological functioning of older preschoolers, especially survivors of prematurity with disabilities involving subtle impairment of neuropsychological functioning. These test batteries are time-consuming and specialized procedures, perhaps best administered to children identified as having difficulties based on previous assessment.

Finally, an indirect approach to be considered is the use of parent-report instruments. For example, the Minnesota Child Development Inventory (Ireton & Thwing, 1972) has been reported to provide relatively reliable developmental screening information for a rather broad high-risk infant population (Eisert, Spector, Shankaran, Faigenbaum, & Szego, 1980).

Working Within the Pediatric Health Care System

Perhaps most important is the integration of psychological testing and intervention into the pediatric health care system. If assessment results are not reported in a useful format, the necessary management, intervention, and follow-up services may not be made available to the family. Establishment of liaison relationships between the psychologist and each pediatric care team, as opposed to consultation services that provide primarily acute response to children exhibiting behavioral or emotional problems, is an appropriate, but at times fiscally difficult, goal for many pediatric centers.

When a genuine, collaborative team approach does evolve, it provides a clear statement that the whole child, not just his or her physical health status, is the management focus of the medical care system. To this end, learning about usual family system functioning and child adaptation as well as understanding each individual child's underlying personality characteristics, strengths, and weaknesses becomes part of the comprehensive care plan, as do interventions that target normalization of child and family routines (Lauria, Whitt, & Wells, 1987; Mattsson, 1972).

A number of clinical and systems issues face psychologists working to collaborate with pediatric health care teams, including the question of how to best implement a time- and cost-efficient response. A clinical protocol can be an effective method to monitor long-term adjustment to chronic childhood physical illness. Repeated, prospective measurement of the multiple variables involved in child and family adaptation to chronic illness often paint a clear picture of the continuities and discontinuities of adaptation to chronic illness. Important illness factors, as well as child and parent coping characteristics, family system functioning, and social support from the community and medical care systems emerge within the context of these results.

Decisions about protocol test selection and intervals for assessment may be difficult. As previously noted, it is important that the protocol not create a rigid approach that blurs the individual differences that often best characterize children and their families. Use of a set of core measures that can be supplemented based on individual child and family characteristics is a useful compromise.

The interval for assessment may also differ from illness to illness: Timing for each subsequent testing may be matched to nodal transition points within the illness course, time since diagnosis, or child age. For example, assessments might be scheduled so as to test children on an annual basis, regardless of age or illness events. On the other hand, one might schedule assessment to correspond with the modal points (e.g., at diagnosis, remission, cure or relapse, or onset of terminal stage for the child with cancer) of the illness course. The more useful protocols are flexible enough to allow triggering of supplemental testing at times when significant changes in the illness experience warrant reassessment.

Children's test responses may be biased by the experience of traumatic procedures, physical effects of medication, association of the psychologist with other doctors, interferences with physical functioning due to IVs, or the need to wear a mask that screens facial expressions as well as protecting against infection. These biases must be accounted for in the interpretation of the tests. Norms that usually guide interpretation of psychological measures must be supplemented by clinical observations regarding the behavioral, emotional, and physical interferences that may impair child functioning.

Other strategies also may facilitate testing efforts. For example, although some psychologists wear white coats in medical centers, it blurs the distinctions between the physicians who provide medical care and mental health professionals who seek to ameliorate psychological distress.

The location for testing young children is an important issue. The child's room may be a haven of safety or, alternatively, the place where painful procedures have occurred. If possible, it is usually better to test the child in a separate space. As straightforward as that recommendation appears, interview space in medical centers is often limited to heavily scheduled conference rooms. Walking to the psychologist's office may be too physically draining for some children. If testing is arranged in a child's hospital room, allowances in interpretation must occur for any factors (e.g., using a bedside table, a bed, an adult-sized chair) that may interfere with test performance. In particular, the bed is a powerful cue for being tired during the examination, inviting escape rather than the best of on-task efforts. Procedures also may need to be adapted for a variety of tubes, wires, and needles, interruptions from scheduled medical treatments or beeping medication pumps, and so on.

It is not necessarily easier to evaluate a child in an outpatient pediatric setting. Outpatient clinics, particularly for the child with chronic illness, also may involve aversive procedures. In addition, the routine of most clinic settings is hectic and may not easily adapt to the time and space demands of psychological assessment. Examination rooms may be even more scarce. Interruptions for psychological assessment procedures may alter the clinic routine to the detriment of family plans. Clearly, the psychologist must be closely involved with the clinic milieu in order to optimize the time for assessment for the child as well as minimize the interference of these testing activities with the health care team.

Communication of results within a medical setting requires sensitivity and awareness of the multiple systems involved with each child. The physician's and parents' questions may not be identical. Leaving written responses to referral questions in the medical chart for communication of results is a time-honored method for consultation services. However, in the absence of personal contact, this strategy runs the risk of misperceptions on the part of the pediatric housestaff, who may then attempt to interpret the results to family members. Although more time-consuming, a team conference that can evolve into a family interpretive or clarify the person(s) responsible for discussing psychological results with the family is often useful. Most tertiary care centers evidence a similar pattern in which the pediatric attending, senior and junior residents, consultation teams, nursing staff members, and support personnel each have relationships with the family that can be used either to reinforce a common set of goals, or to fractionate care through mixed, or even discrepant, messages about test results.

Psychological assessment is a valuable part of the total program of health care that effectively addresses the developmental and emotional needs of chronically ill infants and children and their families. The psychologist's broad understanding of illness variables and the pediatric system, effective collaborative liaison with the pediatric health care team, appropriate use of strategies for gathering psychological data, and thoughtful integration of results into a well-communicated management plan often promote the adaptation of children and families to childhood physical illness.

REFERENCES

Abidin, R.R. (1983). *Parenting Stress Index (PSI)*. Charlottesville, VA: Pediatric Psychology Press.

Achenbach, T., & Edelbrock, C. (1981). Behavioral problems and competencies reported by parents of normal and disturbed children aged 4 through 16. *Monographs of the Society for Research in Child Development, 46*(188).

Achenbach, T.M., & Edelbrock, C. (1983). *Manual for the Child Behavior Checklist and Revised Behavior Profile*. Burlington, VT: University of Vermont, Department of Psychiatry.

Ainsworth, M.D.S., Bell, S.M., & Stayton, D.J. (1971). Individual differences in strange-situation behavior of one-year-olds. In H.R. Schaffer (Ed.), *The origins of human social relations*. London, England: Academic Press.

Allen, M.C., & Jones, M.D. (1986). Medical complications of prematurity. *Obstetrics and Gynecology, 67,* 427–435.

Als, H. (1985). Patterns of infant behavior: Analogues of later organizational difficulties? In F.H. Duffy & N. Geschwind (Eds.), *Dyslexia* (pp. 67–92). Boston: Little, Brown.

Als, H., Lawhon, G., Brown, C., Gibes, R., Duffy, F.H., McAnulty, G., & Blickman, J.G. (1986). Individualized behavioral and environmental care for the very low birth weight preterm infant at high risk for bronchopulmonary dysplasia: Neonatal intensive care unit and developmental outcome. *Pediatrics, 78,* 1123–1132.

Als, H., Lester, B.M., Tronick, E., & Brazelton, T.B. (1982). Manual for the Assessment of Preterm Infants' Behavior (APIB). In H. Fitzgerald, B.M. Lester, & M.W. Yogman (Eds.), *Theory and research in behavioral pediatrics* (Vol. 1, pp. 35–58). New York: Plenum.

Aylward, G.P. (1982). Forty-week full-term and preterm neurologic differences. In L.P. Lipsett & T.M. Field (Eds.), *Infant behavior and development: Perinatal risk and newborn behavior* (pp. 67–83). Norwood, NJ: Ablex.

Aylward, G.P. (1988). Infant and early childhood assessment. In M.G. Tramontana & S.R. Hooper (Eds), *Assessment issues in child neuropsychology* (pp. 225–248). New York: Plenum.

Barnard, K. (1978). *Feeding Scale: Nursing child assessment satellite training.* Seattle: University of Washington.
Bayley, N. (1969). *Bayley Scales of Infant Development: Birth to three years.* San Antonio, TX: Psychological Corporation.
Bergmann, T., & Freud, A. (1965). *Children in the hospital.* New York: International Universities Press.
Bettenburg, A. (1985). *Instruments and procedures for assessing young children.* St. Paul, MN: Minnesota Department of Education.
Bibace, R., & Walsh, M.E. (1980). Development of children's concepts of illness. *Pediatrics, 66,* 912-917.
Bibace, R., & Walsh, M.E. (1981). Children's conceptions of illness. In R. Bibace & M.E. Walsh (Eds.), *Children's conceptions of health, illness, and bodily functions* (pp. 31-48). San Francisco: Jossey-Bass.
Bozynski, M.E.A., Nelson, M.N., Rosati-Skertich, C., Genaze, D., O'Donnell, K., & Naughton, P. (1984). Two year longitudinal follow-up of premature infants weighing < 1,200 grams at birth: Sequelae of intracranial hemorrhage. *Journal of Developmental and Behavioral Pediatrics, 5,* 346-352.
Brantley, H.T., Stabler, B., & Whitt, J.K. (1981). Program considerations in comprehensive care of chronically ill children. *Journal of Pediatric Psychology, 6,* 229-237.
Brazelton, T.B. (1984). *Neonatal Behavioral Assessment Scale* (2nd ed.). Philadelphia: Lippincott.
Brigance, A.H. (1978). *Brigance Diagnostic Inventory of Early Development.* Woburn, MA: Curriculum Associates.
Bzoch, E.R., & League, R. (1970). *The Receptive-Expressive Emergent Language Scale for the Development of Language Scales in Infancy.* Gainesville, FL: Tree of Life.
Caldwell, B., & Bradley, R. (1979). *Home Observation for Measurement of the Environment.* Little Rock, AR: Center for Research on Teaching and Learning.
Cattell, P. (1960). *Cattell Infant Intelligence Scale.* San Antonio, TX: Psychological Corporation.
Chapar, G.N. (1988). Chronic diseases of children and neurological dysfunction. *Developmental and Behavioral Pediatrics, 9,* 221-222.
Cohen, F., & Lazarus, R. (1979). Coping with the stress of illness. In G.C. Stone, F. Cohen, & N.E. Adler (Eds.), *Health psychology* (pp. 217-254). San Francisco: Jossey-Bass.
Drotar, D. (1981). Psychological perspectives in chronic childhood illness. *Journal of Pediatric Psychology, 6,* 211-228.
Eisert, D.C., Spector, S., Shankaran, S., Faigenbaum, D., & Szego, E. (1980). Mothers' reports of their low birth weight infants' subsequent development on the Minnesota Child Development Inventory. *Journal of Pediatric Psychology, 5,* 353-363.
Ellison, P.H., Horn, J.L., & Browning, C.A. (1985). Construction of an infant neurological international battery (INFANIB) for the assessment of neurological integrity in infancy. *Physical Therapy, 65,* 1326-1331.
Epstein, L.G., Sharer, L.E., Oleske, J.M., Connor, E.M., Goudsmit, J., Bagdon, L., Robert-Guroff, M., & Koenigsberger, M.R. (1986). Neurologic manifestations of human immunodeficiency virus infection in children. *Pediatrics, 78,* 678-687.
Eyberg, S.M., & Ross, A.W. (1978). Assessment of child behavior problems: The validation of a new inventory. *Journal of Clinical Child Psychology, 2,* 113-116.
Fagan, J.F. (1986). *Fagan Test of Infant Intelligence.* Cleveland, OH: Infantest Corporation.
Field, T. (1981). Ecological variables and examiner biases in assessing handicapped preschool children. *Journal of Pediatric Psychology, 6,* 155-164.
Forslund, M., & Bjerre, I. (1985). Growth and development in preterm infants during the first 18 months. *Early Human Development, 10,* 201-216.

Fowler, M.G., Whitt, J.K., Redding-Lallinger, R., Nash, K.B., Atkinson, S.S., Wells, R.J., & McMillan, C. (1988). Neuropsychologic and academic functioning of children with sickle cell anemia. *Developmental and Behavioral Pediatrics, 9,* 213-220.

Francis, P.L., Self, P.A., & Horowitz, F.D. (1987). The behavioral assessment of the neonate: An overview. In J.D. Osofsky (Ed.), *Handbook of infant development* (pp. 723-779). New York: Wiley.

Gardner, G.G., & Olness, K. (1981). *Hypnosis and hypnotherapy with children.* New York: Grune & Stratton.

Grant, I., Atkinson, J.H., Hesselink, J.R., Kennedy, C.J., Richman, D.D., Spector, S.A., & McCutchan, J.A. (1987). Evidence for early central nervous system involvement in the acquired immunodeficiency syndrome (AIDS) and other human immunodeficiency virus (HIV) infections. *Annals of Internal Medicine, 107,* 828-836.

Green, M. (1986). Vulnerable child syndrome and its variants. *Pediatrics in Review, 3,* 75-80.

Greenspan, S. (1981). *The clinical interview of the child.* New York: McGraw-Hill.

Greenspan, S.I. (1981). *Psychopathology and adaptation in infancy and early childhood: Principles of clinical diagnosis and preventive intervention.* New York: International Universities Press.

Griffiths, R. (1978). *Griffiths Mental Development Scales.* High Wycombe, England: Test Agency.

Guzzetta, F., Shackelford, G.O., Volpe, S., Perlman, J.M., & Volpe, J.J. (1986). Periventricular intraparenchymal echodensities in the premature newborn: Critical determinant of neurologic outcome. *Pediatrics, 78,* 995-1006.

Harter, S. (1983). *Supplementary description of the Self-Perception Profile for Children (revision of the Perceived Competence Scale for Children).* Unpublished manuscript, University of Denver, Denver, CO.

Hendricks-Munoz, K.D., & Walton, J.P. (1988). Hearing loss in infants with persistent fetal circulation. *Pediatrics, 81,* 650-656.

Hilgard, J.R., & LeBaron, S. (1984). *Hypnotherapy and pain in children with cancer.* Los Altos, CA: Kaufmann.

Holmes, D.L., Reich, J.N., & Pasternak, J.F. (1984). *The development of infants born at risk.* Hillsdale, NJ: Erlbaum.

Hooper, S.R. (1988). Neuropsychological assessment of the preschool child: Issues and procedures. In B.A. Bracken (Ed.), *Psychoeducational assessment of preschool children* (pp. 465-485). Orlando, FL: Grune & Stratton.

Hunt, J.McV. (1979). Longitudinal research: A method for studying the intellectual development of high-risk preterm infants. In T. Field, A.M. Sostek, & H.H. Shuman (Eds.), *Infants born at risk: Behavior and development* (pp. 443-460). New York: SP Medical and Scientific Books.

Ireton, H., & Thwing, E. (1972). *Minnesota Child Development Inventory.* Minneapolis, MN: Behavior Science Systems.

Jensen, E.W., James, S.A., Boyce, W.T., & Hartnett, S.A. (1982). *The Family Routines Inventory: Development and validation.* Unpublished manuscript, University of North Carolina, Chapel Hill.

Johnson, M.R. (1979). Mental health interventions with medically ill children: A review of the literature, 1970-1977. *Journal of Pediatric Psychology, 4,* 147-163.

Johnson, M.R., Gershowitz, M., & Stabler, B. (1981). Children with cystic fibrosis: Analysis of self-concept as influenced by maternal compliance. *Journal of Developmental and Behavioral Pediatrics, 2,* 5-8.

Johnson, M.R., & Helm, J.M. (1988, September). *Parental perceptions of the intensive care nursery experience in preterm and fullterm births.* Paper presented at the meeting of the International Association for Infant Mental Health, Providence, RI.

Johnson, M.R., Whitt, J.K., & Martin, B. (1987). The effect of fantasy facilitation on anxiety in chronically ill and healthy children. *Journal of Pediatric Psychology, 12,* 273-284.

Kaufman, A.S., & Kaufman, N.L. (1983). *Kaufman Assessment Battery for Children (K-ABC).* Circle Pines, MN: American Guidance Service.

Kitchen, W.H., Ford, G.W., Rickards, A.L., Lissenden, J.V., & Ryan, M.M. (1987). Children of birth weight < 1000 g: Changing outcome between ages 2 and 5 years. *Journal of Pediatrics, 110,* 283-288.

Klein, N., Hack, M., Gallagher, J., & Fanaroff, A.A. (1985). Preschool performance of children with normal intelligence who were very low-birth-weight infants. *Pediatrics, 75,* 531-537.

Kleinknecht, C., Broyer, M., Huot, D., Marti-Henneberg, C., & Dartosis, A. (1983). Growth and development of undialyzed children with chronic renal failure. *Kidney International, 24,* S40-S47.

Knobloch, H., Stevens, F., & Malone, A.F. (1980). *Manual of developmental diagnosis.* Hagerstown, MD: Harper & Row.

Lansky, L.L., List, M.A., Lansky, S.B., Cohen, M.E., & Sinks, L.B. (1985). Toward the development of a play performance scale for children (PPSC). *Cancer, 56,* 1837-1840.

Lauria, M.M., Whitt, J.K., & Wells, R.J. (1987). Protocol for survival in childhood cancer: Family system interventions. In *Proceedings of the Fifth National Conference on Human Values and Cancer.*

Lazarus, R.S. (1981). The costs and benefits of denial. In J.J. Spinetta & P. Deasy-Spinetta (Eds.), *Living with childhood cancer* (pp. 50-67). St. Louis: Mosby.

Magrab, P.H., & Lehr, E. (1982). Assessment techniques in pediatric psychology. In J.M. Tuma (Ed.), *Handbook for the practice of pediatric psychology* (pp. 67-109). New York: Wiley.

Maisto, A.A., & German, M.L. (1986). Reliability, predictive validity, and interrelationships of early assessment indices used with developmentally delayed infants and children. *Journal of Clinical Child Psychology, 15,* 327-332.

Mattsson, A. (1972). Long-term physical illness in childhood: A challenge to psychosocial adaptation. *Pediatrics, 50,* 801-811.

McCarthy, D. (1972). *McCarthy Scales of Children's Abilities.* San Antonio, TX: Psychological Corporation.

Minde, K., & Minde, R. (1986). *Infant psychiatry: An introductory textbook.* Beverly Hills, CA: Sage.

Moos, R.H. (1974). *The Family Environment Scale preliminary manual.* Palo Alto, CA: Consulting Psychologists Press.

Moss, H., Nannis, E., & Poplack, D. (1981). The effects of prophylactic treatment of the CNS on the intellectual functioning of children with acute lymphocytic leukemia. *American Journal of Medicine, 71,* 47-52.

Mullen, E.M. (1984). *Mullen Scales of Early Learning (MSEL).* Cranston, RI: T.O.T.A.L. Child.

Olson, D.H. (1986). Circumplex model VII: Validation studies and FACES III. *Family Process, 25,* 337-351.

Page, K.A. (1986). Predictors of outcome of low birth weight infants: A review of the literature and methodological issues. *Physical Therapy, 66,* 1252-1254.

Parcel, G.S., & Meyer, M.P. (1978). Development of an instrument to measure children's health locus of control. *Health Education Monographs, 6,* 149-159.

Patterson, J.M., & McCubbin, H.I. (1983). Chronic illness: Family stress and coping. In C.R. Rigley & H.I. McCubbin (Eds.), *Stress and the family: Volume II. Coping with catastrophe* (pp. 21-36). New York: Brunner/Mazel.

Perrin, E.C., & Gerrity, P.S. (1981). There's a demon in your belly: Children's understanding of illness. *Pediatrics, 67,* 841–849.

Pizzo, P.A., Eddy, J., Falloon, J., Balis, F.M., Murphy, R.F., Moss, H., Wolters, P., Brouwers, P., Jarosinski, P., Rubin, M., Broder, S., Yarchoan, R., Bruneti, A., Maha, M., Nusinoff-Lehrman, S., & Poplack, D.G. (1988). Effect of continuous intravenous infusion of zidovudine (AZT) in children with symptomatic HIV infection. *New England Journal of Medicine, 319,* 889–896.

Pless, I.B., & Pinkerton, P. (1975). *Chronic childhood disorders: Promoting patterns of adjustment.* Chicago: Year Book Medical Publishers.

Pless, I.B., & Roghmann, K.J. (1971). Chronic illness and its consequences: Observations based on three epidemiological surveys. *Journal of Pediatrics, 79,* 351–359.

Reitan, R.M. (1969). *Manual for administration of neuropsychological test batteries for adults and children.* Indianapolis, IN: Reitan Neuropsychology Laboratory.

Rhodes, L., & Bayley, N. (1984). *Supplement to the manual for the Bayley Scales of Infant Development.* San Antonio, TX: Psychological Corporation.

Ross, D.M., & Ross, S.A. (1988). *Childhood pain: Current issues, research, and management.* Baltimore: Urban & Schwarzenberg.

Rossetti, L.M. (1986). *High-risk infants: Identification, assessment, and intervention.* Boston: Little, Brown.

Rotundo, A., Nevins, T.E., Lipton, M., Lockman, L.A., Mauer, S.M., & Michael, A.F. (1982). Progressive encephalopathy in children with chronic renal insufficiency in infancy. *Kidney International, 21,* 486–491.

Routh, D.K. (Ed.). (1988). *Handbook of pediatric psychology.* New York: Guilford.

Sattler, J.M. (1988). *Assessment of children* (3rd ed.). San Diego, CA: Author.

Siegel, L. (1983). Correction for prematurity and its consequences for the assessment of the very low birth weight infant. *Child Development, 54,* 1176.

Siegel, L.S. (1983). The prediction of possible learning disabilities in preterm and full-term children. In T. Field & A. Sostek (Eds.), *Infants born at risk* (pp. 295–315). New York: Grune & Stratton.

Sigman, M., Cohen, S.E., Beckwith, L., & Parmelee, A.H. (1981). Social and familial influences on the development of preterm infants. *Journal of Pediatric Psychology, 6,* 1–14.

Simeonsson, R.J. (1986). Psychometric assessment. In R.J. Simeonsson (Ed.), *Psychological and developmental assessment of special children* (pp. 63–95). Newton, MA: Allyn & Bacon.

Simeonsson, R.J., Buckley, L., & Monson, L. (1979). Conceptions of illness causality in hospitalized children. *Journal of Pediatric Psychology, 4,* 77–84.

Sparrow, S.S., Balla, D.A., & Cicchetti, D.V. (1984). *Vineland Adaptive Behavior Scales.* Circle Pines, MN: American Guidance Service.

Stein, R.E.K., & Riessman, C.K. (1980). The development of an impact-on-family scale: Preliminary findings. *Medical Care, 18,* 465–472.

Stewart, A.L., Reynolds, E.O.R., Hope, P.L., Hamilton, P.A., Baudin, J., Costello, A.M. de L., Bradford, B.C., & Wyatt, J.S. (1987). Probability of neurodevelopmental disorders estimated from ultrasound appearance of brains of very preterm infants. *Developmental Medicine and Child Neurology, 29,* 3–11.

Telzrow, R.W., Kang, R.R., Mitchell, S.K., Ashworth, C.D., & Barnard, K.E. (1982). An assessment of the behavior of the preterm infant at 40 weeks conceptional age. In L.P. Lipsett & T.M. Field (Eds.), *Infant behavior and development: Perinatal risk and newborn behavior.* Norwood, NJ: Ablex.

Terman, L.M., & Merrill, M.A. (1973). *Stanford-Binet Intelligence Scale, Form L-M.* Chicago: Riverside.

Thorndike, R.L., Hagen, E.P., & Sattler, J.M. (1986). *Stanford-Binet Intelligence Scale: Fourth Edition.* Chicago: Riverside.
Tramontana, M.G., & Hooper, S.R. (1988). *Assessment issues in child neuropsychology.* New York: Plenum.
Tuma, J. (1982). *Handbook for the practice of pediatric psychology.* New York: Wiley.
Ultmann, M.H., Diamond, G.H., Belman, A.L., Ruff, H.A., Novick, B.E., Rubenstein, A., & Cohen, H.J. (1987). Developmental abnormalities in children with acquired immune deficiency syndrome (AIDS) and AIDS-related complex: A follow-up study. *International Journal of Neuroscience, 32,* 661–667.
Uzgiris, I.C., & Hunt, J.McV. (1975). *Ordinal Scales of Psychological Development.* Urbana, IL: University of Illinois Press.
Varni, J.W., & Wallander, J.L. (1988). Pediatric chronic disabilities: Hemophilia and spina bifida as examples. In D.K. Routh (Ed.), *Handbook of pediatric psychology* (pp. 190–221). New York: Guilford.
Vernon, D.T.A., Foley, J.M., Sipowicz, R.R., & Schulman, J.L. (1965). *The psychological responses of children to hospitalization and illness.* Springfield, IL: CC Thomas.
Vohr, B.R., & Garcia Coll, C.T. (1985). Neurodevelopmental and school performance of very low-birth-weight infants: A seven year longitudinal study. *Pediatrics, 76,* 345–350.
Weaver, S.J. (Ed.). (1984). *Testing children: A reference guide for effective clinical and psychoeducational assessments.* Austin, TX: PRO-ED.
Whitt, J.K. (1982). Children's understanding of illness: Developmental considerations and pediatric intervention. In M. Wolraich & D.K. Routh (Eds.), *Advances in behavioral pediatrics* (Vol. 3, pp. 163–201). Greenwich, CT: JAI.
Whitt, J.K. (1984). Children's adaptation to chronic illness and handicapping conditions. In M.G. Eisenberg, L.C. Sutkin, & M.A. Jansen (Eds.), *Chronic illness and disability through the lifespan: Effects on self and family* (pp. 69–102). New York: Springer.
Whitt, J.K., Dykstra, W., & Taylor, C.A. (1979). Children's conceptions of illness and cognitive development. *Clinical Pediatrics, 18,* 327–339.
Whitt, J.K., Wells, R.J., Lauria, M.M., Wilhelm, C.L., & McMillan, C.W. (1984). Cranial radiation in childhood acute lymphocytic leukemia: Neuropsychologic sequelae. *American Journal of Diseases of Children, 138,* 730–736.
Wilhelm, C., Johnson, M., & Eisert, D. (1986). Assessment of motor-impaired children. In R.J. Simeonsson (Ed.), *Psychological and developmental assessment of special children* (pp. 241–278). Newton, MA: Allyn & Bacon.
Wilson, W.M. (1987). Age adjustment in psychological assessment of children born prematurely. *Journal of Pediatric Psychology, 12,* 445–450.
Willis, D.J., Elliott, C.H., & Jay, S. (1982). Psychological effects of physical illness and its concomitants. In J. Tuma (Ed.), *Handbook for the practice of pediatric psychology* (pp. 28–66). New York: Wiley.
Yu, V.Y.H., Orgill, A.A., Lim, S.B., Bajuk, B., & Astbury, J. (1983). Growth and development of very low birthweight infants recovering from bronchopulmonary dysplasia. *Archives of Diseases in Childhood, 58,* 791–794.

12

Assessment of Attention-Deficit Hyperactivity Disorder in Young Children

TERRI L. SHELTON, PH.D. & RUSSELL A. BARKLEY, PH.D.

Since the turn-of-the-century appearance of an early paper (Still, 1902) describing symptoms resembling Attention-Deficit Hyperactivity Disorder (ADHD), ADHD has become one of the most common referral problems to child guidance centers in this country. This fact, along with the increasing interest in assessing and treating very young children because Public Law 99-457 has mandated developmental services for this age group, makes an examination of ADHD's special challenges and considerations in preschoolers and young children particularly timely.

HISTORICAL OVERVIEW

The conceptualization of ADHD has changed over the years. A review of the different "labels" of this disorder parallels these changes in conceptualization as well as those in treatment and research. In that early article, Still (1902) described symptomatology in children that closely resembles the current diagnostic criteria for ADHD (American Psychiatric Association, 1987). These children were found to experience "defects in moral control" and "volitional inhibition" that seemed independent of intellectual deficits or an inadequate environment. However, it wasn't until the late 1940s that any additional attention was directed toward these children. Around that time, researchers began to notice the similarity between the behavioral characteristics of children with ADHD and those with brain injury. Because children with brain damage often displayed overactivity, distractibility, and inattention, professionals falsely assumed that youngsters demonstrating these characteristics had some type of underlying brain impairment. Despite the absence of hard neurological evidence (Strauss & Lehtinen, 1947), it was this false assumption that gave rise to labeling this constellation of symptoms as *minimal brain damage* or *minimal brain dysfunction* (MBD; Clements & Peters, 1962; Wender, 1971).

As the accumulating evidence increasingly failed to support this relationship (Routh & Roberts, 1972; Ullman, Barkley, & Brown, 1978; Werry, Weiss, & Douglas, 1964), the emphasis shifted in the 1960s and 1970s from this brain damage concept to a focus on hyperactivity as the primary symptom of the disorder (Chess, 1960; Clements, 1966). As such, the *Diagnostic and Statistical Manual of Mental Disorders* (DSM-II) of the American Psychiatric Association (1978) referred to this disorder as the "Hyperkinetic Reaction of Childhood." However, continued research and observation by Douglas and others (Douglas, 1972, 1980, 1983; Douglas & Peters, 1979) revealed that while overactivity was one component of this disorder, these children also evidenced even more significant problems in sustained attention and impulse control. This new conceptualization and supportive research led to still another revision in the name applied.

DSM-III (American Psychiatric Association, 1980) introduced the terms Attention Deficit Disorder with or without Hyperactivity, with three primary symptoms identified as characterizing the disorder: inattention, impulsivity, and overactivity. However, research supporting the clinical utility of the subclassification of Attention Deficit Disorder without Hyperactivity was lacking. Therefore, the most current terminology in the latest revision of the DSM (DSM-III-R; American Psychiatric Association, 1987) reflects a single disorder identified as Attention-Deficit Hyperactivity Disorder. There is another diagnostic category, Undifferentiated Attention Deficit Disorder, reserved for those children whose symptoms are consistent with the diagnosis of ADHD but the number of symptoms is not sufficient to warrant the ADHD diagnosis.

Definition and Diagnostic Criteria

The current set of ADHD symptom descriptors has been revised and combined in the DSM-III-R into the following list of 14 criteria, with a child needing to demonstrate at least 8 of these for a period of 6 months or more in order to qualify for a diagnosis (the cutoff score of 8 was established through clinical field trial):

1. Has difficulty remaining seated when required to.
2. Often fidgets with hands or feet or squirms in seat.
3. Has difficulty playing quietly.
4. Often talks excessively.
5. Often shifts from one uncompleted activity to another.
6. Has difficulty sustaining attention to tasks and play activities.
7. Has difficulty following through on instructions from others (not due to oppositional behavior or failure of comprehension); for example, fails to finish chores.
8. Is easily distracted by extraneous stimuli.
9. Often interrupts or intrudes on others; for example, butts into other children's games.
10. Often blurts out answers to questions before they have been completed.
11. Has difficulty waiting turn in games or group situations.
12. Often engages in physically dangerous activities without considering possible consequences (not for the purpose of thrill-seeking); for example, runs into street without looking.
13. Often loses things necessary for tasks or activities at school or at home (e.g., toys, pencils, books, assignments).
14. Often doesn't seem to listen to what is being said to him or her.

Additional qualifiers include onset before age 7 and that the child does not meet the criteria for Pervasive Developmental Disorder.

In summary, children with ADHD are characterized as displaying developmentally inappropriate levels of inattention, impulsivity, and overactivity. These symptoms develop early in childhood, are chronic, are pervasive across settings and/or caregivers, and are not attributable to obvious developmental disabilities (i.e., mental retardation, severe language delay), neurological diseases such as severe epilepsy, or disorders such as autism. Additional difficulties that are hypothesized include deficits in self-directed instruction (Kendall & Braswell, 1985), self-regulation of arousal to meet environmental demands (Douglas, 1983), or rule-governed behavior (Barkley, 1987a). In many ways the thinking about ADHD has come full circle, with the current conceptualization very close to Still's 1902 article.

Barkley (1982) has proposed a list of criteria that are similar to those in DSM-III-R with the following modifications:

1. Deviance in symptoms must be established using standardized parent and/or teacher child behavior rating scales with adequate norms.
2. Duration of symptoms must be 12 rather than 6 months.
3. Onset must occur by 6 rather than 7 years.
4. Symptoms must be pervasive across settings.
5. Child must have an intelligence quotient greater than 85 or, if between 70 and 85, behavior must be inappropriate when compared to children of same mental or developmental age.

Using these definitions, the occurrence of ADHD in the population is generally accepted as 3% to 5% (American Psychiatric Association, 1980). Boys are reported as having the disorder more often than girls, with ratios ranging from 4:1 to 9:1 across studies, with a generally accepted ratio of 6:1 (Ross & Ross, 1976) in clinical samples. However, epidemiological studies seem to suggest that a ratio of 3:1 is more typical in the general population (Trites, Dugas, Lynch, & Ferguson, 1980).

Individual differences in attention, impulsivity, and activity are thought to lie along a continuum (Barkley, 1988a; Werry, 1985), with deficits defined by using somewhat arbitrary cutoff points along this continuum. This concept of a continuum is an important one, particularly for those children whose deficits fall into a borderline range, and it certainly affects the prevalence estimates. While ADHD is generally chronic, with a high degree of stability over the child's development (Campbell, Schleifer, & Weiss, 1978), those children whose symptoms lie nearest the cutoff point may move into or out of the class over time as individual scores fluctuate. Furthermore, although the basic ADHD symptoms of inattention, impulsivity, and overactivity are often described as if they were unitary constructs, they are in fact multidimensional (Barkley & Ullman, 1975; Douglas & Peters, 1979; Milich & Kramer, 1985; Ullman et al., 1978; Zettle & Hayes, 1982) and as such can be assessed in numerous ways.

Associated Characteristics

The presence of ADHD does not preclude the fact that these children may experience other difficulties as well (e.g., Oppositional-Defiant Disorder, Conduct Disorder). In fact, these disorders and others are observed with some frequency in children with ADHD. More specifically, some of the difficulties that have been observed include deficits in general intelligence (Safer & Allen, 1976; Tarver-Behring, Barkley, & Karlsson, 1985); academic achievement (Cantwell & Satterfield, 1978; Safer & Allen, 1976); depression and low self-esteem (Weiss, Hechtman, & Perlman, 1978); and poor peer acceptance (Johnston, Pelham, & Murphy, 1985; Pelham & Bender, 1982). Other difficulties include a greater incidence of accidental poisonings and injuries (Hartsough & Lambert, 1985; Stewart, Thach, & Freidin, 1970); allergies (Trites, Tryphonas, & Ferguson, 1980); motor incoordination (Denckla & Rudel, 1978); enuresis and encopresis (Safer & Allen, 1976); and vision, language, and chronic general health problems (Hartsough & Lambert, 1985).

As mentioned, many children with ADHD will also demonstrate difficulties in aggressiveness and oppositionality. Because of the high degree of overlap in diagnostic categories, there has been much controversy about whether ADHD is in fact a separate disorder from conduct problems, oppositional behavior, or learning disabilities. At present there appears to be enough research to suggest that the disorders are in fact distinct (American Psychiatric Association, 1987; Barkley, 1982). As mentioned, ADHD appears to be a deficit in sustained attention, impulse control, and restlessness that is very similar to other developmental disabilities in early onset, pervasiveness across settings, and chronicity. Although interventions can reduce the severity of symptoms, many of the behaviors do not fall under the child's direct control. In contrast, both oppositional and defiant behaviors are learned and more amenable to complete remediation if addressed early and in a comprehensive fashion. Oppositional disorder is characterized by defiant, negative, hostile, and verbally and physically aggressive behaviors. Conduct disorder, which often evolves from oppositional behavior, refers to frequent violations of the rights of others or antisocial acts. Finally, learning disabilities refer to significant delays in reading, spelling, math, handwriting, or language that cannot be attributed to intellectual delays, cultural deprivation, or lack of educational opportunity. Although these disorders may coexist, they are not synonymous. A more thorough discussion of ADHD, its related characteristics, the developmental course and predictors of outcome, and current thinking about the various potential causes can be found, for example, in Anastopoulos and Barkley (1988), Barkley (1981, 1988a), Ross and Ross (1976), and Weiss and Hechtman (1986).

THE ASSESSMENT PROCESS

Implications

The concept of a symptom continuum plus the range of characteristics often associated with ADHD present some important issues in the assessment of this disorder. First, there must be a comprehensive assessment of the primary symptoms to determine whether the difficulties even fit the diagnostic criteria. This assessment must include the use of measures with normative data that will allow one to determine that the behaviors observed are, in fact, deviant from what would be expected from other children of similar age and sex. This is particularly true among preschoolers and young children, where it may be difficult to define symptomatic behavior, to separate ADHD from discipline problems and aggression, and to determine whether the restlessness, inattention, or oppositionality may be difficult but age-appropriate exploration and independence seeking (Campbell, 1985; Campbell, Ewing, Breaux, & Szumowski, 1986; Campbell, Szumowski, Ewing, Gluck, & Breaux, 1982).

This assessment must include information from a variety of sources as, by definition, ADHD is pervasive, occurring in multiple settings with a variety of caregivers/adults. Second, there must be a thorough evaluation or documentation of other factors, such as mental retardation, autism, or health problems, that may give rise to similar, but not ADHD, symptomatology. Third, because of the frequency with which other characteristics are associated with ADHD, the assessment must thoroughly evaluate the presence and severity of any other existing difficulties, such as Oppositional-Defiant Disorder or Conduct Disorder, as well as the parents' reactions to these behaviors. As such, the evaluation of ADHD in children incorporates multiple assessment methods, relying on several informants, inquiring into the nature of the child's difficulties across multiple situations. Among the appropriate assessment methods are parent and teacher rating scales of child behavior and developmental data; perhaps parent self-report measures of relevant psychiatric conditions, to review prior to the actual evaluation; parent, child, and teacher interviews; laboratory measures of ADHD symptoms; and direct observational techniques.

Finally, the cutoff score, duration of symptoms, and age of onset now recommended for clinical practice in the DSM-III-R were established on elementary school-aged children, usually aged 6 to 11, making them of questionable validity for preschool children. Given the relatively high rates of behavioral problems or concerns in preschool children that decline significantly with age, a common cutoff score of 8 of 14 symptoms across all ages fails to correct for this fact. In fact, such a cutoff score likely overidentifies preschool children as having ADHD. Hence, it should be considered as a crude first cutoff in *screening* for ADHD, to confirm more rigorously by rating scales with preschool norms. The duration criterion of 6 months is problematic in ages birth to 2 years, where the symptoms of interest often may not manifest long enough to meet this requirement, particularly given that a mean age of onset for ADHD is usually 3 to 4 years. In short, DSM guidelines are not very appropriate for preschoolers and should serve only as loose guidelines. Below the age of 2 years, no diagnosis should be given.

Behavior Rating Scales

Parent rating scales. Child behavior checklists and rating scales have become an essential element in the evaluation and diagnosis of ADHD in children. Although fewer are available with normative data for very young children and preschoolers, several do apply to this age group. However, while over 50% of children with ADHD have begun to manifest behavioral problems, particularly overactivity, short attention span, and noncompliant behavior, by ages 3 to 4, not many currently available checklists extend to children under 3.

One class of behavioral ratings assesses the concept of temperament. Temperament, or behavioral style, refers to the *how* of behavior, as opposed to the what (content) or why (motivation). Temperament assessment captures both the stylistic manner in which individuals carry out behavior and the way in which this affects their interaction with the environment and significant others. The most widely recognized and used such system in clinical research and practice derives from the work of Thomas, Chess, and associates in the New York Longitudinal Study (NYLS; Thomas, Chess, Birch, Hertzig, & Korn, 1963). These researchers have identified nine temperamental characteristics: activity level, rhythmicity, approach-withdrawal, adaptability, intensity of reaction, mood, distractibility, sensory threshold, and persistence.

Certain constellations of these characteristics (e.g., easy, difficult, slow to warm up) as well as particular individual temperament qualities have been found useful in predicting later outcome. For example, Carey and McDevitt (1978) associated high activity and negative mood with children who remain in the difficult temperament group through early childhood. A clinical description of hyperactive infants and preschoolers reported by Ross and Ross (1982, pp. 28–32) noted that these infants are typically active, restless, and difficult to feed and settle down to sleep. As preschoolers they still appear more active but are also described as more talkative, more prone to accidents, less compliant, more aggressive, and more inattentive than normal children. Not all active and difficult infants go on to have ADHD, of course, nor do all children with ADHD always demonstrate these characteristics as infants or young children, but the presence of these symptoms could be thought of as placing the child at risk of ADHD. Although there are no direct environmental measurements of temperament, there are many standardized interview techniques and questionnaires. Hubert, Wachs, Peters-Martin, and Gandour (1982) provide a comprehensive review of temperament scales and their psychometric properties.

The Bayley Scales of Infant Development (Bayley, 1969) provide a rating of behavior for infants from birth through 30 months. The Infant Behavior Rating Record assesses style of interaction with examiner and parent, activity level, interest in toys and activities, and attention span, among other dimensions. The major drawback here is the absence of normative data. However, this record can provide a method for organizing behavioral observations of very young children.

Achenbach and Edelbrock's (1983) Child Behavior Checklist (CBCL) is one of the most rigorously developed and standardized child behavior ratings scales currently available for ages 4–16. The CBCL consists of 20 items comprising a Social Competence scale and 118 items comprising a Behavior Problems scale. The Social Competence scale generates three scores (Activities, Social, and School), which are plotted on one of six profiles depending on the child's age (4–5 years, 6–11 years, and 12–16 years) and sex. The Behavior Problems scale profiles consist of eight or nine factors (depending on the child's age) examining various behavioral, social, emotional, and physical problems. Test-retest reliability, stability, and interparent agreement are good, and research has shown that the CBCL discriminates children with ADHD from non-ADHD children or those with other psychiatric problems (Mash &

Johnston, 1983). There is a similar checklist available for children ages 2 to 3, although current normative data are less comprehensive. This 100-item version yields four dimensions sampling behaviors related to social interaction, depression, sleep problems, somatic problems, aggressiveness, and destructiveness. Items related to hyperactivity seem to load most frequently on the Aggression subscale.

The Conners Parent Rating Scale–Revised (CPRS-R; Goyette, Conners, & Ulrich, 1978), along with the teacher version of this scale, offers one of the most commonly used rating scales in research and in the clinical assessment of children with ADHD. Both the original 96-item scale and an abbreviated 10-item form (the Conners Abbreviated Symptom Questionnaire; ASQ) are available, but the more recent 48-item revision has the most satisfactory normative data and is appropriate for ages 3 to 17. The latter yields five factor scales: Conduct Problems, Learning Problems, Psychosomatic, Impulsive-Hyperactive, and Anxiety. Information on test-retest reliability has not been published, and the validity of the CPRS-R is not as well studied as the original. Nevertheless, the scale has been shown not only to discriminate between children with ADHD and those without, but also to be sensitive to stimulant drug effects (Barkley, Fischer, Newby, & Breen, 1988); parent training in child management (Barkley, 1987c; Pollard, Ward, & Barkley, 1983); and self-control training of hyperactive children (Horn, Ialongo, Popovich, & Peradotto, 1984). Though many of the items overlap with the CBCL, the CPRS-R is a useful addition to an assessment protocol because (a) there is a substantial research literature using the scale with ADHD children, (b) the CBCL does not have a separate Hyperactivity scale on its profile for 4- to 5-year-olds, which the CPRS-R does, and (c) the CPRS-R is briefer and more easily repeated over short time intervals to assess treatment effects.

The Home Situations Questionnaire (HSQ; Barkley, 1981) was developed in order to evaluate *where* children display their behavioral problems as opposed to what type they have. The HSQ contains 16 situations typically found in the home and in public (e.g., when asked to do homework, at bedtime, in church, when visiting others). Parents answer yes or no as to whether their child has difficulty in a particular area and, if so, rate the severity of the problems using a scale ranging from 1 (mild) to 9 (severe). Normative data address both the number of problem situations and the mean severity rating of these problems for children ages 4 to 12 years (Barkley & Edelbrock, 1987). The scale significantly differentiates children with ADHD from those without, and it is sensitive to parent training and stimulant drug interventions (Barkley, Karlsson, Pollard, & Murphy, 1985; Pollard et al., 1983).

Another scale widely used in the evaluation of ADHD in children and preschoolers is the Werry-Weiss-Peters Activity Rating Scale (WWPARS). The original 31-item version (Werry & Sprague, 1968) was developed as a means of quantifying activity level in children, especially as a dependent measure for research in psychopharmacology. A modified 22-item version was reported by Routh, Schroeder, and O'Tuama (1974) in which school-related items were deleted. Despite some controversy over whether the scale measures hyperactivity and inattention or other situationally inappropriate behavior (see Ross & Ross, 1982, for a discussion), the WWPARS has been employed in numerous studies as a parent report of activity level and offers normative data for ages 2–9 years (Barkley & Ullman, 1975; Campbell et al., 1986;

Campbell et al., 1978; Prior, Leonard, & Wood, 1983; Routh & Schroeder, 1976; Ullman et al., 1978). However, the norms derive from a small sample of children of upper middle class university-employed parents and may not be appropriate for clinical use.

The Louisville Behavior Checklist (LBCL; Miller, 1984) assesses children's difficulties along the following factors: aggression, inhibition, learning disability, infantile aggression, hyperactivity, antisocial behavior, social withdrawal, sensitivity, fear, academic disability, and immaturity. There are three separate forms for 4- to 6-year-olds, 7- to 12-year-olds, and 13- to 17-year-olds. Although the normative data are limited by small, unrepresentative samples, and the scale has not been widely adopted in research, the LBCL does provide some assessment of academic or learning disability that may prove useful in certain situations where this is of concern.

The 36-item Eyberg Child Behavior Inventory (ECBI; Eyberg, 1980) offers a parent report of the child's difficulties in the areas of conduct disorders and oppositional behavior. Two scores are obtained: an Intensity score, reflecting the sum of the ratings (1-7) across all items, and a Problems score, comprised of the number of items the parent endorsed as a problem. The inventory has produced adequate reliability and validity data, and, although somewhat restrictive, there are normative data for ages 2-7 and 13-16 years. The ECBI scores have been found to relate significantly to direct observational measures of noncompliance and negative parent-child interactions, as well as to child activity level and temperament (Robinson & Eyberg, 1981; Webster-Stratton & Eyberg, 1982). The scale also shows sensitivity to treatment effects from parent training in child behavior management skills (Eyberg & Robinson, 1982; Eyberg & Ross, 1978; Packard, Robinson, & Grove, 1983; Webster-Stratton, 1984). Given the frequency with which children with ADHD also evidence difficulties with oppositional behavior or conduct problems, and the relative lack of behavior rating scales available for children under the age of 4, the ECBI may be a helpful adjunct to an assessment battery.

Teacher rating scales. The Teacher's Report form of the Child Behavior Checklist is quite similar to the parent version discussed above. It contains two scales: Adaptive Functioning and Behavior Problems. The Adaptive Functioning scale is based on eight categories of information obtained from the teacher, from which six scores are derived: School Performance, Working Hard, Behaving Appropriately, Learning, Happy, and Summary. The 113-item Behavior Problems scale yields scores on the following factors: Anxious, Social Withdrawal, Unpopular, Self-Destructive, Obsessive-Compulsive, Inattentive, Nervous-Overactive, and Aggressive. The latter scale does discriminate children with ADHD from those without (Edelbrock, Costello, & Kessler, 1984).

Also derived from the Behavior Problems Scale is the Edelbrock Child Attention/Activity Profile (CAP; Edelbrock, 1986). This 12-item measure specifically assesses a child's difficulty with overactivity and inattention, and it is helpful both in assessing ADHD and for repeated assessments in evaluating change due to treatment, such as stimulant medication. Unfortunately the normative data for both the CBCL teacher form and the CAP are available only for children ages 6 to 16, making it inappropriate for preschoolers. However, these instruments can be very helpful in the long-term follow-up of young children at risk for or diagnosed as having ADHD.

The Preschool Behavior Questionnaire (PBC; Behar, 1974) does offer a rating of hostile-aggressive, anxious, and hyperactive-distractible behavior among preschoolers ages 3–6 years. Though the Conners Teacher Rating Scales (see below) are used more widely, the PBC can provide a helpful short screening because many teacher rating scales do not have normative data down to 3 years.

There are at least four versions of the Conners Teacher Rating Scales in current use: (a) the original (Conners, 1969, 1973); (b) the revised Conners Teacher Rating Scale (Goyette et al., 1978); (c) the Abbrevated Symptom Questionnaire, or Hyperactivity Index (Goyette et al., 1978); and (d) the Iowa Conners Teacher Rating Scale (Loney & Milich, 1981). Only the original and revised editions will be discussed here; for more information on the other two scales, the reader is directed to a review of these and other rating scales in Barkley (1987a, 1987b).

The 39-item original Connors scale is the most widely used teacher rating scale for research with children with ADHD, and it provides normative data for children as young as 4 years of age. Items are scored to yield six factor scales, using the normative data from Trites, Blouin, and Laprade (1982): Hyperactivity, Conduct Problem, Emotional-Overindulgent, Anxious-Passive, Asocial, and Daydreams/Attendance Problem. The 28-item revised teacher rating scale is similar to the revised parent version in its format and scoring. Items are scored to yield three factors: Conduct Problem, Hyperactive, and Inattentive-Passive. The advantage of this scale over the original version is that it offers normative data for children as young as 3, it is shorter, and the items focus primarily on the symptoms associated with ADHD. The disadvantage is that it is not as useful for evaluating internalizing, neurotic, depressive, or anxious symptoms. Though both have some overlap with the CBCL, because they do offer information on younger age groups, the CTRS and the CTRS-R can be helpful in assessing ADHD and associated characteristics in preschoolers.

The ADD-H: Comprehensive Teacher's Rating Scale (ACTeRS; Ullman, Sleator, & Sprague, 1984) was developed for the assessment of children with ADHD and for monitoring their response to treatment. This 24-item scale assesses difficulties related to oppositional behavior, attention, hyperactivity, and social problems, and it can be used with children ages 5–12. The ACTeRS needs both additional research and more refined normative data, and its advantage over the Conners scales is not yet clear. Nevertheless, this scale has been shown to differentiate children with ADHD from those without and from those with learning disabilities (Ullman, 1984; Ullmann et al., 1984).

Like the HSQ described earlier, the School Situations Questionnaire (SSQ; Barkley, 1981) assesses a child's behavioral difficulties in 12 common school situations (e.g., in the hallways, in the bathroom, during lectures, during small-group work). As with the HSQ, the SSQ yields two scores: the number of problem settings and their mean severity ratings. Normative data are available for ages 6 to 11 (Barkley & Edelbrock, 1987), and the scale has been shown to discriminate children with ADHD from those without and to be sensitive to stimulant drug treatment (Barkley et al., 1988). Although some of the school situations tapped may not be as reflective of preschool settings, the SSQ can be very helpful when used in conjunction with other teacher rating scales.

Clinical Interviews

Parent interview. After reviewing the results of the previously chosen ratings scales, the examiner begins to develop some idea of the child's difficulties and strengths. However, any assessment data are useful only when interpreted in the context of the child's personal and family history as well as the larger environment in which these behaviors are observed. An indispensable part of the clinical assessment of children is an interview with the child's parent(s) or primary caregiver(s). Interviewing that focuses on the specific complaints and functional parameters of a child's difficulties provides the cornerstone on which one builds the remainder of the evaluation and its interpretation.

After obtaining the routine demographic data concerning the child and family, the interview should proceed next to the major referral concerns of the parents and of the professional referral source where appropriate. A thorough behavioral interview provides a useful framework for approaching this task (Gross, 1984; Morganstern, 1976). Because of the diagnostic criteria for ADHD as well as those for diagnosing or ruling out other psychiatric disorders, it is essential that the interview probes for the specific nature, frequency, age of onset, and chronicity of the behaviors under concern, as well as their situational and temporal variations.

The professional also should obtain thorough developmental, medical, school, and family histories. The developmental history should focus on the attainment of important milestones as well as any concerns in the gross and fine motor, speech and language, intellectual, adaptive, emotional, behavioral (e.g., temperament and activity level), and social functioning domains. The medical history should include the child's birth history, any prenatal or perinatal problems, the child's current physical status, and any other health/medical or neurological conditions or concerns. Information obtained during this part of the interview will help determine whether a referral to a physician or medical specialist is needed. Regarding the school history, the very young child or toddler may not have one per se. However, many children do have some involvement with day care, early intervention, preschool, or some other setting in which impressions of the child's interaction with other children and his or her behavior in a more structured setting can be obtained. The family history should include any concerns regarding the development or behavior of any siblings; the identified child's interaction with siblings; any attentional, learning, psychiatric, or health problems present in the parents or any extended family members; and any major recent psychosocial stressors in the family (e.g., moves, employment problems, marital difficulties). Some of these difficulties can result in the child manifesting behavioral disturbances that appear similar to ADHD but are qualitatively different, requiring in some instances different treatment. They also may be useful in predicting responsiveness to or compliance with therapy.

Inquiry also should be made regarding the presence or history of tics or Tourette's disorder in the child or the immediate biological family members. Where present, this would result in a recommendation either against the use of stimulant medication in the treatment of such a child or at the very least for cautious use of low dosages to preclude exacerbating the child's potential for a tic disorder (Comings &

Comings, 1984; Golden, 1983). With parental consent, contact with the child's pediatrician can help identify further the early history of problems or important family circumstances.

All of this information has a significant bearing on (a) making a differential diagnosis; (b) choosing specific laboratory measures and/or additional rating scales or interviews to conduct; and (c) making recommendations for treatment. To accomplish this requires that the examiner have an adequate knowledge of the diagnostic features of other childhood disorders, particularly those that may present superficially as ADHD. For instance, many children with Pervasive Developmental Disorder (Childhood Onset or Atypical) may be viewed by their parents and others as having attentional problems or other behavioral concerns similar to ADHD. Parents as well as day-care workers or preschool teachers are more likely to have heard about ADHD than Pervasive Developmental Disorder and thus may be more likely to refer the child for an evaluation of ADHD. As such, questioning about inappropriate thinking, affect, social relations, and sensory or motor peculiarities may reveal that the child is experiencing a more serious and pervasive developmental disorder.

This type of comprehensive interview usually yields enough initial information for determining the presence or absence of the diagnostic criteria for ADHD as well as for ruling in or out any other disorder. Where this information is lacking, some specific questions in these areas would be in order. Following the interview, the examiner should pursue more details about the nature of parent-child interactions surrounding how the child follows rules. All children with ADHD have problems to some extent with complying or sustaining compliance with certain types of commands, directions, and assigned tasks. This is particularly true when the child perceives the task as boring, effortful, and one in which there is little or no immediate consequence for him or her. More than 60%, however, also have acquired a repertoire of oppositional, defiant, and coercive behaviors, which further contribute to difficult interactions with their parents and are often of greatest distress to them. Parents should be questioned about the child's ability to accomplish commands and requests in a satisfactory manner, to demonstrate self-control (rule following) appropriate to his or her age in the absence of adult supervision, and to adhere to rules of conduct governing behavior. Of particular interest is the settings in which difficulties occur, the specific type of noncompliance the child shows (e.g., stalling, starting the task but failing to finish it, outright opposition and defiance, etc.), and the particular management style the parents employ to address the noncompliance. The Home Situations Questionnaire (described earlier) can serve as a framework for conducting this part of the interview.

This interview also may reveal that one parent, typically the mother, has more difficulty managing the child than the other. Often because the mother is the one who issues the majority of commands, there is a greater probability that she will experience more of the child's noncompliance. However, other characteristics, such as the way commands are issued and the consequences provided for compliance or noncompliance, can lead to these behavioral differences. One should take care to discuss differences in the parents' approaches to management and any difficulties within the family this may have caused. Such difficulties in child management often lead to decreased satisfaction with one's role as a parent, to reduced leisure and recreational opportunities due to time demands or the unavailability of babysitters, and possibly to increased marital or familial conflict.

Woven throughout the interview or at the very least at its conclusion should be a discussion of the child's positive characteristics and attributes as well as potential rewards and desirable reinforcers. This is particularly helpful not only in planning treatment recommendations but in maintaining a balanced view of the child. Some parents of children with ADHD have had such chronic and pervasive management problems that the majority of their interactions and subsequent perception may be quite negative. Enabling parents to begin thinking of positive attributes actually constitutes an initial step toward treatment, as effective parent training techniques often incorporate focusing on and attending to desirable child behaviors (Barkley, 1988a; Forehand & McMahon, 1981).

Child interview and observation. Some time should always be spent directly interacting with the child. Though the direct administration of tests affords some opportunity for behavioral observation, a brief discussion with the child or observation of behavior in a relatively nonstructured setting would be helpful. Obviously the length and content of this interview will depend greatly on the child's age, intellectual level, and language abilities; with very young examinees, the time may serve merely to become acquainted and reduce any anxiety about the testing situation.

Although these observations are important, professionals must guard against drawing any diagnostic conclusions from those instances where the child does not demonstrate behavioral difficulties. It is not uncommon for children with ADHD not to misbehave in a clinician's office. The setting is a novel one, often with frequently changing activities, it provides the child with a one-on-one interaction, and the child probably does not have a previous history of misbehaving in that setting. A heavy reliance on such observations, particularly in the absence of or in direct conflict with evidence derived from the rating scales, interview, and direct measures, would lead one to falsely rule out a diagnosis of ADHD (Sleator & Ullmann, 1981). In some instances, the child's actions and demeanor with the parents in the waiting area and in transition from one room to another may be a better indication of his or her behavior.

Laboratory Tests and Procedures

Knowledge of the diagnostic criteria coupled with the information obtained from the rating scales and clinical interview will be helpful in determining the choice of measures to administer in the clinic. As with the behavioral rating scales, there are few measures currently available for preschoolers in general and even fewer with normative data for examinees under 3. For these children, behavioral observations, possibly obtained during a developmental evaluation or in a day-care setting, may prove the most helpful. Nevertheless, there are a few tests developed rather recently that begin to address the more objective assessment of ADHD symptomatology.

Vigilance and sustained attention. Probably one of the most widely used measures of attention span or vigilance in the research literature on ADHD is the Continuous Performance Test (CPT; Rosvold, Mirsky, Sarason, Bransome, & Beck, 1956). Though there are many variations on this task, the most common format requires the child to observe a screen while individual letters or numbers are projected onto it at a rapid pace. The task involves pressing a button when a certain stimulus or pair of stimuli in sequence appear. The measures derived from the method are usually the number correct, the number of stimuli missed (errors of omission), and the number of incorrect stimuli to which the child responded (errors of commission). The number of correct and number of omissions are believed to assess vigilance or sustained attention, while the number of commissions may reflect both sustained attention and impulse control. This method has been shown to discriminate children with ADHD (Douglas, 1983), to be sensitive to stimulant drug effects (Barkley, 1977a), and to correlate significantly with the inattention and hyperactivity factors from the Conners Teacher Rating Scale, the Coding and Arithmetic subtests of the Wechsler Intelligence Scale for Children-Revised (WISC-R; Wechsler, 1974) and the Latency and Error scores of the Matching Familiar Figures Test (Kagan, Rosman, Day, Albert & Philips, 1964; Klee & Garfinkel, 1983).

Gordon (1983) has developed a small, solid-state, child-proofed computerized device known as the Gordon Diagnostic System (GDS) for assessing vigilance as well as impulse control (to be described later). In the preschool version, the child is asked to press a small button whenever a "1" appears on the screen. Normative data are available for subjects aged 3 to 16. The GDS has been shown to discriminate children with ADHD from those without (Gordon, 1985) and to be sensitive to stimulant drug treatment (Barkley et al., 1985). Klee and Garfinkel (1983) have developed a similar program using sequences of letters rather than numbers, but normative data are not available. Both measures require recognizing numbers or letters, which may be a problem when testing very young children.

Impulse control. Two methods of assessing impulsivity in children who may have ADHD have shown promise for clinical practice. The first, the previously mentioned Matching Familiar Figures Test (MFFT), was developed by Kagan in 1966. On this task the examiner presents a picture of a recognizable object and then asks the child to choose the one picture that matches this sample from an array of other very similar pictures. The task involves 12 such sets, and the child's score is the mean time taken to the first response (latency) and the total number of errors (incorrectly identified pictures). Both measures (latency and the total number of errors) have been found to discriminate children with ADHD from those without (Campbell, Douglas, & Morganstern, 1971) and aggressive and nonaggressive children with ADHD (Milich, Landau, & Loney, 1981); to correlate with clinic playroom measures of activity level and attention (Milich et al., 1981); and to be sensitive to stimulant drug effects (Barkley, 1977a). Normative data have been reported for ages 5 through 12 years (Salkind & Nelson, 1980) on a version where the child was asked to choose from an array of six alternatives. There also is a preschool version, which requires the child to choose from among only four alternatives.

The second test of interest in measuring impulsivity in these children is the Delay Task from the Gordon Diagnostic System described earlier. In this task, the child sits before the device and is told to wait, then press a blue button. If the child waits long enough, he or she earns a point. The child is not told how long to wait before pushing the button, merely to wait, press the button, then wait again, then press the button. The task is comparable to a direct reinforcement of latency (DRL) procedure and may assess a different form of impulsivity than tasks such as the MFFT. The child's performance is evaluated along three dimensions: the number of rewards (correct responses), the number of button presses (total responses), and the ratio of rewards to button presses (efficiency ratio). All three measures have been found to differentiate children with ADHD from those without and to correlate significantly with ratings from the Conners original teacher and parent rating scales (Gordon, 1979).

Activity level. As with attention span and impulsivity, activity level is a multidimensional construct and has been measured in a variety of ways in the study of children with ADHD. In general, most research on activity level in children with ADHD has focused on the movement of arms and legs to total body motion or locomotor movements as well as the more global concepts of "fidgetiness" and "out-of-seat" behaviors. (These last two behaviors are most commonly assessed using direct observational procedures and will be discussed later.)

Researchers have applied a wide array of devices to the measurement of activity level. Modified self-winding wristwatches, called "actometers," have been used to measure wrist and ankle activity (Barkley, 1977b; Barkley et al., 1988; Tryon, 1984), as have pedometers attached to the waist, wrist, or ankle (Barkley, 1977a). Studies also have used motion transducers with small mercury switches attached to various locations on the child's body (Tryon, 1984). Other such devices have included a solid-state acceleration monitor (Porrino et al., 1983); pneumatic pads on a playroom floor (Montague & Swarbrick, 1975); grid-marked floors (Routh & Schroeder, 1976); and stabilimetric seat cushions (Barkley, 1977a; Tryon, 1984). Although helpful in research and able to provide more objective data about a child's behavioral difficulties, these approaches have not been as widely used by clinicians due to lack of normative data, concerns about reliability, and issues of validity concerning the type of "hyperactivity" being measured.

Direct observation. As mentioned, fidgetiness or restlessness, as well as other ADHD behaviors, often have been evaluated through the use of direct observational procedures. Almost all of the measures employ an interval sampling procedure during which the presence or absence and frequency of a variety of behaviors is recorded. The Hyperactive Behavior Code, developed by Jacob, O'Leary, and Rosenblad (1978), records the following behaviors in a natural classroom setting: Solicitation (seeks interaction with teacher), Aggression, Refusal, Change of Position, Daydreaming, and Weird Sounds (nonspeech vocalizations or noises). These measures are collapsed into a single score representing hyperactive behavior.

Another observational system, again focusing on classroom behavior, was developed by Abikoff, Gittelman-Klein, and Klein (1977). This system contains 14 behavioral categories pertaining to off-task behavior, movement, and other behaviors that occur more often in children with ADHD.

Roberts has developed a code for use in clinic playroom analogue settings (Milich, Loney, & Landau, 1982; Milich, 1984; Roberts, 1979). Over a 15-minute period, observers continuously record grid crossings, out-of-seat behavior, fidgeting, vocalization, on-task behavior, and attention shifts in both a restricted academic setting and a free-play situation. In the academic setting the child is asked to complete a series of worksheets similar to the WISC-R Coding subtest and not to play with any of the toys in the room. In this setting, the time spent touching toys and the number of worksheet items completed also are recorded. Although the academic setting may not be appropriate for very young children, and the play situation may present some problem for those who will not separate from their parents, the method does seem promising for objectively recording ADHD behaviors, discriminating between those children with ADHD and those without, and detecting those children with ADHD who may have additional problems with aggression.

A variation on the Milich/Roberts procedure has been used by Barkley (1988b) and Barkley et al. (1988), the coding form for which is shown in Figure 12.1. In brief, using a clinic playroom with a one-way observation mirror, the examiner places the child and his or her mother in the playroom with instructions to play freely with toys for a short period of time (5 minutes). Then the examiner returns and instructs the mother to have her child sit at a small table and complete some mathematics problems. During this task the mother is to sit on a sofa across the room and read a magazine. This situation lasts 15 minutes or more, during which the examiner records the initial occurrence of eight behaviors during 30-second intervals: off-task, fidgeting, vocalization, talks to mother, plays with objects, out-of-seat, negative behavior for the child, and mother commands.

Although the task may need to be modified for the younger child, this format does allow the parent to be present, which may be very helpful for toddlers or preschoolers who may have difficulty with separation during the testing situation. This measures does differentiate children with ADHD from those without (Breen, 1985), is quite sensitive to drug and dose effects of stimulant medication (Barkley et al., 1985), and the coding procedure is easily learned. Barkley (1988b) now recommends that older preschool children be observed without their mothers present to obtain a purer measure of ADHD behaviors that are less confounded by oppositional behavior. All of these procedures, however, do require that the clinician have access to facilities (e.g., one-way observation room) that will support this type of assessment.

Parent-child interactions. Because many children with ADHD have difficulties with noncompliance and with completing assigned tasks, and demonstrate oppositional or deviant behaviors, it may be useful to evaluate the child's interaction with his or her parents or other adults. Several systems are available that focus primarily on recording the child's noncompliant and negative behaviors plus the parents' commands and other controlling behaviors. These include the coding system for recording noncompliance in parent-child interactions in a clinic playroom (Forehand & McMahon, 1981); the Response-Class Matrix (Mash, Terdal, & Anderson, 1973; reviewed by Mash & Barkley, 1986); and the coding of parent-child interactions particularly in children with conduct problems (Patterson, 1982; Robinson & Eyberg, 1981; Wahler, House, & Stambaugh, 1976).

Barkley (1987c) has developed a modified coding system for recording children's noncompliance that is easy to use in a clinic situation. (The coding sheet appears in Figure 12.2.) The parent goes into a playroom with the child and is given a list of 10 or more commands to give to the child. Within each minute of observation, the coder records the occurrence of each new command (C) issued; how often it is repeated (R); whether the child initiates (Cpy) or fails to initiate compliance (Ncpy) in 10 seconds; any oppositional behavior (Neg); and parental responses of approval (A) or disapproval (PNeg) in response to the child. Although as yet lacking in adequate normative data, this system can reveal glaring problems in child compliance or

FIGURE 12.1. Academic situation code sheet.

Interval #:	1	2	3	4	5	6	7	8	9	10	11	12	13	14	15	16	17	18
Off Task																		
Fidgeting																		
Vocalizing																		
Plays w/ Object																		
Out of Seat																		

Interval #:	19	20	21	22	23	24	25	26	27	28	29	30	Total	Scoring	
Off Task														/30 =	%
Fidgeting														/30 =	%
Vocalizing														/30 =	%
Plays w/ Object														/30 =	%
Out of Seat														/30 =	%
													Total ADD Behavior	/150 =	%

Child's name _____ Coder initials _____ Date: _____

Session: _____ Init. _____ Wk1 _____ Wk2 _____ Wk3 _____   Is this a reliability check? YES   NO
If so, with whom? _____

Comments:

	1			2			3			4			5		
min.	Par.	Child	Par.	Par.	Child	Par.	Par.	Child	Par.	Par.	Child	Par.	Par.	Child	Par.
1	C R R R R R R R R	Cpy Ncpy Neg	A PNeg	C R R R R R R R R	Cpy Ncpy Neg	A PNeg	C R R R R R R R R	Cpy Ncpy Neg	A PNeg	C R R R R R R R R	Cpy Ncpy Neg	A PNeg	C R R R R R R R R	Cpy Ncpy Neg	A PNeg
2	C R R R R R R R R	Cpy Ncpy Neg	A PNeg	C R R R R R R R R	Cpy Ncpy Neg	A PNeg	C R R R R R R R R	Cpy Ncpy Neg	A PNeg	C R R R R R R R R	Cpy Ncpy Neg	A PNeg	C R R R R R R R R	Cpy Ncpy Neg	A PNeg
3	C R R R R R R R R	Cpy Ncpy Neg	A PNeg	C R R R R R R R R	Cpy Ncpy Neg	A PNeg	C R R R R R R R R	Cpy Ncpy Neg	A PNeg	C R R R R R R R R	Cpy Ncpy Neg	A PNeg	C R R R R R R R R	Cpy Ncpy Neg	A PNeg
4	C R R R R R R R R	Cpy Ncpy Neg	A PNeg	C R R R R R R R R	Cpy Ncpy Neg	A PNeg	C R R R R R R R R	Cpy Ncpy Neg	A PNeg	C R R R R R R R R	Cpy Ncpy Neg	A PNeg	C R R R R R R R R	Cpy Ncpy Neg	A PNeg
5	C R R R R R R R R	Cpy Ncpy Neg	A PNeg	C R R R R R R R R	Cpy Ncpy Neg	A PNeg	C R R R R R R R R	Cpy Ncpy Neg	A PNeg	C R R R R R R R R	Cpy Ncpy Neg	A PNeg	C R R R R R R R R	Cpy Ncpy Neg	A PNeg
6	C R R R R R R R R	Cpy Ncpy Neg	A PNeg	C R R R R R R R R	Cpy Ncpy Neg	A PNeg	C R R R R R R R R	Cpy Ncpy Neg	A PNeg	C R R R R R R R R	Cpy Ncpy Neg	A PNeg	C R R R R R R R R	Cpy Ncpy Neg	A PNeg
7	C R R R R R R R R	Cpy Ncpy Neg	A PNeg	C R R R R R R R R	Cpy Ncpy Neg	A PNeg	C R R R R R R R R	Cpy Ncpy Neg	A PNeg	C R R R R R R R R	Cpy Ncpy Neg	A PNeg	C R R R R R R R R	Cpy Ncpy Neg	A PNeg
8	C R R R R R R R R	Cpy Ncpy Neg	A PNeg	C R R R R R R R R	Cpy Ncpy Neg	A PNeg	C R R R R R R R R	Cpy Ncpy Neg	A PNeg	C R R R R R R R R	Cpy Ncpy Neg	A PNeg	C R R R R R R R R	Cpy Ncpy Neg	A PNeg
9	C R R R R R R R R	Cpy Ncpy Neg	A PNeg	C R R R R R R R R	Cpy Ncpy Neg	A PNeg	C R R R R R R R R	Cpy Ncpy Neg	A PNeg	C R R R R R R R R	Cpy Ncpy Neg	A PNeg	C R R R R R R R R	Cpy Ncpy Neg	A PNeg
10	C R R R R R R R R	Cpy Ncpy Neg	A PNeg	C R R R R R R R R	Cpy Ncpy Neg	A PNeg	C R R R R R R R R	Cpy Ncpy Neg	A PNeg	C R R R R R R R R	Cpy Ncpy Neg	A PNeg	C R R R R R R R R	Cpy Ncpy Neg	A PNeg

Abbreviations: Par. = parent; C = parent original command; R = parent repeat command; Cpy = compliance within 10 seconds; Ncpy = noncompliance (failure to comply in 10 seconds); Neg = child negative behavior; A = parent approval and praise; PNeg = parent negative behavior.

FIGURE 12.2. Coding form for recording parent-child interactions.

can monitor change due to parent training or other interventions. Research using similar systems and categories (Mash & Barkley, 1986) find most children without behavioral difficulties will comply with over 90% of these commands.

Again, such a direct observational measure has the advantage of assessing the child's behavior in a more or less naturalistic atmosphere and thus may be more ecologically valid. In particular, the coding of parent-child interactions may yield important information that can be used in treatment recommendations and parent training regarding the types of parent behaviors that may be exacerbating the child's behavioral difficulties. Although there is some limitation in the availability of normative data (which could be overcome by clinics establishing local norms) and such procedures do require facilities that may not be available to all clinicians, the direct assessment of the child's behavior nevertheless can be a helpful adjunct to the pen-and-pencil measures and clinical interview.

INTERPRETATION OF TEST FINDINGS

The rating scales, clinical interview, and any laboratory or direct measures should be chosen and administered to yield a comprehensive picture of the child's physical, intellectual, developmental, social, emotional, and behavioral characteristics. The battery should reflect the multidimensional nature of ADHD and enable the clinician to begin to make a differential diagnosis. For example, the developmental, intellectual, and physical information will be particularly important in establishing that the behavioral difficulties observed cannot be attributed to general developmental delay, a language disorder, some type of developmental disorder (e.g., Autism or Pervasive Developmental Disorder), or a physical disorder (e.g., cerebral palsy, significant head injury). The analysis and integration of the data require a knowledge of relevant research and clinical literature (Barkley, 1981; Ross & Ross, 1976, 1982; Weiss & Hechtman, 1986); knowledge of other childhood disorders; skilled clinical judgment in sorting out the pertinent issues; and sufficient resources to obtain multiple types of information from multiple sources (e.g., parents, extended family members, child, teacher, day-care provider, babysitter). In analyzing and integrating the information obtained, the professional has some important factors to consider.

The first is an awareness of the way one conceptualizes ADHD (Barkley, 1987a). If ADHD is viewed as a categorical disorder, where one looks for the mere presence or absence of symptomatology, then the analysis of the findings is relatively straightforward; the examiner, for example, would examine the assessment results for the presence of at least 8 of the 14 DSM-III-R characteristics. However, if ADHD is viewed as a multidimensional disorder lying on a continuum with normal child behavior, then the evaluator must demonstrate not only the presence of symptomatology, but that it occurs with sufficient frequency and severity to distinguish it from the behavior one typically expects from same-age peers. As mentioned earlier in this chapter, this view requires some type of designation regarding the extremes of these continua. Though the behavioral characteristics of many children may be so extreme that they would be classified as deviant regardless of the scale or cutoff points used, others may fall into a borderline range that makes diagnosis more difficult.

Another critical issue is the degree to which symptomatology must be documented in all major environments. Again, if one accepts an all-or-none approach, then the absence of significant behavioral difficulties in all settings (e.g., home, day care/preschool, laboratory) would rule out the diagnosis. Or the variation in the symptoms might be attributed to rater/clinician inexperience or the insensitivity of the measures themselves. In contrast, one may hypothesize that situational variation may occur in children with ADHD and this variation is important in understanding the disorder and in making treatment recommendations (Barkley, 1987a, 1987b). For instance, Barkley (1981, 1982, 1988a) has argued that children with ADHD have difficulties in settings where the consequences for following rules are delayed or infrequent. If one takes this view, then it is important to assess and interpret the child's behavioral difficulties in this manner. Often differences in the child's behavior with one parent or the other can be explained along these lines.

These dilemmas are particularly evident in the diagnosis of ADHD in very young children where (a) there are fewer assessment measures available in this age range; (b) the differentiation of abnormal levels of activity, impulsivity, and attention from typical levels is difficult; and (c) there is a lack of information about the child's behavior in settings other than home and from sources other than the parent.

Establishing that the symptoms are extreme and have been present for longer than 6 months presents another difficulty in this young age group, especially for children aged 3 and younger. For instance, though the symptoms currently present in a 3-year-old may be identified as extreme, can they be distinguished reliably from the "terrible twos" or the "typical boy behavior" that was in evidence 6 months earlier? Determining that the behavior is in fact deviant also may be problematic for parents with a firstborn only child.

In these cases, it may be more appropriate to withhold a diagnosis. Stating that the child demonstrates behaviors indicating that he or she is at risk for developing ADHD may be more accurate. The initial evaluation then would provide a good baseline from which the child's status and the applicability of the diagnosis can be reviewed. In many cases, the diagnosis of risk does not preclude treatment recommendations to reduce the severity of the symptoms. The success or failure of these interventions and any changes in symptoms in the future can be a very helpful piece of information in further refining the diagnosis and treatment plan.

DEVELOPMENT OF TREATMENT RECOMMENDATIONS

Just as ADHD and its assessment are multidimensional, treatment recommendations must be multidimensional as well. Usually recommendations will address those areas that are (a) most salient or severe, (b) of the most significant concern to the parent and/or some other individual making the referral, (c) interfering the most with the child's current functioning, or (d) having the greatest impact on later adjustment (e.g., presence of a conduct disorder). Though numerous treatments have been used with children with ADHD (Barkley, 1981; Ross & Ross, 1982; Silver, 1987), only some of them have proven effective. A few of the most promising treatment options with very young children are reviewed here.

Stimulant Medication

Overwhelming evidence exists for the efficacy of stimulant medication in the treatment of childhood ADHD, with approximately 75% of children over 5 responding positively to the medication (Barkley, 1977a, 1977b; Barkley et al., 1988). The primary effects of the stimulants (e.g., Ritalin, Dexedrine, Cylert) are improved attention span, decreased impulsivity, diminished task-irrelevant activity, and generally decreased disruptive behavior. Secondary effects include increased compliance to commands and instructions (Barkley & Cunningham, 1980); increased productivity on academic assignments (Rapport, Stoner, DuPaul, Birmingham, & Tucker, 1985); increased peer acceptance; decreased parent and teacher reprimands, supervision, and punishment (Barkley, 1985); and occasionally improvements in handwriting. The behavioral action of the medication is short-lived (e.g., ranging from 3 to 8 hours), and thus it must be given more than once a day.

Though the addition of medication to the therapeutic plan can be quite helpful, used alone it cannot remedy all of the many difficulties that these children may experience. Because of this and the fact that many youngsters under the age of 5 do not respond as well to the medication (Barkley et al., 1988), stimulant medication should be used in combination with other treatments or these other treatments should be used alone.

A decision whether to initiate a trial of stimulant medication should be based on (a) the age of the child and the duration and severity of the presenting problems; (b) the history and success of prior treatment efforts; (c) the absence of a personal or family history of tics or Tourette's syndrome; (d) the presence of symptoms of anxiety, which can be determined through rating scales and the use of clinical interviews; (e) parental motivation for such treatment; (f) absence of stimulant abuse in the parents; and (g) the likelihood that parents will employ the medication responsibly and in compliance with physician directions. Ideally, any use of medication should begin with a controlled trial, preferably in the context of double-blind, drug-placebo format, where the child will take a placebo and two or more doses of medication (1 week trial per condition). Clinical ratings would be obtained from parents and teachers, and if possible, supplemented with observations of child behavior on a weekly basis. A more complete description of these procedures can be found in Barkley (1985, 1988b).

Parent Training in Contingency Management

Many parent training programs exist for teaching parents techniques to manage the behavioral difficulties in children (Dangel & Polster, 1984; Forehand & McMahon, 1981). One such program developed by Barkley (1981; 1987c) is based on the skills taught in the program by Forehand and McMahon (1981). Additional sessions are included to provide information to families about the nature of ADHD, how to establish a token reinforcement program, and how to deal with misbehavior in public places. Briefly, the steps of the program involve

1. an overview of ADHD;
2. the causes of child misbehavior;
3. developing and enhancing parental attending skills;
4. attending to child compliance;
5. implementing the home chip/point system;
6. time out from reinforcement;
7. managing children in public places;
8. coping with future behavior problems; and
9. a 1-month review and booster session.

The decision to employ parent training procedures would be based on the information obtained in the initial evaluation with respect to the child's level of noncompliant, oppositional, or defiant behaviors at home (in addition to the primary ADHD symptoms) and the degree to which the parents are experiencing depression or psychiatric difficulties, stress, or marital discord sufficient to interfere with training. In general, parent training can be helpful for children aged 2 years or less to provide parents with the techniques to prevent future problems from arising. In any case, *all* parents should be thoroughly educated about the nature of ADHD, its course and outcome, and useful treatments. Wender (1987), Ingersoll (1988), and Barkley

(1990) (the latter a videotape prepared for parents) are especially useful in this regard.

Referral to Parent-to-Parent Support

Although perhaps not available in every community, referral to a parent-to-parent support group for mothers and fathers of children with ADHD can be a very helpful part of the overall treatment package. These groups provide not only emotional support but information and advocacy as well. They offer something that professional support or intervention cannot—the perspective of "someone who's been there" (Nathanson, 1985). If a support group for parents of ADHD children is not available, there may be a group for parents of children with learning disabilities. Though not all children with ADHD have learning difficulties, they may require special education or resource assistance, and thus the experience of other parents with the educational system would be very helpful and supportive.

Classroom Management

Given that many young children with ADHD will have difficulties in the structured atmosphere of a school environment, whether it be preschool, day care, or kindergarten, some type of classroom management will comprise an important treatment recommendation. This may involve training the teacher in contingency management methods (Barkley, 1981), increased coordination between home and school, and/or referral for additional psychoeducational testing and resource services (e.g., special classroom for children with behavioral difficulties). Token reinforcement programs, home-based evaluation/reinforcement programs, increased attending by teachers to child compliance, in-class time-out procedures, and behavioral contracts all may be helpful. The degree to which classroom management is needed depends on the success with which parent management impacts on the child's difficulties, the degree to which the child demonstrates difficulties in the classroom, the eligibility of the child for special educational services, and, of course, the degree to which the child is participating in a classroom setting.

An integral part of any treatment plan is periodic reassessment and the evaluation of the treatments/programs recommended. As the toddler or preschooler gets older, other treatment options may be helpful or needed. Other treatments that have been used successfully include social skills training; self-control training; problem-solving therapy; individual therapy, to help the child understand what ADHD is and, if he or she is on stimulant medication, what the effects of the medication are; special education treatment; and, in a few cases, residential treatment.

COMMUNICATION OF RESULTS

The most comprehensive assessment and most thoughtfully developed treatment plan will be wasted unless the results and plans can be communicated effectively to the family and other professionals involved. Ideally the communication of diagnostic information should ensure that (a) parents or other professionals obtain a thorough understanding of the results; (b) they understand how the plan developed from these results; and (c) some attempt is made to address their emotional reactions to the diagnostic information and treatment plan presented.

Whether through a report or during a feedback session, one's choice of language is important. Professional jargon can limit the understanding of the parents or even that of a professional from another discipline. This does not mean professional terminology should be avoided entirely, because the parent is likely to encounter the terms in the future. However, care should be taken to explain any technical language. Likewise, the procedures that were used and the process by which the diagnosis was determined should be explained thoroughly. Actively involving the parents and other professionals in the assessment and the subsequent discussion about treatment can be very helpful in ensuring understanding, an individualized and appropriate treatment plan, and follow-through with the plan.

The feedback session and especially the report should include some statement about the representativeness of the data obtained. For example, does the examiner think that the results obtained during the direct evaluation of the child present a valid and reliable estimate of his or her performance in that setting? If not, what are the reasons for questioning the validity of the results and what are the steps to repeat the testing or use information from other sources?

It also is important to stress the child's positive characteristics. As mentioned earlier, this should be the focus of some of the discussion in the clinical interview. Because children with ADHD have so many problematic interactions with parents, adults, and peers, evaluators must help identify and build on their strengths. This is important for the parent as well, as his or her relationship with the child may be strained because of noncompliance and other ADHD symptoms.

Care should be taken to provide feedback sessions and/or a report to all the individuals with whom the child interacts on a regular basis. Ultimately it is the parents' or legal guardian's decision who receives this information, but the professional should stress the importance of having significant individuals informed about ADHD and the treatment recommendations. This is important for many reasons. First, because there may be some situational variability in the child's behavior, often others do not recognize the degree to which the child has difficulty. Teachers or other family members may try to minimize the child's difficulties or attribute them to inadequate parenting. Although certain parental management styles can exacerbate or diminish the symptoms, poor parenting alone cannot cause ADHD. In addition, children with ADHD have difficulty learning any rules, let alone those applied on an inconsistent basis. A consistent approach by all involved is as important a treatment recommendation as any. Individuals who may need to be informed include other family members, such as grandparents; day-care workers; babysitters; preschool teachers; and the child's physician. Sometimes it is helpful to provide the parents with additional copies of the report so that they can distribute them as the need arises.

While the identification of some reason for the child's behavioral or academic difficulties may bring relief at some level, the diagnosis of any difficulty in a child is upsetting. Furthermore, because ADHD is a chronic disorder, in most cases parents cannot rely on the comfort of having a child outgrow the symptoms. In addition to some discussion about the emotional impact of the diagnosis, a thorough discussion about the emotional reactions to the treatment plan is needed as well. Ideally the treatment plan should have been developed collaboratively with the parents, which should minimize some difficulties. Nevertheless, many potential reactions can interfere with the effectiveness of the treatments recommended. For example, some parents are reluctant to employ tokens as reinforcements because they feel they would be "bribing" their child. Explaining why this type of system often proves so helpful with ADHD is critical if families are to implement such recommendations in an effective way. Some families and/or teachers may be reluctant to use stimulant medication (often because of misinformation), while others, looking for a "quick fix," may want to rely on the medication alone and not implement the other needed treatments. Explaining what medication can and cannot do and the need for additional interventions is extremely important.

Sometimes specific emotional reactions are not clearly identified, or the parents may be still responding to the diagnosis itself rather than thinking about treatment. Scheduling several sessions after the diagnostic feedback may be beneficial. Having the parents think about what factors might prevent them from implementing the recommendations or interfere with their ability to do so may be a productive tact. Whatever the approach, a thorough discussion with the family, other professionals, and, where appropriate, the child is essential to the successful implementation of the treatment plan and, most importantly, to empowering the child to reach his or her full potential.

REFERENCES

Abikoff, H., Gittelman-Klein, R., & Klein, D. (1977). Validation of a classroom observation code for hyperactive children. *Journal of Consulting and Clinical Psychology, 45,* 772–783.

Achenbach, T.M., & Edelbrock, C. (1983). *Manual for the Child Behavior Checklist and Revised Child Behavior Profile.* Burlington, VT: University of Vermont, Department of Psychiatry.

American Psychiatric Association. (1978). *Diagnostic and statistical manual of mental disorders* (2nd ed.). Washington, DC: Author.

American Psychiatric Association. (1980). *Diagnostic and statistical manual of mental disorders* (3rd ed.). Washington, DC: Author.

American Psychiatric Association. (1987). *Diagnostic and statistical manual of mental disorders* (rev. 3rd ed.). Washington, DC: Author.

Anastopoulos, A.D., & Barkley, R.A. (1988). Biological factors in attention deficit-hyperactivity disorder. *The Behavior Therapist, 11,* 47–53.

Barkley, R.A. (1977a). The effects of methylphenidate on various measures of activity level and attention in hyperkinetic children. *Journal of Abnormal Child Psychology, 5,* 351–369.

Barkley, R.A. (1977b). A review of stimulant drug research with hyperactive children. *Journal of Child Psychology and Psychiatry, 18,* 137–165.

Barkley, R.A. (1981). *Hyperactive children: A handbook for diagnosis and treatment.* New York: Guilford.

Barkley, R.A. (1982). Specific guidelines for defining hyperactivity in children (Attention Deficit Disorder with Hyperactivity). In B. Lahey & A. Kazdin (Eds.), *Advances in clinical child psychology* (Vol. 5, pp. 137–180). New York: Plenum.

Barkley, R.A. (1985). The social interactions of hyperactive children: Developmental changes, drug effects, and situational variation. In R. McMahon & R. Peters (Eds.), *Childhood disorders: Behavioral-developmental approaches* (pp. 218–243). New York: Brunner/Mazel.

Barkley, R.A. (1987a). The assessment of attention deficit hyperactivity disorder. *Behavioral Assessment, 9,* 207–233.

Barkley, R.A. (1987b). Child behavior rating scales and checklists. In M. Rutter, A. Tuma, & I.S. Lann (Eds.), *Assessment and diagnosis in child psychopathology* (pp. 113–155). New York: Guilford.

Barkley, R.A. (1987c). *Defiant children: A clinician's manual for parent training.* New York: Guilford.

Barkley, R.A. (1988a). Attention deficit disorder with hyperactivity. In E. Mash & L. Terdal (Eds.), *Behavioral assessment of childhood disorders* (2nd ed., pp. 69–104). New York: Guilford.

Barkley, R.A. (1988b). The effects of methylphenidate on the interactions of preschool ADHD children and their mothers. *Journal of the American Academy of Child and Adolescent Psychiatry, 27,* 336–341.

Barkley, R.A. (1990). *AD/HD Video.* (Available from NEAD, P.O. Box 82, Northboro, MA 01532-0082)

Barkley, R.A., & Cunningham, C.E. (1980). The parent-child interactions of hyperactive children and their modification by stimulant drugs. In R. Knights & D. Bakker (Eds.), *Treatment of hyperactive and learning disordered children* (pp. 219–236). Baltimore, MD: University Park Press.

Barkley, R.A., & Edelbrock, C. (1987). Assessing situational variation in children's problem behaviors: The Home and School Situations Questionnaire. In R.J. Prinz (Ed.), *Advances in behavioral assessment of children and families* (Vol. 3, pp. 157–176). Greenwich, CT: JAI.

Barkley, R.A., Fischer, M., Newby, R., & Breen, M. (1988). Development of a multimethod protocol for assessing stimulant drug responses in ADD children. *Journal of Clinical Child Psychology, 17,* 14–24.

Barkley, R.A., Karlsson, J., Pollard, S., & Murphy, J. (1985). Developmental changes in the mother-child interactions of hyperactive boys: Effects of two dose levels of Ritalin. *Journal of Child Psychology and Psychiatry, 26,* 705–715.

Barkley, R.A., & Ullman, D.G. (1975). A comparison of objective measures of activity and distractibility in hyperactive and nonhyperactive children. *Journal of Abnormal Child Psychology, 3,* 231–244.

Bayley, N. (1969). *Bayley Scales of Infant Development.* San Antonio, TX: Psychological Corporation.

Behar, L. (1974). *Manual for the Preschool Behavior Questionnaire.* Unpublished manuscript, Durham, NC.

Breen, M. (1985). *ADD-H in girls: An analysis of attentional, emotional, cognitive, and academic behaviors and parental psychiatric status.* Manuscript submitted for publication.

Campbell, S.B. (1985). Hyperactivity in preschoolers: Correlates and prognostic implications. *Clinical Psychology Review, 5,* 405–428.

Campbell, S.B., Douglas, V.I., & Morganstern, G. (1971). Cognitive styles in hyperactive children and the effect of methylphenidate. *Journal of Child Psychology and Psychiatry, 12,* 55–67.

Campbell, S.B., Ewing, L.J., Breaux, A.M., & Szumowski, E.K. (1986). Parent-referred problem three-year-olds: Follow-up at school entry. *Journal of Child Psychology and Psychiatry, 27,* 473–488.

Campbell, S.B., Szumowski, E.K., Ewing, L.J., Gluck, D.S., & Breaux, A.M. (1982). A multidimensional assessment of parent-identified behavior problem toddlers. *Journal of Abnormal Child Psychology, 10,* 569–591.

Campbell, S.B., Schleifer, M., & Weiss, G. (1978). Continuities in maternal reports and child behaviors over time in hyperactive and comparison groups. *Journal of Abnormal Child Psychology, 6,* 33–45.

Cantwell, D., & Satterfield, J.H. (1978). The prevalence of academic underachievement in hyperactive children. *Journal of Pediatric Psychology, 3,* 168–171.

Carey, W.B., & McDevitt, S.C. (1978). Stability and change in individual temperament diagnosis from infancy to early childhood. *Journal of the American Academy of Child Psychiatry, 17,* 331–337.

Chess, S. (1960). Diagnosis and treatment of the hyperactive child. *New York State Journal of Medicine, 60,* 2379–2385.

Clements, S.D. (1966). *Task force one: Minimal brain dysfunction in children* (National Institute of Neurological Diseases and Blindness Monograph No. 3). Washington, DC: Department of Health, Education, and Welfare.

Clements, S.D., & Peters, J.E. (1962). Minimal brain dysfunction in the school-age child. *Archives of General Psychiatry, 6,* 185–197.

Comings, D.E., & Comings, D.G. (1984). Tourette's syndrome and Attention Deficit Disorder with Hyperactivity: Are they genetically related? *Journal of the American Academy of Child Psychiatry, 23,* 138–146.

Conners, C.K. (1969). A teacher rating scale for use in drug studies with children. *American Journal of Psychiatry, 126,* 884–888.

Conners, C.K. (1973). Rating scales for use in drug studies with children. *Psychopharmacology Bulletin, 9,* 24–84.

Dangel, R.F., & Polster, R.A. (1984). *Parent training.* New York: Guilford.

Denckla, M.B., & Rudel, R.G. (1978). Anomalies of motor development in hyperactive boys. *Annals of Neurology, 3,* 231–233.

Douglas, V.I. (1972). Stop, look, and listen: The problem of sustained attention and impulse control in hyperactive and normal children. *Canadian Journal of Behavioural Science, 4,* 259–282.

Douglas, V.I. (1980). Higher mental processes in hyperactive children: Implications for training. In R. Knights & D. Bakker (Eds.), *Treatment of hyperactive and learning disordered children* (pp. 65–92). Baltimore, MD: University Park Press.

Douglas, V.I. (1983). Attention and cognitive problems. In M. Rutter (Ed.), *Developmental neuropsychiatry* (pp. 280–329). New York: Guilford.

Douglas, V.I., & Peters, K.G. (1979). Toward a clearer definition of the attentional deficit of hyperactive children. In G.A. Hale & M. Lewis (Eds.), *Attention and the development of cognitive skills* (pp. 173–248). New York: Plenum.

Edelbrock, C. (1986). *The Edelbrock Children's Attention/Activity Problems (CAP) Scale.* Worcester, MA: University of Massachusetts Medical Center.

Edelbrock, C., Costello, E.J., & Kessler, M.D. (1984). Empirical corroboration of attention deficit disorder. *Journal of the American Academy of Child Psychiatry, 23,* 285–290.

Eyberg, S.M. (1980). Eyberg Child Behavior Inventory. *Journal of Clinical Child Psychology, 9,* 22–28.

Eyberg, S.M., & Robinson, E.A. (1982). Parent-child interaction training: Effects on family functioning. *Journal of Clinical Child Psychology, 11,* 130–137.

Eyberg, S.M., & Ross, A.W. (1978). Assessment of child behavior problems: The validation of a new inventory. *Journal of Clinical Child Psychology, 7,* 113–116.

Forehand, R., & McMahon, R. (1981). *Helping the noncompliant child: A clinician's guide to parent training.* New York: Guilford.

Golden, G.S. (1983). Movement disorders in children: Tourette syndrome. *Developmental and Behavioral Pediatrics, 3,* 209–216.
Gordon, M. (1979). The assessment of impulsivity and mediating behaviors in hyperactive and non-hyperactive children. *Journal of Abnormal Child Psychology, 7,* 317–326.
Gordon, M. (1983). *The Gordon Diagnostic System.* Boulder, CO: Clinical Diagnostic Systems.
Gordon, M. (1985, August). *Assessment of ADD/Hyperactivity: Research on the Gordon Diagnostic System.* Symposium presented at the 93rd Annual Meeting of the American Psychological Association, Los Angeles.
Goyette, C.H., Conners, C.K., & Ulrich, R.F. (1978). Normative data for Revised Conners Parent and Teacher Rating Scales. *Journal of Abnormal Child Psychology, 6,* 221–236.
Gross, A.M. (1984). Behavioral interviewing. In T.H. Ollendick & M. Hersen (Eds.), *Child behavioral assessment* (pp. 61–79). New York: Pergamon.
Hartsough, C.S., & Lambert, N.M. (1985). Medical factors in hyperactive and normal children: Prenatal, developmental, and health history findings. *American Journal of Orthopsychiatry, 55,* 190–201.
Horn, W.F., Ialongo, N., Popovich, S., & Peradotto, D. (1984, August). *An evaluation of a multi-method treatment approach with hyperactive children.* Paper presented at the 92nd Annual Meeting of the American Psychological Association, Toronto.
Hubert, N.C., Wachs, T.D., Peters-Martin, P., & Gandour, M.J. (1982). The study of early temperament: Measurement and conceptual issues. *Child Development, 53,* 571–600.
Ingersoll, B. (1988). *Hyperactive children.* New York: Doubleday.
Jacob, R.G., O'Leary, K.D., & Rosenblad, C. (1978). Formal and informal classroom settings: Effects on hyperactivity. *Journal of Abnormal Child Psychology, 6,* 47–59.
Johnston, C., Pelham, W.E., & Murphy, H.A. (1985). Peer relationships in ADDH and normal children: A developmental analysis of peer and teacher ratings. *Journal of Abnormal Child Psychology, 13,* 89–100.
Kagan, J. (1966). Reflection-impulsivity: The generality and dynamics of conceptual tempo. *Journal of Abnormal Psychology, 71,* 17–24.
Kagan, J., Rosman, B.L., Day, D., Albert, J., & Philips, W. (1964). Information processing in the child: Significance of analytic and reflective attitudes. *Psychological Monographs, 78* (1, Whole No. 578).
Kendall, P.C., & Braswell, L. (1985). *Cognitive-behavioral therapy for impulsive children.* New York: Guilford.
Klee, S.H., & Garfinkel, B.D. (1983). The computerized continuous performance task: A new measure of inattention. *Journal of Abnormal Child Psychology, 11,* 487–496.
Loney, J., & Milich, R.S. (1981). Hyperactivity, inattention, and aggression in clinical practice. In M. Wolraich & D.K. Routh (Eds.), *Advances in behavioral pediatrics* (Vol. 2, pp. 113–147). Greenwich, CT: JAI.
Mash, E.J., & Barkley, R.A. (1986). Assessment of family interaction with the Response-Class Matrix. In R. Prinz (Ed.), *Advances in behavioral assessment of children and families* (Vol. 2, pp. 29–67). Greenwich, CT: JAI.
Mash, E.J., & Johnston, C. (1983). Parental perceptions of child behavior problems, parenting self-esteem, and mothers' reported stress in younger and older hyperactive and normal children. *Journal of Consulting and Clinical Psychology, 51,* 68–99.
Mash, E.J., Terdal, L., & Anderson, K. (1973). The Response-Class Matrix: A procedure for recording parent-child interactions. *Journal of Consulting and Clinical Psychology, 40,* 163–164.
Milich, R. (1984). Cross-sectional and longitudinal observations of activity level and sustained attention in a normative sample. *Journal of Abnormal Child Psychology, 12,* 261–276.

Milich, R., & Kramer, J. (1985). Reflections on impulsivity: An empirical investigation of impulsivity as a construct. In K. Gadow & I. Bialer (Eds.), *Advances in learning and behavioral disabilities* (Vol. 3, pp. 36-79). Greenwich, CT: JAI.

Milich, R., Landau, S., & Loney, J. (1981, August). *The inter-relationships among hyperactivity, aggression, and impulsivity.* Paper presented at the 89th Annual Meeting of the American Psychological Association, Los Angeles.

Milich, R., Loney, J., & Landau, S. (1982). Independent dimensions of hyperactivity and aggression: A validation with playroom observation data. *Journal of Abnormal Psychology, 91,* 183-198.

Miller, L.C. (1984). *Louisville Behavior Checklist manual.* Los Angeles: Western Psychological Services.

Montague, J., & Swarbrick, L. (1975). Effect of amphetamine in hyperkinetic children: Stimulant or sedative? A pilot study. *Developmental Medicine and Child Neurology, 17,* 293-298.

Morganstern, K.P. (1976). Behavioral interviewing: The initial stages of assessment. In M. Hersen & A.S. Bellack (Eds.), *Behavioral assessment: A practical handbook* (pp. 51-76). New York: Pergamon.

Nathanson, M. (1985). *Supporting and maintaining parent support groups.* Washington, DC: Association for the Care of Children's Health.

Packard, T., Robinson, E.A., & Grove, D.C. (1983). The effect of training procedures on the maintenance of parental relationship building skills. *Journal of Clinical Child Psychology, 12,* 181-186.

Patterson, G.R. (1982). *Coercive family process.* Eugene, OR: Castalia.

Pelham, W.E., & Bender, M.E. (1982). Peer relationships in hyperactive children: Description and treatment. In K. Gadow & E. Bialer (Eds.), *Advances in learning and behavioral disabilities* (Vol. 1, pp. 365-436). Greenwich, CT: JAI.

Pollard, S., Ward, E.M., & Barkley, R.A. (1983). The effects of parent training on the parent-child interactions of hyperactive boys. *Child and Family Therapy, 5,* 51-69.

Porrino, L.J., Rapoport, J.L., Behar, D., Sceery, W., Ismond, D.R., & Bunney, W.E. (1983). A naturalistic assessment of the motor activity of hyperactive boys. *Archives of General Psychiatry, 40,* 681-687.

Prior, M., Leonard, A., & Wood, G. (1983). A comparison study of preschool children diagnosed as hyperactive. *Journal of Pediatric Psychology, 8,* 191-207.

Rapport, M.D., Stoner, G., DuPaul, G.J., Birmingham, B.K., & Tucker, S. (1985). Methylphenidate in hyperactive children: Differential effects of dose on academic, learning, and social behavior. *Journal of Abnormal Child Psychology, 13,* 227-244.

Roberts, M. (1979). *A manual for the Restricted Academic Playroom Situation.* Iowa City, IA: Author.

Robinson, E.A., & Eyberg, S.M. (1981). The Dyadic Parent-Child Interaction Coding System: Standardization and validation. *Journal of Consulting and Clinical Psychology, 49,* 245-250.

Ross, D.M., & Ross, S.A. (1976). *Hyperactivity: Research, theory, and action.* New York: Wiley.

Ross, D.M., & Ross, S.A. (1982). *Hyperactivity: Current issues, research, and theory* (2nd ed.). New York: Wiley.

Rosvold, H.E., Mirsky, A.F., Sarason, I., Bransome, E.D., & Beck, L.H. (1956). A continuous performance test of brain damage. *Journal of Consulting Psychology, 20,* 343-350.

Routh, D.K., & Roberts, R.D. (1972). Minimal brain dysfunction in children: Failure to find evidence for a behavioral syndrome. *Psychological Reports, 31,* 307-314.

Routh, D.K., & Schroeder, C.S. (1976). Standardized playroom measures as indices of hyperactivity. *Journal of Abnormal Child Psychology, 4,* 199-207.

Routh, D.K., Schroeder, C.S., & O'Tuama, L. (1974). Development of activity level in children. *Developmental Psychology, 10,* 163–168.
Safer, D.J., & Allen, D. (1976). *Hyperactive children.* Baltimore, MD: University Park Press.
Salkind, N.J., & Nelson, C.F. (1980). A note on the developmental nature of reflection-impulsivity. *Developmental Psychology, 16,* 237–238.
Silver, L.B. (1987). The "magic cure": A review of current controversial approaches for treating learning disabilities. *Journal of Learning Disabilities, 20,* 498–512.
Sleator, E.K., & Ullmann, R.K. (1981). Can the physician diagnose hyperactivity in the office? *Pediatrics, 67,* 13–17.
Stewart, M.A., Thach, B.T., & Freidin, M.R. (1970). Accidental poisoning and the hyperactive child syndrome. *Diseases of the Nervous System, 31,* 403–407.
Still, G.F. (1902). Some abnormal psychical conditions in children. *Lancet, 1,* 1008–1012, 1077–1082, 1163–1168.
Strauss, A.A., & Lehtinen, L.E. (1947). *Psychopathology and education of the brain-injured child.* New York: Grune & Stratton.
Tarver-Behring, S., Barkley, R., & Karlsson, J. (1985). The mother-child interactions of hyperactive boys and their normal siblings. *American Journal of Orthopsychiatry, 55,* 202–209.
Thomas, A., Chess, S., Birch, H.G., Hertzig, M.E., & Korn, S. (1963). *Behavioral individuality in early childhood.* New York: New York University Press.
Trites, R.L., Blouin, A.G., & Laprade, K. (1982). Factor analysis of the Conners Teacher Rating Scale based on a large normative sample. *Journal of Consulting and Clinical Psychology, 50,* 615–623.
Trites, R.L., Dugas, F., Lynch, G., & Ferguson, H.B. (1979). Incidence of hyperactivity. *Journal of Pediatric Psychology, 4,* 179–188.
Trites, R.L., Tryphonas, H., & Ferguson, H.B. (1980). Diet treatment for hyperactive children with food allergies. In R. Knights, & D. Bakker (Eds.), *Treatment of hyperactive and learning disordered children* (pp. 151–166). Baltimore, MD: University Park Press.
Tryon, W.W. (1984). Principles and methods of mechanically measuring motor activity. *Behavioral Assessment, 6,* 129–140.
Ullman, D.G., Barkley, R.A., & Brown, H.W. (1978). The behavioral symptoms of hyperkinetic children who successfully responded to stimulant drug treatment. *American Journal of Orthopsychiatry, 48,* 425–437.
Ullmann, R.K. (1984). *Teacher ratings useful in screening learning disabled from attention deficit disordered (ADD-H) children.* Unpublished manuscript, University of Illinois, Urbana.
Ullmann, R.K., Sleator, E.K., & Sprague, R.L. (1984). A new rating scale for diagnosis and monitoring of ADD children. *Psychopharmacology Bulletin, 20,* 160–164.
Wahler, R.G., House, A.E., & Stambaugh, E.E. (1976). *Ecological assessment of child problem behavior.* New York: Pergamon.
Webster-Stratton, C. (1984). Randomized trial of two parent training programs for families with conduct-disordered children. *Journal of Consulting and Clinical Psychology, 52,* 666–678.
Webster-Stratton, C., & Eyberg, S.M. (1982). Child temperament: Relationship with child behavior problems and parent-child interactions. *Journal of Clinical Child Psychology, 11,* 123–129.
Wechsler, D. (1974). *Wechsler Intelligence Scale for Children–Revised.* San Antonio, TX: Psychological Corporation.
Weiss, G., & Hechtman, L. (1986). *Hyperactive children grown up.* New York: Guilford.
Weiss, G., Hechtman, L., & Perlman, T. (1978). Hyperactives as young adults: School,

employer, and self-rating scales obtained during ten-year follow-up evaluation. *American Journal of Orthopsychiatry, 48,* 438–445.

Wender, P.H. (1971). *Minimal brain dysfunction in children.* New York: Wiley.

Wender, P.H. (1987). *The hyperactive child, adolescent, and adult.* New York: Oxford University Press.

Werry, J.S. (1985, June). *Differential diagnosis of ADD and conduct disorders.* Paper presented at the International Workshop on Attention Deficit Disorders, Groningen, The Netherlands.

Werry, J.S., & Sprague, R.L. (1968). Hyperactivity. In C.G. Costello (Ed.), *Symptoms of psychopathology* (pp. 397–417). New York: Wiley.

Werry, J., Weiss, G., & Douglas, V. (1964). Studies of the hyperactive child: I. Some preliminary findings. *Canadian Psychiatric Association Journal, 9,* 120–130.

Zettle, R.D., & Hayes, S.C. (1982). Rule-governed behavior: A potential theoretical framework for cognitive-behavioral therapy. *Advances in cognitive-behavioral research* (Vol. 1, pp. 73–118). New York: Academic Press.

13

Assessment of Children with Autism and Pervasive Developmental Disorder

LEE M. MARCUS, PH.D., MARGARET LANSING, M.ED., & ERIC SCHOPLER, PH.D.

In over two decades of practice and research at Division TEACCH (*T*reatment and *E*ducation of *A*utistic and related *C*ommunication-handicapped *Ch*ildren), the North Carolina statewide program for autistic children, adolescents, and adults and their families (Schopler, Mesibov, Shigley, & Bashford, 1984), the assessment and treatment of the preschool population has been an integral component of both the present program and its predecessor, the Child Research Project (Reichler & Schopler, 1976). With the passage of PL 99–457 and a greater awareness of developmental disabilities in the young child, the TEACCH program has seen a marked increase in the number of preschool referrals. As a result, each year approximately 200 autistic or pervasive developmentally disordered (PDD) young children are evaluated in a TEACCH Center across the state.

Before addressing the specific procedures involved in the assessment of autistic and PDD preschoolers, it is helpful to review some general principles or concepts basic to the TEACCH philosophy (Schopler, 1987). These fundamental concepts are reflected in the clinical and educational methods that will be described later:

1. Autism is best understood as a developmental disability and not an emotional disturbance. The nature of the disorder is such that the cognitive, communicative, and social learning processes are impaired at least to a mild degree and often more seriously. The deviant and maladaptive behaviors manifested by autistic children are the results of such deficits and the absence of environmental adaptation to these deficits.
2. Autism may be the most heterogeneous of the developmental disabilities and thus requires individualization and flexibility in its assessment and treatment.
3. The problems the autistic child has in organizing and understanding his or her world necessitates the use of a structured approach (Schopler, Brehm, Kinsbourne, & Reichler, 1971). This involves the consistent use of a predictable work routine, the physical placement and arrangement of materials, plus a demonstration of the action requested and/or physically helping the child through the activity.
4. Parents and professionals need to work together in a collaborative way, based

on mutual respect and trust. Beginning with the assessment process, the goals are to facilitate the parent-child relationship and to help families cope effectively with this chronic disorder.
5. Staff involved in the assessment of and intervention with autistic children are generalists who are expected to know and, when needed, to help with all aspects of the special problems of these children and their families.
6. An overriding purpose of the program is to improve each child's adaptation in two interacting ways: to enhance the child's skills and competencies, and to help the environment accommodate to the child's deficits.

Issues in Identification and Diagnosis

Professionals often raise the question of the feasibility and appropriateness of making an early diagnosis of autism. Many are concerned that labeling a young child with such a permanent condition may be unfair to the family or perhaps negatively predetermine the child's future. Although the possibility of misdiagnosis certainly exists, and many young children with developmental problems are hard to identify as having autism, our experience is that, with careful evaluation using appropriate methods, a diagnosis of autism can be made reliably. More importantly, parents benefit from this early accurate information for several reasons. First, such information helps the family understand and gain control over their child's situation. Second, an accurate diagnosis avoids confusion, uncertainties, and delays of appropriate services. Families often are confused and annoyed by vague classifications such as "communication disordered with autistic features" or "developmental delays with autistic-like behavior." Third, early diagnosis helps with treatment planning. The principles of structure, individualization, parent involvement, and an emphasis on socialization and communication can be implemented more effectively once the underlying condition has been established.

Can an early diagnosis ever be harmful? If the diagnosis interferes with proper treatment because there has not been a careful assessment and individualization of the child's developmental profile, then problems can arise. If reassessments are not carried out periodically during the early years, a child whose autistic characteristics have significantly diminished may be inappropriately "tracked" and be prevented from receiving more useful services. If the clinician overlooks other possible conditions such as mental retardation or hearing or visual impairments, then making an early diagnosis of autism would be considered harmful. However, negative consequences can be avoided by a thorough understanding of the disorder and a systematic approach to diagnosis and assessment. There have been occasions when a child was misdiagnosed and the child and family have not suffered because of it. This can happen when helpful teaching and behavior management advice has benefitted the child in spite of misdiagnosis. Sometimes when the diagnosis is later changed to one more benign (e.g., language delay), the family usually expresses a sense of relief, while appreciating the direct help they have received. By contrast, parents who have failed to obtain an early diagnosis are often frustrated in their efforts to get needed help and become increasingly cynical about the professional's responsiveness to their situation (Akerley, 1988; Marcus, 1977).

The identification and diagnosis of autism involves the documentation of the major features of the disorder. For the purposes of this chapter, only the key features of the primary deficits are touched on; the reader should consult review articles and related materials for more detailed information (Cohen, Paul, & Volkmar, 1987; Rutter & Schopler, 1987; Schopler, 1983).

Language and Communication

All autistic individuals suffer from severe impairments in communication. Approximately half the population is essentially mute; the large majority of the rest are quite limited in receptive and expressive language (Fay & Schuler, 1980). Those who attain higher levels of communication development continue to have difficulties in processing and using complex reasoning: they tend to be concrete and inflexible in expressing their ideas (Ricks & Wing, 1975). Recent research in both normal child development and autism has highlighted the basic importance of pragmatics or the social functions of communication (Beisler & Tsai, 1983; Bruner, 1975; Watson, Schaffer, Lord, & Schopler, 1989). This area appears to be particularly deficient in autistic persons even when they reach a reasonable level of linguistic competence. Thus, in contrast to a mentally retarded or aphasic child of comparable overall ability, the autistic child lacks an understanding of what is involved in communication and, thus, fails to utilize his or her available language skills.

Social Skills

Related to the problems in communication are the deficits in social development (Schopler & Mesibov, 1986). Described by Kanner (1943) in terms of emotional withdrawal, this impairment is better understood as an inability to grasp the rules of social interaction and reciprocity (Wing & Gould, 1979). Autistic individuals fail to relate adequately to others, not necessarily because of indifference or desired avoidance but because they have been prevented by their disability from learning the essentials of normal human exchange. This becomes evident in observing older autistic children or adolescents, who may stay in close proximity to others and appear to be interested in interacting but either initiate little or act bizarrely. This inability is also apparent in higher level individuals who try to communicate and interact but lack social judgment. They are intrusive, show exaggerated naivete, and are not familiar with the nuances of conversational exchange (Mesibov & Shea, 1980).

Ritualistic Behavior

Autistic individuals tend to relate in unusual ways to objects and events, often perseverating in a behavior or ritualistically repeating a routine. Along with the deficits in language and relatedness, Wing considers the failure of the development of play and imagination to be a hallmark deficit of children with autism, distinguishing this group from nonautistic mentally retarded individuals (Wing & Gould, 1979). This deficit is linked to Kanner's (1943) description of the need to maintain sameness, namely the repetitive and ritualistic play patterns that reflect limited creativity and conceptualization. The combination of perceptual and cognitive disabilities leads to unusually strong reactions to the unanticipated changes in the environment as well as stereotypic use of materials (e.g., repetitive banging, flipping light switches, lining up objects). At higher levels of development, play shows some degree of variety and spontaneity but is typically an elaborated set pattern indicative of limited use of imagination. For example, a child may carry out some pretend play with a toy garage and a car but repeat the same sequence with little variation.

Irregularities in Development and Learning

Historically, the most misunderstood aspect of autism has been the notion that children with this disorder are of normal intellectual potential. The reasons for this belief stemmed from several factors: Autistic children have a typically attractive and "normal" appearance; their gross motor development is usually adequate; their extremes of behavior suggest an "emotional problem" rather than a cognitive one; and the occasional presence of a "peak" skill such as number calculations or excellent motor agility led to the impression of "hidden" intelligence (DeMyer, 1979). The reality is that most autistic individuals are mentally retarded and that only a very small percentage (less than 5%) can be considered to have average or above average ability in all areas (DeMyer, 1979). What is characteristic of this population is unevenness in development, in that certain nonverbal skills, such as visual-spatial, visual memory, and gross motor abilities, are more intact than language, complex problem solving, and sequential processing. A second aspect of the learning disorder is the fluctuations and irregularities in rates of learning over periods of time. The inconsistency of these children, resulting in periods of plateauing alternating with seemingly rapid learning, is a factor to be considered in the planning and implementation of educational services, particularly in the early phases of a program.

In the assessment of autistic individuals the clinician needs to be concerned with severe attentional and organizational problems, unusual sensory responses (e.g., hypersensitivity to sounds), preoccupation with visual or tactile stimuli, or diminished responsiveness to ordinary stimuli.

In diagnosing the young autistic child, the clinician should be aware that there are several courses of development that have been described by parents and researchers (DeMyer, 1979). One course involves generally slow development across all areas of functioning, with increasingly differentiated symptoms of the communication handicap and the lack of relatedness. A second involves apparent normal development until 18–24 months, then a marked regression or at least a failure to continue developing normally. A third pattern is normal development for approximately a year, then a gradual falling off or slowed rate of cognitive and communicative growth.

The Assessment Process

Certain methods and procedures have been found effective for assessing preschool children with autism. In addition to choosing specific developmental, psychological, language, and adaptive behavior instruments, however, professionals also must address prediagnostic staffing, parental involvement, and the interpretive process, as well as the behavior management strategies that are often necessary in testing the autistic preschooler. As background for this process, it is useful to review briefly the major content areas a comprehensive assessment should cover. A detailed discussion of these areas or domains can be found in Watson and Marcus (1988).

Assessment Domains

Social skill development is an essential area to evaluate in the understanding of an autistic preschool child (Olley, 1986). Broadly speaking two components can be assessed: the child's initiation and response to social interaction, and his or her conformity to social rules. Specifically, the clinician should note the child's initiation and attention to gaze, use of and responsiveness to facial expressions, the development of social attachments and peer relations, how the child uses his or her body to initiate or respond to social interactions (e.g., approaches or stands close to others), and the type and level of interfering behavior (e.g., self-stimulatory behavior, complex rituals and repetitive routines, difficulty handling transitions). With respect to conformity to social rules, the clinician should assess the child's awareness and respect of boundaries, the appropriate handling of materials, the use of body, and the appropriateness of vocalizations and verbalizations.

A second area for assessment is communication, another primary deficit in autism. While it is important to assess the structure and semantics of the child's language, it is equally or more important to evaluate how he or she uses language to communicate (Watson et al., 1989). What distinguishes the language of the autistic youngster from other developmentally disabled children is his or her inadequate use of available skills for communication purposes. The assessment process should cover the following functions of communication: communicative intent, means, content, context, and comprehension. Alongside *intent* are the purposes or functions of communication, such as requesting or giving information. The child's *means* may be verbal or nonverbal, appropriate or inappropriate, simple or complex. *Content* involves the type and range of concepts the child communicates, *context* the situations in which communication does or does not occur, such as with specific persons or places. Finally, it is necessary to evaluate the child's *comprehension* of language and communication. Parents and others closely associated with the child commonly will assume more understanding than is actually the case. Difficult, oppositional behavior often is the result of an inability to understand what the adult is saying and is not due to willfulness or negativism.

The third assessment area is cognitive functioning, which, for the preschooler, includes play with objects, imitative abilities, the development of preacademic concepts and skills, and social cognition. The clinician's interest concerns the abstract reasoning and problem solving inferred from the child's use of objects, play, or capacity to imitate. Although cognition cannot be totally independent of language development, it is important to assess the nonverbal components of learning. Relevant for understanding the child's cognitive potential are the indices of spontaneous and imaginative thinking, flexible problem solving, and reasoning as opposed to rote learning. The range and variety of uses of objects are clues to the child's cognitive development. It also is becoming increasingly recognized that there is a strong cognitive component to social development in normal children (Rutter, 1983), and the social deficits in autism consequently reflect underlying cognitive deficiencies. Assessing the child's understanding of social rules, including peer play, helps clarify our understanding of his or her cognitive abilities. In the TEACCH Centers these concepts and issues are applied in the procedures described below.

Prediagnostic Staffing

The meeting to review information prior to the assessment is helpful in preparing the diagnostic team for the main issues to be addressed. In preparation, both the referral source and the family should have been contacted by a clinic staff therapist. The referral source provides information concerning the reasons for requesting the evaluation, such as clarification of diagnosis or need for specialized treatment. Previous diagnostic and treatment reports are obtained and incorporated into the background information that is presented at the staffing.

A telephone interview with the parents, typically the mother, reveals the family's concerns. Usually their questions center around why the child is not talking, how to help him or her behave better, or some aspects of self-help skills like toilet training. In this preliminary contact, the therapist tries to get a sense of how well the parents understand their child's problems, how motivated they are to seek professional guidance, and the nature and degree of stress being experienced.

Parents are asked to complete a history form and an informal open-ended questionnaire. The history form includes (a) demographic data; (b) medical information, including checklists on pregnancy history, birth history, neonatal period, developmental milestones, medical and other professionals who have been involved with the child, illnesses, and medications; and (c) a behavior checklist, which gives a clear picture of the amount of atypical behavioral symptomatology, both historically and currently, that the parents have observed. The history form also covers school history (usually less relevant for the preschooler) and a family tree, listing a wide range of medical and developmental conditions and their relationship to their child.

Complementing the more objective data of the history form is a questionnaire completed separately by both parents. Parents are given ample space to comment on a typical day with their child, their main problems and concerns, what is most distressing, what is most gratifying, effects on other aspects of the parent's life, and what type of help they want and expect from the evaluation. Interestingly, parents often write at length and with considerable candor about their feelings, worries, and hopes. The moving passages provided in these short essays sensitize the diagnostic team to the personal side of the clinical process. The parent perspective is reinforced by this information so that, whatever the findings concerning the child, the staff is reminded that the needs and concerns of the total family are the ultimate focus of the diagnostic day.

The prediagnostic staffing takes approximately a half hour. Participants include the staff involved in the assessment, representatives of the referring agency, psychologists, and other trainees and visitors. Background material is presented by the staff therapist assigned to do the parent interview (at TEACCH this role is called the Parent Consultant; in other settings, it may be the clinic social worker) and is based on the referral reports and completed parent questionnaires. The reason for the referral, previous evaluation data, medical and developmental histories, a summary of the behavioral checklist, and parental concerns and expectations are covered. If present, the representative from the referral agency can clarify questions or supplement the written information.

Schedule of Diagnostic Day

The diagnostic evaluation is completed within one day. Although there are some clinicians who believe that a comprehensive evaluation should be conducted over a lengthy timeframe, including, perhaps, an inpatient stay (e.g., DeMyer, 1979), the experience with the TEACCH program has clearly demonstrated that the process can be carried out within a single day, provided that the assessment involves appropriate test instruments, in-depth interview of parents, and inclusion of relevant observations and reports from other sources. Prior to the TEACCH evaluation, families typically have had one or more contacts with professionals and are aware of the importance of the more specialized evaluation for autism. Their anxiety level is usually high, and it is essential to deal with their questions on the diagnostic day instead of postponing them to a later date. Our experience also has demonstrated that clinic staff are more efficient in assessing and interpreting diagnostic data and then conveying the results to parents if the process is contained within the shorter span of time.

Following the prediagnostic staffing, the parents, staff, and clinic director (or head of the diagnostic team) meet for a brief overview of the schedule and purposes of the evaluation. At this initial meeting, the parents are asked for the questions they hope to have answered by the assessment. Typical questions concern the cause of the child's problems; why he or she does not talk, play, socialize, and so forth like a normal child; the diagnosis; and the future. Not all parents articulate the same concerns; many initially are guarded about their feelings or mistrustful of the professionals because of negative past experiences (Marcus, 1977). The director can help by gently raising issues that would be useful for discussion (e.g., "Do you want us to give our opinion about what problems your child is having?"). Later in the day, during the interpretive conference, these same questions and concerns are answered and discussed.

At TEACCH, the various diagnostic testing and assessment sessions follow this meeting, which involve the developmental-educational evaluation using the Psychoeducational Profile-Revised (Schopler & Reichler, 1979; Schopler, Reichler, Bashford, Lansing, & Marcus, 1990) and the Childhood Autism Rating Scale (Schopler, Reichler, & Renner, 1986); the parent interview, which is problem focused and includes the Vineland Adaptive Behavior Scales (Sparrow, Balla, & Cicchetti, 1984); a medical screening; and the psychological testing. The staff and parent interpretive conferences conclude the diagnostic day. The next sections detail these procedures and provide supplementary information about tests not routinely used at TEACCH but found useful in other programs.

Developmental Testing

Understanding what is both normal and atypical about the autistic child is the underlying principle of assessing developmental functioning. In an earlier section, three major areas for assessment were described that are central to the documentation of the specific developmental irregularities observed in preschool children with autism. The pioneering research and clinical experience of the TEACCH program highlighted the importance of developmental considerations in the diagnostic evaluation of autism (Schopler & Reichler, 1979). As a result, the Psychoeducational Profile or PEP was developed as a method of comprehensively assessing developmental and educational functioning, as well as identifying pathological or atypical behaviors of autistic and other similarly disabled children. It will be described in detail as an example of a test that enables the clinician to gain a thorough understanding of the skills, deficits, learning style, and idiosyncracies of an autistic child.

The administration of any test to an autistic preschooler requires an appreciation of the necessity for structuring and adjusting the test situation to meet the child's atypical responses. The PEP is designed with maximum flexibility in both its scoring and administrative procedures to accommodate to the child.

There are several problems faced by an examiner that require different strategies and responses (Marcus & Baker, 1986). The issue of "testability" (Schopler & Reichler, 1971) usually means that the clinician has chosen an inappropriate test, either too high developmentally or with too much language, or has not taken into account the child's unique deficits and behavioral patterns. These include severe communication deficits; deficits in social judgment and relating to people; problems in attention, organization, and perception; motivational deficits; an uneven pattern of development; and other atypical behaviors such as body stereotypies and perseveration.

By recognizing the major deficits of autism from the testing perspective, the examiner is taking the first step toward the anticipation of problems and preparation for conducting the evaluation successfully. It is important to take the child's viewpoint and understand the reality that he or she has constructed because of cognitive, communicative, and perceptual limitations. The child may not understand our expectations and thus is unable to cooperate rather than deliberately engaging in a battle of wills. The compliance issue often is stated as a "can't versus won't" argument. By assuming that the child *won't* comply, the examiner is forced to rely exclusively on authority and control with a youngster who may be experiencing considerable confusion over expectations. By taking the alternative position, that the child cannot understand, the examiner has many more options to explore. Employing these options can solve the puzzle of untestability. The following general guidelines may help to generate options in assessment methods.

Flexibility in test administration. The optimal test situation is one that combines an appropriate instrument with sensitivity to the child's difficulties regarding communication, attention, and social demands. This may require flexibility in (a) altering sequences of items so that stressful language items are balanced by more enjoyable visual-motor tasks; (b) modifying instructions so that the task is clearly understood; (c) providing frequent breaks when necessary; or (d) simplifying a task to give the child a successful experience. The examiner should not be a slave to test protocol. The observations gathered in interacting with the child and the information obtained from experimenting with test materials and procedures can be as useful as the actual scores.

Establishing an appropriate structure. Most of the management problems encountered in a test situation can be prevented by structuring the environment and establishing a set of rules and routines not dependent on verbal explanations. The room should be cleared of extraneous materials and should have separate work and play areas (for example, a table and chair on one side, a rug or mat with toys on the other). A confused, disorganized youngster can be led through the routine of completing a task, then allowed to go to the play area for a few minutes. The release from task demands can begin to serve as a reinforcer for work and give the child a predictable, orderly routine without the use of language that may not be understood. A finished box can be placed at one end of the table to demonstrate the idea of task completion. Higher level children may be helped by a visual token system that conveys how many tasks have to be performed before a break. The establishment of such structures and routines recognizes and deals with the child's basic deficits in communication and organization.

Alternative methods of communication. As noted above, verbal language may not be sufficient to convey the rules of the testing situation. The examiner should expect to use dramatic gestures, exaggerated affect, manual prompts (sometimes direct physical guidance), or other visual concrete aids as a means of communicating with many autistic children. Verbal language must be kept uncomplicated, free of idiomatic expressions, and limited to the task at hand. If the examining situation provides sufficient time, experimenting with simple manual signs or a picture system may prove useful diagnostically and may help with behavior management.

Increasing motivation. To a lesser degree the diagnostician faces the same frustration experienced by parents, teachers, and clinicians in trying to find a consistent set of incentives or rewards for the autistic child. During an assessment situation the child need only be motivated for a relatively short time; often, if appropriate test selection and environmental structure have been achieved, specially devised reinforcers may not be required. The legitimacy of tangible rewards such as food under certain circumstances has been reviewed by Freeman (1976). However, other more natural contingencies may be equally effective. For example, asking the parents about the child's preferences, such as a favorite object (which may be brought to the session) or activity (being tickled or swung about) can provide information with which to set up a task-reward routine. For children uncomfortable with test demands, being allowed to have a break (or a release from being intruded on) may serve as a reinforcer and help establish a work-then-play routine. Permitting the child to engage in minor self-stimulatory behavior contingent on task effort may be reinforcing.

The examiner may find that for some children the concept of contingent reinforcement has not yet been established and thus the value of any specific reward is marginal. Again, rather than engaging in a battle for control, the examiner should view each child's idiosyncratic behaviors and tendencies as currently essential to his or her coping style and incorporate them into an effective assessment strategy.

Handling attentional problems and atypical behaviors. Attentional problems and other behaviors that interfere with testing (such as hand staring, perseverative play with a material) can occur because of task difficulty or confusion with task demands, or because of some internally determined, organically based factor under the child's limited control. Simplifying the task or instructions, moving back to an easier task, distracting the child by providing a break, or increasing incentives may help if the problem is due to task difficulty.

If the task does not seem too difficult, then the examiner may need to experiment with a variety of intrusive measures or environmental manipulations to gain attention control. These may include (a) presenting test materials at the moment when the child attends; (b) interrupting perseverative responses; (c) repeating test instructions; and (d) refocusing attention to task by snapping fingers, touching the child's hand, or tapping the table. The examiner's timing is often a critical variable. For visual distractibility, presenting materials within the child's visual field and removing potentially distracting materials are useful techniques. Sometimes simply waiting out a period of self-stimulation or inattention is the reasonable strategy.

As noted earlier, the PEP is a test that allows the examiner to provide the necessary structure to get accurate and meaningful information concerning developmental functioning. The PEP has three primary features: it assesses skills in seven areas of development (imitation, perception, fine motor, gross motor, eye-hand integration, cognitive performance, and cognitive verbal), it provides for rating unusual or pathological behavior in five areas (affect, relatedness, play and interest in materials, sensory modes, and language), and it can be used to develop a teaching program through the analysis of its results (Schopler, Reichler, & Lansing, 1980). A unique aspect of the scoring is the category of "Emerging" for those items of which the child has shown a partial understanding, but not complete mastery. A child might obtain an Emerging score if he or she needed help to succeed with a task or completed only a part of a task. For example, on the color matching item, if the child matches only two or three colors the score would be Emerging. On most other tests such a response would earn a failing score. The Emerging score is one basis for developing a beginning teaching program. It is an indication of the general area in which the child has begun to grasp a particular concept or skill.

In addition to facilitating ideas for the content of teaching activities, the PEP yields data that help with the diagnosis of autism. The function areas are based on normative data from ages 1 to 6. The pathology areas are based on the assumption that normal or developmentally disabled children will have no negative scores or, at the very most, a low score. Forty-four items can be scored Absent, Mild, or Severe in the degree of disturbance. The pattern across the five areas along with the severity of the scores provides evidence for a possible diagnosis of autism. The combination of behavioral and developmental measures in a single scale makes the PEP unique among standardized tests in the field of psychology and education.

The age scores on the different functions form a pattern of the developmental profile, characteristically uneven for the autistic child. For the very young autistic child, it is common to have a profile with low scores on imitation and the cognitive performance and verbal functions, and relatively higher scores on the perception, fine and gross motor, and eye-hand integration functions. The preschooler might fail a simple motor imitation item (e.g., tapping a call bell) but pass a developmentally more advanced visual perception item (e.g., letter matching) or visual motor task (e.g., a four-piece puzzle).

The examiner can learn about the child's competence motivation, attention and organization, ability to learn a work-play routine, tolerance for frustration, as well as other aspects of learning style through the course of the PEP session. The test also allows for moments of free play in which the child's use of play materials and social initiation can be assessed. Thus in a relatively brief period (approximately 90 minutes), diagnostic impressions, developmental measures, and educational and treatment intervention strategies can be derived.

Other developmental/behavioral scales specially designed for autistic children include the Evaluation and Prescription for Exceptional Children (EPEC; Flaharty, 1976), the Behavior Evaluation Scale (BES; Kozloff, 1974), the Autism Screening Instrument for Educational Planning (ASIEP; Krug, Arick, & Almond, 1980), and the Behavior Rating Instrument for Autistic and Other Atypical Children (BRIAAC; Ruttenberg, Kalish, Wenar, & Wolf, 1977). These instruments derive from different theoretical or clinical perspectives. The BES and ASIEP are more behaviorally oriented than the BRIAAC, which reflects psychoanalytic concepts, or the EPEC, which is cognitive-developmental in orientation. For more detailed information on these tests, the reader is referred to the individual manuals or to a review in Short and Marcus (1986).

Psychological Tests

Standardized psychological tests are useful adjuncts to the developmental-educational assessment (e.g., PEP). These tests generally enable the clinician to compare the autistic child's skills with those of normal children. In addition, follow-up studies have demonstrated the predictive value of IQ scores for eventual outcome (Bartak & Rutter, 1976; Lotter, 1978). With the preschooler, however, such prognostic indicators should either not be used or used only with considerable caution.

The Bayley Scales of Infant Development (Bayley, 1969) is probably the most useful instrument for assessing children with mental ages of less than 2 years and chronological ages up to 10 years. Item levels range from 2 to 30 months. As the test was developed for infants, the administration of tasks is quite flexible. The tasks are designed to elicit a child's intrinsic interest and do not require a long attention span. Language and social skills can be assessed at a low and simple level. A problem sometimes occurs with autistic children when their interests diverge from those of a normal infant. Particularly for the very young autistic child, this problem may make the Bayley score a low estimate of a child's potential.

For children functioning in the 24-month to late preschool levels, the Merrill-Palmer Scale of Mental Tests (Stutsman, 1948) is often the most useful. This scale's preponderance of visual-matching and visual-motor tasks involve a variety of materials that are often attractive to the child. This measure is best for children with nonverbal skills well into the preschool range but limited language and conceptual skills. Although there are a few language items, mostly at the younger ages, the test does not offer a comprehensive assessment of these skills. Autistic children often score fairly high on the Merrill-Palmer. The clinician must be careful to interpret scores realistically given the emphasis of the test on areas in which autistic children are generally strong. Although a score in the average range is a good prognostic indicator, it does not necessarily imply intellectual potential in the average range in all areas.

The McCarthy Scales of Children's Abilities (McCarthy, 1972) are useful with autistic children whose language and conceptual skills are at or above the 2½- to 3-year level. For them these scales provide a more thorough assessment than does the Merrill-Palmer. For children with lower verbal skills than this, the McCarthy Scales are likely to be confusing and frustrating. The test offers a multiple subtest format similar to the Wechsler scales. Although interpretation of the subtest is somewhat more difficult than with the Wechsler scales, identification of strengths and weaknesses is possible.

The Leiter International Performance Scale (Leiter, 1969) and the Hiskey-Nebraska Test of Learning Aptitude (Hiskey, 1966) are tests developed for use with hearing-impaired children. They tend to deemphasize verbal skills and can be administered without speaking. The Leiter is probably the more useful of the two, as the Hiskey-Nebraska requires a higher degree of behavioral organization and the ability to understand complex nonverbal directions. The Leiter has a highly structured repetitive format. On all tasks, the subject places blocks in a tray stall to match them with a model. The Leiter gives the clinician the opportunity to assess some conceptual skills nonverbally. The format is helpful for many autistic individuals because of the degree of structure that is provided and the lack of need for social cues from the examiner. However, a Leiter administration tends to yield limited information concerning a child's language and social skills, and it tends to overestimate intelligence at younger ages because of the emphasis on visual matching and discrimination. As children grow older, measured IQ on the Leiter usually drops because of increased conceptual demands.

To perform adequately on the Wechsler Preschool and Primary Scales of Intelligence-Revised (WPPSI-R; Wechsler, 1989), an autistic child will need language and conceptual skills at least at the 3- to 4-year level. The division of the WPPSI into Verbal and Performance scales is of obvious value with an autistic child. Although the Verbal IQ is often markedly lower than the Performance IQ in these children, there is a scatter of skills within both the Verbal and Performance scales. Our clinical experience suggests that, as they get older, some high-functioning autistic children are able to score fairly well on most Wechsler subtests and show little interscale scatter. Nonetheless, these children often continue to show subtle deficits in language and social functioning.

The Kaufman Assessment Battery for Children (K-ABC; Kaufman & Kaufman, 1983) is a recently developed intelligence test for children ages 2½ to 12½. The K-ABC is divided into Achievement scales and Mental Processing scales. The former cover school achievement tasks such as reading and arithmetic, but they also include tasks that traditionally have been considered part of the evaluation of intelligence. The Mental Processing scales involve novel tasks and are divided into Sequential and Simultaneous Processing subscales. The theory behind the K-ABC is discussed extensively in the test manual (Kaufman & Kaufman, 1983). Of particular interest in the assessment of autism is the presence of a Nonverbal scale composed of selected Mental Processing subtests. Because of its innovative approach and the presence of a Nonverbal scale, the K-ABC appears to have promise for the assessment of autistic children. More experience with it will be required, though, to assess its value fully.

The Stanford-Binet Intelligence Scale (Terman & Merrill, 1973; Thorndike, Hagen, & Sattler, 1988) is generally not a useful instrument with autistic children because it demands a high level of language from the child and is relatively difficult to interpret with regard to skills in verbal versus nonverbal areas. For children with language at the 3- to 4-year level, the Wechsler, McCarthy, or Kaufman measures are recommended.

Interviewing Parents

Obtaining information from parents is essential for a comprehensive assessment. Not only is such information valuable for understanding how the child behaves, plays, and communicates in his or her natural environment, but engaging the parents in the assessment process lays the groundwork for future collaboration during intervention.

The TEACCH program typically obtains three kinds or sources of information from parents: questionnaires completed prior to the evaluation (discussed in a previous section), a semistructured interview, and more formal data from the Vineland Adaptive Behavior Scales (Sparrow et al., 1984).

The parent interview need not follow a rigid format, but it should be fairly structured and cover relevant areas. It also should allow the parents sufficient time to air out feelings and worries while still providing as objective a view as possible of the child's life at home. Most professionals find it useful to determine initially what the parents' main questions and concerns are and what they hope to gain from the evaluation. The interviewer's manner should be conducive to the establishment of trust. The interviewer also should be sensitive to the difficulty of this experience for the family, and understand that there is a natural tendency for the parents to protect their child. It is helpful to know their expectations of the child's future, their impressions of the child's current level of functioning, and their explanation for his or her problems. Specific areas to review include behavioral problems, communication skills, play skills, relationships with siblings, and daily living and motor skills. Information about informal or formal support networks also helps in planning a program.

The Vineland Adaptive Behavior Scales (Sparrow et al., 1984), the revision of the popular Vineland Social Maturity Scale (Doll, 1965), provides additional objective data in the domains of communication, daily living, socialization, and motor skills (for children under 6 years). The Survey Form yields sufficient detail to assess areas of relative strength and weakness and, if significant gaps are indicated, can facilitate decisions about adaptive and self-help skills to work on.

At the conclusion of a parent interview, the clinician should have a clear picture of the family and its relationship to the handicapped child, its worries and hopes, what resources are available, and what treatment recommendations for the home should be. In addition, the family should be better prepared for the diagnostic and assessment information that will be presented at the interpretive conference.

Diagnostic-Observational Methods

The direct assessment of the child with developmental or psychological tests should be accompanied by formal observational methods. A consideration of the Childhood Autism Rating Scale (CARS; Schopler et al., 1986), a diagnostic instrument developed and used within the TEACCH program, illustrates how the systematic organization of observations of behavioral characteristics can be incorporated into a comprehensive evaluation.

The CARS was developed in the context of direct observation in a clinical setting and serves the purpose of objectifying clinical observations of the behaviors associated with autism and related severe developmental disorders. The scale can be used in different settings (clinic assessment, classroom, report, or observation in the home), the results provide a diagnostic screening in terms of presence or absence of autism, and, if autism is diagnosed, the degree of severity is classified as mild-moderate or severe. The CARS is not intended to be the sole determination of diagnosis, but it has been shown to be a useful measure in conjunction with other relevant assessment data.

The CARS consists of ratings in 15 different areas of functioning significant for autism: Relating to People; Imitation; Emotional Response; Body Use; Object Use; Adaptation to Change; Visual Response; Listening Response; Taste, Smell, and Touch Response and Use; Fear or Nervousness; Verbal Communication; Nonverbal Communication; Activity Level; Level and Consistency of Intellectual Response; and General Impressions. The child's behavior during a TEACCH evaluation is observed during the PEP and rated in each area on a 7-point scale (4 anchor points and 3 half steps). Separate ratings are summed to obtain a total score, for which there are cutoffs for nonautistic, mildly to moderately autistic, and severely autistic. Clear descriptions are provided at each of the four anchor points for each rating. Advantages of the scale include its applicability in a wide range of settings without a requirement for extensive training, generally strong interrater reliability, consideration of the importance of the child's age at the time of evaluation, and the empirical derivation of scoring criteria.

There are other published rating scales that also can be used diagnostically. The BRIAAC (Ruttenberg et al., 1977), based more on psychoanalytic principles, has eight categories rated on a 10-point scale ranging from severe autism to behavior similar to a young normal child. The Autism Behavior Checklist (ABC), part of the previously mentioned ASIEP (Krug et al., 1980), consists of a checklist of 57 behaviors derived from research on autism and organized into five separate scales: Sensory, Relating, Body and Object Use, Language, and Social and Self-help. The Behavior Observation Scale for Autism (BOS; Freeman, Ritvo, Guthrie, Schroth, & Ball, 1978) relies on behavioral observation of 67 objectively defined behaviors. The BOS has been primarily used for research and its practical value for clinical settings has not been established.

Communication Assessment

As mentioned earlier, the important dimensions of communication assessment include communicative purposes or functions, content, means, and context. There are several reasons for choosing communication rather than language as the domain of assessment for this group. First, the majority of autistic children seen in their preschool years are not verbal and thus have no formal language skills to assess. Second, there is no way to predict with certainty which nonverbal children eventually will acquire language skills and which will not. Assessment of language skills is limited in that it does not tell us where to start an intervention program for many children and adolescents with autism.

Although language skills often are not present, rarely is a child totally lacking in the ability to communicate. The assessment of communication is thus more likely to provide some information regarding abilities that can be built upon in intervention. On the other hand, it is widely recognized that autism involves impairment of not only language abilities but of the broad range of communicative abilities, both verbal and nonverbal.

Formal testing, informal and observational assessment, and parental interview all present useful strategies for assessing communication skills. Even though autistic children have a major developmental impairment of language, there are some standardized measures to apply. Among the most useful is the Sequenced Inventory of Communication Development (SICD; Hedrick, Prather, & Tobin, 1975), which covers expressive and receptive skills from 4 months to 4 years. This instrument taps such behaviors as intonation, gesture, and nonverbal and verbal imitation as well as the use and understanding of language. Another appropriate instrument is the Reynell Developmental Language Scales (Reynell, 1978), which measure the receptive and expressive language skills of children from 1 to 7 years of age. For those children who have an understanding of pictures, the Peabody Picture Vocabulary Test–Revised (Dunn & Dunn, 1981) is a satisfactory measure of single-word receptive vocabulary.

The TEACCH Communication Curriculum (Watson, 1985; Watson et al., 1989) includes an observational assessment framework that covers the content described above plus an interview protocol to use with parents. Some elicitation procedures useful in the informal assessment of communication skills are provided in Wetherby and Prutting (1984). Lord (1985) suggested strategies for the assessment of comprehension skills in autistic children and made the clinically helpful point that much of the information gathered in the assessment of other skill areas can be regrouped to give a picture of the child's comprehension skills.

Motor Assessment

As pointed out by DeMyer (1979) and Ornitz, Guthrie, and Farley (1977), autistic children as a group show early and marked delays in motor development. This runs counter to the often-presented picture of these children as physically agile and well coordinated and points to the importance of assessing motor development in children with autism and similar disorders.

The motor area can be assessed both formally and informally. The previously discussed Psychoeducational Profile includes the assessment of both fine and gross motor skills, as well as items designed to assess some of the common disturbances in sensorimotor functioning. Other instruments appropriate for the motor assessment of this age group are the Peabody Developmental Motor Scales (Folio & Fewell, 1983) and the Motor scale of the Bayley Scales of Infant Development. When the child fails to attempt an item, or attends only briefly, then it is important to try to determine whether he or she cannot perform the skill or simply will not perform it in that specific context. Parent interview can provide information regarding the child's interests and more or less comparable behaviors observed at home. This might suggest a different format by which the clinician can informally assess the skill in question. It is also important to integrate information from the cognitive, social, and communication assessments with information from the motor assessment before interpreting results.

Medical Assessment

Although this chapter is concerned mainly with the developmental aspects of autism related to problems in learning and behavior, it is important to recognize the possible medical factors associated with autism. A variety of biological conditions have been documented, including congenital rubella, tuberous sclerosis, certain viral infections, abnormalities in purine metabolism and intestinal absorption, and phenylketonuria. The Fragile X syndrome (Coleman & Gillberg, 1985) and Rett's syndrome (Holm, 1985) have been increasingly reported in conjunction with autism. Although many such conditions do not respond to any specific treatment, some (such as PKU) do require effective intervention and others may have genetic implications for families (e.g., tuberous sclerosis). Other possible impairments such as hearing or visual problems should be assessed. Comprehensive information on the medical aspects of autism can be found in Coleman and Gillberg (1985) and in Schopler and Mesibov (1987).

INTEGRATION AND APPLICATIONS OF ASSESSMENT DATA

The organization, presentation, and practical applications of information gathered in the assessment of an autistic individual is as important as the techniques involved in collecting the data. This process involves several components: the staff conference, in which test results are interpreted and formulated; the parent conference, in which the findings are communicated; and the follow-up phase, in which assessment data are translated into education and treatment recommendations.

Staff Conference

At the staff conference immediately following completion of the testing and interview sessions, each clinician presents relevant assessment results. The initial presentation is that of the parent interview, followed by the medical screening, diagnostic developmental assessment, and psychological testing. The parent data are reviewed first because of the primary importance placed on this information and perspective. The parent consultant briefly describes how comfortable and communicative the parents seemed to be and then reviews in depth the parents' concerns and how the child functions in social, communication, self-help, and other relevant areas. The adaptive behavior data are presented as well as comments on resources and social supports available to the family. Finally the therapist notes if the parents are interested in follow-up teaching and behavior management sessions. The pediatrician then reports on possible etiological factors, health problems, and related medical issues. Any concerns brought up by the parents concerning these factors should be discussed at this time.

The key child presentation in the TEACCH program is the PEP report. The therapist typically begins with general comments about the child's behavior or a performance that stands out, such as unusual qualities, degree of interest In the test, or relationship to the examiner. The Pathology scale is then reviewed in detail covering the main features of autism, if present. The Developmental Function scales are discussed, with estimated age scores and examples of emerging skills. The child's potential for learning and prominent learning or interfering behavior problems are noted. Finally the therapist gives an opinion on the presence or absence of autism. The psychological test report follows the same format, with a behavioral description and test performance including IQ score discussed.

The general discussion that follows the individual presentations should be organized around three topics: the diagnosis, answers to the questions raised by the parents at the initial conference, and other recommendations not covered in the previous topic. Diagnosis is arrived at by consideration of the various observations and reports and the use of an instrument such as the CARS. If the child meets the criteria of autism to whatever degree, that information will need to be passed onto the parents. The parents' questions, which will form the basis for their conference, should be addressed and a consensus opinion or possible responses discussed. Other recommendations may include additional medical tests, a referral to an occupational therapist if there are significant motor problems that need closer examination, and/or referral to a particular school or day program.

Parent Conference

The parent interpretive conference is intended to provide a complete review of the assessment findings, to address the questions raised by the parents, and to make general and specific recommendations. For parents of the young autistic child, the explanation of the diagnosis is often the major topic of the conference. It is helpful to arrive at the specification of diagnosis through answers to the parents' original questions. For example, concerns about why their child is not talking or seems aloof or gets upset when something changes can be discussed as problems typical of children with autism.

Early diagnosis and assessment is the crucial first step in helping parents develop the awareness of what they face as an autistic child's primary caregivers. The manner in which they receive this information is, of course, important, although it is likely that the weight of the news of having a chronically handicapped child cannot be mitigated by any particular approach. Still, that initial conference should be structured in a way that presents the data clearly, descriptively, and sensitively without underplaying the seriousness of the situation (Morgan, 1984; Shea, 1984). The age of the child, the severity of the degree of autism, and the level of intellectual and adaptive impairment to some extent control prognostic implications, but the essential nature of the condition needs to be explained.

During this session, parents need to be told that even though a precise cause may not be known, their child's disorder did not result from improper parenting or related environmental circumstances. Even if parents do not express a prior sense of guilt, there are likely to be many recriminations they attribute to themselves or live with daily. They may feel they have not provided sufficient stimulation or should have identified the problem sooner or sought out help more aggressively. Extended family may be adding to parents' self-imposed pressure by suggesting that they are spoiling the child or worrying unnecessarily. The clinician who is interpreting diagnostic findings to the parents needs to be sensitive to these background factors.

Along with long-range implications of autism, parents need to know of the unique learning patterns of their autistic child. Undoubtedly they have been confused by the atypical pattern of higher skills in motor development and visual memory and deficits in language and abstract problem solving (DeMyer, 1979; Wing, 1976). Like professionals, parents assume that the relative proficiencies suggest normal intelligence and that the child's failure to perform well in the other areas is a temporary phenomenon, a lack of motivation, or an emotional disturbance. Parents need to understand the implications of the uneven developmental profile, in particular that adequate gross motor skills should not be interpreted as potential for normal cognitive and communicative development. One of the first steps in helping parents deal effectively with their child is to establish appropriate expectations. By simplifying language demands and individualizing their approach in teaching their child based on a realistic appraisal of developmental functioning, parents can initiate a process that will facilitate improved behavior as well as basic competencies (Schopler et al., 1984).

Although there are often many questions raised at an interpretive conference and detailed explanations should be provided, parents vary in their understanding and receptivity to the facts and opinions presented. The emotional impact of discovering that their child has a chronic disorder that may involve mental retardation as well as autism should not be underestimated (Akerley, 1975). Although some families can respond with remarkable calm, it is natural to react with worry, anger, or a form of denial. In the clinic, such feelings may not be manifested, but they are likely to emerge over time. Thus, the clinician must be available for follow-up, to continue to discuss the findings and the family response and to plan and help implement an intervention program.

Clinicians should be careful not to destroy the hope and optimism parents need to work with a handicapped child. There is a thin line between making a "realistic prognosis" and undermining a hope, and the professional should be guided by the principle not to disturb parental expectations except when they interfere with appropriate, current management.

From Assessment to Treatment

For autism, education is the treatment of choice and is based on the assessment techniques previously described. In the broadest sense, this educational treatment includes the education of not just the child but also his or her parents, teachers, and home community. For the young child this may include the extended family, day-care workers, preschool teachers, and Sunday school teachers. Treatment plans are discussed more specifically in terms of an Individualized Educational Plan (IEP), one that includes not only specific goals for skills and behavioral change but also teaching techniques specific to the individual autistic child's needs. Through the process of using these techniques and observing their effectiveness, parents and teachers can increase their understanding of the child's autistic characteristics and use this information to educate others in the child's family and community.

Observation of assessment. It is helpful to have parents and teachers observe the child's performance during the assessment. At TEACCH they watch the psychological testing through a one-way window and can give the clinician specific information as to how the child's performance differs from what is more typical at home or in school. This information is used to adjust the educational goals to keep them pertinent to the home/school environment. The subsequent educational recommendations are clearly understood because all parties have observed the same behaviors and have participated in the decisions for next-step goals.

Developing recommendations. The assessment procedures point out the child's strengths and weak areas as well as his or her behavioral characteristics. Information from home and school indicate the first priorities for change in terms of the child's survival in his or her home, school, and community. This information is then organized in the form of answers to the following questions: What is most essential for the child to learn next? What is the child most interested in, good at, and therefore motivated to perform? How does the child perceive his or her environment and understand what others want from him or her? Some typical answers for the preschool autistic child might be (a) he or she needs to learn to wait, to accept change, and to come when called by name; (b) he or she is most interested in lining up small toys in a row, likes food and physical rough-house play, and is good at simple puzzles; or (c) he or she perceives through tactile experiences and visual stimuli and remembers through repetition and visual structure, while auditory perception is inconsistent and verbal language confusing.

The educational recommendations should state the general goals in specific and positive terms; for example, "To come to the adult when called from a distance of 3 feet." The latter would be essential for the child's safety and thus a top priority for his or her parents. As the child will be encouraged to learn by using his or her interests to motivate a response, specific techniques should be suggested that derive from the assessment: "Hold out your arms to show he will get a swing-around when he comes." Some suggestions for visual structure and expected progress also should be given: "Repeat this game several times a day at predictable times, and gradually increase the distance between you as he responds more easily."

A full assessment will point out a number of areas appropriate for educational treatment. These can be organized effectively into the following areas:

1. Language and communication, which includes receptive language and listening attention, expressive verbal and nonverbal language, and the use of spontaneous communication at whatever level the child currently understands.
2. Self-help, leisure play skills, and independence, the goals for which come from the adaptive behavior scale and observations of unstructured play.
3. Fine and gross motor skills.
4. Cognitive and preacademic skills.
5. Social skills, imitation, and social behaviors.
6. Organized work skills, including attention span, task completion, and the recognition of consequences.

Perhaps the most essential point in recommending educational goals and specific suggestions for activities to achieve these goals is to start with skills, behaviors, and concepts the child either already has or shows an emerging ability to understand and achieve. Teaching is most successful when the child can achieve success, can gain his or her reward, fairly easily at the beginning. The assessment information will indicate what is easy for the child, what is slightly new or difficult, and what is clearly above his or her current level. Because the treatment is carried out primarily by parents and teachers, it is important to give recommendations that are clear, specific, and practical enough to carry out in the child's home and school.

Extended diagnostic period. Many preschool children are not familiar with structured teaching sessions and are anxious or confused during the initial evaluation. For this reason we find it helpful to follow up with a few 1-hour teaching sessions called an *extended diagnostic period.* At this time the parents are trained to be their child's teacher and the child's preschool teacher is included when possible. The initial recommendations from the assessment are tried out, modified, and expanded as needed. Teaching techniques, behavioral controls, and visual structure can be specified to meet the needs, interests, and abilities of the parents in the home. Considerations of the home environment include the space, distractions present, and time limits that vary with each family. The same limitations in the preschool classroom also are considered.

During this extended diagnostic period, several other factors emerge that influence successful treatment in the home. We observe and more fully understand the parents' use of language with their child, their energy level, and their ability to adjust demands based on observations of the child's fluctuations in skill and attention (Marcus, Lansing, Andrews, & Schopler, 1978). In addition, we also better grasp the parents' general philosophy of child rearing, their interpretation of the behaviors they observe, and their understanding of normal child developmental sequences.

Case Illustration

The following case study will illustrate the main points of the previously described assessment process. The case is organized around the categories of background information, referral questions, and parental concerns; results of the assessment; and highlights of the parent conference and recommendations, including an initial teaching program.

Background Information

Charlie is a 3½-year-old boy referred to TEACCH by his parents. His former Sunday school teacher, who was also a psychologist, previously had noted unusual behaviors, specifically poor social relationships, and had mentioned autism to the family. The parents were seeking confirmation of the diagnosis and appropriate educational planning. Additional concerns included Charlie's poor language, general intellectual ability, and short attention span. Early medical history indicated a normal and uncomplicated pregnancy, with delivery by caesarean section. As a newborn Charlie was alert and active. He experienced occasional bouts of flu and diarrhea, and at 35 months an accident to his finger required two stitches. Early motor milestones occurred within normal limits, and bladder and bowel training was successful at 35–37 months. The parents first became concerned at 27 months because of Charlie's delayed language development. They also described him as a "solemn" baby who laughed very little.

Results of Assessment

Behavioral observations from the PEP and psychological testing sessions indicated (a) an overall lack of social interest, unresponsiveness to praise, and relating through the activities rather than the relationship; (b) no initiation of any type of interaction, poor eye contact, flat and unexpressive facial expression, occasional inappropriate affect (e.g., becoming giggly during a bead-stringing task), excessive interest in the mirror, some mouthing of objects, and somewhat delayed and inappropriate responses to auditory stimuli; (c) some use of single words to make requests or phrases to label an action or object; (d) speech characterized by singsong quality of intonation, high pitch, and lack of communicative intent; (e) play lacking in creativity and interest in age-related play materials; (f) aimless wandering when left unstructured; (g) general cooperation within the routine and rules of the test structure, with some interest and curiosity regarding certain test materials; (h) an awareness of task difficulty, responding with an anxious humming; and (i) bouts of mild inattentiveness, usually associated with language tasks.

On the PEP Performance scale, Charlie functioned as delayed in all areas of development, with overall skills slightly above a 2-year level. Perceptual abilities, eye-hand integration skills, and good beginning work habits were considered strengths. His weak areas were imitation, fine motor, and cognitive verbal skills, but the high number of emerging items in these areas was encouraging. Examples of these potential learning areas were copying verbal sounds and actions with objects, cutting with scissors and cooperative use of two hands, and labeling of some shapes and letters. On the Merrill-Palmer Scale, Charlie obtained a mental age of 3-2 years and a ratio IQ of 93, which represented a very wide scatter of abilities. His weakest areas were language and imitation, with failures at the 18- to 29-month level; his strengths occurred in visual-spatial and visual-motor skills, with passes at the 54- to 59-month level. This subtest pattern is very typical of young autistic children on the Merrill-Palmer and was consistent with Charlie's PEP performance.

From the parent interview, it was evident that Charlie's parents were an articulate, concerned, and insightful couple. The child's inconsistencies and uneven abilities were confusing to them. Behavior management was an issue, with Charlie's father less patient than his mother and more ready to interpret negative behavior as noncompliance or willfulness. Charlie's communication at home occurred mainly via two-word phrases, with an estimated vocabulary of 250–300 words, although his articulation was sometimes poor. He did not have a consistent yes/no response and did not express his feelings clearly. Echolalia was prominent in his speech, used both functionally and nonfunctionally. His play was characterized by fascination with mechanical devices and copying his parents' actions (e.g., using the vacuum cleaner). Charlie was intrigued by numbers and was attracted to digital clocks. His imaginative play was limited, but the rudiments appeared to be established.

On the Childhood Autism Rating Scale, Charlie was judged to be in the mild-moderate range of autism, with a total score of 34.5. Individual scales that were scored in the high moderate to severe range were Imitation, Relating to People, Verbal Communication, and Unevenness of Intellectual Functioning. Closer to the normal range were Activity Level and Fear and Nervousness.

Parent Conference

The parent conference focused initially on the diagnosis of autism and how this label fit Charlie based on the current evaluation. Charlie was described as having significant deficits in communication, social skills, and play skills, and an uneven profile of abilities. The issue of his apparent stubbornness was discussed and interpreted as indicative of the cognitive disorganization and difficulty with imitation and language on demand so typical of autism. The comment was made that for children like Charlie, it is easier for them to organize their behavior and remain focused when *they* initiate an action than to organize a response to someone else's request. Positive predictor signs were pointed out, including relatively high intellectual abilities, the development of language before the age of 5, and the provision of early and appropriate early intervention. The primary recommendation at this time was for follow-up teaching sessions at the clinic to work on communication, imitation, and organization skills, and to help the parents gain a better understanding of how to help Charlie. A second recommendation was for Charlie's mother to attend a mothers' support group. The recommendation for school supported the parents' plan to have Charlie in a normal preschool with consultation from TEACCH.

The beginning home teaching program that was written for Charlie and his parents is presented in Table 13.1. These activities were demonstrated during the first session, and Charlie's mother worked on them at home daily. These objectives and activities were based on an analysis of the PEP profile and emerging scores plus parent observations and concerns. Having the daily routine of the teaching program helped Charlie in his behavior and overall relatedness to his social environment. His communication, imitation, and organization skills improved. Within a relatively short time, many other activities were added to his program. In addition, the school was given copies of the teaching programs and they were incorporated into Charlie's school day.

The emphasis on understanding both the normal and atypical aspects of development in the early years has guided our work within the TEACCH program and led to the construction of specialized diagnostic and assessment tools for this group of handicapped preschoolers. Appropriate and comprehensive assessment of autism requires specific knowledge of the characteristics, courses of development, and variations of the disorder as well as general knowledge of other problems of early childhood. Above all, the clinician must recognize the importance of the family in the assessment process and bring together and organize the rich and wide range of data that can be generated with a thorough evaluation. Assessment is only the first step of the long road faced by autistic children and their families, but it is a critical beginning that, if properly done, can enhance the child's future success.

TABLE 13.1

Example of a Home Teaching Program

Function Area	Objective	Activity
Imitation	Charlie will imitate the actions of the adult in a nonfamiliar situation.	Have Charlie imitate the actions of the adult using a follow-the-leader type of approach. Using two sets of identical, common objects, have Charlie place them in the same order/orientation as the adult. This could be a building activity with Tinker Toys or a stacking task with common household items (cup, plate, penny, spoon).
Receptive language	Charlie will increase his receptive language skills.	Have Charlie identify common objects amidst a group of items. To make the task more complex, ask Charlie to identify the items by function ("Get the one we brush our teeth with") or have Charlie locate a named object in the room.
Cognitive	Charlie will increase his ability to categorize.	Charlie shows an ability to categorize on the basis of shape. Attempt other categorization tasks using pictures of food, clothes, animals, people, etc.
Organizational skills	Charlie will demonstrate organizational skills while working at a table task.	To increase Charlie's understanding of sequences and provide him with an independent work task, set up a three- or four-step task that demands he follow the steps in a specific order. The task should be clear enough so that Charlie can perform it independently after one demonstration. For example, have Charlie take a pill bottle, put in one penny, put on the top, and place the container in a specified area (such as an egg carton).
Visual-perceptual skills	Charlie will follow the visual cues of a colored pattern.	Have Charlie follow a colored block pattern. Use a sheet of paper on which has been drawn a block pattern using different colored squares. Have Charlie match the actual blocks on the pattern.
Expressive language	Charlie will use words to request objects he wants.	Use simple one-piece puzzles. Give Charlie one of the puzzle outlines and show him two puzzle pieces. Ask him which one he wants and have Charlie verbally choose the piece he needs.

References

Akerley, M. (1975). The invulnerable parent. *Journal of Autism and Childhood Schizophrenia, 5,* 275-281.

Akerley, M. (1988). What's in a name? In E. Schopler & G.B. Mesibov (Eds.), *Diagnosis and assessment in autism* (pp. 59-67). New York: Plenum.

Bartak, L., & Rutter, M. (1976). Differences between mentally retarded and normally intelligent autistic children. *Journal of Autism and Child Schizophrenia, 6,* 109-120.

Bayley, N. (1969). *Bayley Scales of Infant Development.* San Antonio, TX: Psychological Corporation.

Beisler, J.M., & Tsai, L.Y. (1983). A pragmatic approach to increase expressive language skills in young children. *Journal of Autism and Developmental Disorders, 13,* 287-303.

Bruner, J. (1975). The ontogenesis of speech acts. *Journal of Child Language, 2,* 2-19.

Cohen, D.J., Paul, R., & Volkmar, F.R. (1987). Issues in the classification of pervasive developmental disorders and associated conditions. In D.J. Cohen & A.M. Donnellan (Eds.), *Handbook of autism and pervasive developmental disorders* (pp. 20-40). New York: Wiley-Interscience.

Coleman, M., & Gillberg, C. (1985). *The biology of the autistic syndromes.* New York: Praeger.

Doll, E. (1965). *Vineland Social Maturity Scale.* Circle Pines, MN: American Guidance Service.

DeMyer, M.K. (1979). *Parents and children in autism.* New York: Wiley.

Dunn, L.M., & Dunn, L.M. (1981). *Peabody Picture Vocabulary Test-Revised.* Circle Pines, MN: American Guidance Service.

Fay, W., & Schuler, A. (1980). *Emerging language in autistic children.* Baltimore: University Park Press.

Flaharty, R. (1976). EPEC: Evaluation and Prescription for Exceptional Children. In E.R. Ritvo, B.J. Freeman, E.M. Ornitz, & P.E. Tanguay (Eds.), *Autism: Diagnosis, current research and management* (pp. 35-56). New York: Spectrum.

Folio, M.R., & Fewell, R.R. (1983). *Peabody Developmental Motor Scales and Activity Cards.* Allen, TX: DLM Teaching Resources.

Freeman, B.J. (1976). Evaluating autistic children. *Journal of Pediatric Psychology, 1,* 18-21.

Freeman, B.J., Ritvo, E.R., Guthrie, D., Schroth, P., & Ball, J. (1978). The Behavior Observation Scale for Autism: Initial methodology, data analysis, and preliminary findings on 89 children. *Journal of the American Academy of Child Psychiatry, 17,* 576-588.

Hedrick, D.L., Prather, E.M., & Tobin, A.R. (1975). *Sequenced Inventory of Communication Development.* Seattle: University of Washington Press.

Hiskey, M. (1966). *Hiskey-Nebraska Test of Learning Aptitude.* Lincoln, NE: Union College Press.

Holm, V.A. (1985). Rett's syndrome: A progressive developmental disability in girls. *Developmental and Behavioral Pediatrics, 6,* 32-36.

Kanner, L. (1943). Autistic disturbances of affective contact. *Nervous Child, 2,* 212-250.

Kaufman, A.S., & Kaufman, N.L. (1983). *K-ABC: Kaufman Assessment Battery for Children.* Circle Pines, MN: American Guidance Service.

Kozloff, M.A. (1974). *Educating children with learning and behavior problems.* New York: Wiley.

Krug, D.A., Arick, J.R., & Almond, P.J. (1980). *Autism Screening Instrument for Educational Planning.* Portland, OR: ASIEP Educational Co.

Leiter, R.G. (1969). *Leiter International Performance Scale.* Los Angeles: Western Psychological Services.

Lotter, V. (1978). Follow-up studies. In M. Rutter & E. Schopler (Eds.), *Autism: A reappraisal of concepts and treatment* (pp. 475-495). New York: Plenum.

Lord, C. (1985). Autism and the comprehension of language. In E. Schopler & G.B. Mesibov (Eds.), *Communication problems in autism* (pp. 257-281). New York: Plenum.

Marcus, L.M. (1977). Patterns of coping in families of psychotic children. *American Journal of Orthopsychiatry, 47,* 388-399.

Marcus, L.M., & Baker, A. (1986). Assessment of autistic children. In R.J. Simeonsson (Ed.), *Psychological assessment of special children* (pp. 279-304). Newton, MA: Allyn & Bacon.

Marcus, L.M., Lansing, M., Andrews, C., & Schopler, E. (1978). Improvement of teaching effectiveness in parents of autistic children. *Journal of the American Academy of Child Psychiatry, 17,* 625-639.

McCarthy, D. (1972). *McCarthy Scales of Children's Abilities.* San Antonio, TX: Psychological Corporation.

Mesibov, G.B., & Shea, V. (1980, March). *Social and interpersonal problems of autistic adolescents and adults.* Paper presented at the meeting of the Southeastern Psychological Association, Washington, DC.

Morgan, S.B. (1984). Helping parents understand the diagnosis of autism. *Developmental and Behavioral Pediatrics, 5,* 78-85.

Olley, J.G. (1986). The TEACCH curriculum for teaching social behavior to children with autism. In E. Schopler & G.B. Mesibov (Eds.), *Social behavior in autism* (pp. 351-373). New York: Plenum.

Ornitz, E.M., Guthrie, D., & Farley, A.H. (1977). The early development of autistic children. *Journal of Autism and Childhood Schizophrenia, 7,* 207-229.

Reichler, R.J., & Schopler, E. (1976). Developmental therapy: A program model for providing individual services in the community. In E. Schopler & R.J. Reichler (Eds.), *Psychopathology and child development: Research and treatment* (pp. 347-372). New York: Plenum.

Reynell, J.K. (1978). *Reynell Developmental Language Scales, Revised Edition.* Windsor, England: NFER-Nelson.

Ricks, D.N., & Wing, L. (1975). Language, communication, and the use of symbols in normal and autistic children. *Journal of Autism and Childhood Schizophrenia, 5,* 191-222.

Ruttenberg, B.A., Kalish, B.I., Wenar, C., & Wolf, E.G. (1977). *Behavior Rating Instrument for Autistic and Other Atypical Children (BRIAAC).* Philadelphia: Developmental Center for Autistic Children.

Rutter, M. (1983). Cognitive deficits in the pathogenesis of autism. *Journal of Child and Psychiatry, 24,* 513-531.

Rutter, M., & Schopler, E. (1987). Autism and pervasive developmental disorders: Concepts and diagnostic issues. *Journal of Autism and Developmental Disorders, 17,* 159-186.

Schopler, E. (1983). New developments in the definition and diagnosis of autism. In B.B. Lahey & A.E. Kazdin (Eds.), *Advances in clinical child psychology* (Vol. 6, pp. 93-127). New York: Plenum.

Schopler, E. (1987). Specific and nonspecific factors in the effectiveness of a treatment system. *American Psychologist, 42,* 376-383.

Schopler, E., Brehm, S., Kinsbourne, M., & Reichler, R.J. (1971). Effect of treatment structure on development in autistic children. *Archives of General Psychiatry, 24,* 415-421.

Schopler, E., & Mesibov, G.B. (Eds.). (1986). *Social behavior in autism.* New York: Plenum.

Schopler, E., & Mesibov, G.B. (Eds.). (1987). *Neurobiological issues in autism.* New York: Plenum.

Schopler, E., Mesibov, G.B., Shigley, R.H., & Bashford, A. (1984). Helping autistic children through their parents: The TEACCH model. In E. Schopler & G.B. Mesibov (Eds.), *The effects of autism on the family* (pp. 65–81). New York: Plenum.

Schopler, E., & Reichler, R.J. (1971). Problems in the developmental assessment of psychotic children. *Exerpta Medica International Congress Series, 274,* 1307–1311.

Schopler, E., & Reichler, R.J. (1979). *Individualized assessment and treatment for autistic and developmentally disabled children: Vol. 1. Psychoeducational Profile.* Austin, TX: PRO-ED.

Schopler, E., Reichler, R.J., Bashford, A., Lansing, M.D., & Marcus, L.M. (1990). *Individualized assessment and treatment for autistic and developmentally disabled children: Vol. 1. Psychoeducational Profile–Revised (PEP-R).* Austin, TX: PRO-ED.

Schopler, E., Reichler, R.J., & Lansing, M. (1980). *Individualized assessment and treatment for autistic and developmentally disabled children: Vol. 2. Teaching strategies for parents and professionals.* Austin, TX: PRO-ED.

Schopler, E., Reichler, R.J., & Renner, B. (1986). *The Childhood Autism Rating Scale (CARS).* Los Angeles: Western Psychological Services.

Shea, V. (1984). Explaining mental retardation and autism to parents. In E. Schopler & G.B. Mesibov (Eds.), *The effects of autism on the family* (pp. 265–288). New York: Plenum.

Short, A.B., & Marcus, L.M. (1986). Psychoeducational evaluation of autistic children and adolescents. In P. Lazarus & S.S. Strichart (Eds.), *Psychoeducational evaluation of children with low incidence disorders* (pp. 155–180). Orlando, FL: Grune & Stratton.

Sparrow, S.S., Balla, D.A., & Cicchetti, D.V. (1984). *Vineland Adaptive Behavior Scales.* Circle Pines, MN: American Guidance Service.

Stutsman, R. (1948). *Merrill-Palmer Scale of Mental Tests.* Los Angeles: Western Psychological Services.

Terman, L.M., & Merrill, M.A. (1973). *Stanford-Binet Intelligence Scale: 1972 Norms Edition.* Boston: Houghton Mifflin.

Thorndike, R.L., Hagen, E.P., & Sattler, J.M. (1986). *Guide for administering and scoring the Stanford-Binet Intelligence Scale: Fourth Edition.* Chicago: Riverside.

Watson, L.R. (1985). The TEACCH communication curriculum. In E. Schopler & G.B. Mesibov (Eds.), *Communication problems in autism* (pp. 187–206). New York: Plenum.

Watson, L., & Marcus, L.M. (1988). Diagnosis and assessment of pre-school children. In E. Schopler & G.B. Mesibov (eds.), *Diagnosis and assessment in autism* (pp. 271–301). New York: Plenum.

Watson, L.R., Schaffer, B., Lord, C., & Schopler, E. (1989). *Teaching spontaneous communication to autistic and developmentally handicapped children.* Austin, TX: PRO-ED.

Wechsler, D. (1989). *Manual for the Wechsler Preschool and Primary Scales of Intelligence –Revised.* San Antonio, TX: Psychological Corporation.

Wetherby, A., & Prutting, C. (1984). Profiles of communicative and cognitive-social abilities in autistic children. *Journal of Speech and Hearing Research, 27,* 364–377.

Wing, L. (1976). Diagnosis, clinical description, and prognosis. In L. Wing (Ed.), *Early child autism* (2nd ed., pp. 15–64). New York: Pergamon.

Wing, L., & Gould, J. (1979). Severe impairment of social interaction and associated abnormalities in children: Epidemiology and classification. *Journal of Autism and Developmental Disorders, 9,* 11–30.

14

Assessment of the Child with Social and Emotional Disorders

JOHN E. OBRZUT, PH.D. & CAROL A. BOLIEK, PH.D.

The advent of Public Law 99–457 mandated the provision of educational and developmental services to children with special needs prior to their entering public school at the first-grade level. Therefore, school systems across the nation, as well as federal, state, and local agencies, have been and will be developing programs to implement this legislation in the upcoming years. As a result of this law, the need for services to the infant, toddler, and preschool-aged population has increased dramatically.

While the new requirement established in 1987 was for school districts to screen all 3- to 5-year-old children residing within district boundaries, the final implementation of the law will require screening of all infants and toddlers 0–3 years of age as well. The intent of PL 99–457 is to conduct widespread screening of all 0- to 6-year-olds so children who fail screenings/rescreenings can be referred for evaluation to determine whether a handicap exists. Typically most of the emphasis placed on screening and assessment of young children focuses on their learning and cognitive development. However, many of these preschool-aged children experience either mild, moderate, or severe social-emotional disabilities that affect their overall functioning.

Historically, several forces have led to the impetus for involvement in assessment at the preschool level. Boehm and Sandberg (1981) have suggested that one such force was the result of the work accomplished by developmental psychologists. Such psychologists as Piaget and Flavell have focused on the preschool years as a time in which children acquire the basic foundations for later learning. Boehm and Sandberg (1981) also suggest that the development of the Head Start Program and later the implementation of PL 94–142 (Education for All Handicapped Children Act) have had great impact, respectively, on preventing failure among economically disadvantaged children upon entering formal schooling and identifying preschool children at risk for later learning and/or behavioral problems. Although these forces primarily have addressed the need for assessment at the prekindergarten and kindergarten levels (ages 3–5 years), the ultimate aim of the new mandate is one of primary prevention and includes infants and toddlers as well (age span 0–3). Thus, performance areas to be assessed include skills and competencies related to success with the primary school curriculum and to adequate social and emotional functioning as well.

APPROACH TO ASSESSMENT

Regardless of the nature of the presenting problem (i.e., intellectual, educational, social-emotional functioning), the assessment procedure with children from birth to 5 requires ongoing communication among pediatricians, school psychologists, and educators in order to determine academic readiness. Likewise, the assessment process itself should consist of continuous monitoring of behavior as children engage in various activities that reflect how they think, interact, and behave developmentally (Almy & Genishi, 1979). For example, there is some evidence that preschool behavior can predict future psychiatric disorders (Lerner, Inui, Trupin, & Douglas, 1985). These authors found that subjects predicted to be at high risk because of preschool ratings of verbal and physical aggression, hyperactivity-distractibility, social withdrawal, and speech and language problems developed psychiatric disorders and had contact with legal agencies.

The need for the assessment process to be ongoing is vital to ensure correct decision making and minimize the occurrence of "false positives" and "false negatives." This is particularly so when conducting an evaluation to determine social-emotional functioning, given that classifications among disorders are frequently overlapping and difficult to diagnose and that early social-emotional functioning shows excessive variability. Bell and Pearl (1982) noted that psychosocial change occurs in groups of infants and children at risk for various social-emotional disorders, and these individuals are likely to move in and out of "risk" status as far as any given developmental phase is concerned.

Steps to Assessment

Before the actual assessment process takes place, a screening procedure is used to identify those children in need of more thorough diagnosis. For example, screening procedures are essential for "Child Find" as mandated by PL 94-142. At a minimum, the screening instruments selected should be standardized and should screen for (a) hearing, (b) vision, (c) fine/gross motor skills, (d) receptive/expressive communication skills, (e) cognitive development, and (f) socioemotional development. Although screening can identify the need for further assessment, it does not determine the specific type of problem a child might experience. Most screening procedures are used to assess *readiness* for program involvement rather than in-depth testing of performance. Unfortunately many screening instruments do not have adequate statistical reliability and validity. Bradley and Caldwell (1974) argued that a good screening instrument should minimize the occurrence of false positives and false negatives. However, at present the more reliable and valid instruments are those designed to screen difficulties primarily related to academic readiness rather than to social-emotional readiness.

The actual assessment process refers to the entire evaluation process in which there are specific, discrete steps. These include prediagnostic staffing, administration of diagnostic tests and procedures, integration and interpretation of test findings, communication of results with all concerned parties, and a summary statement. Although many of the assessment issues with 0- to 2-year-olds will differ from those of 3- to 5-year-olds, we consider this approach the cornerstone in conducting a systematic and comprehensive assessment on a child with a suspected disability.

When testing very young children, the prediagnostic staffing may prove most crucial in developing an understanding of specific social-emotional disorders. It is at this stage where one must (a) rely on pertinent history (medical, developmental, family, educational, behavioral, prior screening or testing, etc.); (b) rule out or take into consideration physical problems (consultation with other professionals to assess visual acuity, auditory acuity, medication effects, etc.); (c) review the child's presenting symptoms and parent concerns; (d) develop hypotheses about diagnosis and underlying cause(s) of the problem; and (e) develop the appropriate battery of tests and procedures to test the hypotheses. Oftentimes with social-emotional disorders, a complex network of biological and ecological factors impinge simultaneously on the young developing child, which causes undue stress and resultant disability. Thus, it is necessary to consider physical, intellectual, emotional, educational/developmental, and social (P-I-E-E-S) functioning in planning the assessment (Weaver, 1984).

Major Theoretical Models

A large body of theoretical, conceptual, and practical literature related to assessment and diagnosis of socioemotional disorders has developed over the years, and it is useful to categorize various assessment approaches according to their theoretical origins. We believe that the major theoretical models—medical, behavioral, and ecological—guide the assessment and intervention process when working with emotionally handicapped children and allow the clinician to systematically consider the P-I-E-E-S factors in his or her case work. Comprehensive assessments should include detailed information of person, behavior, and environmental dimensions (Reynolds, Gutkin, Elliott, & Witt, 1984). Thus, a brief explanation of each theoretical model will demonstrate its importance in the selection of assessment instruments.

The hallmark of the *medical model* is a primary focus on intrachild variables. The causes of behavior are viewed as intrapsychic or within the individual, and behavioral manifestations of a problem stem from an underlying cause (Rezmierski, Knoblock, & Bloom, 1982). Thus, in terms of assessment, more emphasis would be placed on indirect methods such as structured interviews, including developmental histories and self-report statements, and performance on tasks believed to represent covert thoughts or processes, namely projective techniques. Traditional norm-referenced assessment including intelligence, achievement, and special abilities tests are also viewed from a medical model perspective. Finally, one of the most rapidly growing areas of interest in the evaluation of children from this perspective has been that of neuropsychology. Through the neuropsychological perspective, emotional dysfunction would be addressed by evaluating possible developmental deficits or involvement of the central nervous system and its components.

The *behavioral model* forms on the notion that behavior is strengthened or weakened by its antecedents and it consequences (Kazdin, 1982). One would seek to understand the maintaining conditions (of behavior) in the current environment as the cause of behavior. Behavioral assessment focuses on an individual's environment for the determinants of behavior. Thus, in behavioral assessment more emphasis would be placed on direct methods, such as direct observation, and on recording specific behaviors, both performed in the natural environment. In addition, ratings by others are used because they are either retrospective in nature or present a verbal representation of clinically relevant behaviors that happened at another time or place. However, in contrast to norm-referenced assessment measures, criterion-referenced assessment, which attempts to identify the specific skills a child does or does not have, is perhaps more synonymous with a behavioral model of assessment.

The *ecological model* of behavior is based on the premise that a reciprocal relationship exists between person, behavior, and environment (Bandura, 1978). The causes of behavior are viewed in an interactionist position, that is, behavior as a function of both environmental and personological variables. In contrast to behavioral models, which are concerned with the effects of the environment on thoughts and behavior, the ecological model addresses the reciprocal effects of cognition and behavior upon the environment. The model assumes that each child is unique and that no one strategy or technique will be appropriate across all children, behaviors, or environmental systems (Reynolds et al., 1984).

The proponents of this model (e.g., Lazarus, 1981) would suggest that emotional dysfunction is a product of inept coping as much as it is of environmental demands or stressors. A childhood emotional disorder would be viewed as resulting from stressful episodes confronting the child and the child's appraisal of these episodes as harmful, extreme loss, or threat. These appraisals may produce negatively toned emotions such as fear, anger, and anxiety, to name a few. For example, Bernstein, Jeremy, and Marcus (1986) found at infant age 12 months, mothers' interactive behavior was a significant concurrent predictor of infant functioning.

To understand a child's socioemotional functioning fully and to arrive at accurate diagnostic conclusions, we believe one must thoroughly assess the environments within which children function. Thus, ecological assessment involves direct observation of parent-child interaction and of teacher-child dyadic interaction (Brophy & Good, 1974), sociometric assessment of peer relationships, and assessment of family interactions.

Definition and Classification of Social-Emotional Disorders

According to PL 94-142, the term *seriously emotionally disturbed* is defined as

> a condition exhibiting one or more of the following characteristics over a long period of time and to a marked degree, which adversely affects educational performance: (a) an inability to learn which cannot be explained by intellectual, sensory, or other health factors; (b) an inability to build or maintain satisfactory interpersonal relationships with peers and teachers; (c) inappropriate types of behavior or feelings under normal circumstances; (d) a general pervasive mood of unhappiness or depression; (e) a tendency to develop physical symptoms or fears associated with personal or school problems. (Slenkovich, 1983, pp. 4-5).

The term includes children who are schizophrenic but not those who are socially maladjusted, unless they are determined seriously emotionally disturbed.

Without a doubt the most frequently used system for classifying social-emotional disorders in preschoolers and early childhood is the *Diagnostic and Statistical Man-*

ual of Mental Disorders, now in its revised third edition (DSM-III-R; American Psychiatric Association, 1987). However, a recent review of the clinical case records of 274 3- to 5-year olds led Rescorla (1986) to suggest that current diagnostic taxonomies may require some revision if they are to accurately reflect the patterns of behavior that commonly occur in preschool clinic populations. Regardless of this caution, a child's DSM-III diagnostic grouping has been found to correlate more strongly than other diagnostic data (e.g., face-to-face interviews with primary caregiver) with posttreatment success (Sack, Mason, & Collins, 1987). The following sections will briefly describe social-emotional disorders commonly evidenced in infancy and early childhood as outlined by DSM-III-R, excluding those (e.g., mood disorders, schizophrenia) for which the essential features are the same in children and adults.

Pervasive Developmental Disorders

One of the most common categories of social-emotional disorders is the group labeled Pervasive Developmental Disorders (Axis II). These disorders are characterized by qualitative impairment in the development of reciprocal social interaction, verbal and nonverbal communication skills, and imaginative activity, and a markedly restricted repertoire of activities and interests. The most severe and prototypical form of this category is the Autistic Disorder. However, all other cases that meet the general description of Pervasive Developmental Disorder (PDD) but not the specific criteria for Autistic Disorder are diagnosed as Pervasive Developmental Disorder Not Otherwise Specified (PDDNOS).

In addition to the major characteristics of the PDDNOS syndrome, however, other clinical features likely will be present, including but not limited to (a) abnormalities in the development of cognitive skills; (b) abnormalities of posture and motor behavior; (c) odd responses to sensory input; (d) abnormalities in eating, drinking, or sleeping; (e) abnormalities of mood; and (f) self-injurious behavior. Of interest to note, Levine and Demb (1987) have described children with an atypical pervasive developmental disorder not captured within a diagnostic category in DSM III-R. Its distinguishing characteristics are onset before the age of 3 years, language delay with disordered communication, social relationships characterized by variable relatedness, ritualistic or manneristic behaviors, the likelihood of hyperactivity and/ or short attention span, affective disturbance, excessive anxiety, and a thinking disorder or perseverative behaviors. In general, and according to the DSM-III-R, the younger the child and the more severe the disorder, the more clinical symptoms are likely to be present (APA, 1987).

Although Dahl, Cohen, and Provence (1986) suggest that the hallmark characteristic of both autism and PDDNOS is the nature of the social impairment, the criteria may differ primarily in the age of onset, autism occurring before the age of 30 months (Volkmar, Stier, & Cohen, 1985). The onset of the PDDNOS syndrome is reported to be before the age of 3 in the majority of cases. Manifestations in infancy are more subtle and difficult to define than those exhibited after 2 years of age. Though the exact causes of PDDNOS are not known, a wide variety of prenatal, perinatal, and postnatal conditions causing brain dysfunction are thought to predispose certain individuals to develop this condition.

Attention-Deficit Hyperactivity Disorder

Another common social-emotional disorder in development is Attention-Deficit Hyperactivity Disorder (ADHD), characterized by developmentally inappropriate degrees of inattention, impulsiveness, and hyperactivity. Children with this disorder generally display some disturbance in each of these areas, but to varying degrees. In preschool children the most prominent features include signs of gross motor overactivity, such as excessive running or climbing. Inattention and impulsiveness likely manifest by frequent shifting from one activity to another. In school-aged children, the most prominent features tend to be excessive fidgeting and restlessness rather than gross motor overactivity.

The associated features of ADHD vary as a function of age and include low self-esteem, mood lability, low frustration tolerance, and temper outbursts. "Soft" neurological signs and motor-perceptual dysfunctions (e.g., poor eye-hand coordination) often present as well. Although onset of the disorder generally occurs before age 4, frequently the disorder is not recognized until the child enters school. Academic underachievement and impairment in social functioning is common in most schoolchildren with this disorder. Central nervous system abnormalities such as the presence of neurotoxins, cerebral palsy, epilepsy, and other neurologic disorders are thought to present predisposing factors. (For a comprehensive discussion of ADHD, see chapter 12 in this volume.)

Anxiety Disorders

Two common disorders of early childhood in which anxiety is the predominant clinical feature are Separation Anxiety Disorder and Avoidant Disorder of Childhood. In both disorders the anxiety focuses on specific situations rather than generalizing to a variety of situations.

The major characteristic of Separation Anxiety Disorder is excessive anxiety concerning separation from those to whom the child is attached. Children with this disorder become uneasy when they must function independently from familiar surroundings and people. When separation occurs, the child may experience anxiety to the point of panic, and physical complaints such as headaches, nausea, and vomiting are common, sometimes anticipatory reactions. Associated features of Separation Anxiety Disorder include preoccupation with morbid fears, depressed mood, and personality characteristics described as demanding, intrusive, and in need of constant attention. The age of onset may be as early as preschool years. Although no specific premorbid personality disturbance is associated with this disorder, in most cases separation anxiety develops after some environmental stress, typically a loss (such as the death of a relative or pet), an illness, or a change in the child's environment.

The essential feature of the Avoidant Disorder of Childhood is an excessive withdrawal from contact with unfamiliar people that is of sufficient severity to interfere with social functioning in peer relationships. Children with this disorder are socially withdrawn, embarrassed, and timid when interacting with unfamiliar people and will become anxious when even a trivial demand is made to interact with strangers. Often these children will be unassertive and display a lack of self-confidence. Age-appropriate socialization skills may not develop, with a concomitant severe impairment in social functioning. Although the disorder typically appears during the early school years, when increased opportunities for social contact exists, it may develop as early as age 2½. Specific developmental disorders involving speech and language are thought to comprise predisposing factors.

Elimination Disorders

Elimination disorders first evident in early childhood often may result in social-emotional dysfunction. Two such disorders are Functional Encopresis and Functional Enuresis.

The major feature of Functional Encopresis is repeated involuntary or intentional passage of feces into places not appropriate for that purpose (e.g., clothing or floor). However, the chronological and mental age of the child must be at least 4 years, and physical disorders must be ruled out. Emotionally the child experiences shame or embarrassment and may wish to avoid situations that might lead to embarrassment, such as school. When the incontinence is clearly deliberate, antisocial behaviors are common. The amount of impairment directly attributable to the disorder is primarily a function of the effect on the child's self-esteem; the degree of social isolation by peers; and anger, punishment, and rejection on the part of parents. Inadequate, inconsistent toilet training and psychosocial stress, such as beginning school and the birth of a sibling, are thought to be predisposing factors.

The essential feature of Functional Enuresis is repeated involuntary or intentional voiding of urine, during the day or nocturnally, into bed or clothes, after the age of 5 years. However, similar to Functional Encopresis, physical disorders must be ruled out as the primary cause of this disorder. Although no specific coexisting mental disorder is found in children with Functional Enuresis, the prevalence of encopresis, sleepwalking, and sleep tremor also may be present. As with encopresis, the social-emotional impairment directly attributable to the disorder is primarily a function of the effect on the child's self-esteem and to the degree of social isolation by peers. Delayed or lax toilet training and psychosocial stress, in particular, hospitalization between the ages of 2 and 4, entering school, and the birth of a sibling, are thought to be predisposing factors.

Elective Mutism

Elective Mutism is a childhood disorder characterized by persistent refusal to talk in one or more major social situations, including school, despite ability to comprehend spoken language and to speak. Most commonly the child will not speak at school but will talk normally at home. However, the child with severe Elective Mutism may refuse to speak in nearly all social situations. Children with this disorder generally have normal language skills, though some have delayed language development and abnormalities of articulation.

In addition to the above characteristics, excessive shyness, social isolation and withdrawal, clinging, school refusal, compulsive traits, negativism, temper tantrums, or other controlling or oppositional behavior may be observed. These features may result in severe impairment in social and school functioning. Predisposing factors of Elective Mutism are thought to include maternal overprotection, language and speech disorders, mental retardation, cultural immigration, and hospitalization or trauma before age 3. In support of these predisposing factors, Wilkins (1985) proposed that elective mutism is associated with particular personal and family characteristics and represents a condition different from any recognized emotional disorder. Although the onset usually occurs before age 5, the disorder may be diagnosed simultaneously with school entry.

Reactive Attachment Disorder

A very common social-emotional disturbance of infancy or early childhood is Reactive Attachment Disorder. The essential feature here is markedly disturbed social relatedness in most contexts, presumably due to grossly pathogenic care that preceded the onset of the disturbance. The most common characteristic of this disorder is a persistent failure to initiate or respond in an age-appropriate manner to most social interactions. Some severe forms of this disorder, in which there is lack of weight gain and motor development, have been called "failure to thrive." Infants with this disorder present with poorly developed social responsiveness as evidenced by poor visual tracking and responding to caregiver's voice, as well as absent attention, interest, and gaze reciprocity. These children are often apathetic, and commonly observed symptoms may include staring, weak cry, poor muscle tone, weak rooting and grasping reactions to attempts to feed, and low spontaneous motility. Excessive sleep and a generalized lack of interest in the environment are also manifestations of the Reactive Attachment Disorder. Additionally, feeding disturbances may be present, in particular rumination, regurgitation, and vomiting. Such associated features may relate to psychosocial deprivation and in turn function as a central factor in malnutrition. These children also may experience sleep disturbances and hypersensitivity to touch and sound.

The diagnosis of Reactive Attachment Disorder can be made as early as in the first month of life but generally is not indicated beyond age 5. All factors that interfere with a child's development of early emotional attachment to a primary caregiver can act as predisposing factors to this disorder. In terms of the caregiver, such factors include severe depression, isolation and lack of support systems, impulse-control difficulties, and extreme deprivation or abuse during his or her own upbringing. In terms of the infant or child, factors include "difficult" or lethargic babies, who may frustrate or discourage their caregivers from appropriate behavior; lack of affectionate physical contact between caregiver and child during the first week of life, such as can occur during a prolonged period in an incubator; or other early separations from an adequate caregiver.

METHODS OF PRESCHOOL AND EARLY CHILDHOOD SOCIAL-EMOTIONAL ASSESSMENT

Although interest in the assessment of social-emotional functioning of preschool and school-aged children is rapidly growing, a number of difficulties attend to conducting such assessments. As Martin (1986) has suggested, these problems result from the inability of very young children to comprehend both written and verbal instructions and/or stimuli. For example, because of limited reading skills, written self-report measures are rendered virtually useless. According to Martin (1986), meaningful interviews also are difficult to conduct with very young children because of their limited vocabulary and concept formation. Thus, responses from these subjects to picture stimuli or story-telling tasks tend to be brief and rather concrete, rendering little material for interpretation. Similar problems arise when the examiner uses "questioning" techniques that require more complex information-processing skills on the part of the child. Responses to questions that require long-term recall of positive or negative experiences, or responses that require judgments about certain experiences, are more difficult for very young children.

Another difficulty in the assessment of preschool children, as expressed by Martin (1986), stems from their relative inability to understand the demand characteristics of the assessment situation and their concomitant immaturity in behavior to meet these demands. For example, much of the preschooler's behavior during assessment is controlled by immediate circumstances. Therefore, assessment results may be more affected by impulsivity, short attention span, boredom, fatigue, or separation anxiety.

Because of these difficulties and complexities in the assessment of social-emotional behavior in preschool children, the process should be flexible and varied in nature. Further, the assessment must be based on an understanding of normative expectations and typical social-emotional development across the life span (Knoff, 1986). Therefore, when dealing with children from birth to 5 years of age, it is important to understand the full range of behaviors and social-emotional milestones found within the population of normally developing infants and preschoolers.

When a child's social-emotional development is viewed as dysfunctional, a number of diverse assessment approaches and techniques can be utilized to characterize emotional status, attitudes, behaviors, and reactions to specific situations or environments (Knoff, 1986). The assessment should be viewed as an opportunity to provide a baseline and continuing evaluation of the child's emotional status and the interaction with physiological, cognitive, educational, and social progress. As Knoff (1986) states, assessment is thought to occur continuously with all children and should consist of formal or informal observations, interviews, and/or evaluation processes involving a child's behavior, social-emotional progress, or self-concept formation. Knoff (1986) suggests that an eclectic approach to emotional assessment involving components of all the theoretical models presented earlier will promote a "broad and non-restrictive view of behavior and the many conditions and circumstances under which it occurs" (p. 29).

Interviews and Developmental Histories

During the prediagnostic or preassessment conference, the initial reasons for referring a child should be discussed. This conference offers the child-study team the opportunity to gain a broad understanding of the child's referral problem and a subsequent approach to the assessment process. The goal of this conference should include the presentation of information about the child that led up to the referral, covering the perspectives of the agency professionals who have worked with the child plus those of the child's family, previous intervention strategies (if tried), and the identification of other agencies that may have been involved or are currently in contact with the child or family. The outcomes of the preassessment meeting should include a specific design to guide the assessment process, specific concerns that need to be assessed during the evaluation process, strategies on how to approach and work with the child and his or her family, decisions as to whether immediate intervention is necessary while the evaluation is being conducted and what that intervention would involve, and assignment of responsibilities to each team member in the collection of further diagnostic information. Presumably the results from this meeting will guide the clinician with regard to the type of information needed from the subsequent interviews and developmental history.

The interview process is one of the most widely used methods of gathering information on social-emotional behaviors of young children. Typically interviews would be conducted with the parents, child-care workers, teachers, and sometimes the child, although Barkley (1981) suggests that children younger than 6 are limited in content of information provided. Nuttall and Ivey (1986) discuss two types of interviews: open and structured. The *open interview* is designed to encourage the interviewee to discuss topics freely and at length, the goal being to explore his or her thinking and experience in great depth. This type of interview may be useful when conducted with parents in gaining an in-depth understanding of their perceptions and feelings of themselves, their family, and the targeted child. The open interview can provide information on the dynamics of the family and the parent/child relationship as well as qualitative information on discipline style, level of frustration or stress perceived by the parent, support systems available and utilized by the parent, and the parent's perception of the child's problems, development, and environmental stability. These interviews require a great deal of clinical expertise and training and, because of their open structure have lower interrater reliability than do structured interviews (Nuttall & Ivey, 1986).

The *structured interview* is one in which the interviewer follows a set of standard questions and procedures, such as one finds in a standardized individual achievement or intellectual instrument, and is similar in its objectivity to checklists, rating scales, and paper-and-pencil self-report tests (see Nuttall & Ivey, 1986, for a discussion of reliability and validity of both the open and structured interview methods).

Well-constructed interviews can provide a major source of information required in the assessment of emotional-social issues of young children. Martin (1986) discusses some fundamental parameters to consider when conducting an interview with a parent or teacher. He suggests that the interviewer's task is to build a structure that will produce reliable information by establishing rapport and confirming with the parents that they are participating in a team problem-solving process geared toward helping the child and the family. Their information should be compared to data collected from other sources (e.g., teachers) to determine agreement on the observed set of child behaviors, which will increase the confidence of the information collected.

Interviews with parents also can include a *developmental/medical history* component (see Appendix), not necessarily initiated as a separate questionnaire. Knoff (1986) also outlines several essential components of an interview and developmental history and provides several formats of actual questionnaires. He suggests that the interview and developmental history should include the following: (a) identification information on the child; (b) family information; (c) parental description of the problem(s); (d) pregnancy and prenatal care; (e) perinatal care; (f) feeding; (g) sleeping; (h) toilet training; (i) speech development; (j) motor development; (k) child's health; (l) school history; (m) play activity; (n) expression of feeling; (o) discipline; and (p) relationships (Knoff, 1986, pp. 94–97).

We have found it useful as well to ask specific questions regarding neurological involvement, such as serious falls, head injuries, convulsions, loss of consciousness, epileptic seizures, and evidence of high prolonged fevers, and what the parent likes most about the child and what he or she finds most frustrating. Knoff (1986) and Nuttall and Ivey (1986) also suggest using interview questions pertaining to infant and child temperament, such as whether the child is shy, sociable, moody, even tempered, reserved, or aggressive. If the child is aggressive, to whom does he or she direct the aggression, and how is this handled? In addition, the interviewer should discover the parental attitude towards the child's dependence versus autonomy. We have found it additionally useful to ask what types of discipline were used during the parents' childhood years.

The *parental interview* and the developmental history also can provide the clinician with information about the child's physical status. For example, has the child had a hearing and vision evaluation, and what were the outcomes of his or her last physical examination? If this information is lacking, one should refer the child to a physician, audiologist, and ophthalmologist to rule out physical problems that may be manifesting themselves as well as social-emotional symptoms. Ruling out physical dysfunction is essential in meeting both PL 99-457 and DSM-III-R criteria for social-emotional handicapping conditions. This is particularly critical when dealing with such disorders as hyperactivity, enuresis, and encopresis. The parent interview and developmental history should also provide the clinician with a list of agencies and/or physicians having previous contact with the parent and child, and appropriate release forms can be signed for the purposes of obtaining confidential psychological, educational, or medical information.

Interviews are also important in obtaining information from the primary child care agency if applicable. As Martin (1986) suggests, parental interview information should be cross-checked with other sources. When agreement exists between the parents and the caregiver about a set of child behaviors, more confidence results regarding the factual nature of the observations. The *teacher/caregiver interview* should consist of questions similar to those identified previously for the parent interview. Specifically, the caregiver interview should inquire into the following: (a) motor and speech development; (b) preschool entrance if applicable (separation anxiety, adjustment, attachment to teacher, etc.); (c) play activity; (d) expression of feelings; (e) discipline practice; and (f) relationships to peers. In addition, the interviewer should ask about previous interventions attempted, listing those that were successful and those that failed. The caregiver also should comment on pre-academic progress, structured versus unstructured activities, and the child's reactions to these activities. Additionally, caregivers' feedback should identify their own perceptions of the child's temperament and behaviors that are frustrating and/or positive.

Results from the developmental history, parent, and caregiver interview will offer a beginning point from which to conduct further evaluation. The responses should provide some initial information about the child's referral problem and if the problem is exhibited across several different environments, such as home and day care. Specific assessment instruments, types of observations, and approach to the child can be selected and initiated based on what one learned from the interview. Hypotheses regarding the nature of the social-emotional distress can be formulated and the subsequent attempt to quantify the behaviors initiated. In addition to the previously mentioned referral to physicians, audiologists, and other outside agencies to rule out physical problems, assessment of intellectual functioning should be addressed in order to rule out any cognitive limitation that may confound the manifested behavior, as suggested in the P-I-E-E-S model (Weaver, 1984).

Behavioral Observations

As noted earlier, the limited verbal repertoire of infants, toddlers, and many preschoolers can create limitations when administering self-report or associative testing measures. For this reason observational measures are generally more reliable than rating scales if the observation is systematic and highly structured (see Keller, 1986, for a discussion of reliability and validity of observational data). Behavioral observations with very young children can be very productive because, as Thorndike and Hagen (1977) suggest, youngsters at this age have fewer coping skills and defense mechanisms, thus allowing them to behave naturally even in the presence of an outside observer.

Several issues arise regarding these behavioral observations of young children. First, observations should be conducted over several different times and across a variety of situations. For example, a young child may exhibit different behaviors depending on the time of day, eating and sleeping patterns, and activities presented. In addition, a child may show the same or different behaviors at home as compared to a preschool or day-care situation. Finally, behaviors of young children may change rapidly over time, requiring that observations occur over several occasions.

The five general types of behavioral observations include narrative recording, event recording, duration recording, latency recording, and interval recording. Because these methods are discussed thoroughly elsewhere (see Alberto & Troutman, 1982; Alessi, 1980; Alessi & Kaye, 1983; Keller, 1986), only brief descriptions appear here. Regardless of the observational approach taken, it is important that at least two different observers participate in order to enhance the reliability and validity of results. Finally, observations should be conducted in an actual (rather than simulated) naturalistic environment where targeted behaviors are likely to occur.

A *narrative recording* is a written description of what occurs during the behavioral observation. The observer writes down everything that happens during the session and includes the reactions and behaviors of others in addition to those of the targeted child. The resulting written narrative describing the observational session then must be reorganized into systematic events. Sulzer-Azaroff and Mayer (1977) provide details on the systematic analysis of the narrative recording, which includes breaking the observational data into antecedent events, the child's behavioral response to the events, and the subsequent results or consequences of the behavioral response. Epps (1985) suggests following up with the caregiver or parent after the observation to determine if the behavior tht occurred during the observation was typical of the child, if the child was having a good or bad day, and if the observational period was representative of the child's typical behaviors.

Event recording is designed to measure the frequency with which a behavior occurs during a given time period (i.e., 15 minutes, 30 minutes, morning, all day). In order to perform an event recording observation, targeted behaviors must be identified prior to the observation and must be discrete and definable, with a beginning and ending (i.e., hitting others, throwing objects, screaming outbursts). Event recording entails simply counting (using paper and pencil, counter, etc.) the number of times the target behavior occurs during a set time period (Epps, 1985). Keller (1986) suggests that this type of observation is productive for high- and low-frequency behaviors as well as for behaviors that occur only briefly. Data obtained from event recordings also can provide the observer with information about the products of the observed behaviors, such as number of toys broken, number of teacher/parent consequences employed, and so forth. The event recordings also offer baseline data for measuring behavioral intervention effectiveness.

Duration recording differs from event recording in that the measurement involves the length of a behavior rather than its frequency of occurrence. As it may be important to know how long the behavior lasts before it stops, the targeted behavior must have measurable beginning and ending points. The observer needs a stopwatch to perform duration recording.

Latency recording usually accompanies duration recording and is designed to measure how long it takes from the end of one behavior to the start of another (e.g., from caregiver request to child's compliance or noncompliance). The resulting data can provide the observer with information about a child's responsiveness to environmental structure as well as his or her ability to shift or control behaviors when asked to do so.

Interval recording is a productive observational method for behaviors that are not clearly discrete (Epps, 1985). Epps describes two types of such recording: whole interval and partial interval. In the former, the observer selects a time interval (usually 10 seconds) and scores the behavior if it occurred during the entire time interval (i.e., interactive play with another child). The number of whole interval scores per minute yields an estimate of the behavior's duration as well as a minimal estimate of how much time overall the child spent performing the targeted behavior. Partial interval recordings require that the behavior occurs only for a portion of the 10-second interval in order to receive a score. This recording yields a maximum estimate of the duration of a behavior, and Epps (1985) suggests that the true amount of time in behavior engagement falls somewhere in between the whole and partial estimates.

For each of these types of recording systems, numerous forms can be designed to record behavioral findings (see Epps, 1985, and Keller, 1986, for a variety of samples). If behavioral observations are done with care, the data thus derived can provide the clinician with valuable information about the child and can promote the generation of more in-depth hypotheses regarding his or her social and emotional difficulties. Behavioral observations also can help identify environmental conditions that influence the child's behavior and assist in clarifying the interaction between the child and his or her environment.

Formal observation systems developed to systematically examine behavior in young children often require some type of specific training and/or extensive practice to yield reliable and valid results. Some of these formal systems address social interaction behaviors, as in the case of the Preschool Interaction Code (Todd, Hudsen, & Greenwood, 1978). The latter is a complicated observational design that measures behavior in a free-play setting and yields information on 28 social interaction variables commonly found with preschoolers in such a situation. The Preschool Interaction Code has data on reliability, validity, and norms, and the user gains proficiency through extensive observer training. Other systems have been developed to look at specific emotional disorders. One of these, the Preschool Observation Scale of Anxiety (Glennon & Weisz, 1978), is designed to measure anxiety-related behaviors in an analogue- or experimental-type setting. Still other coding systems have been designed to observe noncompliant and acting out behaviors, often for home observations with preschool children (Martin, 1986).

Behavior Rating Scales

Behavioral rating scales present another widely used means of assessing the young child's social-emotional status. Because the infant and young child is limited in verbal and written skills, self-report scales and direct interviews are not appropriate or productive, nor often are expressive projective techniques (Martin, Hooper, & Snow, 1986). There are some advantages from using rating scales not found with other personality assessment methods. For example, Martin et al. (1986) state that clinicians can use rating scales on very young children and thus avoid inherent problems with self-report measures that require a certain degree of cognitive maturity and the ability to communicate verbally. Another advantage of rating scales is that they allow the clinician to obtain information on the caregiver's reactions to the child's behavior and can be less biased than the child's individual self-ratings. Finally, raters (parents and caregivers) observe the child in his or her natural environment and can comment more readily on the behaviors in these settings. However, the major limitation of behavior rating scales is the response bias of the rater and the variability in the instruments used (see Achenbach & Edelbrock, 1983, and Martin et al., 1986, for a discussion).

Several widely used behavior rating scales are appropriate for use with young children. The Preschool Behavior Questionnaire (PBQ; Behar & Stringfield, 1974), designed for children ages 3–6 years, yields four scores: Hostile-Aggressive, Anxious-Fearful, Hyperactive-Distractible, and Total. The rater is the teacher or agency caregiver. The scale consists of 36 items rated on a 3-point system and takes approximately 10 minutes to complete. The authors report that the purpose of the scale is to validate teacher perceptions and observations and yield information regarding the need for further evaluation. Fox (1985) states that the PBQ fulfills its stated goals and appears to be a valid and reliable measure for screening children with significant emotional difficulties.

Another behavioral rating scale currently utilized for children 3–6 years of age is the Burks' Behavior Rating Scale, Preschool and Kindergarten Edition (Burks, 1977), which can be completed by the parent and/or teacher. The instrument yields 18 separate scales: Self-Blame, Anxiety, Withdrawal, Dependency, Ego Strength, Physical Strength and Coordination, Intellectuality, Attention, Impulse Control, Reality Contact, Identity, Suffering, Control of Anger, Persecution, Aggression, Resistance, and Social Conformity. The test author reports good reliability and validity for the screening of emotional and behavioral disorders in young children.

The California Preschool Social Competence Scale (Levine, Olzey, & Lewis, 1969) is designed for children from age 3 to age 5. Ratings are completed by the child's teacher and yield an overall total score of social competence. Martin (1986) reports that the scoring is easy but the manual is poor, due to insufficient technical and clinical data.

The Martin Temperament Assessment Battery (Martin, 1984), for children 3-7, gathers ratings from parents, teachers, and clinicians, with separate norms for each. The scale is designed to measure activity, adaptability, approach/withdrawal, emotional intensity, distractibility, and persistence. Administration and scoring are moderately difficult, but the technical manual is very good.

The Achenbach Child Behavior Checklist for ages 4-16 (Achenbach & Edelbrock, 1983) and its counterpart for ages 2-3 (Achenbach, Edelbrock, & Howell, 1987) are behavior rating scales designed to be completed by the parent, although teacher forms are also available. The ages 4-16 scale consists of 118 behavior problems and has excellent normative data representing nonreferred children and adolescents, with a good racial distribution. The ages 2-3 version consists of 99 problem items, 57 of which are counterparts to the original ages 4-16 scale. The scales are based on a random sample of 273 nonreferred children. The authors report excellent reliability and validity, including discriminant validity between clinical and nonclinical groups. These scales yield information on areas such as internalization, externalization, withdrawal, depression, immaturity, aggression, hyperactivity, and social competency, and are the most well-developed, standardized such ratings to date.

Table 14.1 lists additional behavior rating scales that include children within the targeted birth to 5-year age range but in some cases extend to higher, even adolescent, age ranges. The reader also should refer to summary tables presented by Martin (1986) and Martin et al. (1986).

Associative Measures of Personality

Associative techniques or projective testing involves presenting the child with pictures, words, objects, or drawing tasks and obtaining responses (associations) from which hypotheses can be made regarding the child's experiences, feelings, attitudes, and imagination (Obrzut & Boliek, 1986; Palmer, 1983). These techniques include word association and sentence completion tests, kinetic drawing tasks, thematic material, and play behavior measures. Using projective techniques with young children requires special consideration and an understanding of several inherent limitations, as discussed previously.

The analysis of play behavior technique has perhaps the greatest potential for providing social-emotional information on young children within an associative framework (Martin, 1986). Most children naturally play with a variety of objects and engage in acting out fantasies through the manipulation of toys and other materials. We have found it useful to expose a child to a variety of materials in a one-on-one situation as well as providing small groups of children with a variety of play activities. As Martin (1986) suggests, the clinician thereby can observe a variety of behaviors and reactions, including exploration, concentrated play, organization, feelings, independent play, and interactive play. A skilled clinician can provide materials that

TABLE 14.1

ADDITIONAL BEHAVIOR RATING SCALES FOR TARGETED AGE GROUP (BIRTH TO 5 YEARS)

Scale	Range
Behavior Problem Checklist (Quay & Peterson, 1983)	5–16 years
Behavior Rating Instrument for Autistic and Other Atypical Children (Ruttenberg, Kalish, Wenar, & Wolf, 1977)	3–4 years
Behavior Rating Scale (Elmore & Beggs, 1975)	Grades K–8
Conners Parent Rating Scale–Revised, and Conners Teacher Rating Scale–Revised (Goyette, Conners, & Ulrich, 1978)	3–17 years
Devereux Elementary School Rating Scale (Swift, 1982)	Grades K–6
Eyberg Child Behavior Inventory (Robinson, Eyberg, & Ross, 1980)	2–16 years
Louisville Behavior Checklist (Miller, 1977)	4–17 years
McDevitt Behavior Style Questionnaire (McDevitt & Carey, 1978)	3–7 years
School Behavior Checklist (Miller, 1972)	4–13 years

will offer the child an avenue for expressing (verbally or nonverbally) his or her views of the environment. Through the play behavior exhibited, the clinician can make some hypotheses regarding general themes the child expresses, stresses he or she is concerned about, and coping skills the child uses or wishes to use when attempting to resolve conflict situations. During the play activities the clinician should also get a sense of the home environment and level of parenting skills. For example, if dolls are employed, young children may act out a situation from home by mimicking family members through the actions of the dolls.

The clinician can choose to initiate an unstructured interview during the play activity or to be a passive observer, noting the behaviors the child exhibits. Little normative or systematic data are available to assist in the interpretation of play behavior, so making direct statements about the meaning of a child's play behavior is risky. However, as play analysis becomes more systematically studied, normative data should become available for the assessment of individual differences (Martin, 1986).

Personality and Family Inventories

When a child is referred for a social-emotional evaluation, it is important to consider the relationship between the child and his or her environment. The presence or absence of family stress, child and family support systems, and environmental constraints should all be considered as part of the evaluation (Brassard, 1986).

The Personality Inventory for Children (PIC; Wirt, Lachar, Klinedinst, & Seat, 1984) is a multidimensional measure of behavior, ability, affect, and family functioning. Designed to be used for children from 3–16, the 420-item questionnaire is completed by the parent, usually the mother, and yields information on 20 scales.

Three scales address the parent's response style and truthfulness; the remainder address the parent's perceptions of the child, which result in four factor scores: Undisciplined/Poor Self-Control, Social Incompetence, Internalization/Somatic Symptoms, and Cognitive Development. A cognitive triad is also provided: Achievement Screening, Intellectual Screening, and Developmental Rate. Other scales derived from the PIC include General Adjustment, Somatic Concern, Depression, Family Relations, Delinquency, Withdrawal, Anxiety, Psychosis, Hyperactivity, and Social Skills. The PIC can be interpreted in several ways, using individual scales, scale patterns, and/or profile types (Lachar, 1982; Lachar & Gdowski, 1979; Lachar, Kline, & Boersman, 1986). The PIC was normed on 2,390 schoolchildren (ages $5\frac{1}{2}$ to $16\frac{1}{2}$) and later sampled 192 preschoolers ($3\frac{1}{2}$ to $5\frac{1}{2}$ years). Reliability fluctuates across scales, and construct validity is questionable at the present time (Reynolds, 1985). However, the PIC holds promise as a good clinical instrument and is currently an excellent research tool. If selected as part of an evaluation, the PIC should be used with caution for making clinical decisions, tapped instead for good screening information regarding social-emotional functioning.

The Family Inventory of Life Events and Changes (FILE; McCubbin & Patterson, 1983) is a 71-item questionnaire completed separately by both members of a couple. If adolescents are in the family, the respondents complete a separate adolescent form. As a family inventory, the FILE does not assess individuals but rather is based on the assumption that a change experienced by one individual will affect the entire family system. Normed on 1,330 husbands and a separate population of 1,410 wives, the FILE yields five scores: Family Readjustment, Family Life Events, Family-Couple Life Events, Family-Couple Discrepancy, and Family Pileup. Nine subscales address intrafamily conflict, marital conflict, pregnancy and childbearing stress, financial stress, work-family transition stress, family illnesses, family losses (separation, health), family transitions (within and outside of the nuclear family), and family legal stress. The test authors report variable reliability across the scales, but the FILE yields good test-retest reliability. Factor analyses revealed good factor structures, and some initial concurrent validity is reported (see Brassard, 1986, for a discussion).

The Family Environment Scale (FES; Moos & Moos, 1981) is a self-report questionnaire completed by family members designed to address social-emotional and family environment perceptions. The 90-item survey yields three domains: Interpersonal Relationships (cohesion, expressiveness, and conflict); Personal Growth (independence, achievement, intellectual, recreational, and moral orientations); and System Maintenance and Change (organization/responsibilities and control). Form R of the FES was normed on 1,125 "normal" families and 500 "distressed" ones. The scales appear to have adequate reliability and validity for purposes of initial screening, but the instrument is relatively new and its use as a diagnostic instrument has not been determined fully. Qualitative information can be derived from Form R and compared to Form E (expected) and Form I (ideal) to identify discrepancies between the family's perception of current situations and their ideal goals and values. In addition, individual behavior can be described in the context of the family system and can provide useful information for intervention programs (Brassard, 1986).

A variety of published and unpublished questionnaires can assess the status of the family system, but many will require further research, standardization, and validation prior to use in diagnosing family or individual social-emotional dysfunctions. The clinician should be aware of the current strengths and limitations of family assessment and therefore is referred to Brassard (1986), Olson, Russell, and Sprenkle (1979), and Olson, Sprenkle, and Russell (1979) for an in-depth discussion.

Professionals also can obtain information about a child's social-emotional functioning from individual standardized diagnostic instruments. Whereas no one individual test can provide an ample basis for diagnosing a social-emotional disorder, the information so gathered can add to the diagnostic database amassed through the techniques previously discussed. Table 14.2 provides a listing of individual testing instruments that assess components of social-emotional development in the birth to age 5 group. Some of the instruments and scales listed are valuable for screening problems and can alert clinicians to the need for a more extensive social-emotional assessment.

CASE STUDY

The following case study is presented using the P-I-E-E-S model and the process of psychological assessment, diagnosis, and intervention as outlined by Weaver (1984).

Prediagnostic Staffing/Administrative Staffing

Jason had just turned 5 when his case was brought to the diagnostic team by his kindergarten classroom teacher. The team consisted of a psychologist, two special educators, a nurse, the school counselor, a parent advocate, members of the teacher assistance team (regular education teachers), and the school principal. The classroom teacher and the teacher assistance team expressed concerns regarding Jason's extreme behavioral and social inappropriateness as well as his emotional stability and self-concept. Presenting behaviors included the following:

1. Inability to remain at his seat for independent tasks (not lasting more than 15 minutes);
2. Kicking, hitting, and throwing items at teachers and peers;
3. Extreme tantrums and screaming episodes when normal limits were applied;
4. Crawling, standing, and jumping on tables and chairs in the classroom;
5. Extreme mood swings from elation to depression, including crying and negative self-statements;
6. Inability to conform to classroom rules;
7. Inappropriate language;
8. Running away from adults and leaving the school grounds; and
9. Stealing money, toys, and other objects from teachers and peers.

Prior to the prediagnostic staffing, the classroom teacher had implemented a variety of behavior modification programs, including token economies, small group counseling (with a certified school counselor), time-out procedures, tangible reinforcement, verbal praise, encouragement, and physical closeness to the teacher.

TABLE 14.2

TESTS AND SCREENING DEVICES FOR MEASURING
SOCIAL-EMOTIONAL DEVELOPMENT (BIRTH TO 5 YEARS)

Instrument	Age Range	Areas Measured
Batelle Developmental Inventory (Newborg, Stock, Wnek, Guidubaldi, & Svinicki, 1988)	0–8 years	Adult interaction, expression of feelings, self-concept, peer interaction, coping, social role, attention, personal responsibility, toileting, self-help skills
Bayley Scales of Infant Development (Bayley, 1969)	2–30 months	Personal/social development, behavior ratings
Brigance Diagnostic Inventory of Early Development (Brigance, 1978)	0–7 years	Socialization, self-help skills
Denver II (Frankenburg & Dodds, 1990)	6 weeks–6.4 years	Personal/social development
Denver Prescreening Developmental Questionnaire (Frankenburg, 1976)	3 months–6 years	Personal/social development
Developmental Profile II (Alpern, Boll, & Shearer, 1980)	6 months–9 years	Self-help skills, socialization
Lexington Developmental Scales (Child Development Centers of the Bluegrass, 1974)	0–6 years	Personal/social development
Minnesota Child Development Inventory (Ireton & Thwing, 1974)	1–6 years	Personal/social development, self-help skills
Neonatal Behavioral Assessment Scale (Brazelton, 1973)	3 days–4 weeks	Temperament and behavioral indicators
Preschool Behavior Questionnaire (Behar & Stringfield, 1974)	3–7 years	Personal/social development
Scales of Independent Behavior (Bruininks, Woodcock, Weatherman, & Hill, 1985)	0–adult	Social interaction problem behavior, self-care
Vineland Social Maturity Scale (Doll, 1965)	0–30 years	Self-help, social maturity, coping skills
Vineland Adaptive Behavior Scales (Sparrow, Balla, & Cicchetti, 1984)	0–18 years	Self-help, socialization, coping skills

The nurse reported that Jason passed both vision and hearing screenings and she had documentation of a recent physical exam, indicating all physical indicators were within normal limits. The counselor presented information about Jason's family and revealed that Jason is an only child being raised by his father (Mr. M.). Mr. M. worked nights and so Jason stayed with a neighbor from early evening until school the next morning. Jason was eating breakfast and lunch at school, and the nutrition he received at home was in question. The counselor also reported that Mr. M. stated he was a recovering alcoholic, and other team members mentioned he had come to school intoxicated several times. The counselor and principal indicated that Mr. M. was a young parent who admitted to having poor parenting skills, but that he had received some initial assistance from community organizations, including AA and local church groups.

The teacher assistance team and the classroom teacher described Jason's academic skills as within normal limits, with strengths in fine motor skills, object manipulation (puzzles, blocks, drawing), and excellent verbal skills. When given an art project, Jason was able to maintain his attention and behavior for approximately 10 minutes. The classroom teacher expressed concerns about his social development, stating that classmates stayed away from Jason and his interactions toward them were hostile and physically threatening. The team commented on Jason's extreme mood swings, indicating that within a 5-minute period he would go from total elation to excessive crying, for no apparent reason and across a variety of classroom activities and situations. This shift in mood was noted at least three times a day during his 2½-hour school program.

Based on the information presented at the prediagnostic staffing, a need for a complete psychological evaluation was determined. All team members assisted in the evaluation process, and the psychologist was appointed to integrate all of the results and present them at the interpretive staffing.

Parent Interview and Developmental History

The psychologist conducted an interview with Mr. M. and at the same time gathered information about Jason's developmental history (using a form similar to that presented in the appendix to this chapter). The results from the interview indicated that the child's biological mother left the family when Jason (an only child) was 3 years old (he had not seen her since the separation). Mr. M. remarried when Jason was 4 and divorced 6 months later. Mr. M. was 28 at the time of the interview and had completed his high school diploma. At that time he was employed full time as a deliveryman, with night hours and little possibility of a shift change. He stated that he was a recovering alcoholic, receiving help from a local AA chapter, and that he was unable to remain sober during times of stress. Mr. M. reported that he was raised by a very strict father and passive mother, and relations with his parents were severed prior to Jason's birth. The child did not know either set of grandparents or other extended family members. Mr. M. reported that he and Jason had moved several times to look for work and that Jason never had the opportunity to establish friendships with children his own age.

Mr. M. also acknowledged that he had difficulty supervising his son's activities and felt that his parenting skills were limited. He stated that at home Jason threw temper tantrums, destroyed household property, ran away when punishment was employed, and often would hit, kick, and push his father and children in the neighborhood. Mr. M. also reported mood swings similar to those observed in school, and he stated that Jason would swear and speak negatively about himself when frustrated. Jason dressed, fed, and bathed himself and was responsible for his own room and toys; in addition, he usually was responsible for fixing his own dinner prior to leaving for the neighbor's house in the evening.

Medical information revealed that all developmental milestones were within normal limits. Mr. M. had taken Jason for a medical/behavioral examination as requested by the school to rule out hyperactivity, and the results were determined as negative prior to the preassessment conference. The father reported one hospitalization for Jason at 2½ years of age when he ingested a bottle of his mother's "mood drugs." Jason's stomach was pumped and he remained in the hospital 2 days for observation. Hospital records were unremarkable. Mr. M. reported that Jason's mother was diagnosed bipolar and was under prescribed medication "to stabilize her emotions." There was no other documented history of family disease or psychopathology.

Mr. M. stated that he enjoyed his son and the company they shared. The behaviors he noted as most frustrating were Jason's "bizarre screaming, throwing fits, and hitting." Mr. M. concluded by saying he wanted to be a better parent and blamed himself for many of Jason's behavioral problems.

Behavioral Observations

Four members of the assessment team conducted event and narrative recordings. The event recordings (1-hour observations over a 1-week period) were compiled, and the behaviors confirmed by all four observers were averaged and converted to percentages (frequency/hour). Table 14.3 presents the results of the event recording data and demonstrates Jason's most frequent behaviors as well as those occurring infrequently. The event recordings indicated that the behaviors occurring most often were out-of-seat behavior, screaming and shouting, throwing objects, destroying materials, and crying. Jason's on-task behavior was the least frequently occurring behavior.

Narrative observations were completed by three team members and resulted in documenting behaviors similar to those obtained during the event recording observations. However, the dynamics between Jason and the classroom environment were better understood. For example, Jason asked to go to the bathroom and, when he got permission, waited 30 seconds before actually leaving the classroom. On returning, he ran across the classroom, stepping on art projects that were placed on the floor as his peers were working on them. He ran back across the room and left the room. The classroom teacher went to get him and asked him to come and join the group. He screamed and stated "I can't do anything and I'm no good." Later, when given a choice of activities, Jason was unable to select from several centers and continued wandering around the classroom. After several minutes he selected the only activity that could be done alone (block designs) and proceeded to dump the entire box of blocks across the table. The classroom teacher explained the activity and demonstrated how the blocks could be put together to make multicolor designs. He worked with the blocks for approximately 30 seconds, began to cry and restate that he was bad at everything, and threw the blocks back into the box. Another observer wrote

Table 14.3

Results from Behavioral Observations of Jason Using Event Recordings

Overt Behavior	Day 1	Day 2	Day 3	Day 4	Day 5
Out-of-seat or out-of-group behavior (includes running, climbing on furniture, crawling, wandering)	40%*	45%	50%	47%	56%
Screaming (includes shouting, loud name calling)	25%	14%	17%	20%	16%
Hitting others	5%	4%	5%	3%	2%
Throwing objects	8%	10%	5%	11%	4%
Tantrums	1%	5%	3%	5%	2%
Destroying materials	10%	11%	9%	6%	9%
Crying	10%	10%	9%	5%	10%
On-task behavior	1%	1%	2%	3%	1%

*Percentages = frequency/time

about Jason's kicking the wall and another child without a prior interaction or confrontation. Observers also noted Jason taking stickers and candy from the teacher's reward jar when she was engaged with the other children. The observations indicated that Jason consistently demonstrated inappropriate behaviors to seek negative attention from the teacher but seemed unconcerned about seeking approval or attention from his peers. The children in the classroom did a very good job of ignoring Jason's explosive episodes and responded to him when he was appropriate. To rule out classroom management issues, the teacher and her students also were observed when Jason was absent. The observer noted complete teacher control of the children, a very organized environment, and excellent on-task behaviors and active learning by her students.

Results from the Devereux Elementary School Behavior Rating Scale (Swift, 1982) and the Behavior Evaluation Scale (McCarney, Leigh, & Cornbleet, 1983) are presented in Table 14.4. Each rating scale was completed by the classroom teacher and indicates significantly deviant scores across a variety of behavioral domains. For example, classroom disturbance was noted as being 2 standard deviations above the mean and indicated that Jason frequently engages in teasing and tormenting his peers. In addition, ratings indicated that Jason annoys or interferes with the work of his peers and often needs a reprimand from the teacher. Jason's ratings were also significant in the area of impatience, indicating that he rushes impulsively through activities and is unwilling to go back over his work once completed. One of the most significant scores relates to deviance and disrespect, indicating the inability to comply with adult requests. Jason also was rated as a child who blames others or situations when things don't go his way. An average level of achievement anxiety and comprehension of new concepts was also noted. Elevated ratings in the areas of inattention and withdrawal

TABLE 14.4

Results from the Devereux Elementary School Behavior Rating Scale and the Behavior Evaluation Scale

DEVEREUX ELEMENTARY SCHOOL BEHAVIOR RATING SCALE

Behaviors Rated	*Scores Attained (in Standard Deviations)*
Classroom disturbance	+2
Impatience	+2
Disrespect-defiance	+2
External blame	+2
Achievement anxiety	0
External reliance	0
Comprehension	0
Inattentive-withdrawn	+2
Irrelevant responsiveness	+2
Creative initiative	0
Needs closeness to teacher	+1
Unable to change tasks	+1
Quits easily	0
Slow to complete work	0

BEHAVIOR EVALUATION SCALE

Scales Measured	*Standard Scores*
Learning problems	7 ($M=10$, $SD=3$)
Interpersonal difficulties	3
Inappropriate behavior	2
Unhappiness/depression	5
Physical symptoms/fears	4
Behavior quotient	59 ($M=100$, $SD=15$)

indicate the wide range of behaviors demonstrated by Jason in his classroom. Depressed scores were derived on scales tapping a general pervasive mood of depression and physiological symptoms of stress. Confirmation between the two behavior rating scales was good, and ratings were congruent with the formal behavioral observations discussed earlier.

It was important to rule out cognitive and achievement difficulties that may have been manifesting themselves in atypical behavior. Jason was given the Wechsler Preschool and Primary Scales of Intelligence (WPPSI; Wechsler, 1967) and the Kaufman Assessment Battery for Children (K-ABC; Kaufman & Kaufman, 1983). The results of these administrations appear in Table 14.5. The clinician noted that Jason's behavior was slightly more appropriate during the individual test sessions. He appeared highly motivated but required tangible reinforcers (stickers) to maintain his persistence throughout the tasks presented. Based on Jason's performance on the WPPSI, he obtained a Full Scale score that fell within the average range of cognitive abilities when compared to others his age. According to his subtest performances, it appeared that Jason did equally well on items tapping verbal comprehension as he did on tasks requiring perceptual organization. However, behaviorally Jason demonstrated greater concentration and effort on tasks that involved manipulatives and visual stimuli. Jason was given the K-ABC to assist in confirming the WPPSI findings and to obtain a measure of academic readiness. On the K-ABC, Jason produced a Mental Processing Composite score that also fell within the average range of cognitive functioning when compared to his agemates. No significant discrepancy emerged between scores on the Sequential and Simultaneous Processing scales.

Achievement measures indicated that Jason's academic skills were also within the average range for his age and grade. He performed very well on tasks tapping math readiness and quantitative concepts and equally so on tasks tapping prereading skills. Jason did less well on tasks tapping a general fund of information and verbal reasoning, but these skill levels were considered within the average range as well. The Brigance Inventory of Early Development (Brigance, 1978) and Inventory of Basic Skills (Brigance, 1983) revealed that Jason was on grade level relative to readiness skills, including gross and fine motor skills, self-help skills, speech and language skills, and general knowledge. Math readiness, listening, and reading readiness were also found commensurate with Jason's kindergarten grade placement.

Jason's father completed the Personality Inventory for Children (PIC), the results for which appear in Table 14.6. The psychologist invited Mr. M. to complete the questionnaire at school in order to ensure that he was physically rested and mentally alert. Interpretation of the PIC results included the analyses of the factor scales, validity scales, and standard scales. Based on the pattern of the lie, frequency, and defensiveness scales, the psychologist determined that Mr. M. was honest and truthful and made no attempt to minimize or deny any problems that Jason might have. The interpretation of the cognitive and academic scales indicated that Jason may become easily distracted away from tasks presented in the classroom. These scales indicated a history of preacademic failure and a poor self-image. Deficient concentration may be impairing Jason's ability to learn and may interfere with his academic performance. Based on the scores from the clinical scales, Jason appeared to be very sensitive to criticism and to fear rejection from peers and adults. Evidence

TABLE 14.5

RESULTS FROM THE WECHSLER PRESCHOOL AND PRIMARY SCALES OF INTELLIGENCE AND THE KAUFMAN ASSESSMENT BATTERY FOR CHILDREN

WECHSLER PRESCHOOL AND PRIMARY SCALES OF INTELLIGENCE

Subtests	*Subtest Standard Scores ($M=10$, $SD=3$)*
Information	7
Vocabulary	9
Arithmetic	11
Similarities	11
Comprehension	10
Sentences	9
Animal House	8
Picture Completion	12
Mazes	11
Geometric Design	10
Block Design	12

Scales	*Standard Scores ($M=100$, $SD=15$)*
Verbal	97
Performance	104
Full Scale	101

KAUFMAN ASSESSMENT BATTERY FOR CHILDREN

Scales	*Standard Scores ($M=100$, $SD=15$)*
Sequential Processing	106
Simultaneous Processing	106
Mental Processing Composite	107
Achievement	91
Faces & Places	86
Arithmetic	102
Riddles	87
Reading/Decoding	96

Table 14.6

Results from the Personality Inventory for Children

Scales	T-Scores (M=50, SD=10)
FACTOR SCALES	
Factor I: Undisciplined/Poor Self Control	99
Factor II: Social Incompetence	68
Factor III: Internalization/Somatic Symptoms	69
Factor IV: Cognitive Development	52
VALIDITY SCALES	
Lie	34
Frequency	63
Defensive	29
STANDARD SCALES	
Adjustment	97
Achievement	99
Intellectual Screening	62
Development	69
Somatic Concerns	37
Depression	86
Family Relations	73
Delinquency	91
Withdrawal	54
Anxiety	76
Psychosis	69
Hyperactivity	88
Social Skills	81

of significantly poor peer relationships, as well as isolation and limited frustration tolerance, also was noted. A general presence of depression and unhappiness was indicated, which may manifest itself in poor sleeping patterns, eating problems, emotional lability, fears, excessive worry, crying, and self-blame.

The PIC scale patterns also indicated that Jason displayed defiant behavior at home and at school and could be observed showing poor judgment and unmodulated hostility. Some evidence for antisocial behavior, such as lying, stealing, destruction of objects, and the need to blame others for current problems, also was apparent. The PIC results also suggested a history of family stress, including marital problems, alcoholism, substance abuse, and inconsistency in parenting skills.

The psychologist interviewed Jason near the end of the evaluation. This procedure was conducted because Jason demonstrated adequate verbal skills and appeared

FIGURE 14.1. Results of Jason's draw-a-person task.

to enjoy the one-on-one attention throughout the individual assessment sessions. During the interview Jason stated that his dad would often come home and "act funny." He described this situation as scary because his dad would walk in and urinate on the floor and then fall asleep on the couch. Jason said it was hard to wake him up sometimes and he worried that his dad might be dead. Jason also stated that no one at school liked him and he felt like running away. He was unable to name any of the children in his classroom and could not say whether any of his peers were friends. During this session, Jason was asked to draw a person. As can be seen in Figure 14.1, Jason's drawing (which depicts a person standing next to an animal) was developmentally appropriate, and the missing elements are not emotionally significant.

Whereas the drawing itself was not extremely revealing, the story Jason told was clinically informative. He stated first that the figure was a "tiny baby" and then that it was himself when he was older (thus the number he said was "31" placed on the forehead). When speaking of the older person, Jason added a mustache. About the animal standing next to this figure Jason stated, "This is my cat, I will play with the cat and then I will tear his legs and paws off and then make fun of it . . . the cat is my mamma or maybe my daddy . . . then I will feel sad about hurting the cat." When asked if he liked to do things with others or alone, Jason responded he liked to do things alone, "like eating, eating makes me feel better, or going to the store and buying toys . . . and guns." When asked about dreams, Jason said he dreamed about strangers coming into his room and beating him up, as well as about eating ice cream with spiders crawling in it, which made him wake up scared. When asked about friends, his response was, "The boy would like to have friends, but he don't . . . no one likes him."

The interview with Jason suggested an unstable home environment and possible exposure to adult substance abuse. Jason also indicated extreme anger directed at his parents and extreme concerns about isolation and rejection. He revealed nightmares and a view of his environment as threatening and insecure. Jason may cope with stress by running away, distancing, or regressing to earlier stages of development.

Interpretive Staffing

The psychologist organized and integrated all of the information gathered during the course of the assessment process. The team met again to discuss the results and to determine a diagnosis and to brainstorm possible intervention strategies and programs. Following Weaver's (1984) P-I-E-E-S model, Jason's current status was discussed. Physiological functioning was assessed through a complete physical exam, and all sensory acuities were within normal limits. Additionally, the possibility of hyperactivity was ruled out by a physician and the behavioral ratings and observations. Jason's intellectual functioning was determined to be within the average range, with no evidence indicating either a processing deficit or learning disability. Regarding educational functioning, Jason's skills in all academic areas were found commensurate with his age and grade. Behavioral observations, behavior ratings, parental inventories, interviews, and limited associative testing addressed the domain of emotional functioning and the results indicated some extreme emotional difficulties, including a general pervasive mood of unhappiness and depression. The social-emotional assessment methods confirmed these impressions and indicated that Jason perceived his environment as hostile and unstable. His reactions to everyday situations were inappropriate and sometimes bizarre and unpredictable.

Jason's social functioning was determined to be maladaptive, as he was unable to establish and maintain meaningful relationships with adults or peers. The assessment revealed that the boy had extreme difficulty trusting others and consequently became isolated both at home and at school. The home environment was identified as unstable, and psychological assistance was recommended for Jason's father.

The team concluded that Jason exhibited an emotional handicap and met three of the federal criteria for emotional involvement, including inability to maintain satisfactory relationships with adults and peers, inappropriate behavior or feelings under normal circumstances, and general pervasive mood of unhappiness or depression. Based on the evaluation, they determined that the least restrictive environment for Jason would be in a self-contained primary-level emotionally handicapped classroom. The intervention program would be designed to meet his emotional and behavioral needs and would involve a behavior level system where privileges and responsibilities would be earned through daily behavior points. Tangible rewards such as stickers, food, and tokens would be given on a variable schedule for any approximation of appropriate behavior. Jason also would be involved in group counseling and individual play therapy provided by the school counselor and school psychologist, respectively. Behaviors would be shaped through academic and nonacademic activities to maintain academic progress. As Jason advanced through the level system, mainstream classes would be considered and targeted for math and physical education, where Jason potentially would be most successful. Jason would be placed with a nurturing female teacher throughout the school day to enhance building a bonding relationship with a female role model. In addition, it was recommended that he participate in a structured/therapeutic play program to enhance social interaction with peers and peer modeling.

Results of the evaluation were discussed with Mr. M. in a smaller meeting with the classroom teacher, the school counselor, and the school psychologist. Mr. M's feelings and concerns were discussed, and referrals to outside agencies were listed and presented. Fortunately Mr. M. was very cooperative and open about needing additional assistance. He followed up with a family HMO plan and began receiving psychological assistance on a weekly basis. He signed release statements so that the results of the evaluation could be sent to the outside agency, and a plan was developed with the therapist and school personnel to ensure consistency in approach to Jason and Mr. M. A 4-week follow-up indicated that Jason was beginning to make progress behaviorally and Mr. M. was attending a group for single parents designed to work on parenting skills and support systems for single-parent families.

The foregoing assessment approaches and case study should serve as a general model for the assessment of young children with social-emotional difficulties. Although there are many types of emotional disorders, the structure of a systematic assessment should follow formats and methodologies similar to those in the case study, for either DSM-III-R or education labeling. Because of the nature of their social-emotional disabilities and their rapid developmental changes, a continuing monitoring system should be implemented, with frequent reevaluations, to assess the social-emotional progress of young children diagnosed as emotionally handicapped. Findings from an impressive meta-analysis involving 108 well-designed outcome studies indicated that identification and treatment of emotional dysfunction in young children yields better social-emotional adjustment and psychological outcomes than treatment of older children and adolescents (Weisz, Weiss, Alicke, & Klotz, 1987). Therefore, a thorough assessment process to identify young children with emotional difficulties indeed may be warranted.

REFERENCES

Achenbach, T.M., & Edelbrock, C.S. (1983). *Manual for the Child Behavior Checklist and Revised Child Behavior Profile.* Burlington, VT: University of Vermont, Department of Psychiatry.

Achenbach, T.M., Edelbrock, C.S., & Howell, C.T. (1987). Empirically based assessment of the behavioral/emotional problems of 2- and 3-year-old children. *Journal of Abnormal Child Psychology, 15,* 629–650.

Alberto, P.A., & Troutman, A.C. (1982). *Applied behavioral analysis for teachers: Influencing student performance.* Columbus, OH: Merrill.

Alessi, G.J. (1980). Behavioral observation for the school psychologist: Responsive-discrepancy model. *School Psychology Review, 9,* 31–45.

Alessi, G.J., & Kaye, J.H. (1983). *Behavior assessment for school psychologists.* Kent, OH: National Association of School Psychologists.

Almy, M., & Genishi, C. (1979). *Ways of studying children* (rev. ed.). New York: Teachers College Press.

Alpern, G.D., Boll, T.J., & Shearer, M.S. (1980). *Developmental Profile II*. Aspen, CO: Psychological Development Publications.

American Psychiatric Association. (1987). *Diagnostic and statistical manual of mental disorders* (rev. 3rd ed.). Washington, DC: Author.

Bandura, A. (1978). The self-system in reciprocal determinism. *American Psychologist, 33,* 344-358.

Barkley, R.A. (1981). Hyperactivity. In E.J. Nash & L.G. Terdal (Eds.), *Behavioral assessment of childhood disorders* (pp. 127-184). New York: Guilford.

Bayley, N. (1969). *Manual for the Bayley Scales of Infant Development*. San Antonio, TX: Psychological Corporation.

Behar, L., & Stringfield, S. (1974). *Manual for the Preschool Behavior Questionnaire*. Durham, NC: Learning Institute of North Carolina.

Bell, R., & Pearl, D. (1982). Psychosocial change in risk groups: Implications for early identification. *Prevention in Human Services, 1,* 45-59.

Bernstein, V.G., Jeremy, R.J., & Marcus, J. (1986). Mother-infant interaction in multiproblem families: Finding those at risk. *Journal of the American Academy of Child Psychiatry, 25,* 631-640.

Boehm, A.E., & Sandberg, B.R. (1981). Assessment of the preschool child. In C.R. Reynolds & T.B. Gutkin (Eds.), *The handbook of school psychology* (pp. 82-120). New York: Wiley.

Bradley, R.H., & Caldwell, B.M. (1974). *Issues and procedures in testing young children* (TM Report No. 37). Princeton, NJ: Educational Testing Services, ERIC Clearinghouse on Tests, Measurement, and Evaluation.

Brassard, M.R. (1986). Family assessment approaches and procedures. In H.M. Knoff (Ed.), *The assessment of child and adolescent personality* (pp. 399-449). New York: Guilford.

Brazelton, T.B. (1973). *Neonatal Behavior Assessment Scale*. Philadelphia, PA: Lippincott.

Brigance, A.H. (1978). *Brigance Diagnostic Inventory of Early Development*. North Billerica, MA: Curriculum Associates.

Brigance, A.H. (1983). *Brigance Diagnostic Comprehensive Inventory of Basic Skills*. North Billerica, MA: Curriculum Associates.

Brophy, J., & Good, T. (1974). Brophy-Good System (Teacher-Child Dyadic Interaction). In A. Simon & E.G. Boyer (Eds.), *Mirrors for behavior*. Philadelphia: Research for Better Schools.

Bruininks, R.H., Woodcock, R.W., Weatherman, R.F., & Hill, B.K. (1985). *Scales of Independent Behavior*. Allen, TX: DLM Teaching Resources.

Burks, H.F. (1977). *Burks Behavior Rating Scales: Preschool and Kindergarten Version—Manual*. Los Angeles, CA: Western Psychological Services.

Child Development Centers of the Bluegrass. (1974). *Lexington Developmental Scales*. Lexington, KY: Author.

Dahl, E.K., Cohen, D.J., & Provence, S. (1986). Clinical and multivariate approaches to the nosology of pervasive developmental disorders. *Journal of the American Academy of Child Psychiatry, 25,* 170-180.

Doll, E. (1965). *Vineland Social Maturity Scale*. Circle Pines, MN: American Guidance Service.

Elmore, P.B., & Beggs, D.L. (1975). *Behavior Rating Scale—Manual*. Carbondale, IL: Southern Illinois University.

Epps, S. (1985). Best practices in behavioral observations. In A. Thomas & J. Grimes (Eds.), *Best practices in school psychology* (pp. 95-111). Kent, OH: National Association of School Psychologists.

Fox, R.A. (1985). Preschool Behavior Questionnaire. In J.V. Mitchell, Jr. (Ed.), *The ninth mental measurements yearbook* (pp. 1189-1190). Lincoln, NE: Buros Institute of Mental Measurements.

Frankenburg, W.K. (1976). *Denver Prescreening Developmental Questionnaire.* Denver, CO: Ladoca Project and Publishing Foundation.

Frankenburg, W.K., & Dodds, J.B. (1990). *Denver Developmental Screening Test.* Denver, CO: Ladoca Project and Publishing Foundation.

Glennon, B., & Weisz, J. (1978). An observational approach to the assessment of anxiety in young children. *Journal of Consulting and Clinical Psychology, 46,* 1246-1257.

Goyette, C.H., Conners, C.K., & Ulrich, R.F. (1978). Normative data on revised Conners Parent and Teacher Rating Scales. *Journal of Abnormal Child Psychology, 6,* 221-236.

Ireton, H.R., & Thwing, E.J. (1974). *Minnesota Child Development Inventory.* Minneapolis, MN: Behavior Science Systems.

Kaufman, A.S., & Kaufman, N.L. (1983). *Kaufman Assessment Battery for Children.* Circle Pines, MN: American Guidance Service.

Kazdin, A.E. (1982). Applying behavioral principles in the schools. In C.R. Reynolds & T.B. Gutkin (Eds.), *The handbook of school psychology* (pp. 501-529). New York: Wiley.

Keller, H.R. (1986). Behavioral observation approaches to personality assessment. In H.M. Knoff (Ed.), *The assessment of child and adolescent personality* (pp. 353-397). New York: Guilford.

Knoff, H.M. (1986). Identifying and classifying children and adolescents referred for personality assessment: Theories, systems, and issues. In H.M. Knoff (Ed.), *The assessment of child and adolescent personality* (pp. 3-31). New York: Guilford.

Lachar, D. (1982). *Personality Inventory for Children (PIC) revised format manual supplement.* Los Angeles: Western Psychological Services.

Lachar, D., & Gdowski, C.L. (1979). *Actuarial assessment of child and adolescent personality: An interpretive guide for the Personality Inventory for Children profile.* Los Angeles: Western Psychological Services.

Lachar, D., Kline, R.B., & Boersman, D.C. (1986). The Personality Inventory for Children: Approaches to actuarial interpretation in clinic and school settings. In H.M. Knoff (Ed.), *The assessment of child and adolescent personality* (pp. 273-308). New York: Guilford.

Lazarus, R.S. (1981). The stress and coping paradigm. In C. Eisdorfer, D. Cohen, A. Kleinman, & P. Maxim (Eds.), *Models for clinical psychopathology* (pp. 177-214). New York: Spectrum.

Lerner, J.A., Inui, T.S., Trupin, E.W., & Douglas, E. (1985). Preschool behavior can predict future psychiatric disorders. *Journal of the American Academy of Child Psychiatry, 24,* 42-48.

Levine, J.M., & Demb, H.B. (1987). Characteristics of preschool children diagnosed as having an atypical pervasive developmental disorder. *Journal of Developmental and Behavioral Pediatrics, 8,* 77-82.

Levine, S., Olzey, F.F., & Lewis, M. (1969). *The California Preschool Social Competence Scale—Manual.* Palo Alto, CA: Consulting Psychologists Press.

Martin, R.P. (1984). *The Temperament Assessment Battery—Interim manual.* Athens, GA: Developmental Metrics.

Martin, R.P. (1986). Assessment of the social and emotional functioning of preschool children. *School Psychology Review, 15,* 216-232.

Martin, R.P., Hooper, S., & Snow, J. (1986). Behavior rating scale approaches to personality assessment in children and adolescents. In H.M. Knoff (Ed.), *The assessment of child and adolescent personality* (pp. 309-351). New York: Guilford.

McCarney, S.B., Leigh, J.L., & Cornbleet, J. (1983). *Behavior Evaluation Scale.* Columbia, MO: Behavior Evaluation Scale Educational Services.

McCubbin, H.I., & Patterson, J.M. (1983). Stress: The Family Inventory of Life Events and Changes. In E.E. Filsinger (Ed.), *Marriage and family assessment: A sourcebook for family therapy* (pp. 275–315). Beverly Hills, CA: Sage.

McDevitt, S.C., & Carey, W.B. (1978). The measurement of temperament in 3–7 year old children. *Journal of Child Psychology and Psychiatry, 19,* 245–253.

Miller, L.C. (1972). School Behavior Checklist: An inventory of deviant behaviors in children. *Journal of Consulting and Clinical Psychology, 38,* 134–144.

Miller, L.C. (1977). *Louisville Behavior Checklist—Manual.* Los Angeles, CA: Western Psychological Services.

Moos, R.H., & Moos, B.S. (1981). *Family Environment Scale manual.* Palo Alto, CA: Consulting Psychologists Press.

Newborg, J., Stock, J.R., Wnek, L., Guidubaldi, J., & Svinicki, J. (1988). *Battelle Developmental Inventory: Examiner's manual.* Allen, TX: DLM Teaching Resources.

Nuttall, E.V., & Ivey, A.E. (1986). The diagnostic interview process. In H.M. Knoff (Ed.), *The assessment of child and adolescent personality* (pp. 105–140). New York: Guilford.

Obrzut, J.E., & Boliek, C.A. (1986). Thematic approaches to personality assessment with children and adolescents. In H.M. Knoff (Ed.), *The assessment of child and adolescent personality* (pp. 173–198). New York: Guilford.

Olson, D.H., Russell, C.S., & Sprenkle, D.H. (1979). Circumplex model of marital and family systems II: Empirical studies and clinical intervention. In J. Vincent (Ed.), *Advances in family intervention, assessment and theory.* Greenwich, CT: JAI.

Olson, D.H., Sprenkle, D.H., & Russell, C.S. (1979). Circumplex model of marital and family systems: I. Cohesion and adaptability dimensions, family types, and clinical application. *Family Process, 18,* 3–28.

Palmer, J.O. (1983). *The psychological assessment of children* (2nd ed.). New York: Wiley.

Quay, H.C., & Peterson, D.R. (1983). *Interim manual for the Revised Behavior Problem Checklist.* Coral Gables, FL: University of Miami.

Rescorla, L.A. (1986). Preschool psychiatric disorders: Diagnostic classification and symptom patterns. *Journal of the American Academy of Child Psychiatry, 25,* 162–169.

Reynolds, C.R. (1985). Personality Inventory for Children. In J.V. Mitchell, Jr. (Ed.), *The ninth mental measurements yearbook* (pp. 1154–1157). Lincoln, NE: Buros Institute of Mental Measurements.

Reynolds, C.R., Gutkin, T.B., Elliott, S.N., & Witt, J.C. (1984). *School psychology: Essentials of theory and practice.* New York: Wiley.

Rezmierski, V.E., Knoblock, P., & Bloom, R.B. (1982). The psychoeducational model: Theory and historical perspective. In R.L. McDowell, G.W. Adamson, & F.H. Wood (Eds.), *Teaching emotionally disturbed children.* Boston: Little, Brown.

Robinson, E.A., Eyberg, S.M., & Ross, A.W. (1980). The standardization of an inventory of child conduct problem behavior. *Journal of Clinical Psychology, 9,* 22–29.

Ruttenberg, B.A., Kalish, B.I., Wenar, C., & Wolf, E.G. (1977). *Behavior Rating Instrument for Autistic and Other Atypical Children—Manual.* Chicago, IL: Stoelting.

Sack, W.H., Mason, R., & Collins, R. (1987). A long-term follow-up study of a children's psychiatric day treatment center. *Child Psychiatry and Human Development, 18,* 58–68.

Slenkovich, J.E. (1983). An analysis of DSM-III diagnoses vis-à-vis special education law. In H.R. Wade (Ed.), *PL 94-142 as applied to DSM-III diagnoses* (pp. 1–18). Cupertino, CA: Kinghorn.

Sparrow, S.S., Balla, D.A., & Cicchetti, D.V. (1984). *Vineland Adaptive Behavior Scales.* Circle Pines, MN: American Guidance Service.

Sulzer-Azaroff, B., & Mayer, G.R. (1977). *Applying behavior-analysis procedures with children and youth.* New York: Holt, Rinehart & Winston.
Swift, M. (1982). *Devereux Elementary School Rating Scale II.* Devon, PA: Devereux Foundation Press.
Thorndike, R.L., & Hagen, E.P. (1977). *Measurement and evaluation in psychology and education* (4th ed.). New York: Wiley.
Todd, N.M., Hudsen, D., & Greenwood, C.R. (1978). *Preschool Interaction Code.* Eugene, OR: University of Oregon Center for Research in the Behavioral Education of the Handicapped.
Volkmar, J.R., Stier, D.M., & Cohen, D.J. (1985). Age of recognition of pervasive developmental disorder. *American Journal of Psychiatry, 142,* 1450–1452.
Weaver, S.J. (1984). Introduction to the psychological assessment process. In S.J. Weaver (Ed.), *Testing children: A reference guide for effective clinical and psychoeducational assessments* (pp. 1–14). Austin, TX: PRO-ED.
Wechsler, D. (1967). *Manual for the Wechsler Preschool and Primary Scales of Intelligence.* San Antonio, TX: Psychological Corporation.
Weisz, J.R., Weiss, B., Alicke, M.D., & Klotz, M.L. (1987). Effectiveness of psychotherapy with children and adolescents: A meta-analysis for clinicians. *Journal of Consulting and clinical Psychology, 55,* 542–549.
Wilkins, P. (1985). A comparison of elective mutism and emotional disorders in children. *British Journal of Psychiatry, 146,* 192–203.
Wirt, R.D., Lachar, D., Klinedinst, J.E., & Seat, P.D. (1984). *Multidimensional description of child personality: A manual for the Personality Inventory for Children* (1984 revision by David Lachar). Los Angeles, CA: Western Psychological Services.

Appendix.
Parent Interview and Developmental History

I. PERSONAL DATA

Child's full name _____ Nickname _____

Home address _____ Telephone _____

Date of birth _____ Age _____

Primary language spoken by the child _____

Primary language spoken in the home _____

Racial/ethnic background _____

Father's name _____ Age _____

    Occupation _____ Education _____

Mother's name _____ Age _____

    Occupation _____ Education _____

Siblings:

Name	Sex	Age	Grade	At home

Child lives with: Both parents _____ Mother _____ Father _____

    Guardian _____ Other _____

Others living in the home: Grandfather, Grandmother, Stepmother,

    Stepfather, Other _____

Parents are: Separated _____ Divorced _____ Remarried _____ Deceased _____

II. DEVELOPMENTAL HISTORY

Describe the pregnancy (target child): _____

_____

Describe the prenatal care received: _____

_____

Any illness or use of medications during pregnancy (describe)? _____

_____

Any complications before, during, or immediately after delivery? _____

_____

Length of gestation: _____

Birth weight and length: _____

Breast or bottle feeding: _____ Any difficulties in appetite: _____

_____ Any difficulties sucking: _____

Weaning: _____ Colic: _____

Infant's general temperament: _____

_____

At what age did the child: roll over? _____

                                 sit unassisted? _____

                                 speak first words? _____

                                 feed self unassisted? _____

At what age was the child toilet trained? _____

What methods were used in training? _____

_____ How did the child respond? _____

_____

Does the child have a peculiar walk, fall, or lose balance easily? _____

_____

Does the child have difficulty grasping objects? _____

Does the child have difficulty blowing up a balloon or blowing out matches? ___

Does the child watch TV or radio turned up excessively loud? _____

Does the child seem to tune in and out of listening situations? _____
_____

Is the child exposed to loud noise consistently? _____

III. MEDICAL INFORMATION

Has the child had any of the following difficulties?

convulsions _____	strep throat _____
unconsciousness _____	high prolonged fever _____
childhood diseases _____	serious falls _____
allergies _____	serious illnesses _____
unusual sleeping habits _____	unusual eating habits _____
seizures _____	diabetes _____

other (please describe) _____
_____
_____
_____

Has the child ever been hospitalized? _____
_____

Has the child ever experienced any traumatic experiences (physical or psychological)? _____
_____

Has the child ever had a psychological evaluation? _____

When? _____ Results? _____

Has the child ever received any outside services (i.e., speech, emotional, social, medical, day care, etc.)? _____
_____

When was the child's last physical exam? _____ Where? _____
                              Results: _____

When was the last hearing exam? _____ Where? _____
                              Results: _____

When was the last vision exam? _____ Where? _____
                              Results: _____

IV. INTERPERSONAL RELATIONSHIPS AND INTERESTS

Feeds self _____ Eats well _____ Dresses self _____ Sleeps well _____

What does the child do in his/her leisure time? _____

_____

Any special interests, toys, or activities? _____

_____

Describe your child's attitude towards the following:

School day care? _____

Teachers, child-care workers? _____

Peers in school, day care? _____

Peers outside of school, day care? _____

Parents? _____

Siblings? _____

Whom does the child prefer to play with? _____

_____

What are the ages of preferred playmates? _____

Does the child relate well to pets? _____

Is he/she oversensitive to being touched or hugged? _____

_____

Describe his/her activity level: _____

Is the child's behavior fairly consistent from day to day? Describe: _____

_____

How does the child express his/her needs? _____

_____

How does the child show anger or frustration? _____

_____

What types of discipline are used at home? _____

_____

Describe the child's general temperament: _____

_____

What is most satisfying about this child? _____

_____

What is most frustrating about this child? _____

_____

V. CHILD CARE AND ACADEMIC HISTORY

Has the child attended a day care, nursery, etc.? _____

Age when outside-of-home care began? _____

How did the child respond? _____

How does the child respond to care now? _____

_____

Additional comments or concerns: _____

_____

_____

_____

Interviewed by: _____ Date completed: _____

Parent/guardian signature _____

VI. INTERVIEWER'S COMMENTS

Brief description of child and impressions of parent-child interactions and environment:

_____

_____

_____

_____

_____

15

Assessing Gifted and Talented Children

JAMES T. WEBB, PH.D. & PATRICIA A. KLEINE, ED.D.

Although retarded children long have been considered appropriate subjects for study, psychologists largely have neglected gifted and talented children—those with substantially above average intelligence or creativity. Even though children defined as gifted (typically the upper 3–5%) comprise generally the same percent of the population as those called retarded, far greater emphasis is placed in clinical training and practice on those functioning 2 or more standard deviations below average. Research efforts and emphasis within the field of psychology have been episodic and small, with the most recent coordinated efforts culminating in the American Psychological Association's 1985 publication of *The Gifted and Talented: Developmental Perspectives* (Horowitz & O'Brien, 1985). This volume attempted to crystallize the scattered information existing about gifted and talented children, and to invigorate psychologists' interest.

In their graduate training, most psychologists' exposure to this topic consists of a brief review of the classic Terman studies (Terman et al., 1925, 1947; Terman & Oden, 1959; Burks et al., 1930; Cox, Gillan, Livesay, & Terman, 1930), with emphasis placed on the research methodology as a prototype of longitudinal study. Most often, the conclusion then offered is that the Terman studies show gifted children generally are physically healthier, socially better adjusted, and mentally and academically superior. The results are taken to imply that these children naturally are better at coping and solving life's problems, or in fact have no problems.

Little attention is given then to the problematic characteristics of children labeled "gifted" or "talented," and even less to the assessment methods or implications for the child and his or her family. Even follow-up reports on the long-term Terman studies (e.g., Coleman, 1980) have minimized the proportion of underachievers and those with emotional problems (some 20%), and only rarely is it noted that the sample selection procedures that Terman used may have biased the results because they tended to exclude children with personal or emotional maladjustments. Indeed, as a result, more than one young psychologist has received advice on the order of, "Beyond IQ 130, intelligence test scores don't matter; you can discontinue testing."

The attitudes of psychologists and other health care professionals appear to reflect the views of current society. The notion prevails that gifted children have no special needs, require little attention, and (like cream) will simply rise to the top if they receive only benign neglect. Despite the Marland (1972) report of the U.S.

383

Department of Education that gifted and talented children are deprived and may suffer psychological damage and permanent impairment of their abilities, a cultural ambivalence exists toward gifted children. That is, although leaders in government, education, and society at large make statements like "We need our brightest minds; they are our nation's greatest resource," simultaneously many such persons protest against special programs or focus being given to children of high potential, lest we become "elitist."

This cultural ambivalence results in substantial numbers of children with unusual talent and ability going unidentified, receiving little (if any) special focus to develop their potential, and indeed being criticized, rejected, and even punished for exhibiting the very characteristics that are part of their high potential (Webb, Meckstroth, & Tolan, 1982). Our country's educational systems most often focus on basic minimal competence and exert subtle pressures to conform to mediocrity (a notable exception to this occurs in school-sponsored athletics). As a result, gifted children are "mainstreamed." Teachers struggle to stimulate and challenge these youngsters adequately in the regular classroom. Families often find the child's creativity, intensity, and curiosity burdensome and irritating. Peers often find the gifted child's interests discrepant and puzzling. Gifted children themselves question why they seem to feel different.

Health care professionals' early screening, identification, and guidance of gifted children and their families is warranted, not only for appropriate educational planning but perhaps more importantly so that the family, through understanding and supportive behaviors, can avoid or ameliorate problems that gifted children might otherwise experience later in childhood or even adult life (Hayden, 1985; Whitmore, 1980). Some of the frequent problems noted for school-aged gifted children are ones of underachievement, peer relation difficulties, intense sibling rivalry, poor self-concept, perfectionism, and depression (Webb et al., 1982). For preschool gifted children, particularly if a child has not been identified as potentially gifted, the problems more often involve family disruptions concerning discipline issues, sibling and peer problems, impatience or intolerance of self and others, hyperactive-like behaviors, and questions of school readiness and early entrance to school. Sometimes the problems are ones of parental enmeshment, where one or both parents overly identify with the child's intellectual and creative behaviors. This problem can, in fact, arise directly from identification of the child as gifted or talented, and caution is needed that this labeling does not result in inappropriate accelerated expectations (Colangelo & Fleuridas, 1986). Most often such enmeshment and inappropriate expectations occur (if at all) in the early stages after the child is identified, and decrease markedly as the parents become more knowledgeable about gifted and talented children.

Definitions

Although individual states have varying definitions of giftedness (Karnes & Johnson, 1986a, 1986b), which generally are calculated to identify approximately 3–5% of their children, all derive basically from the 1972 U.S. Department of Education Marland Report, which stated,

Gifted and talented children are those identified by professionally qualified persons who by virtue of outstanding abilities are capable of high performance. These are children who require differentiated educational programs and services beyond those normally provided by the regular school program in order to realize their contribution to self and society. Children capable of high performance include those with demonstrated achievement and/or potential ability in any of the following areas: 1. general intellectual ability . . . , 2. specific academic aptitude . . . , 3. creative or productive thinking . . . , 4. leadership ability . . . , 5. visual, performing arts, and 6. psychomotor ability . . . . (Marland, 1972, p. 2)

In subsequent rules and regulations, this definition has been adapted and modified to exclude the category of psychomotor ability because it referred primarily to athletes, whose "gifts" already seemed sufficiently recognized and supported by society.

Although in educational and psychological conceptualization the Marland definition may be useful, the focus in practice has been almost exclusively on the first two categories—intellectual ability and specific academic aptitude (Fox, 1981). Thus, "giftedness" is typically treated as though it were synonymous with intelligence test scores and/or academic achievement test scores or educational achievements. Far less attention is given to areas of creativity, leadership, and visual or performing arts except in a few states or local communities. There does, however, seem to be an increasing recognition in psychology and education that giftedness is not necessarily a g factor and that persons are not (and need not be) necessarily gifted in all areas. That is, persons may have unusual potential or ability in only one, two, or several areas and still qualify as "gifted." In the past, such a pattern probably would have been referred to as "talented" rather than "gifted," but more recently the two terms are treated synonymously.

A further limitation of the Marland Report definition and its derivatives is that such definitions are far more applicable to school-aged youngsters than to preschoolers. That is, it makes little sense to talk about the academic achievement of a preschool child, and probably in similar fashion it is difficult to consider creativity, leadership, and so on in children of that age. No agreed upon definition or description of gifted preschool children yet exists.

Despite emerging definitions and the variations in how they are implemented in various locales, and even with the lack of current national standards for operationally defining gifted and talented children (particularly preschoolers), psychologists and other health care professionals have an important professional role. The reader is reminded that the Marland Report definition and derivatives of it use generic language, as in "outstanding abilities," "capable of high performance," and "identified by professionally qualified persons." What these abilities are and who the professionally qualified persons are certainly seem to be appropriate domains for psychology, as well as for educators and other professionals.

As will be discussed subsequently, formal tests of intellect, creativity, leadership, and so on in preschool children have noteable limitations regarding reliability and validity. Although such formal assessment approaches *can* be used (with suitable caution) for screening and identification, professionals usually will find it more helpful to directly consider those behaviors characteristic of gifted preschoolers. Many of these underlie the formal definition listed above and appear to be indicators and precursors of a child's *potential* to meet the requirements of the Marland definition. The following list of behaviors has been adapted from such sources as Webb et al. (1982):

1. Unusually large vocabularies and complex sentence structures.
2. Greater comprehension of subtleties of language.
3. Longer attention span, persistence, and intense concentration.
4. Wide range of interests.
5. Highly developed curiosity and limitless questions.
6. Interest in experimenting and doing things differently.
7. Tendency to put ideas or things together in ways that are unusual or not obvious (divergent thinking).
8. Ability to learn basic skills more quickly with less practice.
9. Largely self-taught reading and writing skills as preschoolers.
10. Retention of much information; unusual memory.
11. Imaginary playmates.
12. Unusual sense of humor.
13. Desire to organize people and things, primarily through devising complex games.

PREEVALUATION CONSIDERATIONS

Background Data

Prior to formal assessment, it is essential to gather information from the child's parents, and probably important to tap his or her preschool teacher or pediatrician as well. Certainly the latter is needed if a visual, motor, or other handicap is also present, as many intellectually gifted children with such physical handicaps are overlooked (Whitmore & Maker, 1985).

In part the background information collected will be the customary developmental milestones such as the Gesell norms (Ames, Gillespie, Haines, & Ilg, 1979); in part it will be the parents' observations concerning these milestones, as well as concerning the presence or absence of the behaviors listed previously. Although more important for counseling than for identification of a child as "gifted," information should be gathered about the parents' expectations and perceptions regarding the relationship between the child's abilities and the behaviors being shown (i.e., Are the child's abilities and behaviors an undue source of pride? a puzzlement to parents? a problem to be squelched? etc.).

The professional should recognize that the statement "Every parent has a gifted child" is a myth, along with the categorical assertion that "Gifted children are a joy to raise." Certainly these statements are true on occasion, but with gifted children clearly are not universal. Some parents indeed are overly enmeshed and ego involved with their preschoolers—particularly firstborns—and are "pushy parents" who produce a "hurried child" (Elkind, 1981). More often the parents of gifted children are surprised, puzzled, and even doubting that their child's behaviors arise from unusual intellectual and creative potential. This difficulty in attributing the behaviors to intellectual or creative precocity seems particularly likely with parents of superior intelligence themselves, as the child's intellectual endeavors often seem "average" to them from their own familial experience.

In their assessments professionals also must realize that most parents (and children) either dislike the term *gifted* and react negatively to it or equate the term with *genius*. Commonly parents are shy about discussing "giftedness," partly due to their internalized reluctance to have a "different" child and partly because often they have developed a history of negative interactions on the subject, where friends and relatives have made disparaging comments when the parents attempted to discuss their child's unusual abilities.

In evaluating a gifted child, it is important for the professional to distinguish between profoundly gifted youngsters and those of "only" superior abilities and potential. The implications for assessment and intervention with a family clearly vary if the child is profoundly gifted. As professionals review the literature, they unfortunately will find that reference most often is made simply to "gifted" children in contrast to "nongifted" ones, as though all gifted children were the same and as though "giftedness" is an either/or state. In fact, it makes no more sense to consider all gifted children the same than it would be to consider all retarded children to be of equal ability and to have identical characteristics.

In IQ terms, a score of 155 or above generally is taken to suggest a child is profoundly gifted (Albert, 1971); an IQ of 130 to 155 is simply called "gifted." Intellectually, the profoundly gifted child—particularly above IQ 165—is so clearly different as to be likely called a prodigy. Behaviorally, the differences appear to be similarly extraordinary, with the previously listed characteristics likely present to a greater, more pervasive, and more intense degree and likely appearing much earlier (Grost, 1970). Profoundly gifted children are ones for whom intellectual stimulation and/or creative expression are clearly emotional needs that may appear to be as intense as the physiological needs of hunger or thirst.

Formal Testing Issues

Ironically, although the concept of profoundly gifted individuals has existed for centuries (Albert, 1971), the scoring norms for most current measures of intelligence typically extend no more than 4 standard deviations above the mean (i.e., an IQ score of 160), thus precluding much detailed information about the extent and types of abilities of those who score above these norms. Despite a widespread belief that such persons are so rare as to be negligible, the experience of the present author and others is bringing this matter into question.

Based on the normal curve, only 1 out of 33,000 individuals should achieve an IQ score of 160 or above, and only 1 in 1,000,000 should reach 180 or above (Sattler, 1988). Instead, field reports are suggesting that approximately twice as many persons as would be expected obtain IQ scores above 160, and more than three times as many above IQ 180. To use a concrete example, in southwestern Ohio the author has tested well over 20 individuals who obtained IQ scores in excess of 160, and an additional 6 who exceeded 180. (Prorating formulas and procedures to exceed the tabled norm values in testing manuals appear in Sattler, 1988, in Reynolds & Clark, 1986, and in the manuals for Terman and Merrill's 1973 Stanford-Binet Intelligence Test, Form L-M. At the time of this writing, the fourth edition of the Stanford-Binet [Thorndike, Hagen, & Sattler, 1986] offered no such provision for extrapolation.) The reason for so many persons surpassing the tabled norm values is unclear, suggesting a range of possibilities from inadequate inclusion in the normative samples to hypotheses that the upper end of the intellectual spectrum may not follow the normal curve smoothness of function. Whatever the underlying reason, there seems to be a "bump" on the normal IQ curve at about 160, and clearly such individuals are not as rare as many professionals believe. (One is less likely to see this phenomenon with several of the newly normed and revised individual intelligence tests due to an artificial ceiling effect that stems from allowing scores only 2 standard deviation units above the mean.)

Because so much of psychologists' training focuses on intelligence tests, such as Wechsler's (1967, 1974) scales and the Stanford-Binet, it seems easy to speak in IQ terms when talking about gifted children. The public's general familiarity with IQ scores further encourages this. However, in the same way that IQ scores are not synonymous with mental retardation, neither should they to be equated with giftedness. For example, measures of creativity show extremely low correlations with measures of intelligence when IQ scores are above about 120 (Amabile, 1983). Similarly, intelligence tests are seldom adequate measures of "talents" in individual areas.

Individual tests of intelligence are particularly hindered in measuring preschoolers' giftedness potential because of developmental spurts and lags (mental and physical) as well as extremely variable motivation and attention factors (day to day and situation to situation). These factors result in low reliabilities for formal test scores. For example, under the age of 24 months, intelligence tests generally correlate less than .50 with later measures of childhood IQ scores (Anastasi, 1988). In some cases the IQ scores increase, while in other cases they decline, sometimes as much as 20 or more points (Roedell, 1980). For gifted children, who are at the extreme of the normal curve distribution, the variability may be even greater from occasion to occasion.

Additionally, recent investigations have raised strong doubts as to the adequacy of current IQ tests to measure "intelligence," because most assess convergent, culturally bound thinking rather than divergent, creative, and innovative mental processes. Perhaps the most salient conceptualization comes from Gardner (1983), who posited at least seven intelligences (linguistic, musical, logical-mathematical, spatial, bodily-kinesthetic, interpersonal, and intrapersonal), only two or three of which are regularly measured by typical psychometric instruments. Admittedly, current IQ tests administered to school-aged children do predict reasonably well how such children will do academically in school settings; however, these tests do not adequately measure intelligence in a broader fashion perhaps more germane to success and overall achievement in life.

When examining the IQ tests of groups of gifted preschoolers, one is struck by the variability across test subdimensions as well as across skill patterns in general (Roedell, 1980). Indeed, preschoolers' early acquisition of advanced academic skills may have a quite small relation to obtained measures of intelligence. Some preschool children with IQ scores above 160 have not yet learned to read, even though most gifted children generally do teach themselves how to read and write prior to entering school. Similarly, certain preschoolers with IQ scores as low as 116 have become fluent readers by the age of 3 (Roedell, 1980). Academic skill levels range more widely among gifted preschoolers than among preschoolers in general, prompting at least one researcher to note that "intraindividual differences among abilities are the rule, not the exception" (Robinson, 1981, p. 72). Even so, "it is highly unlikely, however, that children who are extraordinary in one area of mental functioning will be average or below average in all other areas of functioning" (Sattler, 1988, p. 675). Despite the controversy and the wide range of individual differences, the *g* factor or some other clustering of abilities does seem present in most gifted children.

Some particular idiosyncrasies of frequently used tests of intelligence are noteworthy. On the Wechsler Preschool and Primary Scales of Intelligence (WPPSI; Wechsler, 1967), Verbal IQ scores for gifted children generally are significantly higher than their Performance IQ scores (Speer, Hawthorne, & Buccellato, 1986), and the subtests often present an inadequate level of difficulty (Hawthorne, Speer, & Buccatello, 1986), which results in many reaching a ceiling effect on one or more subtests (Jackson, 1980). This ceiling effect significantly hinders the professional from doing an adequate scatter analysis of the WPPSI profile, as well as obscuring how far above the ceiling that child's performance might have gone (Reynolds & Clark, 1986).

The Kaufman Assessment Battery for Children (K-ABC; Kaufman & Kaufman, 1983) has similar difficulties with ceiling effects, which limits its effectiveness with gifted children. As Sattler (1988) notes, "Over half of the subtests on the Simultaneous and Sequential Processing Scales provide maximum scores that are only two standard deviations or less above the mean. The Achievement Scale also has a restricted range" (p. 303). This ceiling effect appears to be at least one reason why Mental Processing Composite scores from the K-ABC appear generally lower than those of tests such as the Stanford-Binet, Form L-M and the Wechsler Intelligence Scale for Children–Revised (WISC-R; Wechsler, 1974). It is less clear why the K-ABC and the WISC-R correlate only about .65 for fourth-, fifth-, and sixth-grade children (McCallum, Karnes, & Edwards, 1984; Naglieri & Anderson, 1985), and even less so (about .35) with children in kindergarten, first, and second grades (Moreland & Webb, 1988). Thus, the amount of variance in common between the two tests for gifted children appears to range only from about 13% to 45%. For these reasons, one should exercise caution when using the K-ABC with gifted children, whether preschool or school age.

The fourth edition of the Stanford-Binet Intelligence Scale does not appear to have a ceiling effect for preschool children, but questions about its appropriateness have arisen due to the lengthened administration time for these examinees. Further, there are concerns as to whether this test measures the same dimensions as the earlier Form L-M, or whether different and unknown dimensions are being assessed. Correlations between the fourth edition and Form L-M with gifted child samples have ranged from .27 to .55, suggesting less than 30% of the variance is shared for these two tests with samples of gifted children (Harkins & Webb, 1988).

Other frequently used tests for intellectual screening of preschool and primary gifted children have been the Peabody Picture Vocabulary Test–Revised (PPVT-R; Dunn & Dunn, 1981), the Slosson Intelligence Test (SIT; Slosson, 1983) and the McCarthy Scales of Children's Abilities (McCarthy, 1972). None of these appears adequate for routine use in identifying gifted preschoolers, though they might have some use for screening purposes. The PPVT-R not only has lower reliability than such tests as the WISC-R, but gifted children's scores typically are significantly lower than those on tests such as the Stanford-Binet (Bracken, Prasse, & McCallum, 1984; Hayes & Martin, 1986). Similarly, scores on the McCarthy Scales obtained by gifted preschoolers generally are lower than WPPSI and the Stanford-Binet, Form L-M scores (Jackson, 1980). Scores on the Slosson Intelligence Test, on the other hand, tend to be significantly higher for gifted children than those yielded on tests such as the WISC-R (Bondy, Constantino, Norcross, & Sheslow, 1984).

Clearly many questions remain about the adequacy of current intelligence tests with preschool gifted children. The consensus appears to be that prior to age 3, formal tests are of little use. Measures such as the Bayley Scales of Infant Development (Bayley, 1969) have only a moderate predictive correlation with later measures of intelligence (Sattler, 1988) and likely would be helpful only with profoundly gifted children.

Between the ages of 3 and 6 testing may be more useful, but even then these scores have substantially less stability than similar test scores of children beyond age 6 (Anastasi, 1988; Sattler, 1988). Although IQ scores obtained with gifted children at this age often are an underestimate of later test scores, not always is this the case. Jackson's (1980) review of several studies showed that a substantial minority of children who obtained individual test IQ scores above 130 as preschoolers subsequently obtained scores well below this level when retested 2 or 3 years later.

Attempts to measure creativity in preschool children, as distinct from measuring intelligence, has met with even less success. Most of the efforts to measure creativity generally have focused on divergent thinking and behaviors as opposed to convergent thinking or standard achievement. The independence of creativity from academic intelligence has been demonstrated in children of varying ages from kindergarten up, and evidence suggests more than one type of creativity (Wallach, 1970). Formal tests designed expressly for preschool children are few and relatively unvalidated (Piirto, 1992). However, tests such as the 1965 Wallach and Kogan Creativity Battery, which is designed for kindergarten and elementary school children and allows scoring verbal responses for fluency and uniqueness, likely can be used with gifted preschool children. The Torrance Tests of Creative Thinking (Torrance, 1974) are also designed for children in kindergarten and above but can be used with preschoolers. These tests measure creative productive thinking both in verbal and in figural dimensions, and allow scoring on fluency, flexibility, originality, and, in some aspects, elaboration. The predictive validity of both of these tests has been low, however (Jackson, 1980), and has prompted one expert to state that "predictive validity might best be circumvented by considering the quality of the child's responses, rather than simply scoring the number and uniqueness of the answers given" (Crockenburg, 1972, p. 41).

Even more so regarding creativity than in measuring intelligence, the professional is well advised to examine the child's behaviors and to conduct an informal assessment of divergent, creative thinking, rather than attempting to rely on formal testing. Sattler (1988) has suggested a compendium of tasks selected from various measures of creativity, and some of these are listed below. In using these, the professional must carefully consider "the factors that might contribute to the substantial unreliability . . . such as the emotional atmosphere and time limits of the session, the availability of inspirational cues in the testing room, and so on" (Jackson, 1980, p. 33). Even so, such approaches to creativity, as distinct from measures of intelligence, may provide a fairer assessment of giftedness potential in minority or culturally disadvantaged preschoolers (Sattler, 1988). Appropriate informal creativity measures involve asking the child to, for example,

1. List new ways to use specific common objects.
2. List problems that might arise from a common situation.
3. Suggest ways to improve an object.
4. List different ways in which two things are alike and how they are different.
5. Suggest what the effects would be if an everyday class of objects (e.g., cars) no longer existed.
6. List questions that could be asked about a particular picture, or suggest possible outcomes of the scene in the picture (Sattler, 1988).

Because of the various difficulties in formally testing gifted preschool youngsters, Roedell, Jackson, and Robinson (1980) adopted an approach that is particularly appropriate. They noted that "very young children are rarely so consistently cooperative that they can be relied upon to demonstrate the best performance of which they are capable during all phases of a test session. If a session contains several measures, . . . one's chances of observing evidence of a child's advanced capabilities are greatly increased" (Rodell et al., 1980, p. 38). Thus they adopted a testing philosophy that "the most meaningful aspect of a young child's test performance is not the child's average level of performance across a wide range of tasks, but the most advanced performance demonstrated" (p. 38). Although admittedly an unconventional view, this approach is less likely to overlook a gifted preschool child and is most in keeping with educational philosophies regarding starting at readiness level in various skill areas. In evaluating preschool children, it is better to be overly inclusive than to be inappropriately exclusive.

Thus, when evaluating preschoolers, little emphasis should be given to formally testing gifted youngsters before age 4, and where testing is done, the "best performance" model should be used. An exception should be made when a prodigy apparently is at hand—that is, a child who is clearly functioning in one or more areas at least 5 to 7 years ahead of what would be expected for a child of that age. In such cases, formal testing can provide useful benchmarks of achievement and/or potential for knowing how best to appropriately communicate with the child, for choosing the appropriate sorts of enrichment activities, and for planning educational activities and placement that would best match the child's competence.

With gifted preschool children, however, behavioral observations and reports from parents, pediatricians, and preschool teachers are generally more important than test scores. It is interesting to note in this regard that when parents are educated as to the general characteristics of gifted children, they are able to identify their preschool children as gifted at least as accurately as such tests as the Woodcock-Johnson Psycho-Educational Battery (Woodcock & Johnson, 1977) or Raven's (1960) Progressive Matrices (Hanson, 1984).

Referral Questions

Seldom is a gifted preschooler referred simply for assessment of intellectual or creative potential. Far more often he or she is referred for behavioral problems, ostensibly related to "immaturity," with creativity or intelligence rarely mentioned by the parents or professionals making the referral. Some of the more common presenting complaints follow:

"High activity level; low impulse control."
"Seems too serious for child that age; raises moral, ethical or philosophical questions."
"Always into things; takes things apart."
"Perfectionistic; expects too much of self."
"Needs very little sleep, but has extremely vivid dreams."
"Seems too emotional; gets intensely frustrated when unable to accomplish a goal; throws temper tantrums at such times."
"Can't seem to complete tasks or stay on track."
"Seems narcissistic and overly self-absorbed."
"Has difficulty relating to age peers; wants to boss them, doesn't share interests expected for that age, spends much time thinking or alone or with older peers."
"Continually asking questions, interrupting others, showing off knowledge."
"Seems ahead of developmental norms."
"People keep telling me that I have an unusual child."

All of these may be real problems in their own right, and perhaps could be handled in a narrow, circumscribed fashion without considering the concepts of gifted and talented. Our experience, however, suggests it is far more effective to explore the extent to which these behaviors are accompaniments and outgrowths of unusually high intellect or creativity, lest these behaviors be explained incorrectly as part of some other diagnostic entity (such as a behavior or conduct disorder). Indeed, in the absence of such information, parents and children alike construct their own rationale for these behaviors.

Parents in particular seem prone to label the above characteristics as problems in discipline, immaturity, or socialization, or occasionally simply as inborn temperament difficulties. When they learn that these behaviors are normal for many—perhaps most—gifted children, parents are able to "reframe" the problem behaviors, allowing them to act more appropriately, offering support and guidance to shape these behaviors rather than to punish or attempt to extinguish them.

It is important to note that these characteristics that may be problematic in childhood are the very ones that we want and expect our creative adults to possess and demonstrate. The problems arise primarily because (a) these children do not fit our expectations for children of that age, (b) they enter and pass through developmental and mental stages more quickly than our programs are designed to handle, and (c) due to lack of life experience, their judgment, wisdom, and empathy lag significantly behind their intellect, creativity, and intensity.

THE ASSESSMENT

Interviews

In parental interviews as well as in observations and formal testing, attention should be given to the child's behavior in the following areas:

1. Cognitive/language abilities
2. General motor ability
3. Fine motor ability
4. Interpersonal relations
5. Persistence, intensity, concentration

Developmental tests such as the Gesell Developmental Schedule (Ames et al., 1979) or even the widely used Denver Developmental Screening Test (Frankenburg, Dodds, Fandal, Kazuk, & Cohrs, 1975; Fish & Burch, 1985) can be used to guide the conceptualization and to provide norms for comparison, even though such developmental schedules were not specifically designed for the task of identifying gifted children. In general, gifted preschool children are about 30% more advanced developmentally than the norm, though wide variability exists (Brink, 1982). For example, the average child speaks three words (other than "mama" or "dada") at about 14 months. Most gifted children achieve this milestone at about 9 to 10 months, though some will have accomplished this task as early as 6 months and will be speaking in complete sentences of 5 to 10 words (or more) by the end of the first year (Fish, 1984). Gifted children above IQ 150 begin reading on the average at $4\frac{1}{2}$ years, with some starting to read at age 2 (Kincaid, 1969).

The first three areas listed—cognitive/language, general motor ability, and fine motor ability—can be assessed using a checklist such as that presented in Table 15.1. Generally, gifted children are advanced in all three areas, although their development unlikely will be equal in all three. This table, developed by Hall and Skinner (1980) specifically to assess in parent interviews whether a preschool child might be gifted, is based on information compiled from such sources as the Gesell Developmental Schedule and the Bayley infant scales. Children need not be advanced by 30% in all of the areas listed. Indeed, most gifted children are not equally advanced in all areas due to the developmental spurts and lags noted earlier. However, if a child is advanced by 30% or more in most of the items, particularly in cognitive/language, informational, or mathematical skill areas (Jackson, 1980), then it is likely that he or she later will be categorized as gifted.

A pattern that is particularly frustrating to the child occurs in some gifted

TABLE 15.1
DEVELOPMENTAL GUIDELINES FOR IDENTIFYING GIFTED PRESCHOOLERS

General Motor Ability	Normal Months	30% More Advanced	Fine Motor Ability	Normal Months	30% More Advanced	Cognitive Language	Normal Months	30% More Advanced
Lifts chin up when lying stomach down	1	0.7	Grasps handle of spoon but lets go quickly	1	0.7	Social smile at people	1.5	1.05
Holds up both head and chest	2	1.4	Vertical eye coordination	1	0.7	Vocalizes four times or more	1.6	1.12
Rolls over	3	2.1	Plays with rattle	3	2.1	Visually recognizes mother	2	1.4
Sits up with support	4	2.8	Manipulates a ball, is interested in detail	6	4.2	Searches with eyes for sound	2.2	1.54
Sits alone	7	4.9	Pulls string adaptively	7	4.9	Vocalizes two different sounds	2.3	1.61
Stands with help	8	5.6	Shows hand preference	8	5.6			
Stands holding on	9	6.3	Holds object between fingers and thumb	9	6.3	Vocalizes four different syllables	7	4.9
Creeps	11	7.7						
Stands alone well	11	7.7	Holds crayon adaptively	11	7.7	Says "da-da" or equivalent	7.9	5.53
Walks alone	12.5	8.75	Pushes car alone	11	7.7	Responds to name, "no-no"	9	6.3
Walks, creeping is discarded	15	10.5	Scribbles spontaneously	13	9.1	Looks at pictures in book	10	7.0
			Drawing imitates stroke	15	10.5	Jabbers expressively	12	8.4
Creeps up stairs	15	10.5	Folds paper once imitatively	21	14.7	Imitates words	12.5	8.75
Walks up stairs	18	12.6				Has speaking vocabulary of three words (other than "ma-ma" and "da-da")	14	9.8
Seats self in chair	18	12.6	Drawing imitates V stroke and circular stroke	24	16.8			
Turns pages of book	18	12.6						
Walks down stairs one hand held	21	14.7	Imitates V and H strokes	30	21.0	Has vocabulary of four to six words including names	15	10.5
			Imitates bridge with blocks	36	25.2			

GIFTEDNESS 395

Milestone	Normal (months)	Gifted (months)
Walks up stairs holds rail	21	14.7
Runs well, no falling	24	16.8
Walks up and down stairs alone	24	16.8
Walks on tiptoe	30	21.0
Jumps with both feet	30	21.0
Alternates feet when walking up stairs	36	25.2
Jumps from bottom step	36	25.2
Rides tricycle using pedals	36	25.2
Skips on one foot only	48	33.6
Throws ball	48	33.6
Skips alternating feet	60	42.0
Draws person with two parts	48	33.6
Draws unmistakable person with body	60	42.0
Copies triangle	60	42.0
Draws person with neck, hands, clothes	72	50.4
Points to one named body part	17	11.9
Names one object (What is this?)	17.8	12.46
Follows direction to put object in chair	17.8	12.46
Has vocabulary of 10 words	18	12.6
Has vocabulary of 20 words	21	14.7
Combines two or three words spontaneously	21	14.7
Jargon is discarded, three-word sentences	24	16.8
Uses *I, me, you*	24	16.8
Names three or more objects on a picture	24	16.8
Is able to identify five or more objects	24	16.8
Gives full name	30	21.0
Names five objects on a picture	30	21.0
Identifies seven objects	30	21.0
Is able to tell what various objects are used for	30	21.0
Counts (enumerates) objects to 3	36	25.2
Identifies the sexes	36	25.2

Note: From *Somewhere to Turn: Strategies for Parents of the Gifted and Talented* (Perspectives on Gifted and Talented Education Series) by E. G. Hall and N. Skinner, 1980, New York: Teachers College Press.

children when the general motor or fine motor development lags significantly behind the cognitive development. In such situations the child can visualize a desired behavior but is unable to accomplish the task due to poor motor skills.

Of the other two areas listed—interpersonal relations, and intensity, concentration, and persistence—it appears that the interpersonal relations aspect is fairly similar to the personal-social dimension on the Denver Developmental Screening Test, the Battelle Developmental Inventory (Newborg, Stock, & Wnek, 1984), or other similar inventories. As with the earlier dimensions, the 30% advancement over average should be used with regard to the general interpersonal skills (e.g., progression from parallel play to interactive play) tapped by these instruments.

There are, however, some behavioral and interpersonal dimensions that should be examined but are not typically included in standard assessment instruments. In particular, the aspects of intensity, concentration, and persistence are seldom represented, though they clearly have been recognized as signs of advanced intelligence that appear quite early in life (Kolata, 1987; Webb et al., 1982). Most often these characteristics can be estimated by a professional based on parental report. Gifted preschool children typically have a broad range of interests but also spend unusually long periods deeply involved in the project at hand, sometimes literally hours, to the point that those around clearly recognize the difference from average.

An exception arises with the gifted child who also suffers from attention-deficit disorder (ADD). These children show extremely high skill levels in various areas and wide ranging interests, but they have great difficulty with impulse control or in staying on task when distracting or competing stimuli are present. Because the presence or absence of an attention-deficit disorder is extremely important in the recommendations to follow, care should be taken to rule out this disorder if possible.

Whether the preschool gifted child has an attention-deficit disorder or not, one of the most universal characteristics among gifted children (and perhaps the most difficult to define) is intensity. Perhaps one mother's description of her child will suffice when she said, "My child's life motto seems to be 'anything worth doing is worth doing to excess!'" Indeed these children do seem to be excessive personalities, and their intensity permeates virtually everything, from their behaviors to their emotions. It appears they are overly intense in every respect, even in thinking and sleeping. As a result of the lack of modulation in the behaviors of gifted preschoolers, their emotional and interpersonal characteristics usually are distinctly florid and excessive, often to the point of causing problems for those around them.

In addition to the preceding general guidelines, the following behavioral characteristics have been reported consistently by professionals and parents alike as being relatively unique characteristics of gifted preschool children; professionals should inquire specifically about them:

1. Does the child use humor, particularly in riddles, incongruities, or puns?
2. Does the child prefer older playmates?
3. When playmates are not easily available, does the child create games with imaginary playmates?
4. Does the child attempt to modify, improve on, create, or organize games being played with others?

5. Does the child who is capable of interactive play spend substantial amounts of time in solitary play involving manipulating or creating objects?
6. Does the child maintain unusually long periods of focused attention when involved in an area of interest?
7. Does the child repeatedly seek complex tasks and challenges even though experiencing frustration?
8. Does the child show unusually intense feelings (sensitivities) in areas such as the arts or regarding social inequities or moral dilemmas?
9. Does the child experience keen impatience or frustration when peers do not share interests, or when others cannot seem to grasp solutions to problems?
10. Does the child seem to need significantly less sleep or significantly more sleep than others?
11. Does the child have a wide range of interests, such that there seem not to be enough hours in the day?
12. Is the child highly competitive, disliking losing intensely?

If the answer to a majority of these questions is "yes," a strong likelihood exists that the child will fall in the gifted category. In addition to the above checklists and guidelines, a few other findings have emerged with greater frequency among gifted children and their families. They do not, however, usually appear to be of significant help in making clinical decisions and are noted here only for completeness. Gifted children tend to have greater birth weights and head circumferences (Fish, Bilek, Horrobin, & Change, 1976; Perigo-Moore, 1981), mothers beyond age 40 appear more likely to have a profoundly gifted child (Mathieson, 1980), and boys with IQ scores above 140 appear to show significantly higher activity levels and more difficulties with impulse control than boys below IQ 140 (Shaywitz, Shaywitz, Jamner, Towle, & Barnes, 1986).

Observations

Where possible, the examinee should be observed and interacted with individually. Typically the behavioral characteristics noted above become quickly apparent when the child is asked to perform such tasks as drawing a picture, telling a story, constructing three wishes, or talking about family and daily activities. It is *not* helpful to ask children directly whether they think they might be gifted. Seldom are gifted children aware that the way they see and do things differs significantly from others. They have grown up seeing the world through their eyes, and to them that is "normal" or average. Instead, they often puzzlingly find themselves feeling out of step, without being able to explain why others their age seem not to share their interests or skills. Thus, it is more appropriate to ask them about their activities and the quality of their interactions with peers, shared interests and games, and so forth.

Formal Testing

As noted previously, individually administered tests of intelligence or creativity are generally no more likely to be accurate than interview and observation, and the added professional time and expense of formal individual tests are probably not warranted until age 6 or so. The administration of group tests appears even less warranted due to their far lower reliability and validity (Sattler, 1988).

Some situations, however, do warrant formal testing, particularly when a learning disability is suspected or when there are limitations on the usefulness of interview or observation methods, such as in children with speech, hearing, or motor difficulties that interfere. The professional should bear in mind, though, that the child's handicap itself may have made the testing situation more stressful, may have reduced the child's exposure to experiences that would have contributed to knowledge, or may hinder the child's ability to perceive or respond to the test instructions. "Thus, a handicapped child who earns the same score as a non-handicapped child may actually be demonstrating a more unusual performance and greater capacity for future learning" (Jackson, 1980, p. 51). In such cases it is frequently necessary to adapt the standardized administration procedures so that the child can have a reasonable opportunity to demonstrate abilities and skills. Of course, this means that the professional then must use clinical judgment in interpreting the meaning of scores, as interpretation according to the typical norms can no longer be done in straightforward fashion. Here the "best performance" model of Roedell et al. (1980) is particularly appropriate, not only as a measure of potential but also to identify areas of strength that can be built upon in educational planning.

In cases where learning disability or developmental disabilities in motor development is suspected, tests such as Beery's (1982) Developmental Test of Visual-Motor Integration or the Bender Visual-Motor Gestalt Test (Bender, 1938) may be helpful (Sattler, 1988). Typically these are administered in conjunction with whatever portions of individual intelligence tests one can use. Though these tests do not measure "giftedness" per se, they are relevant for many gifted children who can see in their "mind's eye" what they would like to do with a task, even though their muscular coordination does not cooperate. Often this frustration mirrors similar experiences that the child has at home or is likely to have at school, where the child's frustration culminates in temper tantrums that otherwise are inexplicable to surrounding adults.

An overall comment is needed about preschool gifted children suspected of learning disability. The professional should be extremely reluctant to diagnose a gifted preschooler as learning disabled without truly compelling evidence. Instead, consideration should be given to the more likely phenomenon of a developmental lag. Gifted children, like others their age, do not develop smoothly across various skill areas. Indeed, the relative discrepancies are likely to be greater simply because the total potential range of their skills is so great. It is not unusual to find discrepancies between Verbal and Performance IQ scores of 20, 30, or even 40 IQ points. Among scaled scores, differences of 5 to 7 points are not uncommon. Experience suggests that these variations most often reflect temporary developmental anomalies rather than persistent characteristics. Although recommendations can still be made to parents about remediational efforts, caution should be exercised in giving a label of "learning disabled" to a gifted child below age 7.

Often formal testing of gifted children also differs in other respects. Testing generally takes longer because examinees do not reach the ceiling as quickly as other children. The testing should be scheduled over two or even three occasions so an accurate measure of functioning can be obtained, otherwise fatigue quite likely will be a factor. In addition, the gifted child's playfulness and sense of humor may inhibit straightforward progression through the test, and some allowance must be made to adequately consider this both in administration and in interpreting the results. Paradoxically, self-evaluation and self-criticism is also more likely than in other children and can hinder the testing because of the child's reluctance to guess. Even so, most gifted children find the experience of testing to be enjoyable, at least if it is presented as a fun set of challenges that will help the family to plan for school entrance. Most gifted children can readily comprehend such a description and are already extremely anxious to enter school; they can hardly wait to get to the place that has the "rest of the answers." Thus the testing can be construed to them in ways that they find to be in their own self-interest.

In the scoring and interpretation of tests, professionals must not confuse high intelligence with wisdom. In gifted children, judgment lags significantly behind intellect (Roedell, 1980; Webb et al., 1982), not because the child is not smart but because many aspects of life cannot be "reasoned out" and can be understood only through the accumulation of experiences. This lag in judgment often is quite frustrating to parents, who begin to expect the child to "act" in keeping with his or her intelligence. Most often the social and interpersonal judgment is only slightly ahead of the child's chronological age, but significantly lagging behind his or her "mental age." Similarly, caution is particularly needed in interpreting "age equivalent" or "grade equivalent" scores that gifted children obtain on such tests as the Wide Range Achievement Test (Jastak & Jastak, 1978) or the Peabody Individual Achievement Test (Dunn & Markwardt, 1970). Sometimes tests such as these are used for "out of level" testing, to obtain some estimate of a child's reading, spelling or arithmetic level, and for making early entrance or grade placement decisions. Such an "out of level" testing is an appropriate approach, but one must exercise caution in interpreting what these scores mean. Certainly they do *not* necessarily indicate that the child is ready to enter a specific grade, or that he or she functions at that age level in all respects. The sampling in such tests occurs in specific domains only, and many other foundation skills that are taught in specific grades of school are not measured by them. Parents in particular often need this distinction made for them in order to allow appropriate planning.

RECOMMENDATIONS TO PARENTS

Although the professional hopefully will want to learn more about gifted children and their families through reading and other continuing education activities, the following brief descriptions represent a distillation of insights gained from the author's decade of working with these young ones and their families. Further information, including bibliographies of books, magazines, and journals, and names of relevant national associations, can be found in sources such as Webb et al. (1982).

In reviewing assessment results with the parents of gifted children, the professional should expect that they initially will be uncomfortable—most often they expect that you (as the professional) will have found something that they did wrong as parents. Although the parents of preschoolers generally may be somewhat insecure, the mothers and fathers of gifted preschoolers typically are more so, as they characteristically seek professional counsel because they are puzzled by their child's behavior. In addition, as noted previously, most parents of gifted children have already acquired a history of negative interactions with others who have accused them of bragging or overstating their child's abilities. Expect these parents also to be frustrated with many aspects of their gifted child, whose intensity (combined with the other characteristics noted previously) have caused at least one mother to say, "Having a gifted child doesn't change the family's life-style; it destroys it!"

Parents of such children typically are overjoyed and grateful to discover a professional who is willing to listen to them, to take their situation seriously, and to help them plan for the future. Some parents will worry that being gifted inevitably will lead to emotional problems. It is important to offer assurances that such is *not* the case, particularly when gifted children are understood and supported by their parents and school systems. Thus, interactions with the psychologist or other professional should be cast in the light of enhancing human potential and preventing potential difficulties rather than viewed from a psychopathology model. Parents find this approach reassuring, though they usually are less pleased to discover that insurance reimbursement seldom covers such professional services unless there is also a coexisting or derivative problem, such as anxiety or depression.

Future Planning Issues

Most parents soon bring up questions that revolve around enrichment activities, early entrance to school, finding the "right" school, peer relationships, sibling rivalry, developing impulse control, and self-management skills. Some of these questions can be answered simply, others require more detailed information and extended effort by the parents and the child.

Enrichment should follow the child's lead, rather than forcing development on the child. Parents should give the child a broad array of stimulating experiences and provide more in-depth exposure when he or she expresses interest. Museums, libraries, zoos, junkyards—all can be exciting wonderlands for gifted preschool children. It is important to help parents understand when a child might be through with an activity. That is, parents of gifted children often feel that a child should carry all activities through to completion in order to learn responsibility. However, for gifted children, particularly preschoolers, the complexity of the task undertaken and/or the diversity of the child's interests may preclude completion, though the child may have learned much that is stimulating in the process. Parenthetically, yet another characteristic of gifted children is that they often set unrealistic goals because their imagination is so great, only to experience keen disappointment if they find that these goals cannot be met.

Early entrance to school is a common consideration as most gifted youngsters do better with such an approach, in contrast to situations where they feel chronically bored and unchallenged (e.g., if the curriculum is inflexibly lock-step; Webb et al., 1982). Such a decision must involve consideration not only of the child's intelligence and achievement in academic areas but also of sociological variables. If the child's community has a preponderance of gifted children in its school system, then he or she likely will find suitable support and enrichment without early admission. Of course, this is not as often true for profoundly gifted children, who even then generally seem to require 1 year's advanced placement. Occasionally a radically advanced placement of 2 or more years is warranted, but only after considerable study of the individual situation, only if the family is highly informed and supportive, and only after attempts have been made to effect less radical solutions.

Given our society's present sex-role expectancies, boys probably should be in the upper 50% of the growth chart before early entrance to school is seriously considered. In some school systems, and in many school readiness schemas, adequate fine motor coordination is likewise considered a necessity for early entrance. Usually this is operationally defined through such tasks as tying one's shoes, using scissors, or coloring and staying within the lines. The lack of such skills is *not* an adequate reason to deny gifted youngsters early entrance, because these children quickly learn compensatory ways to work around these temporary deficits, which are not barriers to learning.

Parents of gifted preschool children should be encouraged to approach the school system at least a few months prior to the child entering kindergarten or as much as a year before he or she enters first grade. The contact initially should be with the coordinator of gifted education programs for that school system, or perhaps with the principal. Parents commonly report that if they initially contact the regular classroom teacher, they are quite often met with open or implied disbelief, or at least a reserved "wait and see" attitude.

The professional should encourage parents to give permission to send a report of the assessment findings to the school. Having a professional's opinion that the child may be intellectually or creatively gifted assists school personnel in more seriously considering that this child may be different from the average youngster for whom uniform school systems are characteristically designed. Although most U.S. school systems have special, differentiated educational programs for gifted children beginning only in the third grade (and then usually only for a few hours per week), modifications can be made within the regular classroom setting even in the first school years to nurture and develop intellectual abilities as well as the child's sense of integrity and self-concept. It is important for parents to develop an alliance with the school, to be seen by school personnel as helpful rather than as complaining adversaries. More information on how to do this, along with information concerning what expectations parents and schools should have of each other, can be found in such resources as Karnes and Marquardt (1991a, 1991b), Webb et al. (1982), and Clark (1992).

Parents need particular support from professionals if the gifted preschooler is female or is from a cultural minority or disadvantaged setting. Socialization factors begin quite early in life to shape family and self attitudes concerning the acceptability of creative and intellectual behaviors. Gifted girls learn very early that they should camouflage their brightness and lower their overt aspirations (Kerr, 1985). Cultural minority and disadvantaged gifted preschoolers often find themselves confronted with lowered, often prejudicial, expectancies about their abilities, and they may belong to subcultures that place far less value on intellect and creativity (Colangelo & Zaffran, 1979). Counseling with parents can be of particular help in both instances because these gifted preschoolers are far more likely to differ from the norm in ways that will become increasingly obvious as they mature, and which can result in emotional and interpersonal difficulties unless the differences are anticipated.

At home it is important that the parents not be so awed by their gifted preschooler that they allow him or her to rule the family or become its virtual exclusive focus. Similarly, they must not allow being a gifted child to become a liability rather than an asset by overly controlling, limiting, or criticizing gifted child behaviors so that the child feels unaccepted and unacceptable.

Adults who are awed by gifted children often fall into the trap of treating them like "walking heads." These persons often are so struck in their interactions with a gifted preschooler by the child's precocity that they comment quite openly about it, whether visiting relatives or in a grocery checkout line. Such reinforcement of intellectual, creative, or artistic skills, though pleasing to the child or the parents, runs the risk of focusing undue attention on what the child can do. Such children are at risk for subsequently feeling that they can be value *only* if they are producing something, not simply for themselves. Not only is it hazardous to hang one's sense of identity on a single hook (i.e., intellect), but also such a singular focus interferes with the child's ability to relate to others.

Behavioral Concerns

With gifted children as with all youngsters, limits on behaviors are needed. However, because of the gifted child's intensity and creativity, and because he or she is so often "out of step" with age peers and the systems and expectancies for children of his or her age, the likelihood is increased that he or she will be criticized for many of the very behaviors that are inherently a part of being gifted. It is extremely easy for parents to become engaged in power struggles that serve only to create distance between parent and child. An example would be the gifted child who needs only 6 hours' sleep at age 5, or the 4-year-old who asks incessant questions of everyone around. Instead of attempting to stifle such behaviors—at the expense of one's relationship with the child—it is more beneficial to recognize that they are to be expected in many gifted preschool children. The axiom to impart to parents is that of "Flowing with, rather than fighting against." Though it is important to shape and mold the behaviors, most need not become the source of power struggles or criticisms of the child's intensity, creativity, curiosity. Later in life these children will encounter more than their share of persons who feel a need to "take them down a peg" or to "show them they're not as smart as others say they are."

Though as few limits as possible should be set on gifted preschool children, parents should be consistent in their enforcement. Our experience has been that the natural or logical consequences approach of Dreikurs and Soltz (1964) works particularly well with most of these preschoolers, and their book *Children: A Challenge* is recommended for parents along with *Guiding the Gifted Child* (Webb et al., 1982). The exception involves attention deficit disordered–gifted children, who benefit from frequent, tightly enforced limits and close monitoring of all behavioral aspects. These children give the appearance of incredible cunning in violating house rules and appear almost immune to usual reinforcement schedules because they habituate so quickly to new discipline approaches.

For most gifted preschoolers, however, positive reinforcement is quite effective and can be used to ameliorate or prevent several common problems that otherwise may occur. Because these children often have such wide interests, they may have great difficulty staying "on task." As this is an area of importance to school personnel, parents thus should use successive rewarding of small increments to promote this skill.

Similarly, cooperative, rather than competitive, play can be reinforced. Though such a comment might seem applicable to all preschoolers, the intense orientation toward mastery within most gifted preschoolers orients them disproportionately toward games and activities that are competitive and where they can "win." Needless to say, this does not always make for the most harmonious sibling or peer relationships, and will need the parents' focused attention to help the child develop alternate styles of interacting. Role-modeling cooperative and noncompetitive activities is particularly helpful, as is role-playing to help develop empathy for another's viewpoint.

A related and very powerful technique is that of "special time," wherein the parent gives each child in the family 5 minutes of undivided attention to jointly do whatever the child chooses (except for competitive activities). Such special time creates an opportunity for the child to experience sharing and cooperative ventures while removing competitive ones. Webb et al. (1982) describe this and other related techniques in detail.

Above Average Versus Gifted

Finally, the professional will encounter some parents who believe their preschool child is gifted when, in fact, this is not the case even when using a "best performance" approach. Most often this occurs in children who are above average in intelligence, usually with IQ scores of 120 to 125. At the outset many of these parents ardently desire for their child to be formally designated as "gifted," and they may refuse to believe the professional who attempts to tell them otherwise. A helpful approach in such situations is to suggest that the child may fall in the range of "optimum intelligence," though not at this time in the range called "gifted." The concept of optimum intelligence (in IQ terms about 120 to 145) was formulated by Hollingworth (1942/1975) to represent that intelligence level where tasks are mastered easily, but where one is not so different from society's mainstream as to have an increased risk of being noticeably different. Most of our cultural leaders come from this group, and clearly it represents sufficient general intelligence to comfortably complete college-level academic work or beyond yet still retain a sense of belonging to those around. Upon understanding this, most such parents are both satisfied and relieved.

Most of all, the professional should suggest to parents of apparently gifted preschoolers that they treat their children as though they were gifted, at least until such time as more reliable and accurate estimates can be obtained (usually at about age 8 or 9). Encourage them to talk to other parents, to join local discussion groups, to share child-rearing recipes and parenting experiences, and to read the literature on gifted and talented children. If their child subsequently turns out to be gifted, this approach will have helped significantly. If not, it will have done no harm, and the additional information gained will have prevented them from placing inappropriate expectations on their child in later years.

References

Albert, R.S. (1971). Cognitive development and parental loss among the gifted, the exceptionally gifted and the creative. *Psychological Reports, 29,* 19-26.
Amabile, T.M. (1983). *The social psychology of creativity.* New York: Springer-Verlag.
Ames, L.B., Gillespie, B.S., Haines, J., & Ilg, F.L. (1979). *The Gesell Institute's child from one to six: Evaluating the behavior of the preschool child.* New York: Harper & Row.
Anastasi, A. (1988). *Psychological testing* (6th ed.). New York: Macmillan.
Bayley, N. (1969). *Manual for the Bayley Scales of Infant Development.* San Antonio, TX: Psychological Corporation.
Beery, K.E. (1982). *Revised administration, scoring, and teaching manual for the Developmental Test of Visual-Motor Integration.* Cleveland, OH: Modern Curriculum Press.
Bender, L. (1938). A visual motor gestalt test and its clinical use. *American Orthopsychiatric Association Research Monographs* (No. 3).
Bondy, A.S., Constantino, R., Norcross, J.C., & Sheslow, D. (1984). Comparison of Slosson and McCarthy scales for exceptional preschool children. *Perceptual and Motor Skills, 59*(2), 657-658.
Bracken, B.A., Prasse, D.P., & McCallum, R.S. (1984). Peabody Picture Vocabulary Test-Revised: An appraisal and review. *School Psychology Review, 13*(1), 49-60.
Brink, R.E. (1982). The gifted preschool child. *Pediatric Nursing, 9,* 299-302.
Burks, B.S., Jensen, D.W., & Terman, L.M., assisted by Leahy, A.M., Marshall, H., & Oden, M.H. (1930). *Genetic studies of genius: Vol. 3. The promise of youth.* Stanford, CA: Stanford University Press.
Clark, B. (1992). *Growing up gifted: Developing the potential of children at home and at school.* New York: Macmillan.
Colangelo, N., & Fleuridas, C. (1986). The abdication of childhood. *Journal of Counseling and Development, 64*(9), 561-563.
Colangelo, N., & Zaffran, R.T. (1979). *New voices in counseling the gifted.* Dubuque, IA: Kendall-Hunt.
Coleman, D. (1980, February). 1528 little geniuses and how they grew. *Psychology Today,* pp. 28-43.
Cox, C.M., assisted by Gillan, L.O., Livesay, R.H., & Terman, L.M. (1926). *Genetic studies of genius: Vol. 2. The early mental traits of three hundred geniuses.* Stanford, CA: Stanford University Press.
Crockenberg, S.B. (1972). Creativity tests: A boon or boondoggle for education. *Review of Educational Research, 42,* 27-45.
Dreikurs, T., & Soltz, V. (1964). *Children: A challenge.* New York: Hawthorne Books.
Dunn, L.M., & Dunn, L.M. (1981). *Peabody Picture Vocabulary Test-Revised.* Circle Pines, MN: American Guidance Service.
Dunn, L.M., & Markwardt, F.C., Jr. (1970). *Peabody Individual Achievement Test.* Circle Pines, MN: American Guidance Service.
Elkind, D. (1981). *The hurried child: Growing up too fast too soon.* New York: Addison-Wesley.
Fish, L. (1984). The role of the health-care provider with the gifted child. *Roper Review, 6,* 201-204.
Fish, L.J., & Burch, K.J. (1985). Identifying gifted preschoolers. *Pediatric Nursing, 12,* 125-127.
Fish, R., Bilek, M., Horrobin, J., & Change, P. (1976). Children with superior intelligence at seven years of age. *American Journal of Diseases in Children, 130,* 481-487.
Fox, L.H. (1981). Identification of the academically gifted. *American Psychologist, 36*(10), 1103-1111.

Frankenburg, W.K., Dodds, J.B., Fandal, A.W., Kazuk, E., & Cohrs, M. (1975). *Denver Developmental Screening Test* (rev. ed.). Denver: Ladoca Project and Publishing Foundation.

Gardner, H. (1983). *Frames of mind: The theory of multiple intelligences.* New York: Basic Books.

Grost, A. (1970). *Genius in residence.* Englewood Cliffs, NJ: Prentice-Hall.

Hall, E.G., & Skinner, N. (1980). *Somewhere to turn: Strategies for parents of the gifted and talented* (Perspectives on Gifted and Talented Education Series). New York: Teachers College Press.

Hanson, I. (1984). A comparison between parent identification of young bright children and subsequent testing. *Roeper Review, 7*(1), 44–45.

Harkins, D.E., & Webb, J.T. (1988). *A comparison of the Stanford-Binet Form L-M and Fourth Edition among gifted children.* Unpublished manuscript.

Hawthorne, L.W., Speer, S.K., & Buccellato, L. (1983). Appropriateness of the Wechsler Preschool and Primary Scales of Intelligence for gifted children. *Journal of Consulting and Clinical Psychology, 51*(3), 463–464.

Hayden, T. (1985). *Reaching out to the gifted child: Roles for the health care professions.* New York: American Association for Gifted Children.

Hayes, F.B., & Martin, R.P. (1986). Effectiveness of the PPVT-R in the screening of young gifted children. *Journal of Psychoeducational Assessment, 4*(1), 27–33.

Hollingworth, L.S. (1975). *Children above 180 IQ.* New York: Arno Press. (Reprint of 1942 edition)

Horowitz, F.D., & O'Brien, M. (1985). *The gifted and talented: Developmental perspectives.* Washington, DC: American Psychological Association.

Jackson, N.E. (1980). Identification of gifted performance in young children. In W.C. Roedell, N.E. Jackson, & H.B. Robinson (Eds.), *Gifted young children* (pp. 27–65). New York: Teachers College Press.

Jastak, J.R., & Jastak, S. (1978). *The Wide Range Achievement Test* (rev. ed.). Wilmington, DE: Jastak Associates.

Karnes, M.B., & Johnson, L.J. (1986a). Identification and assessment of gifted/talented handicapped and nonhandicapped children in early childhood. *Journal of Children in Contemporary Society, 18*(3–4), 35–54.

Karnes, M.B., & Johnson, L.J. (1986b). Identification and programming for young gifted/talented handicapped. *Topics in Early Childhood Special Education, 6*(1), 50–61.

Karnes, F.A., & Marquardt, R.G. (1991a). *Gifted children and legal issues in education: Parents' stories of hope.* Dayton, OH: Ohio Psychology Press.

Karnes, F.A., & Marquardt, R.G. (1991b). *Gifted children and the law: Mediation, due process and court cases.* Dayton, OH: Ohio Psychology Press.

Kaufman, A.S., & Kaufman, N.L. (1983). *K-ABC: Kaufman Assessment Battery for Children.* Circle Pines, MN: American Guidance Service.

Kerr, B.A. (1985). *Smart girls, gifted women.* Columbus: Ohio Psychology Publishing.

Kincaid, D. (1969). A study of highly gifted elementary pupils. *Gifted Child Quarterly, 13,* 264–267.

Kolata, G. (1987). Early signs of school age IQ. *Science, 23,* 774–775.

Marland, S. (1972). *Education of the gifted and talented* (U.S. Commission on Education, 92nd Congress, 2nd Session). Washington, DC: U.S. Government Printing Office.

Mathieson, A. (1980, October 30). Gifted children. *Nursing Mirror,* pp. xv–xvii.

McCallum, R.S., Karnes, F.A., & Edwards, R.P. (1984). The test of choice for assessment of gifted children: A comparison of the K-ABC, WISC-R, and the Stanford-Binet. *Journal of Psychoeducational Assessment, 2,* 57–63.

McCarthy, D. (1972). *McCarthy Scales of Children's Abilities.* San Antonio, TX: Psychological Corporation.
Moreland, K.M., & Webb, J.T. (1988). *Comparison of the K-ABC and WISC-R with elementary gifted children.* Manuscript submitted for publication.
Naglieri, J.A., & Anderson, D.F. (1985). Comparison of the WISC-R and the K-ABC with gifted students. *Journal of Psychoeducational Assessment, 3,* 175–179.
Newborg, J., Stock, J.R., & Wnek, L. (1984). *Battelle Developmental Inventory.* Allen, TX: DLM Teaching Resources.
Perigo-Moore, L. (1981). *Does this mean my kid's a genius?* New York: McGraw-Hill.
Piirto, J.N. (1992). *Understanding those who create.* Dayton, OH: Ohio Psychology Press.
Raven, J.C. (1960). *Guide to using the Standard Progressive Matrices.* London: H.K. Lewis.
Reynolds, C.R., & Clark, J.H. (1986). Profile analysis of standardized intelligence test performance of very high IQ children. *Psychology in the Schools, 23*(1), 5–12.
Robinson, H.B. (1981). The uncommonly bright child. In M. Lewis & L.A. Rosenblum (Eds.), *The uncommon child: Genesis of behavior* (Vol. 3, pp. 57–81). New York: Plenum.
Roedell, W.C. (1980). Characteristics of gifted young children. In W.C. Roedell, N.E. Jackson, & H.B. Robinson (Eds.), *Gifted young children* (pp. 66–89). New York: Teachers College Press.
Roedell, W.C., Jackson, N.E., & Robinson, H.B. (Eds.). (1980). *Gifted young children.* New York: Teachers College Press.
Sattler, J.M. (1988). *Assessment of children* (3rd ed.). San Diego, CA: Author.
Shaywitz, S.E., Shaywitz, B.A., Jamner, A.H., Towle, V.R., & Barnes, M.A. (1986). Heterogeneity within the gifted: Boys with higher IQs exhibit increased activity, impulsivity and parenting problems. *Annals of Neurology, 20*(3), 415–416.
Slosson, R.L. (1983). *Slosson Intelligence Test (SIT) and Oral Reading Test (SORT) for children and adults.* East Aurora, NY: Slosson Educational Publications.
Speer, S.K., Hawthorne, L.W., & Buccatello, L. (1986). Intellectual patterns of young gifted children on the WPPSI. *Journal of Education for the Gifted, 10*(1), 57–62.
Terman, L.M., assisted by Baldwin, B.T., Bronson, E., DeVoss, J.C., Fuller, F., Goodenough, F.L., Kelley, T.L., Lima, M., Marshall, H., Moore, A.H., Raubenheimer, A.S., Ruch, G.M., Willoughby, R.L., Wyman, J.B., & Yates, D.H. (1925). *Genetic studies of genius: Vol. 1. The mental and physical traits of a thousand gifted children.* Stanford, CA: Stanford University Press.
Terman, L.M., & Merrill, M.A. (1973). *Stanford-Binet Intelligence Scale: Manual for the Third Revision Form L-M.* Chicago: Riverside.
Terman, L.M., & Oden, M.H. (1959). *Genetic studies of genius: Vol. 5. The gifted group at mid-life.* Stanford, CA: Stanford University Press.
Terman, L.M., & Oden, M.H., in association with Bayley, N., Marshall, H., McNemar, Q., & Sullivan, E.B. (1947). *Genetic studies of genius: Vol. 4. The gifted child grows up.* Stanford, CA: Stanford University Press.
Thorndike, R.L., Hagen, E.P., & Sattler, J.M. (1986). *Guide for administering and scoring the Stanford-Binet Intelligence Scale: Fourth Edition.* Chicago: Riverside.
Torrance, E.P. (1974). *Torrance Tests for Creative Thinking: Gr. K–Graduate Schools.* Los Angeles: Western Psychological Services.
Wallach, M.A. (1970). Creativity. In P.H. Mussen (Ed.), *Carmichael's manual of child psychology* (Vol. 1, pp. 1211–1272). New York: Wiley.
Wallach, M.A., & Kogan, N. (1965). *Modes of thinking in young children.* New York: Holt.
Webb, J.T., Meckstroth, E.A., & Tolan, S.S. (1982). *Guiding the gifted child.* Columbus: Ohio Psychology Publishing.

Wechsler, D. (1967). *Manual for the Wechsler Preschool and Primary Scales of Intelligence.* San Antonio, TX: Psychological Corporation.
Wechsler, D. (1974). *Manual for the Wechsler Intelligence Scale for Children–Revised.* San Antonio, TX: Psychological Corporation.
Whitmore, J.R. (1980). *Giftedness, conflict and underachievement.* Boston: Allyn & Bacon.
Whitmore, J.R., & Maker, C.J. (1985). *Intellectual giftedness in disabled persons.* Rockville, MD: Aspen Systems.
Woodcock, R.W., & Johnson, M.B. (1977). *Woodcock-Johnson Psycho-Educational Battery.* Allen, TX: DLM Teaching Resources.

16

Ethical and Legal Issues

MORGAN P. KELLY, J.D., M.A. & GARY B. MELTON, PH.D.

Until the 1970s, the right to a free public education was still being denied to many members of one group: children with handicapping conditions. Two class action suits resolved in 1972 signaled the end of this practice that had long been supported by state and local regulations. Parents were on the winning sides in *Pennsylvania Association for Retarded Children (PARC) v. Pennsylvania* (1972) and in *Mills v. Board of Education* (1972), both of which affirmed the right of every child to educational services regardless of the scope of their needs.

In spite of the holdings of these and other cases, and of state legislation designed to ensure educational rights to all children, Congress found in 1975 that

1. Over 1.75 million U.S. children with handicaps were being excluded entirely from receiving a public education solely on the basis of their handicap.
2. Over half of the estimated eight million handicapped children in this country were not receiving the appropriate educational services they needed and/or were entitled to.
3. Many other children with handicaps were still being placed in inappropriate educational settings because their handicaps were undetected or because of a violation of their individual rights (Abeson & Zettel, 1977, p. 121).

In response, Congress made universal access to public education into federal law in 1975 by approving PL 94–142, the Education for All Handicapped Children Act (now known as the Individuals with Disabilities Education Act [IDEA]). The impact of this legislation and the amendments that followed in 1983 and 1986 shapes major aspects of assessing young children for all of the professions involved.

THE STATUTORY FRAMEWORK

The major source of federal authority in the area of preschool assessment is found in 20 U.S.C. §§ 1401–1485, which is the codification of several acts, including PL 94–142, PL 98–199, and PL 99–457.

In general, PL 94–142, the Education for All Handicapped Children Act of 1975, is designed to meet the rights and unique needs of handicapped children and their parents and to assist the states and localities in the provision of education for all handicapped children. More specifically, this law guarantees all handicapped children between the ages of 3 and 21 the availability of a free appropriate public education. The passage of the Education of the Handicapped Act Amendments of 1983 (PL 98-199) primarily sought to expand and improve services to handicapped preschoolers (including infants at birth). Both of these laws represent major steps toward ensuring that "Child Find" and comprehensive assessment methods for preschoolers are extended beyond mere identification of handicapped preschoolers, so that they serve instead as guides to individualized educational plans (Paget & Nagel, 1986). The Act stops short, however, of requiring the best education possible (*Board of Education v. Rowley,* 1982).

"Special education" under PL 94-142 is education specifically designed to meet the needs of a handicapped child, at no cost to the parents, including classroom instruction, instruction in physical education, home instruction, and instruction in hospitals and institutions. "Related services" are those such as transportation and other developmental, corrective, and supportive services that assist a handicapped child to benefit from special education (e.g., speech pathology, audiology, psychological services, physical and occupational therapy, recreation, early identification and assessment of disabilities in children, counseling services, medical services for diagnosis or evaluation only, school health services, school social work, and parent counseling and training). Although PL 94-142 emphasizes special education and related services, the Act creates a strong presumption for mainstreaming.

The Act was amended again in 1986 by PL 99-457 (The Education of the Handicapped Act Amendments of 1986) to extend its scope to the families of infants and toddlers from birth to age 3. Whereas PL 94-142 and PL 98-199 mandate Individualized Education Plans (IEPs) for ages 3 to 21, PL 99-457 mandates Individualized Family Service Plans (IFSPs) for infants and toddlers.

Criteria for Eligibility

Different criteria are used to determine qualification for the benefits of these Acts. To receive special educational benefits under PL 94-142, a child (aged 3 to 21) must meet the Act's definition of "handicapped." To qualify, the child must have one of the following physical or mental conditions: mental retardation, hearing impairment or deafness, speech impairment, visual handicap, serious emotional disturbance, orthopedic impairment, other health impairment, specific learning disability, or multiple handicaps. Moreover, as the Supreme Court held in *Board of Education v. Rowley* (1982), PL 94-142 does not recognize a child who has such a disability as a "handicapped child" unless the child needs special education in order to progress in school. If the child is not handicapped within the meaning of the law, then the child is entitled to neither special education nor "related services," including psychological services (cf. *Irving Independent School District v. Tatro,* 1984).

Under PL 99-457, infants and toddlers up to age 3 qualify for benefits if they are either experiencing developmental delay or have a diagnosed physical or mental condition with a high probability of resulting in developmental delay. The areas of delay that the Act covers include cognitive development, physical development, language and speech development, psychosocial development, and self-help skills (Secs. 672[1][A], [B]).

Services for Individual Children

Under PL 94-142, each handicapped child must have an Individualized Education Plan (IEP). The IEP includes a statement of the child's present levels of educational performance and states annual goals, including short-term instructional objectives. In addition, it specifies the special education and related services to be provided and the extent to which the child will be able to participate in regular education programs. The IEP sets dates for the initiation and the duration of services. Finally, the plan specifies appropriate objective criteria and evaluation procedures for determining, on at least an annual basis, whether the short-term instructional objectives are being achieved (34 C.F.R. § 300.346).

Analogously, the heart of PL 99-457 is the Individualized Family Service Plan (IFSP). Each infant or toddler and her or his family is entitled to a written and periodically reviewed IFSP. The IFSP must be derived by a multidisciplinary assessment team (which includes the parents) that determines the unique needs of the infant or toddler and the family and identifies the services appropriate to meet those needs (Secs. 677[a], [b]).

The plan must state the infant's or toddler's present levels of physical development, cognitive development, language and speech development, psychosocial development, and self-help skills. The IFSP must delineate the family's strengths and needs with regard to improving the development of the handicapped infant or toddler. The IFSP must state (a) the major outcomes the infant or toddler and the family are expected to achieve, (b) the criteria, procedures, and timelines used to assess progress toward achieving the outcomes, and (c) whether modifications or revisions of the outcomes or services are necessary. The IFSP must specify the early intervention services necessary to meet the unique needs of the infant or toddler and the family, including the frequency, intensity, and method of delivering services, along with the projected dates for initiation and anticipated duration of services. The IFSP names the responsible case manager from the profession most relevant to the infant's or toddler's and family's needs who will implement the plan and coordinate with other agencies and persons. The IFSP outlines the steps necessary to support the transition of the handicapped toddler to services provided under part B to the extent such services are considered appropriate (Sec. 677[d]).

The Act provides that early intervention services are free or are provided on a sliding fee scale to meet the needs of the infant or toddler (Secs. 672[2][A], [B], [C]). Those services, which must be provided by qualified personnel (i.e., special educators, speech and language pathologists and audiologists, occupational therapists, physical therapists, psychologists, social workers, nurses, and nutritionists [Secs. 672(2)(F)(i)-(viii)]), include (a) family training, counseling, and home visits; (b) special instruction; (c) speech pathology and audiology; (d) occupational therapy; (e) physical therapy; (f) psychological services; (g) case management services; (h) medical services for the purpose of diagnosis or evaluation; and (i) early identification, screening, and assessment (Secs. 672[2][E][i]-[ix]). Furthermore, the infant or toddler is entitled to any health services necessary to benefit from the other early intervention services (Sec. 672[2][E][x]).

Procedural Safeguards

Both PL 94-142 and PL 99-457 have procedural safeguards to protect the rights of parents and children. In addition, ethical standards for psychologists require that no action should be taken that would violate or diminish the legal or civil rights of clients (American Psychological Association, 1981, Principle 3c). The procedural safeguards include an administrative hearing that may be appealed to a state or federal district court, the right to confidentiality of personally identifiable information, the opportunity for parents and a guardian to examine records relating to assessment, screening, and eligibility determinations, and the development and implementation of the Individualized Family Service Plan. Prior written notice must be given to the parents of the handicapped infant or toddler, in the parents' native language, whenever the state agency or service provider proposes to initiate or change, or refuses to initiate or change, the identification, evaluation, placement, or provision of appropriate early intervention services to the handicapped infant or toddler (Sec. 680). Procedural violations alone warrant rejection of an IEP (*Bonadonna v. Cooperman*, 1985), a holding presumably applicable to IFSPs.

An integral component to the procedural requirements, as written into the regulations pertinent to PL 94-142, is parental consent (the federal rules implementing PL 99-457 have yet to be promulgated but will probably be very similar). Consent is needed prior to an evaluation for a child who is thought to be handicapped and in need of some sort of special education or related service (34 C.F.R. § 300.504). The schools, however, may overcome parental refusal. For example, some states' laws provide either an administrative or a judicial mechanism for obtaining an authorization to conduct a psychological assessment without parental permission. The administrative mechanism, which is the same for parents challenging the school's decisions regarding the IEP, entails a hearing before an impartial hearing officer in a setting where both parents and the school may have attorneys. Each side has the opportunity to present evidence and confront, cross-examine, and compel the attendance of witnesses. After the hearing is complete, the hearing officer issues a written decision that is appealable to a state hearing panel and ultimately to the courts.

One other important provision reflects the fundamental principle that consent is legally sufficient only when it is obtained after full disclosure of all material information by the person from whom consent is sought (Pryzwansky & Bersoff, 1978). Before evaluation and placement, the school system must tell parents all of the procedural safeguards available to them, describe the action the school proposes to take with regard to the student, and describe any options the school considered and the reasons why those options were rejected (34 C.F.R. § 300.505). Of special importance is paragraph (a)(3) under section 300.505, which requires that parents be given "a description of each evaluation procedure, test, record, or report the agency uses as a basis for the proposal." The significance for psychologists is that they must anticipate which instruments or other modes of assessment will be used and describe, not merely list, their purposes (Pryzwansky & Bersoff, 1978).

Practical Difficulties in Conforming to the Law

Competence in Interpretation

A primary source of difficulty with conforming to the mandates of PL 99–457 is the assumptions the law makes about psychologists' competent use of assessment devices in the evaluation of infants and toddlers. The Act requires both descriptive and predictive uses of these instruments in the context of the particular child's family and environmental settings. The Act further requires written discussions of the child's developmental status across many domains, and mandates that the IFSP specifically outline what is going to be done to bring the child's performance to a specified level. In short, the Act mistakenly assumes both the existence of many reliable and valid assessment devices and the availability of many psychologists well trained in their use.

The law also assumes that nonpsychologists will be expert users of psychological evaluations of children in an age group about which many psychologists themselves are not expert. In such a situation, the law apparently presumes that other team members will weigh the assessment results with due attention to the limitations of the evaluation. Even if the psychologist is expert, the other team members must possess some measure of competence in interpretation of psychological test results. Otherwise, sound conclusions and recommendations can be overridden (or unsound opinions affirmed) by the majority vote of a multidisciplinary team, of which the psychologist is only one among equals (Paul, 1981).

Realism in Goal Setting

Educational personnel naturally are concerned with the possible negative impact on their professional credibility with peers and parents if students fail to reach the goals stated in the IEP or IFSP. Unfortunately, one solution too often seems to be setting achievement goals too low in order to ensure success (Reynolds, Gutkin, Elliott, & Witt, 1984). In anticipation of this problem, the federal rules that implement PL 94–142 state expressly that no agency, teacher, or other person will be held accountable if a child does not achieve the growth projected in the annual goals and objectives (34 C.F.R. § 300.349). The comment to that section states that the rule is intended to relieve concerns that the IEP constitutes a guarantee by the public agency and the teacher that a child will progress at a specified rate. Thus those responsible for the IEP should recognize that there is no legal trap waiting for those who meet their ethical duty to appraise needs and set standards for the child honestly. The lack of a guaranteed result for an IFSP does not abrogate all responsibility, though. The comment to section 300.349 emphasizes that agencies and teachers are not relieved from making good faith efforts to assist the child in achieving the objectives and goals listed in the IEP.

Frequency of Review

Another problem results from the law's specification that each IEP and IFSP need be reviewed only on an annual basis (Reynolds et al., 1984; PL 99–457, Sec. 677[b]). Although more frequent review is advocated by the law, there remains the tendency to review IEPs and IFSPs less frequently than may be optimal for the child because of the time and effort required of many different professionals. A narrow reading of the rules allows this result in that 34 C.F.R. § 300.346(e) states that the IEP must include appropriate objective criteria for determining, on "at least an annual basis, whether the short term instructional objectives are being achieved." A slightly broader reading of the comment to 34 C.F.R. § 300.349 may result in a different conclusion. As already noted, the comment includes a statement that agencies are not relieved from making good faith efforts to assist the child in achieving the objectives and goals listed in the IEP. Therefore, a good faith effort (in the most meaningful sense of the phrase) on the part of the agency to assist a child to achieve short-term instructional objectives would necessarily require some inquiry about his or her short-term progress. Without this review, it is possible that a child's failure to reach his or her short-term objectives will not be discovered until the end of the year at the annual IEP review (Reynolds et al., 1984).

The significance of the frequency of required review is obvious when one considers the nature of development in early childhood. One of the most distinguishing features of young children is rapid developmental change (Ollendick & Meador, 1984; Culbertson & Gyurke, 1990). Infant tests cover a period of development in which important, rapid, qualitative changes occur. One of the difficulties in the testing of infants is that some may be prone to developmental spurts and lags, resulting in a decrease in test score reliability (Sattler, 1982). The wide variability in the experiential backgrounds of young children (i.e., exposure to preschool environments and adults outside the home) requires the psychologist to be vigilant to individual differences and responsive to potential problems with shyness, verbal facility, and interpersonal discomfort—problems that sometimes can be observed in the most socially competent preschoolers. Moreover, rapid developmental changes and behavioral fluctuations characteristic of this age require a good understanding of normal preschool development (Ulrey & Rogers, 1982). In making diagnostic decisions, psychologists must understand the importance of emerging skills as extensions of and complements to acquired skills, and learning processes as vital adjuncts to products of learning (Barnett, 1984).

Limitations in the State of the Art

It must be recognized that preschool-aged children comprise a unique population, qualitatively different from their school-aged counterparts, and that the requisite assessment skills for very young children are not just downward extensions of those used with older examinees (Ulrey & Rogers, 1982). Important differences exist between the interpretation of preschool children's (and infants') test performance and that of school-aged children's performances (Rogers, 1986). The difference in emphasis concerns the theoretical understanding of intelligence as defined by intelligence tests—a type of reasoning and problem-solving ability that requires a certain maturity of thought, an ability to understand and use the abstract symbol system that formal academic education requires.

Infant and preschool psychological tests do not measure these capacities, largely because psychologists do not believe they are present in preschoolers' cognitive repertoire (e.g., Flavell, 1985). Instead, preschoolers use very different cognitive processes, those that emphasize perceptual, rather than conceptual, discrimination and judgments. Preschool tests measure perceptual judgments, spatial reasoning, visual-motor skills, and concrete use of language—areas of functioning that are thought to be more linked to neurodevelopmental maturation than to "intellectual" abilities in the above sense (Rogers, 1986). Because preschool tests emphasize different skills than tests for school-aged children and adults, the tests for school-aged children cannot be modified downward, and the resulting scores of the two cannot be equated.

The scope of the evaluation required by the regulations thus also is problematic. Cognitive development is not the only domain in which the state of the art of preschool assessment is limited. Assessment of socioemotional development may be even more problematic (Martin, 1988), because young children often lack the verbal fluency required by most personality tests and clinical interview techniques.

Even when developmentally appropriate standardized tasks are available, young children often do not understand the demand characteristics of the assessment situation and sometimes cannot control their behaviors even if they understand these demands (Martin, 1988; Rogers, 1986; Sattler, 1982). Whereas many older children understand that they should try hard to answer questions in an interview with a psychologist, can manifest motivated and attentive behavior for an hour or more, and may also understand the significance of the assessment, preschoolers find this almost impossible. Their behavior is controlled by immediate stimuli, and if they become fatigued, fearful (because of separation from a parent), or bored, this directly affects their behavior, contributing to the instability of preschool assessment results (Rogers, 1986; Martin, 1988).

Such instability across time and settings makes concern about reliability and validity central to any discussion of preschool assessment (Boehm & Sandberg, 1982). Developmental change, behavioral fluctuation, emerging skills, and situational variables have direct impact on the reliability and validity of procedures used at the preschool level and, even more so, in infancy. Given this rapid change, the question arises as to how one would make predictions from this period to a later period. Similarly, it can be asked whether an aggregate of several days' scores is more stable and predictive. These types of questions have not been answered, and until they are, the validity of measurement for any one day and the meaning and usefulness of normative comparison remain unclear (Martin, 1988).

These problems should not be viewed as ruling out the professional and scientific usefulness of assessment of young children. Instead, they are problems inherent to preschool assessment of the scope and validity envisioned by the drafters of federal special education law. Clinicians involved in evaluations for possible special educational placement of young children must make practical judgments about the application of the competing values present in special education law: (a) a mandate to "do something" to assist handicapped children (in this instance, to render opinions about the nature of a child's handicap and the educational intervention most likely to alleviate it), and (b) an obligation to avoid error in placement decisions and, in particular, to refrain from procedures that might result in undue stigma and segregation. When evaluators balance such considerations in their everyday work with young children, they are making legal and ethical judgments informed by their knowledge of the limitations of their assessment techniques.

THE BABY DOE ISSUE

The legal and ethical significance of the technical problems of preschool assessment is illustrated most starkly when life or death hinges at least in part on an evaluator's predictions about an infant's future welfare. One of the most unfortunate positions in which mental health professionals can find themselves is confronting the parents with the results of the assessment of a severely handicapped newborn, one with a life-threatening condition. Mental health professionals know that their predictions about the infant's quality of life very likely will be used by the parents to make a life choice (e.g., withhold life-saving treatment from an infant with Down's syndrome or spina bifida).

Pediatric professionals—and society as a whole—have several options: (a) advocate treatment of all neonates, regardless of prognosis, (b) terminate (or acquiesce in the termination of) the lives of selected "non-persons," (c) advocate parental discretion with regard to treatment, (d) advocate treatment according to a "quality of life" projection, or (e) advocate treatment be withheld if not in the child's best interest. Little ethical sensitivity is needed to recognize both that the ethical dilemmas involved are profound and that the resolution of those dilemmas is not within the expertise of health professionals qua health professionals. To the extent that the judgments required are "expert" ones, they are within the province of theologians and moral philosophers, not psychologists and physicians. Nonetheless, even if health professionals make clear to parents and others that the ultimate judgments are ethical, not scientific or clinical ones, clinicians cannot escape the problem. Clinicians who give an opinion about a child's prognosis are acting within the limits of their expertise, but the level of uncertainty that they will tolerate before giving such an opinion will be affected by their assessment of the ethical costs of various kinds of error.

Similarly, the law gives no means of avoidance of the difficult decision whether to involve a third party in the relationship between a clinician and the parents of a handicapped child. The Child Abuse Prevention and Treatment Act (PL 93-247) was amended to create a new category of child abuse/neglect that includes the withholding of medically indicated treatments from disabled infants (PL 98-457). States that receive federal funds for research and intervention related to child abuse and neglect must have state laws in place that are consistent with federal definition. Federal regulations define the term *withholding medically indicated treatment* as the failure to provide treatment (including appropriate nutrition, hydration, and medication) that, in the treating physician's reasonable medical judgment, will be most likely to be effective in ameliorating or correcting all conditions threatening a child's life. The exceptions to the treatment requirement occur when, in the treating physician's reasonable judgment, any of the following apply:

1. The infant is chronically and irreversibly comatose.
2. The provision of such treatment would merely prolong dying, not be effective in ameliorating or correcting all of the infant's life-threatening conditions, or otherwise be futile in terms of the survival of the infant.
3. The provision of such treatment would be virtually futile in terms of the

survival of the infant and the treatment itself under such circumstances would be inhumane (45 C.F.R § 1340.15 [b][2]).

The potential legal difficulties for a mental health professional in this situation are several. First, just as the physician may be liable for child abuse in the form of medical neglect, a mental health professional involved in counseling the parents may be liable for conspiracy in that neglect. In other words, if the mental health professional counsels the parents to withhold treatment, or merely acquiesces in the decision not to treat, and takes no steps to save the child, he or she may be liable for conspiracy to homicide, or manslaughter, plus liability for failure to report the child abuse, usually a misdemeanor.

The misdemeanor/manslaughter rule is a common law rule that states that if a misdemeanor causes death of another, one is guilty of manslaughter (Robertson & Fost, 1976). Thus, if an infant dies as a result of medical neglect, and a physician or mental health professional knowingly has failed to report the decision not to treat, that professional may be liable both for the misdemeanor of failing to report and manslaughter for the infant's death.

There is also liability for homicide by omission, which occurs when failure to discharge a legal duty to care for another person causes the death of that person (LaFave & Scott, 1972). The legal duty of the physician is one of either caring for the child or finding someone who will. The sources of the duty include the child abuse reporting statutes (which impose a duty to report abuse or neglect), the law of contract, tort law, and law relating to placing one in peril (Robertson & Fost, 1976). A physician's failure to report his or her neglect of a defective newborn could lead to the infant's death, a homicide by omission. These theories of homicide liability would survive parental refusal of consent because the physician-patient relationship has already attached, given that the patient could be substantially harmed by withdrawal of treatment.

Another theory of homicide liability is based on the law of contract. The physician and the parents have contracted for services that include the newborn infant as beneficiary of all necessary medical care, with the physician's duty beginning before or at birth. Under the law of third-party beneficiary contracts, the parties contracting for services to another cannot terminate the obligation to a minor if termination would substantially harm the minor (Robertson, 1975). Therefore, a physician who has begun to treat an infant at the request of its parents is under a legal duty of care that can only be discharged by taking such steps as are necessary to protect the infant's interests.

In addition to the contractual duty, physicians still have a legal duty to care for the child on the traditional tort doctrine that one who assumes the care of another, whether gratuitously or not, cannot terminate such care if the third person would be hurt thereby. The notion is that had this person not already begun the care, someone else would have come to the aid of the needy person (LaFave & Scott, 1972).

Lastly, a person who puts another in peril, even innocently and without malice, incurs a legal duty to act to protect the imperiled person. Therefore, a physician or mental health professional has a duty to protect an infant whom he or she imperils by informing the handicapped infant's parents of the economic and psychological burdens they might face if the infant lives (LaFave & Scott, 1972).

Another theory of liability is as an accessory, one who "counsels, encourages or aids or abets another to commit a felony" (LaFave & Scott, 1972). This type of liability is clearest in a case in which a physician or mental health professional counseled or encouraged the parents to withhold treatment (Robertson, 1975).

There are several defenses, including the fact that there is no duty to extend care beyond extraordinary means, that death may have occurred anyway, or that withholding treatment was necessary to avoid the greater harm of an unbearably difficult life.

As the law stands now, the potential for a successful prosecution is clearly present. However, the likelihood of such a prosecution seems now to be very low, given that almost no cases have been brought using any of the theories of liability. Be that as it may, one should be aware of the winds of political change, and of politically motivated prosecutors. If mental health professionals find themselves in a situation where they are called upon to evaluate an infant who is in a life-threatening condition, they should consider consulting an attorney.

Regardless of one's legal position, though, the point should not be obscured that the ethical dilemma is profound. Most fundamentally, the clinician must make an ethical judgment whether to assert his or her own values against those that other possible decision makers might apply. Even if one takes the position that the decision in Baby Doe cases ultimately belongs properly to the child's parents, the problem does not end. In the latter context, the clinician must decide how to present information amid uncertainty so that the least risk of grievous error (however defined) is present. In deciding, for example, the degree of confidence with which such information is presented, the clinician is making both scientific and ethical judgments with potential life-and-death consequences. Although such questions of survival rarely occur in mental health, clinical judgments do often have major personal consequences for clients. In the case of young children, such issues are of special concern because of the possibility of loss of opportunities for the whole life span and the particular uncertainty attached to opinions derived from assessment of infants and toddlers.

GUIDELINES IN PROFESSIONAL ETHICAL CODES

As the Baby Doe example illustrates vividly, ethical problems, like problems of technical merit (indeed, to some extent because of such scientific issues), are rampant in assessment of young children. Such ethical issues can be approached at two levels. First, in some situations, a consensus has arisen in the professions about *normal* ethics, the standards of conduct that are customary among their members (see Reece & Fremouw, 1984). Such principles are formalized in the ethical codes of professional organizations that serve as the authority for adjudicating complaints against members who may be subject to disciplinary action by their peers. As such, professional ethical codes are analogous to law and can be interpreted at least to some extent apart from the *normative* principles on which they purportedly are based.

Second, one can look to such normative principles. Regardless of the level of morality that is "normal" for psychologists, their behavior, collectively and individually, can be evaluated by looking to moral-philosophical analysis to discover how psychologists *should* behave. Even if psychologists conform their conduct to the requirements of the law and professional codes, their judgment may not be ethical in the normative sense. (Conversely, sophisticated ethical judgment occasionally may result in disobedience of the law or professional codes.) To use an example familiar to psychologists, deception is permitted under some circumstances by Principle 9e of the Ethical Principles of Psychologists (APA, 1981), even though most moral philosophers believe that such lying shows disrespect for research participants and thus violates normative principles (e.g., see Bok, 1978).

Having described the application of law to the assessment of young children, we turn now to another "legalistic" topic: the guidelines for assessment that are embedded in professional codes. Similar guidelines appear in the codes of several organizations, three of which would be pertinent to discuss here: the American Psychological Association's Ethical Principles of Psychologists (APA, 1981), the National Association of School Psychologists Principles of Professional Ethics (NASP, 1985), and the Standards for Educational and Psychological Testing, as adopted by the American Educational Research Association, the American Psychological Association, and by the National Council on Measurement in Education (AERA, APA, & NCME, 1985). In the following discussion, these codes will be referred to as APA, NASP, and SEPT, respectively.

The use of these ethical codes in litigation may be inevitable because they help define the professional standard of care in negligence and malpractice cases. However, in legal proceedings and elsewhere, professional judgment based on the accepted body of knowledge *always* plays an essential role in determining the relevance of particular standards in particular situations.

Standards for Assessment

When considering instruments used in the assessment of young and/or handicapped children, special considerations regarding the reliability and validity of those instruments come to the fore. As mentioned earlier, many of the instruments used with these children are of questionable (or as yet unascertained) reliability. Therefore, there is substantial risk of harm to the child as a result of erroneous diagnosis.

Those who use tests and those who interact professionally with potential test takers with handicapping conditions should (a) possess the information necessary to make an appropriate selection of alternate measures, (b) have current information regarding the availability of modified forms of the test in question, (c) inform individuals with handicapping conditions, when appropriate, about the existence of modified forms, and (d) make these forms available to test takers when appropriate and feasible (SEPT, 14.7). Evaluators also should give due consideration to individual integrity and individual differences by the selection and use of procedures and assessment techniques appropriate for the client (NASP).

Those who modify tests for handicapped people should have the requisite psychometric expertise and knowledge of the effects of various handicapping conditions on test performance (SEPT, 14.1). "When feasible, the validity and reliability of tests administered to people with various handicapping conditions should be investigated and reported by the agency or publisher that makes the modification" (SEPT, 14.6).

In addition to providing competent test administration and interpretation, psychologists must take steps to ensure that their assessments are not misused (APA, Principle 8). In reporting assessment results, psychologists should indicate any reservations that exist regarding validity or reliability because of the circumstances of the assessment or the inappropriateness of the norms for the person tested (NASP; APA, Principle 8c). "Clinicians should not imply that interpretation of test data is based on empirical evidence of validity unless such evidence exists for the interpretation given" (SEPT, 7.1). "When validity is appraised by comparing the level of agreement between test results and clinical diagnoses, the diagnostic terms or categories employed should be carefully defined or identified, and the method by which a diagnosis was made should be specified" (SEPT, 7.2). "When differential diagnosis is needed, the user should choose, if possible, a test for which there is evidence of the test's ability to distinguish between the two or more diagnostic groups of concern rather than merely to distinguish abnormal cases from the general population" (SEPT, 7.3).

Professional Responsibility

Psychologists bear an especially heavy social responsibility whenever their actions may alter the lives of others (APA, Principle 1e). Therefore, a basic ethical principle is that a professional should perform only those services for which he or she has acquired a recognized level of competency (NASP). In practice, psychologists must recognize the boundaries and the limitations of their techniques and training. In areas where there are as yet no recognized standards, psychologists must take whatever precautions are necessary to protect the welfare of their clients (APA, Principle 2). Therefore, psychologists must understand the intricacies of psychological and educational measurement, validation problems, and test research (APA, Principle 2e). In educational, clinical, and counseling applications, test administrators and users should not attempt to evaluate test takers whose special characteristics (such as age or handicapping condition) are outside the range of their academic training or supervised experience (SEPT, 6.10). If a psychologist is presented with a situation outside her or his range of competence, the psychologist should seek consultation with (SEPT, 6.10), or should refer the client to, another qualified professional (NASP).

Informed Consent and Confidentiality

Psychologists must inform consumers (i.e., parents and children) fully about the purpose and nature of an evaluative, educational, or treatment procedure (APA, Principle 6). When performing assessments, psychologists must recognize their client's right to a full explanation of the nature and purpose of the assessments in language that he or she can understand, unless an explicit exception to this right has been agreed upon in advance (APA, Principle 8a). The exceptions to this requirement occur when testing without consent is (a) mandated by law or governmental regulation, (b) conducted as a regular part of school activities (e.g., group achievement testing), or (c) clearly implied (e.g., an employment application) (SEPT, 16.1).

The comment following SEPT 16.1 elaborates on the duty imposed in meeting the requirements of informed consent:

> Informed consent implies that the test takers or representatives are made aware, in language that they can understand, of the reasons for testing, the types of tests to be used, the intended use and the range of material consequences of the intended use, and what testing information will be released and to whom. When law mandates testing but does not require informed consent, test users should exercise discretion in obtaining informed consent, but test takers should always be given relevant information about a test when it is in their interest.
>
> Young test takers should receive an explanation of the reasons for testing. Even a child as young as two or three and many mentally retarded test takers can understand a simple explanation as to why they are being tested. For example, an explanation such as "I'm going to ask you to try to do some things so that I can see what you know how to do and what things you could use some more help with" would be understandable to such test takers.

Special professional skill is demanded to overcome possible difficulties associated with young children's normal dependent relationship with adults, lack of language facility, and limited experiences (NASP).

The need for using multiple tests, and the legal requirement for multidisciplinary assessment teams, will require heightened vigilance on the part of assessors. Not only will the nature and purpose of each test or assessment instrument need to be explained, but so will the special need for using many instruments in order to overcome the individual weaknesses of each. Consumers also should be informed that the use of many tests is no guarantee that scores may converge to yield a more confident classification.

Informed consent also requires disclosure of the limits of confidentiality of any information gleaned from the professional encounter. That explanation, which is owed to the child and the parents, includes information about the range of error of clinical interpretations (APA, Principle 8; SEPT, 7.5), the rationale for sharing the information, the uses to be made of the information, procedures for collecting the information, persons who will receive specific information, and any obligations the psychologist has for reporting specified information (APA, Principle 8; NASP). A concomitant duty incumbent upon the psychologist is to assure that this psycho-educational information reaches only authorized, responsible persons, is adequately interpreted for proper usage, and is maintained in a confidential status (NASP).

As already noted, clinicians should provide full disclosure to the child subjects themselves of the reasons for an assessment, its nature, and the limits of confidentiality. To be clear, though, it should be emphasized that such disclosure is rarely legally sufficient or even legally required. The present authors are aware of no instance, other possibly than nontherapeutic research, in which young children are legally recognized participants in clinical decision making. However, respect for children as persons demands honesty about the nature of the relationship in which they find themselves. Therefore, clinicians should be careful to explain the evaluative situation to child clients. Within that context, when children have no real choice (as is normally the case in their assessment), it is disrespectful to imply that they can decide whether to participate. Similarly, it is disrespectful to describe the assessment as private when parents and other third parties have access to information from the evaluation, as they almost always do.

Screening and Labeling

Some of the ethical issues in assessment rest more on their potential consequences than the here-and-now aspects of the relationship between evaluator and client. Preschool screening programs are designed to locate children at risk for developmental delay, behavior disorders, learning disabilities, and so on. The applied interest in preschool assessment often centers on the prediction of problems in order that remedial steps may be taken to reduce the risk. Such screening programs are based on assumptions that have not gone unquestioned. For example, Keogh and Becker (1973) stated that early identification is often based on the assumptions of a disease model, which holds that (a) the condition to be identified is already present, (b) the recognition or diagnosis of the condition leads to a specific prescription for treatment, (c) the sooner treatment is begun, the greater the likelihood of having a positive effect on the condition, and (d) early intervention may prevent the development of related deleterious conditions.

Keogh and Becker (1973) argued that these assumptions do not necessarily hold in psychology and education. For example, early identification in education or mental health should be viewed as more of a hypothesis than a confirmation of a condition now present. Further, there are often no specific treatments or interventions that are implied by the hypothesis, even if the hypothesis is correct. Merely being placed in a treatment program can cause a child's parents much anxiety over the child's label (Cadman et al., 1987); furthermore, labeling may be a common side effect of mass screening (Cadman et al., 1987). Also, there is the ever-present problem of the self-fulfilling prophecy (Rosenthal & Jacobson, 1968).

Keogh and Becker (1973) did not argue against early screening. Instead, they offered guidelines for screening that require assessment programs to specify precisely what behavioral criteria are being predicted and how far into the future predictions are made. They also argued for screening for competence, as well as for the weaknesses and risks of problematic outcomes.

Keogh and Becker's (1973) arguments find support in the professional standards for psychological and educational testing. "In school, clinical, and counseling applications, a test taker's score should not be accepted as a reflection of lack of ability with respect to the characteristic being tested for without consideration of alternate explanations for the test taker's inability to perform on that test at that time" (SEPT, 6.11). Furthermore,

> in school, clinical and counseling applications, tests developed for screening should be used only for identifying test takers who may need further evaluation. The results of such tests should not be used to characterize a person or to make any decision about a person, other than the decision for referral for further evaluation, unless adequate reliability and validity for these other uses can be demonstrated. (SEPT, 6.12)

Finally, "test users should not imply that empirical evidence exists for a relationship among particular test results, prescribed educational plans, and desired student outcomes unless such evidence is available" (SEPT, 8.11).

Overarching Ethical Principles

Both the law and ethical codes offer some guidance to professionals involved in assessing young children. In the end, though, it is useful to consider the significance of broad ethical analysis in such applications. As reflected in the Belmont Report of the National Commission for the Protection of Human Subjects of Biomedical and Behavioral Research (1978; see also Beauchamp & Childress, 1983), ethical decision making in health care ultimately is best informed by consideration of the implications of meta-ethical principles, such as respect to persons, beneficence, and justice. Most ethical problems involve instances in which such principles come into conflict and ethical codes do not provide "the answer."

Consider, for example, the duty embodied in professional ethical codes not to exceed one's competence. Such an obligation has firm grounding in moral-philosophical analysis. When one presents an opinion as if based on specialized knowledge when really it is not, there is an implicit misrepresentation of the foundation for one's opinion. Such deceptive behavior is a violation of the implied contract between the professional and the client and indeed between the professional and society as a whole. Such lack of fidelity to professional role is tantamount to lying and "dehumanizes" the relationship by treating consumers of information as objects to be manipulated.

Besides connoting disrespect for persons, exceeding the bounds of competence often violates the principle of justice, by intruding into the province of decision makers who have been duly designated through democratic processes. A common example of such a violation occurs when psychologists draw conclusions about ultimate legal and moral questions (e.g., the best interests of the child) in child custody and maltreatment cases (Melton & Limber, 1989; Melton, Petrila, Poythress, & Slobogin, 1987; Weithorn & Grisso, 1987).

Less subtly, incompetent professional behavior is usually nonbeneficent. It subjects clients to needless risk of harm, and it effectively may deprive them of a benefit that would accrue if they contracted with more careful or knowledgeable practitioners.

Although readers may not frame the problem intuitively in philosophical terms, the proposition that it is wrong to practice incompetently is unlikely to attract a dispute. Nonetheless, as a practical matter, fulfillment of the obligation to provide services competently often is neither easy nor even necessarily the most ethical course of action. As the forensic example indicates, monitoring one's competence itself often requires a substantial level of sophistication. Moreover, as we and other authors in this volume have noted, the state of the art of preschool assessment still leaves much to be desired. Even when the technology is available, few clinicians, even among those who specialize in work with children, have expertise in the assessment of *young* children. In many communities, no one with such a subspecialty is present. Given such a context and the potential deleterious effects of both erroneous treatment and no treatment, is it better to "do something" than to ensure that one does not exceed the bounds of competence? Apart from questions of beneficence and nonmaleficence, would such behavior result in a more equitable and just distribution of scarce resources? Is failure to do one's best, even if the best is not fully competent, as disrespectful of persons as infidelity to professional role through provision of off-the-cuff interventions? (One way out of the dilemma may be to recognize a duty to be trained, apart from a duty to treat, when services are needed but no competent clinician is available to provide them; see Melton, 1988.)

Other issues arise because of conflicts of interest more than conflicts of principle. Although issues of young children's personal autonomy are much less likely to color ethical decisions about them than those involving older children and adolescents, problems still often remain of questions about the identity of interest among child, family, and state. If a clinician believes that a parent's decision in seeking an evaluation or in consenting to or refusing treatment for the child is not in the child's best interest, what duties accrue? Note the potential conflict between respect for the personhood of the child (in this instance, protection of the child's personal integrity and welfare) and analogous respect for the personhood of parents (reflected in respect for their autonomy in child rearing) and the privacy of families. Such ethical analysis is complicated in many instances by the lack of certainty about empirical assumptions involved in the analysis. In what direction should errors lie?

The answers to none of these questions are simple, and they underscore the ultimate necessity of thoughtful approaches to ethical decision making in work with young children. At the same time, the point should not be lost that the proliferation of statutes governing early childhood special education and codes regulating professional behavior in general have resulted in enormous change in the context in which such decisions are made. Clinicians who become involved in the assessment of young children commonly have not only a new technology to learn, but also a whole array of legal and ethical rules to absorb and issues to consider if their clients' welfare is to be protected and their personhood respected.

REFERENCES

Abeson, A., & Zettel, J. (1977). The end of the quiet revolution: The Education for All Handicapped Children Act of 1975. *Exceptional Children, 44,* 114–128.
American Educational Research Association, American Psychological Association, & National Council on Measurement in Education. (1985). *Standards for educational and psychological testing.* Washington, DC: American Psychological Association.
American Psychological Association. (1981). Ethical principles of psychologists. *American Psychologist,* 36, 633–638.
Barnett, D.W. (1984). An organizational approach to preschool services: Psychological screening, assessment, and intervention. In C. Maher, R. Illback, & J. Zins (Eds.), *Organizational psychology in the schools: A handbook for practitioners* (pp. 53–82). Springfield, IL: CC Thomas.
Beauchamp, T., & Childress, J.F. (1983). *Principles of biomedical ethics* (2nd ed.). New York: Oxford University Press.
Board of Education v. Rowley, 458 U.S. 176 (1982).
Boehm, A., & Sandberg, D. (1982). Assessment of the preschool child. In C.R. Reynolds & T.B. Gutkin, (Eds.), *Handbook of school psychology* (pp. 82–120). New York: Wiley.

Bok, S. (1978). *Lying: Moral choice in public and private life.* New York: Pantheon.
Bonadonna v. Cooperman, 619 F. Supp. 401 (D.N.J. 1985).
Cadman, D., Chambers, L.W., Walter, S.D., Ferguson, R., Johnston, N., & McNamee, J. (1987). Evaluation of public health preschool child developmental screening: The process and outcomes of a community program. *American Journal of Public Health, 77,* 45–51.
Culbertson, J.L., & Gyurke, J. (1990). Assessment of cognitive and motor development in infancy and childhood. In J. Johnson & J. Goldman (Eds.), *Developmental assessment in clinical child psychology: A handbook* (pp. 100–131). New York: Pergamon.
Flavell, J.H. (1985) *Cognitive development.* Englewood Cliffs, NJ: Prentice-Hall.
Irving Independent School District v. Tatro, 468 U.S. 883 (1984).
Keogh, B.K., & Becker, L.D. (1973). Early detection of learning problems: Questions, cautions, and guidelines. *Exceptional Children, 40,* 5–11.
LaFave, W., & Scott, A. (1972). *Handbook of criminal law.* St. Paul, MN: West.
Martin, R.P. (1988). *Assessment of personality and behavior problems: Infancy through adolescence.* New York: Guilford.
Melton, G.B. (1988). Ethical and legal issues in AIDS-related practice. *American Psychologist, 43,* 941–947.
Melton, G.B., & Limber, S. (1989). Psychologists' involvement in cases of child maltreatment: Limits of role and expertise. *American Psychologist, 44,* 1225–1233.
Melton, G.B., Petrila, J., Poythress, N.G., & Slobogin, C. (1987). *Psychological evaluations for the courts: A handbook for mental health professionals and lawyers.* New York: Guilford.
Mills v. Board of Education. 348 F.Supp. 866 (D.D.C. 1972).
National Association of School Psychologists. (1985). *Principles for professional ethics.* Washington, DC: Author.
National Commission for the Protection of Human Subjects of Biomedical and Behavioral Research. (1978). The Belmont report: Ethical principles and guidelines for the protection of human subjects of research. *Federal Register, 44,* 23192–23197.
Ollendick, T.H., & Meador, A.E. (1984). Behavioral assessment of children. In G. Goldstein & M. Hersen (Eds.), *Handbook of psychological assessment* (pp. 351–368). New York: Pergamon.
Paget, K.D., & Nagel, R.J. (1986). A conceptual model of preschool assessment. *School Psychology Review, 15,* 156–165.
Paul, R.E. (1981). Legal requirements for assessing handicapped children. In C. Lidz (Ed.), *Improving assessment of schoolchildren* (pp. 146–159). San Francisco: Jossey-Bass.
Pennsylvania Association for Retarded Children (PARC) v. Pennsylvania. 343 F.Supp. 279 (E.D.Pa. 1972).
Pryzwansky, W.B., & Bersoff, D.N. (1978). Parental consent for psychological evaluations: Legal, ethical, and practical considerations. *Journal of School Psychology, 16,* 274–281.
Reece, H.W., & Freemouw, W.J. (1984). Normal and normative ethics in behavioral sciences. *American Psychologist, 39,* 863–876.
Reynolds, C.R., Gutkin, T.B., Elliott, S.N., & Witt, J.C. (1984). *School psychology: Essentials of theory and practice.* New York: Wiley.
Robertson, J.A. (1975). Involuntary euthanasia of defective newborns: A legal analysis. *Stanford Law Review, 27,* 213–248.
Robertson, J.A., & Fost, N. (1976). Passive euthanasia of defective newborn infants: Legal considerations. *Journal of Pediatrics, 88,* 883–890.
Rogers, S.J. (1986). Assessment of infants and preschoolers with low-incidence handicaps. In P. Lazarus & S. Strichart (Eds.), *Psychoeducational evaluation of children and adolescents with low-incidence handicaps.* Orlando, FL: Grune & Stratton.

Rosenthal, N., & Jacobson, L. (1968). *Pygmalion in the classroom: Teacher expectation and pupils' intellectual development.* New York: Holt, Rinehart & Winston.

Sattler, J.M. (1982). *Assessment of children's intelligence and special abilities.* Boston: Allyn & Bacon.

Ulrey, G., & Rogers, S.J. (1982). *Psychological assessment of handicapped infants and young children.* New York: Thieme-Stratton.

Weithorn, L.A., & Grisso, T. (1987). Psychological evaluation in divorce custody: Problems, principles, and procedures. In L.A. Weithorn (Ed.), *Psychology and child custody determinations: Knowledge, roles, and expertise* (pp. 157–181). Lincoln: University of Nebraska Press.

Appendix: Test Directory and Index

Note: This listing describes only the commercially available tests discussed in the preceding chapters. Additional instruments cited by the authors are included in the General Index. A publisher directory follows this appendix so that interested readers may inquire about test prices and ordering information.

Refer to page(s)	Test Title
243, 248, 253	**AAMD ADAPTIVE BEHAVIOR SCALE–RESIDENTIAL AND COMMUNITY EDITION** *Kazuo Nihira, Ray Foster, Max Shellhaas, & Henry Leland* Assesses the social and daily living skills of children and adults who are mentally retarded or emotionally disturbed. Used for planning education, training and habilitation programs. A two-part 110-item paper-and-pencil scale. Part One covers skills in 10 domains: Independent Functioning, Physical Development, Economic Activity, Language Development, Numbers and Time, Domestic Activity, Vocational Activity, Self-Direction, Responsibility, and Socialization. Part Two measures 14 maladaptive behaviors: Violent and Destructive Behavior, Antisocial Behavior, Rebellious Behavior, Untrustworthy Behavior, Withdrawal, Stereotyped Behavior and Odd Mannerisms, Inappropriate Interpersonal Manners, Unacceptable Vocal Habits, Unacceptable or Eccentric Habits, Self-Abusive Behavior, Hyperactive Tendencies, Sexually Aberrant Behavior, Psychological Disturbances, and Use of Medications. Examiner required. Not suitable for group use. Administration untimed (30 minutes). Examiner evaluated. *Publisher:* PRO-ED, Inc.
174, 256	**AAMD ADAPTIVE BEHAVIOR SCALE–SCHOOL EDITION** *Nadine M. Lambert, Myra Windmiller, Linda Cole, & Deborah Tharinger* Assesses the social and daily living skills of children whose adaptive behavior indicates possible mental retardation, emotional disturbance, or other learning handicaps. Used for screening and instructional planning. A 95-item paper-and-pencil scale measuring the social and daily living skills and behaviors of children. The instrument groups 21 scale domains into five factor scores: Personal Self-Sufficiency, Community Self-Sufficiency, Personal-Social Responsibility, Personal Adjustment, and Social Adjustment. Examiner required. Not suitable for group use. Administration untimed (30 minutes). Examiner evaluated; may be computer scored. *Publisher:* PRO-ED, Inc.

Refer to page(s)	Test Title
174	**ADAPTIVE BEHAVIOR INVENTORY FOR CHILDREN** *Jane R. Mercer & June F. Lewis* Measures a child's social role performance in his or her family, peer group, and community. A 242-item inventory presented in an interview format to measure six aspects of adaptive behavior: family, community, peer relations, nonacademic school rules, earner/consumer, and self-maintenance. Items are divided into two sections; the first applies to all children, and the second consists of age-graded questions. The ABIC is one component of the System of Multicultural Pluralistic Assessment (SOMPA). Examiner required. Not suitable for group use. Manual includes questions in both English and Spanish. Administration untimed (45 minutes). Hand key; examiner evaluated. *Publisher:* The Psychological Corporation.
298	**ADD-H: COMPREHENSIVE TEACHER'S RATING SCALE** *Rina K. Ullmann, Ester K. Sleator, & Robert L. Sprague* Aids in diagnosing attention deficit disorder with or without hyperactivity. Used as a screening device to differentiate between ADD-H children and those who may be otherwise learning disabled, to help determine children who may benefit from therapeutic intervention, and to monitor medication dosages. A 24-item paper-and-pencil or computer-administered multiple-choice test assessing behavior relevant to the diagnosis of attention deficit disorder. The four scales are Attention (6 items), Hyperactivity (5 items), Social Skills (7 items), and Oppositional (6 items). Examiner required. Not suitable for group use. Administration untimed (15 minutes). Self-scored; computer scored. *Publisher:* PRO-ED, Inc.
174	**ASSESSMENT OF CHILDREN'S LANGUAGE COMPREHENSION** *Rochana Foster, Jane J. Giddan, & Joel Stark* Identifies receptive language difficulties in young children in order to provide guidelines for remediation of language disorders. A 41-item verbal test of language comprehension measuring understanding of core vocabulary and combination of language elements. The test uses 50 common words combined into two-, three-, and four-element phrases. Each of the 41 spiral-bound stimulus cards is presented to the child, who points to an appropriate picture in response to a word or phrase from the examiner. A 17-item group form is available for classroom screening. Examiner required. Available in Spanish. Administration timed (10–15 minutes). Examiner evaluated. *Publisher:* Consulting Psychologists Press, Inc.

Refer to page(s)	Test Title

329, 332	**AUTISM SCREENING INSTRUMENT FOR EDUCATIONAL PLANNING** *David A. Krug, Joel R. Arick, & Patricia J. Almond* Assesses the behavioral, social, and educational development of autistic, mentally retarded, deaf/blind, and emotionally disturbed students. Used to establish IEPs, evaluate program effectiveness, and monitor student progress. A multiple-item paper-and-pencil observational inventory consisting of five subtests: Autism Behavior Checklist, Sample of Vocal Behavior, Interaction Assessment, Educational Assessment, and Prognosis of Learning Rate. The observational methods involved in each allow all students to be "testable." Examiner required. Not suitable for group use. The Autism Behavior Checklist is available in Spanish. Administration untimed (varies). Examiner evaluated. *Publisher:* PRO-ED, Inc.
84, 92	**BANKSON LANGUAGE SCREENING TEST-2** *Nicholas W. Bankson* Measures psycholinguistic and perceptual skills. Determines the need for further diagnostic assessment. Used to plan language intervention programs. A multiple-item oral response test measuring three general categories of a child's language competence: Semantic Knowledge, Morphological/Syntactical Rules, and Pragmatics. A 20-item short form is available for screening purposes. Examiner required. Not suitable for group use. Administration untimed (varies). *Publisher:* PRO-ED, Inc.
83, 87, 176, 363, 396	**BATTELLE DEVELOPMENTAL INVENTORY** *Jean Newborg, John R. Stock, Linda Wnek, John Guidubaldi, & John Svinicki* Evaluates the development of children from infant to primary levels. Screens and diagnosis developmental strengths and weaknesses. Used to establish IEPs and aid in placement and eligibility decisions. A multiple-item test assessing key developmental skills in five domains: Personal-Social, Adaptive, Motor, Communication, and Cognition. Information is obtained through structured interactions, observation, and interviews with parents, caregivers, and teachers. Various modifications are required when administering the test to handicapped children. A screening examination is included or is available separately. Examiner required. Suitable for group use if the station procedure is used. Administration untimed (screening 10–30 minutes; diagnostic 1–2 hours). Examiner evaluated. *Publisher:* DLM Teaching Resources.
5, 20, 154, 182, 183, 242, 248, 276, 278, 279, 280, 281, 295, 329, 333, 363, 390, 393	**BAYLEY SCALES OF INFANT DEVELOPMENT** *Nancy Bayley* Assesses mental, motor, and behavioral development. Used for assessing developmental progress, comparison with peers, and providing an objective basis for determining eligibility for special services.

Refer to page(s)	Test Title
	A two-scale test of infant mental and motor development. The Mental scale assesses sensory-perceptual behavior, learning ability, and early communication attempts. The Motor scale measures general body control, coordination of large muscles, and skills in fine-muscle control of hands. Materials include stimulus items and the Infant Behavior Record for noting qualitative aspects of behavior. Examiner required. Not suitable for group use. Administration untimed (45 minutes). Examiner evaluated. *Publisher:* The Psychological Corporation.
366, 367	BEHAVIOR EVALUATION SCALE–2 *Stephen B. McCarney & James E. Leigh* Assesses the behavioral problems of students. Used by school personnel to make decisions about eligibility, placement, and programming for students with behavior problems. A multiple-item paper-and-pencil observational inventory assessing the behavioral problems of students regardless of primary handicapping conditions. The instrument may be used with students who have learning disabilities, mental retardation, physical handicaps, or other handicapping conditions. Examiner/self-administered. Not suitable for group use. Administration untimed (varies). Examiner evaluated. *Publisher:* PRO-ED, Inc.
329, 332, 360	BEHAVIOR RATING INSTRUMENT FOR AUTISTIC AND OTHER ATYPICAL CHILDREN *Bertram A. Ruttenberg, Beth I. Kalish, Charles Wenar, & Enid G. Wolf* Evaluates the status of low-functioning, atypical, and autistic children of all ages. Used to evaluate children who will not or cannot cooperate with formal testing procedures. A paper-and-pencil inventory of observations collected over a 2-day period assessing present level of functioning and measuring behavioral change in eight areas: relationship to an adult, communication, drive for mastery, vocalization and expressive speech, sound and speech reception, social responsiveness, body movement (passive and active), and psychobiological development. Examiner required. Not suitable for group use. Administration untimed (2 days). Examiner evaluated. *Publisher:* Stoelting Company.
176	BENDER VISUAL MOTOR GESTALT TEST *Lauretta Bender* Assesses visual-motor functions. Also used to evaluate developmental problems, learning disabilities, mental retardation, psychosis, and organic brain disorders. A test consisting of nine gestalt cards. Examiner presents cards to the subject one at a time, in order, and the subject reproduces on paper the configuration or design shown on the card. Responses are scored according to the development of the concepts of form, shape, and pattern and orientation in space. Examiner required. Slides may be used for group administration. Administration untimed (15–20 minutes). Examiner evaluated; scoring service available. *Publisher:* American Orthopsychiatric Association.

Refer to page(s)	Test Title
205, 206	BOSTON NAMING TEST *Edith Kaplan, Harold Goodglass, & Sandra Weintraub*

Assesses learning disabled, brain-damaged, dementing, and aphasic populations.

A 60-item wide-range picture naming test used as part of language assessment in populations at risk for brain damage. The 60 pictures are contained in a single test booklet. Examiner required. Not suitable for group use. Available in Spanish. Administration untimed (30 minutes). Examiner evaluated. *Publisher:* Lea & Febiger.

176, 179	BRACKEN BASIC CONCEPT SCALE *Bruce A. Bracken*

Measures a child's acquisition of basic concepts. Used with both regular and special education populations.

A 258-item verbal "point to" test using picture stimuli to evaluate 11 categories of basic concept acquisition: color, shape, size, quantity, counting, letter identification, direction/position, time/sequence, texture, comparisons, and social/emotional responses. The instrument is available as a complete diagnostic scale and as a screening test. Alternate forms facilitate pre- and posttest assessment. Examiner required. Not suitable for group use. Administration untimed (20–40 minutes). Hand key. *Publisher:* The Psychological Corporation.

368	BRIGANCE DIAGNOSTIC COMPREHENSIVE INVENTORY OF BASIC SKILLS *Albert H. Brigance*

Measures attainment of basic academic skills. Used to meet minimal competency requirements, develop IEPs, and determine academic placement.

A test of 203 skill sequences arranged in 22 sections: Readiness, Speech, Word Recognition Grade Placement, Oral Reading, Reading Comprehension, Listening, Functional Word Recognition, Word Analysis, Reference Skills, Graphs and Maps, Spelling, Writing, Math Grade Placement, Numbers, Number Facts, Computation of Whole Numbers, Fractions and Mixed Numbers, Decimals, Percents, Word Problems, Metrics, and Math Vocabulary. Assessment method may vary to accommodate different situations (parent interview, teacher observation, etc.). Alternate forms for pre- and posttesting are available, as is a videotape for in-service training. Examiner required. Many sections suitable for group use. Administration untimed (varies). Examiner evaluated. *Publisher:* Curriculum Associates, Inc.

176, 179, 280, 363, 368	BRIGANCE DIAGNOSTIC INVENTORY OF EARLY DEVELOPMENT *Albert H. Brigance*

Measures the development of children functioning below the developmental age of 7 years. Diagnoses developmental delays and monitors progress over time. Used to develop IEPs.

Refer to page(s)	Test Title

An inventory of 200 paper-and-pencil oral-response and direct observation assessments measuring psychomotor, self-help, communication, general knowledge and comprehension, and academic skill levels. Items are arranged in developmental sequential order in the following major skill area: preambulatory, gross motor, fine motor, prespeech, speech and language, general knowledge and comprehension, readiness, basic reading, manuscript writing, and basic math skills. Examiner required. Not suitable for group use. Administration untimed (varies). Examiner evaluated. *Publisher:* Curriculum Associates, Inc.

176   **BRUININKS-OSERETSKY TEST OF MOTOR PROFICIENCY**   *Robert H. Bruininks*

Determines a child's level of motor proficiency. Used for educational placement, assessing neurological development, and evaluating motor training programs.

A 46-item physical performance and paper-and-pencil battery grouped into eight subtests: Running Speed and Agility, Balance, Bilateral Coordination, Strength;, Upper-Limb Coordination, Response Speed, Visual-Motor Control, and Upper-Limb Speed and Dexterity. A 14-item short form is also available, which yields a single score of general motor proficiency. Examiner required. Not suitable for group use. Administration untimed (short form 15–20 minutes; complete battery 45–60 minutes). Examiner evaluated. *Publisher:* American Guidance Service.

182, 358   **BURKS' BEHAVIOR RATING SCALES, PRESCHOOL AND KINDERGARTEN EDITION**   *Harold F. Burks*

Identifies patterns of behavior problems in children ages 3–6. Used to aid differential diagnosis.

A 105-item paper-and-pencil inventory used by parents and teachers to rate a child on the basis of descriptive statements of observed behavior. The inventory contains 18 subscales: Excessive Self-Blame, Anxiety, Withdrawal, Dependency, Suffering, Sense of Persecution, Aggressiveness, Resistance, Poor Ego Strength, Physical Strength, Coordination, Intellectuality, Attention, Impulse Control, Reality Contact, Sense of Identity, Anger Control, and Social Conformity. This is a downward extension of Burks' Behavior Rating Scale. Examiner required. Not suitable for group use. Administration untimed (15–20 minutes). Hand key. *Publisher:* Western Psychological Services.

207   **BZOCH-LEAGUE RECEPTIVE-EXPRESSIVE EMERGENT LANGUAGE SCALE**   *Kenneth Bzoch & Richard League*

Assesses emerging factors of expressive and receptive language in children. Identifies children needing further evaluation.

A 132-item paper-and-pencil inventory measuring the development of language infants. The child's overt speech and response behaviors are rated as present or absent by a parent or individual

Refer to page(s)	Test Title

who has daily contact with the child. Three expressive and three receptive factors are measured for each of 22 age levels. Examiner required. Not suitable for group use. Administration untimed (varies). Examiner evaluated. *Publisher:* PRO-ED, Inc.

359   CALIFORNIA PRESCHOOL SOCIAL COMPETENCE SCALE   *Samuel Levine, Freeman F. Olzey, & Mary Lewis*

Assesses the social competence of preschool children. Used by teachers for diagnosis, placement, or measurement of the development of young children.

A 30-item paper-and-pencil rating scale providing objective, numerical evaluation of the social competence of preschoolers. The items designate specific interpersonal behaviors and the degree to which subjects assume social responsibility. Examiner required. Not suitable for group use. Administration untimed. Hand key. *Publisher:* Consulting Psychologists Press, Inc.

248, 253   CALLIER-AZUSA SCALE: G EDITION   *Robert Stillman*

Assesses the development of deaf-blind and severely and profoundly handicapped children. Used to plan developmentally appropriate activities and to evaluate a child's developmental progress, particularly at the lower developmental levels.

A multiple-item paper-and-pencil observational inventory measuring 18 developmental subscales in five developmental areas: motor development (postural control, locomotion, fine motor, and visual motor); perceptual abilities (visual, auditory, and tactile development); daily living skills (undressing and dressing, personal hygiene, development of feeding skills, and toileting); cognition, communication, and language (cognitive development, receptive communication, expressive communication, and development of speech); and social development (interactions with adults, peers, and the environment). Examiner required. Not suitable for group use. Administration untimed (varies). Examiner evaluated. *Publisher:* Callier Center for Communication Disorders.

174   CARROW ELICITED LANGUAGE INVENTORY
Elizabeth Carrow-Woolfolk

Measures the productive control of grammar in young children and diagnoses expressive language delays and disorders. Used to obtain data on a child's grammatical structures.

A 52-item test of oral stimuli (51 sentences and 1 phrase) eliciting imitation of a sequence of sentences that include basic construction types and specific grammatical morphemes. Responses are recorded and transcribed from the tape onto a scoring/analysis form in order to analyze errors of substitution, addition, omission, transposition, and reversal. Examiner required. Not suitable for group use or nonverbal subjects. Administration untimed (25 minutes). Examiner evaluated. *Publisher:* DLM Teaching Resources.

Refer to page(s)	Test Title

183, 242–243, 281

CATTELL INFANT INTELLIGENCE SCALE *Psyche Cattell*

Assesses the mental development of infants.

Test of early development rating infant verbalizations and motor control, such as the manipulation of cubes, pencils, pegboards, and other stimulus items. The test has been modified with items from the Gesell, Minnesota Preschool, and Merrill-Palmer scales and is applicable to a younger age range than the Stanford-Binet. Examiner required. Not suitable for group use. Administration untimed (20–30 minutes). Examiner evaluated. *Publisher:* The Psychological Corporation.

85, 95, 117, 118, 182, 201, 243, 269, 295–296, 297, 359

CHILD BEHAVIOR CHECKLIST AND REVISED CHILD BEHAVIOR PROFILE *Thomas M. Achenbach & Craig Edelbrock*

Assesses the behavioral problems and competencies of children and adolescents.

A set of paper-and-pencil multiple-choice inventories evaluating child behavioral problems from four perspectives: Child Behavior Checklist (assesses behavior from the parents' point of view), Teacher's Report Form (assesses the child's classroom behavior), Direct Observation Form (an experienced observer rates the child on the basis of several 10-minute observation periods), and Youth Self-Report (gathers information directly from children ages 11–18). Self-administered (except for the Direct Observation Form). All self-administered forms suitable for group use. Available in many languages. Administration untimed (varies). Examiner evaluated; computer scoring programs available. *Publisher:* University of Vermont.

325, 331–332, 335, 339

CHILDHOOD AUTISM RATING SCALE *Eric Schopler, Robert J. Reichler, & Barbara Rochen Renner*

Diagnoses children with autism syndrome and distinguishes them from nonautistic developmentally handicapped children. Used for psychological, medical, or educational evaluations.

A 15-item behavior rating scale covering relating to people; imitation; emotional response; body use; object use; adaptation to change; visual response; listening response; taste, smell, and touch response and use; fear or nervousness; verbal communication; nonverbal communication; activity level; level and consistency of intellectual response; and general impression. Examiner required. Not suitable for group use. Administration untimed (varies). Examiner evaluated. *Publisher:* Western Psychological Services.

257

CHILDREN'S APPERCEPTION TEST *Leopold Bellak & Sonya Sorel Bellak*

Assesses children's personality. Used for clinical evaluation and diagnosis.

A 10-item oral-response projective test measuring the traits, attitudes, and psychodynamics at work in the personalities of chil-

Refer to page(s)	Test Title

dren ages 3–10. Items consist of pictures of animals in human social contexts, through which the child becomes involved in conflicts, identities, roles, and family structures. Examinees are required to tell a story about each picture. Examiner required. Not suitable for group use. Available in several languages. Administration untimed (20–30 minutes). Examiner evaluated. *Publisher:* C.P.S., Inc.

204, 205, 206   **CLINICAL EVALUATION OF LANGUAGE FUNDAMENTALS–REVISED**   *Eleanor Semel, Elisabeth H. Wiig, & Wayne Secord*

Diagnoses language skill deficits (semantics, syntax, and memory) in school-aged children. Used to qualify students for placement and to develop IEPs.

A battery of 11 subtests yielding measures of performance in six receptive and five expressive language areas. Subtests sample a variety of language skills, including oral directions, formulated sentences, sentence assembly, and semantic relationships. Examiner required. Not suitable for group use. Administration untimed (45–60 minutes). Hand or computer scored. *Publisher:* The Psychological Corporation.

174   **COGNITIVE SKILLS ASSESSMENT BATTERY, SECOND EDITION**   *Ann E. Boehm & Barbara Slater*

Assesses the progress of preschoolers and kindergartners relative to teaching goals in cognitive and physical-motor areas. Used for curriculum planning and to match classroom goals with cognitive skills.

A 64-item verbal test measuring orientation toward environment, discrimination of similarities and differences, comprehension and concept formation, coordination, and immediate and delayed memory. Easel cards introduce the child to the required tasks, which are similar to the content taught at the prekindergarten and kindergarten level. Examiner required. Administration untimed (20–25 minutes). Examiner evaluated. *Publisher:* Teachers College Press.

256   **COLOURED PROGRESSIVE MATRICES**   *J.C. Raven*

Assesses the mental ability of young children and older adults who are mentally below normal or impaired. Used for school and clinical counseling and research.

A 36-item paper-and-pencil nonverbal test consisting of design and pattern problems printed in several colors, including the two easiest sets from the Standard Progressive Matrices. The subject is presented with a pattern or figure design with a missing part and must select one of six possibilities as the missing element. Examiner required. Suitable for group use above age 8. U.S. norms available. Administration untimed (15–30 minutes). Hand key. *Publisher:* H.K. Lewis & Co. Ltd., distributed in the U.S. by The Psychological Corporation.

Refer to page(s)	Test Title
171, 183	COLUMBIA MENTAL MATURITY SCALE *Bessie B. Burgemeister, Lucille Hollander Blum, & Irving Lorge*

Assesses children's mental ability. Used with preschoolers, kindergartners, or children with physical or verbal impairments.

A 92-item test of general reasoning abilities. Items are arranged in a series of eight overlapping levels; the level administered is determined by the child's chronological age. The examinee responds by selecting from among a series of drawings presented on cards the one that does not belong. Examiner required. Not suitable for group use. Administration untimed (15–20 minutes). Examiner evaluated. *Publisher:* The Psychological Corporation. |
| 85, 94, 95, 117, 118, 296, 298, 302, 303, 360 | CONNERS PARENT AND TEACHER RATING SCALES *C. Keith Conners*

Measures hyperactivity and other patterns of child behavior.

A paper-and-pencil or computer-administered instrument used to evaluate children's problem behaviors as reported by teachers, parents, or other caregivers. Scales on the 28- or 39-item Teacher Version include Hyperactivity, Conduct Problem, Emotional Overindulgent, Anxious-Passive, Asocial, and Daydream Attendance Problem. The 48- or 93-item Parent Version includes Conduct Disorder, Psychosomatic, Learning Problem-Immature, Impulsive-Hyperactive, Fearful-Anxious, Obsessional, Hyperactive-Immature, Impulsive-Hyperactive, and Antisocial scales. Self-administered. Not suitable for group use. Administration untimed (varies). Hand or computer scored. *Publisher:* Multi-Health Systems Inc. |
| 22, 79, 83, 85–87, 92, 93, 116, 117, 174, 243, 363 | DENVER II *W.K. Frankenburg, J. Dodds, P. Archer, B. Bresnick, P. Maschka, N. Edelman, & H. Shapiro*

Evaluates a child's personal, social, fine and gross motor, language, and adaptive abilities as a means of identifying possible problems and screening for further evaluation.

A 125-item test in which the stimuli are blocks, a bell, a ball, a bottle, raisins, a rattle, yarn, a pencil, blank paper, a cup, and a doll with feeding bottle. Age-appropriate items are presented to the child to establish a basal and a ceiling. Age-related criteria determine the child's developmental status (normal, abnormal, or questionable) in comparison to other children to detect those who are showing delays. Examiner required. Not suitable for group use. Administration untimed (10–20 minutes). *Publisher:* Denver Developmental Materials, Inc. |
| 204, 205, 206 | DETROIT TESTS OF LEARNING APTITUDE–PRIMARY *Donald D. Hammill & Brian R. Bryant*

Measures general and specific aptitudes of children. Identifies deficiencies in general and specific aptitudes and serves as a standardized instrument in research. |

Refer to page(s)	Test Title

A 130-item battery yielding eight subtest scores (Verbal Quotient, Nonverbal Quotient, Conceptual Quotient, Structural Quotient, Motor-Enhanced Quotient, Motor-Reduced Quotient, Attention-Enhanced Quotient, and Attention-Reduced Quotient) and one total score (General Intelligence Quotient). Intended to provide a detailed profile of students' abilities and deficiencies. Examiner required. Not suitable for group use. Administration untimed (15–40 minutes). Computer scored. *Publisher:* PRO-ED, Inc.

174 DEVELOPMENTAL ACTIVITIES SCREENING INVENTORY–II *Rebecca R. Fewell & Mary Beth Langley*

Detects early developmental disabilities in children.

A 67-item oral response and task performance test assessing 15 developmental skills categories, including sensory intactness, means-end relationship, and causality to memory, seriation, and reasoning. Items may be administered in different sequences in one or two sittings, and instructions are given either verbally or visually. Each item includes adaptations for use with visually impaired children. Examiner required. Not suitable for group use. Administration untimed (varies). Examiner evaluated. *Publisher:* PRO-ED, Inc.

83, 88, 89, 176, 178, 363 DEVELOPMENTAL PROFILE II *Gerald D. Alpern, Thomas Boll, & Marsha Shearer*

Evaluates the age-equivalent physical, social, and mental development of normal or handicapped children. Used for counseling, school planning, and research.

A 186-item paper-and-pencil or computer-administered interview covering five areas: physical, self-help, social, academic, and communication. Developmental age information is derived by interviewing a parent or through teacher observation. A computer report is available through mail-in service or on-site if the computer version is used. Examiner required. Suitable for group use. Administration untimed (20–40 minutes). Examiner evaluated; may be computer scored. *Publisher:* Western Psychological Services.

84, 94, 176, 180, 398 DEVELOPMENTAL TEST OF VISUAL-MOTOR INTEGRATION, THIRD REVISION *Keith E. Beery & Norman A. Buktenica*

Identifies children with visual perception, hand control, and eye-hand coordination problems. Used with children ages 3–18 and developmentally delayed adults.

A multiple-item paper-and-pencil test measuring the integration of visual perception and motor behavior. Test items, arranged in order of increasing difficulty, consist of geometric figures that examinees look at and then are asked to copy. The short form (15 figures) is used with subjects aged 2–8; the long form (24 figures) is used with children aged 2–15 and adults with developmental delays. Examiner required. Suitable for group use. Administration untimed (varies). Examiner evaluated. *Publisher:* PRO-ED, Inc.

Refer to page(s)	Test Title

360, 366, 367

DEVEREUX ELEMENTARY SCHOOL BEHAVIOR RATING SCALE *Marshall Swift*

Assesses problem behaviors that interfere with classroom performance. Used for screening procedures, group placement decisions, and assessment of progress in response to specific programs or procedures.

A 52-item paper-and-pencil inventory assessing symptomatic classroom behavior patterns. The classroom teacher rates each item according to how the subject's behavior compares to that of normal children. The test yields 10 behavior factors—Work Organization, Creative Initiative/Involvement, Positive Toward Teacher, Need for Direction in Work, Socially Withdrawn, Failure Anxiety, Impatience, Irrelevant Thinking/Talk, Blaming, and Negative/Aggressive—and 4 behavior clusters—Perseverance, Peer Cooperation, Confusion, and Inattention. Self-administered. Not suitable for group use. Administration untimed (10–15 minutes). Examiner evaluated. *Publisher:* Devereux Foundation Press.

174

DIFFERENTIAL ABILITY SCALES *Colin Elliott*

Measures conceptual and reasoning abilities of children aged 2½ to 17. Used in school and clinical settings as well as in research.

A battery of core and diagnostic subtests divided into two overlapping levels, Preschool (Block Building, Early Number Concepts, Verbal Comprehension, Naming Vocabulary, Picture Similarities, Pattern Construction, Copying, Recall of Digits, Recognition of Pictures, Matching Letter-Like Forms, Recall of Objects) and School-Age (Word Definitions, Similarities, Matrices, Sequential and Quantitative Reasoning, Recall of Designs, Pattern Construction, Basic Number Skills, Spelling, Word Reading, Recall of Digits, Recall of Objects, Speed of Information Processing). This is the U.S. adaptation of the British Ability Scales. Examiner required. Not suitable for group use. Administration untimed (varies). Examiner evaluated. *Publisher:* The Psychological Corporation.

83, 89

EARLY CHILD DEVELOPMENT INVENTORY *Harold Ireton*

Measures developmental level, symptoms, and behavioral problems. Used as a screening instrument to identify children with problems that may interfere with the ability to learn.

An 88-item paper-and-pencil questionnaire for obtaining a parental report of a child's current functioning. Items are divided into six sections: General Development (60 items covering seven developmental areas), Possible Problems (24 items covering symptoms and behavior problems), Child Description (parents' brief description of the child), Problems or Disabilities (parents' report of major obstacles/handicaps to child's learning), Questions and Concerns (parents' report of their concerns/questions about the child), and Parents' Functioning (asks parents how they are doing,

Refer to page(s)	Test Title

as parents or otherwise). Examiner required. Suitable for group use. Administration untimed (varies). *Publisher:* Behavior Science Systems, Inc.

84, 92–93   EARLY LANGUAGE MILESTONE SCALE   *James Coplan*

Screens language development in children from birth to 36 months. Used by physicians, nurses, teachers, psychologists, speech/language pathologists, and infant development specialists.

A 42-item screening instrument for detecting speech or language delay from any cause, including hearing loss, mental retardation, developmental language disorder, oromotor apraxia, and dysarthria. Scale items are arranged in three divisions: Auditory Expressive, Auditory Receptive, and Visual. Performance on most items may be ascertained by parental report. Examiner required. Not suitable for group use. Administration untimed (1–3 minutes). Examiner evaluated. *Publisher:* PRO-ED, Inc.

90   EXPRESSIVE ONE-WORD PICTURE VOCABULARY TEST   *Morrison F. Gardner*

Assesses a child's verbal intelligence. Used to screen for possible speech defects, to evaluate bilingual student fluency in English, and to determine preschool placement.

A 110-item verbal test of definitional and interpretational skills. The test consists of 100 pictures presented one at a time to the examinee, who names each picture while the examiner records the response. Examiner required. Not suitable for group use. Available in Spanish. Administration untimed (20 minutes). Hand key. *Publisher:* Academic Therapy Publications.

148, 268, 361   FAMILY ENVIRONMENT SCALE   *Rudolph H. Moos*

Assesses characteristics of family environments. Used for family therapy.

A 90-item paper-and-pencil scale measuring 10 dimensions of family environments (cohesion, expressiveness, conflict, independence, achievement orientation, intellectual-cultural orientation, active-recreational orientation, moral-religious emphasis, organization, and control) grouped into relationship, personal growth, and system maintenance categories. Three alternate forms (R, I, E) elicit respondents' perceptions of real, ideal, or expected family environments. Examiner required. Suitable for group use. Examiner evaluated. *Publisher:* Consulting Psychologists Press, Inc.

204, 212   GOLDMAN-FRISTOE-WOODCOCK AUDITORY SKILLS TEST BATTERY   *Ronald Goldman, Macalyne Fristoe, & Richard W. Woodcock*

Diagnoses an individual's ability to hear clearly under difficult conditions. Used for instructional planning.

A battery of 12 subtests measuring auditory selective attention (ability to attend under increasingly difficult listening conditions),

Refer to page(s)	Test Title

diagnostic auditory discrimination (ability to discriminate between specific speech sounds), auditory memory (recognition memory, memory for content, and memory for sequence), and sound-symbol skills (abilities underlying the development of written language skills). The examiner presents a test plate to the subject and records his or her response. Examiner required. Not suitable for group use. Administration untimed (15 minutes per subtest). Examiner evaluated. *Publisher:* American Guidance Service.

204   GOLDMAN-FRISTOE-WOODCOCK TEST OF AUDITORY DISCRIMINATION   *Ronald Goldman, Macalyne Fristoe, & Richard W. Woodcock*

Assesses an individual's ability to discriminate speech sounds in quiet and in noise.

A two-part screen for deficiencies in speech-sound discrimination that may contribute to learning difficulties. The examiner presents a test plate containing four drawings to the subject, who responds to a stimulus word presented via audiocassette by pointing to one of the drawings on the plate. Examiner required. Not suitable for group use. Administration untimed (20–30 minutes). Examiner evaluated. *Publisher:* American Guidance Service.

302–303   GORDON DIAGNOSTIC SYSTEM   *Michael Gordon*

Assesses attention deficits and impulsiveness. Used by clinicians, educators, and physicians.

A computer-based assessment aiding in the diagnosis of attention deficits, especially ADHD/hyperactivity and AIDS dementia complex, and providing information about examinees 'ability to sustain attention and exert self-control. The Vigilance Task requires responding to a particular combination of numbers embedded in a random digit series. The Distractibility Task is a more complex version of the Vigilance Task. The Delay Task requires examinees to inhibit responses to earn points. Examiner required. Not suitable for group use. Administration timed (9 minutes per task). Computer scored. *Publisher:* Gordon Systems, Inc.

242, 280   GRIFFITHS MENTAL DEVELOPMENT SCALES   *Ruth Griffiths*

Measures cognitive/intellectual development infants and children. Used to assess need for remedial treatment and to assess progress.

A multiple-item test of intellectual development measuring social development, fine and gross motor skills, hearing, eye-hand coordination, and speech. The test is available in two levels (birth to age 2; ages 2 to 8), and different materials are required for each. Examiner required. Not suitable for group use. Available in several languages. Administration untimed (varies). Examiner evaluated. *Publisher:* The Test Agency Ltd.

Refer to page(s)	Test Title

256 HALSTEAD-REITAN NEUROPSYCHOLOGICAL TEST BATTERY FOR CHILDREN *Reitan Neuropsychology Laboratory*

Evaluates brain function and dysfunction in children. Used for clinical evaluations.

A battery of tests assessing children's neuropsychological functioning, including the Halstead Neuropsychological Test Battery, the Wechsler Intelligence Scale for Children, the Trail Making Test, the Reitan-Indiana Aphasia Screening Test, various tests of sensory-perceptual functions, and measures of academic achievement. Components are available separately. Examiner required. Not suitable for group use. Administration timed/untimed (varies). Examiner evaluated. *Publisher:* Reitan Neuropsychology Laboratory.

205, 206, 212, 219, 330 HISKEY-NEBRASKA TEST OF LEARNING APTITUDE *Marshall S. Hiskey*

Evaluates learning potential of deaf children and those with hearing, speech, or language handicaps.

A battery of 12 nonverbal subtests measuring visual-motor coordination, sequential memory, visual retention or stimuli in a series, visual discrimination and matching, and awareness of environment. Tests include Bead Patterns, Memory for Color, Picture Identification, Picture Association, Paper Folding Patterns, Visual Attention Span, Block Patterns, Completion of Drawings, Memory for Digits, Puzzle Blocks, Picture Analogies, and Spatial Reasoning. Examiner required. Not suitable for group use. Administration untimed (50–60 minutes). Examiner evaluated. *Publisher:* Hiskey-Nebraska Test.

153 HOME ENVIRONMENT QUESTIONNAIRE *Jacob O. Sines*

Assesses behaviorally relevant dimensions of children's psychosocial environments. Used to investigate sources of environmental stress.

A true/false paper-and-pencil test completed by the mother of the child being studied. The measure can be scored for 10 dimensions of the psychosocial environment that exert pressure on the child: p(ress) achievement, p aggression-external, p aggression-home, p aggression-total, p supervision, p change, p affiliation, p separation, p sociability, and p socioeconomic status. Two forms are available (for use with one- or two-parent families). Examiner/self-administered. Suitable for group use. Administration untimed (15–20 minutes). Hand key. *Publisher:* Psychological Assessment and Services, Inc.

131, 155–156, 257, 268, 278 HOME OBSERVATION FOR MEASUREMENT OF THE ENVIRONMENT *Bettye M. Caldwell & Robert H. Bradley*

Assesses the quality and quantity of support available in the home environment for a child's cognitive, social, and emotional

Refer to page(s)	Test Title

development. Used to identify home environments that pose a risk for development, to evaluate programs designed to improve parenting skills, and to assist research.

An observation and semistructured interview conducted in the home with the parent and child. There are three versions of the inventory: Infant and Toddler (45 items, 6 subscales), Early Childhood (55 items, 8 subscales), and Middle Childhood (59 items, 8 subscales). Each inventory is available in versions for use with children with learning, visual, orthopedic, and mental impairments. Examiner required. Not suitable for group use. Administration untimed (1 hour). Hand key. *Publisher:* Center for Research on Teaching and Learning.

257   HOUSE-TREE-PERSON (H-T-P TECHNIQUE)   *John N. Buck*

Assesses personality disturbances in individuals aged 3 and older in psychotherapy, school, and research settings. May be used with culturally disadvantaged, educationally deprived, mentally retarded, and aged subjects.

A multiple-item paper-and-pencil and oral response measure providing a projective study of personality. The technique consists of two steps: The first (nonverbal, creative, and almost completely unstructured) requires the subject to make a freehand drawing of a house, a tree, and a person. The second (verbal, apperceptive, and more formally structured) asks the subject to describe, define, and interpret the drawings and their respective environments. Examiner required. Not suitable for group use. Administration untimed (15–20 minutes). Hand key; examiner evaluated. *Publisher:* Western Psychological Services.

174   HOUSTON TEST FOR LANGUAGE DEVELOPMENT   *Margaret Crabtree*

Assesses verbal and nonverbal communication abilities in children. Used to plan specific intervention procedures and to monitor a child's progress.

A multiple-item verbal and nonverbal measure of communication abilities. The Infant Scale presents an observational checklist of linguistic and prelinguistic skills characteristic of normal infants up to 18 months. The 2–6 Year Test contains 18 subtests covering both verbal and nonverbal tasks: Self-Identity, Vocabulary, Body Orientation, Gesture, Auditory Judgments, Oral Monitoring with Toys, Sentence Length, Temporal Content, Syntax, Prepositions, Serial Counting, Counting Objects, Imitates Linguistic Structure, Imitates Prosodic Patterns, Imitates Designs, Drawing, Oral Monitoring While Drawing, and Telling About Drawing. Examiner required. Not suitable for group use. Administration untimed (30 minutes). Examiner evaluated. *Publisher:* Stoelting Company.

Refer to page(s)	Test Title
203, 204, 205, 206, 210, 212, 219	**ILLINOIS TEST OF PSYCHOLINGUISTIC ABILITIES** *Samuel A. Kirk, James J. McCarthy, & Winifred D. Kirk*

Assesses specific psycholinguistic abilities and disabilities in young children. Facilitates the assessment of a child's abilities for purposes of remediation.

A 300-item test evaluating a child's cognitive and perceptual abilities in three areas: communication, psycholinguistic processes, and levels of organization. There are 12 subtests: Auditory Reception, Visual Reception, Auditory Association, Visual Association, Verbal Expression, Manual Expression, Grammatic Closure, Visual Closure, Auditory Sequential Memory, Visual Sequential Memory, Auditory Closure, and Sound Blending. Examiner required. Not suitable for group use. Available in Spanish (from the author). Administration untimed (1 hour). Hand key. *Publisher:* University of Illinois Press.

64, 173, 174, 178, 179, 204, 205, 206, 256, 281, 330, 368, 369, 389	**KAUFMAN ASSESSMENT BATTERY FOR CHILDREN** *Alan S. Kaufman & Nadeen L. Kaufman*

Measures children's intelligence and achievement. Used for psychological and clinical assessments (especially with children who are learning disabled, mentally retarded, gifted, preschoolers, or members of minority groups) and for neuropsychological research.

A battery of 16 subtests of mental processing skills and achievement. Three tests cover sequential processing, seven tap simultaneous processing, and six measure achievement (acquired knowledge, reading, and arithmetic). Stimulus items are presented via test plates. Directions may be administered in the child's native language or with gestures for the hearing impaired. Examiner required. Not suitable for group use. Administration untimed (varies). Examiner evaluated; may be computer scored. *Publisher:* American Guidance Service.

84, 93	**KERBY LEARNING MODALITY TEST, REVISED** *Maude L. Kerby*

Measures the learning abilities of children in terms of visual, auditory, and motor activity skills. Used to identify children with learning disabilities, to plan teaching strategies, and to comply with PL 94-142.

A multiple-item paper-and-pencil test measuring strengths and weaknesses in three primary learning modalities: visual, auditory, and motor activity. Eight subtests cover a variety of classroom work samples: visual and auditory discrimination, visual and auditory closure, visual and auditory memory, and visual and auditory motor coordination. Kits are available for three age levels. Examiner required. Suitable for group use. Administration timed (15 minutes). Hand key. *Publisher:* Western Psychological Services.

Refer to page(s)	Test Title
171, 253, 330	**LEITER INTERNATIONAL PERFORMANCE SCALE** *Russell G. Leiter*

Measures intelligence and mental age for individuals aged 2–18, including those who are deaf, cerebral palsied, non-English-speaking, and culturally disadvantaged.

A multiple-item nonverbal task assessment requiring the subject to match blocks with corresponding characters in a wooden frame (difficulty increases at each level). The categories measured are Concretistics (matching of specific relationships), Symbolic Transformation (judging relationships between two events), Quantitative Discriminations, Spatial Imagery, Genus Matching, Progression Discriminations, and Immediate Recall. Examiner required. Not suitable for group use. Administration untimed (45 minutes). Examiner evaluated. *Publisher:* Stoelting Company.

363	**LEXINGTON DEVELOPMENTAL SCALES** *Child Development Centers of the Bluegrass, Inc.*

Assesses the development of handicapped and nonhandicapped preschool children and identifies their needs and abilities. Used to plan programs and evaluate the effectiveness of classroom and child instruction.

A multiple-item observational inventory assessing development in gross and fine motor, language, personal and social, and cognitive areas. Two forms are available: a 2-hour in-depth assessment (LDS Long Form) and a 30- to 45-minute screening tool (LDS Short Form). Examiner required. Not suitable for group use. Administration untimed (varies by form). *Publisher:* Child Development Centers of the Bluegrass, Inc.

297, 360	**LOUISVILLE BEHAVIOR CHECKLIST** *Lovick C. Miller*

Measures a comprehensive range of social and emotional behaviors indicative of psychopathological disorders in children and adolescents. Used as an intake device.

A 164-item paper-and-pencil or computer-administered true/false inventory eliciting parental report of a child's behaviors. Areas assessed include aggression, hyperactivity, sensitivity, fear, inhibition, normal irritability, withdrawal, intellectual or academic disabilities, and neurotic, antisocial, psychotic, somatic, and sexual behaviors. The inventory is available in three forms: E1 (20 scales, ages 4–6), E2 (19 scales, ages 7 12), and E3 (13 scales, ages 13–17). Examiner required. Not suitable for group use. Administration untimed (20–30 minutes). Hand key; may be computer scored. *Publisher:* Western Psychological Services.

APPENDIX 445

Refer to page(s)	Test Title

243   MAXFIELD-BUCHOLTZ SOCIAL MATURITY SCALE FOR BLIND PRE-SCHOOL CHILDREN   *Kathryn E. Maxfield & Sandra Bucholtz*

Measures the social maturity of blind children

A multiple-item paper-and-pencil observational inventory and parent interview guide assessing the developmental skills and social maturity of blind infants and preschoolers. The objective is to find a means of comparing the present status and/or the progress of a blind child's acquisition of personal and social independence and competence with that of same-age peers. This scale is an adaption of the Vineland Social Maturity Scale. Examiner required. Not suitable for group use. Administration untimed (varies). Examiner evaluated. *Publisher:* American Foundation for the Blind.

14, 64, 71, 89, 171, 173, 174, 178, 180, 202, 203, 204, 205, 206, 210, 211, 212, 215–216, 219, 242, 256, 276, 281, 329, 330, 390   McCARTHY SCALES OF CHILDREN'S ABILITIES   *Dorothea McCarthy*

Assesses children's intellectual and motor development.

A measure of five aspects of children's thinking, motor, and mental abilities. The subtests are Verbal Ability, Short-Term Memory, Numerical Ability, Perceptual Performance, and Motor Coordination. The verbal, numerical, and perceptual performance scales combine to yield a general cognitive index. Examiner required. Not suitable for group use. Administration untimed (45–60 minutes). Examiner evaluated. *Publisher:* The Psychological Corporation.

173, 174   McCARTHY SCREENING TEST   *Dorothea M. McCarthy*

Predicts a child's ability to cope with schoolwork in the early grades. For use in early identification of children at risk for school problems.

A six-task test measuring the following mental abilities: right-left orientation, verbal memory, draw-a-person, numerical memory, conceptual grouping, and leg coordination. The tasks are taken from the McCarthy Scales of Children's Abilities. Examiner required. Not suitable for group use. Administration untimed (20 minutes). Examiner evaluated. *Publisher:* The Psychological Corporation.

183, 329–330, 339   MERRILL-PALMER SCALE   *Rachel Stutsman*

Measures intelligence in children.

A task assessment and oral response scale measuring language skills, motor skills, dexterity, and matching. The 19 subtests are Stutsman Color Matching Test, Wallin Pegboards A & B, Stutsman Buttoning Test, Stutsman Stick and String, Scissors, Stutsman Language Test, Stutsman Picture Formboards, Seguin-Goddard Formboard, Pintner-Manikin Test, Decroly Matching Game, Stutsman Nested Cubes, Woodworth-Wells Association Test, Stutsman Copying Test, Stutsman Pyramid Test, Stutsman Little Pink Tower Test, and Kohs Blocks. Examiner required. Not suitable for group use. Administration untimed (not available). Examiner evaluated. *Publisher:* Stoelting Company.

Refer to page(s)	Test Title
83, 88–89, 96, 116, 117, 176, 282, 363	**MINNESOTA CHILD DEVELOPMENT INVENTORY** *Harold Ireton & Edward Thwing*

Measures the development of a young child based on the mother's observations. Used for clinical evaluation.

A 320-item paper-and-pencil or computer-administered yes/no inventory completed by the mother to assess the child's current level of development. The inventory measures general development, gross motor, fine motor, expressive language, comprehension-conceptual, situation-comprehension, self-help, and personal-social skills. Examiner required. Suitable for group use. Administration untimed (20–30 minutes). Hand key; may be computer scored. *Publisher:* Behavior Science Systems, Inc. |
| 83, 89 | **MINNESOTA INFANT DEVELOPMENT INVENTORY**   *Harold Ireton & Edward Thwing*

Assesses infant development in the first 15 months. Used for pediatric review, infant screening, and educating parents about a child's development.

A 75-item paper-and-pencil inventory completed by the mother to measure the child's development in five areas: gross motor, fine motor, language, comprehension, and personal-social. The test does not yield scores; it provides a framework for making professional judgments and a guide for interviewing. Examiner required. Suitable for group use. Administration untimed (10 minutes). Hand key; may be computer scored. *Publisher:* Behavior Science Systems, Inc. |
| 83, 89 | **MINNESOTA PRE-KINDERGARTEN INVENTORY**   *Harold Ireton & Edward Thwing*

Measures a child's readiness for kindergarten. Used by educators, psychologists, physicians, and other professionals.

A 150-item paper-and-pencil inventory assessing a child's current development, readiness skills, social and emotional adjustment, and symptoms. The measure includes self-help, fine motor, expressive language, comprehension, memory, letter recognition, number comprehension, immaturity, hyperactivity, behavior problems, emotional problems, motor, language, somatic, and sensory symptoms. Self-administered. Suitable for group use. Administration untimed (15 minutes). Hand key. *Publisher:* Behavior Science Systems, Inc. |
| 14, 83, 89 | **MINNESOTA PRESCHOOL INVENTORY**   *Harold Ireton & Edward Thwing*

Determines children's readiness to enter preschool.

A multiple-item paper-and-pencil inventory completed by the mother to review a child's development, adjustment, and symptoms. Examiner required. Not suitable for group use. Administration untimed (not available). Examiner evaluated. *Publisher:* Institute of Psychological Research, Inc. |

APPENDIX   447

Refer to page(s)	*Test Title*

84, 94, 176, 180

MOTOR-FREE VISUAL PERCEPTION TEST   *Ronald P. Colarusso & Donald D. Hammill*

Assesses visual perception in children and older individuals who have motor problems. Used for screening and diagnostic and research purposes, especially with individuals who are learning disabled, motorically impaired, physically handicapped, or mentally retarded.

A 36-item test in which the subject is shown a line drawing and asked to match the stimulus by pointing to one of a multiple-choice set of other drawings. Examiner required. Not suitable for group use. Administration untimed (10 minutes). Hand key. *Publisher:* Academic Therapy Publications.

281

MULLEN SCALES OF EARLY LEARNING   *Eileen M. Mullen*

Assesses the learning abilities and learning patterns of children. Identifies learning disabilities, mental retardation, the manner in which both a child learns and should be taught.

A multiple-item oral response and task performance measure covering four areas of visual and language abilities: Visual Receptive Organization (visual discrimination, organization, sequencing, visual concepts, and short-term visual memory), Visual Expressive Organization (unilateral and bilateral fine motor development and writing), Language Receptive Organization (listening, listening/looking, sequencing, verbal concepts, general knowledge, and short- and long-term auditory memory), and Language Expressive Organization (verbal ability, visual and oral vocabulary, abstract and practical reasoning, and short- and long-term auditory memory). Examiner required. Not suitable for group use. Administration untimed (45 minutes). Examiner evaluated. *Publisher:* T.O.T.A.L. Child.

16, 22, 280, 363

NEONATAL BEHAVIORAL ASSESSMENT SCALE
T. Berry Brazelton

Evaluates selected reflexes, motor responses, and interactive behavioral responses of newborn infants. Used by medical professionals and paraprofessionals to teach parents about the newborn's state changes, temperament, and individual behavior patterns and to improve early health and developmental care.

A 47-item paper-and-pencil assessment measuring neonatal reflex responses in a behavioral context. Twenty-seven items measure the infant's inherent neurological capacities as well as responses to certain sets of stimuli. A second section of 20 items assesses specific elicited reflexes and movements on a 3-point scale (hypoactive, normal, and hyperactive). Examiner required. Not suitable for group use. Administration untimed (20–30 minutes per assessment). Examiner evaluated. *Publisher:* MacKeith Press, distributed in the U.S. by Lippincott/Harper Publishers, Inc.

Refer to page(s)	Test Title

281

ORDINAL SCALES OF PSYCHOLOGICAL DEVELOPMENT *Ina C. Uzgiris & J. McVicker Hunt*

Assesses the psychological and cognitive development of infants in the first 2 years of life. Used with severely retarded and handicapped individuals and to compare different populations of children.

A set of six paper-and-pencil observational scales assessing an infant's psychological and cognitive development: The Development of Visual Pursuit and the Performance of Objects, The Development of Means for Obtaining Desired Environmental Events, The Development of Imitation, The Development of Operational Causality, The Construction of Object Relations in Space, and The Development of Schemes for Relating to Objects. Examiner required. Not suitable for group use. Administration untimed (varies). Examiner evaluated. *Publisher:* University of Illinois Press.

85, 95, 96, 117, 118, 121, 122, 156, 243, 253, 257, 268, 269, 278

PARENTING STRESS INDEX *Richard R. Abidin*

Identifies emotional pathology in children ages 1 month to 11 years and parent-child systems under stress and at risk for dysfunctional parenting. Used for intervention, education, treatment planning, research, child abuse risk assessment, and forensic evaluations for child custody.

A 101-item paper-and-pencil screening and diagnostic instrument yielding a total index of stress and scores associated with child characteristics (adaptability, acceptability, demandingness, mood, hyperactive/distractibility, reinforces parent), parent characteristics (depression, attachment, restriction of role, sense of competence, social isolation, relationship with spouse, parental health), and life stress events. The test is suitable for use with visually, physically, mentally, and hearing impaired individuals. Examiner required. Suitable for group use. Administration untimed (20 minutes). Hand key; may be computer scored. *Publisher:* Pediatric Psychology Press.

333

PEABODY DEVELOPMENTAL MOTOR SCALES AND ACTIVITY CARDS *M. Rhonda Folio & Rebecca R. Fewell*

Assesses the motor development of children during the first 7 years of life. Identifies those whose gross or fine motor skills are delayed or abnormal. Used to establish IEPs.

A multiple-item task performance test consisting of a comprehensive sequence of gross and fine motor skills from which the child's relative developmental skill level can be determined. The test may be used to analyze a wide range of skills identified as questionable by prior screening or to diagnose specific characteristics of a motor problem. Examiner required. May be administered individually or to groups of children using a station-testing procedure. Administration untimed (20–30 minutes per scale). Examiner evaluated. *Publisher:* DLM Teaching Resources.

Refer to page(s)	Test Title
399	**PEABODY INDIVIDUAL ACHIEVEMENT TEST–REVISED** *Lloyd M. Dunn & Frederick C. Markwardt, Jr.*

Provides an overview of individual scholastic achievement. Used in schools for academic achievement screening, instructional program planning, and program evaluation, and in research for measuring levels of achievement.

An oral response "point to" measure comprising five subtests: General Information (100 items), Reading Recognition (100 items), Reading Comprehension (100 items), Mathematics (100 items), and Spelling (100 items). Optional subtests include Written Expression, Level I (18 items) and Written Expression, Level II (2 prompts). This instrument may be used with individuals with physical and mental disabilities. Examiner required. Not suitable for group use. Administration untimed (1 hour). Examiner evaluated. *Publisher:* American Guidance Service.

90–91, 173, 174, 179, 181, 205, 206, 253, 333, 390	**PEABODY PICTURE VOCABULARY TEST–REVISED** *Lloyd M. Dunn & Leota M. Dunn*

Measures receptive vocabulary for Standard American English, estimates verbal ability, and assesses academic aptitude. Used with ESL, mentally retarded, and gifted students.

A 175-item "point to" response test measuring receptive vocabulary in English. Test items, arranged in order of increasing difficulty, consist of plates of four pictures. Subjects shown the plates are asked to point to the picture corresponding to a stimulus words. Available in two forms, L and M. Examiner required. Not suitable for group use. Administration untimed (10–20 minutes). Examiner evaluated. *Publisher:* American Guidance Service.

83, 87	**PEDIATRIC EXAMINATION OF EDUCATIONAL READINESS** *Melvin D. Levine*

Detects high prevalence, low severity disabilities in young children that are critical to success in school. Used for diagnosis, screening, research, and professional training.

A verbal paper-and-pencil show-tell measure of six developmental areas: orientation, gross motor, visual-fine motor, sequential, linguistic, and preacademic skills. The child is asked to identify pictures and copy some of them with a pencil. Examiner required. Not suitable for group use. Administration untimed (1 hour). Examiner evaluated. *Publisher:* Educators Publishing Service, Inc.

117, 119, 201, 360, 368, 370	**PERSONALITY INVENTORY FOR CHILDREN, REVISED FORMAT** *Robert D. Wirt, David Lachar, James E. Klinedinst, Philip D. Seat, & William E. Broen, Jr.*

Evaluates the personality attributes of children and adolescents. Used by professionals for counseling and identification of psychopathology, developmental problems, and social disabilities.

A 280-item paper-and-pencil true/false inventory completed

Refer to page(s)	Test Title
	by a parent producing a profile of 16 scales: Intellectual Screening, Family Relations, Hyperactivity, Somatic Concern, Social Skills, Achievement, Development, Depression, Delinquency, Withdrawal, Psychosis, Anxiety, Lie, Frequency, Defensiveness, and Adjustment. A 420-item version is available for higher scale reliabilities, and a 131-item version is available for screening. Examiner required. Not suitable for group use. Administration untimed (not available). Hand key; may be computer scored. *Publisher:* Western Psychological Services.
171, 205, 206, 210, 212, 253, 256	**PICTORIAL TEST OF INTELLIGENCE** *Joseph L. French* Measures children's general ability. Used for curriculum planning and evaluation. A multiple-item oral picture test in six sections, measuring Picture Vocabulary, Information and Comprehension, Form Discrimination, Similarities, Size and Number, and Immediate Recall. The examiner presents picture cards on which four possible answers are represented and asks questions of the child. The cards are designed so that the examiner, by observing eye movement, also can determine the response of children who are physically handicapped. Examiner required. Not suitable for group use. Administration untimed (45 minutes). Hand key. *Publisher:* Institute of Psychological Research, Inc.
174	**PRESCHOOL LANGUAGE SCALE** *Irla Lee Zimmerman, Violette G. Steiner, & Robert Evatt Pond* Provides a diagnostic measure of receptive and expressive language. A multiple-item test assessing both auditory comprehension and verbal ability. Items measure sensory discrimination, logical thinking, grammar and vocabulary, memory and attention span, temporal/spatial relations, and self-image at most age levels in each of the two domains. Examiner required. Not suitable for group use. Available in Spanish. Administration untimed (20 minutes). Examiner evaluated. *Publisher:* The Psychological Corporation.
325, 326, 328, 329, 332, 333, 334–335, 339, 340	**PSYCHOEDUCATIONAL PROFILE–REVISED** *Eric Schopler, Robert J. Reichler, Ann Bashford, Margaret D. Lansing, & Lee M. Marcus* Measures the learning abilities and characteristics of autistic and related developmentally disordered children. Used to establish individualized special education curricula or home programs for developmentally disabled children previously regarded as untestable. A multiple-item task performance test assessing the learning abilities of autistic and developmentally disabled children. The resulting profile translates into an appropriately individualized special education curriculum or home program according to teaching strategies presented in the manual. Examiner required. Not suitable for group use. Administration untimed (varies). Examiner evaluated. *Publisher:* PRO-ED, Inc.

Refer to page(s)	Test Title

206

PURDUE PEGBOARD TEST *Purdue Research Foundation*

Measures hand-finger-arm dexterity.

Multiple-operation manual test of gross and fine motor movements of hands, fingers, arms, and tips of fingers. Examinees use a test board with two vertical rows of holes and four storage wells holding 50 pegs, 40 washers, and 20 collars. Tasks assess right hand, left hand, and both hands together. Examiner required. Suitable for group use. Administration timed (5–10 minutes). Hand key. *Publisher:* SRA/London House.

176, 180

PURDUE PERCEPTUAL-MOTOR SURVEY
Eugene G. Roach & Newell C. Kephart

Identifies children with perceptual-motor disabilities by tracing development to the point where developmental dysfunction occurs. Assists teachers in developing remedial programs.

A 22-item task assessment measuring laterality, directionality, and perceptual-motor matching skills. The walking board and jumping tests measure balance and posture. The body image and differentiation tests include naming 10 parts of the body, imitation of movements, obstacle course, the Krauss-Weber test, and angels in the snow. A chalkboard test for rhythmic writing, ocular control, and form perception measures perceptual-motor matching skills. Examiner required. Not suitable for group use. Administration untimed (varies). Examiner evaluated. *Publisher:* The Psychological Corporation.

282

REITAN-INDIANA NEUROPSYCHOLOGICAL TEST BATTERY FOR CHILDREN *Ralph M. Reitan and others*

Assesses brain-behavior functioning in children. Used for clinical evaluation.

A battery of tests assessing the neurological functioning of young children, including the Wechsler Intelligence Scale for children, sensory-perceptual tests, and modifications of the Reitan-Indiana Aphasia Screening Test and A Neuropsychological Test Battery, which includes a number of tests (Color Form Test, Target Test, Matching Pictures Test, Progressive Figures Test, Marching Test, and Individual Performance Tests). The battery is related to the Halstead-Reitan batteries for adults and older children but contains a number of adaptations for the age 5–8 group. The components may be purchased separately. Examiner required. Not suitable for group use. Administration untimed (varies). Examiner evaluated. *Publisher:* Reitan Neuropsychology Laboratory.

360

REVISED BEHAVIOR PROBLEM CHECKLIST
Herbert C. Quay & Donald R. Peterson

Assesses the nature of problem behavior. Used in educational, mental health, pediatric, and correctional settings as well as for research.

Refer to page(s)	Test Title

An 85-item paper-and-pencil observational inventory consisting of statements about problem behaviors commonly seen in children and adolescents. Each item is rated by a knowledgeable observer (parent, teacher, child-care worker, correctional staff member). Scores are provided for six subscales: Conduct Disorder, Socialized Aggression, Attention Problems-Immaturity, Anxiety-Withdrawal, Psychotic Behavior, and Motor Excess. Examiner required. Not suitable for group use. Administration untimed (15 minutes). Hand key. *Publisher:* Herbert C. Quay, Ph.D.

84, 92, 333   REYNELL DEVELOPMENTAL LANGUAGE SCALES–SECOND REVISION   *Joan Reynell*

Assesses expressive language and verbal comprehension. Used for evaluation of language development.

Two scales (Verbal Comprehension and Expressive Language) comprise multiple-item performance tests of expressive and receptive language development. The test is suitable for use with hearing impaired children. Not suitable for group use. Administration untimed (1 hour). Examiner evaluated. *Publisher:* NFER-Nelson Publishing Company Ltd.

242   REYNELL-ZINKIN DEVELOPMENTAL SCALES FOR YOUNG VISUALLY HANDICAPPED CHILDREN   *Joan Reynell & P. Zinkin*

Assesses the development of blind and partially sighted babies and young children. Used for planning management and early education programs.

A performance test of intellectual development with subscales covering social adaptation, sensorimotor understanding, exploration of environment, response to sound and verbal comprehension, and expressive language and communication. Examiner required. Not suitable for group use. Administration untimed (not available). Examiner evaluated. *Publisher:* NFER-Nelson Publishing Company Ltd.

84, 93   RILEY PRESCHOOL DEVELOPMENTAL SCREENING INVENTORY   *Clara M. Riley*

Measures readiness to attend school and identifies children most likely to need assistance adjusting to normal school situations. Used for counseling and to meet the requirements of PL 94-142.

A multiple-item observational test providing a child's developmental age and self-concept and determining serious developmental and maturational problems. The instrument can be administered at the beginning of preschool, kindergarten, or first grade. Examiner required. Suitable for group use. Test instructions in both English and Spanish. Administration untimed (15–20 minutes). Examiner evaluated. *Publisher:* Western Psychological Services.

Refer to page(s)	Test Title

174, 181, 363

SCALES OF INDEPENDENT BEHAVIOR   *Robert H. Bruininks, Richard W. Woodcock, Richard F. Weatherman, & Bradley K. Hill*

Measures adaptive and problem behaviors. Used in school, community, and institutional settings to determine eligibility for special services, program planning, and individual and program evaluation.

A multiple-item structured interview guide with 14 subtests assessing motor skills, social interaction and communication skills, personal independence skills, and problem behaviors. Four maladaptive behavior indexes measure the frequency and severity of problem behaviors. Information also may be obtained from the parent, caregiver, or teacher. There are five administration options: full battery, short form, early development scale, individual clusters, and a problem behavior scale. Examiner required. Not suitable for group use. Administration untimed (complete battery 45–60 minutes). Examiner evaluated; may be computer scored. *Publisher:* DLM Teaching Resources.

197

SCREENING TEST FOR DEVELOPMENTAL APRAXIA OF SPEECH   *Robert W. Blakeley*

Assists in the differential diagnosis of developmental apraxia of speech.

A multiple-item test diagnosing developmental apraxia of speech through eight subtests: Expressive Language Discrepancy, Vowels and Diphthongs, Oral Motor Movement, Verbal Sequencing, Motorically Complex Words, Articulation, Transpositions, and Prosody. Examiner required. Not suitable for group use. Administration untimed (10 minutes). Examiner evaluated. *Publisher:* PRO-ED, Inc.

207, 333

SEQUENCED INVENTORY OF COMMUNICATION DEVELOPMENT, REVISED EDITION   *Dona Lea Hedrick, Elizabeth M. Prather, & Annette R. Tobin*

Evaluates the communication abilities of normal and retarded children functioning between the ages of 4 months and 4 years. Used for remedial programming by speech/language pathologists, audiologists, psychologists, and teachers trained in speech and language assessment techniques.

A 210-item inventory assessing and diagnosing language disorders in young children. The receptive language section (92 items) includes behavioral items that test sound and speech discrimination and awareness and understanding. The expressive language section (18 items) includes three types of expressive behaviors (imitating, initiating, and responding) and measures verbal output for length, grammatical and syntactic structure, and articulation. Examiner required. Not suitable for group use. A Cuban Spanish edition is available. Administration untimed (varies). Examiner evaluated. *Publisher:* University of Washington Press.

Refer to page(s)	Test Title

84, 94

SLOSSON DRAWING COORDINATION TEST
Richard L. Slosson

Screens for serious forms of brain dysfunction or damage and aids in the diagnosis of visual-perceptual or visual-motor coordination problems. Also indicates the possibility of severe emotional disturbances.

A multiple-item paper-and-pencil screening test identifying individuals suffering from serious forms of brain dysfunction or damage in which eye-hand coordination is involved. The subject is given 12 figures and asked to make three freehand copes of each figure. Examiner required. Suitable for group use. Administration untimed (10–15 minutes). Hand key. *Publisher:* Slosson Educational Publications, Inc.

91, 390

SLOSSON INTELLIGENCE TEST   *Richard L. Slosson*

Measures the mental age, IQ, and reading level of children and adults. Used by psychologists, guidance counselors, special educators, learning disability and remedial reading teachers to provide a quick assessment of mental abilities.

A 195-item oral screening instrument consisting of questions arranged on a scale of chronological age from $1/2$ month to 27 years. The results can be used to predict reading achievement, plan educational programs, predict success and acceptance in college, screen students for reading disabilities, and determine the IQs of blind subjects. Examiner required. Not suitable for group use. Administration untimed (10–20 minutes). Examiner evaluated. *Publisher:* Slosson Educational Publications, Inc.

392

STANDARD PROGRESSIVE MATRICES   *J.C. Raven*

Measures an individual's mental ability through assessment of nonverbal abstract reasoning tasks. Used for school and vocational counseling and placement.

A 60-item paper-and-pencil nonverbal test presented in five sets of 12 problems each. The subject is presented with a pattern or figure design with a missing part and must select one of six possibilities as the solution. The patterns are arrayed from simple to complex. U.S. norms are available. Examiner required. Suitable for group use. Administration untimed (45 minutes). Hand key; may be machine scored. *Publisher:* H.K. Lewis & Co. Ltd., distributed in the U.S. by The Psychological Corporation.

64, 173, 174, 178, 202, 204, 256, 281, 330, 388

STANFORD-BINET INTELLIGENCE SCALE, FOURTH EDITION   *Robert L. Thorndike, Elizabeth P. Hagen, & Jerome M. Sattler*

Measures an individual's mental abilities. Used to substantiate questionable scores from group tests, to provide more comprehensive assessment, and to assess examinees with physical, language, or personality disorders that prevent group testing.

Refer to page(s)	Test Title

A verbal and nonverbal performance test assessing mental abilities in four areas: verbal reasoning (Vocabulary, Comprehension, Verbal Relations, Absurdities), abstract/visual reasoning (Pattern Analysis, Matrices, Paper Folding and Cutting, Copying), quantitative comprehension (Quantitative, Number Series, Equation Building), and short-term memory (Memory for Digits, Memory for Objects, and Bead Memory). Examiner required. Not suitable for group use. Administration untimed (45–90 minutes). Examiner evaluated. *Publisher:* Riverside Publishing Company.

359 **TEMPERAMENT ASSESSMENT BATTERY FOR CHILDREN** *Roy P. Martin*

Measures the basic personality-behavioral dimensions or temperaments of children.

A multiple-item paper-and-pencil test assessing six temperamental variables: Activity, Adaptability, Approach/Withdrawal, Intensity, Distractibility, and Persistence. The 48-item Parent Form describes the child's behavior at home. The 48-item Teacher Form reflects the child's classroom behavior. The Clinician Form is a questionnaire used by professionals involved in the child's psychoeducational evaluation. Examiner required. Not suitable for group use. Administration untimed (12 minutes). Hand key; examiner evaluated. *Publisher:* Clinical Psychology Publishing Company, Inc.

174 **TEST FOR AUDITORY COMPREHENSION OF LANGUAGE–REVISED EDITION** *Elizabeth Carrow-Woolfolk*

Measures children's auditory comprehension.

A multiple-item response test assessing auditory understanding of word classes and relations, grammatical morphemes, and elaborated sentence constructions. The test requires no oral response. Examiner required. Not suitable for group use. Administration untimed (10–20 minutes). Examiner evaluated; may be computer scored. *Publisher:* DLM Teaching Resources.

84, 92, 174 **TEST OF EARLY LANGUAGE DEVELOPMENT** *Wayne P. Hresko, D. Kim Reid, & Donald D. Hammill*

Measures content and form in the receptive and expressive language abilities of children. Used to identify problems, document progress, conduct research, and guide instructional practices.

A 38-item oral response and "point to" test using a variety of semantic and syntactic tasks to asses different aspects of receptive/expressive language. Not suitable for group use. Administration untimed (15 minutes). Examiner evaluated. *Publisher:* PRO-ED, Inc.

Refer to page(s)	Test Title

174

TEST OF LANGUAGE DEVELOPMENT–2 PRIMARY
Phyllis L. Newcomer & Donald D. Hammill

Assesses the expressive and receptive abilities of children. Used as a language achievement test and to identify children with language problems, including mental retardation, learning disabilities, reading disabilities, speech delays, and articulation problems.

A 190-item oral response and "point to" test consisting of seven subtests measuring different components of spoken language: Picture Vocabulary (35 items) and Oral Vocabulary (30 items) assess the understanding and meaningful use of spoken words; Grammatic Understanding (25 items), Sentence Imitation (30 items), and Grammatic Completion (30 items) assess different aspects of grammar; Word Articulation (20 items) and Word Discrimination (20 items), which are supplemental tests, measure the ability to pronounce words correctly and distinguish between words that sound familiar. Examiner required. Not suitable for group use. Administration untimed (40 minutes). Examiner evaluated; computer scored. *Publisher:* PRO-ED, Inc.

204

TOKEN TEST FOR CHILDREN   *Frank G. DiSimoni*

Measures functional listening ability in children and identifies receptive language dysfunction. Used in language therapy.

A 61-item test in which the child arranges wooden tokens in response to the examiner's oral directions. The results can be used to indicate a need for further testing of lexicon and syntax or to rule out language impairment in a child with reading difficulties. The test is not appropriate for deaf subjects. Examiner required. Not suitable for group use. Administration untimed (10 minutes). Examiner evaluated. *Publisher:* DLM Teaching Resources.

390

TORRANCE TESTS OF CREATIVE THINKING
E. Paul Torrance

Assesses the ability to visualize and transform words, meanings, and patterns. Used to identify gifted, creative individuals.

A multiple-task paper-and-pencil measure of individual creativity, assessing four mental characteristics: fluency, flexibility, originality, and elaboration. The test is available in two equivalent forms (A and B) in two editions: Verbal, which uses seven word-based exercises, and Figural, which use three picture-based exercises. Examiner required. Suitable for group use. Administration timed (Figural 30 minutes; Verbal 45 minutes). Examiner evaluated. *Publisher:* Scholastic Testing Service, Inc.

174

UTAH TEST OF LANGUAGE DEVELOPMENT–3
Merlin J. Mecham

Identifies children with language-learning disabilities who may need further assistance.

Refer to page(s)	Test Title
	A 51-item task assessment oral response test measuring receptive semantic language, expressive semantic language, receptive sequential language, and expressive sequential language factors. Test items are arranged in developmental order. Examiner required. Not suitable for group use. Administration untimed (20–30 minutes). Examiner evaluated. *Publisher:* PRO-ED, Inc.
116, 117, 174, 181, 183, 201, 207, 248, 256, 269, 325, 331, 363	**VINELAND ADAPTIVE BEHAVIOR SCALES** *Sara S. Sparrow, David A. Balla, & Dominic V. Cicchetti* Measures personal and social sufficiency from birth to adulthood. Used to assess individuals with mental retardation or handicaps. A multiple-item inventory in three forms (Interview Edition, Survey Form; Interview Edition, Expanded Form; and Classroom Edition) assessing adaptive behavior in four domains: Communication (receptive, expressive, and written), Daily Living Skills (personal, domestic, and community), Socialization (interpersonal relationships, play and leisure time, and coping skills), and Motor Skills (gross and fine). An optional Maladaptive Behavior domain is included in the Interview Edition, Survey and Expanded Forms. Examiner required. Not suitable for group use. Various materials available in Spanish. Administration untimed (varies by form). Examiner evaluated. *Publisher:* American Guidance Service.
42, 64, 81, 182, 183, 256	**WECHSLER INTELLIGENCE SCALE FOR CHILDREN–THIRD EDITION** *David Wechsler* Assesses intellectual ability in children ages 6 years to 16 years, 11 months. Thirteen subtests (including supplementary measures) make up two major divisions: Verbal (Information, General Comprehension, Arithmetic, Similarities, Vocabulary, and Digit Span) and Performance (Picture Completion, Picture Arrangement, Block Design, Object Assembly, Coding, Mazes, and Symbol Search). Some portions of the scale require verbal responses and other require the subject to manipulate test materials in order to demonstrate performance ability. Examiner required. Not suitable for group use. Administration untimed (1 hour). Examiner evaluated. *Publisher:* The Psychological Corporation.
42, 90, 173, 174, 178, 181, 183, 202, 203, 204, 205, 206, 212, 256, 330	**WECHSLER PRESCHOOL AND PRIMARY SCALES OF INTELLIGENCE–REVISED** *David Wechsler* Assesses intelligence in young children ages 3 years to 7 years, 3 months. Twelve subtests (including supplementary measures) make up two major divisions: Verbal (Information, Vocabulary, Arithmetic, Similarities, Comprehension, and Sentences) and Performance (Animal Pegs, Picture Completion, Mazes, Geometric Design, Block Design, and Object Assembly). Selected subscales require verbal responses, and others require the subject to manipulate test materials in order to demonstrate performance ability. Examiner

Refer to page(s)	Test Title
	required. Not suitable for group use. Administration untimed (1 hour). Examiner evaluated. *Publisher:* The Psychological Corporation.
399	**WIDE RANGE ACHIEVEMENT TEST–REVISED** *Sarah Jastak and Gary S. Wilkinson* Measures the basic educational skills of word recognition, spelling, and arithmetic, and identifies individuals with learning difficulties. With children, used for educational placement and measuring school achievement. Three paper-and-pencil subtests (50–100 items each) assessing coding skills: Reading (recognizing and naming letters and pronouncing printed words), Spelling (copying marks resembling letters, writing name, and printing words), and Arithmetic (counting, reading number symbols, oral and written computation). The test consists of two levels, I (ages 5–11) and II (ages 12–adult). Optional word lists for both levels of the reading and spelling tests are offered on plastic cards, and a recorded pronunciation of the lists is available on cassette tape. Examiner required. Spelling and Arithmetic suitable for group use; Reading must be individually administered. Large-print edition available. Administration timed (10 minutes per subtest). Examiner evaluated. *Publisher:* Jastak Associates, Inc.
392	**WOODCOCK-JOHNSON PSYCHO-EDUCATIONAL BATTERY** *Richard W. Woodcock & Mary Bonner Johnson* Evaluates individual cognitive ability, scholastic achievement, and interest level. Used to diagnose learning disabilities, for instructional planning, and in research. A 39-test battery comprising two parts. Part One tests seven factors (long-term memory, short-term memory, processing speed, auditory processing, visual processing, comprehension knowledge, and fluid reasoning). Part Two (available in Forms A and B) tests achievement in five academic areas (reading, mathematics, written language, knowledge, and skills). Examiner required. Not suitable for group use. Available in Spanish. Administration untimed (varies). Examiner evaluated; may be computer scored. *Publisher:* DLM Teaching Resources.

Test Publisher/Distributor Directory

ACADEMIC THERAPY PUBLICATIONS, 20 Commercial Boulevard, Novato, California 94949; (415)883-3314

AMERICAN FOUNDATION FOR THE BLIND, 15 West 16th Street, New York, New York 10011; (212)620-2000

AMERICAN GUIDANCE SERVICE, Publisher's Building, Circle Pines, Minnesota 55014; (800)328-2560, in Minnesota (612)786-4343

AMERICAN ORTHOPSYCHIATRIC ASSOCIATION, INC., 19 West 44th Street, Suite 1616, New York, New York 10036; (212)354-5770

BEHAVIOR SCIENCE SYSTEMS, INC., P.O. Box 1108, Minneapolis, Minnesota 55458; (612) 929-6220

CALLIER CENTER FOR COMMUNICATION DISORDERS, The University of Texas at Dallas, 1966 Inwood Road, Dallas, Texas 75235; (214)905-3106

CENTER FOR RESEARCH ON TEACHING AND LEARNING, College of Education, University of Arkansas at Little Rock, 33rd and University, Little Rock, Arkansas 72204; (501)569-3422

CHILD DEVELOPMENT CENTERS OF THE BLUEGRASS, INC., 465 Springhill Drive, P.O. Box 8003, Lexington, Kentucky 40503; (606)278-0549

CLINICAL PSYCHOLOGY PUBLISHING COMPANY, INC., 4 Conant Square, Brandon, Vermont 05733; (802)247-6871

CONSULTING PSYCHOLOGISTS PRESS, INC., 577 College Avenue, P.O. Box 60070, Palo Alto, California 94306; (415)857-1444

C.P.S., INC., P.O. Box 83, Larchmont, New York 10538; (914)833-1633

CURRICULUM ASSOCIATES, INC., 5 Esquire Road, North Billerica, Massachusetts 01862-2589; (800)225-0248, in Massachusetts (617)667-8000

DENVER DEVELOPMENTAL MATERIALS, INC., P.O. Box 6919, Denver, Colorado 80206-0919; (303)355-4729

DEVEREUX FOUNDATION PRESS, 19 South Waterloo Road, P.O. Box 400, Devon, Pennsylvania 19333; (215)296-6905

DLM TEACHING RESOURCES, One DLM Park, Allen, Texas 75002; (800)527-4747, in Texas (800)442-4711

EDUCATORS PUBLISHING SERVICE, INC., 75 Moulton Street, Cambridge, Massachusetts 02238-9101; (800)225-5750, in Massachusetts (800)792-5166

GORDON SYSTEMS, INC., P.O. Box 746, DeWitt, New York 13214; (315)446-4849

HISKEY NEBRASKA TEST, 5640 Baldwin, Lincoln, Nebraska 68507; (402)466-6145

INSTITUTE OF PSYCHOLOGICAL RESEARCH, INC., 34 Fleury Street West, Montreal, Quebec H3L 1S9, Canada; (514)382-3000

JASTAK ASSOCIATES, INC., P.O. Box 4460, Wilmington, Delaware 19807; (800)221-9278

LEA & FEBIGER, 600 Washington Square, Philadelphia, Pennsylvania 19106; (215)922-1330

LEWIS, H.K., & CO. LTD., 136 Gower Street, London WC1E 6BS, England; (01)387-4282

LIPPINCOTT/HARPER PUBLISHERS, INC., Journals Division, 2350 Virginia Avenue, Hagerstown, Maryland 21740; (800)638-3030

MACKEITH PRESS, 5A Netherhall Gardens, London NW3 5RN, England; (01)794-9859

MULTI-HEALTH SYSTEMS INC., 95 Thorncliffe Park Drive, Suite 100, Toronto, Ontario M4H 1L7, Canada; (416)424-1700

NFER-NELSON PUBLISHING COMPANY LTD., Darville House, 2 Oxford Road East, Windsor, Berkshire SL4 1DF, England; (0753)858961

PEDIATRIC PSYCHOLOGY PRESS, 320 Terrell Road West, Charlottesville, Virginia 22901; (804)296-8211

PRO-ED, INC., 8700 Shoal Creek Boulevard Austin, Texas 78758; (512)451-3246

PSYCHOLOGICAL ASSESSMENT AND SERVICES, INC., P.O. Box 1031, Iowa City, Iowa 52240; (319)338-9316

PSYCHOLOGICAL CORPORATION, THE, A Subsidiary of Harcourt Brace Jovanovich, Inc., 555 Academic Court, San Antonio, Texas 78204; (800)228-0752

QUAY, HERBERT C., PH.D., P.O. Box 248074, University of Miami, Coral Gables, Florida 33124; (305)284-5208

REITAN NEUROPSYCHOLOGY LABORATORY, 1338 East Edison Street, Tucson, Arizona 85719; (602)795-3717

RIVERSIDE PUBLISHING COMPANY, THE, 8420 Bryn Mawr Avenue, Chicago, Illinois 60631; (800)323-9540, in Alaska, Hawaii, or Illinois call collect (312)693-0040

SCHOLASTIC TESTING SERVICE, INC., 480 Meyer Road, P.O. Box 1056, Bensenville, Illinois 60106-8056; (312)766-7150

SLOSSON EDUCATIONAL PUBLICATIONS, INC., P.O. Box 280, East Aurora, New York 14052; (800)828-4800, in New York (716)652-0930

SRA/LONDON HOUSE, Business Test Group, 1550 Northwest Highway, Park Ridge, Illinois 60068; (708)298-7311

STOELTING COMPANY, 620 Wheat Lane, Wood Dale, Illinois 60191; (708)860-9700

TEACHERS COLLEGE PRESS, Columbia University, 1234 Amsterdam Avenue, New York, New York 10027; (212)678-3929

TEST AGENCY LTD., THE, Cournswood House, North Dean, High Wycombe, Bucks HP14 4NW, England; (024)3384

T.O.T.A.L. CHILD, INC., 244 Deerfield Road, Cranston, Rhode Island 02920; (401)942-9955

UNIVERSITY OF ILLINOIS PRESS, 54 East Gregory Drive, Champaign, Illinois 61820; (217)333-0950

UNIVERSITY OF VERMONT, College of Medicine, Department of Psychiatry, Section of Child, Adolescent, and Family Psychiatry, 1 South Prospect Street, Burlington, Vermont 05401; (802)656-4563

UNIVERSITY OF WASHINGTON PRESS, P.O. Box 50096, Seattle, Washington 98145; (206)543-4050, business department (206)543-8870

WESTERN PSYCHOLOGICAL SERVICES, A Division of Manson Western Corporation, 12031 Wilshire Boulevard, Los Angeles, California 90025; (213)478-2061

Names Index

Abbs, J., 201, 223
Abernathy, V., 47, 50
Abeson, A., 408, 423
Abidin, R.R., 95, 97, 118, 124, 156, 161, 243, 259, 268, 284
Abikoff, H., 303, 312
Accardo, P.J., 8, 9
Achenbach, T., 243, 259, 269, 284
Achenbach, T.M., 95, 97, 105, 118, 124, 182, 184, 201, 223, 262, 284, 295, 312, 358, 359, 373
Adams, K., 241, 261
Adams, W., 252, 254, 259
Adelberg, T., 47, 52
Afton, A.D., 48, 54
Ainsworth, M.D.S., 41, 50, 268, 284
Akerley, M., 320, 336, 342
Albert, J., 302, 315
Albert, R.S., 387, 404
Alberto, P.A., 356, 373
Alessi, G.J., 356, 373
Alicke, M.D., 373, 377
Allen, D., 293, 317
Allen, D.A., 195, 196, 198, 225
Allen, D.R., 46, 51
Allen, D.V., 192, 223
Allen, M.C., 270, 284
Allen, V.L., 40, 52
Allport, G., 30, 50
Almond, P.J., 329, 332, 342
Almy, M., 346, 374
Alper, M.H., 16, 27
Alpern, G.D., 88, 89, 97, 178, 184, 363, 374
Alpert, R., 38, 53
Als, H., 272, 280, 284
Altman, I., 152, 161
Amabile, T.M., 388, 404
Ames, L.B., 386, 393, 404
Anastasi, A., 56, 57, 58, 59, 60, 61, 66, 68, 69, 71, 72, 388, 390, 404
Anastopoulos, A.D., 293, 312
Anderson, D.F., 389, 406
Anderson, E., 255, 259

Anderson, K., 121, 126, 304, 315
Anderson, L.W., 29, 50
Andersson, O., 108, 125
Andrews, C., 338, 343
Appelbaum, M., 150, 151, 164
Aram, D.M., 192, 194, 195, 198, 223, 225, 226
Archer, P., 79, 85, 98
Arick, J.R., 329, 332, 342
Ascione, F.R., 121, 124
Asher, K.N., 88, 89, 97
Ashworth, C.D., 272, 288
Askenasy, A., 146, 162
Astbury, J., 271, 289
Atkinson, J.H., 272, 286
Atkinson, R., 150, 164
Atkinson, S.S., 269, 286
Aufseeser, C., 76, 99
Aylward, G.P., 78, 97, 272, 280, 284
Ayres, A.J., 180, 184
Baer, D.M., 39, 51
Bagdon, L., 270, 285
Bajuk, B., 271, 289
Baker, A., 326, 343
Baker, L., 210, 223
Baldwin, A.L., 31, 32, 34, 38, 50
Baldwin, B.T., 383, 406
Baldwin, D.V., 121, 126
Balis, F.M., 270, 272, 288
Ball, J., 332, 342
Balla, D.A., 116, 126, 181, 186, 201, 226, 248, 261, 269, 288, 325, 331, 344, 363, 376
Bandura, A., 38, 39, 50, 348, 374
Bankson, N.W., 92, 97
Barber, T.E., 57, 58, 72
Barbera-Stein, L., 47, 53
Barker, R., 153, 161
Barkley, R., 118, 121, 124, 293, 317
Barkley, R.A., 290, 292, 293, 296, 297, 298, 301, 302, 303, 304, 306, 307, 308, 309, 310, 312, 313, 315, 316, 317, 354, 374

Barlow, S., 201, 223
Barnard, K., 268, 285
Barnard, K.E., 272, 288
Barnes, M.A., 397, 406
Barnett, D.W., 413, 423
Barraga, N., 242, 243, 259
Barrera, M., 133, 134, 135, 136, 161
Barrett, K.C., 3, 10
Bartak, L., 329, 342
Barton, E.J., 121, 124
Basham, R.B., 138, 165
Bashford, A., 319, 336, 325, 344
Bauchner, H.C., 86, 97
Baudin, J., 271, 288
Bauman, E., 142, 164
Baumrind, D., 41, 50, 151, 161
Bax, M., 106, 125
Bayley, N., 5, 9, 19, 20, 27, 28, 151, 161, 182, 184, 242, 259, 280, 285, 288, 295, 313, 329, 342, 363, 374, 383, 390, 404, 406
Beauchamp, T., 422, 423
Beck, L.H., 301, 316
Becker, L.D., 421, 424
Beckwith, L., 278, 288
Beery, K.E., 94, 97, 180, 184, 398, 404
Beggs, D.L., 360, 374
Behar, D., 303, 316
Behar, L., 106, 119, 124, 298, 313, 358, 363, 374
Beisler, J.M., 321, 342
Beitchman, J.H., 210, 223
Bell, R., 156, 165, 346, 374
Bell, S.M., 268, 284
Bellak, L., 2578, 259
Bellak, S.S., 257, 259
Belle, D., 144, 161
Belman, A.L., 270, 289
Belsky, J., 47, 50, 129, 161
Bender, L., 184, 398, 404
Bender, M.E., 293, 316
Bennett, S., 47, 53
Bentler, P., 146, 164
Benton, A.L., 193, 223
Berenberg, S.R., 201, 223
Bergan, J., 149, 150, 151, 153, 163

461

462 NAMES INDEX

Bergmann, T., 265, 285
Bernstein, V.G., 348, 374
Berry, M.F., 194, 223
Bersoff, D.N., 411, 424
Bettenburg, A., 263, 285
Bibace, R., 264, 285
Bierman, J., 129, 166
Bilek, M., 397, 404
Billings, A.G., 43, 52
Birch, H.G., 295, 317
Birch, J.W., 168, 186
Birmingham, B.K., 308, 316
Birnbaum, J., 240, 261
Bjerre, I., 279, 285
Black, A., 151, 161
Black, M.M., 3, 9
Black-Van Santen, L., 196, 223
Blakeley, R.W., 197, 223
Blehar, M.C., 41, 50
Blickman, J.G., 272, 284
Bliss, L.S., 192, 223
Block, J.H., 40, 50
Block, M., 43, 53
Bloom, B., 128, 131, 140, 149, 153, 161
Bloom, R.B., 347, 376
Bloss, J., 255, 256, 260
Blouin, A.G., 94, 98, 100, 298, 317
Blum, L.H., 171, 183, 184
Bluma, S., 178, 184
Boehm, A., 414, 423
Boehm, A.E., 169, 184, 345, 374
Boersman, D.C., 361, 375
Boggs, S.R., 120, 124
Bok, S., 418, 424
Boliek, C.A., 359, 376
Boll, T.J., 88, 89, 97, 178, 184, 363, 374
Bondy, A.S., 390, 404
Boring, E.G., 22, 27
Borowitz, K.C., 86, 97
Boundy, B.E., 108, 124
Bowlby, J., 128, 161
Boyce, W.T., 268, 286
Bozynski, M.E.A., 271, 285
Bracken, B.A., 179, 184, 390, 404
Bradford, B.C., 271, 288
Bradley, R., 128, 131, 140, 148, 149, 150, 151, 152, 153, 155, 161, 162, 163, 268, 285
Bradley, R.H., 346, 374
Brandt, B.J., 89, 99
Bransome, E.D., 301, 316
Brantley, H.T., 263, 285

Brassard, M.R., 360, 361, 362, 374
Braswell, L., 292, 315
Brazelton, T.B., 16, 22, 27, 280, 284, 285, 363, 374
Breasted, J.H., 193, 223
Breaux, A.M., 294, 296, 313, 314
Breen, M., 296, 298, 303, 304, 308, 313
Brehm, S., 319, 343
Breitenbucker, M., 144, 163
Bresnick, B., 79, 85, 98
Brigance, A.H., 179, 184, 280, 285, 363, 368, 374
Brink, R.E., 393, 404
Briskin, H., 255, 256, 260
Broder, S., 270, 272, 288
Broderick, J.E., 45, 46, 52
Brody, G., 46, 51
Broen, W.E., Jr., 201, 226
Bromwich, R., 154, 162
Bronfenbrenner, U., 129, 162
Bronson, E., 383, 406
Brooks, J., 17, 21, 27
Brophy, J., 348, 374
Brouwers, P., 270, 272, 288
Brown, C., 272, 284
Brown, H.W., 290, 292, 297, 317
Brown, W.U., 16, 27
Browning, C.A., 281, 285
Broyer, M., 270, 287
Bruhn, J.,133, 162
Bruininks, R.H., 181, 184, 363, 374
Bruner, J., 321, 342
Bruneti, A., 270, 272, 288
Buccatello, L., 389, 405, 406
Bucholtz, S., 243, 260
Buck, J.N., 257, 259
Buckley, L., 264, 288
Bullard, B., 242, 259
Bunney, W.E., 303, 316
Burch, K.J., 393, 404
Burgemeister, B.B., 171, 183, 184
Burgess, D.B., 88, 89, 97
Burks, B.S., 383, 404
Burks, H.F., 182, 184, 358, 374
Burns, R.C., 257, 259
Byrne, D., 134, 146, 164
Byrne, J.M., 89, 97
Bzoch, E.R., 278, 285
Bzoch, K., 207, 223
Cadman, D., 421, 424
Caldwell, B., 128, 131, 140, 149, 150, 151, 152, 153, 155, 161, 162, 163, 268, 285

Caldwell, B.M., 346, 374
Campbell, J., 255, 256, 260
Campbell, S.B., 292, 294, 296, 302, 313, 314
Campos, J.J., 3, 10
Cantwell, D., 293, 314
Cantwell, D.P., 210, 223
Capute, A.J., 8, 9
Carey, W.B., 295, 314, 360, 376
Carr, J., 75, 97
Carrieri, V.L., 136, 164
Carrow, E., 184
Casey, P., 140, 153, 162
Cassidy, J., 238, 259
Cattell, P., 183, 185, 243, 259, 281, 285
Chamberlin, R.W., 102, 106, 107, 124
Chambers, L.W., 421, 424
Chandler, M., 129, 165
Chandler, M.J., 4, 10
Change, P., 397, 404
Chapar, G.N., 269, 285
Chase, J., 157, 163, 241, 259, 261
Chernoff, R., 76, 87, 99
Chess, S., 40, 50, 106, 109, 111, 124, 126, 246, 259, 290, 295, 314, 317
Childress, J.F., 422, 423
Christensen, A., 44, 45, 46, 50
Cicchetti, D.V., 116, 126, 181, 186, 201, 226, 248, 261, 269, 288, 325, 331, 344, 363, 376
Clark, B., 401, 404
Clark, J.H., 388, 389, 406
Clark, R., 150, 164
Clarke, A.D., 128, 162
Clarke, A.M., 128, 162
Clarke-Stewart, A., 151, 152, 162
Clements, S.D., 290, 314
Cobb, J.A., 121, 126
Cobb, S., 47, 51
Coddington, R.D., 142, 162
Cohen, D.J., 321, 342, 349, 374, 377
Cohen, F., 263, 285
Cohen, H.J., 270, 289
Cohen, L., 142, 159, 165
Cohen, M.E., 268, 287
Cohen, S., 135, 140, 162
Cohen, S.E., 278, 288
Cohrs, M., 22, 27, 173, 185, 393, 405
Colangelo, N., 384, 401, 404
Colarusso, R.P., 94, 98, 180, 185

NAMES INDEX 463

Cole, L., 256, 260
Cole, L.J., 185
Cole, R.E., 44, 51
Coleman, D., 383, 404
Coleman, M., 334, 342
Colligan, R.C., 89, 98
Collins, M., 243, 259
Collins, R., 349, 376
Collins-Moore, M.S., 242, 259
Comings, D.E., 299, 314
Comings, D.G., 300, 314
Conners, C.K., 94, 98, 118, 124, 125, 296, 298, 314, 315, 360, 375
Connor, E.M., 270, 285
Constantino, R., 390, 404
Cooper, C., 157, 163
Cooper, C.S., 157, 159, 163
Coplan, J., 92, 98
Cornbleet, J., 366, 376
Costello, A.J., 120, 124
Costello, A.M. de L., 271, 288
Costello, E.J., 297, 314
Court, J.H., 256, 260
Covitz, F., 151, 166
Cowen, E.L., 45, 51
Cox, C.M., 383, 404
Cox, M., 43, 44, 45, 47, 51
Cox, R., 43, 44, 45, 47, 51
Crabtree, M., 185
Craighead, W.E., 49, 50, 52
Cramer, B.B., 3, 10
Cravioto, J., 128, 162
Crockenberg, S.B., 390, 404
Culatta, B., 255, 260
Culbertson, J., 194, 223
Culbertson, J.L., 5, 6, 7, 8, 10, 238, 261, 413, 424
Cullen, K.J., 108, 124
Cunningham, A.E., 23, 28
Cunningham, C.E., 308, 313
Currier, S.K., 89, 99
Curtis, S., 186
Dahl, E.K., 349, 374
Dalby, M.A., 193, 223
Dangel, R.F., 309, 314
Darby, J.K., 194, 197, 207, 224
Dartosis, A., 270, 287
Daste, M.R., 88, 89, 97
Davé, R., 150, 153, 162
Davidson, P., 237, 240, 241, 242, 243, 246, 248, 249, 252, 254, 259, 260, 261
Davis, C., 242, 260
Day, D., 302, 315
de Ajuriaguerra, J., 195, 224
Dean, A., 135, 140, 162
Dean, R.S., 88, 98
Decker, S.N., 193, 224

DeFries, J.C., 23, 24, 27, 193, 224
DeLicardie, E., 128, 162
DeLong, R., 193, 224
Demb, H.B., 349, 375
DeMyer, M.K., 322, 325, 333, 336, 342
Denckla, M.B., 293, 314
Dennis, W., 149, 152, 162
DeVoss, J.C., 383, 406
DiSimoni, F.G., 206, 224
Diamond, G.H., 270, 289
Dishion, T.J., 121, 126
Dodds, J.B., 22, 27, 79, 85, 98, 116, 125, 173, 185, 243, 260, 363, 375, 393, 405
Dodds, M., 144, 163
Dohrenwend, B., 141, 163
Dohrenwend, B.P., 146, 162
Dohrenwend, B.S., 146, 162
Dolan, A.B., 182, 186
Doll, E., 185, 331, 342, 363, 374
Dorman, R., 128, 165
Doucet, H.J., 88, 89, 97
Douglas, E., 346, 375
Douglas, V., 290, 318
Douglas, V.I., 291, 292, 302, 313, 314
Dreikurs, T., 402, 404
Drillien, C., 128, 163
Drotar, D., 263, 285
Dubowitz, L., 16, 27
Dubowitz, V., 16, 27
Duffy, F.H., 272, 284
Dugas, F., 292, 317
Dumas, J.E., 48, 50
Duncan, D., 140, 164
Duncan-Jones, P., 134, 146, 164
Dunn, J., 201, 226
Dunn, L(eota) M., 90, 98, 173, 185, 206, 224, 253, 260, 333, 342, 390, 404
Dunn, L(loyd) M., 90, 98, 173, 185, 206, 224, 253, 260, 333, 342, 390, 399, 404
Dunst, C., 136, 138, 157, 163, 166
Dunst, C.J., 133, 134, 157, 159, 163, 164
DuPaul, G.J., 308, 316
Dye, H., 149, 165
Dye, H.B., 15, 28
Dykstra, W., 264, 289
Earls, R., 108, 124
Earp, J., 136, 165
Easp, J.A., 47, 53
Eastman, J., 109, 126

Eddy, J., 270, 272, 288
Edelbrock, C., 94, 95, 97, 98, 118, 120, 124, 182, 184, 201, 223, 243, 259, 269, 284, 295, 296, 297, 298, 312, 313, 314
Edelbrock, C.S., 358, 359, 373
Edelman, N., 79, 85, 98
Edwards, R.P., 389, 405
Egeland, B., 144, 151, 163
Eichel, V., 241, 260
Eisenberg-Berg, N., 112, 126
Eisert, D., 238, 261, 277, 289
Eisert, D.C., 88, 98, 282, 285
Elardo, R., 149, 150, 151, 155, 163
Elkind, D., 386, 404
Ellenberg, J.H., 200, 225
Elliott, C.D., 185
Elliott, C.H., 263, 289
Elliott, S.N., 347, 348, 376, 412, 413, 424
Elliott, S.W., 30, 53
Ellison, P., 88, 99
Ellison, P.H., 281, 285
Elmore, P.B., 360, 374
Emery, R.E., 45, 46, 50, 52
Engel, M., 151, 163
Epps, E.G., 57, 58, 72
Epps, S., 356, 357, 374
Epstein, L.G., 270, 285
Erikson, E.H., 37, 38, 50
Ewing, L.J., 294, 296, 313, 314
Exner, J.E., 33, 34, 50
Eyberg, S., 95, 98, 119, 125
Eyberg, S.M., 94, 99, 116, 118, 120, 121, 124, 126, 269, 285, 297, 304, 314, 316, 317, 360, 376
Eysenck, H.J., 30, 31, 51
Eysenck, M.W., 30, 31, 51
Fagan, J., 254, 260
Fagan, J.F., 281, 285
Faigenbaum, D., 282, 285
Falloon, J., 270, 272, 288
Fanaroff, A.A., 278, 287
Fandal, A.W., 22, 27, 173, 185, 393, 405
Farley, A.H., 333, 343
Fay, W., 321, 342
Felner, R.D., 45, 51
Ferb, T., 76, 99
Ferguson, H.B., 292, 293, 317
Ferguson, L.R., 46, 51
Ferguson, R., 421, 424
Fernandez, P., 246, 259
Feshbach, S., 112, 124
Fewell, R.R., 185, 333, 342
Field, T., 279, 285

Figueroa, R.A., 57, 72
Fischer, M., 296, 298, 303, 304, 308, 313
Fischler, R.S., 76, 80, 98
Fish, L., 393, 404
Fish, L.J., 393, 404
Fish, R., 397, 404
Fisher, L., 44, 51
Flaharty, R., 329, 342
Flavell, J.H., 32, 51, 413, 424
Fleuridas, C., 384, 404
Flynn, J.R., 70, 72
Foley, J.M., 263, 289
Folio, M.R., 333, 342
Ford, G.W., 277, 278, 287
Forehand, R., 43, 45, 46, 47, 51, 53, 112, 124, 301, 304, 309, 314
Forslund, M., 279, 285
Fost, N., 416, 424
Foster, R(ay), 243, 248, 260
Foster, R(ochana), 185
Fotheringham, J.B., 168, 185
Fowler, M.G., 269, 286
Fox, L.H., 385, 404
Fox, N.L., 88, 89, 99
Fox, R.A., 358, 375
Fraiberg, S., 240, 244, 260
Francis, P.L., 280, 286
Frankenburg, W.K., 22, 27, 79, 85, 88, 98, 116, 125, 173, 185, 243, 260, 363, 375, 393, 405
Freeland, C.A., 89, 98
Freeman, B.J., 327, 332, 342
Freeman, D.J., 23, 28
Freeman, M., 151, 164
Freemouw, W.J., 417, 424
Freidin, M.R., 293, 317
French F., 129, 166
French, J., 47, 51
French, J.L., 171, 185, 206, 210, 224, 253, 260
Freud, A., 265, 285
Freud, S., 33, 34, 35, 51
Friedman, F., 241, 261
Fristoe, M., 206, 224
Frohman, A., 178, 184
Frumkin, B., 194, 224
Fuller, F., 383, 406
Funderburk, B., 95, 98, 119, 125
Funk, S.G., 89, 100
Furey, W.M., 43, 46, 47, 51
Furman, W., 109, 111, 112, 125
Gabarino, J., 47, 51
Gabel, S., 116, 125
Gaes, G., 76, 87, 99
Gallagher, J., 278, 287

Gallahue, D., 180, 186
Gandour, M.J., 295, 315
Garber, J., 48, 51
Garcia Coll, C.T., 278, 289
Gardner, G.G., 264, 286
Gardner, H., 388, 405
Gardner, M.F., 91, 98
Garfinkel, B.D., 302, 315
Garner, P.W., 87, 99
Garvey, M., 193
Gdowski, C.L., 361, 374
Genaze, D., 271, 285
Genishi, C., 346, 374
Gerrity, P.S., 264, 288
Gershowitz, M., 266, 286
Gibes, R., 272, 284
Gibson, W.C., 193, 224
Giddan, J., 185
Gillan, L.O., 383, 404
Gillberg, C., 334, 342
Gillespie, B.S., 386, 393, 404
Gittelman-Klein, R., 303, 312
Glascoe, F.P., 86, 97
Glasgow, R.E., 44, 45, 46, 50
Glennon, B., 358, 375
Gluck, D.S., 294, 314
Golden, G.G., 197, 220, 225, 300, 315
Goldenberg, D., 168, 185
Goldman, R., 206, 224
Goldsmith, H.H., 3, 10
Goldstein, H., 237, 260
Good, T., 348, 374
Goodenough, F.L., 383, 406
Goodglass, H., 206, 224
Goodwin, T., 142, 166
Goolsby, E., 109, 126
Gordon, B.N., 102, 106, 109, 112, 113, 116, 120, 125, 126
Gordon, I., 151, 163
Gordon, J.S., 48, 54
Gordon, M., 303, 315
Gottfried, A., 152, 163
Gottfried, A.W., 88, 98
Goudsmit, J., 270, 285
Gould, J., 321, 344
Goyette, C.H., 94, 98, 118, 125, 296, 298, 315, 360, 375
Graham, P., 94, 99, 108, 125
Graham, P.J., 106, 126
Grant, I., 272, 286
Green, J.A., 89, 100
Green, M., 277, 286
Greenspan, S., 268, 286
Greenspan, S.I., 274, 286
Greenwood, C.R., 358, 377
Greer, S.W., 86, 97

Griest, D.L., 45, 46, 51, 53
Griffiths, R., 242, 260, 280, 286
Grisso, T., 422, 425
Gross, A.M., 120, 125, 299, 315
Grossman, H.J., 168, 181, 185
Grossman, L., 76, 87, 99
Grost, A., 387, 405
Grove, D.C., 297, 316
Gruen, G., 129, 149, 151, 152, 166
Guerin, D., 88, 98
Guerney, B.G., 43, 52
Guidubaldi, J., 87, 99, 363, 376
Guignard, F., 195, 224
Guthrie, D., 332, 333, 342, 343
Gutkin, T.B., 30, 53, 347, 348, 376, 412, 413, 424
Guzzetta, F., 271, 286
Gyurke, J., 5; 6, 10, 413, 424
Gyurke, J.S., 178, 185
Hack, M., 278, 287
Hagen, E.P., 64, 72, 173, 186, 202, 206, 226, 256, 261, 281, 289, 330, 344, 356, 377, 406
Haggerty, R., 140, 163
Haines, J., 386, 393, 404
Hall, E.G., 393, 405
Hamilton, P.A., 271, 288
Hammill, D.D., 92, 94, 98, 180, 185, 186, 206, 224
Hanson, I., 392, 405
Hanson, M., 76, 99
Hanson, R., 151, 613
Harder, D.W., 44, 51
Hardy, W.G., 193, 224
Harig, P.T., 108, 126
Harkins, D.E., 389, 405
Harper, D.C., 89, 98
Harris, L.H., 142, 164
Hart, H., 106, 125
Harter, S., 269, 286
Hartnett, S.A., 268, 286
Hartsough, C.S., 293, 315
Hartup, W.W., 112, 125
Hastings, J., 131, 161
Hathaway, S.R., 33, 51
Hatwell, Y., 240, 241, 260
Hauser, S.L., 193, 224
Hauser-Cram, P., 1, 3, 10
Hawk, B., 112, 116, 120, 126
Hawthorne, L.W., 389, 405, 406
Hayden, T., 384, 405
Hayes, F.B., 390, 405
Hayes, S.C., 292, 318
Haywood, H.C., 23, 26, 27, 28

Hebel, J.R., 88, 89, 99
Hebert, E., 255, 256, 260
Hechtman, L., 293, 307, 317
Hedrick, D.L., 207, 224, 333, 342
Heller, K., 138, 165
Helm, J.M., 266, 286
Henderson, R., 149, 150, 151, 153, 163
Henderson, S., 134, 146, 164
Hendricks-Munoz, K.D., 278, 286
Herbert, E.W., 39, 51
Herjaniz, B., 43, 53
Herman, J.L., 240, 261
Hersen, M., 101, 112, 116, 126
Hertzig, M.E., 295, 317
Hesselink, J.R., 272, 286
Hetherington, E.M., 39, 43, 44, 45, 47, 51
Hilgard, J.R., 264, 286
Hill, B.K., 181, 184, 363, 374
Hillam, S.M., 47, 54
Hingst, A.G., 112, 125
Hiskey, M., 330, 342
Hiskey, M.S., 206, 224
Hoekelman, R., 249, 259, 261
Hogarty, P., 150, 151, 164
Holden, E.W., 43, 54, 238, 246, 261
Holland, C.J., 120, 125
Hollingworth, L.S., 403, 405
Holly, L., 138, 166
Holm, V.A., 334, 342
Holmes, D.L., 270, 278, 286
Holmes, T.H., 140, 164
Honzik, M.P., 22, 27
Hooker, D., 15, 27
Hooper, S., 358, 359, 375
Hooper, S.R., 263, 282, 286, 289
Hope, P.L., 271, 288
Horn, D., 255, 260
Horn, J.L., 281, 285
Horn, W.F., 296, 315
Horowitz, F.D., 280, 286, 383, 405
Horrobin, J., 397, 404
House, A.E., 304, 317
Howell, C.T., 359, 373
Hresko, W.P., 92, 98, 185
Huba, G., 146, 164
Huber, C., 131, 165
Hubert, N.C., 295, 315
Hudsen, D., 358, 377
Hughey, J.B., 48, 54
Hunker, C., 201, 223
Hunt, J., 128, 149, 152, 153, 164, 166

Hunt, J.McV., 277, 281, 286, 289
Huot, D., 270, 287
Hurt, M., 149, 150, 151, 153, 163
Hussey, M., 142, 166
Hynd, G.W., 12, 16, 17, 27
Iacoviello, J.M., 226
Ialongo, N., 296, 315
Ilg, F.L., 386, 393, 404
Ingersoll, B., 309, 315
Ingle, M., 142, 166
Inglis, S., 149, 152, 166
Ingram, D., 194, 225
Ingram, T.T.S., 193, 224
Inui, T.S., 346, 375
Ireton, H., 88, 89, 98, 99, 116, 125, 185, 282, 286
Ireton, H.R., 363, 375
Ismond, D.R., 303, 316
Ivey, A.E., 354, 355, 376
Jackson, N.E., 389, 390, 391, 393, 398, 405, 406
Jacob, R.G., 303, 315
Jacob, T., 120, 121, 125
Jacobson, L., 421, 425
Jaeggi, A., 195, 224
James, D.S., 47, 54
James, S.A., 268, 286
Jamner, A.H., 397, 406
Jarosinski, P., 270, 272, 288
Jastak, J.R., 399, 405
Jastak, S., 399, 405
Jay, S., 263, 289
Jeffries, V., 47, 53, 136, 165
Jenkins, S., 106, 125
Jenkins, V., 133, 134, 157, 163
Jensen, D.W., 383, 404
Jensen, E.W., 268, 286
Jensen, L.C., 35, 51
Jeremy, R.J., 348, 374
Johnson, J.H., 144, 165
Johnson, L.J., 384, 405
Johnson, M., 238, 261, 277, 289
Johnson, M.B., 392, 407
Johnson, M.R., 263, 265, 266, 286, 287
Johnson, S.B., 120, 126
Johnson, S.M., 39, 44, 45, 46, 50, 51, 52
Johnston, C., 293, 296, 315
Johnston, N., 421, 424
Jones, J.D., 186
Jones, M.D., 270, 284
Justice, B., 140, 164
Kagan, J., 149, 151, 164, 302, 315
Kahn, H., 238, 260

Kalish, B.I., 329, 332, 343, 360, 376
Kamhi, A., 194, 224
Kamphaus, R.W., 63, 68, 72, 178, 179, 180, 185
Kang, R.R., 272, 288
Kanner, L., 321, 342
Kanoy, K., 102, 106, 109, 112, 126
Kaplan, E., 206, 224
Kappelman, M., 76, 87, 99
Karlsson, J., 293, 296, 302, 304, 313, 317
Karnes, F.A., 389, 401, 405
Karnes, M.B., 384, 405
Kaufman, A.S., 14, 27, 56, 60, 64, 72, 172, 173, 178, 185, 206, 224, 256, 260, 281, 287, 330, 342, 368, 375, 389, 405
Kaufman, N.L., 56, 60, 64, 72, 172, 173, 178, 185, 206, 224, 256, 260, 281, 287, 330, 342K, 368, 375, 389, 405
Kaufman, S.H., 257, 259
Kavanagh, J.F., 201, 224
Kaye, J.H., 356, 373
Kazdin, A.E., 102, 125, 347, 375
Kazuk, E., 22, 27, 173, 185, 393, 405
Keane, W., 151, 163
Keeves, J., 153, 164
Keller, H.R., 356, 357, 375
Kelley, T.L., 383, 406
Kelso, J., 46, 52
Kendall, P.C., 49, 50, 52, 292, 315
Kennedy, C.J., 272, 286
Kenny, T.J., 76, 78, 87, 88, 89, 97, 99
Kent, R.N., 46, 52
Keogh, B.K., 421, 424
Kephart, N.C., 180, 186, 206, 225
Kerby, M.L., 93, 99
Kerr, B.A., 401, 405
Kertesz, A., 194, 224
Kessler, M.D., 297, 314
Keyser, D.J., 68, 72
Kidd, K.K., 44, 52
Kincaid, D., 393, 405
King, H.R., 112, 124
Kinsbourne, M., 195, 226, 319, 343
Kirk, S.A., 203, 206, 224
Kirk, W.D., 203, 206, 224
Kitchen, W.H., 277, 278, 287
Klee, S.H., 302, 315

Klein, D., 303, 312
Klein, N., 278, 287
Kleinknecht, C., 270, 287
Kline, R.B., 361, 375
Klinedinst, J.E., 119, 127, 201, 226, 360, 377
Klotz, M.L., 373, 377
Knobloch, H., 21, 27, 88, 99, 185, 281, 287
Knoblock, P., 347, 376
Knoff, H.M., 353, 354, 355, 375
Knorring, A.L., 108, 125
Kocher, F., 195, 224
Koenigsberger, M.R., 270, 285
Kogan, N., 390, 406
Kohlberg, L., 109, 125
Kokes, R.F., 44, 51
Kolata, G., 396, 405
Koppitz, E.M., 42, 52
Korn, S., 295, 317
Korpela, J.W., 102, 125
Kozloff, M.A., 329, 342
Kramer, J., 292, 316
Krasnoff, L., 146, 162
Krauss, M.W., 3, 10
Kriegsman, E., 149, 152, 166
Krug, D.A., 329, 332, 342
LaBuda, M.C., 23, 27
Lachar, D., 119, 127, 201, 226, 360, 361, 374, 375, 377
LaCrosse, J., 109, 125
LaFave, W., 416, 417, 424
Laing, J., 153, 164
Lamb, M.E., 3, 10
Lambert, N.M., 185, 256, 260, 293, 315
Landau, S., 302, 303, 316
Langley, M.B., 185
Lann, I.S., 105, 116, 126
Lansing, M., 328, 338, 343, 344
Lansing, M.D., 325, 344
Lansky, L.L., 268, 287
Lansky, S.B., 268, 287
Lapouse, R., 109, 125
Laprade, K., 94, 100, 298, 317
Lauria, M.M., 272, 282, 287, 289
Lavee, Y., 157, 165
Lawhon, G., 272, 284
Lazarus, P.J., 19, 28
Lazarus, R., 263, 285
Lazarus, R.S., 265, 287, 348, 375
League, R., 207, 223, 278, 285
Leahy, A.M., 383, 404
LeBaron, S., 264, 286
LeBrun, Y., 193, 224

Leet, H.E., 157, 159, 163, 164
Legouri, S., 237, 240, 241, 242, 243, 248, 260
Lehr, E., 262, 275, 287
Lehr, S., 240, 261
Lehtinen, L.E., 290, 317
Leigh, J.L., 366, 376
Leiter, R.G., 171, 185, 253, 260, 330, 343
Leland, H., 243, 248, 260
Leonard, A., 297, 316
Leonard, L.B., 194, 224
Lerner, J., 168, 185
Lerner, J.A., 346, 375
Lerner, R., 129, 152, 164
Lerner, R.M., 49, 50, 52
Lester, B.M., 280, 284
Levin, H., 47, 53
Levine, H.M., 138, 165
Levine, J.M., 349, 375
Levine, M., 76, 87, 99
Levine, S., 359, 375
Levitt, E., 241, 260
Levitt, M., 241, 260
Lewis, J.F., 186
Lewis, M., 359, 375
Liddell, T.N., 88, 98
Lidz, C.S., 56, 59, 72
Lieberman, M.A., 140, 165
Lifschitz, M.H., 87, 99
Lim, S.B., 271, 289
Lima, M., 383, 406
Limber, S., 422, 424
Lindsey, A.M., 136, 164
Linn, N., 135, 140, 162
Liptak, G., 255, 256, 260
Lipton, M., 270, 288
Lissenden, J.V., 277, 278, 287
List, M.A., 268, 287
Livesay, R.H., 383, 404
Lobitz, C.W., 39, 52
Lobitz, G.R., 44, 45, 51
Lockman, L.A., 270, 288
Loda, F.A., 47, 53, 136, 165
Loehlin, J.C., 24, 27
Lomonaco, S., 240, 261
Loney, J., 298, 302, 303, 315, 316
Lorch, E., 255, 260
Lorch, R., Jr., 255, 260
Lord, C., 321, 323, 333, 342, 344
Lorge, I., 171, 183, 184
Lotter, V., 329, 343
Lowell, E., 150, 164
Lucas, A.R., 43, 53
Ludlow, C., 195, 225
Lyman, H., 64, 66, 72
Lynch, G., 292, 317

Lyon, M.A., 173, 178, 185
Maccoby, E.E., 38, 39, 41, 47, 52, 53
MacDonald, J.D., 186
MacPhee, D., 129, 165
Magnusson, D., 40, 52, 108, 125
Magrab, P.H., 262, 275, 287
Maha, M., 270, 272, 288
Maisto, A.A., German, M.L., 280, 287
Majer, L., 76, 87, 99
Maker, C.J., 386, 407
Malone, A., 88, 99
Malone, A.F., 281, 287
Maquard, M., 195, 224
Marcus, J., 348, 374
Marcus, L.M., 320, 322, 325, 326, 329, 338, 343, 344
Mardell-Czudnowski, C., 168, 185
Marjoribanks, K., 149, 150, 152, 153, 164
Markwardt, F.C., Jr., 399, 404
Marland, S., 383, 385, 386, 405
Marquardt, R.G., 401, 405
Marshall, H., 383, 404, 406
Marti-Henneberg, C., 270, 287
Martin, B., 39, 44, 45, 51, 265, 287
Martin, R.P., 352, 353, 355, 358, 359, 360, 375, 390, 405, 414, 424
Martin, S.L., 102, 119, 125
Maschka, P., 79, 85, 98
Mash, E., 119, 125
Mash, E.J., 121, 126, 295, 304, 306, 315
Maslow, A.H., 40, 52
Mason, R., 349, 376
Masters, J.C., 48, 52
Matheny, A.P., Jr., 182, 186
Mathieson, A., 397, 405
Mattis, S., 197, 220, 225
Mattison, R.E., 210, 223
Mattsson, A., 263, 282, 287
Maudaus, G., 131, 161
Mauer, S.M., 270, 288
Maxfield, K., 243, 260
Mayer, G.R., 356, 377
McAnulty, G., 272, 284
McAskie, M., 23, 27
McCall, R., 150, 151, 164
McCallum, R.S., 178, 186, 389, 390, 404, 405
McCarney, S.B., 366, 376
McCarthy, D., 64, 72, 89, 99, 171, 173, 186, 202, 206, 225, 242, 260, 281, 287, 329, 343, 390, 406

NAMES INDEX

McCarthy, J.J., 203, 206, 224
McCartney, K., 24, 28
McClelland, D., 150, 164
McClenaghan, B., 180, 186
McCord, J., 45, 52
McCord, W., 45, 52
McCubbin, H.I., 142, 157, 164, 263, 287, 361, 376
McCutchan, J.A., 272, 286
McDevitt, S.C., 295, 314, 360, 376
McGinnis, M.A., 193, 195, 225
McHenry, L.C., 193, 225
McKinley, J.C., 33, 51
McLanahan, S., 47, 52
McMahon, R., 301, 304, 309, 314
McMahon, R.J., 46, 51
McMillan, C., 269, 286
McMillan, C.W., 272, 289
McNamee, J., 421, 424
McNemar, Q., 383, 406
Meador, A.E., 413, 424
Mecham, M.J., 186
Meckstroth, E.A., 384, 386, 396, 399, 400, 401, 402, 403, 406
Meisels, S.J., 3, 4, 10
Mellits, D., 194, 226
Melton, G.B., 422, 423, 424
Mendez, O., 111, 126
Menkes, J., 238, 257, 260
Mercer, J.R., 186
Merrill, M.A., 91, 100, 242, 261, 281, 288, 330, 344, 388, 406
Mertens, R., 238, 261
Mertens, R.A., 8, 10
Mesibov, G., 109, 126
Mesibov, G.B., 319, 321, 334, 336, 343
Meyer, C., 88, 98
Meyer, M.P., 269, 287
Michael, A.F., 270, 288
Milich, R., 292, 302, 303, 304, 315, 316
Milich, R.S., 298, 315
Miller, J.F., 207, 225
Miller, L.C., 297, 316, 360, 376
Mills, B., 149, 152, 166
Minde, K., 280, 287
Minde, R., 280, 287
Minuchin, S., 43, 52
Mirsky, A.F., 301, 316
Mitchell, R., 46, 52
Mitchell, S.K., 272, 288
Monk, M.A., 109, 125
Monson, L., 264, 288

Montague, J., 303, 316
Montalvo, B., 43, 52
Moore, A.H., 383, 406
Moore, D.R., 47, 52
Moore, T., 150, 152, 164
Moorhead, W., 238, 260
Moos, B.S., 361, 376
Moos, R., 148, 164
Moos, R.H., 43, 52, 268, 287, 361, 376
Morehead, D.M., 194, 225
Moreland, K.M., 389, 406
Morgan, S.B., 335, 343
Morganstern, G., 302, 313
Morganstern, K.P., 299, 316
Morley, M.E., 193, 194, 225
Morris, S., 201, 225
Moscovitch, M., 195, 226
Moss, H., 270, 272, 287, 288
Mullen, E.M., 281, 287
Murphy, H.A., 293, 315
Murphy, J., 296, 302, 304, 313
Murphy, R.F., 270, 272, 288
Murray, D.J., 185
Murray, H., 153, 164
Murray, S., 196, 226
Mussen, P., 112, 126
Mutton, D.E., 193
Myklebust, H.R., 193, 195, 225
Nagel, R.J., 409, 424
Naglieri, J.A., 389, 406
Nannis, E., 272, 287
Nash, K.B., 269, 286
Nathanson, M., 310, 316
Nation, J.E., 192, 194, 195, 198, 223, 225, 226
Naughton, P., 271, 285
Needleman, J., 201, 225
Nelson, C.F., 302, 317
Nelson, J., 153, 162
Nelson, K.B., 200, 225
Nelson, M.N., 271, 285
Nevins, T.E., 270, 288
Newborg, J., 87, 99, 186, 363, 376, 396, 406
Newby, R., 296, 298, 303, 304, 308, 313
Newcomb, M., 146, 164
Newcomer, P.L., 186
Newman, B.M., 39, 52
Newman, P.R., 39, 52
Nihira, K., 243, 248, 260
Nitko, A., 69, 70, 72
Norbeck, J.E., 136, 164
Norbeck, J.S., 136, 146, 164
Norcross, J.C., 390, 404
Novick, B.E., 270, 289
Nusinoff-Lehrman, S., 270, 272, 288

Nuttall, E.V., 354, 355, 376
Oberklaid, F., 76, 99
O'Brien, M., 383, 405
Obrzut, J.E., 12, 27, 359, 376
Oden, M.H., 383, 404, 406
O'Donnell, K., 271, 285
Offord, D.R., 43, 52
O'Leary, K.D., 45, 46, 52, 53, 120, 126, 303, 315
Oleske, J.M., 270, 285
Oliver, J.E., 44, 52
Ollendick, T.H., 101, 112, 116, 126, 413, 424
Olley, J.G., 323, 343
Olness, K., 264, 286
Olson, D.H., 156, 157, 165, 268, 287, 362, 363, 376
Oltman, P., 241, 261
Oltmanns, T.F., 45, 46, 52
Olzey, F.F., 359, 375
O'Neill, J., 173, 186
O'Quinn, A.N., 201, 226
Orgill, A.A., 271, 289
Oritt, E.J., 136, 165
Ornitz, E.M., 333, 343
Orton, S.T., 193, 225
Orvaschel, H., 44, 52
Osborn, K.N., 242, 259
O'Tuama, L., 296, 317
Owen, F.W., 201, 225
Packard, T., 297, 316
Page, K.A., 270, 287
Paget, K.D., 56, 57, 58, 59, 60, 61, 62, 72, 409, 424
Palfrey, J., 76, 99
Palmer, D.J., 87, 99
Palmer, J.O., 29, 53, 359, 376
Paparella, C., 256, 261
Parcel, G.S., 269, 287
Parke, R., 152, 165
Parmelee, A.H., 278, 288
Pasamanick, B., 21, 27
Pascoe, J.M., 47, 53, 136, 165
Pasternak, J.F., 270, 278, 286
Pastor, D., 144, 163
Patterson, G.R., 41, 53, 121, 126, 304, 316
Patterson, J.M., 142, 157, 164, 263, 287, 361, 376
Paul, R., 321, 342
Paul, R.E., 412, 424
Paul, S.C., 136, 165
Pearl, D., 346, 374
Pearlin, L.I., 140, 165
Pearson, L.S., 185
Pederson, F., 150, 151, 152, 154, 166
Peed, S., 112, 124
Pelham, W.E., 293, 315, 316

Peloquin, L.J., 246, 260
Peradotto, D., 296, 315
Perigo-Moore, L., 397, 406
Perkins, P., 44, 51
Perlman, J.M., 271, 286
Perlman, T., 293, 317
Perrin, E.C., 264, 288
Peters, J.E., 290, 314
Peters, K.G., 291, 292, 314
Peters-Martin, P., 295, 315
Peterson, D.R., 360, 376
Petrila, J., 422, 424
Philips, B., 133, 162
Philips, I., 181, 186
Philips, W., 302, 315
Phillips, J., 138, 166
Phillips, S., 44, 45, 46, 50
Piaget, J., 31, 53
Piazza, C., 256, 261
Piercy, M., 194, 226
Piirto, J.N., 390, 406
Pinkerton, P., 263, 288
Pizzo, P.A., 270, 272, 288
Pless, I.B., 263, 288
Plewis, I., 255, 259
Plomin, R., 23, 24, 27
Pollard, S., 296, 302, 304, 313, 316
Polster, R.A., 309, 314
Pond, R.E., 187
Poplack, D., 272, 287
Poplack, D.G., 270, 272, 288
Popovich, S., 296, 315
Porrino, L.J., 303, 316
Porter, B.P., 45, 53
Portner, J., 156, 157, 165
Poythress, N.G., 422, 424
Prasse, D.P., 390, 404
Prather, E.M., 207, 224, 333, 342
Prior, M., 297, 316
Procidano, M.E., 138, 165
Provence, S., 349, 374
Prutting, C., 333, 344
Pryzwansky, W.B., 411, 424
Quay, H.C., 360, 376
Radin, N., 153, 165
Rahe, R.H., 140, 164
Ramey, C., 129, 165
Ramey, C.T., 24, 28
Rancurello, M., 94, 98
Rapin, I., 193, 194, 195, 196, 197, 198, 220, 224, 225
Rapoport, J.L., 303, 316
Rappoport, L., 32, 33, 34, 35, 38, 53
Rapport, M.D., 308, 316
Rau, L., 38, 53
Raubenheimer, A.S., 383, 406

Raven, J., 256, 260
Raven, J.C., 256, 260, 392, 406
Ray, R.S., 121, 126
Reardon, K., 88, 89, 97
Redding-Lallinger, R., 269, 286
Reece, H.W., 417, 424
Reich, J.N., 270, 278, 286
Reichler, R.J., 319, 325, 326, 328, 331, 343, 344
Reid, D.K., 92, 98, 185
Reid, J.B., 121, 126
Reid, J.F., 193, 224
Reis, J., 47, 53
Reitan, R.M., 282, 288
Renner, B., 325, 331, 344
Reschly, D.J., 181, 186
Rescorla, L.A., 349, 376
Revell, G., 255, 256, 260
Reynell, J., 92, 99, 242, 261
Reynell, J.K., 333, 343
Reynolds, C.R., 30, 31, 53, 178, 179, 180, 185, 347, 348, 361, 376, 388, 389, 406, 412, 413, 424
Reynolds, E.O.R., 271, 288
Reynolds, W.M., 91, 99
Rezmierski, V.E., 347, 376
Rhodes, L., 280, 288
Riccuiti, H., 128, 165
Richardson, S.A., 24, 27
Richman, D.D., 272, 286
Richmond, N., 94, 99, 106, 126
Rickards, A.L., 277, 278, 287
Ricks, D., 109, 125
Ricks, D.N., 321, 343
Ridberg, E.H., 45, 51
Riedel, S., 135, 138, 166
Riessman, C.K., 268, 288
Riley, C.M., 93, 99
Risenberg, H., 88, 99
Risucci, D., 226
Risucci, D.A., 196, 198, 217, 225, 226
Ritvo, E.R., 332, 342
Roach, E.G., 180, 186, 206, 225
Robert-Guroff, M., 270, 285
Roberts, M., 303, 304, 316
Roberts, R.D., 290, 316
Robertson, J.A., 416, 417, 424
Robins, L.N., 43, 53
Robinson, E.A., 94, 99, 118, 121, 124, 126, 297, 314, 304, 316, 360, 376
Robinson, H.B., 23, 27, 389, 391, 398, 406
Robinson, N.M., 23, 27
Rock, S., 151, 152, 153, 162
Rockowitz, R., 249, 259, 261

Rodgers, W., 47, 51
Roedell, W.C., 388, 391, 398, 399, 406
Rogers, S.J., 413, 414, 424, 425
Rogers, T.R., 45, 53
Roghmann, K.J., 263, 288
Rohner, R., 151, 165
Rolf, J.E., 108, 126
Rosati-Skertich, C., 271, 285
Rosenbaum, A., 241, 260
Rosenberg D., 144, 163
Rosenblad, C., 303, 315
Rosenthal, N., 421, 425
Rosman, B.L., 43, 52, 302, 315
Rosman, P., 193, 224
Ross, A.W., 94, 99, 112, 118, 124, 126, 269, 285, 297, 314, 360, 376
Ross, D.M., 264, 288, 292, 293, 295, 296, 307, 308, 316
Ross, S.A., 264, 288, 292, 293, 295, 296, 307, 308, 316
Rossetti, L.M., 279, 280, 288
Rosvold, H.E., 301, 316
Roth, S., 195, 224
Rotundo, A., 270, 288
Routh, D., 131, 165
Routh, D.K., 102, 106, 109, 111, 112, 126, 263, 288, 290, 297, 303, 316, 317
Rowan, A.J., 197, 220, 225
Rubenstein, A., 270, 289
Rubenstein, J., 150, 151, 152, 154, 166
Rubin, M., 270, 272, 288
Ruch, G.M., 383, 406
Rudel, R.G., 293, 314
Ruff, H.A., 270, 289
Russell, C.S., 362, 376
Ruttenberg, B.A., 329, 332, 343, 360, 376
Rutter, M., 45, 48, 53, 94, 99, 101, 105, 109, 112, 116, 120, 126, 321, 323, 329, 342, 343
Ryan, M.M., 277, 278, 287
Sabatino, D.A., 43, 53
Sack, W.H., 349, 376
Safer, D.J., 293, 317
Salkind, N.J., 302, 317
Sameroff, A., 129, 165
Sameroff, A.J., 4, 10, 78, 99
Sandberg, B.R., 169, 184, 345, 374
Sandberg, D., 414, 423
Sandler, I.N., 43, 53
Sanford, A., 248, 261
Sanford, A.R., 186

NAMES INDEX 469

Sarason, B.R., 138, 165
Sarason, I., 301, 316
Sarason, I.G., 138, 144, 165
Sarason, S., 55, 57, 58, 72
Satir, V., 45, 53
Satterfield, J.H., 293, 314
Sattler, J.M., 58, 60, 61, 62, 64, 72, 168, 169, 173, 178, 181, 183, 186, 202, 206, 226, 256, 261, 263, 281, 288, 289, 330, 344, 387, 388, 389, 390, 391, 398, 406, 413, 414, 425
Saylor, C.F., 89, 99
Saylor, W., 76, 87, 99
Scanlon, J.W., 16, 27
Scarr, S., 23, 24, 28
Scarr-Salapatek, S., 23, 27
Sceery, W., 303, 316
Schaefer, E., 151, 161
Schaffer, B., 321, 323, 333, 344
Scharf, L., 241, 261
Schellenbach, C.J., 5, 10
Schleifer, M., 292, 296, 314
Schmid, E., 195, 224
Schneider, E.A., 87, 99
Schopler, E., 319, 321, 323, 325, 326, 328, 331, 333, 334, 336, 338, 343, 344
Schroeder, C., 252, 254, 259
Schroeder, C.S., 102, 106, 109, 111, 112, 113, 116, 120, 125, 126, 297, 303, 316, 317
Schroth, P., 332, 342
Schuler, A., 321, 342
Schulman, J.L., 263, 289
Schumer, F., 43, 52
Scott, A., 416, 417, 424
Sears, R.R., 38, 47, 53
Seat, P.D., 119, 127, 201, 226, 360, 377
Secord, W., 206, 226
Self, P.A., 280, 286
Semel, E.M., 206, 226
Sexton, M.J., 88, 89, 99
Shackelford, G.O., 271, 286
Shaffer, D., 201, 226
Shankaran, S., 88, 90, 282, 285
Shapiro, H., 79, 85, 98
Sharer, L.E., 270, 285
Shaw, C.R., 43, 53
Shaw, D.A., 121, 126
Shaywitz, B.A., 397, 406
Shaywitz, S.E., 397, 406
Shea, V., 321, 335, 344
Shearer, M., 178, 184
Shearer, M.S., 88, 89, 97, 178, 184, 363, 374

Shellhaas, M., 243, 248, 260
Sheppard, J.J., 201, 226
Sherard, E.S., Jr., 21, 27
Sheslow, D., 390, 404
Shigley, R.H., 319, 336, 343
Shonkoff, J., 1, 10
Shonkoff, J.P., 3, 10
Short, A.B., 329, 344
Shrout, P., 141, 163
Siegel, J.M., 144, 165
Siegel, L., 279, 288
Siegel, L.S., 280, 288
Sigman, M., 278, 288
Sillen, J., 111, 126
Silver, L.B., 308, 317
Simeonsson, R.J., 263, 264, 280, 288
Simner, M.L., 182, 186
Sines, J., 153, 164
Singer, L., 254, 260
Sinks, L.B., 268, 287
Sipowicz, R.R., 263, 289
Skeels, H., 149, 165
Skeels, H.M., 15, 28
Skinner, N., 393, 405
Slater, B.R., 184
Sleator, E.K., 94, 100, 298, 301, 317
Slenkovich, J.E., 348, 376
Sloan, W., 168, 186
Slobogin, C., 422, 424
Slocumb, P.R., 173, 186
Slosson, R.L., 91, 94, 100, 390, 406
Smith, D.K., 173, 178, 185
Smith, K., 46, 51
Smith, R., 133, 166
Smith, R.D., 75, 76, 80, 87, 100
Snow, J., 358, 359, 375
Snyder, K., 157, 163
Soltz, V., 402, 404
Sparrow, S.S., 116, 126, 181, 186, 201, 226, 248, 261, 269, 288, 325, 331, 344, 363, 376
Spector, S., 88, 98, 282, 285
Spector, S.A., 272, 286
Speer, S.K., 389, 405, 406
Spencer, J.E., 88, 98
Sprague, R.L., 94, 100, 296, 298, 309, 317, 318
Sprenkle, D.H., 362, 376
Sroufe, A., 151, 163
Sroufe, L.A., 48, 53
Stabler, B., 263, 266, 285, 286
Stambaugh, E.E., 304, 317
Stangler, S., 131, 165
Stanovich, K.E., 23, 28
Stark, J., 185

Stark, R., 194, 226
Stayton, D.J., 268, 284
Steffan, J.E., 88, 98
Stein, R.E.K., 268, 288
Steinberg, L., 152, 165
Steiner, V.G., 187
Stenberg, C., 3, 10
Stephens, E., 75, 97
Stevens, F., 88, 99, 281, 287
Stevenson, J., 94, 99
Stevenson, J.E., 106, 126
Stewart, A.L., 271, 288
Stewart, D., 135, 138, 166
Stewart, M.A., 46, 52, 293, 317
Stier, D.M., 349, 377
Still, G.F., 290, 292, 317
Stillman, R., 248, 261
Stock, J.R., 87, 99, 186, 363, 376, 396, 406
Stolberg, A., 45, 51
Stoner, G., 308, 316
Stouwie, R., 45, 51
Strauss, A.A., 193, 226, 290, 317
Strichart, S.S., 19, 28
Stringfield, S., 106, 119, 124, 358, 363, 374
Sturner, R.A., 89, 100
Stutsman, R., 183, 186, 329, 344
Sullivan, E.B., 383, 406
Sulzer-Azaroff, B., 356, 377
Svinicki, J., 87, 99, 363, 376
Swarbrick, L., 303, 316
Swearingen, E., 142, 159, 165
Sweetland, R.C., 68, 72
Swift, M., 360, 366, 377
Switzky, H.N., 23, 26, 27, 28
Szego, E., 282, 285
Szumowski, E.K., 294, 296, 313, 314
Tallal, P., 186, 194, 226
Tancer, M., 76, 80, 98
Tardy, C., 135, 166
Tarver-Behring, S., 293, 317
Taylor, C.A., 264, 289
Taylor, R.L., 173, 186
Tedesco, L., 128, 149, 162
Telzrow, C.F., 167, 173, 178, 186
Telzrow, R.W., 272, 288
Tennenbaum, D.L., 120, 121, 125
Terdal, L., 304, 315
Terdal, L.G., 121, 126
Terman, L.M., 91, 100, 242, 261, 281, 288, 330, 344, 383, 388, 404, 406
Thach, B.T., 293, 317

Tharinger, D., 185, 256, 260
Thomas, A., 40, 50, 106, 109, 111, 124, 126, 295, 317
Thomas, P.D., 89, 100
Thompson, R.J., Jr., 201, 226
Thomson, B., 138, 166
Thorndike, R.L., 21, 28, 64, 72, 173, 186, 202, 206, 226, 256, 261, 281, 289, 330, 344, 356, 377, 388, 406
Thwing, E., 88, 89, 98, 99, 116, 125, 185, 282, 286
Thwing, E.J., 363, 375
Tizard, J., 112, 126
Tobin, A.R., 207, 224, 333, 342
Todd, N.M., 358, 377
Tolan, S.S., 384, 386, 396, 399, 400, 401, 402, 403, 406
Toler, S., 76, 87, 99
Tomkins, S.S., 30, 53
Tonge, W.L., 47, 54
Torgesen, J.K., 169, 186
Torrance, E.P., 390, 406
Tortolani, B.C., 196, 226
Towle, V.R., 397, 406
Tramontana, M.G., 263, 289
Trickett, E., 46, 52
Trites, R.L., 94, 100, 292, 293, 298, 317
Trivette, C., 136, 138, 157, 163, 166
Trivette, C.M., 133, 134, 157, 163
Trohanis, P., 1, 4, 10
Tronick, E., 280, 284
Troutman, A.C., 356, 373
Trupin, E.W., 346, 375
Tryon, W.W., 303, 317
Tryphonas, H., 293, 317
Tsai, L.Y., 321, 342
Tucker, S., 308, 316
Tulkin, S., 151, 166
Tuma, A.J., 105, 116, 126
Tuma, J., 263, 289
Turner, A., 255, 261
Tyler, D., 252, 254, 259
Ullman, D.G., 290, 292, 296, 297, 313, 317
Ullman, R.K., 94, 100, 298, 301, 317
Ulrey, G., 413, 425
Ulrich, R.F., 94, 98, 118, 125, 296, 298, 315, 360, 375
Ultmann, M.H., 270, 289
Upshur, C.C., 3, 10
Uzgiris, I., 149, 166
Uzgiris, I.C., 281, 289

Van Doornick, W.J., 88, 98
Vance S.D., 157, 159, 163
Vance, B., 256, 261
Varni, J.W., 263, 289
Vaux, A., 135, 138, 166
Vernon, D.T.A., 263, 289
Vohr, B.R., 278, 289
Volkmar, F.R., 321, 342
Volkmar, J.R., 349, 377
Volpe, J.J., 271, 286
Volpe, S., 271, 286
Vygotsky, L., 152, 166
Wachs, T., 129, 149, 150, 151, 152, 154, 166
Wachs, T.D., 295, 315
Wahler, R.G., 48, 50, 54, 112, 127, 304, 317
Wallach, M.A., 390, 406
Wallander, J.L., 263, 289
Walsh, M.E., 264, 285
Walter, S.D., 421, 424
Walters, R.H., 39, 50
Walton, J.P., 278, 286
Ward, E.M., 296, 316
Waters, E., Wall, S., 41, 50
Watson, L., 322, 344
Watson, L.R., 321, 323, 333, 344
Watts, J., 150, 153, 166
Weatherman, R.F., 181, 184, 363, 374
Weaver, S.J., 7, 10, 116, 127, 263, 289, 347, 356, 362, 372, 377
Webb, J.T., 384, 386, 389, 396, 399, 400, 401, 402, 403, 405, 406
Webb, K., 196, 226
Webster-Stratton, C., 48, 54, 297, 317
Wechsler, D., 23, 28, 42, 54, 64, 71, 72, 81, 90, 100, 173, 187, 202, 206, 226, 256, 261, 302, 317, 330, 344, 368, 377, 388, 389, 407
Wedemeyer, N., 47, 52
Weeldreyer, J., 157, 163
Weinberg, R.A., 23, 28
Weintraub, M., 17, 21, 27
Weintraub, S., 206, 224
Weiss, B., 373, 377
Weiss, G., 290, 292, 293, 296, 307, 314, 317, 318
Weiss, J.B., 16, 27
Weissman, M., 44, 52
Weisz, J., 358, 375
Weisz, J.R., 373, 377
Weithorn, L.A., 422, 425

Wells, K.C., 46, 51
Wells, R.J., 269, 272, 282, 286, 287, 289
Wenar, C., 329, 332, 343, 360, 376
Wender, P.H., 290, 318
Werner, E., 20, 28, 129, 133, 166
Werry, J., 290, 318
Werry, J.S., 292, 296, 309, 318
West, P., 43, 53
Wetherby, A., 333, 344
Wheeler, F., 217, 226
White, B., 150, 153, 166
White, S., 89, 100
Whitehead, L., 46, 54
Whitmore, J.R., 384, 386, 407
Whitmore, K., 112, 126
Whitt, J.K., 262, 263, 264, 265, 269, 272, 282, 285, 286, 287, 289
Wiig, E.H., 206, 226
Wilde, W. (1853), 193, 226
Wilhelm, C., 238, 261, 277, 289
Wilhelm, C.L., 272, 289
Wilkins, P., 352, 377
Willerman, L., 241, 260
Williams, D., 138, 166
Williams, H., 187
Williamson, W.D., 87, 99
Willis, D.J., 8, 10, 43, 54, 238, 246, 261, 263, 289
Willis, W.G., 16, 17, 27
Willoughby, R.L., 383, 406
Wills, T., 135, 140, 162
Wilson, B.C., 193, 194, 196, 198, 199, 217, 225, 226
Wilson, G.S., 87, 99
Wilson, J., 254, 261
Wilson, J.J., 217, 226
Wilson, L.R., 142, 157, 164
Wilson, R.S., 182, 186
Wilson, W.M., 279, 289
Windmiller, M., 185, 256, 260
Wing, L., 321, 336, 343, 344
Wirt, R.D., 119, 127, 201, 226, 360, 377
Witkin, H., 240, 241, 261
Witt, J.C., 30, 53, 347, 348, 376, 412, 413, 424
Wnek, L., 87, 99, 186, 363, 376, 396, 406
Wohlwill, J., 152, 154, 161, 166
Wolf, E.G., 329, 332, 343, 360, 376
Wolf, R., 153, 166
Wolfus, B., 195, 226
Wolman, B.B., 22, 28

Wolpaw, T., 192, 226
Wolters, P., 270, 272, 288
Wood, G., 297, 316
Woodcock, R.W., 181, 184, 206, 224, 363, 374, 392, 407
Wortham, B., 140, 162
Wright, H., 153, 161
Wulbert, M., 149, 152, 166
Wyatt, J.S., 271, 288
Wyke, M.A., 194, 226

Wyman, J.B., 383, 406
Yarchoan, R., 270, 272, 288
Yarrow, L., 150, 151, 152, 154, 166
Yates, D.H., 383, 406
Yeates, K., 129, 165
Yeaworth, R., 142, 166
Yoder, P., 112, 124
York, J., 142, 166
Yu, V.Y.H., 271, 289
Zaffran, R.T., 401, 404

Zaidel, E., 193, 226
Zangwell, C., 193, 224
Zelman, J.G., 186
Zeskind, P.S., 24, 28
Zettel, J., 408, 423
Zettle, R.D., 292, 318
Zigler, E., 23, 28
Zimmerman, I.L., 187
Zinkin, P., 242, 261
Ziring, P., 238, 241, 246, 261

General Index

academic achievement/development, 89, 293
activity level, 303
actometers, 303
adaptive behavior, 85, 86, 87, 116, 168, 180, 181, 241, 242, 243, 247, 248, 253, 255, 256
adjustment, 241, 242, 247, 238, 263-269
Adolescent Family Inventory of Life Events and Changes, 142
Adolescent Life Change Events Scale, 142
adoption/foster care, 103, 107
aggression, 36, 41, 46, 108, 112, 182, 183, 265, 293, 294, 296, 297, 298, 303, 346, 358
AIDS, 269, 272. *See also* human immunodeficiency virus (HIV)
American Academy of Pediatrics, 75
American Association on Mental Deficiency (AAMD), 168, 181
American Educational Research Association, 418-420
American Psychiatric Association, 290, 293, 349
American Psychological Association, 383, 411, 418-420
antisocial behavior, 105, 109, 297. *See also* social skills
anxiety disorders, 104, 350-351. *See also* specific disorders
anxiety, 45, 49, 58, 109, 113, 118, 171, 241, 253, 265, 267, 271, 279, 296, 297, 298, 301, 309, 348, 349, 358, 361, 400
aphasia, 193, 220, 321
apraxia, 207
Arizona Social Support Interview Schedule, 134
arthrogryposis, 257
Assessment of Preterm Infant Behavior, 280
assessment: communicating results of, 8-9, 213, 216, 259, 283-284, 310-312, 335, 336, 340, 399-400; conceptual planning of, 59; caregivers present during, 15, 62, 70, 241, 242, 304; creating interest and motivation in, 60; environmental characteristics of, 55, 58-59, 63, 248, 283; establishing rapport in, 55, 59, 60, 158, 241-242, 247, 256; examinee characteristics in, 55, 56, 70, 170-171; examiner characteristics in, 6, 55, 57-58, 169-170, 283; factors influencing, 4, 5, 6, 8, 21, 56-59; interpreting/ integrating results of, 8, 244, 248, 258-259, 283, 306-308, 334-336, 339, 372-373, 412, 419; keeping examinee on task in, 60, 61-62; modifying procedures during, 5-6,
8, 20, 61, 62, 63, 173, 178, 237, 251, 252, 253-254, 258, 273, 326, 391, 398, 418-419; motivation of examinee in, 56; multidisciplinary team approach to, 7, 8, 77-78, 96, 256, 97, 168, 181, 200, 276, 278, 410, 412, 420; of infants, 62-63; problems in the process of, 62; serial, 170, 171, 248, 253; theoretical implications for, 30-31, 36, 38, 39, 40, 41. *See also* specific constructs
asthma, 262
at risk: for attention-deficit hyperactivity disorder, 297; for abnormal adjustment/ behavior, 253; for academic failure, 180; for cognitive deficits, 91; for developmental delay or physical handicap, 263, 266, 409; for developmental disorder, 74-75; for learning disabilities, 169, 173, 179; for maladaptive behavior, 181; for psychiatric disorders, 210, 346
ataxia, 252
athetosis, 251, 252
attachment disorders, 266
attention-deficit hyperactivity disorder (ADHD), 94, 104, 396: assessment process for, 293-306; characteristics of, 293, 350; classroom management in, 310; conceptualization of, 290-291; continuum concept of, 292, 293; diagnostic criteria for, 292- 292, 300, 301; in gifted children, 402; multidimensional nature of, 307; parent training in, 309-310; predisposing factors to, 350; secondary to prematurity, 270; treatment recommendations for, 308-310
attention span, 20, 21, 87, 170, 182, 254, 268, 272, 294-295, 298, 301-302, 303, 349, 388
audiology, 210, 244, 199, 409, 410
auditory acuity/functioning, 199, 242, 243-244. *See also* deaf- blind; hearing impairments
auditory cognition, 202, 204, 210, 212
auditory comprehension, 179, 196-197, 198, 199
auditory discrimination, 179, 202, 204, 211, 212
auditory memory abilities, 202, 204, 210, 212
auditory perception, 14, 199, 202, 204, 212
autism, 104, 112, 192, 193, 200, 214, 218, 220, 245, 292, 294, 307, 349; communication impairments in, 321; development rates within, 322; developmental testing in, 325-329; extended diagnostic period sessions, 338; identification and diagnosis

473

of, 320-322; prediagnostic staffing in assessment of, 324; receptive and expressive language skills in, 321, 333; ritualistic behaviors in, 321-322; social skills deficits in, 321; treatment recommendations in, 336-338; unique deficits and behavioral patterns in, 326. *See also* pervasive developmental disorder (PDD)
autism, assessing: adaptive behavior skills, 331; alternative methods of communication, 327; basic TEACCH philosophy, 319- 320; cognitive functioning, 323; communication, 313, 323, 332- 333; development, 331, 333; domains, 323, 332; handling attentional problems and atypical behaviors, 327-328; increasing motivation, 327; social skills development, 323, 331; structuring the testing environment, 326; using standardized psychological tests, 329-330
Autism Behavior Checklist, 332
Autistic Disorder, 349
autistic-like features, 246
Avoidant Disorder, 104, 350

Baby Doe issue, 415-417
Bandura, Albert, 38
Barker-Wright methodology, 153
Bayley, Nancy, 18-19
bed wetting, 17, 108, 112. *See also* enuresis
behavior problems: adoption/foster care and, 103; areas to assess in, 108-116; as a reflection of family problems 95; as predictors of future adjustment/ maladjustment, 109; bad habits and, 103; classification of, 102-106; death and, 103; developmental delays and, 103; divorce/ separation and, 44, 103; fears and, 103; handicaps as risk factors in, 108, 116; moving and, 103; parental negativity and, 103; personality problems and, 103; secondary to giftedness, 103, 392; secondary to handicapping conditions, 237, 238; social context of, 110, 111, 114; sex-related problems and, 103; sibling/peer problems and, 103; significance of age of occurrence of, 109; sleep problems and, 103; somatic complaints and, 103; toileting, 103; transient, 101. *See also* specific assessment constructs
Behavior Rating Scale, 360
behavior rating scales, 116, 118, 294-298, 301, 358-359
behavioral management techniques, 179
behavioral observations, 7, 86, 101, 121, 122, 153, 168, 171, 172, 180, 197, 199, 201, 222, 237, 243, 248, 253, 258, 262, 268, 273, 274, 294, 297, 301, 303, 304, 306, 331-332, 333, 336, 347, 356-358, 365-366, 368, 370-372, 397, 398

Belmont Report of the National Commission for the Protection of Human Subjects of Biomedical and Behavioral Research, 422
Berkeley Growth Study, 19
Bessel, Friedrich Wilhelm, 13
"best performance" model, 391, 398, 403
Binet, Alfred, 14, 18, 22, 90
birth weight, 129, 238, 270, 397
blindisms, 241
blindness, 237, 238; accompanied by sensorineural deafness, 241; causes of, 241; effect of age at occurrence, 241. *See also* visual impairment
Board of Education v. Rowley, 409
Bonadonna v. Cooperman, 411
brain damage, 277, 290. *See also* head injury
bronchopulmonary dysplasia (BPD), 262, 266, 270, 271, 273

cancer, 262, 264, 265, 272
cardiac problems, 262
Carolina Curriculum for Handicapped Infants, 280
Cattell, James M., 14
cerebral palsy, 8, 20, 90, 168, 193, 238, 241, 249-254, 265, 271, 276, 307, 350
child abuse/neglect, 35, 36, 266, 352, 415, 416
Child Abuse Prevention and Treatment Act. *See* PL 93-247
Child Find programs, 2, 76, 77, 346, 409
Child Research Project, 319
cleft palate, 255
coding forms, 305, 306
coercion, 41, 48, 112, 300; model of, 41
cognitive skills, 2, 12-15, 21, 31-33, 44, 87, 88, 89, 90-91, 116, 168, 172-179, 180, 181, 242, 247, 248, 253, 256, 277, 322, 328, 349, 368, 393, 396, 409, 414. *See also* auditory cognition; development
communication disorders/skills, 85, 86, 87, 89, 91-93, 116, 192, 202-203, 204-206. *See also* speech/language skills
conduct disorders/problems, 44, 118, 269, 293, 294, 296, 298, 304
confidentiality, 419-421
conflict of interest, 423
Conners Abbreviated Symptom Questionnaire, 296
consent, 411, 419-421
Continuous Performance Test, 301-302
Coping Health Inventory for Parents, 157
coping skills, 27, 33, 35, 36, 39, 152, 160, 264, 268, 275
counseling, 129, 372, 401, 409, 410
creativity, 390-391, 397
cultural bias, 15
cultural deprivation, 293
cultural immigration, 351
cultural minorities, 401

cultural values, 111
cystic fibrosis, 262, 266

daily living skills. *See* adaptive behavior skills
Darwin, Charles, 13, 17
deaf-blind, 246, 248
death, 43, 45, 107, 112, 350
defiant behavior, 300, 309, 370
denial, adaptive, 265
Denver Developmental Screening Test (DDST), 22, 78, 80, 85, 86, 88, 89, 92, 173, 393, 396
Denver Prescreening Developmental Questionnaire, 363
depression, 44, 45, 95, 118, 152, 156, 222, 271, 293, 296, 298, 309, 350, 352, 361, 372, 384, 400
desensitization, 49
development: cognitive, 2, 19, 21, 31-33, 44, 277, 409, 349; continuous vs. discontinuous, 29-30; ecological model of, 129, 130; effects of environment on, 78; effects of parental support network on, 46-48; factors associated with deviations from normal, 43-48, 246; general, 88, 90, 91, 116, 178; guidelines for identifying gifted preschoolers, 394-395; impact of illness and medical interventions on, 269-275; interactional/systems model of, 40-41; interference of emotional and/or behavioral problems with, 101; language and speech, 2, 17, 78, 91, 409; life-span theory of, 39-40; models of, 29-41; motor, 16-17, 21, 78, 91; neurobehavioral, 16-17; normal course in infants and young children, 15-17; normal postnatal, 16-17; normal prenatal, 15-16; personality, 36-38; physical, 2; psychosocial, 2, 118, 409; relationship between early attainments and later ones, 19; secondary to chronic physical illness, 262; self-help skills, 2; sensory, 16; social learning theory of, 38-39; socioemotional, 29, 44, 33- 36, 414; stage format of, 36; stimulus-response learning theory of, 38. *See also* developmental delays; developmental milestones; specific constructs/domains
developmental delays, 21, 74, 106, 107, 108, 179, 180, 182, 208, 270, 271, 275, 292, 351, 388, 393, 398, 409; and concurrent behavior problems, 19-20; definition of, 168; secondary to illness, 80, 267, 269; secondary to treatment interference, 262; secondary to visual loss, 244; states' definition of, 2, 3; vs. deficits, 91
developmental disabilities, 104, 112, 238, 271. *See also* specific disorders and disabilities
developmental dysphasia, 192
developmental language disorder (DLD): characteristics of, 194; classification of, 194-199; definition of, 193; neuropsychological assessment of, 199-201; origins of, 193-194; precursors to, 207-209
developmental milestones, 39, 80, 91, 101, 112, 121, 122, 172, 180, 200, 207, 208, 209, 214, 218, 239, 245, 250, 254, 272, 299, 353, 365, 386
developmental preschool, 277
diabetes, 262
Diagnostic and Statistical Manual of Mental Disorders (DSM-III-R), 102, 104-105, 220, 221290-291, 348-349, 355, 373
diplegia, 250
direct reinforcement of latency (DRL), 302
discipline, 46, 123, 132, 151, 267, 271, 277, 294, 392, 402
distractibility, 271, 298, 346, 290, 358
divergent thinking, 390, 391
divorce, 29, 43, 44, 45, 107, 112
Down's syndrome, 75, 132, 415
drugs: AZT, 272; effects of, 118, 262, 283; ototoxic, 200, 207; seizure, 271; steroid, 271-272; stimulant, 20, 171, 296, 299, 302, 304, 308-309, 312
duty to protect, 416-417
dynamometer, 14
dysarthria, 251
dyslexia, 193

ear infections, 179. *See also* serous otitis media
ear tubes, 179. *See also* myringotomies
Early Intervention Developmental Profile, 176
early intervention services, 2-4, 74, 244, 276, 299, 410, 421. *See also* intervention
Early Neonatal Neurobehavioral Scale, 16
Early Periodic Screening, Diagnosis & Treatment (EPSDT), 128
early school entrance, 400, 401
eating disorders/problems, 104, 107, 108, 370, 349. *See also* feeding disorders; pica; rumination
Edelbrock Child Attention/Activity Profile, 297
Education for All Handicapped Children Act. *See* PL 94-142
Education of the Handicapped Act Amendments of 1983. *See* PL 98-199
Education of the Handicapped Act Amendments of 1986. *See* PL99-457
educational services, children's right to, 408
elective mutism, 351-352
elimination disorders, 105, 351. *See also* bed wetting, encopresis, enuresis
emotional lability, 253, 271, 350, 362, 370
emotional disorders/problems. *See* social-emotional disorders
encopresis, 105, 293, 351, 355. *See also* elimination disorders
enmeshment, 384, 386
enuresis, 105, 293, 351, 355. *See also* bed

wetting, elimination disorders
environment: and behavior problems, 102; as a predictor of development, 22; caregiving, 198; child's relationship with, 170, 360; collecting and using information about, 131–133; demands of, 292; empirical appraisal of, 26; enriched, effects of, 15; extent of child's interaction with and concomitant problems, 108, 180–181; familiar, observation in, 172; influences of on cognitive ability, 22; influences of on development, 1, 4, 32, 97, 128, 129, 272; inputs of, 148; natural, responses in, 18; nature of child's interaction with, 49; processes of, 148, 149, 150, 154–156; rationale and model for assessing, 128–130; stimulation in the, 74, 149–150; sustaining social and emotional problems, 347; unstable, 372
environmental deprivation, 108, 168, 193
Environmental Language Inventory, 174
environmental measures, evaluating program or treatment effectiveness with, 132
epilepsy, 262, 269, 271, 292, 350, 355. *See also* seizures
Erikson, Erik, 29
esotropia, 240
ethical standards, principles, and codes, 411, 417–423
Ethical Principles of Psychologists (APA), 418–420
Evaluation and Prescription for Exceptional Children, 329
excitability, 253
exotropia, 240
expressive and receptive language, 181; deficits, 214; disorder, 197, 216; skills, 92, 93, 199. *See also* speech/language skills
Eyberg Child Behavior Inventory, 85, 94–95, 117, 118, 121, 122, 269, 297
eye movement disorders, 243, 246, 247. *See also* specific disorders

FACES II, FACES III. *See* Family Adaptability and Cohesion Evaluation Scales
Fagan Test of Infant Intelligence, 254, 258, 281
failure to thrive, 352
Family Adaptability and Cohesion Evaluation Scales, 156–157, 159, 268
Family Inventory of Life Events and Changes (FILE), 361
Family Inventory of Life Events, 157
Family Inventory of Resources for Management, 157
Family Needs Scale, 157
Family Resource Scale, 157
Family Routines Inventory, 268
Family Satisfaction Scale, 157
Family Strengths Scale, 157

Family Support Scale, 134, 157
family systems, issues and assessment of, 1, 2, 4, 6, 40, 45, 74, 101, 107, 112, 156–157, 158–160, 243, 255, 256, 410. *See also* parenting; sibling issues; socioeconomic status, effects of
fear, 5, 107, 108, 113, 297, 348, 350, 370, 358, 414
feeding disorders, 255, 269, 271, 273, 275, 352. *See also* eating disorders
fidgeting, 303, 304, 350
firstborns, 308, 386
Fragile X syndrome, 113, 334
Freud, Sigmund, 29
frustration tolerance, 370

Gall, Joseph, 12
Galton, Francis, 13
gender identity disorders, 104
Gesell Developmental Schedule, 18, 21, 176, 386, 393
Gesell Developmental Screening Inventory, 281
Gesell, Arnold, 17, 18
gifted: profoundly, 387, 400–401; vs. above average, 403; vs. talented, 385
giftedness, 70, 90, 107; attention-deficit disorder and, 402; behavioral characteristics and concerns in, 383, 386, 396–397, 402–403; common problems of, 384; definitions of, 384–386; emotional and interpersonal characteristics in, 396; enrichment activities for, 391, 400; formal testing issues in, 387–392; terms used with, 387; future planning issues in cases of, 400–402; physical handicaps and, 386
graphomotor skills, 202, 206, 211
Gross Motor Assessment for Children in Early Childhood, 176, 180
Guilford, J.P., 22

halo effect, 58
handicapped, definition of, 409
Harvard Preschool Project, 153
Haurte, Juan, 13
Hawaii Early Learning Profile, 280
Hayes-Binet Intelligence Test, 242
head injury, 172, 307, 355. *See also* brain damage
Head Start program, 93, 128, 345
hearing impairments, 199, 252, 320, 409. *See also* auditory acuity/functioning
hemiplegia, 251
hemophilia, 262, 264, 265, 270, 271
high risk infants, 88, 278, 280, 281, 282
history data, 7, 86, 113, 179, 197, 199–201, 240, 246, 252, 256, 268, 278, 299, 324, 347, 353–356, 364–365, 386–387
hit rate, 81–82
home environment, 148–149, 150–152, 278; scales, 153–154

Home Situations Questionnaire, 296, 300
Home Start program, 128
home visits, 132, 158, 409, 410
hospitalization, effects of, 262, 351. *See also* medical treatment, side effects of
human immunodeficiency virus (HIV), 270, 271, 272. *See also* AIDS
Human Interaction Scale, 153
hydrocephalus, 73, 254, 255, 263, 271, 358
Hyperactive Behavior Code, 303
hyperactivity, 89, 94, 118, 201, 253, 298, 346, 349, 350, 355, 361, 365, 372; hyperactivity, 298, 303; self-control training in, 296
hypersensitivity, 352
hypothesis-testing approach, 7, 111, 113, 119, 123, 171-172, 178, 268, 199
hypotonia, 251, 252
hypoxia, 240

immaturity, 89, 170, 297, 392
Impact of Illness Scale, 268
impulsivity, 49, 118, 291, 292, 296, 302-303, 350, 400
inattention, 94, 118, 290, 291, 292, 294, 297, 298, 303, 302, 350, 366. *See also* attention-deficit hyperactivity disorder
incidence and prevalence rates: adjustment problems, 94; attention- deficit hyperactivity disorder, 292; behavior problems, 94, 101, 104-105, 106-108; developmental disorders, 74; developmental language disorders, 192; giftedness, 383; prematurity and low birth weight, 239; retinopathy of prematurity, 239; visual and motor disabilities, 237-239
incontinence, bladder/bowel, 254, 255
Individualized Educational Plan (IEP), 4, 76, 336, 409, 410, 411, 412-413
Individualized Family Service Plan (IFSP), 2, 3, 6, 132, 409, 410, 411, 412-413
Individuals with Disabilities Education Act, 408. *See* PL 94-142
Infant Neurological International Battery, 281
inhibition, 297
intelligence: and cognition, 90-91; concepts and theories of, 13, 22-26, 41-42, 68, 90, 385, 388; controversy over measuring, 14-15; deficits in, 293; definitions of, 22-23, 413; environmental influences on, 23, 24; environmental model of, 23; *g* factor of, 22, 385; genotype-environment interactions in, 24; models of, 22-26; polygenetic endowment theory of, 23; psychometric models of, 41-42; specific patterns of and effects on personality test responses, 42; transactional model of, 23-24; types of, 388; verbal and performance theory of, 22. *See also* specific assessment instruments
interactional/systems theory, 49

interpretation of test findings. *See* assessment
Interview Schedule of Social Interaction, 134
interviews, 7, 111, 116, 119, 121, 120, 168, 171, 172, 180, 188- 191, 268, 294, 299, 301, 324, 331, 333, 347, 353-356, 360, 364-365, 372, 378-382, 393, 396-397, 397, 398
intervention, 48, 76, 110, 115, 129, 131, 132, 154, 169, 172, 192, 195, 244, 262, 274, 275, 296, 308, 336, 353, 415. *See also* early intervention services; treatment
Inventory of Social Support, 136
Inventory of Socially Supportive Behavior, 136
Irving Independent School District v. Tatro, 409
Isle of Wight study, 112
item response theory, 68

Junior High Life Experiences Survey, 142, 159
juvenile rheumatoid arthritis, 238, 257, 262

Kauai, children of, 129
Kaufman Short McCarthy Scales of Children's Abilities, 173, 174
kinetic drawing tasks, 42, 257, 359, 371. *See also* projective techniques

latch key children, 152
latent trait methodology, 68
Learning Accomplishment Profile, 176, 248, 280
learning disabilities, 24, 74, 118, 167, 168, 173, 214, 255, 293, 296, 297, 398, 409; language-based, 173; neurobiological-sociobehavioral model of, 24-26; PL 94-142 definition of, 169; measuring, 172-179, 297; profile of, 178; secondary to chemotherapy, 272; secondary to chronic illness, 269; secondary to prematurity, 270
legal liability, 416, 417
leukemia, 266. *See also* cancer
Life Event Record, 142
Life Events: Stressors & Stress, 144
life events, 43-44, 142-147, 361. *See also* specific events
Life Experiences Survey, 144
life stress, 140-148
Life Stress Scale, 144
List of Recent Experiences, 146
locus of control measures, 268
low birth weight. *See* birth weight; prematurity
lupus cerebritis, 269
lying, 109

magnetic resonance imaging (MRI), 254
marital relationship, 45-46, 95, 129, 156, 301, 309, 370. *See also* divorce
Marland Report of the Department of Education, 383-384, 385
Maslow's motive hierarchy, 40
masturbation, 111
Matching Familiar Figures Test, 302

Maternal Social Support Index, 136
McDevitt Behavior Style Questionnaire, 360
Measuring Scale of Intelligence, 14
medical treatment, side effects of, 271–272
medications. *See* drugs
memory skills, 85, 87, 197–198, 199, 281
meningitis, 200
mental retardation, 19, 35, 70, 74, 81, 90, 104, 112, 116, 167, 192, 193, 200, 209, 218, 220, 244, 246, 252, 257, 276, 292, 294, 320, 321, 336, 383, 388, 409; assessment in cases of, 180–183; concurrent with behavior problems, 182; definition of, 168; secondary to chronic illness, 269
Mills v. Board of Education, 408
minimal brain damage/minimal brain dysfunction (MBD), 290
Minnesota Multiphasic Personality Inventory, 33, 44, 119
minorities, linguistic, 57
minority groups, 178
mood disorders, 105, 269, 349
motivation, 40, 388
Motor Control Process Checklist, 176, 180
motor skills, 16–17, 21, 35, 78, 85, 86, 87, 88, 89, 91, 93, 104, 116, 168, 178, 180, 181, 202, 206, 211, 237, 252, 269, 277, 281, 293, 322, 328, 333, 349, 393, 396. *See also* visual-motor skills
moving, 107, 112
Multidimensional Assessment of Stressful Life Events Among Adolescents, 146
multidisciplinary team, 7, 8, 77–78, 96, 256, 97, 168, 181, 200, 276, 278, 410, 412, 420
multisensory impairment, 237, 245–249
muscular dystrophy, 238, 257, 262
mutism, elective, 105
myelomeningocele 254, 255. *See also* spina bifida
myringotomies, 210, 213. *See also* ear tubes

National Association of School Psychologists, 418–420
National Council on Measurement in Education, 418–420
need-press theory, 153
negative behaviors, 103, 107, 121, 351
neonatal intensive care unit (NICU), 16, 270, 271, 272, 273, 276, 280
neurodevelopmental status of infants, assessing, 22
Neurological Assessment of the Preterm and Full-Term Newborn Infant, 16
neurological dysfunction, 193, 244
neuropsychological assessment, 256, 282
neuroticism, 298
New York Longitudinal Study (NYLS), 295
nightmares, 112. *See also* sleep disturbances
noncompliance, 122, 179, 181, 295, 297, 300, 304, 309
Norbeck Social Support Questionnaire, 136
nystagmus, 245, 252

Object Interaction Scale, 153
observation. *See* behavioral observations
obsessive-compulsive, 297, 351
occupational therapy, 180, 182, 249, 250, 258, 276, 278, 335, 409, 410
oppositional behavior, 5, 121, 291, 293, 294, 298, 300, 309, 351
oppositional defiant disorder, 104, 293, 294
orthopedic impairment, 255, 409. *See also* specific disorders
osteogenesis imperfecta, 257
out-of-level testing, 399
overactivity, 290, 291, 292, 294
overanxious disorder, 104
overdependence, 109

paraplegia, 250–251
Parent Behavior Progression, 154
parent-child interaction, 39, 107, 121, 122, 123, 242, 297, 304, 348
parent conference, 213, 216, 259, 335–336, 340, 399–400
parent daily log, 119, 120, 122
parent report, 86, 88, 94, 95, 253, 294, 396. *See also* specific instruments
parent training, 296, 309, 409
parental psychopathology, 44
parenting: behaviors, 151; process model of the determinants of, 129–130; skills, 37, 41, 44, 62, 129, 311, 360, 364, 370; style, 265–267, 300, 311
parents, single, 43–44
passivity, 94, 118, 265, 298
pediatric health care system, 282–283
pediatric intensive care unit (PICU), 266, 275
pediatricians, 75–76, 96, 116, 172, 181, 209, 218, 240, 244, 247, 250, 276, 278, 300, 346, 386, 391
peer interaction/relationships, 106, 107, 264, 267, 293, 350, 370, 384, 400, 403. *See also* sibling issues; social skills
Pennsylvania Association for Retarded Children v. Pennsylvania, 408
Perceived Social Network Inventory, 136
Perceived Social Support: PSS-Fa for Families and PSS-Fr for Friends, 138
perception of illness, 264
perceptual motor skills, 17, 35, 178, 269
perceptual-performance skils, 281
perceptual skills, 252, 414
periventricular leucomalacia (PVL), 271
Perkins-Binet Tests of Intelligence for the Blind, 242
perseveration, 326, 327, 328, 349
Personal Network Matrix, 138

personality issues and assessment, 30–31, 107, 268, 360–362
pervasive developmental disorder (PDD), 104, 192, 193, 218, 220, 221, 246, 292, 300, 307, 319–320, 349; communication impairments in, 321; identification and diagnosis, 320–322; ritualistic behaviors in, 321–322; social skills deficits in, 321; uneven development and learning in, 322. *See also* autism
phenylketonuria (PKU), 334
phrenology, 13
physical therapy, 76, 237, 258, 271, 273, 276, 278, 409, 410
Piaget, Jean, 29, 31–33, 345
pica, 104
PL 93-247, 415
PL 94-142, 74, 76, 77, 78, 169, 172, 345, 408, 409, 410, 411, 412
PL 98-199, 408, 409
PL 98-457, 415
PL 99-457, 1–4, 74, 77, 78, 132, 192, 290, 319, 345, 355, 408, 409, 410, 411, 412
play behavior technique, 359–360
play setting, 243, 248, 304
play therapy, 372
Portage Guide to Early Education, 176, 178, 179
praxis, 202, 206
preacademic skills, 89, 178, 180, 181
prematurity, 75, 80, 200, 239, 270–271, 273, 277, 278, 279, 282
Preschool Attainment Record, 176
Preschool Behavior Questionnaire, 117, 119, 298, 358
Preschool Interaction Code, 358
Preschool Observation Scale of Anxiety, 358
Preschool Performance Questionnaire, 232–235
prescreening, 80, 85, 96
Principles of Professional Ethics (NASP), 418–420
prodigy. *See* giftedness
programming, educational or developmental, 8, 87, 180, 182, 237
projective techniques, 42, 257, 347, 359–360, 371, 372. *See also* kinetic drawing tasks
Psychiatric Epidemiology Research Interview, 146
psychometric issues, 13, 20–22. *See also* assessment; hit rate; reliability; scores; test sensitivity and specificity; validity
psychopathology, 44, 48–50, 275. *See also* specific disorders
psychosis, 361
Purdue Home Stimulation Inventory, 154

quadriplegia, 249, 250
Quality of Life (scale), 157, 160

rapport, establishing. *See* assessment

reaction time tasks, 14
Reactive Attachment Disorder, 105, 352
reading problems, precursors to, 169
reading readiness skills, 180
referral questions/issues, 107, 110, 111, 114, 199, 355, 392–393
referral source, 59, 111, 172
reinforcement, 39, 41, 132, 170, 310, 312, 327, 362, 368, 372, 402–403
reliability, 20–21, 68–70, 79, 81, 87, 91, 92, 93, 120, 295, 296, 297, 303, 356, 357, 358, 359, 361, 385, 388, 398, 413, 414, 418, 419, 421
remediation, 172, 195, 398. *See also* intervention; treatment
renal disease, 262, 265, 269–270, 275
Resource Scale for Teenage Mothers, 157, 159
respiratory distress syndrome (RDS), 239, 240
retinoblastoma, 241
retinopathy of prematurity (ROP), 239, 244, 270
retrieval skills, 199
retrolental fibroplasia. *See* retinopathy of prematurity (ROP)
Rett's syndrome, 334
Revised Denver Preschool Developmental Questionnaire, 83
Revised Life Event Questionnaire, 146
Revised Prescreening Developmental Questionnaire, 88
Reye's syndrome, 269
ritualistic behavior, 241, 321–322, 323, 349
Rorschach, 33, 42
rubella, 238, 241, 245, 334
rumination, 104, 273, 274, 352

schizophrenia, 105, 108, 112, 218, 348
school problems, 101, 103, 107
school readiness, 87, 93, 346, 401
School Situations Questionnaire, 298
scoliosis, 251, 255
scores: Apgar, 239, 250; age equivalent, 63, 66, 87, 90, 181, 399; age of norms in, 70; developmental quotient (DQ), 128; distribution of, 81; floor and ceiling effects, 70–71, 242, 256, 389, 398; gain/difference, 71; grade equivalents, 66–67, 399; IQ, 24, 89, 90, 92, 167, 181, 182, 213, 242, 277, 292, 329, 330, 383, 387, 388–389, 390, 393, 398; item content differences, 71; latent trait, 68; median, 13; mental age, 63, 66, 182, 242, 399; normal curve equivalents, 64; percentiles, 13, 64–66, 90, 203, 207, 236; practice effects, 71; rating, 87; raw, 63, 66, 67, 70; scaled, 64, 203; standard, 63–64, 66, 87, 90, 181; stanine, 90; T, 64; z, 203, 207, 236
screening tests, 82–95. *See also* specific constructs/domains; specific test titles
screening, 73, 173, 346, 385, 410; cost--

effectiveness of, 79–80, 95, 96; developmental, 73, 75–78; environmental, 131; ethical issues of, 421–422; for academic readiness, 93; for behavioral problems and adjustment, 94–95; for hyperactivity, 94; for school readiness, 82; for visual-motor skills, 93–94; goals of, 80–82; mass, 77, 79, 345; model for comprehensive, 95
seizure medications. *See* drugs
seizures, 168, 171, 181, 200, 217, 218, 252, 254, 355. *See also* epilepsy
self-abusive behaviors, 20, 349
self-concept, 362, 384
self-control, 49, 271, 400
self-esteem, 37, 40, 157, 267, 293, 350, 351, 370
self-help skills, 2, 88, 89, 181, 241, 254, 255, 324, 400, 409
self-stimulation, 268, 323, 327, 328
sentence completion tests, 359
separation and individuation, 264
separation anxiety, 104, 304, 350
sequential processing skills, 322
serous otitis media, 200, 209. *See also* ear infections
services. *See* early intervention services; educational services
sexual abuse, 35
shunt, 254, 255, 271
shyness, 171, 351, 413
sibling issues, 101, 106, 107, 351, 384, 400, 403
sickle cell disease, 262, 264, 265, 269
sign language, 209, 213, 221, 222
Simon, Théodore, 14, 90
sleep problems, 102, 106, 107, 108, 109, 269, 296, 349, 351, 352, 370
sleepwalking, 351
Snellen acuity, 14, 240
social-emotional disorders/skills, 2, 29, 35, 85, 86, 87, 88, 89, 95, 116, 118, 181, 242, 243, 253, 257, 296, 298, 361, 372, 393, 396, 409: as reflections of family problems, 95; assessment of, 89, 297, 298, 346–348, 352–362; behavioral model of, 347–348; definition and classification of, 348–352; ecological model of, 348; medical model of, 347; secondary to handicapping conditions, 238. *See also* peer interaction/relationships; socialization
social isolation, 47–48, 156, 370
social learning theory, 49
social maturity scales, 269
social skills. *See* social-emotional disorders/skills
social support, 46–48, 133–139, 157, 159, 160, 263, 280
Social Support Appraisals, 138
Social Support Behaviors Scale, 138
Social Support Questionnaire, 138
socialization, 29, 38–39, 116, 180, 181, 350, 392

socioeconomic status, effects of, 80, 88
somatic complaints, 107, 266, 296, 350, 361
Southern California Sensory Integration Tests, 176, 180
spasticity, 251, 252
Spearman, Charles, 14–15
special education, 76–77, 90, 167, 179, 244, 409, 411
speech/language disorders, 104, 105, 112, 196–197, 216, 346, 351, 409. *See also* specific disorders
speech/language skills, 2, 17, 32, 74, 78, 85, 86, 87, 89, 91–93, 116, 168, 178, 179–181, 199, 214, 247, 252, 255, 281, 322, 393, 398, 414
speech/language pathologists, 55, 77, 96, 97, 173, 180, 182, 199, 247, 249, 409, 410
speech/language therapy, 28, 76, 179, 213, 217, 221, 237, 276
Speech-Language Inventory Questionnaire, 196, 211, 216, 227–231
spina bifida, 238, 249, 254–257, 265, 415
staffing conferences, 8, 334, 346, 347, 353, 362, 364
Standards for Educational and Psychological Testing (AERA, APA, & NCME), 418–420
Stanford-Binet Intelligence Scale, Form L-M, 242, 281, 389
stereotypies, 241, 243, 246, 326
strabismus, 240
stress, 29, 33, 36, 43, 44, 95, 101, 112, 118, 133, 159, 192, 210, 253, 255, 263, 309, 348, 350, 351, 361, 370
stuttering, 91, 105
sudden infant death syndrome (SIDS), 273
Support Functions Scale, 138, 157
support groups/systems, 132, 310, 352
Sutter-Eyberg Student Behavior Inventory, 85, 117, 119

TEACCH, Division, 319, 323, 324, 325, 331, 334, 336, 338
temper tantrums, 106, 179, 181, 246, 248, 266, 268, 350, 351, 362, 365, 366, 398
temperament, 40, 109, 118, 265, 295, 297, 299, 392
test sensitivity and specificity, 81–82, 86, 88, 89, 95
testability, 326
thematic material, 359. *See also* projective techniques
tic disorders, 105, 214, 299, 309. *See also* Tourette's disorder.
timidity, 109
toilet training, 17, 34, 101, 106, 113, 324, 351, 355
toileting, 102, 107, 108
Total Communication program, 213, 221
Tourette's disorder, 105, 299, 309
treatment, 8, 46, 49, 118, 131, 237, 271–272,

275, 299, 300, 301, 308, 310, 312, 320, 336, 415–416, 421. *See also* intervention
tuberous sclerosis, 334

University of Rochester Child and Family Study, 44

validity, 14, 21, 22, 79, 81, 86, 91, 92, 93, 118, 120, 155, 296, 297, 303, 356, 357, 358, 359, 361, 385, 390, 398, 414, 418, 419, 421
Vernon, Philip, 22
Vineland Social Maturity Scale, 331, 363
Virginia EMI, 280
visual cognitive skills, 202, 205, 211, 212
visual confrontation naming, 202
visual discrimination, 202, 205, 212
visual functioning/impairment, 237, 239–245, 247–248, 320, 409
visual memory skills, 202, 205–206, 211, 212, 322
visual-motor skills, 93–94, 144, 173
visual-perceptual skills, 92, 328, 168, 180

visual-semantic retrieval, 205, 212
visual-spatial skills, 202, 205, 212, 322
vulnerable child syndrome, 277

Wallach and Kogan Creativity Battery, 390
Weber, Ernst Heinrich, 13
Wechsler Adult Intelligence Scale-Revised, 42
Wechsler, David, 22
well-child examinations, 73, 76, 96, 245
Werry-Weiss-Peters Activity Rating Scale, 296–297
Williams Preschool Motor Development Checklist, 176
withdrawal, 171, 222, 265, 268, 297, 346, 350, 351, 361, 366
Women, Infants, & Children (WIC) program, 128
word association tests, 359
word retrieval, 202, 204
Wundt, Wilhelm, 13

Yale Clinic of Child Development, 18

About the Contributors

RUSSELL A. BARKLEY, PH.D. is Director of Psychology and Professor of Psychiatry and Neurology at the University of Massachusetts Medical Center. He received his Ph.D. in clinical psychology from Bowling Green State University in Ohio, where he was the recipient of the Distinguished Dissertation Award for his extensive studies of hyperactive children. Dr. Barkley is a Diplomate in both Clinical Psychology and Clinical Neuropsychology from the American Board of Professional Psychology, Inc. He is a past president of the Section on Clinical Child Psychology, Division 12, of the American Psychological Association. A clinical practitioner, scientist, and educator, Dr. Barkley has authored 3 books, more than 17 book chapters, and over 42 scientific papers on Attention Deficit-Hyperactivity Disorder, stimulant drug therapy, parent training in child management, and child neuropsychology.

CAROL A. BOLIEK, PH.D. is an Assistant Research Scientist in the Center for Neurogenic Communication Disorders at the University of Arizona in Tucson. She earned her doctorate in school psychology in 1986 from the University of Northern Colorado and subsequently was awarded a postdoctoral fellowship from Southern Illinois University, where she studied electrophysiology and developmental neuropsychology. Dr. Boliek's prior experience includes work at Johns Hopkins Hospital, where she conducted developmental and cognitive assessments for terminally ill and neurologically impaired children from birth to adolescence.

ROBERT H. BRADLEY, PH.D. serves as Director of the Center for Research on Teaching and Learning at the University of Arkansas at Little Rock, Adjunct Professor of Pediatrics at the University of Arkansas for Medical Sciences, and Associate Director of the University of Arkansas Affiliated Program in Developmental Disabilities. He is the codeveloper, along with Bettye Caldwell, of the HOME Inventory. His primary research interests involve the relationship between children's environments (home, day care, and school) and their development. Dr. Bradley has been involved in several longitudinal studies of children who are disabled or at risk for developmental problems. He also has conducted numerous program evaluations.

JUDITH A. BRISBY, PH.D. is a Research Associate at the Center for Research on Teaching and Learning at the University of Arkansas at Little Rock. She currently serves as Coordinator of the Little Rock site of the National Study of Children's Lives. She has conducted hundreds of home visits as part of the Center's studies of handicapped and high-risk children and was a primary assessor for the Little Rock site of the Infant Health and Development Project, a multisite study of a model program for premature, low birth weight children and their families. She earned her doctorate in art education and at present is involved in the application of art therapy techniques for children with disabilities.

JAN L. CULBERTSON, PH.D. is Associate Professor in the Department of Pediatrics and Director of Child Neuropsychology Services at the University of Oklahoma Health Sciences Center. She is editor of the *Journal of Clinical Child Psychology,* past editor of the *Child, Youth, and Family Services Quarterly,* and past president of the Section on Clinical Child Psychology, Division 12, American Psychological Association. Dr. Culbertson has published and taught nationally in the areas of child abuse prevention, neuropsychological assessment of learning disabled children and those with Attention-Deficit Hyperactivity Disorder, sudden infant death syndrome, and child advocacy.

PHILIP W. DAVIDSON, PH.D. earned his doctorate from George Washington University in experimental psychology at the Division of Disorders of Development and Learning, University of North Carolina at Chapel Hill. He is Professor of Pediatrics and Psychiatry (Psychology) and Director, Strong Center for Developmental disabilities, Department of Pediatrics, University of Rochester School of Medicine and Dentistry.

MERELYN DOLINS, PH.D., R.P.T. is a physical therapist in private practice. She holds a doctorate in developmental psychology from Yeshiva University.

JANNA DRESDEN, M.A. earned a master's degree in education from the University of Chicago and presently is a doctoral student in the Department of Educational Psychology at the University of Georgia. She has worked as a teacher in preschools and child-care centers, as an educational coordinator at a social service agency, and as a university instructor teaching courses in child development, child guidance, and educational psychology.

BETTY N. GORDON, PH.D. is Associate Professor of Psychology at the University of North Carolina at Chapel Hill, where she specializes in clinical child psychology. She teaches graduate-level courses in child assessment, an undergraduate course in personality, and supervises graduate student clinical practicum work. Dr. Gordon earned her Ph.D. in 1978 from the University of Washington, where she received training in developmental psychology and developmental disabilities. She has been involved clinically in the assessment and treatment of victims of child sexual abuse. Her research interests include factors that influence children's memory for autobiographical events and their abilities to provide accurate testimony in child abuse cases. She has coauthored with Carolyn S. Schroeder the text *Assessment and Treatment of Childhood Problems: A Clinician's Guide*.

GEORGE W. HYND, ED.D. is Research Professor of Special Education and Psychology and Chair, Division for Exceptional Children, at the University of Georgia, and Clinical Professor of Neurology at the Medical College of Georgia. He also is the Director of the University of Georgia Center for Clinical and Developmental Neuropsychology. He received his doctorate in psychology from the University of Northern Colorado and completed a postdoctoral fellowship in clinical neuropsychology. In addition to authoring and editing books in pediatric neuropsychology, he has published numerous chapters and articles dealing with the neurological basis of dyslexia and learning disabilities and on neuropsychological assessment with children.

RANDY W. KAMPHAUS, PH.D. is Associate Professor of Educational Psychology, Coordinator of School Psychology Training, and Director of the School Psychology Clinic at the University of Georgia. He is a licensed psychologist and certified school psychologist. Dr. Kamphaus has published widely in the area of children's assessment and has numerous articles, books, and book chapters to his credit. His previous work includes the two-volume *Handbook of Psychological and Educational Assessment of Children* with Cecil R. Reynolds.

ALAN S. KAUFMAN, PH.D. is Research Professor of School Psychology at The University of Alabama. He worked closely with David Wechsler in the revision of the WISC and supervised the standardization of the WISC-R and the McCarthy Scales. Dr. Kaufman is author of *Intelligent Testing with the WISC-R* and the recent *Assessing Adolescent and Adult Intelligence*. He is the coauthor, with his wife Nadeen, of *Clinical Evaluation of Young Children with the McCarthy Scales* and of several psychological and educational tests, including the Kaufman Assessment Battery for Children (K-ABC), the Kaufman Test of Educational Achievement (K-TEA), and the Kaufman Brief Intelligence Test (K-BIT).

MORGAN P. KELLY, J.D., M.A. serves as quality assurance coordinator and statistical analyst for the Eastern Nebraska Office of Community Mental Health (ENOCMH) in Omaha. He received his J.D. and M.A. degrees from the University of Nebraska at Lincoln, where he is an advanced doctoral student in the Law/Psychology Program. Mr. Kelly is interested in the development of mental health regulatory systems, especially as they affect child and family clients.

THOMAS J. KENNY, PH.D. is Professor of Pediatrics and Director of Pediatric Psychology at the University of Maryland School of Medicine. He received his Ph.D. from the Catholic University of America. He has served as President of the Society of Pediatric Psychology and received the Society's Distinguished Contributions Award in 1984. Dr. Kenny is a Fellow of the American Psychological Association, and his publications include 13 books or book chapters as well as over 75 research publications. Among the latter are articles on developmental screening, including "Developmental Follow-Up: Inherent Problems and a Conceptual Model" and "Developmental Screening Using Parent Report."

PATRICIA A. KLEINE, ED.D. is Assistant Professor in the College of Education and Human Services at Wright State University in Dayton, Ohio. She is the former director of the Gifted and Talented and Gifted Handicapped Program at the University of Maine in Orono, where she was a faculty member in the College of Education. A former teacher and elementary school principal, Dr. Kleine also holds her superintendent's certificate. She is a member of the National Association for Gifted Children, the Council of Exceptional Children, the American Association for Curriculum Development, the American Educational Research Association, and the American Association of School Administrators, as well as a former member of the National Council of State Directors of Programs for the Gifted. Previously she was a researcher and consultant to the Center for the Study of Social Policy in Washington, D.C., where she conducted ethnographic research on at-risk children.

MARGARET LANSING, M.ED. is a psychoeducational therapist with the TEACCH program (Treatment and Education of Autistic and related Communication handicapped Children) in North Carolina. A former teacher, she taught normal Grades 1 through 3 before specializing in learning and behavioral problems in the normal preadolescent group. Following her work as a teacher/therapist in child psychiatric clinics, she obtained a master's degree in emotional disturbance and neurological handicaps and was the educational director for the diagnostic classroom at Dartmouth Psychiatric Department. She has lectured nationally and internationally and contributes to TEACCH publications and research.

LEE M. MARCUS, PH.D. is Clinical Director of the Piedmont TEACCH Center and Associate Professor and Director of Psychology Training in the Department of Psychiatry, University of North Carolina School of Medicine. He received his Ph.D. from the University of Minnesota in 1972 and completed a 2-year postdoctoral fellowship in clinical child psychology at the University of Rochester School of Medicine. He has written extensively in the area of autism, including journal articles and book chapters on assessment of autistic children, collaborative work with families, and the development of model service programs based on his experience in the TEACCH program in North Carolina.

GARY B. MELTON, PH.D. is Carl Adolph Happold Professor of Psychology and Law at the University of Nebraska at Lincoln, where he also directs the Center on Children, Families, and the Law and the Law/Psychology Program. Dr. Melton is past president of the American Psychology-Law Society, a past president of the Division of Child, Youth, and Family Services of the American Psychological Association, and vice chair of the U.S. Advisory Board on Child Abuse and Neglect. In 1985 he received the American Psychological Association's Award for Distinguished Contributions to Psychology in the Public Interest. He is the author or editor of nearly 200 publications, including *Psychological Evaluations for the Courts: A Handbook for Mental Health Professionals and Lawyers.*

ABOUT THE CONTRIBUTORS

JOHN E. OBRZUT, PH.D. is Professor in the Department of Educational Psychology at the University of Arizona. He received his doctoral degree in school psychology from the University of Minnesota and has completed postdoctoral study in neuropsychology at the Minneapolis Veterans Administration Center. Dr. Obrzut is a Fellow of the American Psychological Association, the American Psychological Society, and the International Academy for Research in Learning Disabilities. He has coedited a number of books, and his research has appeared in a variety of psychology journals.

MARY L. PEERY, PH.D. is a licensed psychologist affiliated with Cornerstone Psychiatry. She received her Ph.D. in 1988 from the School Psychology Program at Texas A&M University. She currently practices in Houston, Texas.

MELISSA RAMIREZ-JOHNSON, PH.D. is a pediatric psychologist at Wake Medical Center, where she directs a Developmental Team serving both inpatient pediatric and high-risk infant follow-up clinic populations, and Clinical Assistant Professor of Pediatrics, Psychology, and Psychiatry at the University of North Carolina at Chapel Hill. She received her doctorate in clinical psychology at UNC and completed an internship at North Carolina Memorial Hospital. She has presented and published on psychological aspects of childhood chronic illness and on methods for assessment and intervention in pediatric settings. Dr. Ramirez-Johnson is certified in the Brazelton Neonatal Behavioral Assessment Scale and Assessment of Preterm Infant Behavior, and is a trainer in the Neonatal Individualized Developmental Care and Assessment Program (NIDCAP).

CECIL R. REYNOLDS, PH.D. is Professor of Educational Psychology at Texas A&M University and director of psychology at Sandstone Hospital, where he also has a clinical practice. Dr. Reynolds earned his doctorate in 1978 at the University of Georgia. He is the editor of *Archives of Clinical Neuropsychology*.

ERIC SCHOPLER, PH.D. is Professor of Psychology and Psychiatry and Director of Division TEACCH (Treatment and Education of Autistic and related Communication handicapped Children) at the University of North Carolina School of Medicine. He is the author of numerous texts, chapters, and articles in the field. Dr. Schopler is the editor of the *Journal of Autism and Developmental Disorders* and is editorially involved with six other related professional journals. Among his advisory activities is his involvement with the Work Group to revise the *Diagnostic and Statistical Manual of Mental Disorders* (DSM-III-R).

CAROLYN S. SCHROEDER, PH.D. is Clinical Professor of Pediatrics and Psychiatry at the University of North Carolina Medical School, Research Professor in the Department of Psychology at UNC, and a pediatric psychologist at Chapel Hill Pediatrics. She received her Ph.D. in clinical psychology from the University of PIttsburgh in 1968. Dr. Schroeder has developed a model program for psychologists doing clinical service, teaching, and research in a primary health care setting. She has coauthored with Betty N. Gordon the text *Assessment and Treatment of Childhood Problems: A Clinician's Guide*.

MARGARET SEMRUD-CLIKEMAN, PH.D. is Assistant Professor in the Department of Educational Psychology at the University of Washington at Seattle. She was a school psychologist in Wisconsin for 13 years, specializing in early childhood education. Dr. Semrud-Clikeman received her Ph.D. from the University of Georgia with a specialization in child neuropsychology. She previously was affiliated with Massachusetts General Hospital, where she completed a neuroscience fellowship.

TERRI L. SHELTON, PH.D. is Assistant Professor in the Departments of Psychiatry and Pediatrics at the University of Massachusetts Medical Center, and Assistant Professor in the Department of Psychology at Assumption College. She received her Ph.D. in clinical psychology from Purdue University and completed an internship in pediatric psychology at the University of Oklahoma Health Sciences Center. Dr. Shelton has presented over 100 lectures and workshops and authored several articles and book chapters on early intervention, assessment of young children with developmental delays, apnea and sudden infant death syndrome, child behavior management, and parent/professional collaboration in the treatment of children with chronic illness. She is first author on a monograph entitled *Family-Centered Care for Children with Special Health Care Needs.*

JAMES T. WEBB, PH.D. is Professor and Assistant Dean for Special Programs, and Director of the Supporting Emotional Needs of Gifted (SENG) program, at the Wright State University School of Professional Psychology in Dayton, Ohio. He is a former board member of the National Association for Gifted Children and is a past president of the American Association for Gifted Children. A Fellow of the American Psychological Association and Diplomate in Clinical Psychology, he has served on the Association's Council of Representatives. He is the senior author of *Guiding the Gifted Child: A Practical Source for Parents and Teachers,* which in 1982 won the national media "Best Book" award of the American Psychological Foundation.

J. KENNETH WHITT, PH.D. is Associate Professor of Psychology in the Departments of Psychiatry and Pediatrics at the University of North Carolina School of Medicine, where he directs Pediatric Psychology Programs and is Chief Clinical Child Psychologist in the Division of Child Psychiatry. He received his Ph.D. in clinical psychology from the University of Texas at Austin in 1976, with internship specialization in pediatric and clinical child psychology at North Carolina Memorial Hospital. His clinical research interests include child and family adjustment to chronic illness (especially childhood cancer, epilepsy, renal disease, and hemophilia) and neuropsychological sequelae of pediatric illness and treatment. Dr. Whitt is a member of the Society of Pediatric Psychology, serves on the *Journal of Pediatric Psychology* editorial board, and provides editorial consultation to numerous professional journals.

DIANE J. WILLIS, PH.D. is Professor of Medical Psychology, Department of Pediatrics, University of Oklahoma Health Sciences Center, and Director of Psychological Services at the university's Child Study Center. She received her Ph.D. from the University of Oklahoma. She is a member of the U.S. Advisory Board on Child Abuse and Neglect and has spent all of her professional life working with young children who are chronically ill, abused, or disabled and their families. She is a past president of Division 12, Sections 1 and 5 (Clinical Child Psychology and Society of Pediatric Psychology), and of Division 37 (Children, Youth, and Families) of the American Psychological Association. Dr. Willis is past editor of the *Journal of Clinical Child Psychology* and the *Journal of Pediatric Psychology,* and is the author of numerous articles and book chapters.

BARBARA C. WILSON, PH.D. is Director of the Center for Neuropsychological Services in the Department of Neurology at North Shore University Hospital–Cornell University Medical College, Associate Professor in the Department of Neurology at Cornell University Medical College, and Adjunct Professor of Psychology at Queens College, City University of New York. She has published widely on neuropsychological assessment, language disorders in preschool children, and on other topics in child neuropsychology. She is a founding member of the International Neuropsychological Society and of the American Board of Clinical Neuropsychology (ABPP), and was among the first neuropsychologists in North America to earn the Diplomate in Clinical Neuropsychology. Dr. Wilson is president-elect of the International Neuropsychological Society, slated to take office in 1993.